Dynamic Choice and Asset Markets

Dynamic Choice and Asset Markets

Sumru Altuğ
University of Minnesota
Minneapolis

Pamela Labadie
Graduate School of Business
Columbia University
New York

Academic Press

San Diego   New York   Boston   London   Sydney   Tokyo   Toronto

Copyright © 1994 by ACADEMIC PRESS, INC.
All Rights Reserved.
No part of this publication may be reproduced or transmitted in any form or by any means, electronic or mechanical, including photocopy, recording, or any information storage and retrieval system, without permission in writing from the publisher.

Academic Press, Inc.
A Division of Harcourt Brace & Company
525 B Street, Suite 1900, San Diego, California 92101-4495

United Kingdom Edition published by
Academic Press Limited
24-28 Oval Road, London NW1 7DX

Library of Congress Cataloging-in-Publication Data

Altug, Sumru.
    Dynamic choice and asset markets / Sumru Altug, Pamela Labadie.
        p.   cm.
    Includes index.
    ISBN 0-12-055455-0
    1. Capital assets pricing models.   2. Investments--Mathematical models.   I. Labadie, Pamela H.   II. Title.
    HG4636.A45   1994
    332.6'01'5118--dc20   94-25749
                                                 CIP

PRINTED IN THE UNITED STATES OF AMERICA
94 95 96 97 98 99 QW 9 8 7 6 5 4 3 2 1

To my father S. A.

To my parents   P. L.

Contents

Preface

The purpose of this book is to provide an integrated treatment of a variety of models of dynamic optimization and dynamic equilibrium and to examine their empirical implications. In this text, we consider the implications of dynamic equilibrium frameworks for the behavior of individual choices and asset prices. As we describe each theoretical framework, we also derive econometric and numerical methods that can be used to study its implications.

We provide an extended discussion of methods and results related to the empirical testing of asset pricing relations. More theoretical texts in finance that cover some of the topics we do include the texts by Duffie [102, 104], Dothan [100], Huang and Litzenberger [201], and Jarrow [206]. There is some overlap between the topics we consider in this book and other texts dealing with dynamic general equilibrium models, such as the texts by Malliaris and Brock [244], Harris [180], Sargent [299], and Stokey and Lucas with Prescott [317]. The feature that differentiates our text from most others is that we describe the empirical implications of these models and discuss methods for testing them. As an example, we present an extended discussion of how to test equilibrium models using panel data. We also cover new topics such as methods for formulating and estimating dynamic discrete choice models and models with private information. As part of this discussion, we describe numerical solution methods for asset pricing models, growth models, and dynamic discrete choice models.

A unifying feature of our discussion is that many of the dynamic equilibrium models that we consider can be formulated as dynamic programming problems and solved using a contraction mapping approach. Rather than introduce explicit measure-theoretic considerations for analyzing dynamic stochastic models, we describe uncertainty in terms of Markov uncertainty in a discrete-time setting. In Chapter 1, we provide a review of some results from functional analysis that we use in later chapters. For a review of basic results from functional analysis, we refer the reader to Kreyszig [223] and Naylor and Sell [267], and to Papoulis [274] for a review of probability theory and stochastic processes.

Throughout this text, we have employed what one of our review-ers has described as a "basics first, then applications" approach. For example, in Chapter 2 where we introduce the Lucas representative con-sumer asset pricing model, we provide a detailed description of the basic version of this model, including proofs for the existence of the consumer's value function, proofs of its properties such as concavity and differentia-bility, and proofs for the existence of the equilibrium asset pricing func-tions. In later sections, we describe how this model can be extended in a number of different directions, such as allowing for durable consumption goods, habit persistence, nonexpected utility preferences, or growing en-dowment, and we indicate how the proofs of the basic model must be modified to handle these cases. Likewise, in Chapter 4 where we discuss models with production, we initially analyze the properties of the one-sector stochastic optimal growth model and then extend this model to allow for distorting taxes, adjustment costs, and irreversible investment, to name a few.

Alongside our discussion of alternative theoretical frameworks, we describe various econometric methods that can be used to examine the empirical implications of these models, including Euler equation estima-tion methods, ARCH-type modeling, methods for implementing max-imum likelihood estimation, and panel data estimation methods. We also provide a review of some of the quantitative results that have been obtained from empirical testing of dynamic equilibrium models. Our discussion of alternative econometric methods assumes that the reader already possesses a knowledge of econometrics available at the introduc-tory graduate level. For a useful review, see the text by Greene [161].

The notation conventions that we follow are standard. For example, we let $\mathbb{R}$ denote the real line. For any positive integer n, $\mathbb{R}^n$ denotes the set of n-tuples of of the form $(x_1, \ldots, x_n)$ with x_i in $\mathbb{R}$ for all i. For any n-tuple $(x_1, \ldots, x_n)$ with x_i in X for all i, the conventions for inequalities are: (i) $x \geq 0$ means that x is nonnegative; for x in $\mathbb{R}^n$, this is equivalent to $x \in \mathbb{R}^n_+$; (ii) $x > 0$ means that x is nonnegative and not zero but not necessarily strictly positive in all coordinates; (iii) $x \gg 0$ means that x is strictly positive in all coordinates. For x in $\mathbb{R}^n$, this is equivalent to $x \in \mathbb{R}^n_{++}$. With these conventions, a function f defined on $\mathbb{R}^n$ is increasing if $f(x) \geq f(y)$ whenever $x \geq y$ and strictly increasing if $f(x) > f(y)$ whenever $x > y$.

We have provided a set of detailed exercises at the end of each chapter. These exercises are intended to introduce some new topics at the same time that they allow the student to apply the methods described earlier.

We developed this book from our teaching of graduate financial economics and macroeconomics at Duke University, the University of Minnesota, the University of Wisconsin, and Columbia University. It reflects our desire to provide a unified treatment of material that we could not find in one place. For teaching purposes, this text can be used as the basis for a graduate macroeconomics or financial economics course. We hope that this text will also prove useful to students and practitioners in the fields of macroeconomics, finance, applied general equilibrium modeling, and structural econometrics.

We have received helpful comments from various colleagues, including Erdem Başci, Tom Cooley, Scott Freeman, Christian Gilles, Jeremy Greenwood, Steve LeRoy, Bruce Smith, Anne Sibert, Allan Stockman, Steve Williamson, the participants of the International Workshop at the University of Rochester and of a series of seminars at Bilkent University in Ankara, Turkey. We are grateful to Buz Brock, Darrell Duffie, and Robert Miller for providing comments that led to improvements in successive versions of this manuscript. We thank Zhenyu Wang for many helpful comments and the numerical calculations. We are grateful to John Easton, Eric Rantapaa, and the Social Science Research Facilities Center at the University of Minnesota for making LaTeX available at all times. Finally, we are grateful to Kari Wangen and Wendy Williamson for helping to compile our references, providing editorial comments, and assisting with other aspects of the production of this manuscript.

1

Introduction

In competitive asset markets, consumers make intertemporal choices in an uncertain environment. Their attitudes toward risk, production opportunities, and the nature of trades that they can enter into determine equilibrium quantities and the prices of assets that are traded. The intertemporal choice problem of a consumer in an uncertain environment yields restrictions for the behavior of individual consumption over time as well as determining the form of the asset pricing function used to price random payoffs.

We begin by describing the simplest setup in which individual choices can be made, namely, a complete contingent claims equilibrium. As a precursor of the material to follow, we discuss the relationship of the complete contingent claims equilibrium to security market equilibrium and describe its implications for asset pricing and individual choices. We then provide a brief description of arbitrage and its implications for asset pricing. Two important approaches to asset pricing have been the partial equilibrium approaches of the capital asset pricing model (CAPM) and the arbitrage pricing theory (APT). Although our focus is on general equilibrium asset pricing, the CAPM and APT provide useful background material. We provide a description of risk aversion and some related concepts such as absolute risk aversion and discuss alternative measures of increasing risk such as mean-preserving spreads that are useful for conducting comparative dynamics exercises.

Because we deal so frequently with a "representative consumer," it is useful to highlight the conditions under which aggregation is valid. We discuss exact aggregation as well as the existence of a "composite consumer" that can be constructed in a complete contingent claims equilibrium. When agents are heterogeneous and markets are complete, we have complete risk-sharing; we discuss the implications of full insurance.

The remainder of the chapter is devoted to an introduction to dynamic programming, which is a useful approach when studying dynamic and recursive economies.

1. Equilibrium: Some Introductory Concepts

In this section, we present some introductory concepts related to equilibrium in economies under uncertainty, including definitions of a complete contingent claims equilibrium and security market equilibrium and the derivation of asset pricing relations. Throughout our discussion, we consider economies with one date and a finite number of states.

1.1. Complete Contingent Claims Equilibrium

We begin by describing the simplest setup in which consumer choices are made and asset prices determined, namely, a complete contingent claims equilibrium. In such an equilibrium, a consumer can trade claims to contracts with payoffs that depend on the state of the world, for all possible states.

There is a finite set of consumers $\{1, \ldots, I\}$ in this economy. There are $s \in \{1, \ldots, S\}$ possible states of the world, where S is finite. Each consumer associates the probability π_s^i to state s occurring, where $0 < \pi_s^i < 1$ and $\sum_{s=1}^{S} \pi_s^i = 1$. We assume that there are M commodities, one of which may be leisure. The quantity $c_{s,m}^i$ denotes the consumption of commodity m by consumer i contingent on the state s occurring. Then $c^i \equiv (c_{1,1}^i, \ldots, c_{S,M}^i)'$ is an element of $\mathbb{R}_+^{SM}$, which denotes the commodity space or space over which consumption choices are made. When there are a finite number of states (or dates) and a finite number of commodities at each state (or date), we say that the commodity space is finite-dimensional.

Each consumer has an endowment ω^i in $\mathbb{R}_+^{SM}$ and a utility function u_i such that $u_i : \mathbb{R}_+^{SM} \to \mathbb{R}$. Notice that the function u_i describes consumer i's preferences over alternative consumption bundles indexed by the type of commodity m and the state s. If the utility function can be written as:

$$u_i(c^i) = \sum_{s=1}^{S} \pi_s^i U_i(c_{s,1}^i, \ldots, c_{s,M}^i), \tag{1.1}$$

where $\pi_s^i > 0$ denotes the probability of state s occurring, then we say that consumer i has *expected utility* preferences. Notice that expected utility preferences are additive across states.

An I-tuple $(c^1, \ldots, c^I)$ describing the consumption of each consumer in this economy is an *allocation*. We say that an allocation $(c^1, \ldots, c^I)$ is *feasible* if

$$\sum_{i=1}^{I}(c^i_{s,m} - \omega^i_{s,m}) = 0, \quad s = 1,\ldots,S, \quad m = 1,\ldots,M. \tag{1.2}$$

A feasible allocation $(c^1,\ldots,c^I)$ is *Pareto optimal* if there does not exist another feasible allocation $(\hat{c}^1,\ldots,\hat{c}^I)$ such that $u_i(\hat{c}^i) \geq u_i(c^i)$ for all i and with $u_i(\hat{c}^i) > u_i(c^i)$ for some i.

Since there are S states and M commodities in each state, a total of $S \times M$ contingent claims will be traded in this economy. For each state and commodity, let $p_{s,m}$ denote the price of a claim to a unit of consumption of the m'th commodity to be delivered contingent on the s'th state occurring. Define the set of prices $p_{s,m}$, $s \in \{1,\ldots,S\}$ and $m \in \{1,\ldots,M\}$, as the *price system*. The price function p assigns a cost to any consumption c^i and a value to any endowment ω^i; in our application $p : \mathbb{R}^{SM}_+ \to \mathbb{R}_+$ has an inner product representation:

$$p \cdot c \equiv \sum_{s=1}^{S}\sum_{m=1}^{M} p_{s,m} c_{s,m}.^1$$

The markets for contingent claims open before the true state of the world is revealed. Afterwards, deliveries of the different commodities are made according to the contracts negotiated before the state is realized and then consumption occurs.

A *complete contingent claims equilibrium* is a nonzero price function p on $\mathbb{R}^{SM}_+$ and a feasible allocation $(c^1,\ldots,c^I)$ such that c^i solves

$$\max_c u_i(c) \quad \text{s.t.} \quad p \cdot c \leq p \cdot \omega^i \tag{1.3}$$

for all i. The complete contingent claims equilibrium allows us to specify a competitive equilibrium under uncertainty by assuming that prices exist for consumption in each possible state of the world.

The First Welfare Theorem states that the complete contingent claims equilibrium is Pareto optimal. The Second Welfare Theorem states that under some regularity conditions and with a redistribution of the total endowment, a Pareto optimum can be supported as an equilibrium. The existence of equilibrium and the welfare theorems are discussed by Debreu [88], who provides an introduction to competitive equilibrium when the commodity space is finite-dimensional. Early proofs of the existence of

---

[1]Notice that $p \cdot (\alpha x + \beta y) = \alpha(p \cdot x) + \beta(p \cdot y)$ for any $\alpha, \beta \in \mathbb{R}$ and $x, y \in \mathbb{R}^{SM}$ so that the price function is *linear*.

a competitive equilibrium are by Arrow and Debreu [18] and McKenzie [255].

To provide a simple proof of the First Welfare Theorem, assume that u_i are strictly increasing. Suppose that $(c^1, \ldots, c^I, p)$ is a complete contingent claims equilibrium and $(\hat{c}^1, \ldots, \hat{c}^I)$ is a feasible allocation such that $u_i(\hat{c}^i) \geq u_i(c^i)$ for all i, with at least one strict inequality for agent j. If $u_j(\hat{c}^j) > u_j(c^j)$, it must be case that

$$p \cdot \hat{c}^j > p \cdot c^j, \tag{1.4}$$

otherwise c^j would not have been chosen by consumer j in a complete contingent claims equilibrium. Furthermore, if for some i, it is the case that $\epsilon \equiv p \cdot c^i - p \cdot \hat{c}^i > 0$, then we could define

$$\bar{c}^i = \hat{c}^i + \frac{\epsilon}{p \cdot p} p$$

so that $p \cdot \bar{c}^i = p \cdot c^i$. Since u_i are strictly increasing and $p > 0$, we would have $u_i(\bar{c}^i) > u_i(c^i)$, which cannot occur since $(c^1, \ldots, c^I)$ is an equilibrium allocation. Thus, we have

$$p \cdot \hat{c}^i \geq p \cdot c^i, \quad i = 1, \ldots, I. \tag{1.5}$$

Combining Equations (1.4) and (1.5) and using the feasibility of the allocation $(c^1, \ldots, c^I)$ implies the contradiction,

$$\sum_{i=1}^{I} p \cdot \omega^i \geq \sum_{i=1}^{I} p \cdot \hat{c}^i > \sum_{i=1}^{I} p \cdot c^i = \sum_{i=1}^{I} p \cdot \omega^i,$$

proving the result.

The proof of the Second Welfare is more involved. Debreu [88, pp. 95–96] provides a proof when the commodity space is finite-dimensional. The relationship between valuation equilibrium and Pareto optimum when the commodity space is infinite-dimensional (which occurs for economies with an infinite number of dates and states of the world) has been studied by Debreu [87]. The equivalence between a Pareto optimum and competitive equilibrium can be used to characterize competitive equilibrium in infinite-horizon economies under uncertainty by solving for a Pareto optimal allocation. We illustrate this approach in Chapter 4 in a representative consumer model with production and capital accumulation.[2]

---

[2]Mehra [256] applies the result in Debreu [87] directly to show that an optimal allocation in a pure endowment economy can be supported as an equilibrium. See also Harris [180, Ch. 3] and Stokey and Lucas [317, Ch. 15].

1.2.   Security Market Equilibrium

In actual asset markets, we observe individuals trading in securities that are claims to random payoffs denominated in units of account, not in commodities. We now describe how to formulate an equilibrium with such securities.

Suppose that there are N securities and let $d_{n,s}$ denote the dividend denoted in units of account, say dollars, paid by security n in state s. Let $q = (q_1, \ldots, q_N)$ in $\mathbb{R}^N$ denote the vector of security prices and define D as the $N \times S$ matrix of dividends. Securities are sold before the state s is realized so that their prices are independent of the realized state. After the security markets close, agents trade in spot markets for the M commodities. Let $\bar{p}_{s,m}$ denote the unit price of the m'th commodity in state s and define $\bar{p}_s$ in $\mathbb{R}^M$ as the vector of spot prices in state s.

The i'th agent chooses a portfolio $\theta^i \equiv (\theta_1^i, \ldots, \theta_N^i)$ in $\mathbb{R}^N$ of securities to purchase and a consumption vector c^i in $\mathbb{R}_+^{SM}$. Given the security and spot prices $(q, \bar{p})$, the i'th agent solves the problem:

$$\max_{c^i, \theta^i} u_i(c)$$

subject to

$$[d_{1s}, \ldots, d_{Ns}]$$

$$\theta^i \cdot q \;\leq\; 0, \tag{1.6}$$

$$\bar{p}_s \cdot c_s^i \;\leq\; \bar{p}_s \cdot \omega_s^i + \theta^i \cdot d_s \quad \text{for } s = 1, \ldots, S, \tag{1.7}$$

where $\theta^i \cdot d_s$ is the dollar payoff on the portfolio in state s and c_s^i in $\mathbb{R}_+^M$ is the consumption vector in state s.

We define an equilibrium as a collection $((\theta^1, c^1), \ldots, (\theta^I, c^I), (q, \bar{p}))$ such that, given $(q, \bar{p})$, (θ^i, c^i) solves the problem for agent i; and markets clear:

$$\sum_{i=1}^I \theta_n^i = 0 \quad \text{for } n = 1, \ldots, N, \tag{1.8}$$

$$\sum_{i=1}^I (c_{s,m}^i - \omega_{s,m}^i) = 0 \quad \text{for } s = 1, \ldots, S, \; m = 1, \ldots, M. \tag{1.9}$$

Since spot markets open after securities trading has occurred, we can also refer to this equilibrium as a *security-spot market equilibrium*.

Notice that the consumer faces a separate budget constraint for each state of the world. The consumer's wealth in each realized state s is given by his endowment ω_s^i in that state plus the payoff on his portfolio of assets. Unlike the complete contingent claims equilibrium, the consumer cannot purchase claims to consumption for each possible state subject to a single budget constraint that constrains the value of his consumption to be less than the value of his endowment across all possible states. Instead, his feasible consumption in state s is constrained by his realized wealth at that state. This suggests that the consumption allocation in a security market equilibrium may differ from the allocation in a complete contingent claims equilibrium. However, Arrow [16] has shown that if the number of securities equals the number of states, then the allocation in a complete contingent claims equilibrium can be attained in a security market equilibrium. $S = N$

To show how this is done, denote the allocation and prices in a complete contingent commodity markets equilibrium by $(c^1, \ldots, c^I, p)$. We will consider $N = S$ number of securities and define the dividend vector as:

$$d_{n,s} = \begin{cases} 1 & \text{if } s = n \\ 0 & \text{otherwise,} \end{cases} \qquad D = \begin{bmatrix} 1 & & 0 \\ & \ddots & \\ 0 & & 1 \end{bmatrix}$$

for $s = 1, \ldots, S$ and $n = 1, \ldots, S$. Let the security price vector be $q = (1, \ldots, 1) \in \mathbb{R}^N$ and the spot price of commodities be equal to the contingent claims prices, namely, $\bar{p}_{s,m} = p_{s,m}$. Also define the portfolio weights so that the number of units of the s'th security that is held by consumer i is equated to the cost of the net consumption choice by i in state s:

$$\theta_s^i = \bar{p}_s \cdot (c_s^i - w_s^i). \tag{1.10}$$

Notice that (θ^i, c^i) is feasible for consumer i in the security market equilibrium:

$$\theta^i \cdot q = \sum_{s=1}^{S} p_s \cdot (c_s^i - w_s^i) = p \cdot c^i - p \cdot w^i \leq 0,$$

$(1. \cdots 1)$

and

$$\bar{p}_s \cdot c_s^i = \bar{p}_s \cdot w_s^i + \theta_s^i = \bar{p}_s \cdot w_s^i + \theta^i \cdot d_s \quad \text{for } s = 1, \ldots, S.$$

complete market

To show that (θ^i, c^i) solves the consumer's problem, assume that $(\phi, \hat{c})$ also satisfies the budget constraints and $u_i(\hat{c}) > u_i(c)$. Since c^i is optimal for consumer i in the complete contingent claims equilibrium, we have that $p \cdot \hat{c} > p \cdot c^i$; otherwise c^i would not have been chosen. If $(\phi, \hat{c})$ satisfies the consumer's budget constraints, then $\phi_s = \phi \cdot d_s \geq p_s \cdot (\hat{c}_s - w_s^i)$ and

↑ for each s

$\phi \cdot q \geq \sum_{s=1}^{S} p_s(\hat{c}_s - \omega_s^i)$ since $q = (1, \ldots, 1)$. But $p \cdot \hat{c} > p \cdot c^i$ implies that $\phi \cdot q > 0$ which contradicts Equation (1.6).

Spot markets clear because $(c^1, \ldots, c^I)$ is feasible. Security markets clear since $\sum_{i=1}^{I} \theta^i = \sum_{i=1}^{I} \sum_{s=1}^{S} p_s(c_s^i - \omega_s^i) = \sum_{s=1}^{S} p_s \sum_{i=1}^{I}(c_s^i - \omega_s^i) = 0$.

Recall that we defined each security to have a unit payoff if state $s = n$ occurs and zero otherwise. We can show that a complete contingent claims allocation can be attained in a security market equilibrium with an arbitrary security matrix D whose columns are linearly independent. When the columns of D span $\mathbb{R}^S$, we say that markets are *complete*. With such spanning securities, we can show that a security market equilibrium can be converted into a contingent claims equilibrium. Since the complete contingent claims equilibrium allocation is Pareto optimal, the allocation in the security market equilibrium will also be Pareto optimal. In the absence of spanning, markets are *incomplete* and a security market equilibrium may exist but the equilibrium allocation is not necessarily Pareto optimal.

Now suppose there is only one commodity in each state so that $M = 1$. Without loss of generality, assume that the spot price of consumption in each state is unity, $\bar{p}_s = 1$. Notice from Equation (1.7) that $\theta^i \cdot d_s = c_s^i - \omega_s^i$. Suppose we choose the security price q_n as:

$$q_n = \sum_{s=1}^{S} d_{n,s} p_s, \tag{1.11}$$

where p_s is the price of a contingent claim that pays off in state s. Then (θ^i, c^i) is feasible for consumer i since

$$\theta^i \cdot q = \sum_{n=1}^{N} \theta_n^i \sum_{s=1}^{S} d_{n,s} p_s$$

$$= \sum_{s=1}^{S} p_s \sum_{n=1}^{N} \theta_n^i d_{n,s} = \sum_{s=1}^{S} p_s(c_s^i - \omega_s^i) \leq 0,$$

and

$$c_s^i = \omega_s^i + \theta_s^i = \omega_s^i + \theta^i \cdot d_s \quad \text{for } s = 1, \ldots, S.$$

The remainder of the proof is identical to the previous case. Notice that Equation (1.11) yields a simple representation for the price of the n'th security in terms of the price function for the complete contingent claims equilibrium. In our subsequent discussion, we will make use of the relationship in Equation (1.11) when analyzing the behavior of pricing functions that emerge with and without complete markets.

1.3. Arbitrage and Asset Valuation

In the theoretical finance literature, the absence of arbitrage opportunities in securities trading has been exploited by Ross [286], Harrison and Kreps [181], Chamberlain and Rothschild [68], and others to show the existence of a pricing function that is used to value random payoff streams and to characterize its properties. We now illustrate their approach for the simple setup that we have been studying. We assume that there is one date, S states, and one commodity in each state. As a consequence, spot commodity prices can be normalized as unity.

We now drop the i index and consider an arbitrary portfolio of securities θ in $\mathbb{R}^N$. For any vector of security prices q in $\mathbb{R}^N$, a portfolio θ has market value $q \cdot \theta$ and payoff $D^T \theta$. An *arbitrage* is a portfolio θ in $\mathbb{R}^N$ with

$$q \cdot \theta \leq 0 \quad \text{and} \quad D^T \theta > 0,$$

or

$$q \cdot \theta < 0 \quad \text{and} \quad D^T \theta \geq 0.$$

From the definition of the agent's problem in the security market equilibrium, we see that an arbitrage implies that a zero endowment yields a nonnegative, nonzero consumption allocation. In other words, if $q \cdot \theta \leq 0$, then $\bar{p}_s \cdot c_s \leq \theta \cdot d_s$ is satisfied with $c_s > 0$ for some s if $D^T \theta > 0$, which is equivalent to $\theta \cdot d_s > 0$ for some s. Likewise, if $q \cdot \theta < 0$ and $D^T \theta \geq 0$, then the agent can guarantee a strictly positive consumption at date zero, $c_0 = -q \cdot \theta > 0$. Thus, we can show that if utility functions are strictly increasing, an arbitrage does not exist in equilibrium.

Define a *state-price vector* as a vector ψ in $\mathbb{R}^S_{++}$ with $q = D\psi$. Notice that it is a strictly positive price vector that is used to assign a price to the random payoffs or dividends paid by each security n. If a complete contingent claims equilibrium exists, then the state-price vector is defined as the price function p. Clearly, if a state-price vector exists, then there is no arbitrage. We can also prove the converse.

Theorem 1.1 *There is no arbitrage if and only if there is a state-price vector.*

PROOF

Suppose the payoff of the first N_1 securities are linearly independent with payoff matrix D_1 and the payoff on the other $N_2 = N - N_1$ securities are linear combinations of the first N_1 securities with payoff matrix D_2.

Then there exists an $N_2 \times N_1$ matrix K such that $D_2 = K D_1$. Thus, we can decompose the payoff matrix D as $D^T = (D_1^T, D_1^T K^T)^T$. Let q_1 be the price vector associated with the first N_1 securities and q_2 the price vector associated with the other N_2 securities. Then $q = (q_1^T, q_2^T)^T$.

First, we prove that if there is no arbitrage, then there must be a state-price vector $\psi \in \mathbb{R}^S_{++}$ such that $q_1 = D_1 \psi$. Suppose not. We define $A \equiv \{D_1 \psi : \psi \in \mathbb{R}^S_{++}\}$ and $B \equiv \{\lambda q_1 : \lambda \in \mathbb{R}_+\}$, then $A \cap B$ is empty. It follows from the Separating Hyperplane Theorem, Luenberger [237, p. 133], that there exists a nonzero $\theta_1 \in \mathbb{R}^{N_1}$ such that $\lambda \theta_1^T q_1 \leq \theta_1^T D_1 \psi$ for all $\lambda \in \mathbb{R}_+$ and $\psi \in \mathbb{R}^S_{++}$. This implies that $\theta_1^T q_1 \leq 0$ and $\theta_1^T D_1 \geq 0$. Since D_1 has full rank, there is no $\theta_1 \neq 0$ such that $\theta_1^T D_1 = 0$ and thus we must have $\theta_1^T D_1 > 0$. Let $\theta^T = (\theta_1^T, 0)^T$, then $\theta^T q = \theta_1^T q_1 \leq 0$, and $\theta^T D = \theta_1^T D_1 > 0$, which implies that θ is an arbitrage.

Second, we prove that $q_2 = D_2 \psi$, where ψ was proven to exist in the previous paragraph. Suppose $q_2 \neq D_2 \psi$, then there exists a $\theta_2 \in \mathbb{R}^{N_2}$ such that $\theta_2^T(q_2 - D_2 \psi) < 0$. Let $\theta_1 = -K^T \theta_2$ and $\theta^T = (\theta_1^T, \theta_2^T)$, then $\theta^T D = \theta_1^T D_1 + \theta_2^T K D_1 = 0$, and $\theta^T q = \theta_2^T (q_2 - D_2 \psi) < 0$. Thus, θ is an arbitrage.

Therefore, we have that $q = D\psi$ with $\psi \in \mathbb{R}^S_{++}$. Finally it is easy to check that if a state-price vector exists, then there is no arbitrage. ∎

Notice that we can use the state-price vector to derive an alternative representation of security prices. Given a state-price vector, define $\bar{\psi}_s = \psi_s/\pi_s$, where $\pi_s > 0$ is the probability of state s occurring. Then

$$q_n = \sum_{s=1}^{S} d_{ns}\psi_s = \sum_{s=1}^{S} \pi_s d_{ns}\bar{\psi}_s,$$

which implies that

$$q = E(D\bar{\psi}). \tag{1.12}$$

This asset valuation formula says that security prices are determined as the expected discounted value of future dividends or payoffs, with the elements of the strictly positive vector $\bar{\psi}$ used to discount the payoff that occurs at each state.

This approach provides a powerful way for studying the problem of asset pricing that is discussed in many standard texts in finance. Our approach in this book is to start from an explicit economic environment and deduce implications for asset prices and the form of the asset pricing functions from the equilibrium in these environments.

1.4.   Asset Pricing Relations

Consider a two-period version of the model under uncertainty with one commodity in which the state is revealed in the second period. The commodity space is $\mathbb{R}_{+}^{S+1}$. Let $(c_0, c_1, \ldots, c_S)$ represent c_0 units of consumption in the first period and c_s represent units of consumption contingent on the state s occurring, $s \in \{1, \ldots, S\}$. Suppose preferences satisfy expected utility:

$$u_i(c) = U_i(c_0) + \sum_{s=1}^{S} \pi_s^i V_i(c_s),$$

where $\pi_s^i > 0$ denotes the probability of state s occurring and U_i and V_i are strictly increasing, strictly concave, and differentiable functions.

Suppose $(c^1, \ldots, c^I, p)$ is a complete contingent claims equilibrium where $p \in \mathbb{R}_{+}^{S+1}$. Without loss of generality, let us normalize $p_0 = 1$. Using the problem in Equation (1.3), the first-order necessary and sufficient conditions for c^i to be an optimal plan are:

$$\frac{\partial u_i(c^i)}{\partial c_0^i} = \lambda_i, \tag{1.13}$$

$$\frac{\partial u_i(c^i)}{\partial c_s^i} = \lambda_i p_s, \quad s = 1, \ldots, S, \tag{1.14}$$

where λ_i is a Lagrange multiplier. For any two states k and l, a consumer i chooses consumption satisfying:

$$\frac{\pi_k^i V_i'(c_k^i)}{\pi_l^i V_i'(c_l^i)} = \frac{p_k}{p_l}. \tag{1.15}$$

This condition says that the ratio of the contingent claims prices for any two states is equal to the ratio of the marginal utilities of consumption in those states weighted by the probability of occurrence of those states. We can also derive an expression for the price of a contingent claims contract that pays off in state s as:

$$p_s = \frac{\pi_s^i V_i'(c_s^i)}{U_i'(c_0^i)}. \tag{1.16}$$

Now consider the security market equilibrium. Suppose that there are $N \geq S$ securities with dividends $d_{n,s}$ for $n = 1, \ldots, N$ and $s = 1, \ldots, S$. Without loss of generality, assume that the spot price of consumption is unity for each $s \in \{0, 1, \ldots, S\}$. The budget constraints for the consumer's problem are given by:

$$c_0^i + \theta^i \cdot q \leq w_0^i,$$

$$c_s^i \leq w_s^i + \theta^i \cdot d_s, \quad 1 \leq s \leq S.$$

Let μ_0^i and μ_s^i, $s = 1, \ldots, S$, denote the Lagrange multipliers for the consumer's budget constraints. The first-order conditions with respect to c_0^i, c_s^i, and θ^i are:

$$U'(c_0^i) = \mu_0^i,$$

$$\pi_s^i V'(c_s^i) = \mu_s^i, \quad s = 1, \ldots, S,$$

$$\mu_0^i q_n = \sum_{s=1}^{S} \mu_s^i d_{n,s}, \quad n = 1, \ldots, N.$$

We can use these conditions to solve for the price of the n'th security as:

$$\begin{aligned} q_n &= \sum_{s=1}^{S} \frac{\pi_s^i V'(c_s^i)}{U'(c_0^i)} d_{n,s} \\ &= E\left[\frac{V_i'(c_s^i) d_{n,s}}{U_i'(c_0^i)}\right]. \end{aligned} \tag{1.17}$$

In Section 1.2, we showed that a complete contingent claims equilibrium allocation can be attained in a security market equilibrium in which the spot price of consumption is normalized as one and the price of the n'th security is defined in Equation (1.11). Using the definition of p_s given by Equation (1.16), notice that this yields an asset pricing relation that is identical to Equation (1.17). The price of a security in Equation (1.17) is determined as the expected discounted value of its future dividend, the discount factor defined as the intertemporal marginal rate of substitution (MRS) in consumption for consumer i. Since the individual MRSs are equated across consumers in a complete contingent claims equilibrium, the discount factor used to price random payoffs in Equation (1.17) can be evaluated using the MRS for *any* consumer i. Based on the representation in Equation (1.17), the intertemporal MRS in consumption is sometimes called the *stochastic discount factor*. As we examine alternative dynamic equilibrium frameworks and derive restrictions for individual choices, we will also derive restrictions for the stochastic discount factor.

1.5. Complete Markets and the Composite Consumer

In the economies we examined so far, individuals can differ with respect to their beliefs, their tastes, and their initial endowment or wealth. We refer to such differences as *ex ante* heterogeneity . Notice that the asset pricing relation that we derived in Equation (1.17) is evaluated using the preferences of individual consumers. One approach to deriving asset pricing relations in the presence of population heterogeneity is to contruct a so-called *composite consumer*, as suggested by Constantinides [75] and others. The existence of this composite consumer is based on the Pareto optimality of the complete contingent claims equilibrium. We first derive such a composite consumer and then discuss its usefulness for asset pricing.

Let $\eta = (\eta^1, \ldots, \eta^I) \in \mathbb{R}_+^I$ denote a vector of agent weights and consider the problem of maximizing the weighted sum of individual utilities subject to an aggregate feasibility constraint:

$$\max_{(c^1,\ldots,c^I)} \sum_{i=1}^{I} \eta_i u_i(c^i) \text{ s.t. } c^1 + \ldots + c^I \leq \omega^1 + \ldots \omega^I. \tag{1.18}$$

We will use this problem to contruct a hypothetical composite consumer. Assume that u_i are strictly increasing and concave for all i. Define the function $U_\eta : \mathbb{R}_+^{S+1} \to \mathbb{R}$ by:

$$U_\eta(x) \equiv \max_{(c^1,\ldots,c^I)} \sum_{i=1}^{I} \eta_i u_i(c^i) \text{ s.t. } c^1 + \ldots + c^I \leq x. \tag{1.19}$$

First, notice that a feasible allocation that is Pareto optimal solves the problem in Equation (1.19) with a set of positive weights $\eta \in \mathbb{R}_+^I$ and $c^1 + \ldots + c^I = \omega$. This follows as an application of the Separating Hyperplane Theorem. (See Exercise 1.) Second, notice that if $(c^1, \ldots, c^I)$ solves the problem in Equation (1.19), then it is Pareto optimal.

Suppose markets are complete. Let $(c^1, \ldots, c^I, p)$ denote a complete contingent claims equilibrium and let $((\theta^1, c^1), \ldots, (\theta^I, c^I), q)$ denote the associated security market equilibrium. We now demonstrate that if markets are complete, the no-trade allocation $(0, \omega)$ is optimal for the composite consumer whose preferences are defined in Equation (1.19) and that security prices can be expressed using these preferences, evaluated at the aggregate endowment ω.

Consider the problem that consumer i solves in a complete contingent claims equilibrium. Since the utility function u^i is strictly concave and p is strictly positive, the Kuhn-Tucker Theorem, Luenberger [237, p. 249], states that there exists a set of weights $\lambda_i \geq 0$ such that the equilibrium consumption for consumer i, c^i, solves:

$$\max_{c \in \mathbb{R}_+^{S+1}} u_i(c) + \lambda_i(p \cdot \omega^i - p \cdot c). \tag{1.20}$$

Since u_i is strictly increasing, $\lambda_i > 0$. Define $\eta_i = 1/\lambda_i$. Now for any feasible allocation $x^1, \ldots, x^I$, we have that

$$\sum_{i=1}^I \eta_i u_i(c^i) = \sum_{i=1}^I \eta_i u_i(c^i) + \eta_i \lambda_i(p \cdot \omega^i - p \cdot c^i) \geq \sum_{i=1}^I \eta_i u_i(x^i).$$

Thus, the equilibrium allocation $(c^1, \ldots, c^I)$ solves the problem in Equation (1.19). We can also show that the no-trade allocation $(0, \omega)$ is optimal for the composite consumer with preferences U_η and endowment ω. (We leave this as an exercise.)

The first-order conditions for the problem in Equation (1.20) are given by Equations (1.13) and (1.14). As before, the contingent claims price in state s can be expressed as:

$$p_s = \frac{\partial u_i(c^i)/\partial c_s^i}{\partial u_i(c^i)/\partial c_0^i},$$

where we normalize the price of a contingent claim at date 0 as unity. Dividing both sides of Equations (1.13) and (1.14) by λ_i, summing over i, and then using Equation (1.11) yields:

$$q_n = \sum_{s=1}^S \frac{\partial U_\eta(\omega)/c_s}{\partial U_\eta(\omega)/c_0} d_{n,s}, \tag{1.21}$$

where $\partial U_\eta(\omega)/c_s = \sum_i \eta_i \partial u_i(\omega^i)/\partial c_s^i$ and $U_\eta(\omega)/c_0 = \sum_i \eta_i \partial u_i(\omega^i)/\partial c_0^i$.

Notice that the expression for security prices in Equation (1.21) has been expressed using the preferences of the composite consumer defined in Equation (1.19). However, these indirect preferences depend on the entire distribution of individual characteristics (as captured by the agent weights η_i), the individual utility functions u_i, and the equilibrium distribution of the consumption allocation. As a result, they are not useful for interpreting observed quantities and prices because they require information on the distribution of exogenous and endogenous forms of heterogeneity throughout the population. In Section 3, we derive a set of exact aggregation conditions such that asset pricing relations can be written as a function of a small set of summary variables, namely, per capita consumption and some composites of individual characteristics.

1.6. CAPM and APT

The asset pricing relations that we described above are derived from a general equilibrium framework. In the empirical finance literature, asset pricing relations have typically been modeled using a partial equilibrium approach based on the risk-return relationship implied by the static capital asset pricing model (CAPM) of Sharpe [303], Lintner [229], and others or the factor structure imposed by the arbitrage pricing theory (APT) proposed by Ross [284]. Here we describe briefly these alternative asset pricing frameworks.

1.6.1. The Capital Asset Pricing Model

The CAPM is essentially a static model that describes asset returns in terms of a risk-return relationship. This relationship can be derived under alternative sets of sufficient conditions. Here we consider a simple derivation of this model that relies on assuming that the utility function is quadratic.

Suppose that there are N securities where securities $1, \ldots, N-1$ are risky and security N is risk-free. Also suppose that there are I different investors, each with initial wealth W_0^i, who maximize the expected value of utility from end-of-period wealth $W_s^i = \sum_{j=1}^{N} z_j^i d_{j,s}$ by choosing the portfolio $z^i = (z_1^i, \ldots, z_N^i)$. Let the payoff on security j in state s be denoted $d_{j,s}$ and let the price in the current period for security j be denoted q_j. Investor i solves

$$
\max_{\{z_j^i\}_{j=1}^{N}} E\left[U\left(\sum_{j=1}^{N} z_j^i d_{j,s} \right) \right] \quad \text{s.t.} \quad \sum_{j=1}^{N} q_j z_j^i \leq W_0^i.
$$

Define $R_{j,s} \equiv d_{j,s}/q_j$ as the return on security j. The first-order conditions can be expressed as:

$$
E\left[U'\left(\sum_{j=1}^{N} z_j^i d_{j,s} \right) (R_{l,s} - R_N) \right] = 0, \quad l = 1, \ldots, N-1. \tag{1.22}
$$

Now assume that utility is quadratic or $U(c) = c^2/2$ and define $h_j^i \equiv (z_j^i q_j)/W_0^i$; then Equation (1.22) can be expressed as

$$
E\left[W_0^i \left(\sum_{j=1}^{N} h_j^i R_{j,s} \right) (R_{l,s} - R_1) \right] = 0. \tag{1.23}
$$

Divide both sides of Equation (1.23) by W_0^i and sum over the investors $i = 1, \ldots, I$. Let the return on the *market portfolio* be defined as:

$$R_m \equiv \sum_{i=1}^{I} \sum_{j=1}^{N} h_j^i R_{j,s}.$$

for each s

(handwritten: $\frac{1}{\sum_{i=1}^{I}} E\left[\left(\sum_{j=1}^{N} h_j^i R_{js}\right) \cdot (R_{ls} - R_N)\right]$)

(handwritten: $E[R_{ms}(R_{ls} - R_N)]$)

Using the covariance decomposition, the first-order conditions can be rewritten as: *(handwritten: $Cov(x \cdot y) = E[xy] - E[x] \cdot E[y]$)*

$$\mathrm{Cov}(R_{m,s}, R_{l,s} - R_1) = -E(R_{m,s})E(R_{l,s} - R_1) \tag{1.24}$$

for $l = 1, \ldots, N - 1$. One of our securities can be defined as the market portfolio, in which case Equation (1.24) becomes $\mathrm{Cov}(R_{m,s}, R_{m,s} - R_1) = -E(R_{m,s})E(R_{m,s} - R_1)$ so that

$$E(R_{m,s} - R_1) = -\mathrm{Var}(R_{m,s})/E(R_{m,s}). \tag{1.25}$$

We are now in a position to define the β-coefficient of a security and provide an interpretation of that coefficient. Define β_j as:

$$\beta_j \equiv \mathrm{Cov}(R_{m,s}, R_{j,s})/\mathrm{Var}(R_{m,s}).$$

(handwritten: $E[R_{ls} - R_1] = \frac{Cov(R_{ms}, R_{ls} - R_1)}{-E[R_{ms}]}$)

We can use this definition and substitute Equation (1.25) in Equation (1.24) to express the expected excess return on security l as:

$$E(R_{l,s} - R_1) = \beta_l E(R_{m,s} - R_1). \tag{1.26}$$

(handwritten: $= -\beta \frac{Var[R_{ms}]}{E[R_{ms}]}$)
(handwritten: $= -\frac{Cov(R_{ms}, R_{ls})}{E[R_{ms}]} \downarrow 1.25$)
(handwritten: $= \beta E[R_{ms} - R_1]$)

This says that the expected excess return on the security is proportional to the covariance of the excess return with the end-of-period wealth or equivalently, the market portfolio. Since the expected return depends on the risk-free rate and the return on the market portfolio, this model is known as the two-factor CAPM. Although the CAPM is widely used in the empirical finance literature to describe asset returns, it has been criticized on the grounds that the return on the market portfolio is not observable. (See Roll [282].)

1.6.2.   Arbitrage Pricing Theory

The arbitrage pricing theory (APT) proposed by Ross [284] assumes that the excess returns on assets that are in net zero supply or that are claims to the dividends of N technologies have the factor structure:

$$R_{i,s} = \bar{R}_i + \sum_{k=1}^{K} \beta_{i,k}\delta_{k,s} + \epsilon_{i,s}, \quad i = 1, \ldots, N, \tag{1.27}$$

where $R_{i,s}$ denotes the return on the i'th security in state s, $\delta_{k,s}$ is systematic risk from factor k, $\epsilon_{i,s}$ is unsystematic or idiosyncratic risk specific to asset i, and $\bar{R}_i$ and $\beta_{i,k}$ are constants. We assume that $E(\delta_{k,s}) = 0$, $E(\epsilon_{i,s}) = 0$, $\mathrm{Var}(\delta_{k,s}) = \sigma_k^2$, and $\mathrm{Var}(\epsilon_{i,s}) = \sigma_i^2$ for each k and i so that the random variables denoting systematic and idiosyncratic risk have mean zero and finite variance and they are mutually uncorrelated so that $E(\epsilon_{i,s}\delta_{k,s}) = 0$ for each k and i. Finally, the idiosyncratic risks $\epsilon_{1,s}, \ldots, \epsilon_{N,s}$ are mutually independent. The notion behind the APT is that asset returns can be explained in terms of a small number of factors so that $K < N$.

Notice that $\bar{R}_i$ is the expected return on asset i. Let the N'th security be the risk-free security so that $R_{1,s} = \bar{R}_1$ for all s. If we substitute the expression for returns into Equation (1.22), we have

$$E\left[U'(W_s)\left(\bar{R}_i + \sum_{k=1}^{K} \beta_{i,k}\delta_{k,s} + \epsilon_{i,s} - \bar{R}_1\right)\right] = 0,$$

where $W_s \equiv \sum_{j=1}^{N} z_j^i d_{j,s}$. This can be rewritten as:

$$\bar{R}_i - \bar{R}_1 = \sum_{k=1}^{K}\left\{\frac{E[-U'(W_s)\delta_{k,s}]}{E[U'(W_s)]}\right\}\beta_{i,k} + \frac{E[-U'(W_s)\epsilon_{i,s}]}{E[U'(W_s)]}. \tag{1.28}$$

If all diversifiable risk is eliminated, then the $\epsilon_{i,s}$ term drops out. The excess return on any asset i relative to the risk-free rate is linear in the factor loadings, $\beta_{i,k}$, $k = 1, \ldots, K$. Ross [284] shows that these results can also be derived from no-arbitrage arguments.

2.   Risk Aversion

In an environment under uncertainty, consumer preferences reflect their attitudes toward risk. These attitudes affect equilibrium asset prices and the nature of the equilibrium allocation. In this section, we provide some measures of risk aversion and show their relationship to consumers' optimal portfolio choices. We also discuss such concepts of increasing risk as stochastic dominance and a mean-preserving spread, which make precise the idea that a given situation under uncertainty is more risky relative to another.

2.1.   Measures of Risk Aversion

We say that a consumer is strictly risk averse if she is unwilling to accept an actuarially fair gamble. As an example, an actuarially fair gamble is a random variable $\tilde{\epsilon}$ that has a positive return ϵ_1 with probability p and a negative return ϵ_2 with probability $(1 - p)$ and satisfies $E\tilde{\epsilon} = p\epsilon_1 + (1 - p)\epsilon_2 = 0$, which requires that $p/(1 - p) = -\epsilon_2/\epsilon_1$. Suppose that the consumer has a strictly increasing and strictly concave utility function U defined on wealth W. Using the definition of the actuarially fair gamble, the expected utility of receiving W plus the expected value of an actuarially fair gamble is:

$$U[W + E(\tilde{\epsilon})] = U[W + p\epsilon_1 + (1 - p)\epsilon_2].$$

When the consumer is risk averse, the utility of receiving the sure thing $W + E(\tilde{\epsilon})$ is greater than the utility of receiving $W + \epsilon_1$ with probability p and $W + \epsilon_2$ with probability $1 - p$:

$$U[W + E(\tilde{\epsilon})] > pU(W + \epsilon_1) + (1 - p)U(W + \epsilon_2). \tag{1.29}$$

Under the assumption that the utility function has only one argument, strict risk aversion implies that the utility function is strictly concave.

We can use Jensen's Inequality to show that concavity of the utility function implies risk aversion. Jensen's Inequality states that for a random variable x with mean $E(x)$ and a convex (concave) function $g(\cdot)$, $E[g(x)] > g[E(x)]$ $(E[g(x)] < g[E(x)])$. Because U is concave, it follows that

$$E[U(W + \tilde{\epsilon})] < U[W + E(\tilde{\epsilon})] = U(W). \tag{1.30}$$

Hence, under the assumption that utility is a function of a single argument, strict concavity implies that the agent is risk averse, using Jensen's Inequality.

We now study some measures of risk aversion. Let W_s denote the consumer's wealth if state s occurs and define $\tilde{\epsilon} \equiv W_s - E(W_s)$ as the difference between the realized and expected value of wealth W_s. Implicitly define $\rho > 0$ by $U[E(W_s) - \rho] = E[U(W_s)]$. Intuitively, ρ measures the amount by which certain wealth must be decreased to attain the same expected utility when wealth is risky. Expand both sides of the equation around $E(W_s)$ to result in

$$U[E(W_s) - \rho] \simeq U[E(W_s)] - \rho U'[E(W_s)]$$

and

$$E[U(W_s)] \simeq E\{U[E(W_s)] + \tilde{\epsilon}U'[E(W_s)] + \frac{1}{2}\tilde{\epsilon}^2 U''[E(W_s)]\}.$$

Setting these approximations equal and solving for ρ, we have

$$\rho = \frac{1}{2}\mathrm{Var}(\tilde{\epsilon})\left(-\frac{U''[E(W_s)]}{U'[E(W_s)]}\right).$$

We can define the concept of *absolute risk aversion* using the function:

$$\mathcal{A}(W) \equiv -U''(W)/U'(W). \tag{1.31}$$

For U concave and increasing, $\mathcal{A}(W) \geq 0$. For small risks, ρ measures the intensity of an agent's dislike for risk. Absolute risk aversion is decreasing if $\mathcal{A}'(W) < 0$, constant if $\mathcal{A}'(W) = 0$, and increasing if $\mathcal{A}'(W) > 0$, where the sign is determined by the sign of $[(U'')^2 - U'''U']$. When $\mathcal{A}'(W) < 0$ so that $U''' > 0$, the implication is that as an agent's wealth increases, her aversion to risk decreases which is intuitively plausible. This is a measure that was first defined by Arrow [17]. The properties of the coefficient of absolute risk aversion are described by Pratt [275].

Another measure of risk aversion is provided by relative risk aversion, which considers risk as a proportion of assets or wealth. We define the coefficient of *relative risk aversion* by the function:

$$\mathcal{R}(W) \equiv -U''(W)W/U'(W). \tag{1.32}$$

We can derive this function using the same steps described above by considering risks $\tilde{\epsilon}$ that are measured as a proportion of assets.

We now demonstrate the effects of risk aversion on a consumer's optimal portfolio choices. For this purpose, we consider an economy with two dates and S states at each date. The consumer can allocate her present wealth denoted W_0 among present consumption, a risk-free security, and a risky security. The risk-free security has the rate of return r^f and the risky security has the rate of return r_s if the state s is realized. Let α denote the proportion of initial wealth net of consumption allocated to the risk-free security and $1 - \alpha$ the proportion allocated to the risky security. Notice that wealth in state s is defined by $W_s = (W_0 - c_0)[1 + \alpha r^f + (1 - \alpha)r_s]$.

The consumer has expected utility preferences, $U(c_0) + E[V(W_s)]$, so that utility is additively separable over consumption and future wealth. We assume that U and V are strictly increasing and strictly concave. We denote by $\pi_s > 0$ the probability that the consumer attaches to the occurrence of state s. Substituting for W_s in preferences, notice that the necessary and sufficient conditions for an optimum include the conditions:

$$U'(c_0) = (1 + r^f)\sum_{s=1}^{S}\pi_s V'(W_s), \tag{1.33}$$

$$\sum_{s=1}^{S} \pi_s V'(W_s)(r_s - r^f) = 0. \tag{1.34}$$

Suppose the expected return on the risky securities equals the return on the risk-free security, $E(r_s) = r^f$. In this case, will the risk-averse consumer hold both assets? Notice that $E(W_s) = (W_0 - c_0)(1 + r^f)$, which is equal to the second period wealth when the consumer holds only the risk-free security. From Jensen's Inequality, the strict concavity of V implies that $V[E(W_s)] > E[V(W_s)]$ so that the agent will hold only the risk-free security if $r^f = E(r_s)$. For the consumer to hold willingly both assets, it must be the case that $E(r_s) - r^f > 0$. The quantity $E(r_s) - r^f$ is called the *risk premium* because it provides a measure of the compensation that a risk-averse agent requires to hold the risky asset.

We can relate the risk premium to the measure of absolute risk aversion that we defined earlier. Define $S_0 \equiv W_0 - c_0$ and recall that $E(W_s) = S_0[1 + r^f + (1 - \alpha)(E(r_s) - r^f)]$. As before, $\rho > 0$ is implicitly defined by:

$$V\{S_0[1 + r^f + (1 - \alpha)(E(r_s) - r^f)] - \rho\} =$$
$$EV\{S_0[1 + r^f + (1 - \alpha)(r_s - r^f)]\}.$$

If we expand both sides of this equation around $E(W_s)$, we can show that the properties of an agent's absolute risk aversion determine whether the risky security is a normal or an inferior good. When utility is a function of one argument, Pratt [275] and Sandmo [296] show that decreasing absolute risk aversion is a sufficient condition for the risky asset to be a normal good. As noted above, the sign of absolute risk aversion depends on the sign of the third derivative of utility, which determines whether marginal utility is concave or convex. The concavity or convexity of marginal utility has also been studied by Kimball [218] who defines a measure of "prudence" which shows how precautionary savings varies as wealth increases.

2.2.   Measures of Increasing Risk

We now turn to a discussion of some concepts of increasing risk. The first concept is first-order stochastic dominance (FSD). Consider a family of distribution functions $F(x, \theta)$ where x is a random variable $x : \Omega \to X$ where $X \equiv [\underline{x}, \bar{x}]$ and θ is a parameter. Suppose that $\theta_2 > \theta_1$ and that $F(x, \theta_2)$ is derived from $F(x, \theta_1)$ such that

$$F(\underline{x}, \theta_1) \quad = \quad F(\underline{x}, \theta_2) = 0, \tag{1.35}$$

$$F(\bar{x}, \theta_1) \;=\; F(\bar{x}, \theta_2) = 1, \tag{1.36}$$

$$F(x, \theta_2) \;\leq\; F(x, \theta_1), \tag{1.37}$$

for all $x \in X$. Then $F(x, \theta_2)$ is said to have *first-order stochastic dominance* over $F(x, \theta_1)$.

A second concept of increasing risk is a mean-preserving spread, which describes an increase in the riskiness of a random variable, holding its mean constant. We consider the family of distribution functions $F(x, \theta)$ indexed by the parameter θ defined earlier and suppose that $F(x, \theta_2)$ is derived from $F(x, \theta_1)$ by taking probability mass from the center of the distribution and shifting it to the tails in such a way that the mean is unchanged. Intuitively, $F(x, \theta_2)$ represents a riskier situation than $F(x, \theta_1)$.

A *mean-preserving spread* satisfies two conditions:

$$\int_X [F(x, \theta_2) - F(x, \theta_1)] dx = 0, \tag{1.38}$$

which ensures that the processes have the same mean, and there exists an $\hat{x}$ such that

$$F(x, \theta_2) - F(x, \theta_1) \leq (\geq) 0 \quad \text{when} \quad x \geq (\leq) \hat{x}, \tag{1.39}$$

which ensures that the two distributions cross only once. For "small" changes in riskiness, the conditions are summarized by:

$$\int_X F_\theta(x, \theta) dx \;=\; 0, \tag{1.40}$$

$$T(y, \theta) = \int_{\bar{x}}^{y} F_\theta(x, \theta) dx \;\geq\; 0 \quad \text{for} \quad \underline{x} \leq y \leq \bar{x}, \tag{1.41}$$

where $F_\theta(x, \theta)$ is the derivative of the probability distribution function with respect to the parameter θ. A mean-preserving increase in risk is defined and applied by Rothschild and Stiglitz [287, 288]. The effects of a mean-preserving spread on the behavior of risk averse consumers is discussed by Diamond and Stiglitz [93].

Now consider the effect of an increase in the random variable θ that satisfies the conditions for first-order stochastic dominance (FSD). We consider the problem of a consumer who lives for two periods and starts the initial period with wealth W_0 and receives no exogenous wealth in the second period. All consumption in the second period is financed by savings, which pays a random return $\tilde{r}$ that takes values on $R \equiv [\underline{r}, \bar{r}]$ where $\underline{r} > 0$ and $\bar{r} < \infty$, and has a probability distribution function

$F(r, \theta)$ parameterized by θ. The associated probability density function is denoted $f(r, \theta)$. The consumer solves the problem:

$$\max_{c_0} \left\{ U(c_0) + \int_R V[(W_0 - c_0)(1 + r)] f(r, \theta) dr \right\}. \tag{1.42}$$

where the budget constraint $c_1 = S_0(1 + r)$ with $S_0 = W_0 - c_0$ has already been substituted into the objective function. Assume that U and V are increasing and strictly concave. The first-order condition is

$$0 = U'(c_0) - \int_R V'(c_1)(1 + r) f(r, \theta) dr \tag{1.43}$$

Notice that $U'(c_0)$ is strictly decreasing and that $-V'(c_1)$ is strictly decreasing in c_0 so that there is a solution to this equation, $c_0^* \equiv c^*(W_0, \theta)$.

   To start, implicitly differentiate Equation (1.43) with respect to θ and solve for $\partial c^* / \partial \theta$ to result in

$$\frac{\partial c^*(W_0, \theta)}{\partial \theta} = -\frac{\int_R V'(c_1)(1 + r) f_\theta(r, \theta) dr}{U''(c_0) + E[V''(c_1)(1 + r)]}. \tag{1.44}$$

We are assuming that the probility density function is differentiable in the parameter θ. The denominator of the right side is negative so that the sign of the left side is the same as the sign of the numerator on the right side. Using integration by parts on the numerator, we have

$$\int_R V'(c_1)(1 + r) f_\theta(r, \theta) dr = V'(c_1)(1 + r) F_\theta(r, \theta) \mid_{\underline{r}}^{\bar{r}}$$

$$- \int_R [V''(c_1)c_1 + V'(c_1)] F_\theta(r, \theta) dr$$

$$= - \int_R [V''(c_1)c_1 + V'(c_1)] F_\theta(r, \theta) dr,$$

where $F_\theta(r, \theta)$ is the derivative of the probability distribution function for $\tilde{r}$ with respect to the parameter θ. Notice that $F_\theta(\bar{r}, \theta) = F_\theta(\underline{r}, \theta) = 0$ by Equations (1.35) and (1.36). Hence the sign depends on the sign of $V''(c_1)c_1 + V'(c_1)$, which can be expressed as $V'(c_1)[V''(c_1)c_1/V'(c_1) + 1]$. We can use the coefficient of relative risk aversion to express this as:

$$V''(c_1)c_1 + V'(c_1) = -V'(c_1)[\mathcal{R}(c) - 1].$$

Hence the effect of a parametric change that displays FSD on first-period consumption depends on the size of the coefficient of relative risk aversion. If relative risk aversion is less than one, then current consumption increases while it remains unchanged when relative risk aversion is equal to 1. Finally, current consumption decreases when relative risk aversion is greater than 1.

3.   Aggregation

In the financial economics literature, Rubinstein [290] has shown that
there exist some sets of homogeneity conditions on individual beliefs,
preferences, and wealth such that the asset pricing relations depend on
per capita consumption and some composites of individual characteristics. These exact aggregation conditions are derived for the hyperbolic
absolute risk aversion (HARA) class of preferences and constitute the
basis for many of the recent tests of asset pricing relations such as Euler
equation-based tests that we describe in later chapters.[3]

We now describe these aggregation results for a two-period economy
with a finite number of states but they are valid under more general
circumstances. There are two dates: $t = 0$ and $t = 1$. At date 0, the
state is known with certainty. At date 1, any one of $\{1, \ldots, S\}$ possible
sets can occur. Each individual has a positive amount of wealth W_0^i at
date 0 that she can allocate among present consumption c_0^i or to S state-
contingent securities. Define the price of a contingent claims contract
that pays off if state s occurs by p_s. We can write the consumer's budget
constraint as

$$W_0^i = c_0^i + \sum_{s=1}^{S} p_s W_s^i,$$

which is the standard formulation with complete markets.

The agent has expected utility preferences with $u_i(c_0^i, W_s^i) = U_i(c_0^i) +
\beta_i V_i(W_s^i)$ so that utility is additively separable over consumption and
future wealth and $0 < \beta_i < 1$. We assume that U_i and V_i are strictly
increasing and strictly concave. We specifically assume that they are
from the hyperbolic absolute risk aversion (HARA) class. The HARA
class of preferences is given by:

$$\frac{-U'(c)}{U''(c)} = A + Bc, \tag{1.45}$$

where A and B are fixed parameters. This equation has the following
solutions depending on the value of B:

$$U(c) \quad \sim \quad \frac{b}{1-b}(A + Bc)^{1-b}, \quad B \neq 0, 1, \tag{1.46}$$

$$U(c) \quad \sim \quad \log(A + c), \quad B = 1, \tag{1.47}$$

$$U(c) \quad \sim \quad -A \exp(-c/A), \quad B = 0, \tag{1.48}$$

---

[3]Earlier results on the specification of preferences that admit exact aggregation to
a representative consumer are due to Gorman [155].

where $b = B^{-1}$ and $\sim$ means "is equivalent up to an increasing linear transformation to." This class of preferences contains as special cases: constant absolute risk aversion ($B = 0$), the constant relative risk aversion ($A = 0$), quadratic utility ($B = -1$), and higher order polynomial utility ($B = -1/2, -1/3, \ldots$).

We denote by $\pi_{s,i}$ the subjective probability that an agent attaches to the occurrence of state s. Now the consumer solves:

$$\max_{c_0^i, \{W_s^i\}} \left\{ U_i(c_0^i) + \beta_i \sum_{s=1}^{S} \pi_{s,i} V_i(W_s^i) - \lambda \left[c_0^i + \sum_{s=1}^{S} p_s W_s^i - W_0^i \right] \right\},$$

where λ is a Lagrange multiplier. The necessary and sufficient conditions for an optimum are:

$$U_i'(c_0^i) = (\beta_i \pi_{s,i}/p_s) V_i'(W_s^i) \quad \text{for all } s, \tag{1.49}$$

$$W_0^i = c_0^i + \sum_{s=1}^{S} p_s W_s^i. \tag{1.50}$$

The market-clearing conditions are $\bar{c}_0 = \sum_{i=1}^{I} c_0^i$ and $\bar{W}_s = \sum_{i=1}^{I} W_s^i$.

The next result yields sufficient results to evaluate the first-order conditions described by Equations (1.49) and (1.50) in terms of the consumption and wealth of some average consumer who has a composite of the characteristics and resources of all the consumers in the economy. These are exact aggregation conditions that are derived by aggregating the first-order conditions for all individuals in the economy. Notice that if individuals are alike in all respects in terms of their tastes, beliefs, and resources, then their equilibrium behavior is identical so that $c_0^i = c_0$ and $W_s^i = W_s$ for all $i = 1, \ldots, I$. Thus, the conditions in Equations (1.49) and (1.50) are trivially satisfied at the average allocation $c_0 \equiv \bar{c}_0/I$ and $W_s \equiv \bar{W}_s/I$. The following theorem which is based on Rubinstein [290, pp. 232–233] shows that there are more interesting conditions under which this result holds. We present this theorem to show explicitly the difference between the average or representative consumer derived in this section and the composite consumer that we constructed earlier.

Theorem 1.2 (*Aggregation*) *Consider the following sets of homogeneity conditions:*

o. (Identical individuals) All individuals have the same resources W_0, beliefs $\{\pi_s\}$, and tastes (β, U, V).

i. (Generalized power and logarithmic utility) All individuals have the same beliefs $\{\pi_s\}$, rate of patience β, and taste parameter $B \neq 0$.

ii. (Exponential utility) All individuals have the same taste parameter $B = 0$.

iii. (Generalized logarithmic utility) All individuals have the same resources W_0 and tastes (β, A, B) where $B = 1$.

Equilibrium prices are determined by

$$U'(c_0) = (\beta\pi_s/p_s)V'(W_s) \quad \text{for all } s, \tag{1.51}$$

where $c_0 \equiv \bar{c}_0/I$ and $W_s \equiv \bar{W}_s/I$. Define $\bar{A} \equiv \sum_i A_i$. For economy (i) $A \equiv \bar{A}/I$; for economy (ii)

$$A \equiv \bar{A}/I, \quad \beta \equiv \prod_i \beta_i^{A_i/\bar{A}}, \quad \pi_s \equiv \prod_i \pi_{s,i}^{A_i/\bar{A}};$$

and economy (iii) $\pi_s \equiv \sum_i \pi_{s,i}/I$.

PROOF

o. Described in the text.

i. When $B \neq 0$, $U_i'(c_0^i) = (A_i + Bc_0^i)^{-b}$ and $V_i'(W^i) = (A_i + BW_s^i)^{-b}$ so that the first-order condition in Equation (1.49) is given by $(A_i+Bc_0^i)^{-b} = (\beta\pi_s/p_s)(A_i + BW_s^i)^{-b}$, or

$$A_i + Bc_0^i = (\beta\pi_s/p_s)^{-B}(A_i + BW_s^i).$$

Summing over all individuals

$$\sum_i (A_i + Bc_0^i) = (\beta\pi_s/p_s)^{-B} \sum_i (A_i + BW_s^i).$$

Using the market-clearing conditions for consumption and future wealth and dividing by I yields

$$(A + Bc_0)^{-b} = (\beta\pi_s/p_s)(A + BW_s)^{-b} \quad \text{for all } s, \tag{1.52}$$

where $c_0 \equiv \bar{c}_0/I$, $W_s \equiv \bar{W}_s/I$ and $A \equiv \sum_i A_i/I$. Summing Equation (1.50) and using the market-clearing conditions yields

$$W_0 = c_0 + \sum_{s=1}^{S} p_s W_s, \tag{1.53}$$

where $W_0 \equiv \bar{W}_0/I \equiv \sum_i W_0^i/I$. Notice that Equations (1.52) and (1.53) are the necessary and sufficient conditions for the optimum of a hypothetical consumer with the specified composite resources, beliefs and tastes.

ii. When $B = 0$, $U'_i(c^i_0) = \exp(-c^i_0/A_i)$ and $V'_i(W^i_s) = \exp(-W^i_s/A_i)$ so that from Equation (1.49), $\exp(-c^i_0/A_i) = (\beta_i \pi_{s,i}/p_s)\exp(-W^i_s/A_i)$ which implies that

$$-c^i_0 = -A_i \log(p_s) + A_i \log(\beta_i) + A_i \log(\pi_{s,i}) - W^i_s.$$

Summing over all individuals yields

$$-\sum_i c^i_0 = -\sum_i A_i \log(p_s) + \log\left(\prod_i \beta_i^{A_i}\right) + \log\left(\prod_i \pi_{s,i}^{A_i}\right) - \sum_i W^i_s.$$

Using the market-clearing conditions and dividing by I implies

$$c_0 = -A \log(p_s) + \log\left(\prod_i \beta_i^{A_i/I}\right) + \log\left(\prod_i \pi_{s,i}^{A_i/I}\right) - W_s$$

where $c_0 \equiv \bar{c}_0/I$, $W_s \equiv \bar{W}_s/I$ and $A = \sum_i A_i/I$. Dividing by A and defining

$$\beta \equiv \prod_i \beta_i^{A_i/\bar{A}} \quad \text{and} \quad \pi_s \equiv \prod_i \pi_{s,i}^{A_i/\bar{A}}$$

yields

$$\exp(-c_0/A) = (\beta \pi_s/p_s)\exp(-W_s/A). \tag{1.54}$$

The market-clearing conditions yield

$$W_0 = c_0 + \sum_{s=1}^{S} p_s W_s \tag{1.55}$$

where $W_0 \equiv \bar{W}_0/I$. Now Equations (1.54) and (1.55) are the necessary and sufficient conditions for the optimum of a hypothetical consumer with the specified composite resources, beliefs, and tastes.

iii. When $B = 1$, $U'_i(c^i_0) = (A + c^i_0)^{-1}$ and $V'_i(W^i_s) = (A + W^i_s)^{-1}$. Then Equation (1.49) becomes

$$A + W^i_s = (\beta \pi_{s,i}/p_s)(A + c^i_0).$$

Summing over states and using the constraint in Equation (1.50) yields an expression for the consumption of individual i as:

$$c^i_0 = (1 + \beta)^{-1}\left[A \sum_{s=1}^{S} p_s - A\beta + W_0\right].$$

Notice that this expression does not depend on i; therefore, $c_0^i = c_0 \equiv \bar{c}_0/I$. Using this in the first-order condition and summing over I yields

$$IA + \sum_i W_s^i = \left(\beta \sum_i \pi_{s,i}/p_s\right)(A + c_0).$$

Dividing by I and using the market-clearing yields

$$A + W_s = (\beta\pi_s/p_s)(A + c_0), \tag{1.56}$$

where $W_s \equiv \bar{W}_s/I$ and $\pi_s \equiv \sum_i \pi_{s,i}/I$. Using the market-clearing condition in Equation (1.50) yields

$$W_0 = c_0 + \sum_{s=1}^{S} p_s W_s. \tag{1.57}$$

As before, Equations (1.56) and (1.57) are the necessary and sufficient conditions for the optimum of a hypothetical consumer with the specified resources, beliefs, and tastes. ∎

4.   Risk-Sharing

In the previous sections, we described some of the implications of the complete contingent claims equilibrium for asset pricing. We now describe its implications for the behavior of individual consumption in a heterogeneous population.

Returning to Section 1.2, notice that Equation (1.14) can be written as:

$$\frac{\pi_s^i V_i'(c_s^i)}{\lambda_i} = p_s, \quad s \in \{1,\dots,S\}, \tag{1.58}$$

where λ_i is the individual-specific Lagrange multiplier on the budget constraint. This condition says that the weighted marginal utility of consumption is equated across consumers. We refer to this feature of the complete contingent claims equilibrium as *complete risk-sharing* or *full insurance*. Wilson [342] was one of the first to note that optimal sharing of risk by members of a risk-averse group is equivalent to the existence of a set of individual-specific weights such that individuals' marginal utility satisfies a version of Equation (1.58).[4]

---

[4]See Wilson [342, pp. 123-24].

We can rewrite Equation (1.58) in an equivalent manner:

$$\frac{\pi_k^i V_i'(c_k^i)}{\pi_l^i V_i'(c_l^i)} = \frac{p_k}{p_l}. \tag{1.59}$$

This says that the marginal rate of substitution of consumption for any two states k and l multiplied by the ratio of probabilities for those states is equated to the ratio of the contingent claims prices. Suppose that the state of the economy $s = k$ is defined to include realizations of shocks that only affect the preferences or opportunities for a given individual i. Then the condition in Equation (1.59) says that an individual can purchase claims that pay off for each possible realization of such idiosyncratic shocks so that she cannot increase her utility by substituting consumption across different states.

In an intertemporal context, one of the most widely studied models of individual behavior is the *permanent-income hypothesis* postulated by Friedman [137]. This says that individuals determine their consumption as a function of their permanent income or wealth. The implications of this hypothesis have been frequently taken to mean that changes in individual consumption should be independent of changes in current income. To determine the conditions under which this result holds, suppose that individuals' utility function is given by $U_i(c_0^i) = -A_i \exp[-(c_0^i - \theta_0^i)/A_i]$ and $V_i(c_s^i) = -A_i \exp[-(c_s^i - \theta_s^i)/A_i]$ where θ_0^i and θ_s^i are preference shifters. Also assume that individuals have the same beliefs, $\pi_s^i = \pi_s$. Then Equation (1.58) implies

$$\exp[-(c_s^i - \theta_s^i)/A_i] = \lambda_i p_s/\pi_s.$$

Taking logarithms implies

$$-(c_s^i - \theta_s^i) = A_i \log(\lambda_i) + A_i \log(p_s) - A_i \log(\pi_s). \tag{1.60}$$

We can aggregate this condition over all individuals in the economy as

$$-(c_s - \theta_s) = \log\left(\prod_{i=1}^I \lambda_i^{A_i/I}\right) + A \log(p_s) - A \log(\pi_s), \tag{1.61}$$

where $A \equiv \sum_i A_i/I$, $c_s \equiv \sum_i c_s^i/I$ and $\theta_s \equiv \sum_i \theta_s^i/I$. Define $\lambda \equiv \log\left(\prod_i \lambda_i^{A_i/I}\right)$ and subtract Equation (1.61) from Equation (1.60):

$$c_s^i - c_s = (A_i - A)\log(\pi_s) - (A_i - A)\log(p_s)$$

$$-[\log(\lambda_i^{A_i}) - \lambda] + (\theta_s^i - \theta_s). \tag{1.62}$$

Now suppose $A_i = A$ for all i. Then notice that the terms involving $\log(p_s)$ and $\log(\pi_s)$ all drop out so that individual consumption varies one-to-one with aggregate consumption and two other terms involving individuals' marginal utilities of wealth, λ_i, and idiosyncratic taste parameters, θ_s^i. In a multiperiod context, an implication of the above representations is that changes in consumption, $c_t^i - c_{t-1}^i$, should be independent of changes in endowments, $\omega_t^i - \omega_{t-1}^i$. Another implication is that, at the aggregate level, if there is *ex ante* heterogeneity among consumers, individual consumption for a complete contingent claims equilibrium can vary over time even if there are no aggregate shocks and all idiosyncratic risk is insured against.

What are some situations in which the optimal risk-sharing arrangements described by Equation (1.58) break down? When markets are incomplete, there do not exist claims that pay off for each possible state of the world. In this case, consumers do not face a single budget constraint. Instead they face a set of budget constraints, one for each state (and date) of the world. As a result, marginal rates of substitution in consumption across different states are not equated across consumers and full insurance does not occur.

Private information considerations are typically given as the rationale for market incompleteness and the absence of full insurance opportunities. Individuals may have private information about their characteristics, which can give rise to adverse selection due to asymmetric information. Alternatively, the private actions of individuals may affect the probability distribution of future outcomes. This is known as moral hazard arising from the unobservability of actions and it is commonly assumed to characterize delegated decision making, labor contracting, and insurance markets. In this case, it is not possible to issue claims that pay off in each possible state of the world because such payments cannot be enforced. Thus, markets are incomplete and the optimal risk-sharing rule defined by Equation (1.58) no longer holds. Typically, the second-best risk-sharing rule implies that some risk must be imposed on the privately informed party to ensure that she will undertake the right action.

We discuss tests of risk-sharing in Chapter 7. In that chapter, we also study private information models and discuss the determination of the second-best risk-sharing rule in the context of the principal-agent problem.

5. Dynamic Programming

In the previous sections, we described the implications of static or simple two-period optimization and equilibrium frameworks. In this section, we introduce dynamic programming methods that allow us to formulate infinite-horizon dynamic optimization and dynamic equilibrium problems using a recursive approach.

5.1. A Consumption and Savings Problem

We consider a simple savings and consumption decision problem for this purpose. We now assume the agent lives for an infinite number of periods and has preferences over sequences of consumption $\{c_t\}_{t=0}^{\infty}$ given by:

$$E_0 \left\{ \sum_{t=0}^{\infty} \beta^t U(c_t) \right\}, \quad 0 < \beta < 1, \tag{1.63}$$

where β is the discount factor, $E_0(\cdot)$ denotes expectation conditional on information available at date zero, and the utility function $U : \mathbb{R}_+ \to \mathbb{R}$ is bounded, strictly increasing, strictly concave, and continuously differentiable with $\lim_{c \to 0} U'(c) = \infty$.

At the beginning of period t, the agent has wealth W_t that can be allocated between consumption c_t or savings A_t. Suppose that the return to savings is a random variable that takes on a discrete set of values, $r_t \in R \equiv \{r_1, \ldots, r_S\}$ for each t. Define the *transition probability* or the probability that the return next period is r_j when the return today is r_i by:

$$\pi_{i,j} \equiv \Pr(r_{t+1} = r_j | r_t = r_i), \quad i, j = 1, \ldots, S. \tag{1.64}$$

Notice that the only information at time t that is useful for forecasting the random return next period is the current return. According to this formulation, the random variable r_t evolves as a discrete first-order Markov chain with range $\{r_j\}$ and transition probabilities $\pi_{i,j}$.

Suppose the consumer chooses savings equal to A_t at the beginning of period t. The amount of wealth available for spending on consumption and savings next period is $W_{t+1} = A_t(1 + r_{t+1})$, where $r_{t+1} \in R$ is the return in period $t+1$. The consumer chooses sequences for consumption and savings to maximize Equation (1.63) subject to a sequence of budget constraints and the law of motion for wealth. We first formulate this problem as an infinite-horizon dynamic optimization problem.

Consider the problem:

$$\sup_{\{c_t, A_t\}_{t=0}^{\infty}} E_0 \left\{ \sum_{t=0}^{\infty} \beta^t U(c_t) \right\}, \tag{1.65}$$

subject to

$$A_t + c_t \;\; \leq \;\; W_t, \tag{1.66}$$

$$W_{t+1} \;\; = \;\; (1 + r_{t+1})A_t, \tag{1.67}$$

$$c_t \geq 0, \, A_t \geq 0, \tag{1.68}$$

given the initial conditions W_0 and r_0. In this expression, sup denotes supremum (to allow for the fact that a maximum may not exist) and the expectation in Equation (1.65), which is conditional on the realization of the return at date zero, is evaluated using the transition probabilities in Equation (1.64).

Suppose we could solve the problem described by Equations (1.65) through (1.68) for all possible values of W_0 and r_0. Then we could define a function $V : \mathbb{R}_+ \times R \to : \mathbb{R}$ by taking $V(W_0, r_0)$ as the maximized value of the objective function (Equation 1.65), for each $W_0 > 0$ and given the initial return r_0. The function V is known as the *value function*. If the function V were known, we could evaluate the maximum utility that can be attained with initial wealth W_1 and the initial return r_1 by $V(W_1, r_1)$. Define the set of feasible consumption and savings allocations at time 0 by $\Gamma(W_0) \equiv \{c_0, A_0 : c_0 \geq 0, A_0 \geq 0, A_0 + c_0 \leq W_0\}$. Notice that this is a compact set. Using the function V, we can replace the dynamic optimization problem described by Equations (1.65) through (1.68) with the problem:

$$\max_{c_0, A_0 \in \Gamma(W_0)} \{U(c_0) + \beta E_0[V(W_1, r_1)]\}, \tag{1.69}$$

given Equation (1.67). If the function V were known, we could use Equation (1.69) to define the functions $g : \mathbb{R}_+ \times R \to \mathbb{R}_+$ and $h : \mathbb{R}_+ \times R \to \mathbb{R}_+$ as follows. For each W_0 and r_0, let

$$c_0 = g(W_0, r_0) \;\; \text{and} \;\; A_0 = W_0 - g(W_0, r_0) = h(W_0, r_0)$$

be the values that attain the maximum in Equation (1.69). The functions g and h are the *policy functions*; they describe the optimal choice of consumption and savings as a function of the *state variables*, W_0 and r_0, in this case.[5] Given the functions g and h, we can describe the evolution of the consumer's consumption, savings, and wealth for all $t \geq 0$.

We assumed above that V shows the maximized value of the objective function for the problem described by Equations (1.65) through (1.68). If the function V in Equation (1.69) also solves that problem, then it must be the case that

$$V(W_0, r_0) = \max_{c_0, A_0 \in \Gamma(W_0)} \{U(c_0) + \beta E_0[V(W_1, r_1)]\}, \qquad (1.70)$$

conditional depend on r_0.

given Equation (1.67). This equation is known as the *Bellman equation* and it is a functional equation in the unknown function V. The study of dynamic optimization problems through the analysis of such functional equations is termed *dynamic programming*. Loosely speaking, we motivate the study of Equation (1.70) by noting that the solution to this functional equation is the supremum function for Equation (1.65). One issue that must addressed is whether the problem described by Equations (1.65) through (1.68) is well defined, that is, does the supremum exist? We address this issue in applications that we consider in later chapters.

Notice that we can drop the time subscripts on all variables in Equation (1.70) because the problem has now been reduced to a two-period problem: choose the best level of savings, hence determining consumption today and initial wealth tomorrow through the budget constraint and law of motion of wealth, under the assumption that initial wealth next period is valued according to the function V. We let variables without primes denote current state or choice variables and primed variables future values. Define $S \equiv \mathbb{R}_+ \times R$ and notice that $V : S \to \mathbb{R}_+$. Denote $\mathcal{C}(S)$ as the space of bounded, continuous, real-valued functions equipped with the sup norm. For $V \in \mathcal{C}(S)$, define an operator or mapping T from the right side of Equation (1.70) as:

$$(TV)(W, r) \equiv \max_{c, A \in \Gamma(W)} \{U(c) + \beta E_r[V(W', r')]\} \qquad (1.71)$$

given Equation (1.67), where $E_r(\cdot)$ denotes expectation conditional on the realization of the current return, r. For any function $V \in \mathcal{C}(S)$, $(TV)(W, r)$ assigns a value to the maximum utility that can be attained for each value of (W, r). We define a *fixed point* to this mapping as a function $V^\star$ such that $V^\star = TV^\star$, which means that if we apply T to the function $V^\star$, we obtain the same function $V^\star$. We would like to

---

[5]In many applications, it is sufficient to restrict attention to stationary policy functions, specifically policy functions that do not have the time index as an argument and that is what we assume here.

know under what conditions such a fixed point exists and whether it is
unique. To answer these questions, we need to study the properties of
the mapping T.

5.2.   Mathematical Preliminaries

In this section, we review of some mathematical results that are useful
for solving dynamic programming problems. In our discussion above,
we assumed that the value function V was an element of the space of
bounded, continuous, real-valued functions equipped with the sup norm.
To analyze the properties of such spaces, we begin with definitions of
vector spaces, metric spaces, and normed vector spaces.

A *(real) vector space* X is a set of elements (vectors) together with
two operations, addition and multiplication, such that for all $x, y \in X$,
$x + y \in X$ and for $\alpha \in \mathbb{R}$ and $x \in X$, $\alpha x \in X$, where the operations
obey the usual algebraic laws. A *metric space* is a set X, together with a
metric or distance function $\rho : X \times X \to \mathbb{R}$ such that for all $x, y, z \in X$:

(*i*) $\rho(x, y) \geq 0$ with equality if and only if $x = y$;

(*ii*) $\rho(x, y) = \rho(y, x)$;

(*iii*) $\rho(x, z) \leq \rho(x, y) + \rho(y, z)$.

For vector spaces, we define metrics so that the distance between any two
points is equal to the distance of their differences from the zero point.
This yields the concept of a norm. A *normed vector space* is a vector
space X, together with a *norm* $\| \cdot \| : X \to \mathbb{R}$ such that for all $x, y \in X$
and $\alpha \in \mathbb{R}$:

(*i*) $\|x\| \geq 0$ with equality if and only if $x = 0$;

(*ii*) $\|\alpha x\| = |\alpha| \|x\|$;

(*iii*) $\|x + y\| \leq \|x\| + \|y\|$ (Triangle Inequality).

We can use the distance function ρ to define concepts of continuity
and convergence for elements of the space X. We say that a sequence
$\{x_n\}_{n=0}^{\infty}$ in X *converges* to $x \in X$ if for each $\epsilon > 0$, there exists N_ϵ such
that

$$\rho(x_n, x) < \epsilon \quad \text{for } n \geq N_\epsilon,$$

and that $\{x_n\}_{n=0}^{\infty}$ is a *Cauchy sequence* if for each $\epsilon > 0$, there exists N_ϵ
such that

$$\rho(x_n, x_m) < \epsilon \quad \text{for } n, m \geq N_\epsilon.$$

We say that a mapping $T : X \to X$ is *continuous* at the point $x_0 \in X$ if for every real number $\epsilon > 0$, there exists a real number $\delta > 0$ such that

$$\rho(Tx, Tx_0) < \epsilon \text{ whenever } \rho(x, x_0) < \delta.$$

Define $\mathcal{C}(S)$ as the space of continuous and bounded functions $\{f : S \to \mathbb{R}\}$ equipped with the sup norm. The sup norm is a particular norm function:

$$\|f\| \equiv \sup_{s \in S} |f(s)|. \tag{1.72}$$

The space of bounded, continuous, real-valued functions equipped with the sup norm is a normed, vector space. We can define a metric or distance function ρ for the elements of $\mathcal{C}(S)$ by:

$$\rho(f, g) \equiv \|f - g\| = \sup_{s \in S} |f(s) - g(s)|. \tag{1.73}$$

An important property of the space of bounded, continuous, real-valued functions equipped with the sup norm is that it is a *complete normed, vector space* or a *Banach space*, which means that every Cauchy sequence in $\mathcal{C}(S)$ converges to an element in $\mathcal{C}(S)$.[6]

Returning to Equation (1.71), suppose we choose $V \in \mathcal{C}(S)$. What are some methods for determining the existence and uniqueness of a fixed point to the operator or mapping defined by T? One way is to show that the mapping is a contraction. There are other approaches to studying the properties of a mapping but we discuss only the contraction mapping approach. To define a contraction mapping, let (X, ρ) be a metric space and T be an operator that maps elements of X into itself, $T : X \to X$. We say that T is a contraction or a *contraction mapping* of modulus β if there is a real number β, $0 \leq \beta < 1$, such that

$$\rho(Tf, Tg) \leq \beta \rho(f, g) \text{ for all } f, g \in X. \tag{1.74}$$

Suppose that the set X is the closed interval $[a, b]$ and $\rho(x, y) = |x - y|$. Then we say that $T : X \to X$ is a contraction if for some $0 < \beta < 1$,

$$\frac{|Tx - Ty|}{|x - y|} \leq \beta < 1 \text{ for all } x, y \in X, \text{ with } x \neq y.$$

Thus, T is a contraction if it has slope uniformly less than one in absolute value. The fixed point of T are those elements of X such that $Tx = x$.

---

[6] For a further discussion of complete metric spaces, see Naylor and Sell [267, Ch. 3 and 5].

For this simple example, they can be found as the intersections of Tx with the 45 degree line, which implies that the fixed point of a contraction T defined on the interval $[a, b]$ is unique. The following theorem shows that this result holds more generally.

Theorem 1.3 *(Contraction Mapping Theorem, [237, p. 272]) Let (X, ρ) be a complete metric space and let $T : X \to X$ be a contraction with modulus β. Then (i) T has exactly one fixed point $v \in X$, (ii) for any $v_0 \in X$, $\rho(T^n v_0, v) \leq \beta^n \rho(v_0, v)$, $n = 1, 2, \ldots$*

PROOF

To prove part (i), we define the iterates of T, which are the sequence of mappings $\{T^n\}$, by $T^0 x = x$ and $T^n x = T(T^{n-1}x)$, $n = 1, 2, \ldots$ Choose $v_0 \in X$ and define $\{v_n\}_{n=0}^{\infty}$ by $v_n = T v_{n-1}$ so that $v_n = T^n v_0$. Since T is a contraction,

$$\rho(v_2, v_1) = \rho(T v_1, T v_0) \leq \beta \rho(v_1, v_0).$$

Continuing by induction, we have

$$\rho(v_{n+1}, v_n) \leq \beta^n \rho(v_1, v_0), \quad n = 1, 2, \ldots. \tag{1.75}$$

Hence for any $m > n$,

$$
\begin{aligned}
\rho(v_m, v_n) &\leq \rho(v_m, v_{m-1}) + \cdots + \rho(v_{n+2}, v_{n+1}) + \rho(v_{n+1}, v_n) \\
&\leq [\beta^{m-1} + \cdots + \beta^{n+1} + \beta^n] \rho(v_1, v_0) \\
&= \beta^n [\beta^{m-n-1} + \cdots + \beta + 1] \rho(v_1, v_0) \\
&\leq \frac{\beta^n}{1 - \beta} \rho(v_1, v_0),
\end{aligned}
$$

where the first line uses the Triangle Inequality and the second follows from Equation (1.75). Notice that $\{v_n\}$ is a Cauchy sequence. Since X is a complete metric space, $v_n \to v$ as $n \to \infty$.

To show that $Tv = v$, notice that for all n and all $v_0 \in X$,

$$
\begin{aligned}
\rho(Tv, v) &\leq \rho(Tv, T^n v_0) + \rho(T^n v_0, v) \\
&\leq \beta \rho(v, T^{n-1} v_0) + \rho(T^n v_0, v).
\end{aligned}
$$

But we showed that both terms in the second line converge to zero as $n \to \infty$; therefore, $\rho(Tv, v) = 0$ or $Tv = v$.

To show that the fixed point is unique, suppose to the contrary that $\hat{v} \neq v$ is another solution. Then

$$0 < a = \rho(\hat{v}, v) = \rho(T\hat{v}, Tv) \leq \beta \rho(\hat{v}, v) = \beta a,$$

which cannot hold since $\beta < 1$. This proves part (i).

To prove part (ii), notice that for any $n \geq 1$,

$$\rho(T^n v_0, v) = \rho[T(T^{n-1}v_0), Tv] \leq \beta \rho(T^{n-1}v_0, v),$$

so that (ii) follows by induction. ∎

There are some useful corollaries to the Contraction Mapping Theorem. One additional result we can prove is this: suppose $T : \mathcal{C}(S) \to \mathcal{C}(S)$ is a contraction with a fixed point v, where $\mathcal{C}(S)$ is the space of bounded, continuous functions with the sup norm defined earlier. Suppose $\mathcal{C}'(S)$ is the space of bounded, continuous, concave functions. Notice that $\mathcal{C}'(S)$ is a closed subset of $\mathcal{C}(S)$ and it is a complete normed linear space. If T is a contraction on $\mathcal{C}(S)$ and T maps the space of bounded, continuous, concave functions into itself, then the fixed point v is an element of the smaller space. We have the following corollary.

assume its existence

Corollary 1.1 *Let (X, ρ) be a complete metric space and $T : X \to X$ be a contraction mapping with fixed point $v \in X$. If X' is a closed subset of X and $T(X') \subseteq X'$ (where $T(X')$ is the image of X' under T), then $v \in X'$.*

PROOF
Choose $v_0 \in X'$. Notice that $\{T^n v_0\}$ is a sequence in X' converging to v. Since X' is closed, it follows that $v \in X'$. ∎

This result is useful for verifying some additional properties of the value function, such as concavity. We apply this result in applications described in Chapters 2 and 4. A second corollary of the Contraction Mapping Theorem is given as follows.

Corollary 1.2 *(N-Stage Contraction Mapping Theorem, [237, p. 275])* *Let (X, ρ) be a complete metric space, let $T : X \to X$ and suppose that for some integer N, $T^N : X \to X$ is a contraction mapping with modulus β. Then (i) T has exactly one fixed point in X, (ii) for any $v_0 \in X$, $\rho(T^{kN} v_0, v) \leq \beta^k \rho(v_0, v), k = 0, 1, 2, \ldots .$*

PROOF
$\rho((T^N)^k v_0, v)$

We show that the unique fixed point of T^N is also the fixed point of T. Notice that

$$\rho(Tv, v) = \rho[T(T^N v), T^N v] = \rho[T^N(Tv), T^N v] \leq \beta \rho(Tv, v).$$

Since $0 < \beta < 1$, this implies that $\rho(Tv, v) = 0$ so v is a fixed point of T. To show uniqueness, note that any fixed point of T is also a fixed point of T^N. Part (ii) is established as in the previous theorem. ∎

To apply these results, we need to verify whether a mapping or an operator defines a contraction. We can do this by verifying the condition in Equation (1.74) directly. An alternative method that turns out to be useful in many applications is to verify Blackwell's Sufficient Conditions for a Contraction Mapping [36].

Theorem 1.4 *(Blackwell's Conditions for a Contraction Mapping) Let $\mathcal{B}(S)$ be the space of bounded functions $f : S \to \mathbb{R}$ with the sup norm. Let $T : \mathcal{B}(S) \to \mathcal{B}(S)$ be an operator defined on $\mathcal{B}(S)$ satisfying*

(i) *(Monotonicity) Let $f, g \in \mathcal{B}(S)$. For each $s \in S$, $f(s) \geq g(s)$ implies that $Tf(s) \geq Tg(s)$;*

(ii) *(Discounting) Let $0 < a < \infty$ be a constant. There is some $0 < \beta < 1$ such that, for $f \in \mathcal{B}(S)$, $T(f + a)(s) \leq Tf(s) + \beta a$.*

If $T : \mathcal{B}(S) \to \mathcal{B}(S)$ and satisfies (i)–(ii), then T is a contraction with modulus β.

PROOF
(Left as an exercise.) ∎

Blackwell's conditions and the Contraction Mapping Theorem and its corollaries are key results for proving the existence and uniqueness of a fixed point. We leave their application to problems considered in later chapters.

5.3. Optimal Consumption and Savings Choices

Returning to the problem described by Equation (1.70), suppose that a fixed point $V^\star$ has been found for the mapping in Equation (1.71). How can we use this fixed point to further characterize the simple consumption and savings example? One approach is to analyze the first-order conditions for the optimal choice of consumption and savings. To derive the first-order conditions, suppose that the value function is differentiable.[7] Since the utility function is strictly increasing, the budget constraint holds with equality. Substituting for c in the utility function, the first-order condition for the problem in Equation (1.70) is:

$$U'(W - A) = \beta E_r \left[\frac{\partial V^\star(W', r')}{\partial A} \right]. \tag{1.76}$$

---

[7]We discuss issues related to the differentiability of the value function in the next chapter.

Let the associated policy function for the optimal choice of savings be given by $A = h^\star(W, r)$. Substituting for next period's wealth defined as $W' = (1 + r')h^\star(W, r)$, the first-order condition can be written as:

$$U'[W - h^\star(W, r)] = \beta E_r \left\{ \frac{\partial V^\star[(1 + r')h^\star(W, r), r']}{\partial A} \right\}. \qquad (1.77)$$

Then, using Equation (1.70) evaluated at the optimal policy, we have

$$\frac{\partial V^\star(W, r)}{\partial W} = U'[W - h^\star(W, r)] - \frac{\partial V^\star}{\partial w} \cdot (HV)$$

$$\left\{ U'[W - h^\star(W, r)] - \beta E_r \left(\frac{\partial V^\star(W', r')}{\partial W'}(1 + r') \right) \right\} \frac{\partial h^\star(W, r)}{\partial W}$$

$$= U'[W - h^\star(W, r)],$$

where the bracketed term equals zero using the first-order condition. This is the *envelope condition* which can be used to express the first-order condition at the fixed point as:

$$U'[W - h^\star(W, r)] = \beta E_r \{U'[W' - h^\star(W', r')](1 + r')\}.$$

Provided a fixed point function $V^\star$ exists and it is differentiable, the envelope conditions together with the first-order conditions can be used to characterize the dynamic programming problem under study and to derive implications for the behavior of individual choices and prices.

6.   Exercises

1. This exercise illustrates the application of the Separating Hyperplane Theorem. To state this theorem, we define a *linear functional F* on $\mathbb{R}^n$ as a function $F : \mathbb{R}^n \to \mathbb{R}$ satisfying

$$F(\alpha x + \beta y) = \alpha F(x) + \beta F(y), \quad x, y \in \mathbb{R}^n, \quad \alpha, \beta \in \mathbb{R}.$$

We have the following theorem.

Theorem 1.5 *(Separating Hyperplane Theorem, [237, p.133]) Suppose A and B are convex, disjoint sets in $\mathbb{R}^n$. There is some linear functional F such that $F(x) \leq F(y)$ for each x in A and y in B. Moreover, if x is in the interior of A or y is in the interior of B, then $F(x) < F(y)$.*

Use this result to show that a feasible allocation $(c^1, \ldots, c^I)$ that is Pareto optimal solves the problem in Equation (1.19) with a set of positive weights $\eta \in \mathbb{R}^I_+$ and $c^1 + \ldots + c^I = \omega$.

<u>Hint:</u> Assume that the utility functions u_i are strictly increasing and concave for all i. Define the set $A = \{a \in \mathbb{R}^I : a_i = u_i(x^i) - u_i(c^i), x \leq \omega\}$ and $A' = \{a \in \mathbb{R}^I_+ : a \neq 0\}$. Show that $A \cap A'$ is empty. Show that A is a convex set and that $0 \in A$.

2. Complete Markets and Consumption Inequality

Consider an economy with two consumers. Each consumer lives for two periods. Consumer a has preferences over consumption c_t as:

$$\sum_{t=1}^{2} U^a(c_t^a) = \sum_{t=1}^{2} \frac{(c_t^a)^\gamma - 1}{\gamma}, \quad \gamma < 0.$$

Consumer b is less risk averse than consumer a and has preferences:

$$\sum_{t=1}^{2} U^b(c_t^b) = \sum_{t=1}^{2} \log(c_t^b).$$

Each consumer receives the same endowment in each period, denoted ω_t. There is growth in the economy in that $\omega_1 < \omega_2$.

In a perfect foresight competitive equilibrium for this economy (which is just a special case of the complete contingent claims equilibrium) both consumers solve the problem:

$$\max_{c_1^i, c_2^i} U^i(c_1^i) + U^i(c_2^i) \text{ s.t. } c_1^i + pc_2^i \leq \omega_1 + p\omega_2.$$

where $p \equiv 1/(1 + r)$ and r is the real interest rate.

a) Show that the solution for each consumer's problem is given by

$$c_1^a = \frac{p^{\gamma/(1-\gamma)}(\omega_1 + p\omega_2)}{1 + p^{\gamma/(1-\gamma)}}, \qquad c_1^b = \frac{\omega_1 + p\omega_2}{2}$$

$$c_2^a = \frac{\omega_1 + p\omega_2}{p(1 + p^{\gamma/(1-\gamma)})}, \qquad c_2^b = \frac{\omega_1 + p\omega_2}{2p}.$$

b) Show that if $\gamma < 0$, then $p < \omega_1/\omega_2$, $c_1^a > c_1^b$, and $c_2^a < c_2^b$. Thus, consumer a is compensated with high consumption in the "bad state" which corresponds to date 1 when the endowment is low. Conclude that consumption inequality is increasing in period 2; that is, $| c_1^a - c_1^b | < | c_2^a - c_2^b |$.

3. Consider an economy under uncertainty such that there are T dates and S possible events at each date. Suppose there exists only one type of commodity.

Uncertainty is defined in terms of a random variable s_t that can take on S possible values at each date. The state of the economy is given by the history s^t of realizations of the random variable s_r for $r \leq t$, defined as $s^t \equiv (s_1, \ldots, s_t) = (s^{t-1}, s_t)$. Let $\pi^i(s^t) \in [0,1]$ denote the probability that $s^t \in S^t$ occurs. Notice that $\sum_{t=1}^{T} \sum_{s^t \in S^t} \pi^i(s^t) = 1$.

a) Define the commodity space.

b) Let $p(s^t)$ denote the price of a contingent claim that pays conditional on the history s^t occurring. Define a complete contingent claims equilibrium.

c) Formulate the *social planning problem* for this economy, which is the problem of maximizing a weighted sum of individual utilities subject to an aggregate feasibility constraint defined in Equation (1.18).

d) Compare the first-order conditions for the social planning problem with the optimality conditions in the complete contingent claims equilibrium.

2

Consumption and Asset Pricing

There is a rich array of assets traded in economies with well developed capital markets. We now introduce a simple framework for pricing such assets, including equities which yield a random dividend stream, bonds of different maturities, and options on various underlying assets. This framework is based on the intertemporal capital asset pricing model of Merton [258], Lucas [231], Breeden [42], and others. We assume that there is a representative consumer and output evolves according to an exogenous Markov process.

In Section 1, we demonstrate the existence of a recursive competitive equilibrium for a pure endowment economy based on Lucas [231]. We use this framework to derive the prices for a variety of assets, including pure-discount bonds of various maturities, derivative instruments such as options and forward constracts, and contingent claims contracts. In this section, we also describe asset pricing in a nonstationary environment when endowment is growing. In Section 2, we extend the basic asset pricing model to allow for the effects of past consumption choices on current utility and preferences that satisfy a version of the nonexpected utility hypothesis. We also describe the pricing of durable consumption goods and the service flows from such goods. The final topic of this chapter is a method for numerically solving asset pricing equations that can be expressed in terms of a finite set of exogenous state variables.

1.   A Basic Asset Pricing Model

In this chapter, we consider a pure endowment economy in which there is a representative consumer and output is exogenous. In later chapters, we introduce money into a similar setup. The issue is to derive equilibrium pricing functions under alternative assumptions about preferences, the stochastic properties of output, and the nature of trading arrangements.

As a way of describing uncertainty in this economy, we assume that there are m exogenous shocks, $s_t \in S \subset \mathbb{R}^m$ in each period. The endowment is a function of the shocks or exogenous state variables. The vector of shocks, s_t, follows a first-order Markov process with transition function F. The set S is assumed to be compact and $F : S \times S \to [0, 1]$ such that $F(s, s') \equiv \Pr(s_{t+1} \leq s' | s_t = s)$. We have the following assumption.

Assumption 2.1 *The transition function F has the Feller property so that for any bounded, continuous function $h : S \to \mathbb{R}$, the function $Th(s) = \int_S h(s')F(s, ds')$ is continuous. The process defined by F has a stationary distribution Φ.*

We assume that the endowment is a time-invariant function of the shocks, $y_t \equiv y(s_t)$. Thus, the endowment also follows a stationary first-order Markov process and the evolution of y_t can be described in terms of the transition function F for s_t. The next assumption ensures that the endowment takes values in a compact set.

Assumption 2.2 *Define $\mathcal{Y} \equiv [\underline{y}, \bar{y}]$ with $\underline{y} > 0$ and $\bar{y} < \infty$. The function $y : S \to \mathcal{Y}$ is a continuous function that is bounded away from zero.*

The preferences of the representative consumer over sequences of consumption $\{c_t\}_{t=0}^{\infty}$ are given by:

$$E_0 \left\{ \sum_{t=0}^{\infty} \beta^t U(c_t) \right\}, \tag{2.1}$$

where $0 < \beta < 1$ denotes the subjective discount factor and E_0 is expectation conditional on information available at time zero. Notice that preferences are additively separable with respect to consumption at different dates. The following assumption characterizes the utility function.

Assumption 2.3 *The utility function $U : S \to \mathbb{R}_+$ is continuous, continuously differentiable, strictly increasing, strictly concave with $U(0) = 0$ and $\lim_{c \to 0} U'(c) = \infty$.*

We now describe the nature of securities trading. We begin with the simplest scenario in which consumers can trade in shares to the exogenous output process and also buy and sell real risk-free bonds that are in zero net supply. Let q_t^e denote the price of a share after the dividends on the share have been paid. This price is referred to as the *ex-dividend price*. Let Q_t^1 denote the price at time t of a bond that pays off a sure unit of output at time $t + 1$. This is typically referred to as a *pure discount bond*. Let z_t denote a consumer's beginning-of-period share holdings and

b_t the beginning-of-period bond holdings. Also assume that there is one perfectly divisible outstanding share. The consumer faces the following sequence of budget constraints:

$$c_t + q_t^e z_{t+1} + Q_t^1 b_{t+1} \leq (y_t + q_t^e) z_t + b_t, \quad t = 0, 1, \dots, \tag{2.2}$$

where y_t denotes dividends paid in period t and z_0 and b_0 are given. Prior to any securities trading in period t, the consumer observes the current value of output. She also knows all past values of output, y_r for $r < t$. The consumer takes the sequences for the prices of equities and bonds as given and chooses sequences for consumption and equity and bond holdings to maximize Equation (2.1) subject to Equation (2.2) and the constraints that $c_t \geq 0$, $0 \leq z_{t+1} \leq \bar{z}$ where $\bar{z} > 1$ and $b_{t+1} \geq 0$ for all t.

The market-clearing conditions for $t = 0, 1, \dots,$ are:

$$c_t = y_t, \tag{2.3}$$

$$z_{t+1} = 1, \tag{2.4}$$

$$b_{t+1} = 0. \tag{2.5}$$

We will follow the approach in Lucas [231] to show the existence of a *recursive competitive equilibrium* in which prices can be expressed as time-invariant functions of variables that summarize the current state of the economy. In equilibrium, consumption equals the exogenous output at each date. We begin by establishing that the consumer's expected discounted utility is well defined and finite under this allocation.

Lemma 2.1 *Under Assumptions 2.1 through 2.3, for any consumption sequence $\{c_t\}_{t=0}^{\infty}$ such that $c_t \leq y_t$, then*

$$E_0 \left\{ \sum_{t=0}^{\infty} \beta^t U(c_t) \right\} \leq \mathcal{U} < \infty.$$

PROOF
Notice that for any feasible c_t, $c_t \in [0, \bar{y}]$ where $y_t \leq \bar{y}$. Since U is continuous and takes a compact set into $\mathbb{R}_+$, we can define an upper bound $\mathcal{U} \equiv \sum_{t=0}^{\infty} \beta^t U(\bar{y}) < \infty$. ∎

The Markov nature of uncertainty allows us to formulate the consumer's problem as a stationary dynamic programming problem. The consumer's state is summarized by its beginning-of-period equity holdings, z_t, its beginning-of-period bond holdings b_t, and the current shock s_t. We can show that the consumer's choices take values in a compact set. Because there is one equity share outstanding, z_{t+1} will equal exactly one in equilibrium and so define an interval $Z = [0, \bar{z}]$ where $\bar{z} > 1$ such that $z_{t+1} \in Z$. In equilibrium, $b_{t+1} = 0$ and so define an interval $B = [-b, b]$ where $b > 0$ such that $b_{t+1} \in B$.

We will seek an equilibrium in which the price of equities and the price of the risk-free asset are continuous, strictly positive functions of the exogenous shocks, $q^e : S \to \mathbb{R}_{++}$ and $Q^1 : S \to \mathbb{R}_{++}$. To emphasize the recursive nature of the problem, we let variables without primes denote current state or decision variables and variables with primes denote future values. Define $v(z, b, s)$ as the expected discounted utility of the consumer, given initial equity holdings z, bond holdings b, and the current shock s. By Lemma 2.1, this is well defined and finite. Given the price functions $q^e(\cdot)$ and $Q^1(\cdot)$, the value function for the consumer's problem satisfies:

$$v(z, b, s) = \max_{c, z', b'} \left\{ U(c) + \beta \int_S v(z', b', s') F(s, ds') \right\} \tag{2.6}$$

subject to

$$c + q^e(s)z' + Q^1(s)b' \leq [y(s) + q^e(s)]z + b, \tag{2.7}$$

$$c \geq 0, \quad z' \in Z, \quad b' \in B. \tag{2.8}$$

We have the following definition.

Definition 2.1 *A recursive competitive equilibrium is a set of price functions* $q^e : S \to \mathbb{R}_{++}$ *and* $Q^1 : S \to \mathbb{R}_{++}$ *and a value function* $v : Z \times B \times S \to \mathbb{R}_+$ *such that (i) given* $q^e(s)$ *and* $Q^1(s)$, $v(z, b, s)$ *solves the consumer's problem; (ii) markets clear.*

Notice that the price functions that the consumer takes as given are identical to the equilibrium price functions. This is the property of *rational expectations* which imposes a consistency between subjective beliefs about prices and the objective distributions for prices that arise in equilibrium.

We first study the consumer's problem for given price behavior. Define the set $S \equiv Z \times B \times S$. Let $C(S)$ denote the space of bounded, continuous functions $\{v : S \to \mathbb{R}_+\}$ equipped with the sup norm:

$$\|u\| \equiv \sup_{z,b,s \in S} |u(z, b, s)| \quad \text{for any } u \in C(S).$$

We have the following proposition.

complete

Proposition 2.1 *Under Assumptions 2.1 through 2.3, there exists a unique solution* $v^* : \mathcal{C}(\mathcal{S}) \rightarrow \mathcal{C}(\mathcal{S})$ *to the functional equation defined by Equation (2.6). The function* v^* *is concave, increasing in* (z, b).

PROOF
For $v \in \mathcal{C}(\mathcal{S})$, define the operator T by:

$$(Tv)(z, b, s) = \max_{c, z', b'} \left\{ U(c) + \beta \int_{\mathcal{S}} v(z', b', s') F(s, ds') \right\}$$

subject to Equations (2.7) and (2.8). Since $0 \leq c \leq y$, $z' \in Z$ and $b' \in B$, the constraint set is compact. By Assumption 2.3, the utility function U is continuous in c and the function v is jointly continuous in (z, b, s) since $v \in \mathcal{C}(\mathcal{S})$. Hence, Tv involves maximizing a continuous function over a compact set so that it is well defined; that is, a maximum exists. Since $U(c)$ is bounded for $0 \leq c \leq y$ and $v(z', b', s')$ is bounded, the maximum function Tv is bounded and by the Theorem of the Maximum (see Stokey and Lucas [317, p. 62]), it is continuous. Thus, T maps bounded, continuous functions into the same space, $T : \mathcal{C}(\mathcal{S}) \rightarrow \mathcal{C}(\mathcal{S})$.

Next, notice that T is monotone. Given any two functions $u \in \mathcal{C}(\mathcal{S})$, $w \in \mathcal{C}(\mathcal{S})$ such that $u(z, b, s) \geq w(z, b, s)$ for all $z, b, s \in \mathcal{S}$,

$$\int_{\mathcal{S}} u(z', b', s') F(s, ds') \geq \int_{\mathcal{S}} w(z', b', s') F(s, ds')$$

so that $(Tu)(z, b, s) \geq (Tw)(z, b, s)$. To verify discounting, for any constant a, notice that

$$
\begin{aligned}
T(v + a)(z, b, s) &= \max_{c, z', b'} \left\{ U(c) + \beta \int_{\mathcal{S}} [v(z', b', s') + a] F(s, ds') \right\} \\
&= \max_{c, z', b'} \left\{ U(c) + \beta \int_{\mathcal{S}} v(z', b', s') F(s, ds') \right\} + \beta a \\
&= (Tv)(z, b, s) + \beta a.
\end{aligned}
$$

Hence, T satisfies Blackwell's conditions for a contraction. Since $\mathcal{C}(\mathcal{S})$ is a complete, normed, linear space, the Contraction Mapping Theorem implies that T has a unique fixed point and $\lim_{n \rightarrow \infty} T^n v_0 = v^*$ for any $v_0 \in \mathcal{C}(\mathcal{S})$.

To show that v^* is concave and increasing in (z, b), let $\mathcal{C}'(\mathcal{S})$ be the space of continuous, bounded, increasing, and concave real-valued functions defined on $\mathcal{S}$ equipped with the sup norm. Notice that $\mathcal{C}'(\mathcal{S})$ is a closed subset of $\mathcal{C}(\mathcal{S})$ and it is a complete, normed, linear space. Choose some $w \in \mathcal{C}'(\mathcal{S})$. Notice that for any $w(z_1, b, s) < w(z_2, b, s)$ for $z_1 < z_2$ implies $Tw(z_1, b, s) < Tw(z_2, b, s)$ and similarly for b.

To show that T preserves concavity, let (z_0, b_0) and (z_1, b_1) be given, let $0 \leq \theta \leq 1$, and define $z_\theta = \theta z_0 + (1 - \theta)z_1$ and $b_\theta = \theta b_0 + (1 - \theta)b_1$. Let (c_i, z_i', b_i') attain $(Tw)(z_i, b_i, s)$, $i = 0, 1$. Now, $(c_\theta, z_\theta', b_\theta')$ satisfies the budget constraint because (c_0, z_0', b_0') and (c_1, z_1', b_1') are both feasible. Therefore,

$$(Tw)(z_\theta, b_\theta, s) \geq U(c_\theta) + \beta \int_S w(z_\theta', b_\theta', s')F(s, ds')$$

$$\geq \quad \theta U(c_0) + (1 - \theta)U(c_1) + \theta\beta \int_S w(z_0', b_0', s')F(s, ds')$$

$$+ (1 - \theta)\beta \int_S w(z_1', b_1', s')F(s, ds')$$

$$\geq \quad \theta(Tw)(z_0, b_0, s) + (1 - \theta)(Tw)(z_1, b_1, s).$$

The second line follows by the concavity of U and w while the third line follows since (c_i, z_i', b_i') attains $(Tw)(z_i, b_i, s)$ for $i = 0, 1$. Hence, $(Tw)(z, b, s)$ is concave in (z, b).

Because $\mathcal{C}'(\mathcal{S})$ is a closed subset of $\mathcal{C}(\mathcal{S})$ and we have shown that T is a contraction on $\mathcal{C}(\mathcal{S})$ (so that, for any initial guess $v^0 \in \mathcal{C}(\mathcal{S})$, repeated applications of T result in $v^\star$), we can conclude by Corollary 1.1 that $v^\star$ is an element of $\mathcal{C}'(\mathcal{S})$. ∎

These results establish the existence of a solution to the consumer's problem, given the price functions q^e and Q^1. They also show that the value function is concave, increasing in shares and bond holdings. Intuitively, increases in number of shares and bonds increases the consumer's wealth and hence, the maximum utility that can be achieved.

To derive further results about the nature of the price functions, we study the optimality conditions for this problem, given the fixed point $v^\star$. Define $v_z^\star$ and $v_b^\star$ as the partial derivative of $v^\star$ with respect to z and b, respectively. We have the following proposition.

Proposition 2.2 *[231, p. 1433-1434] For all $(z, b, s) \in \mathcal{S}$, the value function $v^\star$ is differentiable in z and b, with*

$$v_z^\star(z, b, s) \quad = \quad U'(c)[y(s) + q^e(s)], \tag{2.9}$$

$$v_b^\star(z, b, s) \quad = \quad U'(c).^1 \tag{2.10}$$

---

[1] Benveniste and Scheinkman [28] have shown that under fairly general conditions the value function is *once* differentiable. Rather than applying their result, we provide a direct proof under more restrictive conditions that can be adapted to applications we consider in later chapters. For a further discussion of this issue, see Stokey and Lucas [317, pp. 84–85 and 266].

PROOF

Let $W : \mathbb{R}_+ \to \mathbb{R}_+$ be defined by

$$W(x) = \max_{c,z',b'} \{U(c) + \beta E_s[v(z', b', s')]\}$$

↳ depends on s'

subject to $c + q^e(s)z' + Q^1(s)b' \le [y(s) + q^e(s)]z + b \equiv x$ and $c, z', b' \ge 0$, where $E_s(\cdot)$ denotes expectation conditional on the current shock s.

   Note that for each x, $W(x)$ is attained by $c(x)$, $z'(x)$, and $b'(x)$. Since the maximand is strictly concave in c, $c(x)$ is unique and varies continuously with x. If $c(x) > 0$ and if h is sufficiently small, $c(x) + h$ is feasible at "income" $x + h$ and $c(x + h) - h$ is feasible at income x. Thus,

$$\begin{aligned} W(x + h) &\ge U(c(x) + h) + \beta E_s\{v[z'(x), b'(x), s']\} \\ &= U(c(x) + h) - U(c(x)) + W(x) \end{aligned}$$

and

$$\begin{aligned} W(x) &\ge U(c(x + h) - h) + \beta E_s\{v[z'(x + h), b'(x + h), s']\} \\ &= U(c(x + h) - h) - U(c(x + h)) + W(x + h). \end{aligned}$$

Combining these inequalities gives

$$\begin{aligned} U(c(x) + h) - U(c(x)) &\le W(x + h) - W(x) \\ &\le U(c(x + h)) - U(c(x + h) - h). \end{aligned}$$

Dividing by h, letting $h \to 0$ and utilizing the continuity of $c(\cdot)$ gives $W'(x) = U'(c(x))$. Since $x = [y(s) + q^e(s)]z + b$ so that $v(z, b, s) = W(x)$, we have that $v_z^*(z, b, s) = W'(x)(\partial x/\partial z)$ and $v_b^*(z, b, s) = W'(x)(\partial x/\partial b)$, yielding the result. ∎

   Define the policy functions $c^*(z, b, s)$, $z^*(z, b, s)$, and $b^*(z, b, s)$ that are associated with the value function $v^*(z, b, s)$. In equilibrium, $z' = 1$, $b' = 0$, and consumption equals output so that we need to determine the price functions such that the associated policy functions satisfy $c^*(1, 0, s) = y(s)$, $z^*(1, 0, s) = 1$, and $b^*(1, 0, s) = 0$. To determine these price functions, we study the first-order conditions when markets clear:

$$U'(y(s))q^e(s) = \beta \int_S U'(y(s'))[y(s') + q^e(s')]F(s, ds'), \qquad (2.11)$$

$$U'(y(s))Q^1(s) = \beta \int_S U'(y(s'))F(s, ds'). \qquad (2.12)$$

These equations are known as the *intertemporal Euler equations* and they are satisfied for the optimal choice of consumption and equity and bond holdings. In the next chapter, we will describe a test of this model based on such optimality conditions.

Notice that Equation (2.11) defines a functional equation for the unknown equity price $q^e(s)$. To complete the proof of the existence of a recursive competitive equilibrium, we need to show that given the consumer's value function v, there exists a unique solution for the equity price $q^e(s)$. Let $C_q(S)$ denote the space of bounded, continuous functions $\{\phi : S \to \mathbb{R}_+\}$ equipped with the sup norm. Define the function $\gamma : S \to \mathbb{R}_+$ by:

$$\gamma(s) \equiv \beta \int_S U'(y(s'))y(s')F(s, ds').$$

Instead of seeking a solution for the function $q^e(s)$, define the function $\phi(s) \equiv U'(y(s))q^e(s)$. Notice that $y(s)$ is exogenous and U' is strictly decreasing so that finding ϕ is equivalent to finding q^e. Notice that for any $\phi \in C_q(S)$, we can define an operator T_q from the right side of Equation (2.11) as:

$$(T_q\phi)(s) = \gamma(s) + \beta \int_S \phi(s')F(s, ds'). \qquad (2.13)$$

We have the following proposition.

Proposition 2.3 *There is a unique, continuous and bounded solution $\phi^\star$ to $T_q\phi = \phi$. For any $\phi_0 \in C_q(S)$, $\lim_{n\to\infty} T_q^n \phi_0 = \phi^\star$.*

PROOF
The first expression on the right side of Equation (2.13) is nonnegative since U is an increasing function and $y(s) > 0$ for all $s \in S$. Since $y(s)$ takes values in the compact set $\mathcal{Y}$ and U is continuous, we know that U is bounded. We first show that if U is bounded on $\mathcal{Y}$, then $\gamma(s)$ is bounded. By the concavity of U, we have

$$U(y) - U(0) \geq U'(y)(y - 0) = U'(y)y.$$

Thus, there exists a $\bar{U}$ such that $U'(y)y \leq \bar{U}$ for all $y \in \mathcal{Y}$, which implies that $\gamma(s) = \beta \int_S U'(y(s'))y(s')F(s, ds') \leq \beta\bar{U}$. Since ϕ is bounded, T_q maps bounded functions into bounded functions. Assumption 2.1 implies that both terms on the right side of Equation (2.13) are continuous. Thus, the operator T_q maps elements of the space of bounded, continuous functions into itself, $T_q : C_q(S) \to C_q(S)$.

Notice that T_q is monotone since given any $\psi \geq \phi$, $T_q\psi \geq T_q\phi$. For any constant a, notice that

$$T_q(\phi + a)(s) = \gamma(s) + \beta \int_S [\phi(s') + a]F(s, ds')$$

$$= (T_q\phi)(s) + \beta a$$

so that T_q discounts. Thus, T_q satisfies Blackwell's conditions to be a contraction. Since $\mathcal{C}_q(S)$ is a complete normed, linear space, the Contraction Mapping Theorem implies that Equation (2.13) has a unique fixed point. ■

Define the fixed point function by $\phi^\star$. The equilibrium equity price is determined as:

$$q^e(s) = \frac{\phi^\star(s)}{U'(y(s))}. \tag{2.14}$$

There are different methods for finding the unknown function $\phi^\star$. In Exercise 1, we describe the method of *successive approximation* that allows us to numerically compute this function given distributional assumptions for the shocks and a parametric specification of preferences. In Section 3, we also describe *quadrature-based methods* for numerically solving asset pricing equations. Under certain circumstances, we can also calculate exact solutions. We describe how this is done after we have introduced the case with constant relative risk aversion (CRR) preferences and growing endowment.

We now study some other properties of the solution. Define the (gross) real return on the equity by $r_{t+1} \equiv (q^e_{t+1} + y_{t+1})/q^e_t$. Reverting to time subscripts in Equation (2.11), this satisfies

$$1 = \beta E_t\left[\frac{U'(y_{t+1})}{U'(y_t)} r_{t+1}\right], \tag{2.15}$$

where $E_t(\cdot)$ denotes expectation conditional on s_t. Similarly, the bond price is given by:

$$Q^1_t = \beta E_t\left[\frac{U'(y_{t+1})}{U'(y_t)}\right]. \tag{2.16}$$

These conditions show that the intertemporal marginal rate of substitution (MRS) in consumption for the representative consumer is used to price payoffs on all securities traded in this economy. Using our earlier definition, we denote this MRS as the stochastic discount factor.

Define the gross real risk-free rate of interest by $r_t^1 \equiv 1/Q_t^1$. Using a covariance decomposition, we can rewrite equation (2.15) as:

$$E_t(r_{t+1}) = r_t^1 \left[1 - \text{Cov}_t \left(\beta \frac{U'(y_{t+1})}{U'(y_t)}, r_{t+1} \right) \right]. \tag{2.17}$$

We can use the expressions in Equation (2.17) to evaluate the *conditional equity premium* defined as:

$$E_t(r_{t+1}) - r_t^1 = -r_t^1 \text{Cov}_t \left(\beta \frac{U'(y_{t+1})}{U'(y_t)}, r_{t+1} \right). \tag{2.18}$$

This says that the excess return on a risky asset over the risk-free rate, or the *risk premium*, is proportional to the negative of the covariance of the return with the MRS. Thus, an asset is risky if its return covaries negatively with the intertemporal MRS. This is the concept of riskiness suggested by Breeden [42]. Since the relevant pricing function that we have derived depends on the MRS in consumption, this asset pricing model is sometimes referred to as the *consumption-based capital asset pricing (CAPM) model*.

The behavior of the observed equity premium has been studied by Mehra and Prescott [257], among others. These authors assume constant relative risk aversion preferences and growing endowment to determine if a representative consumer model can generate an average equity premium that matches the average equity premium observed in the data. They use annual data for the sample period 1889–1978; in this sample, the average equity premium is 6.18% with a standard deviation of 16.67%. They model endowment growth $\lambda(s_t)$ as a two-state Markov chain. The Markov chain for endowment growth is constructed so that the mean growth and first-order autocorrelation match the appropriate sample moments for annual U.S. data over the 1889–1978 period. They then use the theoretical model and the Markov chain for endowment growth to simulate equity premiums for a variety of values of the risk aversion parameter. They find a simple representative model with CRR preferences and a two-state Markov chain is unable to generate an average equity premium that is close to the observed average equity premium.

This finding has been referred to as the equity premium "puzzle." The equity premium "puzzle" has led to a wide variety of studies seeking to explain the puzzle. One possible resolution is to drop the assumption of time-additive preferences in favor of preferences displaying habit persistence, consumption durability, or to assume a version of nonexpected utility. We describe such preferences in the next section. An alternative direction is to introduce another source of uncertainty such as inflation risk. In Chapter 6, we study the implications of stochastic inflation on asset returns and the equity premium. Another possible resolution is to assume that agents are heterogeneous and subject to borrowing constraints, limiting their ability to smooth consumption. This is briefly discussed in Chapter 7. There are several other explanations that have been offered to explain this puzzle.

The pricing function in this model depends on consumers' attitudes toward risk, their rate of time preference, and the stochastic properties of output or consumption. In Exercise 2, the reader is asked to show that when output is identically and independently distributed over time, the responsiveness of the equity price to changes in output depends on the coefficient of relative risk aversion. In an environment under certainty, we can define the intertemporal elasticity of substitution in consumption. When preferences are additive over time and across states, as we have assumed here, risk aversion and intertemporal substitution cannot be disentangled. Later on, we study preferences where these concepts can be separated.

1.1. Discount Bonds and the Yield Curve

In actual capital markets, we observe many other types of assets being traded, including derivative instruments such as options, futures contracts, and forward contracts. We begin by describing the pricing of risk-free debt instruments and by defining some of the returns and premiums that are associated.

The simplest type of debt instrument is a zero-coupon discount bond, which we defined above. This type of bond pays a fixed amount, which we assume is one unit of the consumption good, at some maturity date and there are no coupons paid before the maturity date. Because there are no payments made to the bondholder before the maturity date, the bond sells for a real price that is below the real amount paid at the maturity date, or the bond sells at a discount. We can also price a coupon bond, which pays a coupon of c at regular intervals and the principal at maturity. Likewise, we could introduce a perpetuity or consol bond, which is a coupon bond with an infinite maturity date. There are many other types of debt instruments traded in actual capital markets.[2]

---

[2]These are typically differentiated in terms of default risk, convertibility provisions (providing the option to convert to another financial instrument), call provisions (allowing debt to be paid off before the maturity date), and other features.

We now determine the prices for a variety of maturity lengths of zero-coupon discount bonds that are risk free. The household's initial wealth consists of the endowment and its portfolio of discount bonds $b_{j,t}$, where $b_{j,t}$ denotes the number of bonds held at the beginning of period t that mature in j periods and pay one unit of the endowment at time $t + j$. The agent's real wealth constraint at the beginning of period t is:

$$c_t + \sum_{j=1}^{N} b_{j,t+1} Q_t^j \leq y_t + \sum_{j=0}^{N} b_{j,t} Q_t^j,$$

where N is the longest maturity issue and $Q_t^0 = 1$. We assume that the discount bonds are in zero net supply so that, in equilibrium, $b_{j,t+1} = 0$ for all j and t. We also have that $c_t = y_t$ so that the equilibrium first-order conditions with respect to bond holdings $b_{j,t+1}$ are:

$$U'(y_t)Q_t^j = \beta E_t \left[U'(y_{t+1}) Q_{t+1}^{j-1} \right], \quad j = 1, \ldots, N. \tag{2.19}$$

Substituting recursively in this condition, we can express the equilibrium price of an indexed discount bond maturing in τ periods by:

$$Q_t^\tau = \beta^\tau E_t \left[\frac{U'(y_{t+\tau})}{U'(y_t)} \right], \tag{2.20}$$

for any $\tau = 1, \ldots, N$. Define the real return on this bond as $r_t^\tau \equiv 1/Q_t^\tau$.

The returns to the bonds at various maturity dates are not directly comparable because the number of periods over which the bond is held is not the same. One way to make the returns comparable is to compute the yield to maturity, i_t^τ, and a particularly convenient way to do this is to define the continuously compounded yield:

$$i_t^\tau = -\frac{1}{\tau} \log Q_t^\tau. \tag{2.21}$$

Given the price Q_t^τ, the yield to maturity i_t^τ at time t on a discount bond maturing τ periods later is the steady rate at which the price should increase if the bond is to be worth one unit of output at $t + \tau$. Thus, i_t^τ satisfies the relation $Q_t^\tau \exp(-\tau i_t^\tau) = 1.00$, which yields Equation (2.21). An alternative method is to define the yield as

$$i_t^\tau = (Q_t^\tau)^{-\frac{1}{\tau}}. \tag{2.22}$$

By defining the yield for bonds of various maturities, we can construct a *yield curve* or *term structure* by varying τ. The *slope* of the yield curve (or the yield spread) is $i_t^\tau - i_t^{\tau-1}$.

We can also derive the prices of *forward contracts* on pure-discount bonds of various maturities. A forward contract on a τ-period pure-discount bond to be delivered at date $t + n$ where $n \leq \tau$ is an agreement to buy or sell the bond at that date, which is called the *maturity date*. We denote the price at date t of such a forward contract by $F_{t,n}^{\tau}$, which is called the *delivery price*. At the time the contract matures, an agent holding the contract must buy or sell the bond at the delivery price. Entering into a forward contract at date t which is to be delivered at some time in the future has no effect on the agent's time t budget constraint. If the agent must deliver the bond (so he has a short position), then he must purchase the bond at the current spot price. He profits if the spot price is less than the delivery price. Similarly, the agent in the long position is obligated to purchase the bond at the delivery price. He profits if the spot price is greater than the delivery price. The net profit of the short and long positions is zero.

The spot price on the bond at time $t + n$ is $Q_{t+n}^{\tau-n}$. The payoff on a long position in a forward contract on one unit of the discount bond at time $t + n$ is $Q_{t+n}^{\tau-n} - F_{t,n}^{\tau}$. In equilibrium, the expected discounted present value of that payoff is equal to zero, or

$$0 = \beta^n E_t \left[\frac{U'(y_{t+n})}{U'(y_t)} (Q_{t+n}^{\tau-n} - F_{t,n}^{\tau}) \right]. \tag{2.23}$$

Define the marginal rate of substitution in consumption between periods t and $t + n$ by $\mathcal{M}_{t,n} \equiv \beta^n U'(y_{t+n})/U'(y_t)$. Notice that the equilibrium delivery price satisfies:

$$F_{t,n}^{\tau} = (E_t \mathcal{M}_{t,n})^{-1} E_t(\mathcal{M}_{t,n} Q_{t+n}^{\tau-n}) = Q_t^{\tau}/Q_t^n, \tag{2.24}$$

where we have made use of Equations (2.19) and (2.20) to obtain the second equality.

The forward price provides information about the expected spot price. To see this, use Equation (2.19) and the conditional covariance decomposition to express the forward rate as:

$$F_{t,\tau-1}^{\tau} = r_t^{\tau-1} \text{Cov}_t \left(\mathcal{M}_{t,\tau-1}, Q_{t+\tau-1}^1 \right) + E_t(Q_{t+\tau-1}^1). \tag{2.25}$$

Clearly, if the conditional covariance between the marginal utility at time $t + \tau - 1$ and the spot price at time $t + \tau - 1$ is positive (negative), then the forward price is greater than (less than) the expected spot price. The *forward premium* is defined as the difference between the expected spot price and the forward price, or $E_t(Q^1_{t+\tau-1}) - F^\tau_{t,\tau-1}$ so that the forward premium is the negative of the conditional covariance in Equation (2.25).[3]

We now turn to the one-period expected *holding return*. This is the expected return to holding a bond for one period and then selling it in the secondary market. The (gross) return to holding a bond maturing in τ periods for one period and selling is:

$$h^\tau_{t+1} \equiv Q^{\tau-1}_{t+1}/Q^\tau_t. \tag{2.26}$$

From the first-order condition and using the conditional covariance decomposition, the expected one-period holding return satisfies:

$$E_t(h^\tau_{t+1}) - r^1_t = -r^1_t \mathrm{Cov}_t(\mathcal{M}_{t,1}, h^\tau_{t+1})$$

where r^1_t is the certain return on a one-period bond. If the conditional covariance is nonzero, then there exists a *term risk premium*. Since the real payoff to the one-period bond is certain, this bond provides a convenient benchmark for measuring riskiness. A bond is risky relative to the benchmark bond if its risk premium is positive. Since the risk premium is proportional to the conditional covariance between the MRS and the bond's return, this measure of riskiness refers to the usefulness of the payoff in smoothing consumption over time. If a payoff is high when consumption is high (so that marginal utility is low), then the covariance is negative and the risk premium is positive because the bond is a poor instrument for smoothing consumption over time.

The (gross) return to holding a bond maturing in τ periods for n period and selling is:

$$h^\tau_{t+n} \equiv Q^{\tau-n}_{t+n}/Q^\tau_t \quad \text{for } 0 < n < \tau. \tag{2.27}$$

This satisfies the relation:

$$1 = E_t\left(\mathcal{M}_{t,n} h^\tau_{t+n}\right), \quad 0 < n < \tau.$$

Using the conditional covariance decomposition, we have

$$E_t(h^\tau_{t+n}) - r^n_t = -r^n_t \mathrm{Cov}_t\left(\mathcal{M}_{t,n}, h^\tau_{t+n}\right), \tag{2.28}$$

where once again, if the conditional covariance on the right side is zero, then expected holding returns on all assets are equalized. Otherwise,

---

[3]This is the premium in the forward price. The premium on the implied return is $1/F^\tau_{t,\tau-1} - E_t(r^1_{t+\tau-1})$, where r^1 is the spot return. Notice that if the conditional covariance in Equation (2.25) is zero, then the forward premium on the return is negative because of Jensen's inequality. Hence, in the case where the covariance is negative, there may be some indeterminacy about the sign of the premium.

there exists a term risk premium and this premium depends on the holding period n as well as the time to maturity τ.

A long-standing hypothesis about the way interest rates of different maturities are determined is given by the *expectations theory* of the term structure of interest rates. Loosely speaking, downward-sloping term structures are taken to indicate expectations of a decline in interest rates and upward-sloping ones of a rise. When the conditional covariance in Equation (2.28) is constant, the slope of the term structure or yield curve depends on changing expectations for future interest rates, as hypothesized by the expectations theory. Shiller [307] describes the empirical evidence that has been obtained on the term premium. Many of these tests are derived by assuming that the conditional covariance on the right side of Equation (2.28) is constant. Under this assumption, all term premia depend only on maturity and not on time.

1.2.   Pricing Derivative Instruments

A derivative security has a value that depends on other underlying securities such as forward contracts, stocks, and bonds. We examine just a few of the derivative securities that are now traded in the market.[4] We begin by describing options pricing.

There are two types of options: the *call option* gives the holder the right to buy the asset by a certain date for a certain price; the *put option* gives the holder the right to sell the underlying asset by a certain date for a certain price. The price of the option is known as the exercise price or *strike price* and the date is known as the *expiration date*. There are two categories of options: the *American option* and the *European option*. The American option can be exercised any time up to the expiration date. The European option can be exercised only on the expiration date. Most of the options that are traded are American. Unlike futures or forward contracts where the holder is obligated to buy or sell, the holder of the option doesn't have to exercise the option; he may simply hold it until it expires. Entering into a futures or forward contract doesn't affect the current budget constraint of the agent while buying or selling an option does affect the current budget constraint.

A *stock option* entitles the consumer to buy (or sell) an equity at a certain date for a certain price. To determine the price of a one-period stock option, we have to determine the price at time t that someone

---

[4]Useful books on derivative securities include Rubinstein and Cox [292], Hull [203], and Stoll and Whaley [318]. Some of our discussion is based on Turnbull and Milne [330]. A useful book on futures markets is by Duffie [103].

would pay to buy an equity at a price $\bar{q}$ at time $t+1$. In equilibrium, the stock price satisfies:

$$q^e(s_t) = \beta \int_S \frac{U'(y(s_{t+1}))}{U'(y(s_t))} [q^e(s_{t+1}) + y(s_{t+1})] F(s_t, ds_{t+1}).$$

What is the price that someone would pay for the option of buying the equity next period for the price $\bar{q}$ — the price of a one-period call option? If the price next period is greater than the strike price $q^e(s_{t+1}) > \bar{q}$, then the agent will exercise the option while if $q^e(s_{t+1}) < \bar{q}$, the agent will not. The equilibrium price of a call option is:

$$
\begin{aligned}
P^c_{s,t} &= \beta \int_{\bar{q} \leq q^e(s_{t+1})} \frac{U('y(s_{t+1}))}{U'(y(s_t))} [q^e(s_{t+1}) - \bar{q}] F(s_t, ds_{t+1}) \\
&\quad + \beta \int_{\bar{q} \geq q^e(s_{t+1})} \frac{U'(y(s_{t+1}))}{U'(y(s_t))} \cdot 0 \cdot F(s_t, ds_{t+1}) \\
&= E_t \left[\mathcal{M}_{t,1} \cdot \max(0, q^e_{t+1} - \bar{q}) \right].
\end{aligned}
\tag{2.29}
$$

The price of the put option is then equal to

$$P^p_{s,t} = E_t \left[\mathcal{M}_{t,1} \cdot \max(0, \bar{q} - q^e_{t+1}) \right]. \tag{2.30}$$

We can also price *interest rate options* using the same approach. Consider now the price of a European option on a pure discount bond that matures in τ periods. Suppose that the expiration date is $t+n$ where $n \leq \tau$ and the strike price is $\bar{Q}$. A European option can be exercised only at time $t+n$. The price of a call option at time t when the expiration date is time $t+n$ is:

$$P^c_{d,t}(n,\tau) = E_t \left[\mathcal{M}_{t,n} \cdot \max(0, Q^{\tau-n}_{t+n} - \bar{Q}) \right], \tag{2.31}$$

where $Q^{\tau-n}_{t+n}$ is the price at time $t+n$ of a discount bond that matures in $\tau - n$ periods.

Now consider an American call option on a pure discount bond that matures in τ periods. This is much more complicated for the obvious reason that the holder can exercise the option at any time up to and including the expiration date. At time $t+n-1$ when there is one period until the option expires, the price of the American option and the European option are the same, or

$$S^c_{1,t+n-1} = E_{t+n-1} \left[\mathcal{M}_{t+n-1,1} \cdot \max(0, Q^{\tau-n}_{t+n} - \bar{Q}) \right].$$

Now consider the choices of the holder of an American call option at time $t+1$. At that time the agent can continue to hold the option, with the value of the option at that time denoted $S^c_{n-1,t+1}$, or he can exercise the option to buy a bond that matures at time $t + \tau$ at the time $t + 1$ at the exercise price of $\bar{Q}$ instead of paying the current price $Q^{\tau-1}_{t+1}$. The value of an n-period call option on a discount bond maturing in τ periods is:

$$S^c_{n,t} = \beta E_t \left[\mathcal{M}_{t,1} \cdot \max(S^c_{n-1,t+1}, Q^{\tau-1}_{t+1} - \bar{Q}) \right]. \tag{2.32}$$

It is also possible to price options on derivative instruments such as a forward or futures contract. Consider the price of an m-period European call option on an n-period forward contract where the underlying asset on which the contract is written is a τ-period discount bond. We have shown that the price of the n-period forward contract written on a discount bond maturing in τ periods at time $t + m$ is $F^\tau_{t+m,n} = Q^\tau_{t+m} / Q^n_{t+m}$. The European call option on the forward contract gives the holder the right to buy the n-period contract in m periods ($m \le n$) at the strike price $\bar{F}$. Because the only time at which the option can be exercised is period $t + m$, the price of the call option is:

$$S^c_{f,t}(m,n) = E_t \left[\mathcal{M}_{t,m} \cdot \max(0, F^\tau_{t+m,n} - \bar{F}) \right]. \tag{2.33}$$

Because the European option cannot be exercised before the date $t + m$, it is straightforward to price.

1.3. Pricing Contingent Claims Contracts

We now describe how to price claims that have payoffs for all possible events that can occur in this economy. We consider a sequential interpretation of the complete contingent claims equilibrium for this purpose.

The consumer lives for τ periods starting at $t = 1$ in an economy where she can trade in one-period securities that payoff for each possible event in period $t+1$. Let $[q(s_{t+1}) + y(s_{t+1})] z_{t+1}$ denote the state-contingent payoff on a portfolio of securities purchased in period t when $s_{t+1} \in S$ occurs in period $t+1$. We assume that $q(s_{t+1}) + y(s_{t+1}) > 0$. We represent the value of a portfolio contingent on $\bar{S} \subseteq S$ occurring in period $t + 1$ as:

$$\int_{\bar{S} \subseteq S} \hat{p}(s_t, s_{t+1}) [q(s_{t+1}) + y(s_{t+1})] z_{t+1} f(s_{t+1}|s_t) ds_{t+1},$$

where $f(s_{t+1}|s_t)$ is the strictly positive probability density function of s_{t+1} given s_t. Notice that the market value of the portfolio is evaluated using the strictly positive conditional "price density" $\hat{p}(s_t, s_{t+1})$. We write the price density at time t as a function of the shock that is realized at time t only because uncertainty evolves as a first-order Markov process. Using this representation, we write the sequence of budget constraints for the consumer in the complete contingent claims equilibrium as:

$$c(s_t) + \int_S \hat{p}(s_t, s_{t+1})[q(s_{t+1}) + y(s_{t+1})]z(s_t, s_{t+1})f(s_{t+1}|s_t)ds_{t+1}$$

$$\leq [q(s_t) + y(s_t)]z(s_t), \tag{2.34}$$

where $[q(s_t)+y(s_t)]z_t$ is the payoff on the portfolio when $s_t \in S$ is realized in period t. We write $z(s_t, s_{t+1})$ to make explicit the fact that at time t, the consumer chooses how much to hold of a security that pays off conditional on the state s_{t+1} occurring in period $t + 1$.

Given strictly positive prices $\hat{p}(s_t, s_{t+1})$ and payoffs $q(s_{t+1}) + y(s_{t+1})$, the consumer chooses consumption $c(s_t)$ and security holdings $z(s_t, s_{t+1})$ for $s_t, s_{t+1} \in S$ and $t = 1, \ldots, \tau$ to maximize

$$E_1 \left\{ \sum_{t=1}^{\tau} \beta^{t-1} U(c(s_t)) \right\},$$

subject to the sequence of budget constraints in Equation (2.34) where E_1 denotes expectation conditional on s_1. In equilibrium, $c(s_t) = y(s_t)$ and $z(s_t, s_{t+1}) = 1$ for $s_t, s_{t+1} \in S$ and $1 \leq t \leq \tau$.

Let $\eta(s_t)$ denote the Lagrange multiplier on the sequence of budget constraints. The consumer's optimal choices satisfy the budget constraints in Equation (2.34) and the first-order conditions:

$$\beta^{t-1} U'(c(s_t)) = \eta(s_t), \tag{2.35}$$

$$\int_S \eta(s_t)\hat{p}(s_t, s_{t+1})[q(s_{t+1}) + y(s_{t+1})]f(s_{t+1}|s_t)ds_{t+1} =$$

$$\int_S \eta(s_{t+1})[q(s_{t+1}) + y(s_{t+1})]f(s_{t+1}|s_t)ds_{t+1}, \tag{2.36}$$

for $s_t \in S$ and $1 \leq t \leq \tau$.

Suppose we set the price of the security equal to:

$$q(s_t) = \int_S \hat{p}(s_t, s_{t+1})[q(s_{t+1}) + y(s_{t+1})]f(s_{t+1}|s_t)ds_{t+1}. \tag{2.37}$$

Since $\hat{p}(s_t, s_{t+1}) > 0$ and $q(s_{t+1}) + y(s_{t+1}) > 0$, we can use Equations (2.35) and (2.36) to show that

$$\hat{p}(s_t, s_{t+1}) = \frac{\beta U'(c(s_{t+1}))}{U'(c(s_t))}. \tag{2.38}$$

If we substitute the result in Equation (2.38) into Equation (2.37), we can proceed as in Chapter 1 to show that the complete contingent claims equilibrium allocation can be attained in a security market equilibrium. The expression for the security price in Equation (2.37) is just a restatement of the asset valuation formula we derived in Chapter 1; when markets are complete, the contingent claims prices can be used to value the payoffs on any security traded in equilibrium. However, when there is a representative consumer, the stochastic discount factor is a function of per capita consumption only and is expressed using the preferences of the representative consumer.

We can derive an alternative version of the consumer's budget constraint by solving the sequence of budget constraints in Equation (2.34) forward. For this purpose, we define a joint "price density" as:

$$p(s_t, s_{t+1}, s_{t+2}, \ldots, s_{t+i}) \equiv \hat{p}(s_t, s_{t+1})\hat{p}(s_{t+1}, s_{t+2}) \cdots \hat{p}(s_{t+i-1}, s_{t+i})$$

which shows the price of consumption in period $t + i$ conditional on the history of shocks $(s_t, s_{t+1}, s_{t+2}, \ldots, s_{t+i})$ occurring. The joint density of this history is given by:

$$g(s_t, s_{t+1}, s_{t+2}, \ldots, s_{t+i}) \equiv f(s_{t+1}|s_t)f(s_{t+2}|s_{t+1}) \cdots f(s_{t+i}|s_{t+i-1}).$$

Denote by $\tilde{s}^{t+i} = (s_t, s_{t+1}, \ldots, s_{t+i})$ the history of shock from time t onwards. Using the definition of p and the fact that s_t is known at time t, the single budget constraint at time t can be written as:

$$c(s_t) + E_t\left\{p(\tilde{s}^{t+1})c(\tilde{s}^{t+1}) + E_{t+1}\left\{p(\tilde{s}^{t+2})c(\tilde{s}^{t+2})\cdots\right\}\right\}$$

$$\leq [q(s^t) + y(s_t)]z(s_t),$$

where $\tilde{s}^t = s_t$. Using an iterated expectation argument and suppressing the arguments in c and p yields the representation $E_t\left\{\sum_{r=t}^{t+\tau} p_r c_r\right\} \leq p_t W_t$, where $W_t \equiv [q(s_t) + y(s_t)]z(s_t)$ is the consumer's wealth at time t.

One of the most widely studied hypotheses in the empirical literature on consumption concerns the *random walk model of consumption* proposed by Hall [171]. This says that if consumers are free to borrow and lend at a constant interest rate and the utility function is quadratic, then current consumption is sufficient to predict future consumption. It is straightforward to derive this model by appropriately redefining the discount factor in the consumer's single budget constraint. One implication of this model is that any other variable known at time t such as income is not useful for predicting future consumption. In Chapter 7, we discuss so-called *excess sensitivity tests* of this hypothesis, which seek to determine whether consumption growth is independent of lagged income growth.

1.4. Portfolio Separation

In a complete contingent claims equilibrium, a consumer can purchase claims that pay off in all possible states of the world or all possible events. It turns out when preferences are of the HARA described in Chapter 1, a consumer will hold only a small number of these securities. In this case, we say that the consumer's optimal portfolio choice problem satisfies a *portfolio separation* property.

We now assume that the consumer lives between t and $t + \tau$ and has initial wealth given by W_t. Define $V(W_t, s_t)$ as the lifetime expected utility of the consumer conditional on the initial state s_t and initial wealth W_t:

$$V(W_t, s_t) \equiv \max_{\{c_r\}_{r=t}^{t+\tau}} \left\{ E_t \sum_{r=t}^{t+\tau} \beta^{r-t} U(c_r) \ \text{ s.t. } \ E_t \sum_{r=t}^{t+\tau} p_r c_r \leq p_t W_t. \right\}.$$

Under the assumption that U is of the HARA class, we will derive explicit expressions for the value function $V(W_t, s_t)$, the consumption choice in the initial period t, and the securities that are held in equilibrium. We have the following proposition.

Proposition 2.4 *The optimal consumption choices at time t are:*

$$c_t = \frac{Ab(\phi_t^\tau - \psi_t^\tau)}{1 + \psi_t^\tau} + \frac{W_t}{1 + \psi_t^\tau}, \quad B \neq 0,$$

$$c_t = \frac{W_t - Aq_t^\tau}{1 + \phi_t^\tau}, \quad B = 0.$$

The corresponding value functions are:

$$V(W_t, s_t) = (1 + \psi_t^\tau)^b \frac{b}{1-b} [A(1 + \phi_t^\tau) + BW_t]^{1-b}, \quad B \neq 0, 1,$$

$$V(W_t, s_t) = \sum_{s=0}^{\tau} \beta^s \log(A(1 + \phi_t^\tau) + W_t), \quad B = 1,$$

$$V(W_t, s_t) = -A(1 + \phi_t^\tau) \exp\left[\frac{-W_t + Aq_t^\tau}{A(1 + \phi_t^\tau)} \right], \quad B = 0,$$

where

$$\psi_t^\tau \equiv E_t \left[\sum_{s=1}^{\tau} (p_{t+s}/p_t)(\beta^s p_t/p_{t+s})^B \right],$$

$$q_t^\tau \equiv E_t \left[\sum_{s=1}^{\tau} (p_{t+s}/p_t) \log(\beta^s p_t/p_{t+s}) \right],$$

$$\phi_t^\tau \equiv E_t \left[\sum_{s=1}^\tau (p_{t+s}/p_t) \right].$$

PROOF

We begin by considering the case with $B \neq 0$. Let η denote the Lagrange multiplier on the single budget constraint. The first-order conditions with respect to $\{c_r\}_{r=t}^{t+\tau}$ are:

$$\beta^{r-t} b(A + Bc_r)^{-b} = \eta p_r, \quad t \leq r \leq t + \tau.$$

Now use these conditions to eliminate the Lagrange multiplier as:

$$(\beta^r p_t / p_{t+r})^B (A + Bc_t) = A + Bc_{t+r} \qquad (2.39)$$

for $1 < r \leq \tau$. Using Equation (2.39) in the budget constraint yields the decision rule for c_t when $B \neq 0$. When $B = 0$, the first-order conditions are:

$$\beta^{r-t} \exp(-c_r/A) = \eta p_r, \quad t \leq r \leq t + \tau,$$

which can be rewritten as

$$c_t = -A \log(\beta p_t / p_{t+r}) + c_{t+r}, \qquad (2.40)$$

for $1 < r \leq \tau$. We can substitute for c_{t+r} in the budget constraint using Equation (2.40) to derive the expression for c_t when $B = 0$. We obtain the expressions for the value functions by using the first-order conditions and the relevant solution for c_t in the utility functions.   ∎

Notice that the form of the valuation functions does not depend on the time horizon τ. Also, the consumption choice at time t and the valuation functions depend on a small number of securities. One of these securities is a risk-free security that pays off one unit in each possible state and date of the economy. The price of this security is ϕ_t^τ defined in Proposition 2.4; this says that the ratio of the contingent claims prices between periods t and $t + s$ is used to discount the constant payoff. The other security has the random payoff stream:

$$(\beta^s p_t / p_{t+s})^B \quad \text{or} \quad \log(\beta^s p_t / p_{t+s}), \quad s = 1, \ldots, \tau, \qquad (2.41)$$

depending on the nature of preferences. In Exercise 6, the reader is asked to prove an alternative statement of the portfolio separation property of the consumer's problem by considering a two-period version of this problem.

1.5.   A Growing Economy

We now describe a version of the basic asset pricing model with unbounded utility and growing endowment. Since expected discounted utility becomes unbounded in this case, we need to modify our approach for
proving the existence and uniqueness of the representative consumer's
value function and the equilibrium asset price functions.

We assume that there are a vector of exogenous shocks to the economy
that satisfy Assumption 2.1. When the endowment is growing, we write
its law of motion as:

$$y_t = \lambda(s_t)y_{t-1}. \tag{2.42}$$

Notice that in general, the growth rate of the endowment depends on the
shock. The following assumption on the λ-process is made.

Assumption 2.4 *Define* $\mathcal{L} \equiv [\underline{\lambda}, \bar{\lambda}]$ *where* $\underline{\lambda} > 0$ *and* $\bar{\lambda} < \infty$. *The set* S
is compact and the function $\lambda : S \to \mathcal{L}$ *is a continuous function that is
bounded away from zero.*

The following assumption characterizes the utility function.

Assumption 2.5 *The utility function is given by* $U(c) = (c^{1-\gamma} - 1)/(1 - \gamma)$ *for* $\gamma \geq 0$.

If $\gamma = 1$, $U(c) = \log(c)$. When $\gamma \leq 1$, the utility function is unbounded
above on $\mathbb{R}_{++}$ and unbounded below when $\gamma \geq 1$. Notice that we have
an unbounded return function and unbounded endowment process. We
have an additional restriction on endowment growth.

Assumption 2.6 *For all* $s \in S$, $\beta \int_S \lambda(s')^{1-\gamma} F(s, ds') < 1$, $\gamma \neq 1$.

Notice that the restriction is on the conditional expectation of $\lambda(s')$ so
that it holds for each $s \in S$. In Chapter 5, we describe how this assumption can be weakened so that discounted utility is less than one on average
and not for every realization of the shock. Because endowment is growing
and prices are measured in units of the endowment good, prices are also
growing. In general, the equity price q^e is a function of the endowment
level $y \in \mathbb{R}_{++}$ and the current shock $s \in S$. We will restrict our attention
to price functions such that the *price-dividend ratio*, defined as $q^e(y, s)/y$,
and risk-free bond price $Q^1(s)$ are functions of s only. Further, we assume
that they are elements of the space of continuous and bounded real-valued
functions defined on S, $q^e(y, s)/y \in \mathcal{C}_q(S)$ and $Q^1(s) \in \mathcal{C}_q(S)$, and that
q^e is continuous with respect to y.

The representative consumer's problem is identical to that described in Section 1.1 aside from the fact that the equity price depends on both the level of the endowment y and the current shock s, $q^e(y, s)$. Feasible consumption levels are those that satisfy $0 \leq c \leq y$. The discounted expected utility from consuming the endowment process by setting $c_t = y_t$ for all t is given by:

$$W(y_0) \equiv \frac{1}{1 - \gamma} E_0 \left[\sum_{t=0}^{\infty} \beta^t y_t^{1-\gamma} \right]$$

$$= \frac{1}{1 - \gamma} y_0^{1-\gamma} E_0 \left[1 + \sum_{t=1}^{\infty} \beta^t \left(\prod_{i=1}^{t} \lambda_i \right)^{1-\gamma} \right], \qquad (2.43)$$

where the constant term $-1/[1 - \gamma)(1 - \beta)]$ has been omitted. Using an iterated expectation argument, notice that:

$$E_0 \left\{ \beta^t \left(\prod_{i=1}^{t} \lambda_i \right)^{1-\gamma} \right\} = E_0 \left\{ \beta \lambda_1^{1-\gamma} \cdots E_{t-1} \left\{ \beta \lambda_t^{1-\gamma} \right\} \right\} \leq \alpha^t,$$

where

$$\alpha = \sup_{s \in S} \left\{ \beta \int_S \lambda(s')^{1-\gamma} F(s, ds') \right\}.$$

Since $\alpha < 1$ by Assumption 2.6, this result shows that the term in square brackets in Equation (2.43) is finite. Consequently, $W(y_0)/y_0^{1-\gamma}$ is finite even though total expected discounted utility is not.

In the previous sections, recall that we defined the consumer's value function to be an element of the space of bounded, continuous functions on the space $Z \times B \times S$. For this application, the value function depends on the level of the endowment. More precisely, given the price functions $q^e(y, s)$ and $Q^1(s)$, the consumer's value function satisfies:

$$V(z, b, s, y) = \max_{c, z', b'} \left\{ U(c) + \beta \int_S V(z', b', s', y') F(s, ds') \right\}$$

subject to

$$c + q^e(y, s)z' + Q^1(s)b' \leq [y + q^e(y, s)]z + b, \qquad (2.44)$$

$$0 \leq c \leq y, z' \in Z, \ b' \in B. \qquad (2.45)$$

Since the endowment is growing, we cannot choose the value function V to be an element of the space of bounded, continuous functions on

$Z \times B \times S$. Instead the result in Equation (2.43) suggests that we should restrict our attention to value functions V that grow no faster than $y^{1-\gamma}$.

To describe the space of such functions, let $\mathcal{Z} = Z \times B \times S \times \mathbb{R}_{++}$ and define $\mathcal{B}$ as the space of functions $g : \mathcal{Z} \to \mathbb{R}$ that are jointly continuous in the arguments (z, b, s, y). Notice that Z, B, S are compact and $y \in \mathbb{R}_{++}$. Define the norm for elements of $\mathcal{B}$ by:

$$\|g\|_\varphi = \sup_{z,b,s,y \in \mathcal{Z}} \left| \frac{g(z,b,s,y)}{\varphi(y)} \right| < \infty,$$

where $\varphi \in \mathcal{B}$; in our case, we choose $\varphi(y) = y^{1-\gamma}$. This function is still an element of $\mathcal{B}$ even though it is not an explicit function of (z, b, s). We say that a function $g \in \mathcal{B}$ is φ-bounded if the φ-norm $\|g\|_\varphi$ is finite. We can show that the space $\mathcal{B}$ is a complete, normed, linear space.

To show the existence of a fixed point to the functional equation above, we use a modification of the Contraction Mapping and Blackwell's conditions, known as the Weighted Contraction Mapping Theorem. (See Boyd [41].) Suppose T is an operator that maps the space $\mathcal{B}$ into itself, where $\mathcal{B}$ is a complete, normed, linear space. According to this theorem, if (i) T is monotone ($f \geq g$ implies that $Tf \geq Tg$ for $f, g \in \mathcal{B}$); (ii) T discounts ($T(g + a\varphi) \leq Tg + \delta a\varphi$ for some constant $0 < \delta < 1$ and $a > 0$) and (iii) $T(0) \in \mathcal{B}$, then T has a unique fixed point in $\mathcal{B}$.

To apply this result for our problem, for $V \in \mathcal{B}$ define the operator T by:

$$(TV)(z, b, s, y) = \max_{c, z', b'} \left\{ U(c) + \beta \int_S V(z', b', s', y') F(s, ds') \right\} \quad (2.46)$$

subject to Equations (2.44) and (2.45). We have the following proposition.

Proposition 2.5 *Under Assumptions 2.1, 2.4, 2.5, and 2.6, there exists a unique solution $V^\star : \mathcal{B} \to \mathcal{B}$ to Equation (2.46).*

PROOF

First, we need to show that the operator T maps the space of bounded, continuous functions with the φ-norm into itself. This requires that for any $V \in \mathcal{B}$, TV is bounded (so that $\|(TV)\|_\varphi < \infty$) and that it is jointly continuous in its arguments.

From the budget constraint, notice that

$$\frac{c}{y} \leq \frac{b}{y} + z \left(\frac{q^e(s,y)}{y} + 1 \right) - z' \frac{q^e(s,y)}{y} - \frac{Q(s)b'}{y}.$$

We have restricted $b' \in B, z' \in Z$ and feasible c such that $0 \leq c \leq y$. For any c such that $0 \leq c \leq y$, current utility (which is continuous in c) is also φ-bounded and continuous. If $v \in \mathcal{B}$, then $\beta E_s[v(z', b', s', y')]$ is φ-bounded because

$$\frac{\varphi(y)}{\varphi(y)}\beta \int_S \varphi(y') \frac{v(z', b', s', y')}{\varphi(y')} F(s, ds')$$

$$= \varphi(y)\beta \int_S \lambda(s') \frac{v(z', b', s', y')}{\varphi(y')} F(s, ds')$$

$$\leq \varphi(y)\bar{B}\beta \int_S \lambda(s')F(s, ds') \leq \varphi(y)\bar{B}$$

since v is φ-bounded and $\beta \int_S \lambda(s')F(s, ds') < 1$. Furthermore, the function $\beta E_s[v(z', b', s', y')]$ is continuous since v is continuous and the transition function has the Feller property. Hence, TV involves maximizing a continuous function over a compact set so that it is well defined; that is, a maximum exists and it is bounded, and by the Theorem of the Maximum, it is continuous. Thus, $T : \mathcal{B} \to \mathcal{B}$.

Next, notice that T is monotone. Given any two functions $u \geq w$, it is straightforward to verify that $Tu \geq Tw$. Furthermore, for any constant $a > 0$,

$$(TV + a\varphi)(z, b, s, y) \leq \max_{c, z', b'} \left\{ y^{1-\gamma} \left[\frac{c^{1-\gamma} - 1}{y^{1-\gamma}(1 - \gamma)} + \right. \right.$$

$$\left. \left. \beta \int_S \lambda(s')^{1-\gamma} \frac{V(z', b', s') + a\varphi(y')}{\varphi(y')} F(s, ds') \right] \right\}$$

$$\leq (TV)(z, b, s, y) + \delta a\varphi(y),$$

where $\delta = \beta \int_S \lambda(s')^{1-\gamma}F(s, ds') < 1$ by Assumption 2.6 so that T discounts. Finally, notice that $T(0) \in \mathcal{B}$ since U is φ-bounded and continuous for $0 \leq c \leq y$. Hence, T satisfies the conditions for a weighted contraction mapping and has a unique fixed point $V^* \in \mathcal{B}$. ∎

In equilibrium, $c = y$, $z' = 1$, and $b' = 0$. The equilibrium first-order conditions are given by:

$$q^e(s, y)U'(y) = \beta \int_S U'(y')[q^e(s', y') + y(s')]F(s, ds'), \qquad (2.47)$$

$$Q^1(s)U'(y) = \beta \int_S U'(y')F(s, ds'). \qquad (2.48)$$

We can use the fact that $U'(y) = y^{-\gamma}$ to derive a functional equation for the equilibrium price-dividend ratio, defined as $\psi(s) \equiv q^e(s, y)/y$. Equation (2.47) can be rewritten as:

$$\psi(s) = \beta \int_S \lambda(s')^{1-\gamma} [1 + \psi(s')] F(s, ds'). \qquad (2.49)$$

Notice that $\psi : S \to \mathbb{R}_+$. When endowment is growing, the equity is a claim to a growing dividend and it is not a stationary variable. However, the price-dividend ratio $\psi(s)$ is a function only of endowment growth $\lambda(s)$ and it is stationary. Under Assumptions 2.1, 2.4, 2.5, and 2.6, it is straightforward to demonstrate that for any $\psi \in C_q(S)$ an operator $T_q\psi$ defined from the right side of Equation (2.49) maps the space of bounded, continuous, real-valued functions into itself and satisfies Blackwell's conditions for a contraction. By the Contraction Mapping Theorem, we can show that there exists a unique fixed point to Equation (2.49). It also follows from the equilibrium first-order conditions that the risk-free bond price is:

$$Q^1(s) = \beta E_s[\lambda(s')^{-\gamma}]. \qquad (2.50)$$

In Exercises 7 and 9, the reader is asked to analyze the properties of the solution to this model under alternative distributional assumptions about dividend growth.

2. Extensions of the Basic Model

The asset pricing relations that we developed above depend on the intertemporal MRS in consumption for the representative consumer. We now describe alternative preference specifications that alter the intertemporal MRS used to price risky payoffs in this model. These include models with consumption durability, habit persistence, and nonexpected utility preferences.

2.1. Habit Persistence and Consumption Durability

Habit persistence and consumption durability are alternative ways of modeling the effect of past consumption choices on current utility. When current utility depends on past consumption, we say that preferences are *nonadditive over time*. Models with consumption durability have been studied by Dunn and Singleton [108] and Eichenbaum and Hansen [111] while habit persistence and asset prices have been studied by Constantinides [77] and Ferson and Constantinides [128], among others.

We first describe a simple model that allows us to show the effects of habit persistence and consumption durability on current preferences. The endowment is determined exogenously and is stationary in levels and there is a single good that is used to produce consumption services in each period. We model the effects of consumption durability as follows:

$$c_t^\star = \sum_{s=0}^{\infty} b_s c_{t-s}, \tag{2.51}$$

where $b_s \geq 0$ for all $s \geq 0$ and $\sum_{s=0}^{\infty} b_s = 1$. This says that new consumption goods acquisitions at time t produce a flow of consumption services $b_\tau c_t$ at time $t + \tau$. The representative consumer derives utility from consumption services $c_t^\star$. Following Ferson and Constantinides [128], we can model habit persistence by assuming that the consumer has preferences over consumption services defined by:

$$E_0 \left\{ \sum_{t=0}^{\infty} \beta^t U \left(c_t^\star - h \sum_{s=1}^{\infty} a_s c_{t-s}^\star \right) \right\}, \tag{2.52}$$

where $a_s \geq 0$ and $\sum_{s=1}^{\infty} a_s = 1$ and $h \geq 0$. The function U is defined as strictly increasing, strictly concave, and differentiable. Notice that the habit parameter h shows the fraction of lagged consumption services that establishes a subsistence level of consumption.

We can write the consumer's preferences as a function of c_t only by noting that

$$c_t^\star - h \sum_{s=1}^{\infty} a_s c_{t-s}^\star = \sum_{s=0}^{\infty} b_s c_{t-s} - h \sum_{\tau=1}^{\infty} \sum_{s=0}^{\infty} a_\tau b_s c_{t-s-\tau}$$

$$= b_0 \sum_{s=0}^{\infty} \delta_s c_{t-s}, \tag{2.53}$$

where $\delta_0 = 1$ and $\delta_s = \left(b_s - h \sum_{i=1}^{s} a_i b_{s-i} \right) / b_0$. Suppose $b_s = (1-b)b^s$ for $0 \leq b < 1$ and $a_s = (1-a)a^{s-1}$ for $0 \leq a < 1$. Then we can write:

$$\delta_s = \left(1 - \frac{(1-a)h}{b-a} \right) b^s + \frac{(1-a)h}{b-a} a^s,$$

for $s \geq 1$. If expenditures are not durable ($b = 0$) then $\delta_s = -(1-a)ha^{s-1}$ and the coefficients δ_s are negative for $s \geq 1$. In the absence of habit persistence but with consumption durability, $\delta_s = b^s$ and δ_s are positive. When both habit persistence and consumption durability are present, the coefficients δ_s are positive or negative depending on the relative magnitudes of the durability parameter b and the habit parameters h and a. If

$b \geq a + h(1 - a)$, the coefficient δ_s is positive for all s. If $b \leq h(1 - a)$ then δ_s is negative for all s. Finally, if $h(1 - a) < b < a + h(1 - a)$, then δ_s is positive for recent lags and negative for distant ones.

2.2.   Pricing Durable Consumption Goods

In this section, we derive asset pricing relations with habit persistence and consumption durability. We also present a framework that allows us to derive pricing relations for durable consumption goods by modifying the model in Eichenbaum and Hansen [111].

There are multiple consumption goods and consumption services are produced using a vector of household capital stocks. Denote by k_{t-1} the m-dimensional vector of household capital stocks brought into period t. Given purchases of m new consumption goods at time t, k_t evolves as:

$$k_t = \Delta k_{t-1} + \Theta c_t, \tag{2.54}$$

where Δ is an $m \times m$ matrix whose eigenvalues are strictly less than one. Consumption services $c_t^\star$ are produced as:

$$c_t^\star = \Gamma k_t, \tag{2.55}$$

for an $m \times m$ matrix Γ. This is a dynamic version of the household service technology proposed by Gorman[156] and Lancaster [227], which views consumption goods as claims to future consumption services. In this more general setup, a vector of consumption goods at time t provides consumption services $\Gamma \Delta^\tau \Theta c_t$ at time $t + \tau$. To simplify the matter further, we assume that Δ, Θ, and Γ are diagonal matrices with diagonal elements δ_j, θ_j and γ_j for $j = 1, \ldots, m$ and that $0 < \delta_j < 1$ and $\theta_j > 0$ and $\gamma_j > 0$.

The output of consumption goods evolves as an exogenous stochastic process defined by $y_t \equiv (y_{1,t}, \ldots, y_{m,t})'$. As before, we assume that each $y_{j,t}$ is a function of an m-dimensional vector of exogenous shocks $s_t \in S \subseteq \mathbb{R}^m$, namely, $y_{j,t} \equiv y_j(s_t)$ for $j = 1, \ldots, m$. The exogenous shocks s_t have a transition function F that satisfies Assumption 2.1. The endowment of each consumption good takes values in a compact set. Let $\mathcal{Y} \equiv [\underline{y}, \bar{y}]$ where $\underline{y} > 0$ and $\bar{y} < \infty$. We assume that $y_j : S \to \mathcal{Y}$ are continuous functions that are bounded away from zero for $j = 1, \ldots, m$.

The representative consumer has preferences over sequences of consumption services $\{c_t^\star\}_{t=0}^\infty$ given by:

$$E_0 \left\{ \sum_{t=0}^\infty \beta^t U(c_t^\star) \right\}, \tag{2.56}$$

where $0 < \beta < 1$ and E_0 denotes expectation conditional on information available at time zero. The utility function $U : S \to \mathbb{R}_+$ is continuous, continuously differentiable, strictly increasing, and strictly concave in c^*. For all $c^* \geq 0$, assume that $U(c^*) \geq 0$. Define $\mathrm{MU}_j(c^*) \equiv \partial U(c^*)/\partial c_j^*$ and assume that $\lim_{c_j^* \to 0} \mathrm{MU}_j(c^*)/\mathrm{MU}_i(c^*) = \infty$ for all i and j. This ensures that all goods are consumed in equilibrium. Finally, the restrictions that $\theta_j > 0$ and $\gamma_j > 0$ imply that past consumption choices have a positive effect on current utility.

Notice that we can derive an alternative expression for the vector of household capital stocks as:

$$k_t = \Theta c_t + \sum_{s=1}^{\infty} \Delta^s \Theta c_{t-s}. \tag{2.57}$$

This is well defined since the diagonal elements of Δ are less than one. The feasible consumption goods purchases satisfy $0 \leq c_{j,t} \leq y_{j,t}$ for $j = 1, \ldots, m$. Since each $y_{j,t}$ is bounded above by $\bar{y}$, the vector of capital stocks takes values in the compact set:

$$\mathcal{K} \equiv [0, (1 - \delta_1)^{-1} \theta_1 \bar{y}] \times \cdots \times [0, (1 - \delta_m)^{-1} \theta_m \bar{y}].$$

We assume that consumers can trade in the market for used capital goods as well as make new purchases of consumption goods. We denote by $p_{j,t}^c$ the price of new capital goods purchases and $p_{j,t}^k$ the price of used capital goods. The first consumption good is the numeraire so that its price is normalized as one. The consumer can also purchase equities that pay off in terms of each consumption good and a risk-free bond that pays off in terms of the numeraire good. We define the consumer's purchases of used capital by k_t^d and the vector of equity prices by $q_t^e \equiv (q_{1,t}^e, \ldots, q_{m,t}^e)'$. Define the aggregate or per capita capital holdings of capital by κ_{t-1}. The consumer's state is summarized by its beginning-of-period capital stocks k_{t-1}, its equity holdings z_t, its beginning-of-period bond holdings b_t, the value of per capita capital stock κ_{t-1}, and the current shock s_t. The state of the economy is summarized by the current shock s_t and the per capita capital holdings, κ_{t-1}.

We seek an equilibrium in which all prices and the law of motion for the per capita capital stock can be expressed as time-invariant functions of the current state, s and κ. Define the strictly positive, continuous price functions $p^c : S \times \mathcal{K} \to \mathbb{R}_{++}^m$, $p^k : S \times \mathcal{K} \to \mathbb{R}_{++}^m$, $q^e : S \times \mathcal{K} \to \mathbb{R}_{++}^m$, and $Q^1 : S \times \mathcal{K} \to \mathbb{R}_{++}$. Assume that the per capita capital stock evolves according to $\kappa' = \bar{\kappa}(s, \kappa)$, where $\bar{\kappa} : S \times \mathcal{K} \to \mathcal{K}$ are strictly positive, continuous functions and define the set of functions $\mathcal{P} \equiv (p^c, p^k, q^e, Q^1)$.

Given $\mathcal{P}$ and the law of motion for capital $\bar{\kappa}$, the valuation function for the consumer's problem satisfies:

$$V(k, z, b, \kappa, s) = \max_{c, k^d, z', b'} \left\{ U(c^\star) + \beta \int_S V(k', z', b', \kappa', s') F(s, ds') \right\}$$

subject to

$$p^c(s, \kappa) \cdot c + p^k(s, \kappa) \cdot k^d + q^e(s, \kappa) \cdot z' + Q^1(s, \kappa) b' \leq$$

$$p^k(s, \kappa) \cdot \Delta k + [y(s) + q^e(s, \kappa)] \cdot z + b, \tag{2.58}$$

$$k' = k^d + \Theta c, \tag{2.59}$$

$$c^\star = \Gamma k', \tag{2.60}$$

$$c \geq 0, \quad z' \in Z, \quad b' \in B, \quad k^d \in \mathcal{K}. \tag{2.61}$$

We can use the approach in Proposition 2.1 to show that there exists a bounded, continuous function $V : \mathcal{K} \times Z \times B \times \mathcal{K} \times S \to \mathbb{R}_+$ that solves the consumer's problem.

The market-clearing conditions require that the goods market clears, $c_j = y_j$ for $j = 1, \ldots, m$, the used capital goods market clears, $k_j^d = \delta_j k_j$ for $j = 1, \ldots, m$, all shares are held $z' = \underline{1}$, and all bonds are held, $b' = 0$. A *recursive competitive equilibrium* for this economy is a set of price functions $\mathcal{P} \equiv (p^c, p^k, q^e, Q^1)$, a value function V, and a law of motion for the per capita capital stock $\bar{\kappa}$ such that (i) given $\mathcal{P}$ and $\bar{\kappa}$, V solves the consumer's problem; (ii) markets clear; (iii) the law of motion for the individual capital stock is equal to the law of motion for the per capita capital stock, $k_j' = \bar{\kappa}_j(\kappa, s)$ for $j = 1, \ldots, m$.

Let $\xi(s, \kappa)$ be the multiplier on the budget constraint. Following the approach in Chapter 1, we can substitute the envelope conditions into the first-order conditions for c, k^d, z' and b' to obtain:

$$\xi(s, \kappa) p_j^c(s, \kappa) = \gamma_j \theta_j \mathrm{MU}_j(c^\star) + \beta E_s[\theta_j \delta_j \xi(s', \kappa') p_j^k(s', \kappa')], \tag{2.62}$$

$$\xi(s, \kappa) p_j^k(s, \kappa) = \gamma_j \mathrm{MU}_j(c^\star) + \beta E_s[\delta_j \xi(s', \kappa') p_j^k(s', \kappa')], \tag{2.63}$$

$$\xi(s, \kappa) q_j^e(s, \kappa) = \beta E_s\{\xi(s', \kappa')[y_j(s') + q_j^e(s', \kappa')]\} \tag{2.64}$$

$$\xi(s, \kappa) Q^1(s, \kappa) = \beta E_s[\xi(s', \kappa')]. \tag{2.65}$$

The conditions in Equations (2.62) and (2.63) imply that the price of used capital goods is proportional to the price of durable consumption goods:

$$p_j^k(s, \kappa) = \frac{1}{\theta_j} p_j^c(s, \kappa), \quad j = 1, \ldots, m.$$

We can use Equation (2.62) to show that the durable consumption goods prices satisfy:

$$\xi(s,\kappa)p_j^c(s,\kappa) = \mathrm{MU}_j(c^\star)\gamma_j\theta_j + \beta\delta_j E_s[\xi(s',\kappa')p_j^c(s',\kappa')]$$

for $j = 1,\ldots,m$. These are functional equations in $\xi(s,\kappa)p_j^c(s,\kappa)$. The vector of capital stocks k' carried into the next period is given once $c_j = y_j(s)$ and $k_j^d = \delta_j k$ are determined. Therefore, solving for an equilibrium involves solving for the asset price functions. Since $\mathrm{MU}_j(c^\star)$ is bounded for any $0 < c^\star \le \Gamma k'$ where $k' \in \mathcal{K}$ and $\beta\delta_j E_s[\xi(s',\kappa')p_j^c(s',\kappa')]$ is bounded and continuous for any bounded, continuous $\xi(s,\kappa)p_j^c(s,\kappa)$ for $j = 1,\ldots,m$, we can find a fixed point for this equation using the Contraction Mapping Theorem. Assuming the fixed point has been found, we revert to time subscripts and solve this forward as:

$$\xi_t p_{j,t}^c = \gamma_j\theta_j E_t\left[\sum_{s=0}^{\infty}(\beta\delta_j)^s\mathrm{MU}_j(c_{t+s}^\star)\right].$$

The price of the first consumption is normalized as one so that

$$\xi_t = \gamma_1\theta_1 E_t\left[\sum_{s=0}^{\infty}(\beta\delta_1)^s\mathrm{MU}_1(c_{t+s}^\star)\right].$$

Substituting for ξ_t from the previous expression yields the price of the j'th consumption good as:

$$p_{j,t}^c = \frac{\gamma_j\theta_j E_t\left[\sum_{s=0}^{\infty}(\beta\delta_j)^s\mathrm{MU}_j(c_{t+s}^\star)\right]}{\gamma_1\theta_1 E_t\left[\sum_{s=0}^{\infty}(\beta\delta_1)^s\mathrm{MU}_1(c_{t+s}^\star)\right]} \tag{2.66}$$

for $j = 1,\ldots,m$. Notice that the price of the j'th durable consumption good is defined in terms of the future discounted value of the services from that good, expressed in units of the numeraire good.

We can also use this framework to derive the implicit price of consumption services. Notice that a claim to the j'th durable consumption good for one period contributes $\gamma_j\theta_j$ units of services at date t so the value of a unit of services denoted $p_{j,t}^{c\star}$ is:

$$p_{j,t}^{c\star} = \frac{1}{\gamma_j\theta_j}\left[p_{j,t}^c - \beta\delta_j E_t\left(\frac{\xi_{t+1}}{\xi_t}p_{j,t+1}^c\right)\right], \tag{2.67}$$

where the second term on the right side shows the expected resale value of the durable good, expressed in units of the numeraire.

We now derive an expression for the risk-free rate and the return on the m risky securities. From Equation (2.65), we have that

$$Q^1(s, \kappa) = \beta E_s[\xi(s', \kappa')/\xi(s, \kappa)].$$

Likewise, the equity prices satisfy the relation:

$$\xi(s, \kappa)q_j^e(s, \kappa) = \beta E_s\{\xi(s', \kappa')[y_j(s') + q_j^e(s', \kappa')]\}, \quad j = 1, \ldots, m.$$

Notice that the relevant stochastic discount factor used to price payoffs on any security in this framework is the marginal rate of substitution for the numeraire consumption good, ξ_{t+1}/ξ_t. Using the expressions derived earlier, we can define this pricing function or stochastic discount factor as:

$$\mathcal{M}_{t,1} \equiv \frac{\beta E_{t+1}\left[\sum_{s=0}^{\infty}(\beta\delta_1)^s \mathrm{MU}_1(c_{t+s+1}^\star)\right]}{E_t\left[\sum_{s=0}^{\infty}(\beta\delta_1)^s \mathrm{MU}_1(c_{t+s}^\star)\right]}. \tag{2.68}$$

The relevant pricing function that is used to value risky payoffs depends on the discounted utility of all future services from consumption goods. Notice that if there is habit persistence as well as consumption durability, then the effect of future consumption services will be positive or negative depending on the sign of the coefficients on $\mathrm{MU}(c_{t+s}^\star)$ (which equal δ_s in the previous setup).

The price of the risk-free bond is given by:

$$Q_t^1 = E_t[\mathcal{M}_{t,1}]. \tag{2.69}$$

Similarly, the return on the j'th risky security $r_{j,t+1} \equiv (y_{j,t+1} + q_{j,t+1}^e)/q_{j,t}^e$ satisfies:

$$1 = E_t[\mathcal{M}_{t,1}r_{j,t+1}]. \tag{2.70}$$

We can also derive expressions for risk-free bonds that mature in τ periods by considering the discount factor $\mathcal{M}_{t,\tau} \equiv \xi_{t+\tau}/\xi_t$ and define holding returns of n periods for bonds of maturing at dates τ for $0 < n < \tau$. In Chapter 3, we describe how a special case of this model can be used to analyze the term structure of real risk-free bonds.

2.3.   The Nonexpected Utility Hypothesis

In Chapter 1, we defined the concept of risk aversion in terms of a consumer's preferences over actuarially fair gambles or lotteries at a point in time. In an intertemporal context, we need to define preferences over temporal consumption lotteries or over random consumption paths.

As Kreps and Porteus [222] have shown, the assumption underlying the expected utility model is that individuals are indifferent to the timing of resolution of uncertainty for such temporal lotteries. When this assumption is relaxed to allow for preference for early versus late resolution of uncertainty, preferences can be represented recursively as:

$$U_t = W\left(c_t, E_t\left[U_{t+1}|I_t\right]\right), \tag{2.71}$$

where U_t denotes lifetime utility at time t, W is an aggregator function (through which current consumption and future utility are aggregated), and $E_t(\cdot)$ denotes expectation conditional on information available at time t. We say that consumers exhibit a preference for early (late) resolution of uncertainty over temporal lotteries depending on whether $W(c, \cdot)$ is convex (concave) in its second argument. When W is linear, we obtain the standard time and state-additive formulation of preferences.

Epstein and Zin [120] and Weil [333] have considered a parametric class of nonexpected utility preferences that satisfy the recursive structure of Equation (2.71). This class of preferences allows us to parameterize risk aversion and aversion to intertemporal substitution as two distinct aspects of a consumer's tastes. Here we use Epstein and Zin's [120] formulation. The aggregator function, W, is defined to be of the CES form:

$$W(c, z) = \left[(1 - \beta)c^\delta + \beta z^\delta\right]^{1/\delta}, \quad 0 \neq \delta < 1, \tag{2.72}$$

$$W(c, z) = (1 - \beta)\log(c) + \beta\log(z), \quad \delta = 0, \tag{2.73}$$

where $c, z \geq 0$ and $\beta = 1/(1 + \rho), \rho > 0$. When future consumption paths are deterministic, this aggregator function results in an intertemporal constant elasticity of substitution utility function with elasticity of substitution $1/(1 - \delta)$ and rate of time preference ρ.

The certainty equivalent function $\mu[U_{t+1}]$, which shows the certain value of the random utility stream U_{t+1} conditional on information available at time t, is specified to be a constant relative risk aversion expected utility function. For some random variable x, μ is given by:

$$\mu[x] = [Ex^\alpha]^{1/\alpha}, \quad 0 \neq \alpha < 1, \tag{2.74}$$

$$\log(\mu) = E\left[\log(x)\right], \quad \alpha = 0, \tag{2.75}$$

where $E(\cdot)$ is the expectation operator. In our application, the random variable is the utility from consuming the uncertain consumption stream $\{\tilde{c}_{t+1}, \tilde{c}_{t+2}, \ldots\}$. Thus, we can derive a recursive specification for intertemporal utility as:

$$U_t = \left[(1-\beta)c_t^\delta + \beta(E_t U_{t+1}^\alpha)^{\delta/\alpha}\right]^{1/\delta}, \quad \alpha \neq 0, \quad \delta \neq 0, \tag{2.76}$$

where $E_t(\cdot)$ is expectation conditional on information available at time t. Notice that when $\alpha = \delta$, Equation (2.76) specializes to the expected utility specification $U_t^\alpha = (1-\beta)E_t\left\{\sum_{j=0}^\infty \beta^j c_{t+j}^\alpha\right\}$.

We now explore the implications for asset pricing using this class of preferences. We consider the optimal portfolio choice problem of some representative consumer who is endowed with an initial stock of the consumption good, A_0, which can either be consumed or invested in assets traded on competitive markets. Suppose there are N assets available for trade. Let r_t denote an N-vector of returns with typical element $r_{j,t}$ which show the gross, real return on an asset held throughout period t. Each $r_{j,t}$ has support $[\underline{r}, \bar{r}]$, $\underline{r} > 0$. We assume that (r_t, s_t) follows a first-order stationary Markov process with transition function F where s_t are variables that help to predict the future. The random vector (r_t, s_t) is observed at the beginning of period t before decisions are made.

When (r_t, s_t) follows a first-order Markov process, the state of the economy is summarized by $I_t \equiv (r_t, s_t)$. The state variables for the individual are her initial wealth and the current state of the economy. The consumer's problem can be formulated as a dynamic programming problem as follows:

$$J(A_t, I_t) \equiv \max_{c_t, \omega_t} \left\{(1-\beta)c_t^\delta + \beta\left[E_t J(A_{t+1}, I_{t+1})^\alpha\right]^{\delta/\alpha}\right\}^{1/\delta} \tag{2.77}$$

subject to $A_{t+1} = (A_t - c_t)\omega_t' r_t$ and $\sum_{j=1}^N \omega_{j,t} = 1$.

The solution for this problem is a plan that expresses consumption and portfolio choices as a function of the state variables (A_t, I_t). Suppose there exists a solution that expresses (c_t, A_{t+1}) as homogeneous functions of the state variables; that is, for all (A_t, I_t), $h_t(1, I_t) = (c_t, A_{t+1})$ implies that $h_t(A_t, I_t) = (c_t A_t, A_{t+1})$. In this case, the consumer's value function is given by:

$$J(A_t, I_t) = \phi(I_t)A_t \equiv \phi_t A_t,$$

where

$$\phi_t A_t = \max_{c_t, \omega_t} \left\{(1-\beta)c_t^\delta + \beta\left[E_t(\phi_{t+1}A_{t+1})^\alpha\right]^{\delta/\alpha}\right\}^{1/\delta} \tag{2.78}$$

subject to $A_{t+1} = (A_t - c_t)\omega_t' r_t$ and $\sum_{j=1}^N \omega_{j,t} = 1$.

The first-order condition with respect to c_t is:

$$\left[\delta(1-\beta)c_t^{\delta-1} - \beta\delta(A_t - c_t)^{\delta-1}\mu^{*\delta}\right] = 0, \tag{2.79}$$

where $\mu^* = [E_t(\phi_{t+1}M_t)^\alpha]^{1/\alpha}$ and M_t is the gross return on the optimal portfolio, $M_t = w_t'r_t$. Notice that the optimal consumption choice satisfies the portfolio separation property and that consumption is proportional to wealth,

$$c_t = \psi_t(I_t)A_t.$$

Using this result in Equation (2.79) to solve for $\mu^{*\delta}$ and simplifying yields the optimality condition for consumption:

$$1 = E_t\left[\beta\left(\frac{c_{t+1}}{c_t}\right)^{\delta-1}M_t\right]^{\alpha/\delta}, \quad \alpha \neq 0, \ \delta \neq 0. \tag{2.80}$$

The optimal portfolio weights w_t can be obtained by solving the problem:

$$\max_{w_t}\left[E_t(\phi_{t+1}w_t'r_t)^\alpha\right]^{1/\alpha} \quad \text{subject to} \quad \sum_{j=1}^{N}w_{j,t} = 1,$$

where $\phi(I_{t+1}) = (1-\beta)^{1/\delta}\psi(I_{t+1})^{(\delta-1)/\delta} = (1-\beta)^{1/\delta}(c_{t+1}/A_{t+1})^{1-1/\delta}$. Define $\gamma \equiv \alpha/\delta$. The first-order conditions with respect to $w_{j,t}$ are:

$$E_t\left[\left(\frac{c_{t+1}}{c_t}\right)^{(\delta-1)\gamma}M_t^{\gamma-1}(r_{j,t} - r_{1,t})\right] = 0, \quad j = 2,\ldots,N. \tag{2.81}$$

Multiplying by $w_{j,t}$, summing over j, and substituting from Equation (2.80) yields:

$$E\left[\beta^\gamma\left(\frac{c_{t+1}}{c_t}\right)^{(\delta-1)\gamma}M_t^{\gamma-1}r_{j,t}\right] = 1, \quad j = 1,\ldots,N. \tag{2.82}$$

Notice that the intertemporal MRS or the stochastic discount factor that is used to price uncertain payoffs in this model is defined as:

$$\mathcal{M}_{t,1} \equiv \left[\beta\left(\frac{c_{t+1}}{c_t}\right)^{\delta-1}\right]^\gamma\left(\frac{1}{M_t}\right)^{1-\gamma}, \tag{2.83}$$

which is a geometric average of the intertemporal MRS from the standard expected utility model and the intertemporal MRS from the logarithmic expected utility model. The weights attached to each MRS are determined by γ. When $\gamma = 1$, consumption growth is sufficient for discounting future payoffs as in the intertemporal asset pricing model with time-additive preferences. When $\gamma = 0$, the market return is sufficient for discounting uncertain payoffs as in the simple static CAPM.

If $\alpha = \delta$ (or $\gamma = 1$), then these first-order conditions become:

$$E_t \left[\beta \left(\frac{c_{t+1}}{c_t} \right)^{\delta-1} r_{j,t} \right] = 1, \quad j = 1, \dots, N,$$

which correspond to the first-order conditions for the expected utility model with constant relative aversion preferences. Another specialization that is of interest is logarithmic risk preferences, which occurs when $\alpha = 0$ but $\delta \neq 0$. Then the counterpart to Equation (2.82) is:

$$E_t \left[M_t^{-1} r_{j,t} \right] = 1, \quad j = 1, \dots, N,$$

which imposes the same restrictions as those implied by the expected utility problem with logarithmic preferences. In this case, the parameter δ, which governs intertemporal substitutability, cannot be identified from these equations. In Chapter 3, we discuss issues of identification and estimation in more detail when we describe how the restrictions of the nonexpected utility model can be tested using data on per capita consumption and asset returns.

3. Solving Asset Pricing Models

We now describe a numerical solution method for solving asset pricing equations that depend on a finite set of exogenous state variables. According to this method, we approximate the continuous Markov process for the exogenous state variables by a discrete Markov chain. Our discussion derives from Tauchen and Hussey [324].

We describe this method for the case with CRR utility and growing endowment. Recall from Section 1.5 that the solution for the price-dividend ratio satisfies the relation:

$$\psi(s) = E_s\{[1 + \psi(s')]\lambda(s')\mathcal{M}(s')\}, \tag{2.84}$$

where $\psi(s) = q^e(s, y)/y(s)$ is the price-dividend ratio, $\lambda(s') = y(s')/y(s)$ is dividend growth, and $\mathcal{M}(s')$ is the intertemporal MRS that is a function of dividend growth, $\lambda(s')^{-\gamma}$. The exogenous shocks s_t follow a first-order Markov process. We now consider the issue of approximating this solution.

Let $f(s_{t+1}|s_t)$ denote the conditional density for s_{t+1} given s_t. Also define $\phi(s') \equiv \lambda(s')\mathcal{M}(s')$. The integral form of the asset pricing equation is:

$$\psi(s) = \int_S [1 + \psi(s')]\phi(s')f(s'|s)ds'. \tag{2.85}$$

This equation is termed a Fredholm equation of the second kind. To describe the solution, rewrite Equation (2.85) by defining $\tau(s') = [1 + \psi(s')]\phi_i(s')$ and letting $I[\tau]$ denote the integral operator given by the right side of this equation as:

$$I[\tau](s) = \int_S \tau(s')f(s'|s)ds'. \tag{2.86}$$

We can rewrite Equation (2.86) as

$$I[\tau](s) = \int \tau(s')\frac{f(s'|s)}{\omega(s')}\omega(s')ds', \tag{2.87}$$

where $\omega(s')$ is some strictly positive weighting function. The idea underlying the technique that Tauchen and Hussey implement is to approximate the integral $\int[\cdot]\omega(s')s'$ in Equation (2.87) using a quadrature rule. This method of solution is known as Nystrom's method or the quadrature method.[5] To describe its implementation, we briefly describe the method of numerical quadrature.

Let $\mathcal{C}(S)$ denote the space of bounded, continuous functions defined on the compact set S equipped with the sup norm. There are different types of quadrature rules. Here we describe the class of Gaussian quadrature rules. We define an N-point numerical quadrature rule for approximating integration of $g \in \mathcal{C}(S)$ against a density $w(s)$ for $s \in \mathbb{R}$ as a set of abscissa $\bar{s}_{Nk}$ and a set of weights w_{Nk} for $k = 1, \ldots, N$ such that:

$$I_N(g) = \sum_{k=1}^{N} g(\bar{s}_{Nk})w_{Nk} \doteq \int_S g(s)w(s)ds = I(g). \tag{2.88}$$

In Gaussian quadrature, the weights $\{w_{Nk}\}$ and abscissa $\{\bar{s}_{Nk}\}$ are chosen such that $I_N(g)$ equals $I(g)$ exactly when g is a polynomial of degree less than or equal to $2N - 1$. In this expression, the weight function w is assumed to be nonnegative and $\int_S w(s)ds = 1$.[6]

---

[5] For further discussion, see, for example, Atkinson [21] or Cryer [79].

[6] Atkinson [21, Ch. 3–5], describes the construction of univariate quadrature rules.

Using this definition, an N-point quadrature rule for approximating the integral in Equation (2.87) is given by a set of abscissa and weights $\bar{s}_k$ and w_k, $k = 1, 2, \ldots, N$ such that

$$I_N[\tau](s) = \sum_{k=1}^{N} \tau(\bar{s}_k) \pi_k^N(s),$$

where

$$\pi_k^N(s) = \frac{f(\bar{s}_k | s)}{k(s)\omega(\bar{s}_k)} w_k, \qquad k = 1, 2, \ldots, N, \tag{2.89}$$

$$k(s) = \sum_{i=1}^{N} \frac{f(\bar{s}_i | s)}{\omega(\bar{s}_i)} w_i. \tag{2.90}$$

Notice that the weights $\pi_k^N(s)$ are obtained by replacing integration against $\omega(s')$ with summation using the quadrature rule and normalizing so that the weights sum to unity. Also notice that the quadrature rule provides a way of approximating the continuous Markov density with a discrete Markov chain.

To obtain an approximate solution for the price-dividend ratio, $\psi(s)$, we evaluate $I_N[\tau](s)$ at each of the quadrature abscissa and solve the implied linear system of equations. Define:

$$\bar{\psi}_{Nj} = \tilde{\psi}_N(\bar{s}_j), \qquad j = 1, \ldots, N,$$

where $\tilde{\psi}_N : \mathbb{R}_+ \to \mathbb{R}$ denotes the (yet to be determined) approximate solution extended to all $s \in S$ and let $\bar{\psi}_{Nj} = \tilde{\psi}_N(\bar{s}_j)$ denote the values of $\tilde{\psi}_N$ at each of the abscissa. In addition, we let $\phi_k = \phi(\bar{s}_k)$ and $\pi_{jk}^N = \pi_k^N(\bar{s}_j)$. Evaluating $I_N[\tau]$ at s's equal to each of the quadrature abscissa $\bar{s}_j$ and remembering the definition of τ yields:

$$\bar{\psi}_{Nj} = \sum_{k=1}^{N} [1 + \bar{\psi}_{Nk}] \phi_k \pi_{jk}^N, \qquad j = 1, \ldots, N. \tag{2.91}$$

The equations above comprise a system of N linear equations in the $\bar{\psi}_{Nj}$ which can be solved directly. Their solution provides the values of the approximate solution to the integral equations at each of the quadrature points. Notice that we have obtained the solution at a finite set of values $\bar{\psi}_{Nj}$ for $j = 1, \ldots, N$ of the state space. The Nystrom extension of the solution states that the solution can be evaluated on the entire domain of $s \in S$ as:

$$\tilde{\psi}_N(s) = \sum_{k=1}^{N} [1 + \tilde{\psi}_N(\bar{s}_k)] \phi(\bar{s}_k) \pi_k^N(s), \qquad s \in S. \tag{2.92}$$

The $\{\bar{\psi}_{Nj}\}_{j=1}^{N}$ defined above are the solutions to the asset pricing equation if one views the law of motion of the state vector as a discrete Markov
chain with range $\{\bar{s}_k\}$ and transition probabilities $\pi_{jk}^N = Pr(s_{t+1} = \bar{s}_k | s_t = \bar{s}_j)$.

Under certain regularity conditions, Tauchen and Hussey, [324, p.
394], show that the approximate solution to the asset pricing equation
converges to the exact solution uniformly. Here we describe a numerical
solution. We assume that the state vector s_t is an element of $S \subseteq \mathbb{R}^2$ and
assume that it has the law of motion:

$$
\begin{bmatrix} s_{1,t} \\ s_{2,t} \end{bmatrix} = \begin{bmatrix} a_{11} & a_{12} \\ a_{21} & a_{22} \end{bmatrix} \begin{bmatrix} s_{1,t-1} \\ s_{2,t-1} \end{bmatrix} + \begin{bmatrix} \epsilon_{1,t} \\ \epsilon_{2,t} \end{bmatrix},
$$

where $s_{1,t} = \log(c_t/c_{t-1})$ and $s_{2,t} = \log(d_t/d_{t-1})$ are logarithmic consumption and dividend growth, and $\epsilon_{i,t}$, $i = 1, 2$ are independent normal
random variables, each with variance σ_i^2. The representative agent's per
period utility function is of the CRR form, $u(c) = c^{(1-\gamma)}/(1-\gamma)$. We
chose $\beta = 0.97$ and $\gamma = 0.03$ and parameterized the law of motion of s_t
as $a_{11} = -0.1$, $a_{22} = 0.1$, $a_{12} = a_{21} = 0$, and $\sigma_i^2 = 0.01$.

Since the state space is multivariate, we need to use a multivariate
quadrature rule which can be defined as the product of a univariate rule
or as a nonproduct rule.[7] In our application, we use a Gauss-Hermite
product rule, which is based on the family of Hermite polynomials. Define
the weight function $w(x) = \exp(-x^2)$ and let $H_n(x)$ be an element of
the Hermite polynomial family. Then $H_n(x)$ is computed recursively by
setting $H_0(x) = 1$, $H_1(x) = 2x$ and

$$
H_{n+1}(x) = 2x H_n(x) - 2n H_{n-1}(x).
$$

It is easy to verify that this is an orthogonal family of polynomials so
that for $n > m$,

$$
\int_{-\infty}^{\infty} H_m(x) H_n(x) \exp(-x^2) dx = 0.
$$

We can derive Gaussian quadrature rules from other orthogonal polynomial families such as Legendre, Chebyshev, Jacobi, or Laguerre polynomials.

In practice, quadrature formula for different N are available from a
variety of different sources.[8] We used the IMSL Math Library routine

---

[7] Stroud [319] discusses the construction of multivariate quadrature formulas.
[8] See the tables of abscissa and weights in Abramowitz and Stegun [5], for example.

Table 2.1. Solution at abscissa points: $\tilde{\psi}_N(\bar{s}_{1,j}, \bar{s}_{2,j})$

	−0.38	−0.24	−0.12	0.00	0.12	0.24	0.38
−0.38	39.18	39.80	40.33	40.85	41.37	41.93	42.58
−0.24	39.33	39.94	40.48	41.00	41.53	42.090	42.74
−0.12	39.46	40.07	40.61	41.14	41.67	42.23	42.88
0.00	39.60	40.20	40.74	41.27	41.80	42.36	43.02
0.24	39.84	40.46	41.01	41.54	42.07	42.64	43.30
0.38	40.00	40.61	41.16	41.69	42.23	42.80	43.46

GAUSSQUADRULE developed by Golub and Welsch [154]. Recall that we require the weights w_{kN} to sum to one but the weights for a Gauss-Hermite rule sum to $\sqrt{\pi}$ so that we need to normalize the computed weights by $\sqrt{\pi}$. In our example, the conditional density $f(s_{t+1}|s_t)$ is just the product of two independent, normal, conditional densities for $s_{1,t}$ and $s_{2,t}$. We chose the weighting function $\omega(s_{1,t}, s_{2,t})$ as the conditional density for s_{t+1} evaluated at $s_t = 0$, $f(s_{1,t+1}, s_{2,t+1}|s_{1,t} = 0, s_{2,t} = 0)$. (Tauchen and Hussey [324] discuss some considerations in the choice of the weighting function.) Given the abscissa and weights for the numerical rule and the expressions in Equations (2.89) and (2.90), it is straightforward to calculate the values π_{jk}^N for $k = 1, \ldots, N$ where $J = 2, 3, \ldots, 8$ and to solve for the discrete price-dividend ratios $\tilde{\psi}_{Nj}, j = 1, \ldots, N$, $N = J^2$. Our solution is displayed in Table 2.1.

In this table, the first column shows the abscissa for an N-point Gauss-Hermite rule with $N = 7$. The weights corresponding to each abscissa are given by 0.548E−03, 0.308E−01, 0.240E+00, 0.457E+00, 0.308E−01, and 0.548E−03. We also calculated the Nystrom extension of the solution at some pre-chosen points that are different from the abscissa points of the quadrature rule using the formula in Equation (2.92). For example, the value of the price-dividend ratio when the current state is $s_{1,t} = 0.08$ and $s_{2,t} = -0.02$ is obtained by multiplying the terms $[1 + \tilde{\psi}_{Nk}]\phi(\bar{s}_k)$ with the discrete conditional probabilities $\pi_k^N(s)$ evaluated at $s_{1,t} = 0.08$ and $s_{2,t} = -0.02$ and summing over $k = 1, \ldots, N$. Since the Nystrom extension can be calculated at any arbitrary set of points, we can use this approach to calculate various moments implied by the model and compare them to those in the data.

4. Exercises

1. Risk-Neutral Pricing

Suppose output evolves as a stationary Markov process with transition function $F(s, s')$ and consumers are risk neutral, $U(c) = ac$. Show that the equilibrium price function satisfies:

$$q^e(y) = \sum_{s=1}^{\infty} \beta^s E(y_{t+s}|y_t = y). \tag{2.93}$$

Suppose y_t evolves as $y_{t+1} = \rho y_t + \varepsilon_{t+1}$ where $|\rho| < 1$ and $E(\varepsilon_t) = 0$, $E(\varepsilon_t^2) = \sigma^2$, and $E(\varepsilon_t \varepsilon_{t-s}) = 0$ for $s > 0$. Show that the equity price is given by $q_t = \beta \rho y_t/(1 - \beta \rho)$. Interpret these results.

2. Independent Output Shocks

Let $\{y_t\}_{t=0}^{\infty}$ be a sequence of independent and identically distributed random variables with cumulative distribution function $\Phi(y)$. Define $\beta E[yU'(y)] \equiv \bar{\phi}$ where $\bar{\phi}$ is a constant. Beginning with $\phi_0(y) = 0$, define the mapping:

$$\phi_n(y) = (T\phi_{n-1})(y) = \bar{\phi} + \beta \int \phi_{n-1}(y')d\Phi(y') = \bar{\phi}\sum_{i=0}^{n-1} \beta^i.$$

a) Show that the equity price can be obtained by using the limit of this mapping as $U'(y)q^e(y) = \bar{\phi}/(1 - \beta)$ where

$$\lim_{n \to \infty} (T^n \phi_0)(y) = \phi(y) = \bar{\phi}/(1 - \beta).$$

b) Derive an expression for the elasticity of price with respect to output and interpret the resulting expression.

3. The Random Walk Model of Consumption

Use the model in Section 1.3 with quadratic utility and a real interest rate that is equal to the rate of time preference $r = \rho$ to derive the random walk model of consumption proposed by Hall [171]:

$$E_t[c_{t+1}] = c_t. \tag{2.94}$$

Let ε_{t+1} denote a forecast error in predicting future consumption that is uncorrelated with all information that is known at time t, $E_t(\varepsilon_{t+1}) = 0$. Derive a test of the random walk model of consumption by using the properties of this forecast error.

4.Pricing Coupon Bonds

Suppose that a coupon bond matures in τ periods at which time it pays one unit of the consumption good. It also pays a coupon equal to c in periods $t+1,\ldots,t+\tau-1$. Show that the price of such a bond satisfies:

$$Q^{\tau}_{c,t} = c \sum_{i=1}^{\tau-1} Q^i_t + Q^{\tau}_t.$$

5. Pricing Forward Contracts on Equities

The owner of an n-period forward contract purchases one share of the equity at the forward price where the forward price has been set such that the initial value of the contract is equal to zero. Let $\bar{S}$ denote the delivery price. The ex-dividend price of the equity at time $t+n$ is $q^e(s_{t+n})$. Derive an expression for the delivery price on the forward contract.

6. Consider the model we considered in Section 1.3 with a complete set of contingent prices and HARA preferences. Assume that the consumer lives for two periods and has the budget constraint:

$$p_t c_t + E_t(p_{t+1} W_{t+1}) \leq p_t W_t,$$

where W_{t+1} is state-contingent wealth in period two. Derive the following expressions for W_{t+1}:

$$W_{t+1} = (1 + r^1_t) \left\{ \frac{A(1-\phi)}{B} \right\} + \frac{(\beta p_t/p_{t+1})^B}{E_t[(p_{t+1}/p_t)(\beta p_t/p_{t+1})^B]} \times$$

$$\left\{ \frac{[A\phi + BW_t] E_t[(p_{t+1}/p_t)(\beta p_t/p_{t+1})^B]}{B\{1 + E_t[(p_{t+1}/p_t)(\beta p_t/p_{t+1})^B]\}} \right\}$$

when $B \neq 0$ and

$$W_{t+1} = (1 + r^1_t) \left\{ \frac{(1-\phi)\{W_t - AE_t[(p_{t+1}/p_t)\log(\beta p_t/p_{t+1})]\}}{\phi} \right\}$$

$$+ \frac{\log(\beta p_t/p_{t+1})}{E_t[(p_{t+1}/p_t)\log(\beta p_t/p_{t+1})]} \{AE_t[(p_{t+1}/p_t)\log(\beta p_t/p_{t+1})]\}$$

when $B = 0$ where $\phi = 1 + E_t(p_{t+1}/p_t)$ and $1 + r^1_t \equiv [E_t(p_{t+1}/p_t)]^{-1}$. Show that the terms in braces each sum to $W_t - c_t$. Using this result, argue that the consumer holds her portfolio in two assets, one of which is risk free.

7. Consider the version of the model with CRR preferences and growing endowment.

a) Show that Equation (2.49) can be solved forward to yield an expression for the price-dividend ratio as:

$$\frac{q_t^e}{y_t} = E_t \left[\sum_{i=1}^{\infty} \beta^i \left(\prod_{j=1}^{i} \lambda_{t+j}^{1-\gamma} \right) \right].$$

b) Suppose that dividend growth satisfies:

$$\lambda_t = \exp(\mu + \varepsilon_t), \quad \varepsilon_t \sim N(0, \sigma^2).$$

Show that the price-dividend ratio is given by:

$$\frac{q_t^e}{y_t} = \frac{\Omega}{1 - \Omega},$$

where $\Omega = \beta \exp[(1-\gamma)\mu + (1-\gamma)^2(\sigma^2/2)]$.

c) Show that the condition for the existence of a recursive competitive equilibrium with growing endowment, $\beta \int_S \lambda(s')^{1-\gamma} F(s, ds') < 1$, is equivalent to the condition that $\Omega < 1$.

8. The Effects of a Mean-Preserving Spread

We now study the effects of a mean-preserving spread in the distribution of dividend growth on the equilibrium price-dividend ratio. We use the example in the previous exercise for this purpose.

a) Show that if the variance of dividend growth $\mathrm{Var}(\lambda_t)$ changes, the mean of dividend growth $E(\lambda_t)$ also changes.

b) To define a mean-preserving spread for this example, let μ be a function of a parameter ξ and similarly let σ^2 be a function also of ξ. Define a mean-preserving spread as a change in ξ such that $-\partial\mu(\xi)/\partial\xi = \partial(\sigma^2(\xi)/2)/\partial\xi$.

Show that a mean-preserving spread satisfying the preceding condition decreases the price-dividend ratio if $\gamma > 1$ and increases it if $\gamma < 1$.

9. Assume that preferences are CRR and consider two alternative time series models for dividend growth. The first time series model is termed the *trend-stationary model* and it assumes that the logarithm of endowment follows a first-order autoregressive stationary process around a deterministic trend:

$$y_t = \exp(\delta_0 + \delta_1 t + \varepsilon_t), \quad \varepsilon_t = \delta_2 \varepsilon_{t-1} + e_t \text{ with } |\delta_2| < 1. \quad (2.95)$$

The disturbance $\{e_t\}$ is assumed to be an i.i.d. normally distributed process with mean zero and variance σ_e^2.

The second model is termed the *difference-stationary model* and it assumes that the difference of the logarithm of the endowment is a stationary autoregressive process. The endowment evolves according to Equation (2.42) while endowment growth has the law of motion:

$$\log \lambda_t = \rho_0 + \rho_1 \log \lambda_{t-1} + u_t \text{ with } |\rho_1| < 1. \quad (2.96)$$

The innovation $\{u_t\}$ is assumed to be an i.i.d. normally distributed process with mean zero and variance σ_u^2.[9]

a) Show that the price of a τ-period bond for the first time series model is given by:

$$Q_t^\tau = A_\tau \exp(a_\tau \varepsilon_t), \quad (2.97)$$

where

$$a_1 = \gamma(1 - \delta_2), \quad a_\tau = a_1 \sum_{i=0}^{\tau-1} \delta_2^i,$$

$$A_1 = \beta \exp[-\gamma \delta_1 + \gamma^2(\sigma_e^2/2)],$$

$$A_\tau = \beta A_{\tau-1} \exp[-\gamma \delta_1 + (a_{\tau-1} - \gamma)^2(\sigma_e^2/2)].$$

b) Show that the price of a τ-period bond for the second time series model is given by:

$$Q_t^\tau = B_\tau \lambda_t^{b_\tau}, \quad (2.98)$$

---

[9]Campbell and Mankiw [62], Eichenbaum and Christiano [110], and Stock [313], among others, discuss the adequacy of these time series models for describing aggregate GNP or output. For an application of these models in an asset pricing context, see Campbell [59].

where

$$b_1 = -\gamma\rho_1, \quad b_\tau = b_1 \sum_{i=0}^{\tau-1} \rho_1^i,$$

$$B_1 = \beta \exp[-\gamma\rho_0 + \gamma^2(\sigma_u^2/2)],$$

$$B_\tau = \beta B_{\tau-1} \exp[(b_{\tau-1} - \gamma)\rho_0 + (b_{\tau-1} - \gamma)(\sigma_u^2/2)].$$

c) Derive an expression for the slope of the yield curve, $i_t^\tau - i_t^{\tau-1}$.

d) Backus, Gregory, and Zin [22] show that the yield curve has a negative slope when the endowment process has a unit root. Demonstrate this result using your answer to part b). Suppose you use the trend-stationary model for the dividend growth. Does the yield curve have a positive or a negative slope?

e) Derive a closed-form solution for the forward premium and show that the time series models predict opposite signs for the premiums.

10. Approximating a Continuous Markov Process

Tauchen [325] proposes a simple method for approximating a continuous Markov process for some exogenous state variable by a discrete Markov model. Suppose the real-valued exogenous state variable s_t follows a first-order autoregressive process:

$$s_t = \rho s_{t-1} + \epsilon_t, \quad |\rho| < 1, \tag{2.99}$$

where ϵ_t is a white noise process with variance σ_ϵ^2 and distribution function given by $\Pr[\epsilon_t \leq u] = F(u/\sigma)$. Here F is a cumulative distribution with unit variance.

Let $\tilde{s}_t$ denote the discrete-valued process that approximates $\{s_t\}$. Suppose the N discrete values that $\tilde{s}_t$ may take are defined to a multiple m of the unconditional standard deviation $\sigma_s = (\sigma_\epsilon^2/(1 - \rho^2))^{1/2}$. Then let $\bar{s}^1 = -\bar{s}^N$ and let the remaining be equispaced over the interval $[\bar{s}^1, \bar{s}^N]$. The transition probabilities $\pi_{j,k} = \Pr[\tilde{s}_t = \bar{s}^k|\tilde{s}_{t-1}^j]$ are calculated as follows. Let $w = \bar{s}^k - \bar{s}^{k-1}$. For each j, if k is between 2 and $N - 1$, set

$$\begin{aligned}
\pi_{j,k} &= \Pr[\bar{s}^k - w/2 \leq \rho\bar{s}^j + \epsilon_t \leq \bar{s}^k + w/2] \\
&= F\left[\sigma_\epsilon^{-1}(\bar{s}^k - \rho\bar{s}^j + w/2)\right] - F\left[\sigma_\epsilon^{-1}(\bar{s}^k - \rho\bar{s}^j - w/2)\right],
\end{aligned}$$

otherwise,

$$\pi_{j,1} = F\left[\sigma_\epsilon^{-1}(\bar{s}^1 - \rho\bar{s}^j + w/2)\right],$$

and

$$\pi_{j,N} = 1 - F\left[\sigma_\epsilon^{-1}(\bar{s}^N - \rho\bar{s}^j - w/2)\right].$$

Compare this method with the quadrature-based method described in Section 3.

3

Tests of Asset Pricing Relations

Empirical testing of asset pricing relations is a very broad area. Models and methods have been developed to study the empirical behavior of stock returns and interest rates, options prices, the prices of forward and futures contracts, and exchange rates.

In this chapter, we describe tests of the equilibrium asset pricing model based on the Euler equations characterizing the representative consumer's optimal portfolio choice problem. As part of this discussion, we describe generalized method of moments estimation (GMM) and the empirical evidence from GMM estimation under a variety of preference specifications, including models with a single good, time additive preferences, and models that allow for time nonadditive and nonexpected utility preferences.

Next, we describe the literature on variance bounds tests. Variance bounds tests are typically derived from a present-value relation linking stock prices and dividends or from versions of the expectations theory of the term structure of interest rates. This literature originates with Shiller [305, 306], Singleton [311], and LeRoy and Porter [228]. We describe the original versions of these tests in Section 3 as well as the modifications that have been implemented.

There are other widely used methods for analyzing asset market data. These methods are not explicitly linked to any underlying economic model. In this respect, we discuss formulation and estimation of ARCH type models, which seek to explain volatility in asset prices and returns in terms of time-varying variances and covariances. This idea dates back to Mandelbrot [245] and Fama [123] and it has generated a voluminous literature associated with it. We review this literature in Section 4. In this section, we also discuss some new methods for testing for nonlinearities in asset prices that derive from the literature on chaos and nonlinear time series. The final topics of this chapter are methods for implementing bootstrap simulations and the application of these methods in an empirical study of stock returns.

1.   Euler Equation-Based Tests

We begin by describing methods that are derived from an underlying economic framework such as the asset pricing model that we studied in Chapter 2. The restrictions implied by this model form the basis for a number of widely used tests, including Euler equation-based tests and variance bounds tests. In this section, we describe tests of asset pricing relations derived from the intertemporal Euler equations. These tests can be implemented using maximum likelihood estimation or GMM estimation. Maximum likelihood-based tests typically require a distributional assumption on the process generating per capita consumption and asset returns. We describe GMM estimation methods, which do not require such distributional assumptions.[1]

We consider a version of the representative consumer asset pricing model that we developed in Chapter 2. Suppose there are m assets that have maturities of n periods for $n \geq 1$. Using the approach in Chapter 2, the intertemporal Euler equations characterizing the behavior of per capita consumption and asset returns are given by:

$$1 = \beta^n E\left[\frac{U'(c_{t+n})}{U'(c_t)} r_{j,t+n} \Big| I_t\right], \quad j = 1, \ldots, m,$$

$$1 \equiv E\left[\mathcal{M}_{t,n} r_{j,t+n} | I_t\right], \tag{3.1}$$

where $r_{j,t+n}$ is the (gross) return on the j'th asset with maturity n and I_t is the consumer's information set at date t, which is generated by current and past values of prices, payoffs, and other variables that are useful for predicting future prices, payoffs, and so on.

We now describe how to derive econometric tests from these conditions without specifying the entire economic environment (as we did in Chapter 2) and without imposing distributional assumptions on asset returns, per capita consumption, and other variables that may be useful for predicting these variables. Notice that we can rewrite Equation (3.1) as:

$$\beta^n \frac{U'(c_{t+n})}{U'(c_t)} r_{j,t+n} - 1 = u_{j,t+n}, \quad j = 1, \ldots, m, \tag{3.2}$$

where $u_{j,t+n}$ is a forecast error that is uncorrelated with variables that are known at time t, $E[u_{j,t+n}|I_t] = 0$. The idea that such a forecast

---

[1] For applications of maximum likelihood estimation of the intertemporal capital asset pricing model, see Hansen and Singleton [178] and Grossman, Shiller, and Melino [169].

error could be used as the disturbance of an econometric model was noted by McCallum [253] in the context of a linear rational expectations model. In what follows, we describe an estimation method that Hansen and Singleton [179] proposed for nonlinear rational expectations models using a similar approach.

To describe this estimation method, we assume that the econometrician's information set at time t, denoted $I_t^\star$, is a subset of agents' information sets, $I_t^\star \subseteq I_t$. The distinction between agents' information sets and the econometrician's information set is a key feature of many of the econometric tests that we describe in this chapter. Define the k-dimensional vector $x_{t+n} = (r_{1,t+n}, \ldots, r_{m,t+n}, c_t^{\star\prime})'$, where $c_t^\star$ is an $n^\star$-dimensional vector containing functions of c_t and c_{t+n} and $k = m + n^\star$. Let b_0 be the ℓ-dimensional vector of unknown parameters in Equation (3.1). Notice that b_0 consists of the discount factor β and the parameters of the utility function, U. Using this notation, define the function $h : \mathbb{R}^k \times \mathbb{R}^\ell \to \mathbb{R}^m$ by:

$$h(x_{t+n}, b_0) = \begin{bmatrix} \beta^n \dfrac{U'(c_{t+n})}{U'(c_t)} r_{1,t+n} - 1 \\ \vdots \\ \beta^n \dfrac{U(c_{t+n})}{U(c_t)} r_{m,t+n} - 1 \end{bmatrix}. \tag{3.3}$$

The restrictions implied by Equation (3.1) can be expressed as:

$$E[h(x_{t+n}, b_0)|I_t] = 0. \tag{3.4}$$

We can define an econometric disturbance using Equation (3.4) as follows:

$$u_{t+n} = h(x_{t+n}, b_0). \tag{3.5}$$

Notice that u_{t+n} is the forecast error in predicting $h(x_{t+n}, b_0)$, conditional on information available at time t. Let z_t be a q-dimensional vector of variables that is observed by agents and by the econometrician at time t, $z_t \in I_t^\star \subseteq I_t$. We can derive an alternative expression for the restrictions in Equation (3.4) as:

$$E[h(x_{t+n}, b_0) \otimes z_t] = 0. \tag{3.6}$$

This is obtained using an iterated expectation argument together with Equation (3.4) as follows:

$$E[h(x_{t+n}, b_0) \otimes z_t] = E\{E[h(x_{t+n}, b_0)|I_t] \otimes z_t\} = 0.$$

The conditions in Equation (3.6) are known as the population *orthogonality conditions*. We will use these conditions to derive an estimator for the unknown parameter vector b_0. There are several points to note about these conditions. First, we require the k-dimensional vector of variables x_{t+n} to be observed by agents and the econometrician as of date $t + n$. This rules out the dependence of the Euler equations on unobservable preference or technology shocks and the presence of measurement error in consumption and asset returns. Second, we require that the covariance matrix for the forecast errors, $E(u_{t+n} u'_{t+n})$, has full rank. Third, we note that the forecast errors u_{t+n} are potentially correlated with the elements of x_{t+n} since x_{t+n} includes consumption and asset returns at date $t + n$. Finally, we note that the error terms u_{t+n} in Equation (3.5) may be serially correlated. Notice that if $n = 1$ for all assets, then $\{u_{t+1}\}_{t=0}^{\infty}$ is a serially uncorrelated process. This is because $u_{t-k} \in I_t$ for all $k \geq 0$, which implies that $E(u_{t+1} u'_{t-k}) = E[E(u_{t+1}|I_t) u'_{t-k}] = 0$. When $n > 1$, the disturbances u_{t+n} are serially correlated because u_{t+n-k} is not necessarily included in I_t for $0 \leq k < n$.

1.1. Stochastic Processes: Basic Concepts

We preface our remaining discussion in this section with a review of some basic properties of stochastic processes. We also provide definitions of some terms that will used in the rest of the chapter.

Let $x_t(\omega)$ denote a real-valued random variable defined on some underlying probability space $(\Omega, \mathcal{F}, \mathcal{P})$ such that $x_t : \Omega \to \mathbb{R}$. Here Ω is called the sample space, $\mathcal{F}$ is a sigma-field of subsets of Ω or the set of all possible events, and $\mathcal{P}$ is a probability measure defined for all possible events in $\mathcal{F}$. Aside from some definitions in this section, we do not make use of the notion of an abstract probability space; for a detailed treatment of these concepts, we refer the reader to Stokey and Lucas [317]. Some of our following discussion is derived from Breiman [43], who provides an excellent treatment of probability theory and stochastic processes.

A *stochastic process* is a collection of random variables $\{x_t\}_{t \in T}$ defined on a common probability space $(\Omega, \mathcal{F}, \mathcal{P})$. In this expression, T is referred to as the index set; when T is the set of all integers or the set of nonnegative integers , we have a discrete-time stochastic process. For any set of times $t_1, t_2, t_3, \ldots, t_n$, we can define the joint probability distribution of $(x_{t_1}, \ldots, x_{t_n})$ by:

$$F_{x_{t_1}, \ldots, x_{t_n}}(\bar{x}_1, \ldots, \bar{x}_n) \equiv \mathcal{P}(\omega : x_{t_1}(\omega) \leq \bar{x}_1, \ldots, x_{t_n}(\omega) \leq \bar{x}_n).$$

A process $\{x_t\}$ is called *stationary* if for any set of times $t_1, t_2, t_3, \ldots, t_n$

and any integer k, the joint probability distribution of $(x_{t_1}, \ldots, x_{t_n})$ is identical with the joint probability distribution of $(x_{t_1+k}, \ldots, x_{t_n+k})$:

$$F_{x_{t_1}, \ldots, x_{t_n}}(\bar{x}_1, \ldots, \bar{x}_n) = F_{x_{t_1+k}, \ldots, x_{t_n+k}}(\bar{x}_1, \ldots, \bar{x}_n). \tag{3.7}$$

We say that $\{x_t\}$ is *weakly stationary* or *stationary* if only the joint moments up to order two of the above probability distributions exist and are identical:

$$E(x_t) = \mu \quad \text{and} \quad E(x_t^2) = \mu_2', \tag{3.8}$$

where μ and μ_2' are constants independent of t. As a result, $\text{Var}(x_t) = \sigma^2$ is also a constant that is independent of t. Furthermore, $E(x_t x_{t-s})$ will be a function only of $(t - s)$ and so will $\text{Cov}(x_t, x_{t-s})$.

We say that $\{x_t\}$ is a *Gaussian* process if the set of random variables $(x_{t_1}, \ldots, x_{t_n})$ has a multivariate normal distribution. Since the multivariate normal distribution is completely specified by its mean and variance-covariance matrix, if $\{x_t\}$ is covariance stationary, then it is strictly stationary. When x_t is a p-dimensional vector of random variables, $\{x_t\}$ is called a *multivariate stochastic process*. Such multivariate processes allow us to examine relationships among different series. In addition to requiring each series to be stationary, we require that the collection of p series are *jointly stationary*; that is, for each i, j, $\text{Cov}(x_{i,t} x_{j,s})$ is a function of $(t - s)$ only.

In most applications in time series analysis, a particular law of motion is assumed to characterize the evolution of the process $\{x_t\}$. As a special case of stochastic processes known as Markov processes, we can define a p'th order autoregressive process as:

$$x_t = c + \sum_{i=1}^{p} \alpha_i x_{t-i} + u_t, \tag{3.9}$$

where $\{u_t\}$ is a sequence of independently and identically distributed random variables with zero mean and constant variance σ^2. In this case, we say that x_t evolves as an $\text{AR}(p)$ process. Define the lag polynomial $\alpha(L) = 1 - \alpha_1 L - \ldots - \alpha_p L^p$. Notice that covariance stationarity for x_t requires that the roots of the polynomial $\alpha(\lambda) = 0$ lie outside the unit circle $|\lambda| = 1$.

We can define a q'th moving average process as:

$$x_t = c + \sum_{i=0}^{q} \beta_i u_{t-i}, \quad \beta_0 = 1, \tag{3.10}$$

where $\{u_t\}$ is a sequence of i.i.d. random variables with zero mean and constant variance σ^2 or a white noise. In this case, x_t evolves as an MA(q) process; if $q = 0$, then $\{x_t\}$ is just white noise. It is straightforward to verify that an MA(q) with $q < \infty$ is always stationary. Furthermore, if the roots of $\alpha(\lambda) = 0$ lie outside the unit circle, then an AR(p) process can be written as a MA(∞) process. A converse of this result is that an MA(q) can be written as an infinite-order autoregressive process or AR(∞) if the roots of the polynomial $\beta(\lambda) = 0$ lie outside the unit circle. This is called the *invertibility condition*.

A mixed moving average autoregressive process of order p, q is defined as:

$$x_t = c + \sum_{i=1}^{p} \alpha_i x_{t-i} + \sum_{i=0}^{q} \beta_i u_{t-i}, \tag{3.11}$$

where $\{u_t\}$ is a white noise and $\beta_0 = 1$. In this case, x_t evolves as an ARMA(p, q). Using lag operator notation, we can write this as:

$$\alpha(L)x_t = c + \beta(L)u_t,$$

where $\beta(L) = 1 + \beta_1 L + \ldots \beta_q L^q$. Using the previous results, if $\{x_t\}$ is a stationary process, then the roots of $\alpha(\lambda) = 0$ lie ouside the unit circle and there is an equivalent MA(∞) representation. Furthermore, if the roots of $\beta(\lambda) = 0$ lie outside the unit circle, then there is an equivalent AR(∞) representation. Thus, a stationary AR process can always be approximated by a high-order MA process and if the invertibility condition holds, then it can also be approximated by a high-order AR process.

In some applications, it is assumed that there is a deterministic component to the process $\{x_t\}$ such as a deterministic trend. We say that a sequence $\{D_t\}$ is *deterministic* if there exists a function of past and current values $\hat{D}_t = H(D_t, D_{t-1}, \ldots)$ such that

$$E\left[(D_{t+1} - \hat{D}_t)^2\right] = 0. \tag{3.12}$$

If the function H is a linear function of current and past D_t, then D_t is called *linearly deterministic*. A result that unifies the study of linear time series models is the *Wold decomposition theorem*, which states that a covariance stationary process $\{x_t\}$ can be uniquely represented as the sum of two mutually uncorrelated processes, $x_t = D_t + y_t$, where D_t is linearly deterministic and y_t is an MA(∞) process.

A generalization of this class of models to allow for nonstationary behavior in $\{x_t\}$ is achieved through the use of *integrated processes*:

$$\alpha(L)(1 - L)^d x_t = c + \beta(L)u_t, \tag{3.13}$$

where $\{u_t\}$ is a zero mean white noise, $\alpha(L)$, $\beta(L)$ are polynomials in L of orders p, q, respectively, and d is an integer. Such a process is denoted an ARIMA(p, q, d) or an autoregressive integrated moving average process of orders p, q, d. It is generally assumed that the roots of $\alpha(\lambda) = 0$ all lie outside the unit circle so that the process obtained by differencing x_t d times, $y_t = (1 - L)^d x_t$, will be a stationary ARMA(p, q) process. In later parts of this chapter, we will describe how the time series models described here may be generalized to deal with multivariate processes.

We already described some examples of such time series models in Chapter 2, Exercise 9, where we described the trend-stationary model, which assumes that the logarithm of x_t is the sum of a deterministic linear trend and a stationary first-order autoregressive process. The difference-stationary model is an ARIMA(p, q, d) for the logarithm of x_t with $p = 1$, $q = 0$ and $d = 1$. The models we have described here are known as *linear time series models* because a linear function of past, current, and possibly future values $\ldots, x_{t-2}, x_{t-1}, x_t, x_{t+1}, x_{t+2}, \ldots$ of the process is used to generate a white noise process, u_t. It is also possible to represent a stationary stochastic process in terms of *nonlinear stochastic models* such as ARCH-type models. We describe such nonlinear stochastic models in later parts of this chapter.[2]

1.2.   Estimation Method

Returning to the problem posed in the first part of this section, define the p-dimensional random vector $(x'_{t+n}, z'_t)'$ where $p = k + q$. We assume that $\{(x'_{t+n}, z'_t)'\}_{t=0}^{\infty}$ is a strictly stationary stochastic process. Define the function f as:

$$f(x_{t+n}, z_t, b_0) = h(x_{t+n}, b_0) \otimes z_t. \tag{3.14}$$

Thus, $f : \mathbb{R}^k \times \mathbb{R}^q \times \mathbb{R}^\ell \to \mathbb{R}^r$, where $r = m \cdot q$. For $z_t \in I_t^\star$, the restrictions in Equation (3.4) can be expressed as:

$$E[f(x_{t+n}, z_t, b_0)] = 0, \tag{3.15}$$

where $E(\cdot)$ is the unconditional expectation operator. Notice that these conditions are just another expression of the population orthogonality conditions in Equation (3.6).

---

[2]There are many references that deal with time series analysis. Harvey [183] provides a good introduction to time series models while Granger and Newbold [159] provide a discussion from the perspective of forecasting. A classic treatment of linear least-squares methods in time series analysis is provided by Whittle [339]. Priestley [276] discusses nonlinear stochastic models.

The generalized method of moments (GMM) estimator for b_0, denoted b_T, is derived by using a sample counterpart of the population orthogonality conditions in Equation (3.6). Define the sample moment:

$$g_T(b) = \frac{1}{T} \sum_{t=1}^{T} f(x_{t+n}, z_t, b). \tag{3.16}$$

Suppose that a law of large numbers can be applied to $g_T(b)$ so that it converges to its population mean for all b with probability one (or almost surely):[3]

$$\lim_{T \to \infty} \frac{1}{T} \sum_{t=1}^{T} f(x_{t+n}, z_t, b) = E[f(x_{t+n}, z_t, b)] \quad \text{a.s.}$$

The GMM estimator b_T is chosen to set the sample counterpart of the population orthogonality conditions in Equation (3.15) as close to zero as possible by minimizing the quadratic form:

$$J_T(b) = g_T(b)' W_T g_T(b) \tag{3.17}$$

with respect to b. In this expression, W_T is a positive definite weighting matrix which converges in probability to a positive definite matrix W_0:

$$\lim_{T \to \infty} W_T = W_0.$$

Under some regularity conditions, the GMM estimator b_T is a consistent estimator of b_0. (See Hansen [173].) The nonlinear instrumental variables estimators discussed by Amemiya [14], Jorgenson and Laffont [210], and Gallant [142] are defined in a similar manner for an appropriate choice of W_T. One difference is that these authors consider the case of serially independent errors.

The asymptotic normality of the GMM estimator is established by making a set of assumptions that provide sufficient conditions for applying a central limit theorem for stationary, ergodic processes. Define a sequence of r-dimensional random vectors as $w_{t+n} = f(x_{t+n}, z_t, b_0)$. Suppose that a central limit theorem can be applied to w_{t+n} so that $(1/\sqrt{T}) \sum_{t=1}^{T} w_{t+n}$ converges to an asymptotically normal random vector with mean zero and covariance matrix S_w as the sample size T gets large, where

$$S_w = \lim_{j \to \infty} \sum_{-j}^{j} E(w_{t+n} w'_{t+n-j}).$$

---

[3]This is a property of ergodic processes. For a further discussion of ergodicity and the ergodic theorem for stationary stochastic processes, see Breiman [43, Ch. 6].

Also define the $\ell \times r$ matrix as $D_0 = E\left[\partial f(x_{t+n}, z_t, b_0)/\partial b\right]$ and assume that D_0 has rank ℓ. Under some regularity conditions, $\sqrt{T}(b_T - b_0)$ is asymptotically normally distributed with mean zero and covariance matrix:

$$\Lambda = (D_0' W_0 D_0)^{-1} D_0' W_0 S_w W_0 D_0 (D_0' W_0 D_0)^{-1'}. \tag{3.18}$$

The condition that D_0 has full column rank ℓ is a population identification condition that is sufficient to ensure that the population orthogonality conditions $E[f(x_{t+n}, z_t, b)]$ have a unique solution at the true parameter vector b_0. When the number of parameters ℓ is equal to the number of orthogonality conditions r, the model is just identified. If $r > \ell$, there are more orthogonality conditions than parameters so the model is overidentified. In this case, the choice of a different weighting matrix gives rise to different GMM estimators. The asymptotically efficient GMM estimator or one which has the smallest covariance among estimators with weighting matrices W_0 is obtained by setting $W_0 = S_w$. In this case, the GMM estimator has asymptotic covariance:

$$\Lambda = (D_0' S_w^{-1} D_0)^{-1}. \tag{3.19}$$

Given a sample of observations $\{(x_{t+n}', z_t')'\}_{t=1}^T$, the GMM estimator is computed as follows:

1. Minimize $g_T(b)' g_T(b)$ with respect to b which sets $W_T = I$. We denote the first round minimizer by $\hat{b}_T$.

2. Estimate $w_{t+n} = h(x_{t+n}, b_0) \otimes z_t$ by setting $\hat{w}_{t+n} = h(x_{t+n}, \hat{b}_T) \otimes z_t$ and form a consistent estimator of S_w, denoted S_T, using the estimated residuals.

3. Minimize $g_T(b)' S_T^{-1} g_T(b)$ with respect to b. The resulting estimator is optimal and it will have asymptotically efficient standard errors given by Equation (3.19).

We can estimate D_0 by

$$D_T = \frac{1}{T} \sum_{t=1}^T \frac{\partial f}{\partial b}(x_{t+n}, z_t, \hat{b}_T).$$

Estimation of S_w is more involved and depends on the serial correlation properties of the disturbances $\{u_{t+n}\}$.

Consider the first case of serially uncorrelated disturbances, that is, $E[u_{t+1}|z_t, u_t, z_{t-1}, u_{t-1}, \cdots] = 0$. It is easiest to view this case in terms of the optimal portfolio choice problem with the maximum maturity date on the different assets equal to $n = 1$. Then we have:

$$E[w_{t+1}w'_{t+1-j}] = E\{E[u_{t+1}|z_t, u_t, z_{t-1}, u_{t-1}, \cdots] \times$$

$$u'_{t+1-j} \otimes z_t z'_{t-j}\} = 0$$

for $j \geq 1$. Thus, S_w is defined as:

$$S_w = E[u_{t+1}u'_{t+1} \otimes z_t z'_t], \tag{3.20}$$

which can be estimated consistently by

$$S_T = \frac{1}{T} \sum_{t=1}^{T} \left(\hat{u}_{t+1}\hat{u}'_{t+1} \otimes z_t z'_t \right),$$

where $\hat{u}_{t+1} \equiv h(x_{t+1}, \hat{b}_T)$. If, in addition, we assume that $\{u_{t+1}\}$ is conditionally homoscedastic, that is, $E[u_{t+1}u'_{t+1}|z_t, u_t, z_{t-1}, u_{t-1}, \cdots] = E[u_{t+1}u'_{t+1}]$, then S_w can be expressed as:

$$S_w = E[u_{t+1}u'_{t+1}] \otimes E[z_t z'_t]. \tag{3.21}$$

A consistent estimate is provided by:

$$S_T = \left(\frac{1}{T} \sum_{t=1}^{T} \hat{u}_{t+1}\hat{u}'_{t+1} \right) \otimes \left(\frac{1}{T} \sum_{t=1}^{T} z_t z'_t \right).$$

Now consider the case with serially correlated disturbances. In some cases, the order of the serial correlation is determined by the model. For example, if the maximum maturity date on assets in the portfolio choice problem described above is known to be $n > 1$, then we have that $E[u_{t+n}|z_t, u_{t+n-k}, z_{t-1}, u_{t+n-k-1}, \cdots] = 0$ for $k \geq n$. Notice that

$$E[w_{t+n}w'_{t+n-j}] = E\{E[u_{t+n}|z_t, u_{t+n-j}, z_{t-1}, u_{t+n-j-1}, \cdots] \times$$

$$u'_{t+n-j} \otimes z_t z'_{t-j}\} = 0$$

for $j \geq n$ since $u_{t+n-j} \in I_t$ for $j \geq n$. Therefore, S_w is defined as:

$$S_w = \sum_{j=-n+1}^{n-1} E[u_{t+n}u'_{t+n-j} \otimes z_t z'_{t-j}]. \tag{3.22}$$

If $E[u_{t+n}u'_{t+n-j}|z_t, u_{t+n-k}, z_{t-1}, u_{t+n-k-1}, \cdots] = E[u_{t+n}u'_{t+n-j}]$ for $k \geq n$ and $0 \leq j < n$, then

$$S_w = \sum_{j=-n+1}^{n-1} E[u_{t+n}u'_{t+n-j}] \otimes E[z_t z'_{t-j}]. \tag{3.23}$$

Finally, consider the case with serially correlated disturbances of unknown order. Define the sample autocovariances of w_{t+n} at lag j by:

$$R_T(j) = \frac{1}{T} \sum_{t=1+j}^{T} f(x_{t+n}, z_t, \hat{b}_T) f(x_{t+n-j}, z_{t-j}, \hat{b}_T)' \qquad (3.24)$$

for $j \geq 0$, where $R_T(j) = R_T(-j)'$ for $j < 0$. The estimators for S_w that have been proposed in the literature are *kernel estimators* of the form:

$$S_T = \frac{T}{T-p} \sum_{j=-T+1}^{T-1} K\left(\frac{j}{\delta_T}\right) R_T(j), \qquad (3.25)$$

where $K(\cdot)$ is a real-valued kernel, δ_T is a bandwidth parameter, and the factor $T/(T-p)$ is a small sample degrees of freedom of adjustment to account for the fact that parameter vector b_0 is estimated. Andrews [15] shows that the Quadratic Spectral kernel defined as:

$$K_{QS}(x) = \frac{25}{12\pi^2 x^2} \left(\frac{\sin(6\pi x/5)}{6\pi x/5} - \cos(6\pi x/5) \right),$$

produces an estimate of S_w that is positive semidefinite in small samples and has the smallest mean square error among the class of estimators defined by Equation (3.25). This estimator can also be used when the order of serial correlation is known as in Equation (3.22).[4]

Recall that the GMM estimator of b_0 is found by setting a set of sample orthogonality conditions as close to zero as possible. In practice, this is accomplished by setting the following ℓ conditions equal to zero:

$$\left[\frac{\partial g_T'(b)}{\partial b} W_T \right] g_T(b) = 0.$$

When the number of orthogonality conditions is greater than the number of parameters, $r > \ell$, there are $r - \ell$ linearly independent remaining orthogonality conditions that are not set to zero during the estimation but should be close to zero if the restrictions of the model are true. This fact provides a way of developing a test of the model under the null hypothesis that all r orthogonality conditions are equal to zero. This test is based on a statistic which is defined as T times the minimized value of the function:

$$T J_T \equiv T g_T(b_T)' S_T^{-1} g_T(b_T). \qquad (3.26)$$

---

[4]Ogaki [273] discusses alternative estimators that have the form in Equation (3.25).

This test may be considered an extension of the specification test in Sargan [297] and Ferguson [127]. Hansen [173] shows that TJ_T converges in distribution to a chi-square random variable with $r - \ell$ degrees of freedom.

In some cases, we can derive orthogonality conditions by stacking the orthogonality conditions that we obtain from different sets of optimality conditions, for example, the optimality conditions associated with agents' intertemporal choices and those associated with intratemporal choices. We can derive a test of the hypothesis that a subset of these orthogonality conditions holds. Let us partition the $r \times 1$ vector $w_{t+n} = u_{t+n} \otimes z_t$ into two subvectors w_{t+n}^1 and w_{t+n}^2. Here, w_{t+n}^1 depends on the ℓ_1 parameters and w_{t+n}^2 depends on (possibly a subset of) these ℓ_1 parameters plus additional ℓ_2 parameters that do not enter the expressions for w_{t+n}^1. Thus, $b_0' = (b_{1,0}', b_{2,0}')$ and $\ell_1 + \ell_2 = \ell$. It is assumed that w_{t+n}^1 is $r_1 \times 1$ with $r_1 \geq \ell_1$ and w_{t+n}^2 is $r_2 \times 1$ where $r_2 = r - r_1$. Let the assumption that $E(w_{t+n}^1) = 0$ and that $E(\partial w_{t+n}^1(b_0)/\partial b) = D_0^1$ has rank ℓ_1 be maintained as true. The elements of w_{t+n}^1 may be chosen to be the orthogonality conditions associated with a particular disturbance vector. We will partition $g_T(b)$ as $g_{1,T}(b_1) = (1/T)\sum_{t=1}^{T} w_{t+n}^1(b_1)$ and $g_{2,T}(b_2) = (1/T)\sum_{t=1}^{T} w_{t+n}^2(b_2)$.

To implement this test, one obtains an estimator of b_0 by minimizing the objective function $g_T(b)'S_T^{-1}g_T(b)$ by choice of b. This estimator uses all of the orthogonality conditions assumed to hold under the null hypothesis. Next, the estimator of $b_{1,0}$ is formed using only the r_1 orthogonality conditions assumed to hold under the alternative. The $r_1 \times r_1$ dimensional weighting matrix $(S_T^{11})^{-1}$, which is obtained by partitioning S_T, is used. Given both estimators, we form the statistic:

$$C_T \equiv Tg_T(b_T)'S_T^{-1}g_T(b_T) - Tg_{1,T}(b_{1,T})'(S_T^{11})^{-1}g_{1,T}(b_{1,T}). \qquad (3.27)$$

Under the null hypothesis, this quantity is asymptotically distributed as $\chi^2_{r-\ell-(r_1-\ell_1)}$.

We can also conduct hypothesis testing in the GMM framework. Suppose we are interested in testing the s nonlinear restrictions:

$$H_0 : R(b_0) = r, \qquad (3.28)$$

where R is an $s \times 1$ vector of functions. The null hypothesis is tested against the alternative that $R(b_0) \neq r$. A likelihood ratio-type test statistic for testing these nonlinear restrictions is:

$$T(J_T(b_T^r) - J_T(b_T^u)), \qquad (3.29)$$

where $J_T(b_T^r)$ and $J_T(b_T^u)$ denote the minimized value of the criterion function with and without the restrictions in Equation (3.28). When estimating the restricted and unrestricted models, the same estimate of the optimal weighting matrix S_T^{-1} is used. Under some regularity conditions, this test statistic has an asymptotic χ^2 distribution with s degrees of freedom.[5] These tests are implemented in the applications we describe below.

1.3.   Empirical Evidence

We now describe the empirical evidence that has been obtained from tests of asset pricing models using GMM estimation methods with time series data. We describe the results of tests using a variety of preference specifications, including those with consumption durability and nonexpected utility preferences.

We begin by describing the study by Hansen and Singleton [178], who provide estimates and tests for a single good, representative consumer model with time-additive preferences. These authors assume CRR preferences with $U(c) = c^\gamma/\gamma$, $\gamma \leq 1$, and consider one-period returns. Two measures of consumption are used: nondurables plus services and nondurables. The monthly consumption series are converted to per capita values by dividing each observation by the corresponding observation on population. The return series consist of the equally weighted average returns on all stocks listed on the New York Stock Exchange (NYSE), the value-weighted average return on stocks on the NYSE, and the equally weighted returns on the stocks of three two-digit SEC industries. In their revised estimates (published as "Errata" in 1984), they also use observations on a one-month, nominal risk-free bond return, which are converted to real returns by dividing by the implicit deflator associated with the measure of consumption. The sample period is February, 1959 to December, 1978.

Following the notation of Section 1.2, define the vector:

$$x_{t+1} = (r_{1,t+1}, r_{2,t+1}, \dots, r_{m,t+1}, c_{t+1}/c_t)'.$$

---

[5]Gallant [143], Gallant and White [145], and Newey and West [270] have proposed Wald and Lagrange multiplier-type tests for hypothesis testing in the GMM framework while other types of specification tests are due to Singleton [312], Ghysels and Hall [147, 148], and Dufour, Ghysels, and Hall [106].

Thus, the function $h(x_{t+1}, b_0)$ is defined as:

$$h(x_{t+1}, b_0) = \begin{bmatrix} \beta(c_{t+1}/c_t)^{\gamma-1} r_{1,t+1} - 1 \\ \vdots \\ \beta(c_{t+1}/c_t)^{\gamma-1} r_{m,t+1} - 1 \end{bmatrix},$$

where m is the number of different assets. With one-period returns, notice that $n = 1$. The instrument vector includes the constant plus one, two, four, or six lagged values of the vector x_{t+1}.

Let us form orthogonality conditions in this framework. When a single return is used, notice that $m = 1$ and $h(x_{t+1}, b_0)$ is a scalar. Suppose we define the instrument vector in this case as $z_t = (1, x_t')' = (1, r_{1,t}, c_t/c_{t-1})'$. Then the function $f(x_{t+1}, z_t, b_0)$ is defined as:

$$\begin{aligned} f(x_{t+1}, z_t, b_0) &= h(x_{t+1}, b_0) \otimes z_t \\ &= [(c_{t+1}/c_t)^{\gamma-1} r_{1,t+1} - 1] \otimes z_t, \end{aligned}$$

and the population orthogonality conditions are given by:

$$E[f(x_{t+1}, z_t, b_0)] = 0.$$

There are two parameters to estimate, β and γ, and three population orthogonality conditions. Thus, there is one overidentifying condition that can be tested using the test procedure described in Section 1.2. If we increase the number of lagged values of x_{t+1} that are used to form the instrument vector z_t, the number of population orthogonality conditions and overidentifying restrictions also increases. Notice also that with one-period returns, the forecast errors $\{u_{t+1}\}$ are serially uncorrelated. Thus, the matrix S_w can be consistently estimated as:

$$S_T = \sum_{t=1}^{T} \hat{u}_{t+1}^2 \otimes z_t z_t',$$

where $\hat{u}_{t+1} = h(x_{t+1}, \hat{b}_T)$ are estimated forecast errors evaluated at the first-round estimates, $\hat{b}_T$. The second-round asymptotically efficient estimates are found by minimizing the value of

$$g_T(b)' S_T^{-1} g_T(b),$$

where

$$g_T(b) = \frac{1}{T} \sum_{t=1}^{T} h(x_{t+1}, b) \otimes z_t.$$

When we use multiple returns $(m > 1)$, then $h(x_{t+1}, b_0)$ is an $m \times 1$ vector and there are $r = m \cdot q$ orthogonality conditions to estimate, where q is the dimension of z_t and depends on the number of lags of x_{t+1} that are included in z_t. Orthogonality conditions are constructed by using value-weighted and equally weighted stock returns separately and also by using the combinations of returns consisting of value-weighted and equally weighted stock returns, value-weighted returns and nominal risk-free bond returns, and the returns on three industry-average stock returns. The revised results show that the estimate of $\alpha = \gamma - 1$ fluctuates considerably in the single return equations, depending on the definition of consumption expenditures and the set of instruments used in estimation. These estimates range from -1.59 to 1.26, with estimates greater than zero implying nonconcave preferences.

The authors find that there is greater evidence against the model when equally weighted returns are used. On the other hand, when the model is estimated with multiple returns, the orthogonality conditions are rejected at the 5 percent level for all sets of returns except for two sets of industry averages. These results indicate that the single good, consumption-based asset pricing model with time-additive preferences cannot rationalize the joint time series behavior of stock and bond returns. In particular, the strong rejections of the model involving stock returns and bond returns imply that the common stochastic discount factor defined as the representative consumer's MRS cannot capture the relative risk structure of stocks versus bonds.

In a different application, Dunn and Singleton seek to determine whether a model with consumption durability can explain the holding returns on Treasury bills of various maturities. The model that they consider is a special case of the model in Chapter 2, Section 2.2.

Let c_t denote purchases of nondurable consumption goods and d_t purchases of durable consumption goods, as defined in the National Income and Product Accounts, respectively. The service flow from nondurable consumption goods is given by:

$$c_t^* = \alpha_0 c_t + \ldots \alpha_m c_{t-m}, \quad m < \infty, \tag{3.30}$$

where $\alpha_j \geq 0$ and $\alpha_0 = 1$. Services from durable consumption goods are proportional to the sum of the stock of durable consumption goods at the beginning of period t (k_{t-1}) and durable goods purchases during period t (d_t):

$$d_t^* = \theta(k_{t-1} + d_t), \quad 0 < \theta < 1.$$

The representative consumer owns the capital stock so that capital carried over into the next period k_t is equal to $(k_{t-1} + d_t)$ less the amount used to produce services: $k_t = (1 - \theta)(k_{t-1} + d_t)$. Substituting in the expression for d_t^* yields:

$$d_t^* = \frac{\theta}{1 - \theta} k_t = \theta \sum_{j=0}^{\infty} (1 - \theta)^j d_{t-j}. \tag{3.31}$$

Preferences over sequences of consumption services c_t^* and d_t^* are given by:

$$E_0 \left\{ \sum_{t=0}^{\infty} \beta^t \frac{\left(c_t^{*\delta} d_t^{*(1-\delta)} \right)^{\gamma} - 1}{\gamma} \right\}, \quad 0 < \delta < 1, \gamma < 1. \tag{3.32}$$

Let $p_{d,t}$ denote the price of durable consumption goods expressed in units of the numeraire good and $b_{j,t+1}$ the quantity of real risk-free bonds that are purchased at date t which mature in j periods. The longest maturity date is N and $Q_t^0 = 1$. The budget constraint for the representative is given by:

$$c_t + p_{d,t} d_t + \sum_{j=1}^{N} b_{j,t+1} Q_t^j \leq y_t + \sum_{j=0}^{N} b_{j,t} Q_t^j, \tag{3.33}$$

where y_t is the endowment of the numeraire consumption good.

The representative consumer chooses sequences for c_t, d_t, and $b_{j,t+1}$, $j = 1, \ldots, N$ and $t \geq 0$ to maximize the objective function in Equation (3.32) subject to the constraints in Equations (3.30), (3.31), and (3.33), given an initial capital stock k_{-1}. We can formulate this problem as a dynamic programming problem using the approach in Chapter 2, Section 2.2. (We leave this as an exercise for the reader.) Let $\{\xi_t\}$ denote the sequence of Lagrange multipliers on the sequence of budget constraints in Equation (3.33). The first-order conditions are given by:

$$\xi_t = \text{MU}(c_t), \tag{3.34}$$

$$\xi_t p_{d,t} = \text{MU}(d_t), \tag{3.35}$$

$$\xi_t Q_t^j = \beta E_t(\xi_{t+1} Q_{t+1}^{j-1}), \quad j = 1, \ldots, N. \tag{3.36}$$

where $\text{MU}(c_t)$ and $\text{MU}(d_t)$ denote the marginal utility from nondurable and durable consumption goods.

Dunn and Singleton examine the implications of this model for holding returns on Treasury bills of various maturities. They consider the one-month holding period returns on one-month Treasury bills, the three-month holding period returns on three-month and six-month Treasury bills, and the three-month returns from rolling over a sequence of three one-month bills. Let $h_{t,n}^k$ denote the gross holding return from following the k'th investment strategy from date t to $t+n$, denominated in terms of the numeraire consumption good. Using the definition of the pure discount bonds described above, the holding return on the first investment strategy is $h_{t,1}^1 = 1/Q_t^1$.[6] Using Equations (3.34) and (3.36), these holding returns satisfy the relation:

$$\beta^n E_t \left[\frac{MU(c_{t+n})}{MU(c_t)} h_{t,n}^k \right] = 1, \quad k = 1, \cdots, K. \tag{3.37}$$

Equations (3.34) and (3.35) yield an expression for the price of durable good $p_{d,t}$ as:

$$p_{d,t} = \frac{MU(d_t)}{MU(c_t)},$$

which is identical to Equation (2.66) in Chapter 2, Section 2.2. This relation is not useful for giving empirical content to the model because $MU(d_t)$ depends on the infinite future of expected durable goods acquisitions. However, if consumers can trade in consumption services, then the price of services from durable consumption goods expressed in units of the numeraire good must equal the ratio of the marginal utility of services from durable consumption goods and the marginal utility of nondurable consumption goods acquisitions:

$$MU(d_t^*) = p_{d,t}^* MU(c_t), \tag{3.38}$$

where $MU(d_t^*)$ denotes the marginal utility with respect to d_t^*. We will show how to construct orthogonality conditions from Equations (3.37) and (3.38).

Using the utility function defined above, notice that:

$$MU(c_t) = E_t \left[\sum_{j=0}^m \alpha_j \delta \beta^{t+j} c_{t+j}^{*\delta\gamma-1} d_{t+j}^{*(1-\delta)\gamma} \right],$$

$$MU(d_t^*) = (1-\delta)\beta^t c_t^{*\delta\gamma} d_t^{*(1-\delta)\gamma-1}.$$

---

[6] For the remaining investment strategies, we have:

$$h_{t,3}^2 = \frac{1}{Q_t^3} \quad \text{or} \quad h_{t,3}^2 = \frac{Q_{t+3}^3}{Q_t^6}, \quad h_{t,3}^3 = \left(\prod_{i=0}^2 \frac{1}{Q_{t+i}^1} \right).$$

In order to evaluate Equation (3.38), we need an observable counterpart for $p_{d,t}^{\star}$. But, as we argued in Chapter 2,

$$p_{d,t}^{\star} = \frac{1}{\theta}\left[p_{d,t} - \beta(1-\theta)E_t\left(\frac{\mathrm{MU}(c_{t+1})}{\mathrm{MU}(c_t)}p_{d,t+1}\right)\right].$$

Using these results and scaling the resulting expressions by $c_t^{\star\delta\gamma-1}d_t^{\star(1-\delta)\gamma}$, we obtain the following relations from Equations (3.37) and (3.38):

$$u_{k,t} \equiv \left[\sum_{j=0}^{m}\alpha_j\beta^j(c_{t+j}^{\star\delta\gamma-1}d_{t+j}^{\star(1-\delta)\gamma})\right.$$

$$\left. -\beta^n\left(\sum_{j=0}^{m}\alpha_j\beta^j(c_{t+j+n}^{\star\delta\gamma-1}d_{t+j+n}^{\star(1-\delta)\gamma})\right)h_{t,n}^k\right]/[c_t^{\star\delta\gamma-1}d_t^{\star(1-\delta)\gamma}], \qquad (3.39)$$

for $k = 1, \ldots, K$. Likewise,

$$u_{K+1,t} \equiv [(1-(1-\theta)\beta L^{-1})\{p_{d,t}\sum_{j=0}^{m}\alpha_j\delta\beta^j c_{t+j}^{\star\delta\gamma-1}d_{t+j}^{\star(1-\delta)\gamma}\}$$

$$-\theta(1-\delta)(c_t^{\star\delta\gamma}d_t^{\star(1-\delta)\gamma-1})]/[c_t^{\star\delta\gamma-1}d_t^{\star(1-\delta)\gamma}]. \qquad (3.40)$$

The disturbances $u_{k,t}$ for $k = 1, \ldots, K+1$ are the disturbances for the econometric model to be estimated by GMM. The unknown parameter consists of $b_0 = (\beta, \theta, \gamma, \delta, \alpha_1, \cdots, \alpha_m)$. Notice that Equations (3.37) and (3.38) have been scaled by the factor $c_t^{\star\delta\gamma-1}d_t^{\star(1-\delta)\gamma}$, which is an element of agents' information set at time t. In Exercise 6, we describe one set of conditions under which this scaling yields disturbances in the econometric model that are stationary.

The population orthogonality conditions and their sample counterparts can be formed as we described earlier by choosing vectors $z_{k,t}$ that are uncorrelated with agents' forecast errors at time t, that is, choose $z_k \in I_t$ such that $E[z_{k,t}u_{k,t}] = E[E_t(u_{k,t})z_{k,t}] = 0$ for $k = 1, \cdots, K+1$. Let $u_t = (u_{1,t}, \ldots, u_{K+1,t})'$ and define Z_t as an $R \times (K+1)$-dimensional diagonal matrix which contains the instrument vector $z_{k,t}$ on its diagonal. Let $z_{k,t}$ be a q_k-dimensional vector. With this notation, there are $R = \sum_{k=1}^{K+1} q_k$ population orthogonality conditions, defined as $E[Z_t u_t] = 0$.

To construct sample orthogonality conditions, we need obtain a consistent estimate of S_w, which depends on the serial correlation properties of the disturbances $\{Z_t u_t\}$. The number of nonzero autocovariances of $Z_t u_t$ depends on the number of periods n over which the k'th return is computed and the degree of nonseparability of preferences, m. Thus,

$u_{k,t}$ is not observed until period $t + n + m$ because $\text{MU}(c_{t+n})$ depends on values of consumption services up to and including period $t + n + m$, namely, $c^{\star}_{t+n+m}$. Using this fact, we can show that $\{Z_t u_t\}$ follows a moving average process of order $(n + m - 1)$. (See Exercise 7.) Thus, we need to use a kernel estimator of the type proposed by Andrews [15] to obtain an estimate of S_w that is positive semidefinite in small samples.

The variables c_t and d_t are measured as the value of real purchases of nondurables and services and real purchases of durable goods deflated by monthly population estimates. The service flow variables $c^{\star}_t$ and $d^{\star}_t$ are computed endogenously using observations on current and past purchases of nondurables and services and durable goods. Computing $d^{\star}_t$ also requires a value for the initial capital stock. Finally, $p_{d,t}$ is computed as the ratio of implicit price deflator for durables and nondurables and services.

The model is initially estimated for each return separately by assuming a single, nondurable consumption good and CRR preferences, $U(c) = c^{\gamma}$, $\gamma \leq 1$. The instrument vector is defined as $(1, c_t/c_{t-1} - 1, c_{t-1}/c_{t-2} - 1, h^k_{t-n,n} - 1, h^k_{t-n-1,n} - 1)'$. Thus there are five orthogonality conditions and two parameters, β and γ, to estimate. The orthogonality conditions are formed as in the first example. The overidentifying restrictions of their model are rejected for all returns. For $h^2_{t,3}$ and $h^3_{t,3}$, the estimate of γ falls outside of the concave region for the parameter space.

The conditions in Equations (3.39) and (3.38) are also estimated jointly for each return, with $m = 1$. The instrument vector corresponding to the disturbance $u_{1,t}$ is set as $z_{1,t} = (1, h^1_{t-n,n}, c_t/c_{t-1} - 1, d_t/d_{t-1} - 1, p_{d,t}/p_{d,t-1} - 1)'$, and $z_{2,t} = z_{1,t}$. There are ten orthogonality conditions and five parameters, $(\beta, \theta, \alpha, \gamma, \delta)$, leaving five orthogonality conditions to test. In this case, the overidentifying conditions associated with the three-month returns are not rejected while the use of $h^1_{t,1}$ provides substantially more evidence against the model. Finally, two returns are considered simultaneously ($K = 2$) and Equation (3.38) is included in the estimation. In this case, the p-values associated with the test statistics for each set of estimates are greater than 0.95. For the case with multiple returns, Dunn and Singleton show that the unconditional risk premia for the excess return on two alternative investment strategies (such as the excess return on $h^2_{t,3}$ versus $h^3_{t,3}$) is too large relative to the covariation with the relevant intertemporal MRS. As in the single good, representative consumer asset pricing model, the model with consumption durability is incapable of rationalizing the relative risk structure of multiple assets, in this case, the term structure of real risk-free bonds.

A third application concerns the model with nonexpected utility preferences proposed by Epstein and Zin [122]. In Chapter 2, we showed that the nonexpected utility model implies restrictions for the joint behavior of consumption growth, asset returns, and the gross return on the optimal wealth portfolio M_t as:

$$E_t\left[\beta\left(\frac{c_{t+1}}{c_t}\right)^{\delta-1}M_t\right]^{\gamma} = 1, \quad \alpha \neq 0, \quad \delta \neq 0, \tag{3.41}$$

$$E_t\left[\beta^{\gamma}\left(\frac{c_{t+1}}{c_t}\right)^{\gamma(\delta-1)}M_t^{\gamma-1}r_{j,t}\right] = 1, \quad j = 1,\ldots,N, \tag{3.42}$$

where $\gamma = \alpha/\delta$. The first condition is the Euler equation for optimal consumption. The second set of equations is derived from the optimal portfolio choice problem of a representative consumer with lifetime preferences described in Chapter 2, Section 2.3.

Epstein and Zin estimate their model using GMM by forming orthogonality conditions from Equations (3.41) and (3.42) with four returns. We will discuss their data set momentarily. First, however, we discuss identification. There are three parameters to estimate, β, α, and δ. When $\alpha = 0$ (which corresponds to logarithmic risk preferences), the parameter δ is not identified from Equation (3.42). However, it can be identified from Equation (3.41). Write this equation as

$$E_t\left[\frac{\{\beta(c_{t+1}/c_t)^{\delta-1}M_t\}^{\gamma} - 1}{\gamma}\right] = 0.$$

As α goes to zero, γ goes to zero and the above expression converges to:

$$\log(\beta) + (\delta - 1)E_t[\log(c_{t+1}/c_t)] + E_t[\log(M_t)] = 0,$$

which can be used to differentiate between the logarithmic expected utility model ($\alpha = \delta = 0$) and the nonexpected utility model with logarithmic risk preferences ($\alpha = 0$, $\delta \neq 0$). Thus, to ensure identifiability of δ, Equation (3.41) is always included as one of the orthogonality conditions. The econometric error terms are defined as:

$$u_{j,t} = \beta^{\gamma}(c_{t+1}/c_t)^{\gamma(\delta-1)}M_t^{\gamma-1}r_{j,t} - 1, \quad j = 1,\ldots,4, \tag{3.43}$$

$$u_{5,t} = \frac{[\beta(c_{t+1}/c_t)^{\delta-1}M_t]^{\gamma} - 1}{\gamma}. \tag{3.44}$$

Equation (3.43) is used with two different sets of four returns. These are given by value-weighted indices of stocks in four broad groups of the standard industrial classification of individual firms, and three of these stock returns and the return on the 30-day Treasury bill return, respectively. The measures of per capita consumption that are used include expenditures on nondurables, nondurables minus shoes and clothing, nondurables and services, and nondurables and services minus clothing, shoes, and medical expenditures. The nominal return on the optimal wealth portfolio, M_t, is measured as the value-weighted index of shares on the NYSE. This measure suffers from the usual problem that it does not reflect the shadow value to human capital. Epstein and Zin use three instruments for each of the five Euler equations. Thus, there are 15 orthogonality conditions and 12 overidentifying restrictions. They consider three alternative sets of instruments. The first includes a constant, and two lags of consumption growth. The second includes a constant, consumption growth lagged once, and the market return lagged once while the third set has twice-lagged values of the variables in the second set. (We leave it as an exercise to the reader to construct the population orthogonality conditions, $E[f(x_{t+1}, z_t, b_0)] = 0$, by appropriately defining all the relevant terms.)

For the first two instrument sets, the parameter estimates vary with the choice of consumption and there is more evidence against the model when the bond return is included than when only stocks are used. The most favorable results for the model are obtained when the vector of returns includes the Treasury bill rate, consumption is measured as nondurables only, and the instrument choice is defined as the third set. However, when stock returns are used and the consumption measure is nondurables and services, although the nonexpected utility model is not rejected, the expected utility model also cannot be rejected. Although some favorable results are obtained with nonexpected utility preferences, they are sensitive to the measure of consumption and the instrument set.

Tests of the representative consumer asset pricing model have also been conducted by allowing for consumption and leisure choices (see Mankiw, Rotemberg, and Summers [249] and Eichenbaum, Hansen, and Singleton [113]), structural breaks (see Ghysels and Hall [147, 148]), alternative sample periods (Brown and Gibbons [55]), the use of seasonally adjusted data (see Ferson and Harvey [129]) or habit persistence (see Ferson and Constantinides [128]). The results from these tests do not alter the conclusion that the representative consumer model cannot rationalize the joint time series of asset returns and, in particular, that it fails to explain the relative risk structure of alternative asset such as the returns on stocks and bonds or the returns on bonds of different maturities.

These findings are related to the equity premium "puzzle" that we described earlier as well as the average real risk-free rate puzzle and the behavior of the term premia that have been studied using the approach proposed by Mehra and Prescott [257]. For example, the average real risk-free rate puzzle says that the average real risk-free return implied by a representative consumer model is too high relative to that in the data, a finding that also accounts for the equity premium puzzle. Constantinides [77] and Epstein and Zin [121] analyze the equity premium puzzle when there is habit persistence and nonexpected utility, respectively. The behavior of the term premia is examined by Backus, Gregory, and Zin [22]. These latter results are typically derived using restrictions for the behavior of unconditional means implied by the model. By contrast, tests of asset pricing models using Euler equation estimation methods rely on conditional second moment restrictions for the MRS and asset returns. Since the underlying economic model constrains all the moments for the endogenous variables, it is not surprising that tests of the model based on the behavior of alternative sets of moments yield similar results.

Various potential explanations have been offered for rejections of the representative consumer asset pricing model. One reason is the representative consumer assumption itself, which imposes strong aggregation conditions on individual preferences and the form of heterogeneity throughout the population. As we described in Chapter 1, even if markets are complete, if there is heterogeneity throughout the population that does not aggregate to a representative consumer, the stochastic discount factor or pricing function cannot be expressed in terms of a representative consumer's MRS. Thus, rejections of the representative consumer asset pricing model may be due to the use of aggregate consumption data and the misspecification that arises from ignoring exogenous and endogenous forms of heterogeneity in the population.

A second reason that has been suggested for these rejections is market incompleteness or market frictions. When markets are complete and there are no frictions such as transactions costs or borrowing constraints, there is a common stochastic discount factor that is used to price all random payoffs, which implies that all asset returns should tend to move together.[7] Yet the empirical evidence appears to be at odds with this requirement. By introducing market incompleteness, borrowing constraints, and other sorts of frictions, some have suggested that this close link can be broken. We briefly discuss this explanation in Chapter 7 when we introduce models with private information.

---

[7]This point has been explored by Barsky [25], among others.

2. Volatility Bounds for MRSs

In the previous sections, we derived restrictions from the optimal portfolio choice problem of some representative or average consumer and showed how such restrictions could be tested by making parametric assumptions about the form of the utility function. We now describe how to derive restrictions for the unconditional mean and variance of the intertemporal MRS without making such parametric assumptions. Such unconditional moment restrictions are described in terms of the mean-standard deviation frontier for intertemporal MRSs, which is related to the mean-standard deviation frontier for asset returns derived by Chamberlain and Rothschild [68]. Here we describe a similar approach that Hansen and Jagannathan [176] develop. We derive volatility bounds assuming that there are no short sales constraints, transactions costs, and other frictions. Volatility bounds with such frictions are studied by Luttmer [238] and He and Modest [187].

We describe the construction of the volatility bounds using a setup that is based on Hansen and Jagannathan, although we have described versions of this framework in Chapters 1 and 2. There are multiple consumers who trade in securities markets and who may differ in terms of their preferences and information sets. Trading takes place at time 0 and the assets or securities pay off in date τ. We let I^j denote the information set of consumer j at time 0 and $I = \cap I^j$, where the intersection is taken over the consumers in the economy who trade securities. We assume that consumers can trade in assets at time zero that have payoffs p denominated in the numeraire good at time τ. Let P denote the set of portfolio payoffs that are traded by consumers. The first-order condition for the portfolio choice problem of consumer j is given by:

$$\pi_I(p) = E(p\mathcal{M}^j | I^j), \quad p \in P. \tag{3.45}$$

In this expression, $\mathcal{M}^j$ is the intertemporal marginal rate of substitution in consumption (MRS) for consumer j and $\pi_I(p)$ is the price at time 0 of a portfolio that pays p units of the numeraire good at date τ. Since consumers know the prices of securities that are traded at time zero, prices are represented as a function $\pi_I(p)$ mapping P into I. We can also define a functional π that maps portfolio payoffs into the expected value of prices; that is, $\pi(p) = E[\pi_I(p)]$.

It follows from an iterated expectation in Equation (3.45) that

$$\pi_I(p) = E\left[E(p\mathcal{M}^j | I^j) | I\right] = E(p\mathcal{M}^j | I), \quad p \in P, \tag{3.46}$$

since security prices are observed by all consumers. Notice that this relationship holds for all consumers j provided they engage in securities trading. Hence, we will drop the j superscript and refer to the intertemporal MRS as $\mathcal{M}$.

We can study the implications of the asset pricing relation in Equation (3.46) by assuming that the payoff space P is defined from a subset of the asset payoffs that are traded by consumers. Suppose first that the asset payoffs at date τ consist of an n-dimensional vector $\boldsymbol{x}$. The time zero prices of these n payoffs is represented with an n-dimensional vector $\boldsymbol{q}$. In this case, the asset pricing relation in Equation (3.46) can be represented as:

$$q = E(\boldsymbol{x}\mathcal{M}|I). \tag{3.47}$$

We can also define the payoff space $P \equiv \{\boldsymbol{c} \cdot \boldsymbol{x} : \boldsymbol{c} \in \mathbb{R}^n\}$ by taking all possible independent linear combinations of the vector $\boldsymbol{x}$. The prices of payoffs in P are given by the corresponding linear combinations of the prices $\boldsymbol{q}$; that is,

$$\pi_I(\boldsymbol{c} \cdot \boldsymbol{x}) \equiv \boldsymbol{c} \cdot \pi_I(\boldsymbol{x}) = \boldsymbol{c} \cdot \boldsymbol{q}.$$

Since $\boldsymbol{q}$ is an element of the common information set I, π_I maps P into I while π maps P into the real line $\mathbb{R}$. Later we also consider payoffs which are found by taking nonlinear combinations of the payoffs in P.

We can express the restrictions in Equation (3.47) by using an iterated expectation argument as follows:

$$E(\boldsymbol{q}) = E(\boldsymbol{x}\mathcal{M}). \tag{3.48}$$

This is just the unconditional counterpart of Equation (3.47). If consumers are nonsatiated in the numeraire good at time τ, then it must be the case that

$$\mathcal{M} > 0. \tag{3.49}$$

Notice that this condition is sufficient to imply the absence of arbitrage opportunities: if $\mathcal{M} > 0$, then nonnegative payoffs that are strictly positive with positive probability conditioned on I have positive prices.

We first derive the implications of the condition in Equation (3.48) for the behavior of intertemporal MRSs denoted $\mathcal{M}$. We begin by constructing random variables in P that have the same mean as $\mathcal{M}$ and that have the smallest variance among all random variables satisfying the unconditional moment restriction in Equation (3.48). We denote such random variables by $\mathcal{M}^*$. Since P is assumed to contain a finite vector of asset payoffs, we can write $\mathcal{M}^*$ as $\mathcal{M}^* = \boldsymbol{x}'\boldsymbol{\alpha}_\mathrm{o}$ where $\boldsymbol{\alpha}_\mathrm{o}$ is in $\mathbb{R}^n$. Using Equation (3.48), we solve for $\boldsymbol{\alpha}_\mathrm{o}$

$$\boldsymbol{\alpha}_\mathrm{o} = E(\boldsymbol{x}\boldsymbol{x}')^{-1}E(\boldsymbol{q}), \tag{3.50}$$

since $E(\boldsymbol{x}\boldsymbol{x}')$ is nonsingular. Thus, given asset market data on the payoffs $\boldsymbol{x}$ and prices $\boldsymbol{q}$ of n assets, we can construct the random variable $\mathcal{M}^*$.

We now consider two cases, when there exists a riskless payoff p in P such that $p = 1$ and when there does not. In the former case, Equation (3.48) implies that $E(\mathcal{M}^*) = \pi(1) = E(\mathcal{M})$, where $\pi(1)$ is the price of the sure payoff. Since both $\mathcal{M}$ and $\mathcal{M}^*$ satisfy Equation (3.48), we have that $E[\boldsymbol{x}(\mathcal{M} - \mathcal{M}^*)] = 0$, which means that the discrepancy between $\mathcal{M}$ and $\mathcal{M}^*$ is orthogonal to the random vector $\boldsymbol{x}$. Thus, $\mathcal{M}^*$ is the least-squares projection of $\mathcal{M}$ onto P, which implies that

$$\sigma^2(\mathcal{M}) = \sigma^2(\mathcal{M}^*) + \sigma(\mathcal{M} - \mathcal{M}^*)^2.$$

This yields the first volatility result, which can be expressed as:

$$\sigma^2(\mathcal{M}) \geq \sigma^2(\mathcal{M}^*), \quad E(\mathcal{M}^*) = E(\mathcal{M}). \tag{3.51}$$

Now suppose there does not exist a riskless payoff in P. Let $\boldsymbol{x}^a$ denote the $(n+1)$-dimensional random vector formed by augmenting $\boldsymbol{x}$ with a unit payoff. Since $E(\boldsymbol{x}\boldsymbol{x}')$ is nonsingular, $E(\boldsymbol{x}^a\boldsymbol{x}^{a'})$ is also nonsingular. Define the augmented payoff space P^a to contain a unit payoff by using $\boldsymbol{x}^a$ in place of $\boldsymbol{x}$. To proceed as before, we must assign a number ν to the expected price of the hypothetical unit payoff; that is, to $\pi(1)$. Such price data may not be available. Thus, we have to examine the implications of Equation (3.48) for an array of such prices. Let ν be a candidate for $\pi(1)$ and π_ν the expected pricing function that corresponds to P^a. Let us construct a random variable $\mathcal{M}_\nu$ in P^a such that $E(\boldsymbol{x}\mathcal{M}_\nu) = E(\boldsymbol{q})$ implies $E(\mathcal{M}_\nu) = \nu$. We get this result because $\mathcal{M}_\nu$ satisfies Equation (3.48) with the unit payoff. Consider any random variable $\mathcal{M}$ that has mean ν and satisfies Equation (3.48). As before, we can show that $\mathcal{M}_\nu$ is the least-squares projection of $\mathcal{M}$ on P^a so that:

$$\sigma^2(\mathcal{M}) = \sigma^2(\mathcal{M}_\nu) + \sigma(\mathcal{M} - \mathcal{M}_\nu)^2,$$

which implies that

$$\sigma^2(\mathcal{M}) \geq \sigma^2(\mathcal{M}_\nu). \tag{3.52}$$

We can replicate the above analysis to construct a set of random variables $\mathcal{M}_\nu$ that satisfy Equation (3.48) and have means ν for all real numbers ν. Define the region:

$$S = \{(\nu, w) \in \mathbb{R}^2 : w \geq \sigma(\mathcal{M}_\nu)\}. \tag{3.53}$$

This set is the set of random variables that have mean ν and variance at least as great as $\mathcal{M}_\nu$. Since this set contains the mean and standard deviation for intertemporal MRSs that satisfy the condition in Equation (3.48), its boundary is called the *mean-standard deviation frontier* for intertemporal MRSs.

Let us now derive an expression for $\mathcal{M}_\nu$. From Equation (3.48), we know that $E(\boldsymbol{x}\mathcal{M}_\nu) = E\left[(\boldsymbol{x} - E\boldsymbol{x})(\mathcal{M}_\nu - \nu)\right] + \nu E(\boldsymbol{x}) = E(\boldsymbol{q})$. By definition, $\mathcal{M}_\nu$ is a linear combination of a unit payoff and the entries of $\boldsymbol{x}$ and $E(\mathcal{M}_\nu)$ is ν so that $\mathcal{M}_\nu = (\boldsymbol{x} - E\boldsymbol{x})'\beta_\nu + \nu$ for some β_ν in $\mathbb{R}^n$. Substituting this expression above yields $\beta_\nu = \Sigma^{-1}[E(\boldsymbol{q}) - \nu E(\boldsymbol{x})]$ where $\Sigma = E[(\boldsymbol{x} - E\boldsymbol{x})(\boldsymbol{x} - E\boldsymbol{x})']$. The standard deviation of $\mathcal{M}_\nu$ is given by:

$$
\begin{aligned}
\sigma(\mathcal{M}_\nu) &= E\left[(\mathcal{M}_\nu - \nu)^2\right]^{1/2} \\
&= \left[(E\boldsymbol{q} - \nu E\boldsymbol{x})'\Sigma^{-1}(E\boldsymbol{q} - \nu E\boldsymbol{x})\right]^{1/2}.
\end{aligned}
\tag{3.54}
$$

For a given ν, $\sigma(\mathcal{M}_\nu)$ depends only on the means of $\boldsymbol{x}$ and $\boldsymbol{q}$ and the covariance matrix of $\boldsymbol{x}$ and can be computed from asset market data. Suppose $\mathcal{M}$ is equal to the value of ν in all states of the world so that there is *risk-neutral pricing*. Then Equation (3.48) implies that expected prices are proportional to expected payoffs, $E(\boldsymbol{q}) = \nu E(\boldsymbol{x})$. The result in Equation (3.54) can be interpreted as saying that for a fixed Σ, the bounds on the variability of $\mathcal{M}$ will be larger for economies with more risk averse agents.

We can extend this analysis to construct minimum variance random variables among the class of nonnegative random variables satisfying the positivity constraint in Equation (3.49) by considering random variables that can be interpreted as either European call or put options on payoffs in P. Recall that when the payoff on the underlying portfolio is p and the strike price is k, a European call option entitles an investor to the payoff $\max\{p - k, 0\}$ and a put option to the payoff $\max\{k - p, 0\}$. These payoffs are nonnegative but they may be nonlinear functions of the payoff vector $\boldsymbol{x}$. There are again two cases, the case when a riskless payoff exists and when it does not. In the former case, finding the minimum variance nonnegative random variable $\tilde{\mathcal{M}}$ satisfying Equation (3.48) is equivalent to finding a vector $\boldsymbol{\alpha}_o$ in $\mathbb{R}^n$ such that

$$E\left[\boldsymbol{x}(\boldsymbol{x}'\boldsymbol{\alpha}_o)^+\right] = E(\boldsymbol{q}), \tag{3.55}$$

where $\tilde{\mathcal{M}} = (\boldsymbol{x}'\boldsymbol{\alpha}_o)^+$. If the constructed $\tilde{\mathcal{M}}$ is positive with probability one, then the volatility bound cannot be sharpened further. This occurs only if $\tilde{\mathcal{M}}$ coincides with $\mathcal{M}^*$.

Define $R = \{p \in P : \pi(p) = 1\}$. When $\boldsymbol{q}$ is nonrandom, R is the collection of (gross) returns on portfolios in P. We cannot solve Equation (3.55) to obtain $\boldsymbol{\alpha}_o$ because it is a nonlinear function of $\boldsymbol{\alpha}_o$. However, we can solve the problem of finding a payoff r in R whose (positive) truncation has the smallest second moment:

$$\min_{r \in R} \|r^+\|^2, \tag{3.56}$$

where $\|r\| \equiv [E(r^2)]^{1/2}$. We scale $\tilde{r}^+$ as $\tilde{\mathcal{M}} = \tilde{r}^+/\|\tilde{r}^+\|$. It can be shown that $\|\tilde{r}^+\|$ must be strictly positive as long as there is one random variable $\mathcal{M}$ satisfying Equations (3.48) and (3.49). It is easy to show that $\tilde{\mathcal{M}}$ satisfies Equation (3.48).

In the case when there does not exist a unit payoff in the payoff space P, the payoff space must be augmented with a unit payoff to form the augmented payoff space, P^a. As before, assign alternative, strictly positive numbers ν to $\pi(1)$ and define R_ν as the set of payoffs with expected prices equal to one. The counterpart to Equation (3.56) is:

$$\delta_\nu \equiv \inf_{r \in R_\nu} \|r^+\|^2, \tag{3.57}$$

If this problem has a solution with $\delta > 0$, denote the minimum variance, nonnegative random variable with mean ν that satisfies Equation (3.48) by $\tilde{\mathcal{M}}_\nu$. The counterpart to the region S given in Equation (3.53) is:

$$S^+ \equiv \left\{(\nu, w) : \delta_\nu > 0 \text{ and } w \geq \sigma(\tilde{\mathcal{M}}_\nu)\right\}. \tag{3.58}$$

Figure 3.1 plots the mean-standard deviation frontiers S and S^+ using data on all the firms in the New York Stock Exchange and the American Exchange for which we have monthly returns between January 1926 and December 1990. Notice that the impact of imposing the strict positivity constraint on the MRS is to reduce the admissible mean-standard deviation region.

The mean-standard deviation region can be used as a diagnostic tool by plotting the unconditional means and standard deviations for the intertemporal MRS implied by alternative asset pricing models and examining whether these means and standard deviations fall within the

Figure 3.1. Frontier for intertemporal MRSs with and without positivity imposed.

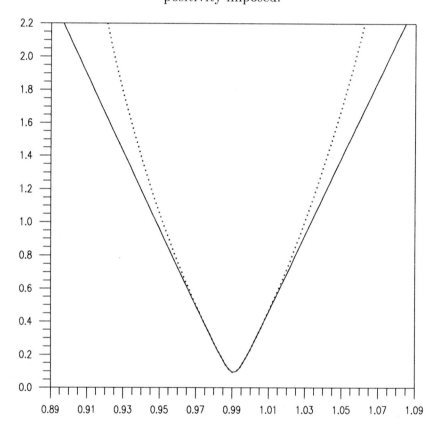

admissible region implied by data on asset returns. As an example, the intertemporal MRS for the model with time-additive, CRR preferences is given by:

$$\mathcal{M}_t \equiv \beta \left(\frac{c_{t+1}}{c_t} \right)^{-\gamma}, \quad \gamma \geq 0.$$

Recall that the MRS for models with consumption durability or nonexpected utility preferences is described by Equations (2.68) and (2.83), respectively. Suppose we are given a sample of observations on consumption $\{c_t\}_{t=1}^T$. For any value of the unknown parameters entering the relevant expression for $\mathcal{M}_t$, we can calculate the sample means and sample standard deviations of $\mathcal{M}_t$ to determine the set of parameters of the underlying economic model that are consistent with data on asset returns. Hansen and Jagannathan [176] and Cochrane and Hansen [72] calculate the mean-standard deviation region for intertemporal MRSs as a way of examining the implications of alternative asset pricing models.

3.   Variance Bounds Tests

We now turn to a discussion of variance bounds tests, which provide an alternative approach for examining the implications of asset pricing relations. Variance bounds tests have been derived by Shiller [305, 306], Singleton [311], and LeRoy and Porter [228]. We start with the framework proposed by LeRoy and Porter.

3.1.   The Present-Value Model

Let p_t denote the price of a share to some stock at the beginning of period t and d_t the dividends paid on this stock during period t. Consider the present-value relation linking the price of a stock to its future stream of dividends:

$$p_t = \sum_{j=0}^{\infty} \beta^j E_t(d_{t+j}), \tag{3.59}$$

where $E_t(\cdot)$ denotes expectation conditional on information at date t. This formula has the intuition that sudden changes in stock prices can be attributed to new information about future dividends or earnings. Notice that it can be derived from the equilibrium asset pricing model that we studied in Chapter 2 by assuming that consumers are risk neutral.

The variance bounds tests derived by LeRoy and Porter are obtained by imposing a joint distribution on the earnings or dividends of a technological process and any other variables that might be useful in predicting dividends, d_t. For this purpose, assume that there exists a vector z_t that is useful for predicting future dividends and that $(d_t, z_t')'$ is generated from the $p \times 1$ multivariate stationary stochastic process as:

$$\begin{bmatrix} d_t \\ z_t \end{bmatrix} = C + \underline{\epsilon}_t + D_1 \underline{\epsilon}_{t-1} + D_2 \underline{\epsilon}_{t-2} + \cdots = C + D(L) \underline{\epsilon}_t, \qquad (3.60)$$

where $\{\underline{\epsilon}_t\}$ is a sequence of serially uncorrelated random vectors with mean zero and positive definite covariance matrix Σ, C is a $p \times 1$ vector, D_i's are $p \times p$ matrices, and L is the lag operator.

The derivation of the variance bounds tests proceeds by assuming that there exist variables z_t which, in addition to past d_t, provide perfect forecasts of d_t. Define the *perfect foresight price* p_t^* as being generated by the relation:

$$p_t^* = \sum_{j=0}^{\infty} \beta^j d_{t+j}. \qquad (3.61)$$

Then, it is easy to see from Equation (3.59) that

$$p_t^* = p_t + \pi_t, \qquad (3.62)$$

where π_t is the discounted sum of forecast errors in predicting future dividends using information available to agents at time t, defined as:

$$\pi_t = p_t^* - p_t = \sum_{j=0}^{\infty} \beta^j [d_{t+j} - E_t(d_{t+j})].$$

Also define the price $\hat{p}_t$ by assuming that only past dividends help forecast future dividends:

$$\hat{p}_t = \sum_{j=0}^{\infty} \beta^j E(d_{t+j} | d_t, d_{t-1}, \ldots). \qquad (3.63)$$

The relations in Equations (3.59) through (3.63) allow a simple derivation of the *variance bounds inequalities*. Recall that $p_t = p_t^* - \pi_t$. Likewise, $\hat{p}_t = p_t^* - \hat{\pi}_t$ and $\hat{\pi}_t \geq \pi_t$. This last inequality follows from the fact that the presence of additional forecasting variables cannot increase the magnitude of the forecast error. Thus, the unconditional variances of $\hat{p}_t$, p_t, and p_t^* satisfy the relation:

$$\mathrm{Var}(\hat{p}_t) \leq \mathrm{Var}(p_t) < \mathrm{Var}(p_t^*). \qquad (3.64)$$

An equivalent representation of the variance bounds inequalities in Equation (3.64) can be obtained by defining the coefficient of dispersion for some random variable y_t as:

$$CD(y_t) \equiv \sqrt{Var(y_t)}/E(y_t).$$

Let c denote the first element of the $p \times 1$ vector of constants C and notice that the unconditional means of p_t, $p_t^\star$, and $\hat{p}_t$ all equal $c/(1 - \beta)$. Then the inequalities in Equation (3.64) can be expressed as:

$$CD(\hat{p}_t) \leq CD(p_t) < CD(p_t^\star). \tag{3.65}$$

To test the *upper bound inequality* $CD(p_t) \leq CD(p_t^\star)$, we form the test statistic:

$$f_1^u = \left[\frac{Var(p_t^\star)}{c/(1 - \beta)} \right]^{\frac{1}{2}} - \left[\frac{Var(p_t)}{c/(1 - \beta)} \right]^{\frac{1}{2}}. \tag{3.66}$$

The null hypothesis is $f_1^u > 0$. Now consider the *lower bound inequality*, $CD(\hat{p}_t) \leq CD(p_t)$. This can be tested using the statistic:

$$f_1^\ell = \left[\frac{Var(p_t)}{c/(1 - \beta)} \right]^{\frac{1}{2}} - \left[\frac{Var(\hat{p}_t)}{c/(1 - \beta)} \right]^{\frac{1}{2}}. \tag{3.67}$$

The null hypothesis is $f_1^\ell \geq 0$.

We evaluate these test statistics by estimating a bivariate and invertible autoregressive moving average (ARMA) representation for p_t and d_t using the method described in Wilson [341]. Let $\underline{\omega}$ be the vector of ARMA parameters (including intercepts and distinct elements of the variance-covariance matrix of the serially uncorrelated shocks to the ARMA representation). Under general conditions, $\hat{\underline{\omega}}$, the quasi-maximum likelihood estimate of $\underline{\omega}$, is asymptotically normally distributed with mean $\underline{\omega}$ and covariance matrix Ω. Given $\hat{\underline{\omega}}$ and an estimate of Ω, the functions $f_i(\underline{\omega})$ described in Equations (3.66) and (3.67) may be evaluated and their standard errors calculated. Since each of the test functions f_i is continuous in $\underline{\omega}$, the ratio of $f_i(\hat{\underline{\omega}})$ to its estimated asymptotic standard error will have a $N(0,1)$ distribution under the null hypothesis.

LeRoy and Porter correct for trends induced by inflation by dividing nominal quantities by the GNP deflator. They correct for retained earnings by calculating a new variable k_t which they argue can be viewed as a quantity index to which corporate equity is title. They set this index equal to unity in the initial period and augment it in proportion to the amount of retained corporate earnings in each quarter as

$$k_t = \begin{cases} 1, & t = 1, \\ k_{t-1} + \frac{E_t - D_t}{P_0}, & t = 2, 3, \ldots, \end{cases}$$

where E_t is real earnings, D_t is real dividends, and P_t is real stock value. Finally, the adjusted earnings and equity value series, d_t and p_t, are calculated as $d_t = E_t/k_t$ and $p_t = P_t/k_t$. The resulting series are treated as stationary.

LeRoy and Porter use data on earnings and price for the Standard & Poor's Composite Index, AT&T, GE, and GM. Their most notable empirical result is that the upper bound test, $f_2^u > 0$, is flagrantly violated for all four data sets. However, the asymptotic variances of the test statistics are very high, with the estimates and asymptotic variances for GE only leading to clear rejection of the null hypothesis. They also construct a test of the relation, $\text{Var}(p^*) = \text{Var}(p_t) + \text{Var}(\pi_t)$, which is derived from Equation (3.62) and is more restrictive than the variance bounds inequalities. In this case, the z-statistic for the hypothesis that this equality holds in the data is rejected for all three firms; for the aggregate index, the test statistic is not statistically different from zero.

Shiller [306] derives variance bounds inequalities for detrended stock prices and dividends. Let g denote the deterministic growth rate in stock prices and dividends and P_t and D_t the real stock price and dividend. Shiller's model of the detrended stock price can be written as:

$$\frac{P_t}{(1+g)^t} = \sum_{k=0}^{\infty} \beta^k E_t \left[\frac{D_{t+k}}{(1+g)^t} \right],$$

or

$$p_t = \sum_{k=0}^{\infty} (\beta\gamma)^k E_t(d_{t+k}) = \sum_{k=0}^{\infty} \bar{\beta}^k E_t(d_{t+k}), \tag{3.68}$$

where $\gamma = 1+g$ and $\bar{\beta} = (1+g)/(1+r)$. Here r is the "real" (or inflation-adjusted) expected rate of return on the stock market and $\beta\gamma < 1$, to guarantee a finite price p_t. The perfect foresight price or the *ex post* rational price, p_t^*, is:

$$p_t^* = \sum_{k=0}^{\infty} \bar{\beta}^k d_{t+k}, \tag{3.69}$$

where $\bar{r} = 1/\bar{\beta} - 1$ is the appropriate discount rate for detrended prices and dividends.

Shiller computes the *ex post* rational price recursively as:

$$p^*_{t|T} = \bar{\beta} p^*_{t+1|T} + d_t, \quad t = 1, \ldots, T-1, \tag{3.70}$$

assuming a terminal value:

$$p^*_{T|T} = \frac{1}{T} \sum_{t=1}^{T} p_t.$$

His test is based on the upper bound inequality, $\text{Var}(p_t) \leq \text{Var}(p^*_t)$. He constructs sample estimates of the variances of p_t and p^*_t as the average squared deviation of each variable from its mean. He uses an annual data set for the period 1871–1979 and measures P_t as the Standard and Poor's Monthly Stock Price Index for January divided by the Bureau of Labor Statistics wholesale price index. The dividend series D_t is measured as total dividends for the calendar year accruing to the portfolio represented by the stocks in the index divided by the wholesale price index for the year. Shiller finds that the standard deviation of actual stock prices exceeds that of the *ex post* rational stock prices by a factor of 5.59. Although he does not report any significance tests, he interprets this result as a rejection of the variance bounds inequalities.

3.2.   Criticisms of Variance Bounds Tests

The variance bounds tests described above have been criticized on a number of grounds, including small sample estimation problems and problems arising from the nonstationarity of dividends and prices. Some of our following discussion derives from Gilles and LeRoy [149], who provide a detailed survey of the econometric problems in variance bounds tests.

Flavin [133] and Kleidon [219] show that small sample estimation problems can bias the variance bounds tests toward violation of the variance bounds. Flavin notes that the variance of p_t and p^*_t are both biased downward in small samples. Furthermore, the bias in estimating the variance of p^*_t is more severe. The reason for the bias occurs because the estimate of the unconditional variance for both p_t and p^*_t requires an estimate of their unconditional means as well. A second criticism that Flavin has of Shiller's implementation of the variance bounds tests is that construction of an observable counterpart for p^*_t, namely, $p^*_{t|T}$, requires that a terminal value $p^*_{T|T}$ must be used. This induces a bias in the estimate of p^*_t, conditional on the sample. Gilles and LeRoy show that an observable counterpart of p^*_t calculated by imposing the terminal condition $p^*_{T|T} = p_T$ will provide an unbiased estimate for p^*_t. But this does not eliminate the bias in the sample variance of the true p_t^* because the calculation of the observable *ex post* rational price sets innovations in dividends occurring after the end of the sample equal to zero. This reduces the estimated variance of the *ex post* rational price.

The assumption of stationarity in the dividends or earnings process has been criticized by Marsh and Merton [252]. They argue that the variance bounds tests are a joint test of the following hypotheses: (i) stock prices reflect investor beliefs which are rational expectations of future dividends; (ii) the "real" or (inflation-adjusted) expected rate of return on the stock market, r, is constant over time (recall constant discounting); and (iii) aggregate real dividends on the stock market can be described by a finite-variance stationary stochastic process with a deterministic exponential trend (or growth rate) denoted by g. They question this last assumption on the grounds that, although there is no theory of optimal dividend policy, empirical observations suggest that firms employ some type of dividend smoothing policy. Marsh and Merton specify an empirical dividend policy which assumes that managers set dividends to grow at an exponential trend g but deviate from this path when changes in permanent earnings or the value of the firm departs from their long-run growth path. Given this process for dividends, Marsh and Merton show that the *ex post* rational price p_t^* can be written as a convex combination of the observed detrended stock prices, in which case the variance bounds inequalities can be reversed.

Kleidon's [220] criticism is also based on the assumption that dividends follow a nonstationary process. He is motivated by Grossman and Shiller's [167] contention that a time series plot of the *ex post* rational price is too smooth relative to the plot of the actual stock price series. These authors claim that agents would have to be extremely risk averse to generate the volatility in the actual stock price. If agents are very risk averse, then a highly variable stock price is consistent with an environment in which agents are trying to smooth their consumption.

If the variance bounds inequalities refer to different replications of the same economy and not to a single realization from a given economy, then the plots presented by Grossman and Shiller do not provide evidence for excess volatility. In other words, if we could observe n replications of the same economy for each t, then the cross-sectional variance bounds inequality defined by:

$$\widehat{\mathrm{Var}}(p_t) = \sum_{i=1}^n \frac{(p_{i,t} - \overline{p}_t)^2}{n-1} \leq \widehat{\mathrm{Var}}(p_t^*) = \sum_{i=1}^n \frac{(p_{i,t}^* - \overline{p}_t^*)^2}{n-1}$$

would be satisfied. This is the observation made by Kleidon, and he further notes that what we observe being contradicted by the data is the time series inequality defined by:

$$\widehat{\mathrm{Var}}(p_t) = \sum_{t=1}^{T} \frac{(p_t - \overline{p})^2}{T-1} \leq \widehat{\mathrm{Var}}(p_t^*) = \sum_{t=1}^{T} \frac{(p_t^* - \overline{p}^*)^2}{T-1}.$$

However, if dividends are nonstationary, then the second inequality is not guaranteed to hold even in large samples. Notice that the present-value relationship implies that $\mathrm{Var}(p_t) \leq \mathrm{Var}(p_t^*)$ for each t, regardless of whether dividends are nonstationary or not. But the nonstationarity of dividends implies that these variances will not be constant over time, and hence, cannot be estimated consistently using a single realization of a given economy.

3.3.   New Developments

New developments in the variance bounds literature include so-called "unbiased" variance bounds tests and methods for dealing with non-stationarity in the measured series. We describe several papers in this literature.

West [336] develops a variance bounds test that is valid even if dividends are nonstationary and does not require a proxy for p_t^*. He assumes that I_t, the information set possessed by the market, is generated by current and past values of a finite number of random variables and that after s differences, all random variables in I_t jointly follow a covariance stationary $\mathrm{ARMA}(q, r)$ process for some finite $s, q, r \geq 0$. Since dividends d_t are assumed to be one of the variables that generates the information set I_t, this assumption differentiates West's analysis from LeRoy and Porter's because dividends are allowed to be nonstationary. Let $\hat{I}_t$ denote a subset of I_t including at least current and past values of d_t. Assume that conditional expectations are equivalent to linear least squares projections denoted $\hat{E}(\cdot | I_t)$. West shows that

$$E\left[\hat{p}_t - \hat{E}\left(\hat{p}_t | \hat{I}_{t-1}\right)\right]^2 \geq E\left[p_t - \hat{E}\left(p_t | I_{t-1}\right)\right]^2. \tag{3.71}$$

Notice that if dividends are stationary, this inequality is equivalent to the lower bound inequality, $f_1^{\ell} \geq 0$ defined in Equation (3.67). To analyze the nonstationary case, West uses the projection formulas in Hansen and Sargent [177] to derive a result similar to that in Equation (3.71). (See Exercise 4 for a simple implementation of this test in the nonstationary case.)

Mankiw, Romer, and Shapiro [247, 248] derive a test statistic for testing stock price volatility where the expected value of the sample statistic
is equal to its population value. They refer to this property of their test
as "unbiasedness" of the test. This is in response to Flavin's criticism
that the sample variance does not provide an unbiased estimate of the
population variance. Let p_t^0 be any variable constructed from information
available to agents at time t. We can interpret p_t^0 as a "naive forecast"
of the actual price. Construct the *ex post* rational price $p_{t|T}^*$ recursively
using the terminal value $p_{T|T}^* = 1/T \sum_{t=1}^T p_t$ and consider the identity:

$$p_{t|T}^* - p_t^0 = (p_{t|T}^* - p_t) + (p_t - p_t^0). \tag{3.72}$$

Now, $E[(p_{t|T}^* - p_t)(p_t - p_t^0)] = 0$, because $p_t - p_t^0$ depends only on infor-
mation available at time t, and $p_{t|T}^* - p_t$ is uncorrelated with any variable
available at time t. Squaring both sides and taking expectations yields:

$$S \equiv E\left[(p_{t|T}^* - p_t^0)^2\right] - E\left[(p_{t|T}^*) - p_t)^2\right] - E\left[(p_t - p_t^0)^2\right] = 0. \tag{3.73}$$

Mankiw *et al.* evaluate the sample counterpart of S, say $\hat{S}$, and find that
it is negative, thus indicating excess volatility. But they do not report
any standard errors.

In three papers, Campbell and Shiller [63, 64, 65] combine the theory
of estimation and testing for cointegrated processes with tests for volatility. In their first paper, they show that the implications of the present-
value model can be tested by using a bivariate autoregression involving
stock prices and dividends. Unlike earlier papers, they derive a test that
is valid when prices and dividends are stationary in first differences. In
[65], they assume that dividends and other variables useful for predicting
dividends form a multivariate log-linear model while in [64], they add
corporate earnings to the autoregression for prices and dividends.

We now describe the approach followed in their first paper. The
present-value relation in Equation (3.59) linking stock prices and dividends is assumed to hold. To derive a test that is valid for the first
differences of prices and dividends, we define the variable S_t as the
"spread" between the stock price and a multiple of dividends:

$$S_t = p_t - \frac{1}{1 - \beta} d_t.$$

Subtracting $1/(1 - \beta)d_t$ from both sides of the present-value relation as

$$p_t - \frac{1}{1 - \beta} d_t = \sum_{i=0}^{\infty} \beta^i E_t(d_{t+i}) - \frac{1}{1 - \beta} d_t$$

and rearranging the right side of the resulting expression yields an equivalent expression for the spread as:

$$S_t = \frac{1}{1-\beta} \sum_{i=1}^{\infty} \beta^i E_t(\Delta d_{t+i}) = \frac{\beta}{1-\beta} E_t(\Delta p_{t+1}), \tag{3.74}$$

where Δ is the first difference operator. Notice that if Δd_t is stationary, then Equation (3.74) implies that S_t is also stationary. Likewise, if S_t is stationary, then from Equation (3.74), Δp_t is also stationary. These results imply that a linear combination of p_t and d_t, namely, S_t, is stationary even though p_t and d_t are stationary in first differences. In the language of Engle and Granger [117], the bivariate process $\{x_t\}$, $x_t \equiv (p_t, d_t)'$, is said to be a *cointegrated process*.

The relationship in Equation (3.74) yields a test of the present-value model according to which one can regress Δp_t on S_{t-1} and other variables. Under the null hypothesis, the coefficient on S_{t-1} should be $(1 - \beta)/\beta$ and the coefficients on the other variables should be zero. We can also derive a test of the present-value relation by considering the bivariate autoregression for S_t and Δd_t as follows:

$$\begin{bmatrix} \Delta d_t \\ S_t \end{bmatrix} = \begin{bmatrix} a(L) & b(L) \\ c(L) & d(L) \end{bmatrix} \begin{bmatrix} \Delta d_{t-1} \\ S_{t-1} \end{bmatrix} + \begin{bmatrix} u_{1,t} \\ u_{2,t} \end{bmatrix}, \tag{3.75}$$

where $a(L)$, $b(L)$, $c(L)$, and $d(L)$ are all of order p and $\{u_t\}$, $u_t \equiv (u_{1,t}, u_{2,t})'$, is a serially uncorrelated process with mean zero and covariance matrix Σ. Stack the above representation into a first-order system:

$$\begin{bmatrix} \Delta d_t \\ \vdots \\ \Delta d_{t-p+1} \\ S_t \\ \vdots \\ S_{t-p+1} \end{bmatrix} = \begin{bmatrix} a_1 & \cdots & a_p & b_1 & \cdots & b_p \\ 1 & & & & & \\ & \ddots & & & & \\ & & 1 & & & \\ c_1 & \cdots & c_p & d_1 & \cdots & d_p \\ & & & 1 & & \\ & & & & \ddots & \\ & & & & & 1 \end{bmatrix} \begin{bmatrix} \Delta d_{t-1} \\ \vdots \\ \Delta d_{t-p} \\ S_{t-1} \\ \vdots \\ S_{t-p} \end{bmatrix} + \begin{bmatrix} u_{1,t} \\ \vdots \\ 0 \\ u_{2,t} \\ \vdots \\ 0 \end{bmatrix},$$

or, in compact notation,

$$z_t = A z_{t-1} + v_t. \tag{3.76}$$

Denote by H_t the information set generated by current and lagged values of p_t and d_t, $H_t = \{p_s, d_s, s \leq t\}$. Notice that H_t is a subset of agents' full information set, I_t.

To derive the full set of restrictions implied by the present-value relation for S_t and Δd_t, we project Equation (3.74) onto the information set H_t:

$$E(S_t|H_t) = E\left[\frac{1}{1-\beta}\sum_{i=1}^{\infty}\beta^i E_t(\Delta d_{t+i})\,|H_t\right], \tag{3.77}$$

which equals S_t since S_t is in H_t. Let $\boldsymbol{g}$ and $\boldsymbol{h}$ denote $2p \times 1$ vectors,

$$\boldsymbol{g} = (0\cdots 0\; 1\cdots 0)' \quad \text{and} \quad \boldsymbol{h} = (1\cdots 0\; 0\cdots 0)'.$$

Then notice that $E(S_t|H_t) = S_t = \boldsymbol{g}'\boldsymbol{z}_t$. Also, $E(\Delta d_{t+i}|H_t) = \boldsymbol{h}'\boldsymbol{A}^i\boldsymbol{z}_t$, since $E(\boldsymbol{z}_{t+i}|H_t) = \boldsymbol{A}^i\boldsymbol{z}_t$ using the first-order Markov nature of $\boldsymbol{z}_t$. To get $E(\Delta d_{t+i}|H_t)$, we just pick off the first element of this projection using the vector $\boldsymbol{h}'$. Thus, Equation (3.77) implies

$$\boldsymbol{g}'\boldsymbol{z}_t = \frac{1}{1-\beta}\sum_{i=1}^{\infty}\beta^i\boldsymbol{h}'\boldsymbol{A}^i\boldsymbol{z}_t. \tag{3.78}$$

But this must hold for all $\boldsymbol{z}_t$. Therefore,

$$\boldsymbol{g}' = \frac{1}{1-\beta}\sum_{i=1}^{\infty}\beta^i\boldsymbol{h}'\boldsymbol{A}^i = \frac{1}{1-\beta}\boldsymbol{h}'\beta\boldsymbol{A}(\boldsymbol{I}-\beta\boldsymbol{A})^{-1},$$

where the second term is obtained by evaluating the infinite sum. Now, postmultiplying both sides of the resulting expression by $\boldsymbol{I} - \beta\boldsymbol{A}$ yields:

$$\boldsymbol{g}'(\boldsymbol{I}-\beta\boldsymbol{A}) = \frac{1}{1-\beta}\boldsymbol{h}'\beta\boldsymbol{A}. \tag{3.79}$$

Using the structure of the $\boldsymbol{A}$ matrix, it can be shown that these constraints imply constraints on the individual coefficients of the form:

$$c_i = -\frac{1}{1-\beta}a_i, \quad i = 1,\cdots,p,$$

and

$$d_1 = \frac{1}{\beta} - \frac{1}{1-\beta}b_1, \quad d_i = -\frac{1}{1-\beta}b_i, \quad i = 2,\cdots,p.$$

We now interpret these restrictions. Since $S_t = c_1\Delta d_{t-1} + \cdots + c_p\Delta d_{t-p} + d_1 S_{t-1} + \cdots + d_p S_{t-p} + u_{2,t}$, we can use the restrictions in Equation (3.79) to derive an alternative expression for the "spread" S_t as:

$$S_t = -\frac{1}{1-\beta}(\Delta d_t - u_{1,t}) + \frac{1}{\beta}S_{t-1} + u_{2,t}.$$

Define the new variable:

$$\xi_t \equiv S_t - \frac{1}{\beta}S_{t-1} + \frac{1}{1-\beta}\Delta d_t = u_{1,t} + u_{2,t}.$$

Since ξ_t is equal to $u_{1,t} + u_{2,t}$, which are the innovations to Δd_t and S_t in the bivariate autoregression, $E(\xi_t|H_t) = 0$. But ξ_t can be written as

$$\begin{aligned} \xi_t &= p_t - \frac{1}{1-\beta}d_t - \frac{1}{\beta}p_{t-1} + \frac{1}{(1-\beta)\beta}d_{t-1} + \frac{1}{1-\beta}(d_t - d_{t-1}) \\ &= p_t - \frac{1}{\beta}(p_{t-1} - d_{t-1}) = p_t - E_{t-1}(p_t). \end{aligned}$$

Thus, ξ_t is the true innovation at time t to p_t; namely, the part of p_t that is unforecastable using agents' full information set I_t.

Campbell and Shiller perform a test of the present-value model based on a Wald test of the restrictions in Equation (3.79). They test for unit roots in p_t and d_t (which they cannot reject) and test for cointegration between prices and dividends (for which they find weaker evidence). They find some statistical evidence against the present-value model for stocks and use alternative measures of volatility to show that *"the spread between stock prices and dividends moves too much and that deviations from the present-value model are quite persistent..."* In their other two papers, they also obtain evidence of excess volatility. For example, in [65] they find that earnings are a strong predictor of dividend growth rates, even conditional on the current log price-dividend ratio. This finding contradicts the present-value model, according to which current price is a sufficient statistic for future dividend growth.

4. Conditional Volatility and Nonlinearity in Asset Prices

The idea that time-varying variances and covariances may be an important source of uncertainty about asset prices was recognized by authors such as Mandelbrot [245] and Fama [123]. Yet, as Bollerslev, Chou and Kroner [39] (hereafter referred to as Bollerslev *et al.*) note in their survey of ARCH and GARCH modeling, it is only recently that researchers have begun modeling time variation in the second or higher moments of speculative prices.

The most widely used method for modeling such time variation is the Autoregressive Conditional Heteroscedasticity (ARCH) model proposed by Engle [115] and its extensions. Paralleling the literature on specification, estimation, and inference in variants of ARCH and GARCH models, there is a large literature associated with empirical applications of these models to financial market data. In this section, we describe some of the most widely used models of conditional volatility. In Section 5, we describe an application.

The recent literature on nonlinear time series and chaos has shown that ARCH-type models are just one type of model in which the distribution of a process depends nonlinearly on the elements of some conditioning set. We briefly review some other classes of models that can give rise to such behavior, including models that display low-dimensional deterministic chaotic dynamics and nonlinear stochastic models.

4.1. Variants of ARCH

In this section, we discuss some of the most commonly used variants of ARCH models as a way of providing background material for applications that we consider in our subsequent discussion. For further details and references, we refer the reader to the excellent survey by Bollerslev *et al.*

Following Engle [115], an ARCH model is given by the discrete time stochastic process $\{u_t\}$ satisfying the relations:

$$u_t = z_t \sigma_t, \tag{3.80}$$

$$z_t \text{ i.i.d.,} \quad E(z_t), \quad \text{Var}(z_t) = 1, \tag{3.81}$$

with σ_t a time-varying, positive function of the elements of the time $t - 1$ information set. Notice that $\{u_t\}$ is a serially uncorrelated process with mean zero but the conditional variance of u_t, which is given by σ_t^2, may be changing over time. Typically, u_t corresponds to the innovation in the mean of some other stochastic process y_t, where

$$y_t = g(x_{t-1}) + u_t, \tag{3.82}$$

and x_{t-1} is an element of the time $t - 1$ information set. Notice that neither the form of the mean function g nor the nature of the innovation u_t is specified according to an underlying economic theory.

The linear ARCH(q) model, due Engle [115], provides one of the simplest ways for parameterizing σ_t^2 by assuming that σ_t^2 can be written as a linear function of past squared values of the process:

$$\sigma_t^2 = c + \sum_{i=1}^{q} \alpha_i u_{t-1}^2 = c + \alpha(L)u_t^2, \tag{3.83}$$

where $c \geq 0$, $\alpha_i \geq 0$, and L is the lag operator. This says that large (small) price changes will be followed by other large (small) price changes but of an unpredictable sign. Under the assumption that z_t is normally distributed, the unknown parameters of the model, including c and α_i, $i = 1, \ldots, q$, can be estimated by the method of maximum likelihood. Engle discusses maximum likelihood-based inference procedures under the above distributional assumptions. ARCH-type models may also be estimated by GMM and Monte Carlo methods may be used to conduct Bayesian inference.

The generalized ARCH model suggested by Bollerslev [38], known as the GARCH(p, q) model, allows for a more flexible lag structure than the ARCH(q) model by specifying the conditional variance to depend on a finite number of lagged values of itself:

$$
\begin{aligned}
\sigma_t^2 &= c + \sum_{i=1}^{q} \alpha_i u_{t-i}^2 + \sum_{i=1}^{p} \beta_i \sigma_{t-i}^2 \\
&= c + \alpha(L)u_t^2 + \beta(L)\sigma_t^2.
\end{aligned} \tag{3.84}
$$

To ensure a well defined process, all the parameters in the infinite order autoregressive (AR) representation $\sigma_t^2 = (1 - \beta)c + (1 - \beta(L))^{-1}\alpha(L)u_t^2$ must be nonnegative, where the roots of the polynomial $1 - \beta(\lambda) = 0$ lie outside the unit circle. For example, for a GARCH(1,1), this is equivalent to requiring that both α_1 and β_1 are nonnegative. Taking unconditional expectations in Equation (3.84) shows that:

$$
\begin{aligned}
\sigma^2 &= E(\sigma_t^2) = c + \sum_{i=1}^{q} \alpha_i E(u_{t-i}^2) + \sum_{i=1}^{p} \beta_i E(\sigma_{t-i}^2) \\
&= c/\left[1 - \sum_{i=1}^{q} \alpha_i - \sum_{i=1}^{p} \beta_i\right] = c/[1 - \alpha(1) - \beta(1)],
\end{aligned}
$$

where $\alpha(1)$ and $\beta(1)$ are the lag polynomials $\alpha(L)$ and $\beta(L)$ evaluated at $L = 1$. Thus, $\{u_t\}$ is a covariance stationary process if and only if $\alpha(1) + \beta(1) < 1$. In this case, the GARCH(p, q) is equivalent to an infinite-order linear ARCH with geometrically declining weights.

A finding that emerges from the empirical literature associated with high-frequency financial data is the persistence in the conditional variance functions. In terms of the GARCH(p, q) model, this implies a unit root in the autoregressive polynomial with $\alpha_1 + \cdots + \alpha_q + \beta_1 + \cdots + \beta_p = 1$. This class of models is referred to as IGARCH(p, q) by Engle and Bollersev [116]. As in random walk models for unconditional means, the effect of current information is important for forecasts of the conditional variance at all horizons. In this case, the unconditional variance for the general IGARCH(p, q) does not exist. Unlike the ARIMA class of models for conditional means, however, the IGARCH model is strictly stationary and ergodic though not covariance stationary.

Another variant of ARCH models is given by nonlinear ARCH proposed by Nelson [269]. In this case, the variance depends not only on the magnitude of u_t but also its sign. In the Exponential GARCH(p, q), or EGARCH(p, q) model, σ_t^2 is an asymmetric function of past u_t^2:

$$\log \sigma_t^2 = c + \sum_{i=1}^{q} \alpha_i \left[\phi z_{t-i} + \alpha \left(|z_{t-i}| - E|z_{t-i}| \right) \right]$$

$$+ \sum_{i=1}^{p} \beta_i \log \sigma_{t-i}^2. \tag{3.85}$$

Unlike the linear GARCH(p, q), there are no restrictions on the parameters α_i and β_i to ensure nonnegativity of the conditional variances. If $\alpha_i \phi < 0$, the variance tends to rise (fall) when u_{t-i} is negative (positive). Provided z_t is i.i.d., it is easy to see that u_t is covariance stationary if all the roots of the autoregressive polynomial $1 - \beta(\lambda) = 0$ are outside the unit circle. Other parametric ARCH models include the logarithm or Multiplicative ARCH model, power transformations of u_t^2 in the nonlinear ARCH model, a threshold ARCH model in which σ_t^2 is a linear piecewise function, and so on. Alternatively, it is possible to follow a nonparametric approach wherein σ_t^2 is estimated as a weighted average of $u_t^2, t = 1, 2, \ldots T$ using kernel methods with typically Gaussian kernels.

ARCH-type models have been used to model time-varying conditional second moments and risk premia in stock and index returns, interest rate data, and foreign exchange data. The ARCH-in-mean model introduced by Engle, Lilien, and Robins [118] is a variant of ARCH models in which the conditional mean is an explicit function of the conditional variance of the process, $y_t = g(x_{t-1}, \sigma_t^2) + u_t$. The ARCH-M model has been used to model the risk-return tradeoff implied by theories in finance. In the last section of this chapter, we provide a comparison of alternative ARCH type models for explaining index returns based on the study by Brock, Lakonishok, and LeBaron [53].

In addition to time-varying conditional variances, high-frequency financial data, such as daily changes in exchange rates or daily holding returns on stock indices, are known to have fatter tails than the normal distribution. Alternative parametric distributions that have been proposed to account for leptokurtosis in the innovations in ARCH and GARCH models include standardized t-distributions with the degrees of freedom being estimated, a normal-Poisson mixture distribution, the power exponential distribution, a normal-lognormal mixture distribution, and a generalized exponential distribution. Alternatively, it is possible to employ a seminonparametric approach for fitting the conditional density for the observed series, y_t. Similar to the approach followed in specifying alternative parameterizations for the conditional variance, the form of these distributions is not derived from an economic model.

Although there is substantial evidence for the presence of ARCH-type effects in the conditional variances of high-frequency financial data, there is less evidence for the sources of such time-varying conditional volatility. One common explanation of ARCH-type effects has been sought in the presence of a *serially correlated news arrival process*, which we describe in Chapter 6 in the context of a model for changes in short-term exchange rates. Even in this case, however, the news arrival process is not derived from an economic model. Other applications seeking the source of ARCH efects in international asset markets include Domowitz and Hakkio [96] and Diebold and Pauly [95], who model time-varying risk premia in the forward exchange market with a univariate ARCH-M model. On the other hand, Giovannini and Jorion [151] use the multivariate ARCH model, which specifies a time-varying covariance matrix for a vector stochastic process $\{u_t\}$, to examine the sources of ARCH in the international CAPM.

Among the few applications that have incorporated ARCH effects into simple general equilibrium frameworks are the papers by Abel [2] and Hodrick [191]. Hodrick constructs a two-country model in which innovations to money growth, endowments, and government expenditures are modeled as ARCH processes. The model he considers is a variant of the two-country asset pricing model with cash-in-advance constraints that we describe in Chapter 6. He uses the solution to this model to show that the conditional variances of the innovations affect risk premia and induce conditional volatility in exchange rates. Although Hodrick's paper provides an interesting modeling attempt, he fails to uncover any significant role for the conditional variances for explaining exchange rate changes. An additional problem in incorporating ARCH effects in general equilibrium models is that aside from data on speculative prices, there is little data on other economic variables that are available at intervals at which ARCH effects are found to be important.

4.2.   Testing for Nonlinearities

In the previous section, we described ARCH-type processes which are examples of processes that, conditional on their past, may be uncorrelated but are not independent. It is now recognized that such patterns of nonlinear dependence can arise from deterministic low-dimensional chaotic dynamics as well as stochastic nonlinear models, of which ARCH-type models are just one example. We begin by discussing models of deterministic chaos. Brock [46, 47] surveys the applications of chaos models in economics and provides further references to the literature on chaos in economics and the physical sciences. Brock, Hsieh, and LeBaron [52] describe how such models can be used to detect patterns of nonlinear dependence in stock returns and exchange rate changes.

A simple example of a system that displays chaotic dynamics is given by the *tent map*:

$$x_{t+1} = F(x_t) = \begin{cases} 2x_t & \text{if } x_t < .5 \\ 2 - 2x_t & \text{if } x_t \geq .5, \end{cases} \qquad (3.86)$$

given an initial condition $x_0 \in (0,1)$. In early applications of time series methods in finance, it was standard practice to compute the autocorrelations at different lags for changes in stock prices as a way of determining whether such changes are independent. Yet if we compare the autocovariances for a time series generated by a tent map, we will be unable to distinguish them from the autocovariances for a white noise (i.i.d.) process. We know that the autocovariances of an i.i.d. process are zero at all lags and leads, that is, $E(x_t x_{t-r}) = 0$ for all r. The time series from a tent map also have this property but they are generated by a deterministic system and can be forecasted perfectly if the initial condition x_0 and the law of motion F are known. This is one property of deterministically chaotic dynamic systems.

Suppose $\{y_t\}$ is defined as the series of monthly returns on the Dow Jones Industrial Average since 1900. We say that $\{y_t\}$ has a *deterministic explanation* if there is some state vector x_t that evolves according to the deterministic law of motion, $x_{t+1} = F(x_t)$, and there is a function $h(x)$ such that $y_t = h(x_t)$ for all t. If the researcher knew the function h and F and could measure x_t perfectly, then future x's and future y's could be forecasted perfectly. Typically, however, the state vector and its law of motion function, F, are unknown. The problem is to use observations on $\{y_t\}$ to determine the form of F or find evidence for the weaker claim that F is deterministic, without knowledge of (h, F, x_0) and, in some cases, the dimension of x_0.

The function h is known as the measurement function and the function F as the deterministic law of motion for the state variable x_t. Notice that in the case of the tent map, the measurement function is just the identity function, $h(x) = x$. We simplify our discussion by assuming that $h(x) = x$ and $\{x_t\}$ is a scalar time series.

One definition of chaos requires that the largest Lyapunov exponent, L, of F is positive. We define the quantity L as:

$$L \equiv \lim_{T \to \infty} \left[\log(\|DF^t(x) \cdot v\|)/t \right], \tag{3.87}$$

where $F^t(x)$ denotes the t'th iterate of F starting at the initial condition x, (that is, $F^t(x)$ is obtained by applying F to x, $F(x)$, $F^2(x)$, and so on), $\| \cdot \|$ denotes a norm (typically chosen to be the sup norm), v is a directional vector, D denotes derivative, and $\cdot$ is scalar multiplication. When the quantity L is positive, the trajectories generated by a chaotic system spread apart at an exponential rate. As an example, for the tent map, $L = \log(2) > 0$.

To test for chaos, we consider the m-histories generated by some time series $\{x_t\}$ as

$$x_t^m \equiv (x_t, \ldots, x_{t+m-1}),$$

and define the *correlation integral*:

$$C_{m,T}(\epsilon) = \sum_{t<s} I_\epsilon(x_t^m, x_s^m) \times [2/(T_m(T_m - 1))], \tag{3.88}$$

where $T_m = T - (m - 1)$ and $I_\epsilon(x_t^m, x_s^m)$ is an indicator function which equals one if $\|x_t^m - x_s^m\| < \epsilon$ and equals 0 otherwise. The correlation integral provides an estimate of the probability that two vectors of length m of the time series $\{x_t\}$ are within ϵ distance of each other. Thus, it is a measure of the spatial correlation of points in m-dimensional space.

We can also define a quantity known as the *correlation dimension in embedding dimension m*:

$$d_m = \lim_{\epsilon \to 0} \lim_{T \to \infty} \log[C_{m,T}(\epsilon)]/\log(\epsilon). \tag{3.89}$$

The *correlation dimension* is defined as:

$$d = \lim_{m \to \infty} d_m. \tag{3.90}$$

Dimension is a measure of complexity. It can be shown that the tent map has dimension equal to 1. On the other hand, an i.i.d. stochastic process (with a nondegenerate distribution function) has correlation dimension

$d = \infty$. The correlation dimension can be used to distinguish deterministic chaos from truly random systems. When the term "low-dimensional chaos" is used, typically correlation dimensions of less than 10, around 5 or 6, are implied. In their empirical study of stock returns and exchange rate changes, Brock, Hsieh, and LeBaron [52] graph $\log(C_{m,T})$ against $\log(\epsilon)$ and use the slopes to estimate the correlation dimension.

Brock, Dechert, and Scheinkman [51] use the correlation integral to derive a test of nonlinearity. First, they show that under the null hypothesis that $\{x_t\}$ is an i.i.d. process with a nondegenerate cumulative distribution function F, for fixed m and fixed ϵ,

$$C_{m,T}(\epsilon) \to C(\epsilon)^m \text{ with probability 1, as } T \to \infty,$$

where $C(\epsilon) = \int[F(z + \epsilon) - F(z - \epsilon)]dF(z)$ and it shows the probability that two m-histories of the $\{x_t\}$ process are within ϵ distance of each other. This result is used to construct a test of nonlinearity based on the so-called BDS test statistic, which is defined by:

$$W_{m,T}(\epsilon) = T^{1/2}[C_{m,T}(\epsilon) - C(\epsilon)^m]/\sigma_{m,T}(\epsilon), \tag{3.91}$$

where $\sigma_{m,T}(\epsilon)$ is an estimate of

$$\sigma_m^2(\epsilon) = 4\left[K(\epsilon)^m + 2\sum_{j=1}^{m-1} K(\epsilon)^{m-j}C(\epsilon)^{2j}\right.$$

$$\left. +(m-1)^2C(\epsilon)^{2m} - m^2K(\epsilon)C(\epsilon)^{2m-2}\right]. \tag{3.92}$$

Here $K(\epsilon) = \int[F(z + \epsilon) - F(z - \epsilon)]^2dF(z)$. We estimate $C(\epsilon)$ by $C_{1,T}(\epsilon)$ and $K(\epsilon)$ by:

$$K_T(\epsilon) = \sum_{t < s < r} h_\epsilon(x_t^m, x_s^m, x_r^m) \times [6/T_m(T_m - 1)(T_m - 2)],$$

where $h_\epsilon(i, j, k) = [I_\epsilon(i, j)I_\epsilon(j, k) + I_\epsilon(i, k)I_\epsilon(k, j) + I_\epsilon(j, i)I_\epsilon(i, k)]/3$. In this expression, I is the indicator function for the event $\|x_t^m - x_s^m\| < \epsilon$. If the null hypothesis is that $\{x_t\}$ is an i.i.d. process, then the BDS test statistic has a limiting standard normal distribution and critical values can be calculated using the standard normal distribution. Brock, Hsieh, and LeBaron [52] also determine the asymptotic distribution of the BDS test statistic under the null hypothesis that $\{x_t\}$ is a weakly dependent process. Since the expressions for the asymptotic variance of the BDS statistic are very complicated in this case, we refer the reader to [52, pp. 44–47] for the relevant expressions.

The BDS statistic is intended to detect nonlinearities in observed series. We already showed how nonlinear dependence can arise from chaotically dynamic systems. However, it can also arise from *nonlinear stochastic models*. These models have been proposed to explain behavior that cannot be generated by linear models. We first consider the ARCH model, which we introduced earlier:

$$x_t = \sigma_t u_t, \quad \sigma_t = (\alpha + \phi x_{t-1}^2)^{1/2},$$

where u_t is i.i.d., $N(0,1)$. We can show that x_t is not autocorrelated but it is clearly not independent of x_{t-1}. Notice that

$$\text{Var}(x_t|x_{t-1}) = E(\sigma_t^2 u_t^2|x_{t-1}) = \alpha + \phi x_{t-1}^2,$$

which varies with x_{t-1}. Thus, the distribution of x_t, conditional on x_{t-1}, varies with x_{t-1} also. On the other hand,

$$\begin{aligned} E(x_t x_{t-1}|x_{t-1}) &= E(\sigma_t u_t x_{t-1}|x_{t-1}) \\ &= E(u_t|x_{t-1})x_{t-1}(\alpha + \phi x_{t-1}^2)^{1/2}, \end{aligned}$$

which equals zero since u_t is independent of x_{t-1}. We can generate similar behavior from other types of nonlinear time series models, such as the nonlinear moving average (NMA) model, the bilinear model, and the threshold autoregressive model (TAR) These models are due, respectively, to Robinson [279], Granger and Andersen [158], and Tong and Lim [327]. The nonlinear moving average (NMA) model is given by:

$$x_t = u_t + \alpha u_{t-1} u_{t-2}.$$

The bilinear model is defined as:

$$x_t = u_t + \alpha x_{t-1} u_{t-1},$$

and the threshold autoregressive model (TAR) is defined by:

$$x_t = \begin{cases} \alpha x_{t-1} + u_t & \text{if } x_{t-1} < 1 \\ \beta x_{t-1} + u_t & \text{if } x_{t-1} \geq 1. \end{cases}$$

In all these examples, u_t is i.i.d., $N(0,1)$. We refer the reader to Brock, Hsieh and LeBaron for a further discussion of the empirical evidence obtained from implementing such tests for nonlinearities in stock return data and changes in exchange rates.

5.   Bootstrapping

The bootstrap method, introduced by Efron [109], is a method to resample the data to derive estimates of variances, confidence intervals, p-values, and other properties of statistics. In econometric applications, resampling methods have been used to analyze the stability of a given estimator by computing it from alternative subsamples or to compute standard deviations of the estimator across subsamples. An early example of resampling methods is the jackknife, which was introduced by Quenoille [277]. The jackknife systematically deletes a fixed number of observations to sample (without replacement). By contrast, the bootstrap samples data randomly.

   The situations in which the bootstrap method can prove useful are as follows. Consider first the case in which the asymptotic theory associated with a given estimator is intractable. In this case, the bootstrap allows us to obtain confidence intervals and other properties of the estimator. These are typically equivalent to the asymptotic theory. Second, suppose that the asymptotic theory is tractable but not very accurate for sample sizes typically encountered in applied work. Then the bootstrap can be used to improve upon the approximations provided by asymptotic theory.

   Following Efron, we can describe the general one-sample bootstrap problem as follows. Let

$$T(Z; F) \tag{3.93}$$

be a random variable of interest, where $Z = (x_1, \ldots, x_n)$ indicates the entire i.i.d. sample and F is distribution from which each x_i is drawn. On the basis of observations on Z, we wish to estimate some aspect of the distribution of the statistic T. For example, we may wish to estimate the population mean $E_F(T)$, or $\Pr_F(T < c)$, where c is some constant. The bootstrap method is implemented for this purpose as follows.

1. Fit the nonparametric maximum likelihood estimator of F, denoted $\hat{F}$, which puts mass $1/n$ at each x_i for $i = 1, \ldots, n$.

2. Draw the bootstrap sample from $\hat{F}$, denoted $Z^\star = (x_1^\star, \ldots, x_n^\star)$, and calculate $T^\star = T(Z^\star; \hat{F})$.

3. Independently repeat step 2 a large number m of times, obtaining bootstrap replications $T_j^\star$, $j = 1, \ldots, m$, and calculate whichever

aspect of T's distribution that is of interest. For example, if we wish to estimate $E_F(T)$, we calculate

$$E_\star(T^\star) = \frac{1}{m} \sum_{j=1}^{m} T_j^\star.$$

Bickel and Freedman [34] and Singh [310] show the consistency of bootstrap estimators of the mean and other sample statistics. Freedman [134, 135] provides asymptotic results for bootstrap estimation in regression models while Freedman [135] shows the asymptotic properties of bootstrap estimators in simultaneous equation models. A useful survey of bootstrap methods in econometrics can be found in Jeong and Madalla [208].

5.1.   Stock Returns and Technical Trading Rules

"Technical analysis" refers to the use of trading techniques that attempt to forecast prices by past prices and some other statistics related to security trading. One justification for studying the properties of such trading rules can be found in the recent literature showing evidence for the predictability of stock returns from past returns.[8] We now describe the study by Brock, Lakonishok, and LeBaron [53], hereafter referred to as Brock *et al.*, who analyze the implications of some simple technical trading rules for the behavior of stock returns using bootstrap methods.

Brock *et al.* consider 90 years of daily data consisting of observations on the Dow Jones Industrial Average from the first trading day in 1897 to the last trading day in 1986. They evaluate two simple trading rules, the moving-average oscillator and trading-range break. The moving average rule generates buy and sell signals using two moving averages of the level of the index — a long-period average and a short-period average. In its simplest form, this strategy implies buying (or selling) when the short-period moving average rises above (or falls below) the long-period moving average and it is often modified by introducing a band around the moving average. The trading-range break-out (TRB) generates a buy signal when the price penetrates the resistance level, which is defined as a local maximum. Conversely, a sell signal is generated when the price penetrates the support level, which is the local minimum price.

Brock *et al.* conduct tests of the variable-length moving average (VMA), which initiates buy (sell) signals when the short moving average

---

[8]See, for example, Fama and French [125].

is above (below) the long moving average by an amount greater than the band, the fixed-length moving average rule (FMA), which generates a buy (sell) signal when the short moving average cuts the long moving average from below (above), and the trading-range break-out (TRB). To evaluate the moving average rules, the sample is divided into buy or sell periods depending on the relative position of the moving averages. They find that the difference between mean daily buy and sell returns is positive and highly significant. Furthermore, the mean buy returns are all positive and the mean sell returns are all negative. The equality of the mean daily buy and sell returns with the unconditional mean return can also be rejected for the different trading rules. These results indicate some evidence for the predictability of stock returns.

The application of bootstrap methods comes into play in the context of this study because the various statistics that are used to conduct the tests either have valid asymptotic distributions under assumptions about the return process that are typically not satisfied in the data (such as normality, stationarity, and the existence of time independent distributions) or because the asymptotic or small distributions of the relevant test statistics are not known.

Notice that each day in the sample can be classified as a buy (b), sell (s), or neutral (n) day according to the trading rules, where the classification is based on information available up to and including day t. The h-day holding return is defined as:

$$r_t^h = \log(p_{t+h}) - \log(p_t).$$

Define the expected h-day return from t to $t + h$, conditional on a buy (sell) signal at date t by:

$$m^i = E(r_t^h | i_t), \quad i = b, s. \tag{3.94}$$

The standard deviation of holding returns, conditional on a buy (sell) signal, are likewise defined as:

$$v^i = \left(E \left[(r_t^h - m^i)^2 | i_t \right] \right)^{1/2}, \quad i = b, s. \tag{3.95}$$

The bootstrap method is used to deliver the distribution of estimates of these moments, under alternative assumptions about the process generating stock returns.

The return process is modeled using four different null models: i.i.d. returns, an AR(1), a GARCH-M, and Exponential GARCH. The first model merely says that the log of stock prices evolves as a random walk with drift so that returns are i.i.d.:

$$r_t = \frac{p_{t+1} - p_t}{p_t} = \exp(\epsilon_{t+1}) - 1, \tag{3.96}$$

where ϵ_t is i.i.d. with distribution F.

We begin by describing the application of bootstrap method under the assumption that returns are i.i.d. We define date t to be a buy signal if

$$p_t > \mathrm{MA}_{t,L} \quad \text{and} \quad p_{t-1} < \mathrm{MA}_{t-1,L}, \tag{3.97}$$

where

$$\mathrm{MA}_{t,L} = \frac{1}{L} \sum_{j=0}^{L-1} p_{t-j}.$$

Define the sample average of the h-day return, conditional on t being a buy signal, as:

$$r_n^b = \frac{1}{n} \sum_{t \in B} r_t^h, \tag{3.98}$$

where B is the set of all buy signals.

Let $Z = (r_1, \ldots, r_n)$ denote the actual sample and write r_n^b as $r_{n;Z}^b$ to show its dependence on the sample.[9] We derive an expression for $r_{n;Z}^b$ using the moving-average rule described in Equation (3.97). Notice that this condition can be rewritten as:

$$\exp(\epsilon_t + \ldots \epsilon_{t-L+2}) >$$
$$[\exp(\epsilon_t + \ldots \epsilon_{t-L+2}) + \ldots + \exp(\epsilon_{t-L+2})] / L,$$

and

$$\exp(\epsilon_{t-1} + \ldots \epsilon_{t-L+1}) <$$
$$[\exp(\epsilon_{t-1} + \ldots \epsilon_{t-L+1}) + \ldots + \exp(\epsilon_{t-L+1})] / L.$$

Thus we can write the indicator function I_B, denoting the event "buy at time t" as a function of $(\epsilon_t, \ldots, \epsilon_{t-L+1})$. Also, h-day returns can be written as:

$$r_t^h = \frac{p_{t+h} - p_t}{p_t} = \exp\left(\sum_{j=1}^{h} \epsilon_{t+j}\right) - 1.$$

---

[9]We can derive a similar expression to estimate the mean holding return, conditional on a sell signal, and other higher conditional moments, such as the conditional variances v^b and v^s defined in Equation (3.95).

We can write Equation (3.98) as:

$$r_{n;Z}^b = \frac{1}{n} \sum_{t=1}^{n} I_B(\epsilon_t, \ldots, \epsilon_{t-L+1})(\exp(\epsilon_{t+1} + \ldots + \epsilon_{t+h}) - 1).$$

Define the vector $\boldsymbol{w}_t = (\epsilon_{t-L+1}, \ldots, \epsilon_{t+h})'$ and the function h in the appropriate way to write:

$$r_{n;Z}^b = \frac{1}{n} \sum_{t=1}^{n} h(\boldsymbol{w}_t) = T(Z; F), \tag{3.99}$$

where T is a random variable that depends on F.

Let $\hat{F}_n$ be the empirical distribution that puts mass $1/n$ on x_i for $i = 1, \ldots, n$. To conduct tests involving the different trading rules, notice that we need to derive an estimate of the cumulative distribution function:

$$\Pr(r_{n;Z}^b < x) = \Pr(T(Z; F) < x). \tag{3.100}$$

We can use bootstrap methods by drawing the bootstrap sample $Z_j = (x_1^\star, \ldots, x_n^\star)$ from $\hat{F}_n$ for $j = 1, \ldots, m$ and computing:

$$\frac{1}{m} \sum_{j=1}^{m} I(T(Z_j; \hat{F}_n) < x). \tag{3.101}$$

Provided $r_{n;Z}^b$ conforms to the standard bootstrap cases (which Brock *et al.* demonstrate) the results in Bickel and Freedman [34], Singh [310], and Freedman [135] can be used to show that the quantities in Equation (3.101) provide consistent estimates of the true probabilities defined in Equation (3.100).

We outline the bootstrap method for the case when returns follow an AR(1) process. In this case, returns can be written as:

$$r_t = c + \rho r_{t-1} + \epsilon_t, \quad |\rho| < 1, \tag{3.102}$$

with $r_0 = \bar{r}_0$ and $\{\epsilon_t\}$ is i.i.d. with distribution F. Suppose that enough conditions have been imposed on F, the unknown distribution of the i.i.d. errors ϵ_t, to yield consistency and asymptotic normality of the OLS estimates of c and ρ. Let $\hat{e}_t$ denote the estimated residuals from OLS estimation of Equation (3.102). Define $\hat{F}_n$ by placing $1/n$ mass on $\hat{e}_t$ for $t = 1, \ldots, n$. Next, generate the bootstrap sample $Z_j = (r_1^\star, \ldots, r_n^\star)$ by drawing $e_t^\star$ from $\hat{F}_n$ and generate $r_t^\star$ recursively from Equation (3.102) using the estimated parameters and $r_0^\star = \bar{r}_0$. Now calculate $r_{n;Z}^b$ using the bootstrap sample and the trading rules. The distribution of $r_{n;Z}^b$ can be calculated by replicating this procedure for $j = 1, \ldots, m$. The asymptotic justification for the bootstrap when $\{r_t\}$ is a stable autoregressive process is provided by Freedman [135].

The remaining models are the GARCH-M model and the Exponential GARCH or EGARCH model. It turns out that none of the proposed models is successful in generating the patterns of conditional means and conditional standard deviations for buy and sell periods implied by the different trading rules. For example, not only do buy signals select out periods with higher conditional means, they also pick out periods with lower volatilities. (The opposite pattern is observed for sell periods.)

6.   Exercises

1. Consider the version of Equation (3.1) with risk-neutral consumers and one-period securities. Then we can express the first-order conditions for the consumer's problem as:

$$E_t(r_{j,t+1}) = 1/\beta, \quad j = 1, \ldots, M.$$

Define $y_{j,t+1} = r_{j,t+1} - 1/\beta$ and consider the l-dimensional vector $X_t \in I_t^\star \subseteq I_t$.

   a) What restrictions does the model with risk-neutral consumers imply for the following regression:

$$y_{j,t+1} = X_t'\gamma_j + u_{j,t+1}, \quad j = 1, \ldots, M,$$

   where $u_{j,t+1}$ is a forecast error that is uncorrelated with elements of the agent's information set, I_t?

   b) Derive the form of the function $h(\cdot, b_0)$ and suggest a choice of instrument vector, z_t that makes GMM equivalent to OLS. What is the form of the sample criterion function that is used to obtain estimates of b_0? How are the standard errors calculated?

2. The Present-Value Model

   a) Let the first row of the multivariate representation for $(d_t, \underline{z}_t')'$ described in Section 3.1 be given by:

$$d_t = c + \underline{\delta}_0'\epsilon_t + \underline{\delta}_1'\epsilon_{t-1} + \cdots = c + \underline{\delta}'(L)\epsilon_t,$$

where $\underline{\delta}'_k$ are $p \times 1$ vectors. Derive an alternative representation for p_t as:

$$p_t = \frac{c}{1-\beta} + \sum_{j=0}^{\infty} \left[\sum_{k=j}^{\infty} \beta^{k-j} \underline{\delta}'_k \right] \underline{\epsilon}_{t-j} = \frac{c}{1-\beta} + \underline{a}'(L)\underline{\epsilon}_t,$$

where $\underline{a}'_j = \sum_{k=j}^{\infty} \beta^{k-j} \underline{\delta}'_k$.

b) Using the definition of π_t, show that

$$\pi_t = \beta \sum_{j=0}^{\infty} \beta^j \underline{a}'_0 \underline{\epsilon}_{t+1+j},$$

and that

$$\mathrm{Var}(\pi_t) = \frac{\mathrm{Var}(\beta p_{t+1} + d_t - p_t)}{1 - \beta^2}.$$

These results show that we can estimate $\mathrm{Var}(p^*_t)$ using observations only on p_t and d_t. Discuss how this result can be used to implement LeRoy and Porter's variance bounds tests.

3.[10] Suppose a stock pays a dividend only at some terminal date T. Take $d_t = \sum_{i=1}^{T} \epsilon_i$, where $\{\epsilon_i\}$ is an identically and independently distributed process with $\mathrm{E}(\epsilon_i) = 0$ and $\mathrm{Var}(\epsilon_i) = 1$.

a) Find expressions for the *ex post* rational price p^*_t and $\mathrm{Var}(p^*_t)$.

b) Find an expression for the actual price p_t and its variance $\mathrm{Var}(p_t)$.

c) Suppose we have one realization of the economy from which p_t and p^*_t are drawn. Plot p_t and p^*_t against time. Which series is "smoother," p_t or p^*_t?

d) Relate your answers to parts a – c to Kleidon's criticisms of variance bounds tests.

4. Let agents' information set I_t consist of current and past values of dividends, d_t, and one other variable, z_t. Let $\hat{I}_t$ consist of current and lagged values of d_t only. Let the bivariate representation for (d_t, z_t) be:

$$\begin{bmatrix} d_t \\ z_t \end{bmatrix} = \begin{bmatrix} \phi & 1 \\ 0 & 0 \end{bmatrix} \begin{bmatrix} d_{t-1} \\ z_{t-1} \end{bmatrix} + \begin{bmatrix} \epsilon_{1,t} \\ \epsilon_{2,t} \end{bmatrix},$$

---

[10]This exercise draws on material from Gilles and LeRoy [149].

where $|\phi| \leq 1$, $\{\epsilon_{1,t}\}$ and $\{\epsilon_{2,t}\}$ are i.i.d. with $E(\epsilon_{1,t}\epsilon_{2,s}) = 0$ for all t and s. Let $E(\epsilon_{1,t}^2) = \sigma_1^2$, $E(\epsilon_{2,t}^2) = \sigma_2^2$. Notice that dividends may be written as $d_t = \phi d_{t-1} + v_t$, where $v_t = \epsilon_{1,t} + \epsilon_{2,t-1}$.

a) As in West's [336] analysis, show that

$$E\left[\hat{p}_t - \hat{E}(\hat{p}_t|\hat{I}_{t-1})\right]^2 \geq E\left[p_t - \hat{E}(p_t|I_{t-1})\right]^2.$$

b) Suppose $\phi = 1$. Calculate the inequalities in part a) under this assumption.

5. Aggregation
   Consider an economy with multiple consumers. Let I_t^i be the information set of consumer i at date t and W_0^i the initial wealth of this consumer. Each consumer has preferences

$$E\left[\sum_{t=0}^{T} \beta^t u^i(c_{i,t})|I_0^i\right], \quad i \in I, \quad 0 < \beta < 1,$$

where u^i has the usual properties and $E(\cdot|I_0^i)$ denotes expectation conditional on the information set of consumer i at date 0.

a) Suppose every consumer has the option of purchasing security $j \in J$ with random payoff $R_{j,\tau}$ at date τ and price $p_{j,t}$ at date t, $t < \tau \leq T$, where $p_{j,t} \in I_t^i$ for $i \in I$ and $j \in J$. Using the portfolio choice problem of consumers, show that the equilibrium price of any security must satisfy the relationship:

$$p_{j,t} = E\left[\mathcal{M}_{t,\tau}R_{j,t}|I_t\right], \quad j \in J, \tag{3.103}$$

where $I_t = \cap_{i \in I} I_t^i$. Define $\mathcal{M}_{t,\tau}$ and show that it is independent of consumers' types.

b) Suppose there are two dates of the world so that $T = 1$ and N states of the world at each date. Suppose that

$$u^i(c_{i,t}) = A_i \exp(-c_{i,t}/A_i), \quad i \in I, \tag{3.104}$$

and markets are complete. Show that (a version of) Equation (3.103) can be derived from the portfolio choice problem of a consumer with initial wealth W_0, consumption c_t, and information set I_t, where

$$W_0 = \sum_{i \in I} W_0^i/I, \quad c_t = \sum_{i \in I} c_{i,t}/I, \quad I_t = \cap_{i \in I} I_t^i.$$

c) Given observations on per capita consumption and the returns on K securities, defined as $r_{j,\tau} \equiv R_{j,\tau}/p_{j,t}$, $j \in K$, how would you test the overidentifying restrictions in Equation (3.103) if individual utilities are given by Equation (3.104)? Be explicit.

6. Consider the model with durable consumption goods estimated by Dunn and Singleton [108]. Suppose purchases of nondurable and durable goods grow over time (possibly at different rates) according to geometric trends:

$$c_t/c_{t-1} = \lambda_c, \quad d_t/d_{t-1} = \lambda_d,$$

where λ_c and λ_d are the (gross) growth rates of c_t and d_t. Also assume that returns $r_{t,n}^k$ and the quantity $c_t^*/(p_{d,t}d_t^*)$ are strictly stationary.

a) Show that the disturbances in the econometric model, $\{u_{k,t}\}$, $k = 1, \ldots, K+1$ defined in Equations (3.39) and (3.40) are strictly stationary processes.

b) Suppose the assumption of stationarity is violated for these disturbances. How would this affect the researcher's ability to apply GMM estimation procedures?

7. Consider the same model as in the previous problem. Suppose consumers engage only in three-period investments at time t so that $n = 3$. Also assume that $c_t^* = c_t + \alpha c_{t-1}$.

a) Using the expressions in Equations (3.37) and (3.39), show that the process $\{Z_t u_t\}$ follows an MA(3) process.

b) Discuss how you would obtain a positive semidefinite estimate of the matrix S_w in small samples.

4

Models with Production and Capital Accumulation

In Chapter 2, we assumed that output is determined according to an exogenous stochastic process. We now study investment and production decisions using the framework provided by the one-sector stochastic optimal growth model. According to this framework, output is affected in each period by random productivity shocks and the economy evolves over time to a stochastic steady state. In recent years, the one-sector optimal growth model has been used to describe cyclical fluctuations in the aggregate economy. In Section 1, we derive the optimal policy functions for consumption and investment. We also describe numerical solution methods for solving growth models and review the empirical evidence.

The one-sector optimal growth model has also been used as the basis for the asset pricing model with production. We describe this model in Section 2 following the discussion in Brock [44, 45], who integrated the growth model and asset markets. In Section 3, we formulate the firm's problem as a present-value maximization problem and prove a Modigliani-Miller theorem about the irrelevance of firms' financial structure to production decisions. We use this framework to discuss the effects of distortionary taxes on firms' cost of capital and optimal financial policies. We also analyze a version of the one-sector optimal growth model with distortionary taxation and derive a version of the $\mathcal{Q}$-theory of investment when there are adjustment costs and irreversibilities in investment.

In many applications involving production and capital accumulation, the assumption that production opportunities can be described in terms of a set of continuous-valued variables is not appropriate. In Section 4, we introduce a framework for modeling discrete choices in a dynamic setting. We first describe a search model due to Weitzman [335]. We also describe methods for solving and estimating dynamic discrete choice models based on Miller [260] and Rust [294].

1.   The One-Sector Optimal Growth Model

The one-sector optimal growth model provides a simple framework for studying production and capital accumulation decisions. We begin by describing how the optimal policy functions for consumption and investment are derived.

1.1.   Optimal Policy Functions

The long-run behavior of the deterministic one-sector optimal growth model has been studied by Cass [66] and Koopmans [221], who showed the existence of a steady state solution. The extension of this model to the uncertainty case is due to Brock and Mirman [48, 49] and Mirman and Zilcha [261]. In describing this model, we analyze the case of independent and identically distributed technology shocks.

The representative consumer has preferences over sequences of consumption given by:

$$E_0 \left\{ \sum_{t=0}^{\infty} \beta^t U(c_t) \right\}, \quad 0 < \beta < 1, \tag{4.1}$$

where c_t denotes consumption of the single good and $E_0(\cdot)$ denotes expectation conditional on information at date zero. The following assumption characterizes the utility function.

Assumption 4.1 *The utility function* $U : \mathbb{R}_+ \to \mathbb{R}$ *is strictly concave, strictly increasing, and continuously differentiable with* $U(0) = 0$, $U'(0) = \infty$ *and* $U'(\infty) = 0$.

There are n production processes in this economy that can be used to produce one type of good that can be consumed or added to the capital stock. Each production process has the form:

$$y_{i,t} = f_i(K_{i,t}, \theta_t), \tag{4.2}$$

where θ_t is the common random productivity shock to the n production processes and $K_{i,t}$ is the capital stock installed in process i.

Let Ω denote the set of possible states of the world and $\theta_t(\omega)$, $\omega \in \Omega$ denote random variables that are independent, identically distributed with $\theta : \Omega \to [\underline{\theta}, \bar{\theta}]$. We have the following assumption.

Assumption 4.2 *The technology shock* $\theta : \Omega \to \Theta$ *where* $\Theta = [\underline{\theta}, \bar{\theta}]$ *is i.i.d. with stationary distribution function* G. *The function* G *has the properties that* $G(\theta) = 0$ *for* $\theta \leq \underline{\theta}$ *and* $G(\theta) = 1$ *for* $\theta \geq \bar{\theta}$. *Also* $dG > 0$ *and* dG *is continuous.*

Let $0 < \delta_i \leq 1$ denote the depreciation rate of capital installed in process i. The per capita feasibility constraint is:

$$c_t + \sum_{i=1}^{n}(K_{i,t+1} - K_{i,t}) \leq \sum_{i=1}^{n}[f_i(K_{i,t}, \theta_t) - \delta_i K_{i,t}]. \tag{4.3}$$

Here, $K_{i,t}$ denotes the aggregate per capita stock allocated to production process i at the beginning of period t, $K_{i,t+1} - K_{i,t}$ denotes net investment in the capital installed in process i, and $f_i(K_{i,t}, \theta_t) - \delta_i K_{i,t}$ is output net of depreciation. We make the following assumption.

Assumption 4.3 *(i) The functions $f_i(\cdot, \theta)$ are continuously differentiable, strictly increasing, and strictly concave on $\mathbb{R}_+$ with $f_i(0, \theta) = 0$, $f_i'(0, \theta) = \infty$, and $f_i'(\infty, \theta) = 0$. (ii) $f_i(K, \theta) - f_i'(K, \theta)K > 0$ for all $K > 0$.*

The second part of this assumption ensures that profits are always positive. Define total output in process i as:

$$F_i(K_{i,t}, \theta_t) \equiv f(K_{i,t}, \theta_t) + (1 - \delta_i)K_{i,t}.$$

Notice that we can rewrite the constraint in Equation (4.3) as $c_t + \sum_{i=1}^{n} K_{i,t+1} \leq \sum_{i=1}^{n} F_i(K_{i,t}, \theta_t)$. Let K_t be the n-dimensional vector with i'th element $K_{i,t}$.

The optimal policy functions for consumption and investment are computed from the *social planning problem* for this economy. We assume that the current realization of the technology shock is observed before any decisions are made. Since there is a representative consumer, the social planning problem involves choosing consumption and investment sequences to maximize Equation (4.1) subject to the constraints on feasibility and information:

$$\max_{\{c_t\}_{t=0}^{\infty}, \{K_{t+1}\}_{t=0}^{\infty}} E_0 \left\{ \sum_{t=1}^{\infty} \beta^t U(c_t) \right\},$$

subject to

$$c_t + \sum_{i=1}^{n} K_{i,t+1} \leq \sum_{i=1}^{n} F_i(K_{i,t}, \theta_t), \tag{4.4}$$

$$c_t, K_{t+1} \geq 0, \tag{4.5}$$

given the fixed initial stocks $K_{0,i}$ for $i = 1, ..., n$ and the current realization of the productivity shock, θ_0.

We now describe how to formulate the social planning problem as a stationary dynamic programming problem. This approach yields solutions that are time-invariant functions of a finite set of state variables. We begin by showing that the set of feasible allocations $\Gamma(K_t, \theta_t)$, defined as pairs (c_t, K_{t+1}) satisfying Equation (4.4) is a compact set because there exists a maximum sustainable capital stock for each production process.

Define $M_i(\theta)$ as $M_i(\theta) \equiv \max_{K_i}[f_i(K_i, \theta) - \delta K_i]$ and let $\hat{K}_i(\theta)$ be the unique solution to $f_i(K_i, \theta) = \delta_i K_i$. Notice that f is increasing and strictly concave so that such a maximum exists. Define $\hat{K}_i \equiv \max_\theta \hat{K}_i(\theta)$ and $M_i \equiv \max_\theta M_i(\theta)$. These quantities are well defined because f_i is continuous and θ takes on values in the compact set $[\underline{\theta}, \bar{\theta}]$. We have the following lemma.

Lemma 4.1 *If $(c_t, K_{i,t+1})$ satisfy Equation (4.4), then $0 \leq K_{i,t+1} \leq B_i$ and $0 \leq c_t \leq \sum_{i=1}^n (B_i + M_i)$ where $B_i = \max(\hat{K}_i + M_i, \bar{K}_{i,0})$ and $\bar{K}_{i,0} = K_{i,0}$.*

PROOF
By assumption, $0 \leq K_{i,t}$ and $0 \leq c_t$. If $K_{i,t} > \hat{K}_i$ then $K_{i,t+1} < K_{i,t}$ and it also follows that $K_{i,t+1} < K_{i,t} + M_i$. The proof that $K_{i,t} < B_i$ is by induction on t. Clearly, $K_{i,0} = \bar{K}_{i,0} \leq B_i$. We must show that this implies $K_{i,t+1} \leq B_i$. If $K_{i,t} \leq \hat{K}_i$, then $K_{i,t+1} \leq K_{i,t} + M_i \leq \hat{K}_i + M_i \leq B_i$. If $K_{i,t} > \hat{K}_i$, then $K_{i,t+1} < K_{i,t} \leq B_i$ by the induction hypothesis, yielding the result. Finally,

$$0 \leq c_t \leq \sum_{i=1}^n F_i(K_{i,t}, \theta_t) \leq \sum_{i=1}^n (M_i + B_i) \quad \text{for all } t,$$

since $F_i(K_{i,t}, \theta_t) = f_i(K_{i,t}, \theta) - \delta_i K_{i,t} + K_{i,t}$. $\blacksquare$

Define B as the $n \times 1$ vector with i'th element B_i and let $\underline{0}$ be an $n \times 1$ vector with i'th element equal to 0; define $\mathcal{K} \equiv [\underline{0}, B]$ so that the constraint set $\Gamma(K_t, \theta_t)$ can be expressed as a mapping $\Gamma : \mathcal{K} \times \Theta \to \mathcal{K}$. We can prove the following.

Lemma 4.2 *Under Assumptions 4.1—4.3, for any sequence $\{c_t, K_{t+1}\}$ such that (c_t, K_{t+1}) satisfy Equation (4.4) and the initial conditions $K_{i,0}$ for $i = 1, \ldots, n$, then*

$$E_0 \left\{ \sum_{t=0}^\infty \beta^t U(c_t) \right\} \leq \mathcal{U} < \infty. \tag{4.6}$$

PROOF

Define $\bar{C} = \sum_{i=1}^{n}(M_i + B_i)$ and note that, for any feasible c_t, $c_t \in [0, \bar{C}]$. Because U is continuous and takes a compact set into $\mathbb{R}_+$, we can define an upper bound $\mathcal{U} \equiv \sum_{t=0}^{\infty} \beta^t U(\bar{C}) < \infty$. ∎

We can also construct an upper (and lower) bound on output. Notice that the vector of capital K_t is determined at time $t-1$ and θ_t is exogenous so the level of output y_t is fixed once θ_t is realized. Let $M \equiv \max_i M_i$ and let $B \equiv \max_i B_i$. Then the finite upper bound on y is $n \times (M + B)$ and we conclude that $y \in \mathcal{Y} \equiv [0, n \times (M + B)]$. The set of feasible allocations can be written $\Lambda(y)$ where $\Lambda(y)$ is the set (c, K') such that $c + \sum_{i=1}^{n} K_i' \leq y$. Clearly, Λ is compact.

In the following discussion, we drop the time subscripts on time t variables and let variables with primes, z', for example, denote variables at time $t + 1$. This notation emphasizes the recursive structure of the problem. Since there is an upper (and lower) bound on the expected discounted present value of utility, the social planner's problem is well defined. The valuation function $W : \mathcal{Y} \to \mathbb{R}_+$ for a dynamic programming problem satisfies the functional equation:

$$W(y) = \max_{(c,K') \in \Lambda(y)} \left\{ U(c) + \beta \int_{\Theta} W(y') dG(\theta') \right\} \tag{4.7}$$

where $y' = \sum_{i=1}^{n} F_i(K', \theta')$. The maximization problem is to choose consumption and next period's capital stock assuming that the value placed on capital next period is summarized by $\beta E_t[W(y_{t+1})]$. Let $\mathcal{C}(\mathcal{Y})$ denote the space of continuous, bounded functions $\{W : \mathcal{Y} \to \mathbb{R}_+\}$ equipped with the sup norm. Define the operator T by:

$$(TW)(y) = \max_{(c,K') \in \Lambda(y)} \left\{ U(c) + \beta \int_{\Theta} W(y') dG(\theta') \right\}. \tag{4.8}$$

We have the following theorem.

Theorem 4.1 *Let $T : \mathcal{C}(\mathcal{Y}) \to \mathcal{C}(\mathcal{Y})$ be defined by Equation (4.8). Under Assumptions 4.1—4.3, the operator is a contraction with unique fixed point $W^\star$, which is bounded, increasing, and concave. Further, there exists unique, bounded, and increasing optimal policy functions,*

$$c = g(y), \tag{4.9}$$

$$K_i' = h_i(y), \quad i = 1, \ldots, n, \tag{4.10}$$

such that $y = g(y) + \sum_{i=1}^{n} h_i(y)$, that satisfy

$$W^\star(y) = U(g(y)) + \beta \int_{\Theta} W^\star(y') dG(\theta'). \tag{4.11}$$

where $y' = \sum_{i=1}^{n} F_i(h_i(y), \theta')$.

PROOF

Notice that U is continuous and $\int_\Theta W(y')dG(\theta')$ is continuous for continuous W. Thus, applying T involves maximizing a continuous function over a compact set so that TW is well defined for any $W \in \mathcal{C}(\mathcal{Y})$. Since $U(c)$ is bounded because c is bounded and U is continuous, TW is bounded and hence, continuous. Thus, for any $W \in \mathcal{C}(\mathcal{Y})$, the operator T takes continuous, bounded functions into continuous, bounded functions. The operator T is monotone; for any $W_1, W_2 \in \mathcal{C}(\mathcal{Y})$ such that $W_1 > W_2$, $TW_1 \geq TW_2$. Because $0 < \beta < 1$, the operator T also discounts, that is, $T(W + a) \leq TW + \beta a$ for $a \geq 0$. Hence, T satisfies Blackwell's conditions for a contraction. Thus, there exists a unique solution, $W^\star(y) = (TW^\star)(y)$.

To prove that $W^\star$ is increasing and concave, choose some $\bar{W} \in \mathcal{C}(\mathcal{Y})$ that is increasing and concave. Denote the space of continuous, bounded, increasing, and concave functions defined on $\mathcal{Y}$ by $\mathcal{C}'(\mathcal{Y})$. Applying the operator T to $\bar{W}$ notice that T preserves these properties so that $T : \mathcal{C}'(\mathcal{Y}) \rightarrow \mathcal{C}'(\mathcal{Y})$. Because the space of continuous, bounded, increasing, and concave functions $\mathcal{C}'(\mathcal{Y})$ is a subspace of the space of continuous and bounded functions $\mathcal{C}(\mathcal{Y})$ and we have shown that T is a contraction, we can conclude that $W^\star$ is increasing and concave. This follows as an application of Corollary 1.1 from Chapter 1.

Because $W^\star$ is concave and U is strictly concave by assumption, we can conclude that the optimal policy (defined by the functions g and h_i for $i = 1, \ldots, n$) is unique and, by the Theorem of the Maximum, conclude that it is continuous and bounded. Finally, by the envelope theorem, we have that $W_y^\star(y) = U'(g(y)) > 0$.   ∎

Since the valuation function $W^\star$ is strictly concave, the necessary and sufficient conditions for an optimum are given by:

$$U'(c) \geq \beta \int_\Theta U'(c')F_i'(K_i', \theta')dG(\theta'), \quad i = 1, \ldots, n, \qquad (4.12)$$

$$c + \sum_{i=1}^n K_i' = y = \sum_{i=1}^n F_i(K_i, \theta). \qquad (4.13)$$

The resource constraint holds with equality because the utility function is strictly increasing. At the optimum, the first-order conditions also hold as equalities, given the conditions on U and F. The optimal consumption policy $g(y)$ and the investment policies $h_i(y)$ for $i = 1, \ldots, n$ are obtained as the solution to the problem in Equation (4.7), given the solution for the valuation function $W^\star$, and they satisfy the first-order conditions in Equations (4.12) and (4.13).

We assumed above that technology shocks were identically and independently distributed. The case with serially correlated shocks is discussed by Donaldson and Mehra [97]. It is also possible to analyze the case with constant relative risk aversion preferences and constant returns to scale production (which yields unbounded returns) using a modification of the approach that we described in Chapter 2, Section 1.5 (see Boyd [41] and Stokey and Lucas [317]). Under some specifications for preferences and the production function, there exist linear solutions for optimal consumption and next period's capital stock as a function of the current state variables. (See Exercise 1.)

Recall that in the asset pricing model of Chapter 2, all state variables were exogenous and have a stationary or invariant distribution by assumption. When there are endogenous state variables such as capital stocks, we need to show that there exists a unique stationary distribution of the capital stock that remains fixed every period and to characterize this distribution. This stationary or invariant distribution can be used to compute unconditional moments for such variables as consumption, investment, and output and describe how such moments vary across different economies. For a derivation of the stationary distribution of output and references to the relevant literature, we refer the reader to Danthine and Donaldson [81] and Stokey and Lucas [317]. We now turn to the empirical evidence.

1.2. The Growth Model and the Data

The literature on "real" models of the business cycle (as opposed to monetary models) uses the one-sector optimal growth model to describe cyclical fluctuations in the aggregate economy. In this section, we describe some of the issues that have been debated in the real business cycle literature.

We begin by describing numerical solution methods, which are typically used to derive solutions for the optimal policy functions. One approach for obtaining numerical solutions is to use *numerical dynamic programming*. This method has also been used for solving dynamic discrete choice models. Another approach for solving growth models is to use a *quadratic approximation* around the deterministic steady state for the model, as proposed by Kydland and Prescott [224]. We will describe both approaches in this section.

Numerical dynamic programming is motivated by the fact that the valuation function characterizing agents' or the social planner's optimum typically satisfies a contraction mapping. The underlying theory is well understood.[1] In what follows, we describe value function iteration with a discretized state space, which is one approach to implementing numerical dynamic programming. We consider a simple parametric example from Donaldson and Mehra [97] that has been widely studied in this literature.

Preferences are assumed to be of the constant relative risk variety, $U(c) = c^\gamma/\gamma$, and the production function displays constant returns to scale with $f(k) = Ak^\alpha\theta$. The following parameter values are considered: $\gamma \in \{-2, -1, 0, 0.25, 0.5\}$ where $\gamma = 0$ is the case $U(c) = \log(c)$, $A = 2/3$, and $\alpha \in \{0.24, .5\}$, and the discount rate takes values in the set $\beta \in \{0.8, 0.9, 0.95\}$. In this example, the productivity shock θ_t is correlated and follows a first-order Markov process. We describe below how the distribution for θ_t is parameterized.

In this problem, the state variables are the per capita capital stock k_t and the current value of the technology shock, θ_t. Both variables take values on continuous intervals. To implement value function iteration, we need to discretize or partition the state space into a finite set of points. This implies that the control variables also take on a finite number of values. In their application, Donaldson and Mehra assume that the technology shock takes values in the set $\theta_t \in \Theta \equiv \{1.5, 1.0, 0.5\}$. Because θ can take on 3 possible values, the transition probability matrix Φ is 3×3 with element $\phi_{i,j} = \text{Prob}(\theta_{t+1} = \Theta_j | \theta_t = \Theta_i)$. They incorporate the persistence of the technology shock by assuming that Φ is symmetric $(\phi_{i,j} = \phi_{j,i})$ and that $\phi_{i,i} = a$ and $\phi_{i,j} = (1 - a)/2$ for $i \neq j$. The identical diagonal elements of the matrix Φ take values from the set $\phi_{i,i} \in \{0.333, 0.5, 0.7, 0.9\}$. As $\phi_{i,i}$ increases, the correlation of the shocks over time increases. Notice that this procedure substitutes a discrete Markov chain for the continuous Markov process for θ_t.

The remaining issue is how to discretize the endogenous state variable k_t. Because this is a recursive model, choosing a set of possible values for k_t also specifies the set of values from which the decision variable k_{t+1} at time t can be chosen; we will call this set $\mathcal{K}$. To determine this set, we first determine the maximum sustainable capital stock. This can be calculated as $k_m = (2/3)k_m^\alpha(1.5)$. We know that $\alpha \leq 1$ and at $\alpha = 1$, the solution is $k_m = 1$. Hence we can conclude that capital takes values on $[0, 1]$. The next step is to define a partition of this range, such as $k_{i+1} - k_i = 0.01$. This creates an evenly spaced grid of 100 possible values for the capital stock and defines our feasible set $\mathcal{K}$.

---

[1]See Bertsekas [29] and Bertsekas and Shreve [30]. Judd [215] provides a discussion with applications in economics. As review of some of this material, Exercise 5 presents an example of a discrete state, discrete control dynamic programming problem.

The problem now becomes one of solving the functional equation:

$$V^n(k_i, \theta_r) = \max_{k_j \in \mathcal{K}} \left[U(Ak_i^\alpha \theta_r - k_j) + \beta \sum_{s=1}^{3} \phi_{r,s} V^{n-1}(k_j, \theta_s) \right] \quad (4.14)$$

subject to $k_j \leq Ak_i^\alpha \theta_r$, where $k_i \in \mathcal{K}$ and $\theta_r, \theta_s \in \Theta$. A computer program can be written along the following lines.

1. Formulate an initial guess of the function V^0. For example, set $V^0 = 0$.

2. For each pair (k_i, θ_r), compute the value function for each point k in the feasible set $\mathcal{K}$ that satisfies the constraint $k_j \leq Ak_i^\alpha \theta_r$; this will limit the set over which the value function must be computed. Given the initial guess V^0, choose the point $k_j^0 \in \mathcal{K}$ that maximizes the right side of Equation (4.14); call this new value function $V^1(k_i, \theta_r)$.

3. Evaluate the value function for all pairs $(\theta_r, k_i) \in (\Theta \times \mathcal{K})$. There are 3×100 points in the range of $V^1(k_i, \theta_r)$ and the associated policy function $k_j^1 = h^1(k_i, \theta_r)$.

4. Repeat steps 2. and 3. until $|V^{n+1}(k_i, \theta_r) - V^n(k_i, \theta_r)| \leq \epsilon_c$ for all $k_i \in \mathcal{K}$ and all $\theta_r \in \Theta$ where ϵ_c is a convergence criterion.

There are different ways of choosing the convergence criterion. One possible convergence criterion is to choose $\epsilon_c = b\|K\|$ where b is a small positive constant and $\|K\|$ is the norm of the capital partition (equal to 0.01 in our example). The convergence criterion should be small but there is a tradeoff in terms of computation time. Notice that the set $(\Theta \times \mathcal{K})$ is compact so that the value function iteration described above is well defined. One problem with this procedure is that we run into the "curse of dimensionality" described by Bertsekas. The accuracy of the solution can be increased by partitioning the state space in terms of a finer grid but at the cost of increased computing time.

Another approach to solving growth models is to use the method of quadratic approximation around a deterministic steady state. This method has been used because it facilitates the computation of decision rules for models that have multiple choice variables and a high-dimensional state space. According to this method, we replace the nonlinear optimization problem described in Section 1.1 by a linear-quadratic dynamic optimization problem. The relationship between the solutions of the original nonlinear problem and the linear-quadratic problem is generally not established. Although the decision rules or optimal policy functions for the linear-quadratic dynamic optimization problem are also obtained iteratively, the corresponding value function and the optimal policy functions can be expressed as known functions of coefficient matrices that enter the quadratic objective function and the linear laws of motion for the state variables.

We now modify the parametric example presented earlier to describe this method. Instead of assuming that depreciation is 100%, we assume that capital depreciates at the rate $0 < \delta < 1$ per period. In this case, the law of motion for the capital stock becomes

$$k_{t+1} = (1 - \delta)k_t + i_t, \tag{4.15}$$

where i_t is investment per period. We also assume that the technology follows a stationary first-order autoregressive process as:

$$\theta_{t+1} = \mu_\theta + \rho\theta_t + \varepsilon_{t+1}, \quad |\rho| < 1, \tag{4.16}$$

where $\varepsilon_t \sim N(0, \sigma_\varepsilon^2)$. The feasibility constraint is given by:

$$c_t + i_t \leq A\theta_t k_t^\alpha.$$

Since the utility function is strictly increasing, consumption plus investment equals output at the optimum. Using this fact, we can substitute for consumption in the utility function to obtain $U(A\theta_t k_t^\alpha - i_t)$.

The quadratic approximation procedure is implemented as follows. First, compute the steady state values for k_t and i_t, assuming that θ_t equals its unconditional mean of $\bar\theta \equiv \mu_\theta/(1 - \rho)$. For this simple model, the steady state values are:

$$\bar{i} = \delta\bar{k}, \quad \bar{k} = \left\{ \frac{1}{A\bar\theta\alpha} \left[\frac{1}{\beta} - (1 - \delta) \right] \right\}^{1/(\alpha-1)}.$$

Next, let $x \equiv (\theta, k, i)$ and $\bar{x} \equiv (\bar\theta, \bar{k}, \bar{i})$. Approximate $U(x)$ near the deterministic steady state $\bar{x}$. The approximate quadratic function is:

$$u(x) = U(\bar{x}) + b'(x - \bar{x}) + (x - \bar{x})'Q(x - \bar{x})$$

for $x, b \in \mathbb{R}^3$ and Q is a 3×3 symmetric matrix. The elements b_i and $q_{i,i}$ are chosen so that the approximation error is zero at the points $\bar{x} - z^i$ and $\bar{x} + z^i$, where $z^i > 0$ correspond to the approximate average deviations of the x_i from their steady state values. (Kydland and Prescott let $z_i^i/\bar{x}_i$ vary according to the percentage standard deviation of the actual series whereas Danthine, Donaldson, and Mehra [84] also consider an equiproportionate deviation scheme such that $z_i^i/\bar{x}_i$ equals some constant, say 0.00001.) For the approximation error to equal zero at $\bar{x} + z^i$ and $\bar{x} - z^i$ requires that:

$$b_i \;=\; [U(\bar{x} + z^i) - U(\bar{x} - z^i)]/2z_i,$$

$$q_{i,i} \;=\; [U(\bar{x} + z^i) - U(\bar{x}) + U(\bar{x} - z^i) - U(\bar{x})]/2z_i^2.$$

The elements $q_{i,j}$, $i \neq j$, are selected to minimize the sum of squared approximation errors at $\bar{x} + z^i + z^j$, $\bar{x} + z^i - z^j$, $\bar{x} - z^i + z^j$, and $\bar{x} - z^i - z^j$. This yields

$$q_{i,j} = [U(\bar{x} + z^i + z^j) - U(\bar{x} + z^i - z^j) - U(\bar{x} - z^i + z^j)$$

$$+ U(\bar{x} - z^i - z^j)]/8z_i z_j, \quad i \neq j.$$

The linear-quadratic dynamic optimization problem is now given by:

$$\max_{\{i_t\}_{t=0}^{\infty}} E_0 \left\{ \sum_{t=0}^{\infty} \beta^t [U(\bar{x}) + b'x_t + x_t' Q x_t] \right\}, \tag{4.17}$$

subject to

$$k_{t+1} \;=\; (1 - \delta)k_t + i_t, \tag{4.18}$$

$$\theta_{t+1} \;=\; \mu_\theta + \rho\theta_t + \varepsilon_{t+1}, \tag{4.19}$$

given k_0, θ_0. The solution for this problem yields next period's capital stock (or investment) as a linear function of the state variables, k_t and θ_t, such that

$$k_{t+1} = \mu_k + \lambda k_t + \xi\theta_t, \quad |\lambda| < 1, \tag{4.20}$$

where λ and ξ depend on the parameters of preferences and technology and exhibit cross-equation restrictions with the law of motion for the technology shock. We can approximate the production function by a first-order Taylor approximation to obtain solutions for optimal output and consumption that are linear functions of k_t and θ_t.

In the real business cycle literature, linear decision rules of this type have been used to match the model with the data. The typical approach in this literature is to "calibrate" models instead of formally estimating and testing them. Calibration involves fixing a number of the unknown parameters at values determined from unconditional first moments for various series or by using estimates from other studies. The remaining values are chosen by matching a small set of moments implied by the model with the corresponding moments in the data. The theoretical moments are computed using the time series for each variable generated from the model for alternative parameter values.

Kydland and Prescott use this approach to analyze the properties of a real business cycle model in which preferences are not separable over time with respect to leisure and there exists a time-to-build feature in investment for new capital goods. The production function displays constant returns to scale with respect to hours worked and a composite capital good. The only exogenous shock to their model is a random technology shock which follows a stationary first-order autoregressive process. They use the quadratic approximation procedure to obtain linear decision rules for a set of aggregate variables and generate time series for the remaining series by drawing realizations of the innovation to the technology shock, $\{\varepsilon_t\}_{t=0}^T$.

They calculate a small set of moments associated with each series to match the model with the data. Because Kydland and Prescott choose the variance of the innovation to the technology shock to make the variability of the output series generated by their model equal to the variability of observed GNP, the model cannot be tested to determine whether *"technology shocks are adequate to generate output, employment, etc. fluctuations of the magnitude actually observed"* (see McCallum [254]). Put differently, it is difficult to identify technology shocks that can generate cyclical fluctuations of magnitudes that are observed in the data (see Summers [320]).

An alternative approach to fitting real business cycle models is to estimate their parameters using the method of maximum likelihood, for example. Altuğ estimates a modified verison of the Kydland and Prescott model for this purpose. She derives a statistical model for a variety of aggregate series by augmenting the linear decision rules implied by a quadratic approximation to the original nonlinear model with i.i.d. errors. The reason for augmenting the original model with additional shocks is that unless there are as many shocks as there are series used in estimation, the stochastic model describing the joint behavior of output, hours, and the other variables will be singular. The approach of augmenting the linear decision rules, which are functions of the unobserved technology shock, with i.i.d. measurement errors yields an unobservable index model of the type studied by Sargent and Sims [300] and others.

We first describe how to formulate unobservable index models in general and then relate them to the model that Altuğ estimates. For this purpose, let $\{\tilde{w}_t\}_{t=0}^{\infty}$ denote an n-dimensional mean zero, covariance stationary stochastic process used to describe observations on the (possibly detrended) values of a set of variables. A k-factor unobservable index model for $\tilde{w}_t$ is given by:

$$\tilde{w}_t = \sum_{s=-\infty}^{\infty} \tilde{H}(s)\tilde{\varepsilon}_{t-s} + \tilde{\nu}_t, \qquad (4.21)$$

where $\{\tilde{H}(s)\}_{s=-\infty}^{\infty}$ is a sequence of $n \times k$-dimensional matrices, $\tilde{\varepsilon}_t$ is a $k \times 1$ vector of common factors, and $\tilde{\nu}_t$ is an $n \times 1$ vector of idiosyncratic shocks that are mutually uncorrelated and uncorrelated with common factors. More precisely, we require that $E(\tilde{\varepsilon}_t\tilde{\nu}_{i,t}) = 0$ for $i = 1, \ldots, n$ and $E(\tilde{\nu}_{i,t}\tilde{\nu}_{j,t}) = 0$ for $i \neq j$. Both the common factors and the idiosyncratic factors may be serially correlated. Under these assumptions, the variances and autocovariances of the observed series $\{\tilde{w}_t\}$ can be decomposed in terms of the variances and autocovariances of a low-dimensional set of unobserved common factors and the idiosyncratic shocks. As described by Sargent and Sims and others, the dynamic factor model can be estimated and its restrictions tested across alternative frequencies using a frequency domain approach to time series analysis.

The unrestricted version of the dynamic factor or unobservable index model does not place restrictions on the matrices $\tilde{H}(s)$, which describe how the common factors affect the behavior of the elements of y_t at all leads and lags. Nor is it possible to identify the common factors with different types of shocks to the economy. In the restricted dynamic factor model that Altuğ derives, there is a single unobservable index that corresponds to the innovation to the technology. Suppose we consider two series: the capital stock and output. Notice that we can express the equilibrium capital stock as:

$$\begin{aligned}
k_{t+1} &= (1 - \lambda L)^{-1}\mu_k + \xi(1 - \lambda L)^{-1}(1 - \rho L)^{-1}(\mu_\theta + \varepsilon_t) \\
&\equiv \mu_{k'} + h_1(L)\varepsilon_t,
\end{aligned}$$

where $\mu_{k'} \equiv (1 - \lambda)^{-1}\mu_k + \xi(1 - \lambda)^{-1}(1 - \rho)^{-1}\mu_\theta$ and where we have used the law of motion for the technology shock to substitute for θ_t in Equation (4.20). Now linearize the production function with respect to θ_t and k_t using a first-order Taylor series approximation near the steady state values $\bar{\theta}$ and $\bar{k}$:

$$\begin{aligned}
y_t &= \alpha_1(\theta_t - \bar{\theta}) + \alpha_2(k_t - \bar{k}) \\
&= \mu_y + \alpha_1(1 - \rho L)^{-1}\varepsilon_t + \alpha_2\xi(1 - \lambda L)^{-1}(1 - \rho L)^{-1}\varepsilon_{t-1} \\
&\equiv \mu_y + h_2(L)\varepsilon_t,
\end{aligned}$$

where $\mu_y \equiv \alpha_1(1-\rho)^{-1}\mu_\theta + \alpha_2\mu_{k'} - \alpha_1\bar{\theta} - \alpha_2\bar{k}$. The restricted unobservable index model is defined as:

$$w_t = \sum_{s=0}^{\infty} H(s)\varepsilon_{t-s} + \nu_t, \qquad (4.22)$$

where $w_t \equiv (k_{t+1} - \mu_{k'}, y_t - \mu_y)'$ and $H(L) \equiv [h_1(L), h_2(L)]'$. The idiosyncratic shocks ν_t are interpreted as i.i.d. measurement errors or idiosyncratic components not captured by the underlying real business cycle model. Unlike the unrestricted factor model which can be estimated frequency by frequency, this model must be estimated jointly across all frequencies because the underlying economic model constrains the dynamic behavior of the different series as well as specifying the nature of the unobserved factor.[2]

Altuğ initially estimates an unrestricted dynamic factor model for the level of per capita hours and the differences of per capita values of durable goods consumption, investment in equipment, investment in structures, and aggregate output. She finds that the hypothesis of a single unobservable factor cannot be rejected at conventional significance levels for describing the joint time series behavior of the variables described above. For the unrestricted model, the overall proportion of variance explained by the single factor is 0.758, 0.59, and 0.610 for the growth rates of consumer durables, investment in structures, and investment in equipment. The single factor also explains 93% of the variance of the growth rate of output. For per capita hours, the common factor has most explanatory power at the low frequencies and explains about 50% of the overall variability of per capita hours. However, when the restrictions of the underlying model are imposed, the model cannot explain the cyclical variation in per capita hours worked.

Other developments in the real business cycle literature include the indivisible labor, lottery models studied by Hansen [172] and Rogerson [280]. The purpose of the indivisible labor models is to devise a framework that explains the stylized fact that aggregate hours vary more than productivity. This is accomplished by assuming that individuals can work all the time or none at all. To account for the nonconvexities introduced by work/nonwork decision, it is assumed that individuals choose the probability of working α_t. A lottery then determines whether an individual actually works. This economy is one in which individuals and a

---

[2]In a recent paper, Watson [331] shows how the approach of adding errors to the stochastic process generated by a theoretical model can be used to derive measures of fit for the underlying economic model which may depend on a low-dimensional vector of shocks.

firm trade a contract that commits the household to work h_0 hours with probability α_t. Since what is being traded is the contract, the individual gets paid regardless of whether he works or not.

Hansen assumes that the single-period utility function is given by:

$$u(c_t, \ell_t) = \log(c_t) + A\log(\ell_t), \quad A > 0,$$

where c_t and ℓ_t are consumption and leisure in period t, respectively. The time endowment is normalized as one so that $\ell_t = 1 - h_t$, where h_t is hours of work. Using the lottery, expected utility in period t is given by $\alpha_t[\log(c_t) + A\log(1 - h_0)] + (1 - \alpha_t)[\log(c_t) + A\log(1)]$. This yields a function $U : \mathbb{R}_+ \times [0, 1] \to \mathbb{R}$ such that

$$U(c_t, \alpha_t) = \log(c_t) + A\alpha_t \log(1 - h_0).$$

Since the fraction α_t of households work h_0 hours and the remainder work zero hours, per capita hours worked in period t is $h_t = \alpha_t h_0$. The aggregate production function is given by $f(\lambda_t, k_t, h_t) = \lambda_t k_t^\theta h_t^{1-\theta}$ where k_t is the capital stock and λ_t denotes a stochastic technology shock with the law of motion $\lambda_{t+1} = \rho\lambda_t + \varepsilon_{t+1}$, $|\rho| < 1$. The capital stock evolves as $k_{t+1} = (1 - \delta)k_t + i_t$, $0 \leq \delta \leq 1$. The social planner's problem for this economy involves maximizing the expected, discounted utility of the hypothetical representative consumer, $E_0\{\sum_{t=0}^\infty \beta^t U(c_t, \alpha_t)\}$, $0 < \beta < 1$, subject to the constraints with respect to aggregate hours, the production function, the laws of motion for capital and the technology shock, and the aggregate resource constraint, $c_t + i_t \leq f(\lambda_t, k_t, h_t)$. Hansen calibrates this model by specifying values for the unknown parameters θ, δ, β, A, ρ and the distribution function F for the innovations to the technology shock, ε_t, using the approach in Kydland and Prescott. He argues that the model with indivisibilities can generate a variability of hours relative to productivity around 2.7 compared to the model without indivisibilities which implies a value near unity.

The purpose of the framework that Hansen and Rogerson consider is to generate the stylized fact with respect to the relative variability of hours versus productivity and it is not intended to incorporate the microeconomic foundations of the labor market. Nevertheless, it has features that are counterfactual to the behavior of actual labor markets. In this model, *ex ante* all individuals are alike but *ex post* they differ because some work while others enjoy leisure. With complete insurance and identical preferences that are separable with respect to consumption and leisure, all individuals have the same consumption but those who work are worse off. Equivalently, the unemployed are better off.

Another recent development concerns models of endogenous growth models considered by Romer [283], Lucas [234], and others. These models have been motivated by observations that growth rates across countries are diverging and countries that exhibit high growth rates may continue to exhibit such growth, whereas slow-growing countries may remain on a path of continued slow growth. To generate sustained growth and divergence of growth based on differences in initial conditions, Romer considers a model with externalities and increasing returns in the production of knowledge, whereas Lucas [234] relies on alternative forms of human capital accumulation. Jones and Manuelli [209] show that the standard deterministic one-sector optimal growth model can also generate sustained growth under the assumption that the marginal productivity of capital is bounded from below. While there have been interesting theoretical developments in this field, there has been little empirical work matching these models to the observations.

2. Asset Pricing with Production

In the previous section, we derived optimal policy functions by solving a social planning problem. We now derive an asset pricing model from this framework based on the analysis in Brock [44, 45]. For this purpose, we decentralize the optimal allocation for the growth model

We assume that households own the initial capital stocks and competitive firms rent capital from households at a market-determined rental rate. The firm issues equity shares, which are claims to its stream of future profits. As in the Lucas asset-pricing model, each firm i has outstanding one perfectly divisible equity share. Ownership of α percent of the equity shares in firm i at date t entitles an individual to α percent of profits of the firm i at date $t+1$. The utility function, technology shock, and the production functions satisfy the conditions of Assumptions 4.1 through 4.3.

The timing of trades and information in this economy is as follows. At the beginning of the period, the household owns the n-dimensional vector of capital stocks k_t. Let K_t denote the vector of per capita aggregate capital stocks. All agents observe the realization of the technology shock θ_t. Firms then rent capital from households at the rate $R_{i,t}$. Notice that households decide how much of each type of capital $k_{i,t}$ to hold at the end of period $t-1$ before observing the rental rates at time t, while firms decide how much capital to rent $k_{i,t}^d$ after observing the realization of the technology shock. Firms sell output, pay rent to the owners of the capital stock, return the undepreciated capital to its owners, and pay dividends $\pi_{i,t}$ to its shareholders. Households decide how much to consume, how much to invest in new capital, how to allocate their capital across the production units, and the number of equity shares $z_{i,t+1}$ to purchase at the price $q_{i,t}$ for $i = 1, \ldots, n$.

The representative household chooses sequences $\{c_t\}_{t=0}^{\infty}$, $\{z_{t+1}\}_{t=0}^{\infty}$, $\{k_{t+1}\}_{t=0}^{\infty}$ to solve:

$$\max \left\{ E_0 \sum_{t=0}^{\infty} \beta^t U(c_t), \right\}$$

subject to

$$c_t + \sum_{i=1}^{n} k_{i,t+1} + q_t \cdot z_{t+1} \leq (\pi_t + q_t) \cdot z_t +$$

$$\sum_{i=1}^{n} [R_{i,t} k_{i,t} + (1 - \delta_i) k_{i,t}], \tag{4.23}$$

$$c_t \geq 0, \quad z_{i,t+1} \geq 0, \quad k_{i,t+1} \geq 0, \quad i = 1, \ldots, n, \tag{4.24}$$

and given the initial conditions $z_{i,0} \equiv 1$, $R_{i,0} \equiv f_i'(k_{i,0}, \theta_0) + (1 - \delta_i)$, $\pi_{i,0} \equiv f_i(k_{i,0}, \theta_0) - f_i'(k_{i,0}, \theta_0) k_{i,0}$, and $k_{i,0} > 0$ for $i = 1, ..., n$.

A firm of type i is assumed to maximize its current period profits:

$$\pi_{i,t} = f_i(k_{i,t}^d, \theta_t) - R_{i,t} k_{i,t}^d \tag{4.25}$$

by choosing the amount of capital $k_{i,t}^d$ to rent at the market-determined rate $R_{i,t}$. Under the assumption that the household owns the capital stocks, the firm solves a simple profit-maximization problem in each period.

The market-clearing conditions require that all shares are held,

$$z_{i,t+1} = 1 \quad \text{for } i = 1, \ldots, n,$$

the goods market clears,

$$c_t + \sum_{i=1}^{n} k_{i,t+1} = \sum_{i=1}^{n} [f_i(K_{i,t}, \theta_t) + (1 - \delta_i) K_{i,t}],$$

and the markets for used capital clear,

$$k_{i,t}^d = K_{i,t} \quad \text{for } i = 1, \ldots, n.$$

We now describe how to formulate a recursive competitive equilibrium for this economy. The economy-wide state variables are (K_t, θ_t). We focus

on equilibria that are time-invariant functions of the state variables. We
assume that rental rates, dividends, and equity prices are determined
as strictly positive, continuous functions of the aggregate capital stocks
and the productivity shock, $R_{i,t} = \bar{R}_i(K_t, \theta_t)$, $\pi_{i,t} = \bar{\pi}_i(K_t, \theta_t)$, and $q_{i,t} = \bar{q}_i(K_t, \theta_t)$. Similarly, we assume that the aggregate capital stocks evolve
as strictly positive, continuous functions of K_t and θ_t, $K_{i,t+1} = \bar{K}_i(K_t, \theta_t)$.
Let $\bar{q} : \mathcal{K} \times \Theta \to \mathbb{R}^n_{++}$, $\bar{\pi} : \mathcal{K} \times \Theta \to \mathbb{R}^n_{++}$, and $\bar{R} : \mathcal{K} \times \Theta \to \mathbb{R}^n_{++}$ be the
vector of functions determining equity prices, dividends, and rental rates,
respectively. Denote by $\bar{K} : \mathcal{K} \times \Theta \to \mathcal{K}$ as the law of motion for the
vector of aggregate capital stocks. Define $\mathcal{P}$ as the set of vector-valued
functions $(\bar{q}, \bar{\pi}, \bar{R})$.

The first-order condition for the firm's problem is:

$$0 = f_i'(k_{i,t}^d, \theta_t) - \bar{R}_i(K_t, \theta_t), \tag{4.26}$$

so that the firm rents capital up to the point where the marginal product
of capital equals its rental rate. Define the firm's optimal choices of
capital by $\hat{k}_{i,t}^d = \hat{k}_i^d(K_t, \theta_t)$. The firm's profits are:

$$\pi_i(\hat{k}_{i,t}^d, K_t, \theta_t) = f_i(\hat{k}_{i,t}^d, \theta_t) - \bar{R}_i(K_t, \theta_t)\hat{k}_{i,t}^d. \tag{4.27}$$

Under Assumptions 4.1—4.3, given the set of functions $\mathcal{P}$, $\bar{K}$, and
the aggregate state (K_t, θ_t), we can formulate a dynamic programming
problem for the representative household. The state variables for an
agent are $(z_t, \theta_t, k_t, K_t)$. The household solves:

$$v(z_t, \theta_t, k_t, K_t) = \max\{U(c_t) + \beta E_t[v(z_{t+1}, \theta_{t+1}, k_{t+1}, K_{t+1})]\}. \tag{4.28}$$

by choosing the vectors z_{t+1}, k_{t+1}, and the level of consumption c_t subject
to the set of constraints in Equation (4.23), the nonnegativity constraints,
initial conditions, and given the set of functions $\mathcal{P}$ and the law of motion
$\bar{K}$. Assume that $z_{i,t+1} \in [0, \bar{z}]$ where $\bar{z} > 1$. In equilibrium, we know
that $z_{i,t+1} = 1$ so that this assumption is not restrictive. We assume that
$0 < \bar{R}_{i,t} < \infty$, $0 < \bar{\pi}_{i,t} < \infty$, and $0 < \bar{q}_{i,t} < \infty$. For an initial capital
stock such that $K_0 \geq 0$, there is a maximum sustainable capital stock so
that output is bounded, as is total income. Let $\Gamma_{\mathcal{P}}(z_t, \theta_t, k_t, K_t)$ be the
set of consumption, equity shares, and capital allocations (c_t, z_{t+1}, k_{t+1})
satisfying the budget constraint. This set is compact. For given price
functions, we can show that there exists a unique value function that
solves Equation (4.28).

Let $\mathcal{S} \equiv [0, \bar{z}] \times \Theta \times \mathcal{K} \times \mathcal{K}$ and define $\mathcal{C}(\mathcal{S})$ as the space of continuous,
bounded functions $\{v : \mathcal{S} \to \mathbb{R}_+\}$ equipped with the sup norm. Define

the operator T_P by:

$$T_P v(z_t, \theta_t, k_t, K_t) \equiv$$

$$\max_{(c_t, z_{t+1}, k_{t+1}) \in \Gamma_P} \{U(c_t) + \beta E_t[v(z_{t+1}, \theta_{t+1}, k_{t+1}, K_{t+1})]\}. \qquad (4.29)$$

We have the following theorem.

Theorem 4.2 *Under Assumptions 4.1—4.3 and given the set of functions $\mathcal{P}$ and $\bar{K}$, let $T_P : \mathcal{C}(\mathcal{S}) \rightarrow \mathcal{C}(\mathcal{S})$ be defined by Equation (4.29). The operator T_P is a contraction with unique fixed point $v^\star$.*

PROOF
For any $v \in \mathcal{C}$, the operator T_P takes continuous, bounded functions into continuous, bounded functions. The operator T_P is monotone; for any $v_1, v_2 \in \mathcal{C}$ such that $v_1 > v_2$, $T_P v_1 \geq T_P v_2$. Because $0 < \beta < 1$, the operator T_P also discounts, that is, $T_P(v + a) \leq T_P v + \beta a$. Hence T_P satisfies Blackwell's conditions for a contraction.   ■

Let λ_t denote the multiplier on the budget constraint in Equation (4.23) and let v_k^i denote the partial derivative of the value function with respect to the i'th component of k_{t+1}, and v_z^i the partial derivative with respect to the i'th component of z_{t+1}. The necessary and sufficient conditions for a solution to the household's problem are:

$$U'(c_t) = \lambda_t, \qquad (4.30)$$

$$\lambda_t = \beta E_t[v_k^i(z_{t+1}, \theta_{t+1}, k_{t+1}, K_{t+1})], \qquad (4.31)$$

$$\lambda_t \bar{q}_i(K_t, \theta_t) = \beta E_t[v_z^i(z_{t+1}, \theta_{t+1}, k_{t+1}, K_{t+1})], \qquad (4.32)$$

where $\lambda_t > 0$ if the budget constraint in Equation (4.23) holds with equality. The envelope conditions are:

$$v_k^i(z_t, \theta_t, k_t, K_t) = \lambda_t[\bar{R}_i(K_t, \theta_t) + (1 - \delta_i)], \qquad (4.33)$$

$$v_z^i(z_t, \theta_t, k_t, K_t) = \lambda_t[\bar{q}_i(K_t, \theta_t) + \bar{\pi}_i(K_t, \theta_t)]. \qquad (4.34)$$

Let the solution be a set of policy functions $c = \hat{g}(z_t, \theta_t, k_t, K_t)$, $z_{i,t+1} = \hat{z}_i(z_t, \theta_t, k_t, K_t)$ and $k_{i,t+1} = \hat{h}_i(z_t, \theta_t, k_t, K_t)$ for $i = 1, \ldots, n$.

We have the following definition.

Definition 4.1 *A recursive competitive equilibrium is a set of functions:*

$$\mathcal{P} \equiv (\bar{q}, \bar{\pi}, \bar{R}), \quad \mathcal{Q} \equiv (\hat{g}, \hat{z}, \hat{h}, \hat{k}^d, \bar{K}),$$

such that (i) given prices $\mathcal{P}$ and the law of motion for the aggregate capital stock $\bar{K}$, the household chooses $c_t = \hat{g}(z_t, \theta_t, k_t, K_t)$, $z_{i,t+1} = \hat{z}_i(z_t, \theta_t, k_t, K_t)$, and $k_{i,t+1} = \hat{h}_i(z_t, \theta_t, k_t, K_t)$ to solve the problem in Equation (4.28); (ii) given $\mathcal{P}$, the firm chooses $\hat{k}_{i,t}^d = \hat{k}_i^d(K_t, \theta_t)$ to solve the problem in Equation (4.25); (iii) markets clear; (iv) the individual's law of motion for capital is identical to the aggregate law of motion for the per capita capital stock, $\hat{h}_i(1, \theta_t, K_t, K_t) = \bar{K}_i(K_t, \theta_t)$.

The last condition is a property of a rational expectations equilibrium, which imposes a consistency between the subjective distribution for the per capita capital stock and the objective distribution generating the per capita capital stock in equilibrium. We now show that the optimal policy functions for the consumer and firm are based on the set of prices $\mathcal{P}$ that actually clear the market and discuss how to construct the equilibrium price functions.

To show the existence and uniqueness of a competitive equilibrium, we take the allocation from the social planner's problem as fixed and construct the equilibrium prices that support this allocation. We now drop the time subscripts and adopt the primed, unprimed notation. Notice that in the competitive equilibrium, $z = 1$ and $k = K$, so that we can define the functions:

$$\bar{g}(K, \theta) = \hat{g}(1, \theta, K, K),$$
$$\bar{h}_i(K, \theta) = \hat{h}_i(1, \theta, K, K), \quad i = 1, \ldots, n.$$

Recall that all households are identical and that the consumption of the representative household in the social planner's problem was a policy function $g(y)$ and investment decisions were determined according to $h_i(y)$ for $i = 1, \ldots, n$. Recall that $y = \sum_{i=1}^{n}[f_i(K_i, \theta) + (1 - \delta_i)K_i]$ and define the equilibrium allocation as:

$$c = \bar{g}(K, \theta) = g(y),$$
$$K_i' = \bar{h}_i(K, \theta) = h_i(y), \quad i = 1, \ldots, n.$$

Take the allocation c and K_i', $i = 1, \ldots, n$, defined from g and h_i, $i = 1, \ldots, n$, as fixed. The supporting equilibrium prices are derived from the relevant marginal rate of substitution conditions in consumption and marginal rate of transformation conditions in production.

We take the equilibrium rental rate to be:

$$\bar{R}_i(K, \theta) = f_i'(K, \theta) + (1 - \delta_i), \tag{4.35}$$

and equilibrium dividends as:

$$\bar{\pi}_i(K,\theta) = f_i(K,\theta) - f'_i(K,\theta)K_i. \tag{4.36}$$

Furthermore, define the equity price $\bar{q}_i(K,\theta)$ to satisfy the condition in Equation (4.32) in which the envelope condition in Equation (4.34) has been substituted. Define $\bar{h}(K,\theta)$ as an n-dimensional vector with element $\bar{h}_i(K,\theta)$. Specifically, $\bar{q}_i$ is defined by:

$$U'[\bar{g}(K,\theta)]\bar{q}_i(K,\theta) = \beta \int_\Theta U' \left\{ \bar{g} \left[\bar{h}(K,\theta), \theta' \right] \right\} \times$$

$$\left\{ \bar{q}_i \left[\bar{h}(K,\theta), \theta' \right] + \bar{\pi}_i \left[\bar{h}(K,\theta), \theta' \right] \right\} dG(\theta'). \tag{4.37}$$

Then it is easy to see that taking as fixed the allocation $c = g(y)$ and $K'_i = h_i(y)$ for $i = 1, \ldots, n$, the solution to the household's problem and the firm's problem and the price functions defined by Equations (4.35), (4.36), and (4.37) satisfy the definition of a recursive competitive equilibrium. Conversely, the functions $\bar{g}$, $\bar{h}_i$, $\bar{R}_i$, $\bar{\pi}_i$, and $\bar{q}_i$ for $i = 1, \ldots, n$ satisfy the valuation function, first-order conditions, and feasibility condition for the social planner's problem given by the conditions in Equations (4.11), (4.12), and (4.13).

The remaining issue is to demonstrate existence and uniqueness of the price functions $\bar{q}_i(K,\theta)$. Define $\phi_i(K,\theta) \equiv U'(\bar{g}(K,\theta))\bar{q}_i(K,\theta)$ and

$$\psi_i(K,\theta) \equiv \beta \int_\Theta U' \left\{ \bar{g} \left[\bar{h}(K,\theta), \theta' \right] \right\} \bar{\pi}_i \left[\bar{h}(K,\theta), \theta' \right] dG(\theta').$$

Define the operator T_i from the right side of Equation (4.37) by:

$$(T_i \phi_i)(K,\theta) \equiv \psi_i(K,\theta) + \beta \int_\Theta \phi_i \left[\bar{h}(K,\theta), \theta' \right] dG(\theta'). \tag{4.38}$$

Let $\mathcal{C}_q$ denote the space of bounded, continuous functions $\{ q_i : K \times \Theta \to \mathbb{R}_+ \}$ equipped with the sup norm. We have the following result.

Theorem 4.3 *Under Assumptions 4.1—4.3, the operator T_i is a contraction and has a unique fixed point $\phi_i^\star$.*

PROOF
Recall that y takes values on a compact set $\mathcal{Y}$ and that, because U is continuous by assumption and takes values on a compact set in $\mathbb{R}$, it is bounded. By the envelope conditions, we know that $U'(\bar{g}(y)) = W^{\star\prime}(y)$. We first show that if U is bounded on $\mathcal{Y}$, then $\psi_i(K,\theta)$ is bounded. By the concavity of U, we have

$$U(y) - U(0) \geq U'(y)(y - 0) = U'(y)y.$$

Thus, there exists a $\bar{U}$ such that $U'(y)y \leq \bar{U}$ for all $y \in \mathcal{Y}$. Define

$$Y(K, \theta, \theta') \equiv \sum_{i=1}^{n} F_i[\bar{h}_i(K, \theta), \theta'].$$

Then, we have that

$$\psi_i(K, \theta) \equiv \beta \int_{\Theta} U'\left\{\bar{g}\left[\bar{h}(K, \theta), \theta'\right]\right\} \bar{\pi}_i\left[\bar{h}(K, \theta), \theta'\right] dG(\theta')$$

$$= \beta \int_{\Theta} W'\left[Y(K, \theta, \theta')\right] Y(K, \theta, \theta') \frac{\bar{\pi}_i\left[\bar{h}(K, \theta), \theta'\right]}{Y(K, \theta, \theta')} dG(\theta')$$

$$\leq \beta\bar{U}$$

since $f_i' \geq 0$ implies that $f_i - f_i'K_i \equiv \bar{\pi}_i \leq f_i$ and
$\bar{\pi}_i\left[\bar{h}(K, \theta), \theta'\right] / Y(K, \theta, \theta') \leq 1$.

Thus, T_i maps the space of bounded functions into the same space. Notice that $\psi_i(K, \theta)$ is continuous and for any continuous $\phi(K, \theta)$,

$$\int_{\Theta} \phi[\bar{h}(K, \theta), \theta'] dG(\theta')$$

is continuous. Hence, $T_i : \mathcal{C}_q \to \mathcal{C}_q$.

For any two elements ϕ_i and γ_i in $\mathcal{C}_q$, consider:

$$|T_i\phi_i - T_i\gamma_i| = \beta \left| \int_{\Theta} \phi_i\left[\bar{h}(K, \theta), \theta'\right] dG(\theta') - \int_{\Theta} \gamma_i\left[\bar{h}(K, \theta), \theta'\right] dG(\theta')\right|$$

$$\leq \beta \int_{\Theta} |\phi_i[\bar{h}(K, \theta), \theta'] - \gamma_i[\bar{h}(K, \theta), \theta']| dG(\theta')$$

$$\leq \beta \int_{\Theta} \sup_{K,\theta} |\phi_i[\bar{h}(K, \theta), \theta'] - \gamma_i[\bar{h}(K, \theta), \theta']| dG(\theta')$$

$$= \beta\|\phi_i - \gamma_i\|. \tag{4.39}$$

Taking the supremum of the left side of Equation (4.39), we obtain:

$$\|T_i\phi_i - T_i\gamma_i\| = \beta\|\phi_i - \gamma_i\|,$$

showing that T_i is a contraction with modulus β. Applying the Contraction Mapping Theorem shows that there is a unique fixed point $\phi_i^\star$ to Equation (4.38). ∎

The equity prices are continuous and bounded functions satisfying

$$\bar{q}_i(K, \theta) = \frac{\phi_i^\star(K, \theta)}{U'(\bar{g}(K, \theta))}, \quad i = 1, \ldots, n. \tag{4.40}$$

This completes our discussion of proving existence and uniqueness of equilibrium in the asset pricing model with production.

3.   Financial Structure, Taxes and Investment

In this section, we formulate the present-value maximization problem of competitive firms who own the physical stocks of capital and who finance new investment by issuing debt and equity. We use this framework to discuss the financial structure of a firm, to derive a Modigliani-Miller theorem about the irrelevance of debt versus equity financing, and to study market returns and risk. Our discussion is based on Brock and Turnovsky [50], who work with a continuous time version of the one-sector growth model.

Next, we study the effects of distortionary taxation on firms' financial structure. We also describe the effects of taxation on capital accumulation decisions using a version of the optimal growth model with distortionary taxation. As the final topic of this section, we derive a version of the $\mathcal{Q}$-theory of investment when there are adjustment costs and irreversibilities in investment.

3.1.   Financial Structure of a Firm

We now assume that firms are the owners of the capital stock and finance investment by retained earnings, equity issue, and debt issue, which we assume takes the form of one-period bonds. There is a single production process that uses labor and capital and that depends on the random technology shock.

The household supplies labor inelastically and chooses sequences for consumption, and bond and share holdings to solve:

$$\max E_0 \left\{ \sum_{t=0}^{\infty} \beta^t U(c_t) \right\} \tag{4.41}$$

subject to

$$c_t + q_t z_{t+1} + b_{t+1}^d \leq w_t l_t^s + (1 + r_t)b_t^d + z_t(q_t + d_t), \tag{4.42}$$

and the restriction that $0 \leq l^s \leq 1$. The household treats the stochastic processes for prices w_t, r_t, q_t, and dividends d_t as given. Let λ_t denote the multiplier for the constraint in Equation (4.42). The first-order conditions are:

$$\lambda_t = U'(c_t), \tag{4.43}$$

$$q_t \lambda_t \geq \beta E_t[\lambda_{t+1}(q_{t+1} + d_{t+1})], \tag{4.44}$$

$$\lambda_t = \beta E_t[\lambda_{t+1}(1 + r_{t+1})]. \tag{4.45}$$

Define $\mathcal{M}_{t,i} \equiv \beta U'(c_{t+i})/U'(c_t)$ as the intertemporal marginal rate of substitution in consumption. We assume that $0 \leq l^s \leq 1$ and because labor causes no disutility, $l^s = 1$ in equilibrium.

On the production side, the firm chooses how much labor to hire, how much to produce, and how much to invest. The production function is given by $F(K_t, l_t, \theta_t)$ and it displays constant returns to scale. The technology shock is i.i.d. and has a distribution that satisfies the conditions of Assumption 4.2. We assume that F is homogeneous of the first degree in its first two arguments so that $f(k_t, \theta) \equiv F(K_t/L_t, 1, \theta_t)$. The function $f(\cdot, \theta)$ is strictly increasing. strictly concave, and differentiable with $f(0, \theta) = 0$, $f'(0, \theta) = \infty$, and $f'(\infty, \theta) = 0$.

The firm sells output to consumers and to other firms for investment. In the absence of adjustment costs, irreversibilities in investment, and other frictions, the relative price of old and new capital equals 1. Thus, the gross profit of the firm equals total sales (which we assume equals its output so that no inventories are held) minus its wage bill, or

$$\pi_t = F(k_t, l_t, \theta_t) - w_t l_t. \tag{4.46}$$

The receipts π_t are disbursed in various ways: either paid out as dividends, $z_t d_t$, as payments on bonds $(1 + r_t b_t)$, or held as retained earnings, RE_t. The following accounting identity holds:

$$\pi_t = RE_t + d_t z_t + (1 + r_t)b_t. \tag{4.47}$$

Because a firm is the owner of the capital stock, it must decide not only how much to invest but also how to finance this investment. A firm finances its investment by borrowing b_{t+1}, by issuing new equity shares $q_t(z_{t+1} - z_t)$, or by its retained earnings. Investment satisfies:

$$k_{t+1} - (1 - \delta)k_t = RE_t + q_t(z_{t+1} - z_t) + b_{t+1}. \tag{4.48}$$

Solving both Equations (4.47) and (4.48) for retained earnings, equating the two resulting expressions, and simplifying, we have:

$$\begin{aligned} N_t &\equiv \pi_t - [k_{t+1} - (1 - \delta)k_t] \tag{4.49} \\ &= d_t z_t + (1 + r_t)b_t + q_t(z_t - z_{t+1}) - b_{t+1}. \end{aligned}$$

In Equation (4.49), N_t is the firm's *net cash flow*. We will relate this to the value of the firm momentarily.

The (ex-dividend) value of the firm, or the value of the firm at the end of the period after all dividend and debt payments have been made, is defined as the value of its equity shares, $q_t z_{t+1}$, plus the value of its outstanding debt, b_{t+1}. The value of the firm at the beginning of period t is the sum of net cash flow in period t and the ex-dividend value:

$$W_t \equiv N_t + W_t^e = N_t + q_t z_{t+1} + b_{t+1}. \tag{4.50}$$

We now show that the value of the firm can be expressed as the expected discounted value of its future cash flows. Now

$$
\begin{aligned}
W_t^e &\equiv q_t z_{t+1} + b_{t+1} \\
&= E_t\{\mathcal{M}_{t,1}[(q_{t+1} + d_{t+1})z_{t+1} + (1 + r_{t+1})b_{t+1}]\},
\end{aligned}
\tag{4.51}
$$

where we have substituted for $q_t z_{t+1}$ and b_{t+1} after multiplying Equations (4.44) and (4.45) by z_{t+1} and b_{t+1}, respectively. Adding and subtracting $q_{t+1}z_{t+2}$ and b_{t+2} from the right side of Equation (4.51) and using the definition of W_{t+1}^e, we have:

$$
\begin{aligned}
W_t^e = E_t\Big\{&\mathcal{M}_{t,1}\Big[W_{t+1}^e + q_{t+1}(z_{t+1} - z_{t+2}) \\
&+ d_{t+1}z_{t+1} + (1 + r_{t+1})b_{t+1} - b_{t+2}\Big]\Big\}.
\end{aligned}
\tag{4.52}
$$

Increase the time subscripts in Equation (4.49) by 1, solve the resulting Equation for $q_{t+1}(z_{t+1} - z_{t+2}) + b_{t+2}$, and substitute into Equation (4.52), to result in

$$
\begin{aligned}
W_t^e &= E_t\Big\{\mathcal{M}_{t,1}\Big[W_{t+1}^e + \pi_{t+1} - k_{t+2} + (1 - \delta)k_{t+1}\Big]\Big\} \\
&= E_t\Big[\mathcal{M}_{t,1}(W_{t+1}^e + N_{t+1})\Big].
\end{aligned}
\tag{4.53}
$$

We can use this expression and solve Equation (4.53) forward to express the (ex-dividend) value of the firm as:

$$W_t^e = E_t\left[\sum_{i=1}^{\infty} \mathcal{M}_{t,i} N_{t+i}\right]. \tag{4.54}$$

The present-value maximization problem solved by the firm is defined as follows. At the beginning of period t, the firm solves:

$$W_t = \max_{\{k_{s+1}\}_{s=t}^{\infty}, \{l_s\}_{s=t}^{\infty}} \left\{N_t + E_t\left[\sum_{i=1}^{\infty} \mathcal{M}_{t,i} N_{t+i}\right]\right\}, \tag{4.55}$$

given k_t. The discount rate is treated parametrically by the firm, although it depends on the representative household's behavior in equilibrium. Hence, we can model a firm as maximizing its value, defined as its expected discounted cash flow. This result holds more generally; if there exist complete contingent claims markets, the discount factor for the firm's problem is also given parametrically but it can be evaluated in terms of the intertemporal MRS in consumption for *any* consumer in the economy, which equals the ratio of the contingent claims prices.[3] In the absence of a representative consumer or the complete markets assumption, we run into the problem of shareholder unanimity explored by Hart [182], Radner [278], and others in terms of determining the criterion function for the firm.

We can derive the Modigliani-Miller theorem regarding the irrelevance of the firm's financing decisions using this framework. (See Modigliani and Miller [263].) Notice that the firm's cash flow depends only on the firm's production decisions, such as how much labor to hire, how much to produce, and how much to invest. It does not depend on the financing decisions made by the firm. In particular, it does not depend on the amount of equity issued, the debt-equity ratio, nor on the amount of retained earnings. In the absence of taxation, bankruptcy, and other distortions, the financing decisions do not affect the value of the firm. In the discussion below, we assume that the firm issues no new equity shares so that $z_{t+1} = 1$ for all t but it is straightforward to allow for new equity share issues by the firm.

3.1.1. The Equity Price and the Equity Premium

We now derive expressions for the equity price, equilibrium dividends, and the equity premium. Since there are no taxes or other distortions, the equilibrium allocation is optimal and can be found by solving the social planning problem. Let the solution take the form of time-invariant policy functions $c_t = g(k_t, \theta_t)$ and $k_{t+1} = h(k_t, \theta_t)$. We will construct supporting prices for the implied allocation.

In equilibrium, all shares are held, $z_{t+1} = 1$, all bonds are purchased, $b_{t+1}^d = b_{t+1}$, and consumption plus investment exhaust output, $c_t + k_{t+1} = F(k_t, 1, \theta_t) + (1 - \delta)k_t$. Notice that the net cash flow, N_t, is equal to the cash that flows from the business sector to the household sector. Since the consumer does not derive utility from leisure, $l_t = 1$ for all t.

The first-order conditions for the firm's maximization problem are:

$$w_t = F_2(k_t, l_t, \theta_t), \tag{4.56}$$

$$1 = E_t \{\mathcal{M}_{t,1} [F_1(k_{t+1}, l_{t+1}, \theta_{t+1}) + (1 - \delta)]\}. \tag{4.57}$$

---

[3]This is just a restatement of the implications of complete contingent claims equilibrium that we derived in Chapter 1.

To determine dividends, notice under the assumption of constant returns to scale, we can rewrite the production function in terms of the capital-labor ratio, k_t/l_t. Since $l_t = 1$ in equilibrium, we define $f(k_t, \theta_t) \equiv F(k_t, 1, \theta_t)$. In this case, gross profits are equal to $\pi_t = f'(k_t, \theta_t)k_t$, or the value of capital, which is the marginal product of capital times the capital stock per capita.

The net cash flow is:

$$N_t = f'(k_t, \theta_t)k_t - [k_{t+1} - (1 - \delta)k_t].$$

If we solve Equation (4.48) for retained earnings and substitute into Equation (4.47) and then solve for d_t, we have

$$d_t = f'(k_t, \theta_t)k_t - [k_{t+1} - (1 - \delta)k_t] + b_{t+1} - (1 + r_t)b_t. \tag{4.58}$$

Increasing the time subscript by 1 in the preceding equation and then substituting for d_{t+1} into Equation (4.44), the equity price satisfies:

$$
\begin{aligned}
q_t = {} & E_t \left\{ \mathcal{M}_{t,1} [q_{t+1} + f'(k_{t+1}, \theta_{t+1})k_{t+1} \right. \\
& \left. - k_{t+2} + (1 - \delta)k_{t+1} + b_{t+2} - (1 + r_{t+1})b_{t+1}] \right\}.
\end{aligned}
\tag{4.59}
$$

Multiplying the first-order condition for the firm's choice of investment described by Equation (4.57) by k_{t+1}, using the resulting expression to substitute for the term $\mathcal{M}_{t,1}f'(k_{t+1}, \theta_{t+1})k_{t+1}$ in Equation (4.59), and adding b_{t+1} to both sides, we have

$$q_t + b_{t+1} = E_t [\mathcal{M}_{t,1}(q_{t+1} + b_{t+2} - k_{t+2} + k_{t+1})],$$

which is a stochastic difference equation with the solution $q_t + b_{t+1} = k_{t+1}$. Hence, we can express the (ex-dividend) value of the firm as the value of the capital stock at the end of the period, or $W_t^e = q_t + b_{t+1} = k_{t+1}$.

Under the assumptions that (i) the firm finances investment by retained earnings; (ii) there is no borrowing ($b_{t+1} = 0$); (iii) there are no new equity shares issued; and (iv) production displays constant returns to scale, the ex-dividend value of the firm is $W_t^e = q_t = k_{t+1}$. The dividend paid by the firm at time $t + 1$ is:

$$d_{t+1} = f'(k_{t+1}, \theta_{t+1})k_{t+1} - [k_{t+2} - (1 - \delta)k_{t+1}]. \tag{4.60}$$

The expression for equity prices in Equation (4.59) implies that:

$$q_t = E_t \left\{ \mathcal{M}_{t,1} [f'(k_{t+1}, \theta_{t+1})k_{t+1} + (1 - \delta)k_{t+1}] \right\}, \tag{4.61}$$

where we have used $q_{t+1} = k_{t+2}$ together with Equation (4.58). Define the equity return as $1 + r^e_{t+1} \equiv (q_{t+1} + d_{t+1})/q_t$. The equity return satisfies:

$$1 = \beta E_t \left[\mathcal{M}_{t,1}(1 + r^e_{t+1}) \right]$$

$$1 = \beta E_t \left\{ \mathcal{M}_{t,1} \left[f'(k_{t+1}, \theta_{t+1}) - (1 - \delta) \right] \right\}. \tag{4.62}$$

Using Equation (4.45), we can show that the risk-free rate of return is given by $1 + r^f_{t+1} = 1/E_t(\mathcal{M}_{t,1})$. Thus, the *conditional equity premium*, which shows the expected value of the difference between the equity return and the return on the risk-free bond, is:

$$E_t(r^e_{t+1}) - r^f_{t+1} = -\frac{1}{E_t(\mathcal{M}_{t,1})} \mathrm{Cov}_t \left[\mathcal{M}_{t,1}, f'(k_{t+1}, \theta_{t+1}) \right]. \tag{4.63}$$

Hence, the equity premium depends on the conditional covariance between the intertemporal marginal rate of substitution in consumption and the marginal productivity of capital.

There are a variety of factors that affect the magnitude of the equity premium, such as consumer's attitudes toward risk, the variability and persistence of productivity shocks, and the marginal product function for capital. Unlike the pure exchange model in which consumption is exogenous, the intertemporal MRS or stochastic discount factor depends on factors that affect both consumption and investment. Using numerical solutions for the parametric example we described earlier, Donaldson and Mehra [97] derive a variety of comparative dynamics results for the behavior of the risk-free rate, the equity return, and the equity premium.

First, they show that the unconditional equity premium rises as agents become more risk averse and the risk-free rate declines. They also find that the average or unconditional equity return first rises and then declines with greater risk aversion. The reason for the eventual decline in the equity return is that the reduced variation in consumption due to increased risk aversion is accompanied by the increased variation in output. Since the equity return is the marginal product of capital, the average equity return falls when the economy operates at higher levels of capital. Finally, increases in the discount factor reduce both the risk-free rate and the equity return. The equity return falls because consumers with higher discount factors invest a larger fraction of output. The risk-free rate falls because consumers who value the future more are willing to pay a higher price for a certain payoff in the future. The links among risk aversion, production, and the equity premium are also discussed in Benninga and Protopapadakis [27].

3.1.2.   Taxes and the Debt-Equity Ratio

The effect of taxation on optimal capital structure has been widely studied in the financial economics literature. In the U.S. tax code, corporations can deduct the interest payments on debt but not dividend payments from taxable corporate income. The "balancing theory" of corporate financial structure states that firms balance the tax advantage of debt against various costs associated with "financial distress."[4] Yet Miller [259] has noted that the usual arguments for the tax advantage of corporate debt relative to corporate equity would be offset by the tax on interest income paid by holders of corporate debt. We now use a version of the model in Brock and Turnovsky with distortionary taxes to demonstrate Miller's equilibrium with debt and taxes and to describe the effects of distortionary taxes on firms' cost of capital.

The government assesses a proportional income tax equal to τ_y on households so that a household's budget constraint becomes:

$$c_t + z_t q_{t+1} + b_{t+1} \leq (1 - \tau_y)[w_t l_t + r_t b_t + z_t d_t] + b_t + z_t q_t. \qquad (4.64)$$

Notice that only interest income and dividend income are taxed; a capital gains tax is studied by Brock and Turnovsky.

The representative household maximizes the objective function in Equation (4.41) subject to the constraint in Equation (4.64) by choosing sequences for c_t, z_{t+1}, and b_{t+1}. The first-order conditions are:

$$U'(c_t) = \lambda_t, \qquad (4.65)$$

$$q_t \lambda_t = \beta E_t \left\{ \lambda_{t+1} [(1 - \tau_y) d_{t+1} + q_{t+1}] \right\}, \qquad (4.66)$$

$$\lambda_t = \beta E_t \left\{ \lambda_{t+1} [1 + r_{t+1}(1 - \tau_y)] \right\}. \qquad (4.67)$$

We'll use these conditions later to determine the value of the firm.

The firm pays taxes on its gross profits but is allowed to deduct interest payments on debt. We assume constant returns to scale in production for convenience. Since the household supplies labor inelastically, the firm's gross profits are:

$$\pi_t = f(k_t, \theta_t) - w_t.$$

The accounting identity in Equation (4.47) is now modified to include tax payments and deductions; the other accounting identity in Equation (4.48) remains unchanged. The gross profits of a firm are distributed as:

$$\pi_t = RE_t + d_t z_t + (1 + r_t)b_t - \tau_p r_t b_t + \tau_p \pi_t. \qquad (4.68)$$

---

[4]See the discussion and references in Kim [217].

Solving Equations (4.68) and (4.48) for retained earnings, we have

$$(1 - \tau_p)\pi_t - d_t z_t - (1 + r_t)b_t + \tau_p r_t b_t =$$

$$k_{t+1} - (1 - \delta)k_t + q_t(z_t - z_{t+1}) - b_{t+1}. \tag{4.69}$$

Define the after-tax net cash flow as N_t^τ:

$$N_t^\tau \equiv (1 - \tau_p)\pi_t - [k_{t+1} - (1 - \delta)k_t] \tag{4.70}$$

$$= d_t z_t + (1 + r_t)b_t - \tau_p r_t b_t + q_t(z_t - z_{t+1}) - b_{t+1},$$

where the equality follows from Equation (4.69). The (ex-dividend) value of the firm, $W_t^e \equiv q_t z_{t+1} + b_{t+1}$, is defined as:

$$W_t^e = E_t \{ \mathcal{M}_{t,1}[(1 - \tau_y)(d_{t+1}z_{t+1} + r_{t+1}b_{t+1})$$

$$+ b_{t+1} + q_{t+1}z_{t+1}] \}, \tag{4.71}$$

where we have substituted for $z_{t+1}q_t$ and b_{t+1} after multiplying Equation (4.66) by z_{t+1} and Equation (4.67) by b_{t+1}. Adding and subtracting $q_{t+1}z_{t+2}$ and b_{t+2} from the right side of Equation (4.71), we have:

$$W_t^e = E_t \{ \mathcal{M}_{t,1}[(1 - \tau_y)(d_{t+1}z_{t+1} + r_{t+1}b_{t+1})$$

$$+ q_{t+1}(z_{t+1} - z_{t+2}) - b_{t+2} + W_{t+1}^e + b_{t+1}] \}. \tag{4.72}$$

Increasing the time subscripts by 1 in Equation (4.69), solving this expression for $q_{t+1}(z_{t+1} - z_{t+2}) - b_{t+2}$, substituting into Equation (4.72) and simplifying, we obtain:

$$W_t^e = E_t \left\{ \mathcal{M}_{t,1}[(\tau_p - \tau_y)r_{t+1}b_{t+1} - \tau_y d_{t+1}z_{t+1} + N_{t+1}^\tau + W_{t+1}^e] \right\}.$$

Define $D_t \equiv b_{t+1}/q_t z_{t+1}$ as the debt-equity ratio and $\Psi_{t+1} \equiv d_{t+1}/q_t$ as the dividend-price ratio so that $q_t z_{t+1} = W_t^e/(1 + D_t)$. The first-order condition in Equation (4.67) can be expressed as $E_t(\mathcal{M}_{t+1}r_{t+1}) = [1 - E_t(\mathcal{M}_{t,1})]/(1 - \tau_y)$. Substituting these definitions and the rewritten first-order condition into the above expression results in

$$W_t^e = \frac{(\tau_p - \tau_y)}{1 - \tau_y}[1 - E_t(\mathcal{M}_{t+1})]\frac{W_t^e D_t}{1 + D_t} + E_t \left\{ \mathcal{M}_{t,1} \left[-\tau_y \frac{W_t^e \Psi_{t+1}}{1 + D_t} \right. \right.$$

$$\left. \left. + N_{t+1}^\tau + W_{t+1}^e \right] \right\}$$

$$= E_t \left[\Omega_{t+1}(N_{t+1}^\tau + W_{t+1}^e) \right], \tag{4.73}$$

where

$$\Omega_{t+1} \equiv \left[\frac{\mathcal{M}_{t,1}}{1 + \frac{D_t}{1+D_t}\frac{\tau_y - \tau_p}{1 - \tau_y}(1 - E_t\mathcal{M}_{t,1}) + \frac{\tau_y}{1+D_t}E_t(\mathcal{M}_{t,1}\Psi_{t+1})} \right].$$

Notice that if $\tau_y = \tau_p = 0$, then $\Omega_{t+1} = \mathcal{M}_{t+1}$. Generally, $\Omega_{t+1} < \mathcal{M}_{t+1}$ which indicates that the cost of capital to the firm, defined as $\rho = 1/\Omega - 1$ when there is taxation and $\rho = 1/\mathcal{M} - 1$ when there is not, increases with distortionary taxation. Notice that the cost of capital now depends on the firm's financial decisions such as the debt-equity ratio and the price-dividend ratio. The cost of capital with distortionary taxation can be expressed as:

$$\rho_{t+1} = \frac{1}{\mathcal{M}_{t,1}} \left[1 + \frac{b_{t+1}}{W_t^e}\frac{\tau_y - \tau_p}{1 - \tau_y}[1 - E_t(\mathcal{M}_{t,1})] \right.$$

$$\left. + \frac{\tau_y q_t z_{t+1}}{W_t^e}E_t\left(\mathcal{M}_{t,1}\Psi_{t+1}\right) - \mathcal{M}_{t,1} \right], \qquad (4.74)$$

which is a weighted average of the cost of debt capital and the cost of equity capital. The Modigliani-Miller theorem no longer holds because clearly the discount rate now depends on the financing decisions made by firms. We can incorporate the effects of distortionary taxation on the value of the firm and the equity return following the steps in Section 3.1.1.

The firm maximizes the present value of future cash flows, $W_t = N_t^{\tau} + W_t^e$, in two steps: first, it minimizes its cost of capital by choosing the optimal debt-equity ratio D_t and the optimal dividend policy. Second, given the minimum cost of capital, it determines the optimal capital and labor sequences $\{k_{t+s}\}_{s=1}^{\infty}$ and $\{l_{t+s}\}_{s=0}^{\infty}$. The optimization can be performed in this way because Ω_{t+1} depends only on the financial variables D_t and Ψ_{t+1} while net cash flow N_t^{τ} depends on the real production variables, k_t and l_t. Brock and Turnovsky study the firm's optimization problem and show that the optimal dividend policy and optimal capital structure will involve a corner solution: either all debt financing or all equity financing. To demonstrate this result, we differentiate the expression for ρ_{t+1} with respect to D_t and Ψ_{t+1}:

$$\text{sgn}\frac{\partial \rho_{t+1}}{\partial D_t} = \text{sgn}\left\{ \frac{\tau_y - \tau_p}{1 - \tau_y}[1 - E_t(\mathcal{M}_{t,1})] - \tau_y E_t\left(\mathcal{M}_{t,1}\Psi_{t+1}\right) \right\},$$

$$\text{sgn}\frac{\partial \rho_{t+1}}{\partial \Psi_{t+1}} = \text{sgn}\left\{ \tau_y E_t\left(\mathcal{M}_{t,1}\right) \right\}.$$

These conditions are similar to those derived by Brock and Turnovsky. Since τ_y is positive, the firm minimizes its cost of capital by minimizing the value of the dividend payout ratio, $E_t(\mathcal{M}_{t,1}\Psi_{t+1})$. Brock and Turnovsky note that in the absence of any constraints, this would involve repurchase of shares. However, this is discouraged under the U.S. tax code. Instead of modeling the legal constraints faced by firms, we assume that the firm minimizes the value of its dividend payments by setting $E_t(\mathcal{M}_{t,1}\Psi_{t+1}) = E_t(\mathcal{M}_{t,1}\tilde{\Psi})$, where $\tilde{\Psi}$ is the minimum payout rate taken to be exogenous. Then, the optimal financial mix is determined as follows:

$$ \text{if } \frac{\tau_y - \tau_p}{1 - \tau_y}[1 - E_t(\mathcal{M}_{t,1})] \; < \; \tau_y E_t\left(\mathcal{M}_{t,1}\tilde{\Psi}\right), \text{ set } D_t = \infty, \quad (4.75) $$

$$ \text{if } \frac{\tau_y - \tau_p}{1 - \tau_y}[1 - E_t(\mathcal{M}_{t,1})] \; > \; \tau_y E_t\left(\mathcal{M}_{t,1}\tilde{\Psi}\right), \text{ set } D_t = 0. \quad (4.76) $$

Notice that $D_t = \infty$ implies all bond financing while $D_t = 0$ involves all equity financing.

We can also derive versions of Equations (4.75) and (4.76) that allow for a capital gains tax τ_c on equities. In this case, if the net after-tax income on bonds exceeds the net after-tax income from equity, where the latter are taxed twice, first as corporate profits and second as personal income to shareholders, no investor will wish to hold stocks and the firm must engage in all debt financing. Otherwise, the firm will engage in equity financing. A sufficient condition for the former to hold is that the corporate profit tax rate τ_p exceeds the personal income tax rate τ_y.

Other explanations of corporate capital structure that are based on conflicts of interest among shareholders, bondholders, and managers have been provided by Myers [266], Jensen and Meckling [207], and others. Firms' financial structure and dividend policy have also been explained in terms of signaling models. In Ross's [284] signaling model, the debt-equity ratio serves as a signaling mechanism to outsiders about the firm's risk and profitability. Likewise, Bhattacharya [33] uses a signaling model to rationalize why firms pay dividends despite the fact that dividends are taxed at a higher rate than capital gains. Although private information considerations and incentive problems are potentially important ways for explaining corporate capital structure and other observed contractual arrangements, the papers cited above do not derive the form of the proposed arrangements as part of an optimal contract. In Chapter 7, we introduce models with private information explicitly and describe how to derive the optimal contract in a model with moral hazard.

3.2. Taxes and Capital Accumulation

We now turn to a discussion of the effects of taxation on capital accumulation. Since output is endogenously determined in this model, distortionary taxes also affect equilibrium asset prices and asset returns. In this section, we describe how a distortionary capital tax can be incorporated into the one-sector growth model.

Following Danthine and Donaldson [82] and Danthine, Donaldson, and Mehra [83], we construct exact solutions for the optimal consumption and investment policies and the equity price; these solutions are then used to discuss the comparative dynamics results associated with a capital income tax. The production function is given by:

$$f(k_t)\theta_t = k_t^\alpha \theta_t, \quad 0 < \alpha < 1, \tag{4.77}$$

where k_t is the capital stock. Under this formulation, there is only one factor of production. We also assume that capital depreciates 100% each period. We assume the stochastic technology shock θ_t is a first-order autoregressive lognormal process of the form:

$$\log(\theta_{t+1}) = \rho_0 + \rho_1 \log(\theta_t) + \epsilon_{t+1}, \quad |\rho_1| < 1, \tag{4.78}$$

where $\epsilon_{t+1} \sim N(0, \sigma^2)$.

In this model, firms take the rental rate on capital R_t as given and choose how much capital to rent from households. Their problem is defined as:

$$\max_{k_t} \pi_t = k_t^\alpha \theta_t - R_t k_t.$$

The first-order condition is:

$$\alpha k_t^{\alpha-1} \theta_t = R_t. \tag{4.79}$$

Households own the stocks of capital which they rent to firms. They also trade in claims to the output produced by firms. They are taxed on their capital income at the rate τ and receive a lump-sum transfer from the government. Their problem can be expressed as follows:

$$\max_{\{c_t\}_{t=0}^\infty, \{k_{t+1}\}_{t=0}^\infty} E\left\{ \sum_{t=0}^\infty \beta^t \log(c_t) \right\}$$

subject to $c_0 + k_1 = y_0$,

$$c_t + k_{t+1} + q_t z_{t+1} = (1 - \tau) R_t k_t + (q_t + d_t) z_t + g_t,$$

where q_t is the ex-dividend price of the equity, d_t is the dividend, g_t is the lump-sum transfer from the government, and y_0 is given. Here k_t denotes the household's holdings of capital at the beginning of period t and z_t and z_{t+1} are its share holdings at the beginning of t and $t + 1$, respectively. We assume that the total number of shares in each period is one.

Let K_t denote the per capita aggregate capital stock. The government taxes capital and then redistributes its revenue in a lump-sum fashion:

$$g_t = \tau R_t K_t = \tau \alpha K_t^\alpha \theta_t. \tag{4.80}$$

In equilibrium the individual holdings of capital equal the per capita holdings so that $k_t = K_t$. Furthermore, $z_{t+1} = z_t = 1$ and consumption plus investment equal total output, $c_t + K_{t+1} = f(K_t)\theta_t$.

When there are distortions such as taxes, the competitive equilibrium is not optimal and we need to solve for the equilibrium directly. For this simple model, we can also formulate a hypothetical social planning problem to solve for the consumption and investment policies with the distortionary tax. (See Exercise 3.) Given the policy functions, the equilibrium rental rate is defined by Equation (4.79); we construct the equity price after solving for the policy functions.

The optimal policy functions satisfy the first-order condition:

$$\frac{1}{c_t} = \beta(1 - \tau)E_t \left[\frac{1}{c_{t+1}} \alpha K_{t+1}^{\alpha-1} \theta_{t+1} \right]. \tag{4.81}$$

Notice that this example falls within the class of problems described in Exercise 1. Hence, we guess that the policy functions for consumption and investment have the form, $c_t = \phi y_t$ and $K_{t+1} = (1 - \phi)y_t$, where $y_t = f(K_t)\theta_t$ and ϕ is a constant to be determined. By our hypothesis,

$$c_{t+1} = \phi K_{t+1}^\alpha \theta_{t+1} = \phi[(1 - \phi)y_t]^\alpha \theta_{t+1}.$$

Substituting these expressions in Equation (4.81) yields:

$$\frac{1}{\phi y_t} = (1 - \tau)\beta E_t \left\{ \alpha[(1 - \phi)y_t]^{\alpha-1}\theta_{t+1} \frac{1}{\phi[(1 - \phi)y_t]^\alpha \theta_{t+1}} \right\}.$$

This can be solved for $\phi = 1 - \alpha\beta(1 - \tau)$, yielding the solutions for c_t and K_{t+1} as:

$$c_t = [1 - \alpha\beta(1 - \tau)]y_t, \tag{4.82}$$

$$K_{t+1} = \alpha\beta(1 - \tau)y_t. \tag{4.83}$$

To derive an expression for the equity price, we substitute for profits equal to $\pi_{t+i} = (1 - \alpha)K_{t+i}^{\alpha}\theta_{t+i}$ and $c_{t+i} = \phi y_{t+i}$ into the equilibrium condition for shares. This yields:

$$\frac{q_t}{y_t} = \beta E_t \left[(1 - \alpha) + \frac{q_{t+1}}{y_{t+1}} \right]. \tag{4.84}$$

We guess that the solution has the form, $q_t = \psi y_t$. Equating coefficients on both sides of Equation (4.84) yields $\psi = \beta(1 - \alpha) + \beta\psi$, or $\psi = (1 - \beta)^{-1}\beta(1 - \alpha)$. Thus, the equity price is given by:

$$q_t = \frac{\beta}{1 - \beta}(1 - \alpha)\theta_t K_t^{\alpha}. \tag{4.85}$$

Notice that consumption, investment, output, and the equity price exhibit persistence because they depend on current capital. When the technology shock is serially correlated, an additional source of persistence is introduced into the behavior of these variables. The capital tax rate also affects the entire time path of the endogenous variables although its effect on the equity price is through its effect on output and capital.

To examine the behavior of long-run averages, substitute recursively for past values of the capital stock using Equation (4.83) to obtain:

$$K_{t+1} = [\alpha\beta(1 - \tau)]^{\sum_{s=0}^{t} \alpha^s} \left(\prod_{s=0}^{t} \theta_s^{\alpha^{t-s}} \right) K_0^{\alpha^{t+1}}. \tag{4.86}$$

We can derive similar expressions for c_t, y_t, and q_t. Taking the limit as $t \to \infty$ yields expressions for the long-run averages as follows:

$$E(c_t) = [1 - \alpha\beta(1 - \tau)][\alpha\beta(1 - \tau)]^{\alpha/(1-\alpha)}\hat{\rho}_0 L,$$

$$E(K_{t+1}) = [\alpha\beta(1 - \tau)]^{1/(1-\alpha)}\hat{\rho}_0 L,$$

$$E(y_t) = [\alpha\beta(1 - \tau)]^{\alpha/(1-\alpha)}\hat{\rho}_0 L,$$

$$E(q_t) = \frac{\beta(1 - \alpha)}{1 - \beta}[\alpha\beta(1 - \tau)]^{\alpha/(1-\alpha)}\hat{\rho}_0 L,$$

where

$$L = \lim_{t\to\infty} E \left[\exp \left(\sum_{s=0}^{t-1} \alpha^s \sum_{r=0}^{t-s-1} \rho_1^{t-s-1-r}\epsilon_{r+1} \right) \right],$$

and

$$\hat{\rho}_0 = \lim_{t\to\infty} \exp \left(\rho_0 \sum_{s=0}^{t-1} \alpha^s \sum_{r=0}^{t-s-1} \rho_1^r \right)^{.5}.$$

It is easy to see that $\partial E(K_{t+1})/\partial \tau < 0$, $\partial E(y_t)/\partial \tau < 0$, $\partial E(q_t)/\partial \tau < 0$, and some manipulation yields $\partial E(c_t)/\partial \tau < 0$. Hence, long-run average consumption, investment, output, and the equity price all increase with a reduction in the tax rate. Notice that the capital income tax enters the equilibrium first-order condition in Equation (4.81) multiplicatively with the discount factor β. Becker [26] and Danthine and Donaldson [82] show more generally that the effects of a reduction in the income tax rate τ are identical to an increase in the discount factor β. Consequently, decreases in the tax rate lead to a decrease in the average equity return and the risk-free rate. When the technology shock is i.i.d., we can also show that the unconditional variances of output, consumption, and investment increase with a reduction in the tax rate. This implies that the benefits of a lower tax rate are associated with greater variability in the economy.

Other studies that analyze the effects of distortionary taxation on capital accumulation include Judd, who uses the perfect foresight model proposed by Brock and Turnovsky to study the effects of cuts in distortionary taxes followed by cuts in spending and a temporary substitution of government debt for distortionary income taxes ([212, 214]) as well as the question of incidence and redistributive effects of factor taxes ([211, 213]). Dotsey [101] studies the effect of production taxes in a stochastic growth model. In his model, the stochastic tax is assessed on the firm's profits and the tax rate is the only source of randomness. Coleman [73] studies the effect of a state-dependent income tax on the capital accumulation process. He also describes a numerical solution procedure called the monotone map method for computing the equilibrium in an economy with a distortionary tax. Bizer and Judd [35] also discuss the effects of distortionary taxation.

---

[5]It is easy to see that $K_0^{\alpha^{t+1}}$ converges to 1 in Equation (4.86). The expressions for L and $\hat{\rho}_0$ are obtained by noting that, conditional on K_0, θ_0:

$$\prod_{s=0}^{t} \theta_s^{\alpha^{t-s}} = \exp\left(\rho_0 \left(\sum_{s=0}^{t-1} \alpha^s\right)\left(\sum_{r=0}^{t-s-1} \rho_1^r\right)\right) \theta_0^{\left(\sum_{s=0}^{t} \rho_1^s \alpha^{t-s}\right)} \times$$

$$\exp\left(\sum_{s=0}^{t-1} \alpha^s \sum_{r=0}^{t-s-1} \rho_1^{t-s-1-r} \epsilon_{r+1}\right).$$

The quantity $\hat{\rho}_0$ exists since the exponent is a monotonically increasing sequence of positive numbers that is bounded above by $[1/(1-\rho_1)][1/(1-\alpha)]$. Likewise, $\sum_{s=0}^{t} \rho_1^s \alpha^{t-s} \to 0$ as $t \to \infty$. Let $\delta = \max(\alpha, \rho_1)$. Then $\sum_{s=0}^{t} \rho_1^s \alpha^{t-s} \le (t+1)\delta^{t+1}$. To show that $(t+1)\delta^{t+1} \to 0$ as $t \to \infty$, we can show that $\sum_{t=0}^{\infty} t\delta^t$ converges using a Ratio Test. Thus, the initial condition θ_0 disappears from the limiting expression.

3.3. The Q-theory of Investment

One of the most widely studied relationships in the empirical investment literature is the relationship between the price of existing capital relative to new capital, a relative price that is called "Tobin's Q," and investment expenditures. The Q-theory of investment says that the firm's demand for new capital goods, as captured by its investment expenditures, should be increasing in the value of capital relative to its replacement cost.

Yet in the version of the one-sector optimal growth model without adjustment costs, irreversibilities in investment, and other frictions, investment is defined as the difference between the current capital stock and next period's desired capital stock and the relative price of investment is always equal to one. To derive a well defined investment demand function, as specified by the Q-theory, it is necessary to introduce such frictions as adjustment costs and irreversibilities in investment. This is the topic that we address now.

Output in this economy is produced according to production function $y_t = f(K_t)\theta_t$, where K_t is measured as per capita. In equilibrium, it turns out that $l_t = 1$ so this causes no problem assuming that the production function displays constant returns to scale. The production function satisfies $f' > 0$, $f'' < 0$, $f'(0) = \infty$, and $f'(\infty) = 0$. The technology shock is i.i.d. and has a distribution that satisfies Assumption 4.2.

Adjustment costs in investment arise because installing new capital goods is disruptive, with the installation or adjustment costs increasing in the amount of new capital installed. Holding factor inputs fixed, the cost of the investment good in terms of the consumption good is increasing as the rate of investment increases. Let i_t/K_t be the ratio of investment to the beginning of period capital stock. As in Lucas [230], Treadway [329], Gould [157], and others, assume that the resources or output required to install i_t units of new capital are given by:

$$i_t[1 + h(i_t/K_t)].$$

Let $x \equiv i/K$. Then h is defined so that $h(0) = 0$, $h' \geq 0$, and $2h'(x) + xh''(x) > 0$ for all $x > 0$.

The per capita capital stock evolves according to:

$$K_{t+1} = i_t + (1 - \delta)K_t, \tag{4.87}$$

where $0 < \delta \leq 1$ is the depreciation rate. The irreversibility of investment is captured by constraining i_t to be nonnegative. Equivalently, investment is constrained to satisfy $K_{t+1} \geq (1 - \delta)K_t$. The resource or feasibility constraint for this economy is given by:

$$c_t + i_t[1 + h(i_t/K_t)] \leq f(K_t)\theta_t. \tag{4.88}$$

Unlike the standard one-sector growth model, the household cannot consume old capital when investment is constrained to be nonnegative. The feasibility constraint also accounts for the resources expended due to the adjustment costs.

We begin by describing the social planning problem. The social planner solves:

$$V(K_t, \theta_t) = \max_{c_t, i_t}\{U(c_t) + \beta E_t[V(K_{t+1}, \theta_{t+1})]\} \tag{4.89}$$

subject to the resource constraint in Equation (4.88), the nonnegativity constraints $c_t, i_t \geq 0$, and given the law of motion for capital in Equation (4.87) and the fixed initial capital stock, K_0. Let λ_t^p denote the multiplier for the resource constraint in Equation (4.88) and let μ_t^p denote the multiplier on the nonnegativity constraint, $i_t \geq 0$. Let $x_t \equiv i_t/K_t$ and $H(x) \equiv 1 + h(x) + xh'(x)$. The first-order conditions are:

$$U'(c_t) = \lambda_t^p, \tag{4.90}$$

$$\lambda_t^p H(x_t) = \beta E_t[V_1(K_{t+1}, \theta_{t+1})] + \mu_t^p. \tag{4.91}$$

The envelope condition is:

$$V_1(K_t, \theta_t) = \lambda_t^p[f'(K_t)\theta_t + (x_t)^2 h'(x_t)]$$
$$+ (1 - \delta)\beta E_t[V_1(K_{t+1}, \theta_{t+1})]. \tag{4.92}$$

Notice that the expected value of the slope of the value function next period enters on the right side of the envelope condition. This term enters through the law of motion for the capital stock. Because of the irreversibility assumption, investment today results in a loss of $1 - \delta$ units tomorrow, discounted to today. Notice that if $\mu_t^p = 0$ for all t, then

$$\lambda_t^p H(x_t) = \beta E_t[V_1(K_{t+1}, \theta_{t+1})],$$

and Equation (4.92) becomes

$$V_1(K_t, \theta_t) = \lambda_t^p[f'(K_t)\theta_t + (x_t)^2 h'(x_t) + (1 - \delta)H(x_t)].$$

In the absence of adjustment costs so that $H(x_t) = 1$ and $h'(x_t) = 0$, this model becomes a model with irreversible investment. The optimal allocation for the social planning problem can be determined using the standard methods for solving dynamic programming problems.

Next, we describe the market economy. We assume that the firm is the owner of the capital stock and is a price-taker. The firm not only participates in the goods market where it sells consumption goods and new capital goods, it also participates in the used capital good market. Used capital sells for a price of $p_{k,t}$ and the value of the capital stock that the firm can sell at the end of the period is $p_{k,t}(1-\delta)k_t$. It also purchases used capital of value $p_{k,t}k_t^d$.

The firm's receipts from selling its output consist of the consumption good sales, c_t^s, and the value of investment goods sold, i_t^s. The firm pays wages w_t, buys used capital $p_{k,t}k_t^d$, and buys investment goods i_t^d. The law of motion for the firm's capital stock is:

$$k_{t+1} = k_t^d + i_t^d. \tag{4.93}$$

The firm's gross profits are:

$$\pi_t = f(k_t)\theta_t - w_t l_t - i_t^d h(i_t^d/k_t),$$

where the cost of installing new capital i_t^d is included. Gross profits are disbursed according to Equation (4.47). Purchases of used and new capital are financed according to:

$$p_{k,t}k_t^d + i_t^d = RE_t + q_t(z_{t+1} - z_t) + b_{t+1}. \tag{4.94}$$

The net cash flow of the firm is defined as:

$$N_t \equiv f(k_t)\theta_t + p_{k,t}(1-\delta)k_t - w_t l_t$$
$$-i_t^d[1 + h(i_t^d/k_t)] - p_{k,t}k_t^d. \tag{4.95}$$

(Compare this expression with Equation (4.49) in which the price of capital is always equal to unity and there are no adjustment costs.) Notice that we can solve Equations (4.47) and (4.94) as before for RE_t, equate the resulting expressions, and use the definition of N_t to express the net cash flow as $N_t = d_t z_t + (1 + r_t)b_t + q_t(z_t - z_{t+1}) - b_{t+1}$.[6]

The household's problem is standard and identical to the problem in Section 3.1. It consists of choosing sequences for c_t, z_{t+1}, and b_{t+1} to maximize the objective function in Equation (4.41) subject to the wealth constraint in Equation (4.42) and given the restriction that $0 \le l_t \le 1$. The first-order conditions are identical to Equations (4.43)–(4.45).

---

[6]This formulation of the firm's problem is similar to Abel and Blanchard [3].

The firm maximizes

$$W(k_t, \theta_t) = N_t + E_t[\mathcal{M}_{t,1}W(k_{t+1}, \theta_t)] \qquad (4.96)$$

subject to $i_t^d \geq 0$ and given k_t by choosing l_t, k_t^d, i_t^d. The first-order conditions are:

$$w_t = f(k_t)\theta_t - f'(k_t)\theta_t, \qquad (4.97)$$

$$p_{k,t} = E_t[\mathcal{M}_{t,1}W_1(k_{t+1}, \theta_{t+1})], \qquad (4.98)$$

$$H(i_t^d/k_t) = \mu_{i,t} + E_t[\mathcal{M}_{t,1}W_1(k_{t+1}, \theta_{t+1})]. \qquad (4.99)$$

The envelope condition is:

$$W_1(k_t, \theta_t) = f'(k_t)\theta_t + \left(i_t^d/k_t\right)^2 h'\left(i_t^d/k_t\right) + (1-\delta)p_{k,t}. \qquad (4.100)$$

We consider the case of $\mu_{i,t} = 0$ first. In this case, investment i_t^d is strictly positive so that Equation (4.99) implies

$$H(i_t^d/k_t) = p_{k,t}. \qquad (4.101)$$

The left side of this expression equals the marginal cost of investment and the right side is the shadow price of installed capital. Since H' is strictly increasing, we can solve Equation (4.101) for i_t/k_t as an increasing function of the shadow price of capital. If we define the replacement cost of new capital to be equal to the price of output (which equals unity in this model), then Equation (4.101) yields a relationship between $\mathcal{Q}$ and investment as hypothesized by Tobin.

Sargent [298] studies a special case of the model described above by assuming that there are no adjustment costs, so that $H(x) \equiv 1$ while retaining the assumption that investment is irreversible. In this case, $\mathcal{Q}_t$ satisfies $\mathcal{Q}_t = p_{k,t}$. When there are no adjustment costs ($H(x_t) = 1$), the first-order conditions reduce to $1 = \mu_{i,t} + p_{k,t}$. Suppose that $\mu_{i,t} > 0$ so that $i_t^d = 0$ in Equation (4.99); then $\mathcal{Q}_t < 1$. If $\mu_{i,t} = 0$, then $\mathcal{Q}_t = 1$. Thus, we obtain a determinate relationship between investment expenditures and the ratio of the shadow price of existing capital to its replacement cost, although this relationship is somewhat complicated. We study this relationship in more detail below.

We now drop the assumption that $H(x) = 1$ to explore the joint effects of adjustment costs and irreversibility in investment. To start, notice that in equilibrium, all equity shares are held, $z_t = z_{t+1} = 1$, all bonds are held, $b_{t+1}^d = b_{t+1}$, all used capital is purchased, $k_t^d = (1-\delta)k_t$, and all output is purchased, $f(k_t)\theta_t = c_t + i_t[1 + h(i_t/k_t)]$. Finally, the aggregate capital stock equals the stock owned by the representative firm, $K_t = k_t$. Let $\hat{c}(K, \theta)$ and $\hat{i}(K, \theta)$ denote the social planner's policy functions for consumption and investment that satisfy the feasibility condition in Equation (4.88), the valuation function in Equation (4.89), and the first-order conditions in Equations (4.90) and (4.91). Let $\mathcal{M}_{t,1} = \beta U'[\hat{c}(\hat{K}_{t+1}, \theta_{t+1}]/U'[\hat{c}(K_t, \theta_t]$ denote the intertemporal MRS under the policy function $\hat{c}$ where $\hat{K}_{t+1} = \hat{i}(K_t, \theta_t) + (1 - \delta)K_t$.

Define the equilibrium rental rate under the policy $\hat{i}$ as:

$$R(\hat{K}_{t+1}, \theta_{t+1}) \equiv f'(\hat{K}_{t+1})\theta_{t+1} + \left[\hat{i}(\hat{K}_{t+1}, \theta_{t+1})/\hat{K}_{t+1}\right]^2 \times$$

$$h'\left[\hat{i}(\hat{K}_{t+1}, \theta_{t+1})/\hat{K}_{t+1}\right].$$

Notice that the quantity $(x_t)^2 h'(x_t)$ is the reduction in the opportunity cost of installation $i_t h(i_t/k_t)$ made possible by an additional unit of capital. Thus, the equilibrium rental rate equals the total marginal product of capital. Using Equations (4.98), (4.99) and (4.100), the equilibrium price of used capital is a function satisfying:

$$p_k(K_t, \theta_t) = \min\left(H\left[\hat{i}(K_t, \theta_t)/K_t\right], E_t\left\{\mathcal{M}_{t,1}\left[R(\hat{K}_{t+1}, \theta_{t+1})\right.\right.\right.$$

$$\left.\left.\left. +(1 - \delta)p_k(\hat{K}_{t+1}, \theta_{t+1})\right]\right\}\right). \tag{4.102}$$

Under the assumption that $E_t[\mathcal{M}_{t,1} R(\hat{K}_{t+1}, \theta_{t+1})] < 1$, we can show that there is a unique price function $p^\star(K_t, \theta_t)$ satisfying Equation (4.102). As noted above, the measure of Q defined from this functional equation will equal one or fall below unity depending on whether investment is strictly positive or not in any given period. We can interpret this as a version of the Q-theory of investment although the implied relationship is an equilibrium relationship between two endogenously determined variables.

Let us assume that the irreversibility constraint is not binding in Equation (4.99). Then we can solve Equation (4.98) after substituting the envelope condition in Equation (4.100) to obtain an expression for $p_{k,t}$ as:

$$p_{k,t} = E_t\left\{\sum_{i=1}^{\infty}(1 - \delta)^i \mathcal{M}_{t,i}\left[f'(k_{t+i})\theta_{t+i} + (x_{t+i})^2 h'(x_{t+i})\right]\right\}, \tag{4.103}$$

which is well defined since the solution to Equation (4.102) is bounded. Thus, the shadow price of capital is the expected discounted value of the future marginal products of capital, the discount rate equal to the product of one minus the depreciation rate and the marginal rate of substitution for consumption between periods t and $t + i$.

When the irreversibility constraint is not binding, we can also show that the value of installed capital at the end of the period, $p_{k,t}k_{t+1}$, is equal to the ex-dividend value of the firm, W_t^e. To show this result, substitute the envelope condition in Equation (4.98) and multiply both sides by k_{t+1} to obtain:

$$p_{k,t}k_{t+1} = E_t \left(\mathcal{M}_{t,1} \left\{ f'(k_{t+1})\theta_{t+1}k_{t+1} + i_{t+1}[x_{t+1}h'(x_{t+1})] \right. \right.$$

$$\left. \left. +(1-\delta)p_{k,t+1}k_{t+1} \right\} \right).$$

Since the production function is linearly homogeneous, the first term is equal to $f(k_{t+1})\theta_{t+1} - f'(k_{t+1})$ which is also equal to output minus wage payments. Add and subtract the term $p_{k,t+1}i_{t+1}$ to the above expression. This yields:

$$p_{k,t}k_{t+1} = E_t \left(\mathcal{M}_{t,1} \left\{ f(k_{t+1})\theta_{t+1} - w_{t+1} + (1-\delta)p_{k,t+1}k_{t+1} \right. \right.$$

$$\left. \left. -i_{t+1}[1 + h(x_{t+1})] - p_{k,t+1}k_{t+1}^d + p_{k,t+1}k_{t+2} \right\} \right),$$

where we obtain $p_{k,t+1}i_{t+1} = p_{k,t+1}(k_{t+2} - k_{t+1}^d)$ by using the law of motion for the firm's capital stock and use Equations (4.98) and (4.99) to simplify $i_{t+1}[x_{t+1}h'(x_{t+1})] - p_{k,t+1}i_{t+1}$ as $i_{t+1}[x_{t+1}h'(x_{t+1})] - H(x_t)i_{t+1} = i_{t+1}[1 + h(x_{t+1})]$. Iterating this expression forward and imposing a terminal condition that the discounted value of the installed capital stock goes to zero as t goes to infinity (which will hold since the price of capital is bounded), we obtain:

$$p_{k,t}k_{t+1} = E_t \left(\sum_{i=1}^{\infty} \mathcal{M}_{t,i} \left\{ f(k_{t+i})\theta_{t+i} - w_{t+i} + (1-\delta)p_{k,t+i}k_{t+i} \right. \right.$$

$$\left. \left. -i_{t+i}[1 + h(x_{t+i})] - p_{k,t+i}k_{t+i}^d \right\} \right)$$

$$\equiv W_t^e. \tag{4.104}$$

Early tests of the $\mathcal{Q}$-theory are due to von Furstenberg [141]. From our discussion above, recall the $\mathcal{Q}$ is the market value of an additional unit of capital relative to its replacement costs but in practice, it is typically measured as the ratio of the market value of capital to its replacement cost. The former quantity is often referred to as *marginal* $\mathcal{Q}$, whereas the latter is referred to as *average* $\mathcal{Q}$. Hayashi [184] shows that average $\mathcal{Q}$ is equal to marginal $\mathcal{Q}$ for a competitive firm that faces a constant returns to scale production function and a linearly homogeneous installation cost function. This is just the result that we derived in Equation (4.104). Abel [1] tests a version using quadratic costs of adjustment in investment. Abel and Blanchard [4] use a version of the relationship in Equation (4.103) to construct a measure of marginal Q that does not rely on stock market data. They find that regressing investment on their measure of marginal Q implies that a large, serially correlated fraction of investment is left unexplained, similar to results from regressions of investment on average Q

This analysis can be extended to other models of investment. Altuğ [11] derives restrictions between the price of new and used capital goods and the term structure of real interest rates for the time-to-build model of investment. Although the empirical work described above is implemented with aggregate data, the theoretical framework constrains the behavior of individual firms. A few recent papers have employed panel data on firms to exploit both cross-sectional and time series variation in prices and quantities. Hayashi and Inoue [186] and Blundell, Bond, Devereux, and Schiantarelli [37] estimate Q models of investment using panel data on firms from Japan and the U.K., respectively. The former find that a tax-adjusted measure of Q is a significant determinant of investment but cash flow variables are also significant in some years while the latter find that the coefficient on Q is significant but small.

4.   Dynamic Discrete Choice

In different versions of the one-sector optimal growth model that we considered above, we made the assumption that all choice variables could be described in terms of continuous-valued variables. Aside from the model with irreversible investment, we did not allow for the possibility of corner solutions or discrete choice sets. Yet many important applications with production and capital accumulation involve discrete choices in a dynamic setting. As an example, we can consider the problem of choosing from a discrete set of risky investment projects.

Another important reason for studying dynamic discrete choice models is the failure of representative consumer models that are estimated using aggregate data. Since most individual decison-making problems involve dynamic discrete choice, it is possible to use disaggregated or panel data to study a rich set of intertemporal optimization and equilibrium problems. Unlike models with continuous interior choices that satisfy first-order conditions with equality, the optimal policy functions for dynamic discrete choice problems are characterized by inequality conditions. Consequently, the Euler equation estimation methods that we described in Chapter 3 cannot be used to estimate dynamic discrete choice models.

One approach to estimating such models is to solve numerically the valuation function characterizing optimal choices and to use these numerical solutions as part of the maximum likelihood estimation of the model. We illustrate these issues in the contexts of the applications by Miller [260] and Rust [294].

As a way of relating the material in this section to the problem of asset valuation, we describe how the valuation functions or solutions to the model of optimal search and the matching model can be used to value random income streams generated by discrete alternatives. In this sense, the models we consider in this section are also models of asset valuation.

4.1. A Search Model

We begin by describing a model of search due to Weitzman [335] as an introduction to dynamic discrete choice models.[7] According to this model, an individual can choose to sample from a discrete set of alternatives with random payoffs. This problem is typically referred to as Pandora's problem because the reward from a given alternative cannot be determined until this alternative is actually sampled. It provides a useful framework for formulating problems in capital accumulation such as oil exploration or choosing among alternative professions in which two or more discrete alternatives cannot be sampled simultaneously.

There are n alternatives. Each alternative or box i has a potential reward with probability distribution function $F_i(x_i)$, which is independent of the other rewards. It costs c_i to open box i and to learn its contents, which become known after t_i periods. At each stage, Pandora must decide whether or not she will continue to search. If she stops, then she collects the maximum reward she has so far uncovered. If she continues to search, then she must decide which box to open next, pay the fee for sampling this box, and wait for the outcome. An initial amount x_0 is available, representing a fallback reward that can be collected if no sampling is undertaken or every sampled reward turns out to be less than x_0. Pandora maximizes the net present value of her rewards. The optimal decision rule for Pandora's sequential decision problem involves determining whether to stop or to continue searching at each stage and if so, which box to sample next.

We will illustrate the nature of the optimal decision rule by formulating this problem as a dynamic programming problem. We denote the

---

[7]For a further discussion of search models more generally, see the text by Devine and Kiefer [90].

collection of n boxes by I and the set of sampled boxes by S. Thus, $I = S \cup \bar{S}$ where $\bar{S}$ is the set of boxes that have not been opened yet. The variable y denotes the maximum reward from the sampled boxes:

$$y = \max_{i \in S \cup \{0\}} x_i. \tag{4.105}$$

Notice that the state of the system is described by the pair $(\bar{S}, y)$; all information about the boxes that were previously opened is contained in y since the rewards are independent. We define $V(\bar{S}, y)$ as the expected discounted present value of following an optimal policy from the current period, given the set of closed boxes $\bar{S}$ and the maximum sampled reward y. The valuation function satisfies the recursive relationship:

$$V(\bar{S}, y) = \max \left\{ y, \max_{i \in \bar{S}} \left\{ -c_i + \beta^{t_i} \left[V(\bar{S} - i, y) \int_{-\infty}^{y} dF_i(x_i) + \right. \right. \right.$$
$$\left. \left. \left. V(\bar{S} - i, x_i) \int_{y}^{\infty} dF_i(x_i) \right] \right\} \right\}, \tag{4.106}$$

where $V(\emptyset, x) = x$. Given the current state $(\bar{S}, y)$, Pandora can choose to stop searching and collect the reward y or she can sample box $i \in \bar{S}$. Her expected discounted reward depends on whether the reward from box i is greater or less than the maximum reward she has collected so far as well as the time lag t_i with which the reward on the i'th box is collected.

Notice that each alternative or box is characterized by the fee for opening it, the time lag for finding out about its contents, and the probability distribution for the reward it contains. Weitzman shows that the optimal decision rule for this problem implies that there is an index or reservation price associated with each box that summarizes all information about that box. This index or reservation price determines which of the unopened boxes to open and when to stop searching.

Suppose now that there are only two boxes, one which is already opened and offers the sure reward z_i. If the searcher elects to stop searching, she receives the sure reward z_i. If she continues searching, she receives the expected reward:

$$-c_i + \beta^{t_i} \left[z_i \int_{-\infty}^{z_i} dF_i(x_i) + \int_{z_i}^{\infty} x_i dF_i(x_i) \right]. \tag{4.107}$$

Notice that the searcher is indifferent between opening the box and taking the sure reward if z_i equals the expression above. This yields the condition:

$$c_i = \beta^{t_i} \int_{z_i}^{\infty} (x_i - z_i) dF_i(x_i) - (1 - \beta^{t_i}) z_i. \tag{4.108}$$

It is possible to derive an alternative interpretation of Equation (4.108) by assuming that there are only type i boxes but there are an infinite number of them. If z_i is defined as the discounted value of following an optimal search policy, then clearly the expression in Equation (4.107) equals z_i. We define z_i as the reservation price associated with alternative i. It is straightforward to show that the formula determining the reservation price is well defined. Define the function $H_i(z)$ from the right side of Equation (4.108). The function $H_i(z)$ is continuous and monotonic. Furthermore, $H_i(-\infty) = \infty$ and $H_i(\infty) = -\infty$ ($= 0$ if $\beta = 1$). Thus, as long as $c_i > 0$ or $\beta < 1$, there exists a solution to z_i to the Equation $c_i = H_i(z_i)$.

The optimal policy for Pandora's problem is characterized as follows: if a box is to be opened, it should be that closed box with highest reservation price, and terminate search whenever the maximum sampled reward exceeds the reservation price of every closed box. A proof of this assertion is provided by Weitzman. We can demonstrate the optimality of this decision rule by considering a version of this problem in which there are two alternatives, denoted A and B, which represent two alternative investment projects at time t.

Project A takes at most m periods to complete and it yields a certain return of a in period $t+m$. However, in each period, there is a probability $\pi_{a,s}$ that the project will yield a return a in period $t+s$, conditional on not having done so in the earlier period. More precisely, $\pi_{a,s} = \Pr(a_{t+s+1,t} = a | a_{t+s,t} = 0)$ for $s = 0, \ldots, m-2$ where $a_{t+s,t}$, $s = 0, \ldots, m-2$ are random variables that show the payoff at time $t + s$ of a project begun at time t. Notice that $\Pr(a_{t,t} = a) = \pi_{a,0}$ and $\Pr(a_{t,t} = 0) = 1 - \pi_{a,0}$. Project B takes at most n periods to complete and yields the reward b with certainty n periods after it is started. In each period, there is a probability $\pi_{b,s}$ for $s = 0, \ldots, n-2$ that it will yield the return b, conditional on this not having occurred in the previous period. The decision problem confronting the investor is which project to choose at time t, given that both projects cannot be undertaken simultaneously.

For this simple example, we can derive the optimal policy by comparing the present value of undertaking project A and then B versus the present value of undertaking B and then A. The former is computed as follows:

$$PV_{A,B} = \pi_{a,0}a + \beta\pi_{a,1}a + \cdots + \beta^{m-1}a +$$
$$\beta^m \pi_{b,0}b + \beta^{m+1}\pi_{b,1}b + \cdots + \beta^{m+n-1}b. \qquad (4.109)$$

The present value of undertaking B first and then A is:

$$PV_{B,A} = \pi_{b,0}b + \beta\pi_{b,1}b + \cdots + \beta^{n-1}b +$$
$$\beta^n\pi_{a,0}a + \beta^{n+1}\pi_{a,1}a + \cdots + \beta^{m+n-1}a. \qquad (4.110)$$

The investor will undertake A first and then B if $PV_{A,B} > PV_{B,A}$. Using the expressions above, this can be expressed as:

$$a(\pi_{a,0} + \beta\pi_{a,1} + \cdots + \beta^{m-1})(1 - \beta^n) >$$
$$b(\pi_{b,0} + \beta\pi_{b,1} + \cdots + \beta^{n-1})(1 - \beta^m).$$

If we divide both sides of this expression by $(1 - \beta^n)$ and $(1 - \beta^m)$ and notice that $\sum_{s=t}^{t+m-1} \beta^s = (1 - \beta^m)/(1 - \beta)$, we obtain the expression:

$$\frac{E_t[\sum_{s=t}^{t+m-1} \beta^{s-t} a_{t+s,t}]}{\sum_{s=t}^{t+m-1} \beta^{s-t}} > \frac{E_t[\sum_{s=t}^{t+n-1} \beta^{s-t} b_{t+s,t}]}{\sum_{s=t}^{t+n-1} \beta^{s-t}}. \qquad (4.111)$$

We can define the quantity that appears on each side of this expression as the dynamic allocation index (DAI) associated with each project. The DAI provides a simple valuation formula for each risky investment in terms of its future expected payoffs. It is straightforward to demonstrate that the DAI satisfies the definition of a reservation price described by Equation (4.108). In this simple example, there is no cost associated with sampling and the investor knows for sure that the project will yield a return after a specific time interval so that there is no choice about terminating search before both alternatives are sampled. In the matching model we present below, this is not the case.

4.2.   A Matching Model

We now describe a version of this model in which the set of alternatives from which an individual chooses at a given date are defined in terms of jobs which yield different future random payoffs. As in Pandora's problem, the individual must choose which job to work in without initially knowing her productivity on the job. She can discover her productivity in a given job only through experience.

The person receives a return denoted $x_{m,t}$ from working on the m'th job at time t chosen from some job set M. The return is not directly observed unless the person works on the job and it is the sum of two components:

$$x_{m,t} = \xi_m + \sigma_m \epsilon_{m,t}. \qquad (4.112)$$

The first is a time-invariant match parameter. The person does not observe ξ_m directly before acquiring any experience on the job but believes it to be normally distributed $N(\gamma_m, \delta_m^2)$. The second component is never observed but σ_m is known and $\epsilon_{m,t}$ is an independent $N(0,1)$ random variable. Thus, the individual cannot determine match quality exactly but forms a guess by using prior information from previous matches combined with the return history from the current match. Notice that this is a generalization of Weitzman's framework because there is learning about the random payoff associated with each discrete alternative.

Let the indicator variable $d_{m,s}$ be unity if the m'th job is chosen and 0 otherwise. Define $\tau_{m,t}$ as the measure of experience the worker has accumulated in the m'th job by time t:

$$\tau_{m,t} = \sum_{s=0}^{t-1} d_{m,s}. \tag{4.113}$$

As the person accumulates experience on a given job, she can use observations on returns $x_{m,t}$ to update her beliefs about the distribution of the match parameter ξ_m using Bayes' rule, which states that the posterior distribution for γ_m is obtained using the prior distribution and the likelihood function for the sample of returns. Using this updating scheme, we can show that a person's beliefs about the mean and variance of the match parameter evolves as:

$$\gamma_{m,t} = \left[\delta_m^{-2} \gamma_m + \sigma_m^{-2} \sum_{s=0}^{t-1} x_{m,s} d_{m,s} \right] / \delta_{m,t}^{-1}, \tag{4.114}$$

$$\delta_{m,t} = \left(\delta_m^{-2} + \tau_{m,t} \sigma_m^{-2} \right)^{-1/2}. \tag{4.115}$$

(See Exercise 7.) Notice that beliefs change only with experience on the job. As the individual gains more experience on the job, the variance of her beliefs about the match parameter falls ($\partial \delta_{m,t}/\tau_{m,t} < 0$). Since each additional observation on returns $x_{m,s}$ is weighted by the inverse of the variance, such additional observations receive a smaller weight in the revised estimate of $\gamma_{m,t}$. Similarly, if σ_m^2 is large, observations on returns receive less weight relative to prior beliefs. One would expect that the more information the individual gets from returns, the more likely she is to leave the job during the initial stages. If learning is fast, the individual will not experience turnover after the initial stages of learning because she can ascertain her match parameter quickly.

Let $d_t = (d_{1,t}, \ldots, d_{M,t})'$ denote the $M \times 1$ vector showing the agent's job choice at time t where $d_{m,t} \in \{0,1\}$ and $\sum_{m=1}^{M} d_{m,t} = 1$. The agent's problem is to solve:

$$\max_{\{d_t\}_{t=0}^{\infty}} E_0\left\{\sum_{t=0}^{\infty}\sum_{m\in M}\beta^t d_{m,t}x_{m,t}\right\}, \tag{4.116}$$

where E_t denotes expectation conditioned on information $\{\gamma_{m,t},\delta_{m,t}\}_{m\in M}$ available at time t.

In the optimal control literature, the problem we described above is known as a multiarmed bandit problem and its solution has been characterized by Gittins and Jones [153]. This solution implies that there is an index associated with each job depending on beliefs about its future returns and the optimal decision is to choose the job with the largest index. Following Miller [260], the dynamic allocation index for the m'th job, $\text{DAI}_m(\gamma_{m,t},\delta_{m,t})$, is defined as:

$$\text{DAI}_m(\gamma_{m,t},\delta_{m,t}) = \sup_{\tau\geq t}\left\{\frac{E_t\left[\sum_{r=t}^{\tau}\beta^{r-t}x_{m,r}\right]}{E_t\left(\sum_{r=t}^{\tau}\beta^{r-t}\right)}\right\}. \tag{4.117}$$

The index can be thought of as a valuation function for the problem of choosing at time t a stopping time τ to maximize the expected return from remaining on the m'th job divided by the current value of receiving a unitary return over that period. It is similar to the reservation price that we characterized for Pandora's problem.

The valuation function for the individual's problem shows the value of optimized lifetime income, which involves comparing the present value of income from each job m. The solution proposed by Gittins and Jones says that an individual will choose the job with the largest dynamic allocation index:

$$\text{DAI}_k(\gamma_{k,t},\delta_{k,t}) = \max_{m\in M}\{\text{DAI}_m(\gamma_{m,t},\delta_{m,t})\}. \tag{4.118}$$

This decision rule greatly simplifies the solution of the dynamic discrete choice problem. In general, the decision rule will depend on the characteristics of all jobs, described by beliefs about the mean and variance of the distribution of match parameters, $(\gamma_{k,t},\delta_{k,t})_{m\in M}$. On the other hand, the decision rule in Equation (4.118) implies that the index associated with a job m depends on the characteristics of that job alone and the problem is to choose the job with the largest index.

We can further simplify this problem by deriving an alternative representation for the dynamic allocation index associated with the m'th job. A job yields two benefits: the expected reward from working in that job and information from future returns. The expected reward is $\gamma_{m,t}$, which is just the updated mean of the match parameter. It turns out that we can define information from future returns using the standard index:

$$D(\sigma_m^2, \beta) \equiv \mathrm{DAI}_m(0, 1).$$

This is the valuation function for a job whose match parameter ξ_m is drawn from a standard normal distribution $N(0, 1)$ and whose return $x_{m,t}$ is perturbed by a normal random variable with variance σ_m^2. Define the information factor associated with job m as $\alpha_m \equiv \sigma_m^2 \delta_m^{-2}$. We have the following proposition.

Proposition 4.1 $\mathrm{DAI}_m(\gamma_{m,t}, \delta_{m,t}) = \gamma_{m,t} + \delta_{m,t} D(\alpha_m + \tau_{m,t}, \beta).$

PROOF
Multiplying and dividing the right side of $\mathrm{DAI}_m(\gamma_{m,t}, \delta_{m,t})$ in Equation (4.117) by $\delta_{m,t}$ and adding and subtracting $\gamma_{m,t}$ to the resulting expression yields

$$\mathrm{DAI}_m(\gamma_{m,t}, \delta_{m,t}) =$$

$$\gamma_{m,t} + \sup_{\tau \geq t} \left\{ \frac{E_t \left[\sum_{r=t}^{\tau} \beta^{r-t} \delta_{m,t}^{-1}(x_{m,r} - \gamma_{m,t}) \right]}{E_t \left(\sum_{r=t}^{\tau} \beta^{r-t} \right)} \right\} \delta_{m,t}.$$

But the definition of $x_{m,r}$ and $\delta_{m,t}$ in Equations (4.112) and (4.115) implies that $\delta_{m,t}^{-1}(x_{m,r} - \gamma_{m,t}) = \delta_{m,t}^{-1}(\xi_m - \gamma_{m,t}) + (\alpha_m + \tau_{m,t})^{1/2} \epsilon_{m,t}$. At time t beliefs about the match parameter are distributed as $N(\gamma_{m,t}, \delta_{m,t})$; thus, beliefs about $\delta_{m,t}^{-1}(\xi_m - \gamma_{m,t})$ are distributed as $N(0, 1)$. Using the definition of the standard index $D(\sigma_m^2, \beta)$ implies that

$$D(\alpha_m + \tau_{m,t}, \beta) = \sup_{\tau \geq t} \left\{ \frac{E_t \left[\sum_{r=t}^{\tau} \beta^{r-t} \delta_{m,t}^{-1}(x_{m,r} - \gamma_{m,t}) \right]}{E_t \left(\sum_{r=t}^{\tau} \beta^{r-t} \right)} \right\},$$

yielding the result. ∎

The previous result shows that evaluating the decision rule in Equation (4.117) depends on evaluating the standard index $D(\alpha_m, \beta)$. For this purpose, define $\mathcal{C}$ as the space of bounded, continuous functions $\{f : (-\infty, \infty) \times (0, \infty) \to \mathbb{R}\}$ and consider the following mapping:

$$T[f(\gamma, \alpha)] = \beta \int_{-\infty}^{\infty} \max \left(0, (1 - \beta)\{\gamma + \epsilon[\alpha(\alpha + 1)]^{-1/2}\} + \right.$$

$$\left. f\{\gamma + \epsilon[\alpha(\alpha + 1)]^{-1/2}, \alpha + 1\} \right) d\Phi(\epsilon), \tag{4.119}$$

where $\Phi(\epsilon)$ is the standard normal cumulative probability distribution. Notice that T maps $\mathcal{C}$ into itself. For any $f \in \mathcal{C}$, T is bounded because it is the maximum of zero and

$$\beta \left(1 - \beta\right)\{\gamma + \sqrt{2\pi}[\alpha(\alpha + 1)]^{-1/2}+$$

$$Ef\{\gamma + \epsilon[\alpha(\alpha + 1)]^{-1/2}, \alpha + 1\}\right),$$

which is bounded. Since f is continuous, Tf is also continuous. We have the following proposition.

Proposition 4.2 *The mapping T is a contraction which has unique fixed point $g(\gamma, \alpha) \in \mathcal{C}$ satisfying $g(\gamma, \alpha) = T[g(\gamma, \alpha)]$. Furthermore, for all $(\alpha, \beta) \in (0, \infty) \times (0, 1)$, the standard index $D(\alpha, \beta)$ can be obtained as the solution of the implicit equation:*

$$D(\alpha, \beta) = (1 - \beta)^{-1}\alpha^{1/2}g[-\alpha^{-1/2}D(\alpha, \beta), \alpha]. \tag{4.120}$$

PROOF

We first show that the mapping T satisfies Blackwell's conditions for a contraction. If $h \geq f$ for some $h \in \mathcal{C}$, $T(h) \geq T(f)$. Furthermore, for some constant a,

$$\begin{aligned}
T(f + a) &= \beta \max\left[0, (1 - \beta)\left(\gamma + \sqrt{2\pi}[\alpha(\alpha + 1)]^{-1/2}+\right.\right. \\
&\qquad\qquad \left.\left. Ef\{\gamma + \epsilon[\alpha(\alpha + 1)]^{-1/2}, \alpha + 1\}\} + a\right)\right] \\
&\leq T(f) + \beta a.
\end{aligned}$$

Thus, T is contraction. Since the space $\mathcal{C}$ is complete, the Contraction Mapping Theorem implies that there is a unique fixed point $g(\gamma, \alpha) \in \mathcal{C}$ satisfying $g(\gamma, \alpha) = T[g(\gamma, \alpha)]$.

To show the second result, we let $\sigma_m^2 = 1$ and define for all $y \in (-\infty, \infty)$ the functions:

$$V(y, \gamma_m, \alpha_m) \equiv \sup_{\tau \geq 0} E_0 \left\{(1 - \beta) \sum_{r=0}^{\tau} \beta^r x_{m,r} + \beta^{\tau+1}y\right\},$$

$$g_1(\gamma_m, \alpha_m) \equiv \beta E_0\{\max[0, V(0, \gamma_{m,1}, \alpha_m + 1)]\}.$$

We will show that $g(\gamma_m, \alpha_m) = g_1(\gamma_m, \alpha_m)$. Now $g_1 \in \mathcal{C}$. Applying T to g_1:

$$\begin{aligned}
T[g_1(\gamma_m, \alpha_m)] &= \beta E_0\{\max[0, (1 - \beta)\gamma_{m,1} + g_1(\gamma_{m,1}, \alpha_m + 1)]\} \\
&= \beta E_0\{\max(0, (1 - \beta)\gamma_{m,1} + \beta E_1 \max[0, V(0, \gamma_{m,2}, \alpha_m + 2)])\} \\
&= \beta E_0\{\max[0, V(0, \gamma_{m,1}, \alpha_m + 1)]\} \equiv g_1(\gamma_m, \alpha_m).
\end{aligned}$$

The first line above is obtained by using the definition of T and $\gamma_{m,1}$.[8] The second line uses the definition of g_1 while the third line is obtained by applying Bellman's principle. Thus, g_1 is the fixed point of T. By the uniqueness of the fixed point, $g_1 = g$. Using Bellman's again, we have that

$$V(0, \gamma_m, \alpha_m) = (1 - \beta)\gamma_m + g(\gamma_m, \alpha_m). \tag{4.121}$$

Now rearrange terms in the expression for the dynamic allocation index in Equation (4.117) to obtain

$$0 = \sup_{\tau \geq t} E_t \left\{ \sum_{r=t}^{\tau} \beta^{r-t} x_{m,r} - \left(\sum_{r=t}^{\tau} \beta^{r-t} \right) \text{DAI}_m(\gamma_{m,t}, \delta_{m,t}) \right\}.$$

But $\sum_{r=t}^{\tau} \beta^{r-t} = (1 - \beta)^{-1}(1 - \beta^{\tau-t+1})$. Making this substitution, multiplying through by $(1 - \beta)$ and adding $\text{DAI}_m(\gamma_{m,t}, \delta_{m,t})$ to both sides yields

$$\text{DAI}_m(\gamma_{m,t}, \delta_{m,t}) =$$

$$\sup_{\tau \geq t} E_t \left\{ (1 - \beta) \sum_{r=t}^{\tau} \beta^{r-t} x_{m,r} + \beta^{\tau-t+1} \text{DAI}_m(\gamma_{m,t}, \delta_{m,t}) \right\}. \tag{4.122}$$

The definition of $V(y, \gamma_m, \alpha_m)$ implies

$$V[\text{DAI}_m(\gamma_m, \alpha_m^{-1/2}), \gamma_m, \alpha_m] =$$

$$\sup_{\tau \geq 0} E_0 \left\{ (1 - \beta) \sum_{r=0}^{\tau} \beta^{r-t} x_{m,r} + \beta^{\tau+1} \text{DAI}_m(\gamma_m, \alpha_m^{-1/2}) \right\}$$

$$= \text{DAI}_m(\gamma_m, \alpha_m^{-1/2})$$

$$= \gamma_m + \alpha_m^{-1/2} D(\alpha_m, \beta), \tag{4.123}$$

The second line in the proof follows from Equation (4.122) and the third line follows from Proposition 4.1. If we use the definition of V and set

---

[8]Notice that $\sigma_m^2 = 1$ implies that $\alpha_m = \delta_m^{-2}$. Using Equations (4.114) and (4.115), $\gamma_{m,1} = (\alpha_m \gamma_m + x_{m,0})/(\alpha_m + 1)$. But $x_{m,0} = \xi_m + \epsilon$. Now ξ_m is a normal random variable with mean γ_m and variance δ_m^2. Thus it can be written as $\xi_m = \gamma_m + \alpha_m^{-1/2}\epsilon$. Substituting these results into the expression for $\gamma_{m,1}$ yields $\gamma_{m,1} = \gamma_m + (\alpha_m^{-1/2}\epsilon + \epsilon)/(\alpha_m + 1)$. The term in parentheses is the weighted sum of two $N(0,1)$ which itself is normal with variance equal to $[(1 + \alpha_m)\alpha_m]^{-1}$. Thus, it can be replaced by the normal random variable $[(1 + \alpha_m)\alpha_m]^{-1/2}\epsilon$.

$\gamma_m = -\alpha_m^{-1/2} D(\alpha_m \beta)$ in Equation (4.123), we have that

$$
\begin{aligned}
0 &= \text{DAI}(\gamma_m, \alpha^{-1/2}) \\
&= V[0, -\alpha^{-1/2} D(\alpha_m, \beta), \alpha_m] \\
&= -(1-\beta)\alpha^{-1/2} D(\alpha_m, \beta) + g[-\alpha^{-1/2} D(\alpha_m, \beta), \alpha_m]. \quad (4.124)
\end{aligned}
$$

The last line follows by using Equation (4.121). We can use the result in Equation (4.124) to show that the standard index $D(\alpha, \beta)$ satisfies Equation (4.120). Notice that a solution exists to Equation (4.120) because the left side is increasing in $D(\alpha, \beta)$ and the right side is decreasing in $D(\alpha, \beta)$. Furthermore, the slope of the left side with respect to $D(\alpha, \beta)$ is unity so these equations cross only once, implying that there exists a solution $D(\alpha, \beta)$. ∎

In what follows, we will use this result to demonstrate how the agent's decision rule can be computed numerically. First, however, we analyze the economic intuition underlying the form of the decision rule in Equation (4.117). As we noted, there are two benefits associated with each job: the expected reward from working in that job defined as $\gamma_{m,t}$ and information from future returns, which is captured by $\delta_{m,t} D(\alpha_m + \tau_{m,t}, \beta)$. Given two jobs with the same informational content, the person will choose the option that yields the highest expected reward. Thus, as $\gamma_{m,t}$ increases, $\gamma_{m,t} + \delta_{m,t} D(\alpha_m + \tau_{m,t}, \beta)$ also increases. Second, if expected rewards are equal, the person will choose the job that embodies the most information. The value of information is affected by various parameters. As the precision of prior information, δ_m^{-2}, increases, an individual is willing to forego less current rewards to find out about the job, implying that $\delta_{m,t} D(\alpha_m + \tau_{m,t}, \beta)$ decreases. If there is a lot of variability in returns (σ_m is large), on-the-job experience is not useful for learning about the match. Thus, as σ_m increases, $D(\alpha_m, \beta)$ falls. Also, as experience on the job $\tau_{m,t}$ increases, the value of additional information falls. Finally, individuals who discount the future more value information less so that reducing β reduces $D(\alpha_m, \beta)$.

4.2.1. Estimation

We now describe how the numerical solution derived from this model can be used as part of maximum likelihood estimation of the model. To fit this model to data, we identify a match m with employment in some job in a given occupation. An occupation is defined as the set of jobs that are characterized by the same set of prior beliefs about the future return stream. More precisely, two jobs m and m' belong to the same occupation if $(\gamma_m, \delta_m, \sigma_m) = (\gamma_{m'}, \delta_{m'}, \sigma_{m'})$.

We begin by defining some concepts that are useful for describing how an individual moves among jobs in a given occupation. Define the conditional probability that an individual will leave a given job m at date t after having worked in that job for $\tau_{m,t} = \tau$ periods as the hazard rate of length τ:

$$h_{m,\tau} \equiv \Pr\left[\gamma_{m,t} + \delta_{m,t} D(\alpha_m + \tau_{m,t}, \beta) < \right.$$

$$\left. \gamma_m + \delta_m D(\alpha_m, \beta)|\tau_{m,t} = \tau\right]. \qquad (4.125)$$

Here we have used the alternative representation of $\mathrm{DAI}(\gamma_{m,t}, \delta_{m,t})$ given by Proposition 4.1. This says that if the expected benefit of working in a job m conditional on experience $\tau_{m,t}$ is less than the expected benefit conditional only on prior information, the person leaves. To describe how the hazard rates are calculated, we begin with the case of $\sigma_m = 0$ so that match quality is revealed perfectly after one period. From Equation (4.117) notice that $\mathrm{DAI}_m(\gamma_{m,1}, \delta_{m,1}) = \mathrm{DAI}_m(\gamma_{m,1}, 0) = \xi_m$. Thus,

$$h_{m,1} = \Pr\left[\xi_m < \gamma_m + \delta_m D(0, \beta)\right] = \Phi[D(0, \beta)],$$

since $\xi_m \sim N(\gamma_m, \delta_m)$. Furthermore, since no information is acquired after working more than one period, $h_{m,\tau} = 0$ for $\tau \geq 1$.

In the more general case with $\sigma_m > 0$ if $\tau_{m,t} = \tau$, then from Equation (4.115), $\delta_{m,t} = \sigma_m(\alpha + \tau)^{-1/2}$. Thus,

$$\begin{aligned}
h_{m,\tau} &= \Pr\left[\gamma_{m,t} + \sigma_m(\alpha_m + \tau)^{-1/2} D(\alpha_m + \tau, \beta) < \right. \\
&\qquad\qquad \left. \gamma_m + \sigma_m \alpha_m^{-1/2} D(\alpha_m, \beta)|\tau_{m,t} = \tau\right] \\
&= \Pr\left[\gamma_{m,t} < \gamma_m + \sigma_m[\alpha_m^{-1/2} D(\alpha_m, \beta) - \right. \\
&\qquad\qquad \left. (\alpha_m + \tau)^{-1/2} D(\alpha_m + \tau, \beta)]|\tau_{m,t} = \tau\right] \\
&= \Psi_{m,\tau}[\alpha_m^{-1/2} D(\alpha_m, \beta) - (\alpha_m + \tau)^{-1/2} D(\alpha_m + \tau, \beta)],
\end{aligned}$$

where $\Psi_{m,\tau}(\rho) \equiv \Pr(\gamma_{m,t} < \gamma_m + \rho\sigma_m|\tau_{m,t} = \tau)$. Furthermore, the probability distribution for transformed means can be computed recursively as follows:

$$\Psi_{m,1}(\rho) = \Phi\left[\rho\alpha_m^{1/2}(\alpha_m + 1)^{1/2}\right], \qquad (4.126)$$

$$\Psi_{m,\tau+1}(\rho) = (1 - h_{m,\tau})^{-1}\left\{\int_{-\infty}^{\infty} \psi_{m,\tau}[\rho - \epsilon(\alpha_m + \tau)^{1/2} \times \right.$$

$$\left. (\alpha_m + \tau + 1)^{1/2}]d\Phi(\epsilon) - h_{m,\tau}\right\}, \qquad (4.127)$$

where $\psi_{m,\tau}$ is the probability density function corresponding to $\Psi_{m,\tau}$. The intuition behind the recursive definition of Ψ_m is as follows. First, the distribution $\Psi_{m,1}(\rho)$ is found by updating the prior transformed mean (of zero) for ξ_m with a realization from the standard normal distribution $\Phi(\epsilon)$. If the transformed posterior mean lies below the critical value $[\alpha_m^{-1/2}D(\alpha_m,\beta) - (\alpha_m + 1)^{-1/2}D(\alpha_m + 1,\beta)]$, the spell ends so that the proportion of spells ending with one period's experience $h_{m,1}$ is $\Psi_{m,1}[\alpha_m^{-1/2}D(\alpha_m,\beta) - (\alpha_m + 1)^{-1/2}D(\alpha_m + 1,\beta)]$. The probability distribution $(1 - h_{m,1})^{-1}[\Psi_{m,1}(\rho) - h_{m,1}]$ now forms the distribution of prior means for beliefs about uncompleted spells with one period's tenure. This shows how the probability distributions $\Psi_{m,\tau+1}(\rho)$ are generated. Notice that the hazard rates can be written as a function of α_m, the information factor for job m, and the person's discount factor β, $h(\alpha_m,\beta)$.

Finally, we can define the unconditional probability of a person with discount factor β working τ periods in a job with information factor α_m before switching to a new job, denoted as $p_\tau(\alpha_m,\beta)$. The unconditional probability is the product of the conditional probabilities of working in the current job for $s = 1,\ldots,\tau - 1$ periods and the probability of leaving this job conditional on having worked there for τ periods:

$$p_\tau(\alpha_m,\beta) \equiv h_\tau(\alpha_m,\beta) \prod_{s=1}^{\tau-1}[1 - h_s(\alpha_m,\beta)]. \tag{4.128}$$

These probabilities enter the likelihood function used to estimate the parameters of this model and to test its restrictions. One problem regarding estimation of this model is that the unconditional probabilities defined above do not have closed-form solutions because the hazard rates and the distributions Ψ are computed recursively. Furthermore, both the hazard rates and the distribution functions Ψ are evaluated at points determined by the unknown function $D(\alpha,\beta)$, which solves an implicit equation defined by the fixed point function g.

Miller provides an algorithm for computing all of these unknown functions numerically as part of the maximum likelihood estimation of his model. First, the algorithm iteratively computes the fixed point $g(\gamma,\alpha)$ by combining value iteration with a method for using cubic splines. To evaluate the map in Equation (4.119), the continuous state variables $(\gamma,\alpha) \in (-\infty,\infty) \times [0,\infty)$ are partitioned in terms of the finite grid $\{\gamma_i\}_{i\in I} \times \{\alpha_j\}_{j\in J}$. For each $(\alpha_j,\beta_k) \in [0,\infty] \times (0,1)$, the functions $f_h(\gamma,\alpha_j - h)$ are defined recursively as follows. First, $f_0(\gamma,\alpha_j) = 0$ and $f_{h+1}(\gamma,\alpha_j - h - 1)$ is a cubic *spline* or piecewise cubic polynomial that joins coordinate pairs to yield a function that is twice differentiable. The coordinate pairs are defined as $[\gamma_i, f_{h+1}(\gamma_i, \alpha_j - h - 1)]$, where γ_i is drawn from a finite set $\{\gamma_i\}_{i \in I}$ and $f_{h+1}(\gamma_i, \alpha_j - h - 1) = T[f_h(\gamma_i, \alpha_j - h)]$. Let ν denote the lowest positive integer for which

$$|f_{\nu+1}(\gamma_i, \alpha_j - \nu) - f_\nu(\gamma_i, \alpha_j - \nu)| \leq 0.001(1 - \beta_k).$$

This inequality bounds the error in approximating each f_ν. Once an approximation to the function g is obtained, for each α_j, β_k the value of the standard index $D_{j,k}$ is computed as the solution to the equation:

$$D_{j,k} = (1 - \beta_k)^{-1}(\alpha_j - \nu)^{1/2} f_\nu[-(\alpha_j - \nu)^{-1/2} D_{j,k}, \alpha_j - \nu].$$

The standard index $D(\alpha, \beta)$ is computed for 230 coordinate pairs (α, β) such that $\alpha \in [0.1, \ldots, 17.1]$ and $\beta \in [0.1, \ldots, 0.95]$. To compute the hazards $h_\tau(\alpha, \beta)$, notice that $\Psi_1(\rho)$ can be computed directly using Equation (4.126). Then the expression for h_1 is obtained by evaluating $\Psi(\rho)$ at the number $[\alpha^{1/2} D(\alpha, \beta_k) - (\alpha + 1)^{1/2} D(\alpha + 1, \beta_k)]$. The expressions for $\Psi(\rho)$ and h_1 are subsituted into Equation (4.127) to obtain $\Psi_2(\rho)$. Evaluating $\Psi_2(\rho)$ at the number $[\alpha^{1/2} D(\alpha, \beta_k) - (\alpha + 2)^{1/2} D(\alpha + 2, \beta_k)]$ yields h_2. Continuing in this manner yields h_3, h_4, and so on.

The estimation of this model is accomplished using a panel data set on N individuals. Associated with each individual n are (n) job spells. Under the null hypothesis that all jobs come from the same occupation, each spell $i \in (n)$ corresponds to a different match. Denote by $\bar{\tau}$ the longest completed employment spell of individuals in the sample and define the indicator variable $i_{n,\tau}$ to equal one if the person has completed an employment spell of τ periods and zero otherwise. Also define the indicator variable $j_{n,\tau}$ to equal one if the person is observed to have a spell of employment continuing for $\{\tau, \tau + 1, \ldots\}$ periods. The likelihood function for the sample of N observations is given by:

$$\mathcal{L} \equiv \prod_{n \in N} \prod_{i \in (n)} \prod_{\tau=1}^{\bar{\tau}} p_\tau(\alpha_i, \beta_n)^{i_{n,\tau}} [1 - p_\tau(\alpha_i, \beta_n)]^{j_{n,\tau}}. \tag{4.129}$$

The matching model relates an individual's job turnover decison to the unobserved match parameters and discount factor. Miller assumes that the information and discount factors are linear mappings of a set of socioeconomic characteristics z_i and z_j:

$$\alpha_i = z_i' a,$$
$$\beta_n = z_n' b,$$

where z_i and z_j include dummy variables for educational attainment levels such as "grade school," "high school," and "college" as well as dummy variables for employment group such as "professional," "manager," "farm owner," and so on. The inclusion of these socioeconomic characteristics allows tests of the hypothesis that educational attainment is associated with different beliefs and learning speeds, generating systematic changes in turnover behavior. For a one-occupation economy, Miller finds that the effect of education on the information factor is nonmonotone. The information factor α equals 7, 4, and 16 for the educational categories "grade school," "high school," and "college." Since $\alpha_m = \sigma_m^2 \delta_m^{-1}$, higher educational attainment may be associated with faster learning about match quality, implying a lower σ_m and higher δ_m. On the other hand, general education may compensate for lower aptitude in determining match quality, lowering δ_m and raising σ_m. The overall effect on α_m is thus ambiguous. Miller also tests to determine whether employment group dummies have a significant impact on match quality. He rejects the hypothesis that the match parameters α_m do not depend on the employment categories.

4.3.   A Model of Replacement Investment

We now describe a final application of dynamic discrete choice models by considering the model of bus engine replacement due to Rust [294]. Rust estimates a structural model of bus engine replacement to derive the demand function for new bus engines by the Madison (Wisconsin) Metropolitan Bus Company. The problem is to choose when to replace a bus engine by minimizing maintenance costs versus unexpected engine failures. Unlike a reduced-form approach that would derive an investment demand function by regressing observations for the replacement decision on replacement costs, the investment demand function is derived from an optimal stopping rule which specifies whether or not to replace the current engine as a function of observed and unobserved state variables.

In this application, we denote by x_t the observed state variable which consists of accumulated mileage (since last replacement) on the bus engine at time t. Expected per period operating costs are defined in terms of an increasing, differentiable function of x_t and some unknown parameters θ_1, $c(x_t, \theta_1)$. Operating costs are the sum of maintenance, fuel, and insurance costs (which are potentially observable) plus estimates of the cost of lost ridership and goodwill due to unexpected breakdowns. In the absence of data on maintenance and operating costs, however, only the total cost function can be identified, not its separate components.

The decision at each date is to (i) perform normal maintenance on the current bus engine and incur operating costs $c(x_t, \theta_1)$ or (ii) scrap the old bus engine for scrap value $\underline{P}$, install a new engine at cost $\bar{P}$, and incur the operating cost $c(0, \theta_1)$. The problem is to choose an optimal replacement policy to minimize the expected discounted costs of maintaining the bus fleet. We let i_t denote the replacement decision at time t, where $i_t = 0$ denotes the decision to keep the current engine and $i_t = 1$ denotes the decision to replace the engine. Define the value function V_θ by:

$$V_\theta(x_t, \epsilon_t) = \sup_\Pi E \left\{ \sum_{j=t}^\infty \beta^{j-t} [u(x_j, f_j, \theta_1) + \epsilon(f_j)] | x_t, \epsilon_t \right\}, \qquad (4.130)$$

where the function $u(x_t, i, \theta_1) + \epsilon(i)$ shows the current cost of undertaking the alternative i and it is defined as:

$$u(x_t, i, \theta_1) + \epsilon(i) = \begin{cases} -(\bar{P} - \underline{P}) - c(0, \theta_1) + \epsilon_t(1) & \text{if } i = 1 \\ -c(x_t, \theta_1) + \epsilon_t(0) & \text{if } i = 0 \end{cases}$$

where $\epsilon(i)$ is a component of utility associated with alternative i that is observed by the agent but not by the econometrician and θ_1 is a vector of unknown parameters to be estimated. In this expression, Π is an infinite sequence of decision rules $\Pi = \{f_t, f_{t+1}, \ldots\}$ chosen to be elements of the choice set $C(x_t)$ when the state is x_t that specify the replacement decision as a function of the observed and unobserved state variables at time t, $i_t = f_t(x_t, \epsilon_t, \theta) \in C(x_t)$. The expectation in Equation (4.130) is taken with respect to the controlled stochastic process (x_t, ϵ_t).

Define $p(x_{t+1}, \epsilon_{t+1} | x_t, \epsilon_t, i_t, \theta_2, \theta_3)$ as the Markov transition density for the state vector (x_t, ϵ_t) when alternative i is selected and θ_2 and θ_3 are unknown parameters to be estimated. The transition probability density for the stochastic process (x_t, ϵ_t) is given by:

$$dp(x_{t+1}, \epsilon_{t+1}, \ldots, x_{t+N}, \epsilon_{t+N} | x_t, \epsilon_t) =$$

$$\prod_{i=t}^{N-1} p(x_{i+1}, \epsilon_{i+1} | x_i, \epsilon_i, f_i(x_i, \epsilon_i), \theta_2, \theta_3). \qquad (4.131)$$

Rust further assumes that transition density of the process (x_t, ϵ_t) factors as:

$$p(x_{t+1}, \epsilon_{t+1} | x_t, \epsilon_t, i, \theta_2, \theta_3) = q(\epsilon_{t+1} | x_{t+1}, \theta_2) p(x_{t+1} | x_t, i, \theta_3). \qquad (4.132)$$

Notice that Equation (4.132) implies that x_{t+1} is a sufficient statistic for ϵ_{t+1}. Second, the probability density of x_{t+1} depends only on x_t and not on ϵ_t. Thus, we can view ϵ_t as noise superimposed on the $\{x_t\}$ process since ϵ_t is drawn according to the density $q(\epsilon_t | x_t, \theta_2)$ given the realization of x_t. Given the Markov nature of uncertainty and some additional regularity conditions, the solution to this problem is given by a stationary decision rule:

$$i_t = f(x_t, \epsilon_t, \theta), \qquad (4.133)$$

which specifies the agent's optimal decision when the state variables are (x_t, ϵ_t) and $\theta \equiv (\theta_1, \theta_2, \theta_3)'$. The inclusion of the unobservable variable ϵ implies that the replacement decision i_t depends on both the observed state variable x_t and the unobserved variable ϵ_t, preventing an exact relationship between observations on the replacement decision i_t and the observed state x_t.

The optimal value function V_θ is the unique solution to the Bellman equation given by:

$$V_\theta(x_t, \epsilon_t) = \max_{i \in C(x_t)} \{u(x_t, i, \theta_1) + \epsilon_t(i) + \beta EV_\theta(x_t, \epsilon_t, i)\},$$

where

$$EV_\theta(x_t, \epsilon_t, i) \equiv \int_y \int_\eta V_\theta(y, \eta) p(dy, d\eta | x_t, \epsilon_t, i, \theta_2, \theta_3),$$

and the optimal control f is defined by

$$f(x_t, \epsilon_t, \theta) \equiv \mathrm{argmax}_{i \in C(x_t)} \{u(x_t, i_t, \theta_1) + \epsilon_t(i) + \beta EV_\theta(x_t, \epsilon_t, i)\}.$$

Under the assumption made in Equation (4.132), however, the calculation of the optimal value function can be simplified considerably. First, notice that EV_θ is not a function of ϵ_t. Second, EV_θ can be determined as the fixed point of a separate contraction mapping on the state space $\Gamma = \{(x, i) | x \in \mathbb{R}, i \in C(x)\}$. Define the function $G([u(x, \theta_1) + \beta EV_\theta(x)] | x, \theta_2)$ by:

$$G([u(x, \theta_1) + \beta EV_\theta(x)] | x, \theta_2) =$$
$$\int_\epsilon \max_{j \in C(x)} \{u(x, j, \theta_1) + \epsilon(j) + \beta EV_\theta(x, j)\} q(d\epsilon | x, \theta_2), \qquad (4.134)$$

which shows the expected cost of making the optimal choice conditional on the observed state x. The function EV_θ is the unique fixed point to a contraction mapping $T_\theta(EV_\theta) = EV_\theta$ defined for each $(x, i) \in \Gamma$ by:

$$E[V_\theta(x, i)] = \int_y G([u(y, \theta_1) + \beta EV_\theta(y)] | y, \theta_2) p(dy | x, i, \theta_3). \qquad (4.135)$$

Under certain distributional assumptions for the unobserved state variables $\{\epsilon(0), \epsilon(1)\}$, we can derive closed-form expressions for the function G and the form of the contraction mapping, $T_\theta(EV_\theta)$. If we assume, as Rust does, that $q(\epsilon|x, \theta_2)$ is given by a bivariate extreme value distribution:

$$q(\epsilon|x, \theta_2) = \prod_{j\in\{0,1\}} \exp[-\epsilon(j) + \theta_2]\exp\{-\exp[-\epsilon(j) + \theta_2]\}, \quad (4.136)$$

where $\theta_2 = 0.577216$ (which is Euler's constant), then the function G is given by:

$$G([u(x, \theta_1) + \beta EV_\theta(x)]|x, \theta_2) =$$

$$\log\left\{\sum_{j\in C(x)} \exp[u(x, j, \theta_1) + \beta EV_\theta(x, j)]\right\}. \quad (4.137)$$

We can define the conditional choice probability (which shows the probability of choosing the alternative $i \in C(x)$ when the state is x) by $P(i|x, \theta) \equiv \Pr\left\{i = \text{argmax}_{j\in C(x)}[u(x, j, \theta_1) + e(j) + \beta EV_\theta(x, j)]|x\right\}$. Under the extreme value distribution assumption, $P(i|x, \theta)$ is given by:

$$P(i|x, \theta) = \frac{\exp\{u(x, i, \theta_1) + \beta EV_\theta(x, i)\}}{\sum_{j\in C(x)} \exp\{u(x, j, \theta_1) + \beta EV_\theta(x, j)\}}. \quad (4.138)$$

Finally, EV_θ is given by the unique solution to the functional equation:

$$EV_\theta(x, i) = \int_y \log\{\sum_{j\in C(x)} \exp[u(y, j, \theta_1)$$

$$+\beta EV_\theta(y, j)]\}p(dy|x, i, \theta_3). \quad (4.139)$$

Given these results, notice that the only unknown function that must be calculated numerically is EV_θ. To do this, Rust discretizes the state variable x which denotes accumulated mileage in terms of 90 intervals of length 5000. Accumulated mileage x_{t+1} evolves as:

$$x_{t+1} = \begin{cases} x_t + u_t & \text{if } i_t = 0 \\ u_t & \text{if } i_t = 1. \end{cases}$$

The sequence of random variables $\{u_t\}$ is assumed to be i.i.d. with a fixed discrete support. In particular, u_t has a multinomial distribution on the set $\{0, 1, 2\}$ corresponding to monthly mileage in the intervals $[0, 5000)$, $[5000, 10000)$, and $[10000, +\infty)$ that is completely characterized by two parameters $(\theta_{3,0}, \theta_{3,1})$ where $\theta_{3,j} = \Pr(x_{t+1} = x_t + j|x_t, i_t = 0)$

for $j = 0, 1$. Rust also assumes that x_t takes on one of a discrete set of values representing fixed-length mileage intervals $x_t \in \{1, 2, \ldots, 90\}$. The cost function is parameterized as (i) polynomial: $c(x, \theta_1) = \theta_{11}x + \theta_{12}x^2 + \theta_{13}x^3$; (ii) exponential: $c(x, \theta_1) = \theta_{11}\exp(\theta_{12}x)$; (iii) hyperbolic: $c(x, \theta_1) = \theta_{11}/(91 - x)$; and (iv) square root: $c(x, \theta_1) = \theta_{11}\sqrt{x}$ and $c(0, \theta_1)$ is normalized as zero. Let $RC \equiv \bar{P} - \underline{P}$. The unknown parameters to be estimated are defined as $\theta \equiv (\theta_1, RC, \theta_3)$.

Suppose we are given observations on the replacement decision and accumulated mileage for M engines over T periods, $\{(i_t^m, x_t^m)\}_{t=0}^T$ for $m = 1, \ldots, M$. Under Equation (4.132), the likelihood function for these observations is given by:

$$\mathcal{L}^f(x_1^m, \ldots, x_T^m, i_1^m, \ldots, i_T^m | x_0^m, i_0^m, \theta) =$$

$$\prod_{t=1}^T P(i_t^m | x_t^m, \theta) p(x_t^m | x_{t-1}^m, i_{t-1}^m, \theta_3), \qquad (4.140)$$

where $P(i_t^m | x_t^m, \theta)$ is the conditional choice probability of choosing the alternative $i_t^m \in C(x_t^m)$ when the state is x_t^m. The numerical solution for the unknown value function EV_θ is used to construct the conditional choice probabilities. The likelihood function for the full panel data set on bus engines consisting of $m = 1, \ldots, M$ is obtained by multiplying the individual likelihoods $\mathcal{L}^f$. As in Miller's application, maximum likelihood estimation is combined with a method for numerically solving a dynamic discrete choice model.

An alternative approach to estimating dynamic discrete choice models that does not rely on the use of discretization procedures has been implemented recently by Hotz and Miller [196] and Hotz, Miller, Sanders, and Smith [198]. According to the approach in the first paper, the conditional choice probabilities that are the outcome of the dynamic discrete choice problem are calculated using nonparametric methods by expressing the valuation function as the product of the utilities that can be attained in each possible state and the conditional choice probabilities associated with that state. This approach is feasible if the number of nodes or states over which utilities must be calculated is not too large. In Hotz, Miller, Sanders, and Smith [198], a simulation estimator is implemented that evaluates expected utilities along a path of future simulated choices as opposed to the expected utilities associated with all feasible future paths.

5.   Exercises

1.[9] Consider the problem of solving

$$\max_{\{c_t, k_{t+1}\}_{t=0}^{\infty}} E_0 \left\{ \sum_{t=0}^{\infty} \beta^t U(c_t) \right\}$$

subject to $c_t + k_{t+1} \le f(k_t)\theta_t \equiv y_t$ given y_0. Assume that $\{\theta_t\}_{t=0}^{\infty}$ is i.i.d. with distribution function G that satisfies Assumption 4.2.

a) Let a be an arbitrary level of output and let x be the optimal level of investment associated with a. Show that the optimal consumption policy $g(a)$ satisfies:

$$U'(g(a)) = \beta f'(x) \int U'\{g(f(x)\theta')\}\theta' dG(\theta'),$$

where θ' denotes next period's shock.

b) Let $U'(\cdot)$ and $f(\cdot)$ be homogeneous of degree $\gamma - 1$ and α, respectively. Show that the optimal consumption and investment policies are linear if and only if $\gamma = 0$ (for all α) or $\alpha = 1$ (for all γ).

Hint: To show this, consider the output level ka, $k \ge 1$. Show that if $g(a)$ and x are optimal relative to a, then $kg(a)$ and kx are optimal relative to ka.

c) Using the result in part b), find the optimal consumption and investment policies when

(i) $U(c) = c^\gamma/\gamma$, $\gamma \le 1$, $f(k)\theta = k\theta$,

(ii) $U(c) = \log(c)$, $f(k) = k^\alpha\theta$, $\alpha < 1$.

2. Consider an economy where the representative consumer has preferences over stochastic consumption c_t and hours worked h_t given by

$$E_0 \left\{ \sum_{t=0}^{\infty} \beta^t [\exp(u_t) \log(c_t) - \gamma h_t] \right\}, \quad \gamma > 0,$$

where $\{u_t\}_{t=0}^{\infty}$ is a mean zero i.i.d. preference shock with variance σ_u^2 and E_0 is expectation conditional on information available at time 0.

---

[9]This exercise is derived from Danthine and Donaldson [81].

Output in this economy is produced according to the production function:

$$f(\theta_t, h_t, k_t) = (\theta_t h_t)^{1-\alpha} k_t^{\alpha}, \quad 0 < \alpha < 1,$$

where k_t is the per capita capital stock and θ_t is a technology shock that follows a logarithmic random walk, $\theta_{t+1} = \theta_t \exp(\epsilon_{t+1})$, where $\{\epsilon_t\}_{t=0}^{\infty}$ is a mean zero i.i.d. innovation to technology with variance σ_{ϵ}^2. We assume that $\{u_t\}_{t=0}^{\infty}$ and $\{\epsilon_t\}_{t=0}^{\infty}$ are mutually uncorrelated.

The capital stock evolves as $k_{t+1} = (1-\delta)k_t + i_t$, where $0 < \delta < 1$ is the depreciation rate and i_t is investment.

Define the following transformed variables:

$$k_t^{\star} \equiv \log(k_t/\theta_t), \qquad i_t^{\star} \equiv \log(i_t/\theta_t)$$

$$c_t^{\star} \equiv \log(c_t/\theta_t), \qquad h_t^{\star} \equiv \log(h_t).$$

a) Show that utility in each period can be written as:

$$U \equiv \exp(u_t)c_t^{\star} + \log(\theta_t)\exp(u_t) - \gamma \exp(h_t^{\star}),$$

and the feasibility constraint as:

$$\exp(c_t^{\star}) + \exp(\epsilon_{t+1})\exp(k_{t+1}^{\star}) - (1-\delta)\exp(k_t^{\star}) \leq$$
$$\exp(h_t^{\star})^{1-\alpha}\exp(k_t^{\star})^{\alpha}.$$

b) Formulate the social planner's problem for this economy in terms of the transformed variables and show that this problem has a stationary solution.

3. Consider the following social planning problem:

$$\max_{\{c_t, k_{t+1}\}_{t=0}^{\infty}} E_0 \left\{ \sum_{t=0}^{\infty} \beta^t (1-\tau)^t U(c_t) \right\}$$

subject to

$$c_t + k_{t+1} = f(k_t)\theta_t,$$

k_0 given. Assume that U, f and the law of motion for θ_t satisfy the assumptions in Section 3.2.

a) Show that the first-order conditions for this problem are equivalent to the first-order conditions that arise in the competitive equilibrium with a capital income tax described in Section 3.2.

b) Suppose U, f and the distribution for θ_t satisfy Assumptions 4.1–4.3 in Section 1.1. Elaborate on how you would construct the optimal policy functions for the social planning problem and construct supporting equilibrium prices.

4. Assume that the model with a capital income tax described in Section 3.2 has an i.i.d. technology shock $\{\theta_t\}_{t=0}^{\infty}$.

a) Show that

$$\text{Var}(k_{t+1}) = [\alpha\beta(1-\tau)^{1/(1-\alpha)}]^2 M,$$

$$\text{Var}(c_t) = \{[1-\alpha\beta(1-\tau)][\alpha\beta(1-\tau)]^{\alpha/(1-\alpha)}\}^2 M,$$

$$\text{Var}(y_t) = \{[\alpha\beta(1-\tau)]^{\alpha/(1-\alpha)}\}^2 M,$$

where $M = \lim_{t\to\infty} \text{Var}(\prod_{s=0}^{t} \theta_{t-s}^{\alpha^s})$.

b) Let $\tau_1 < \tau_2$ and let c_{τ_i} for $i = 1, 2$ denote the optimal consumption policies corresponding to τ_i. Show that $c'_{\tau_1}(y) \leq c'_{\tau_2}(y)$ for all y.

c) Given the result in b), show that

$$\partial\text{Var}(k_{t+1})/\tau < 0, \quad \partial\text{Var}(c_t)/\tau < 0 \quad \text{and} \quad \partial\text{Var}(y_t)/\tau < 0.$$

5. A Discrete State, Discrete Control Problem[10]

Let x_i, $i = 1, \ldots, n$ denote the set of states and u_i, $i = 1, \ldots, m$ the set of controls. We assume that there is also a random disturbance in the model that takes on the finite values defined in terms of the set $\Theta = \{\theta_1, \ldots, \theta_k\}$ and that is identically and independently distributed over time. Let $\pi_{i,j}^l$ denote the transition probability for the state variable defined as:

$$\pi_{i,j}^l \equiv \Pr(x_{t+1} = x_j | x_t = x_i, u_t = u_l).$$

The problem is to solve

$$\max_{\{u_t\}_{t=0}} E_0 \left\{ \sum_{t=0}^{\infty} \beta^t v(x_t, u_t) \right\}, \quad 0 < \beta < 1,$$

subject to the law of motion, $x_{t+1} = f(x_t, u_t, \theta_t)$, $t = 0, 1, \ldots$ and given x_0. To make the problem well defined, we assume that $0 \leq v(x_t, u_t) \leq M < \infty$ for all x_t and u_t.

---

[10]This exercise is derived from Judd [215].

a) Find an expression for $\pi^l_{i,j}$ using the law of motion for the state variable and the known probability distribution for the random shock, $G(\theta_t)$.

b) Let $V_i \equiv V(x_i)$ and $v_{i,l} \equiv v(x_i, u_l)$. Show that the value function satisfies the equation

$$V_i = \max_l [v_{i,l} + \beta \sum_{j=1}^k \pi^l_{i,j} V_j] \equiv (TV)_i. \qquad (4.141)$$

c) Suppose that when the state is x_i, the optimal control is

$$U_i \in \mathrm{argmax}_{u_l} [v_{i,l} + \beta \sum_{j=1}^k \pi^l_{i,j} V_j] \equiv (\mathcal{U}V)_i. \qquad (4.142)$$

If U_i is the control in state x_i, then the return in that state is $S_i \equiv v(x_i, U_i)$. Let $V \equiv (V_1, \ldots, V_n)'$ and $S \equiv (S_1, \ldots, S_n)'$ and define the $n \times n$ matrix Π as the matrix of transition probabilities such that $\Pi_{i,j} = \pi^l_{i,j}$ if and only if $U_i = u_l$. Show that the solution for V is given by

$$V = (1 - \beta \Pi)^{-1} S.$$

d) Describe how you would do *value function iteration* in this problem.

e) *Policy function iteration* is implemented as follows:

$$
\begin{aligned}
\text{(i)} \quad & U^{n+1} &=& \; \mathcal{U}V^n, \\
\text{(ii)} \quad & S^{n+1}_i &=& \; v(x_i, U^{n+1}), \\
\text{(iii)} \quad & \Pi^{n+1} &=& \; \mathcal{P}U^{n+1}, \\
\text{(iv)} \quad & V^{n+1} &=& \; (1 - \beta \Pi^{n+1})^{-1} S^{n+1},
\end{aligned}
$$

where the map $\mathcal{P}U$ is defined as $\Pi_{i,j} = \pi^l_{i,j}$ if and only if $U_i = u_l$ and the remaining maps are defined from the left sides of Equations (4.141) and (4.142). Describe the nature of this algorithm and compare it with value function iteration.

6. Error Bounds for Value Iteration

Let T denote a mapping defined on the space of bounded, continuous functions $\mathcal{C}(S)$ where S is some bounded set. Define the norm on $\mathcal{C}(S)$ as the sup norm, $\| \cdot \| \equiv \sup_{s \in S} |V(s)|$ for all $V \in \mathcal{C}(S)$.

a) Show that if T is a contraction of modulus β, then

$$\|V^n - V_\infty\| \le (1 - \beta)^{-1}\|V^n - V^{n-1}\|, \tag{4.143}$$

where $V^n = T^n(V_0)$ for some $V_0 \in \mathcal{C}(S)$ and V^n converges uniformly to V_∞ as $n \to \infty$.

b) Describe how you would use the result in Equation (4.143) to determine the error in approximating the true value function V_∞ by V^n. How would you compute the error bounds during the successive approximation or value iteration algorithm?

7. Bayesian Updating

Recall that in the matching model of Section 4.2, $\xi_m \sim N(\gamma_m, \delta_m^2)$. Let $X_m \equiv (x_{m,1}, \ldots, x_{m,t-1})'$ denote the random sample of observations on returns from the m'th job and let $f(X_m = x | \xi_m = \xi)$ denote the conditional probability density of $X_m = x$. Following DeGroot [89], the posterior probability density function of $\xi_m = \xi$ given $X_m = x$ is

$$h(\xi | x) = \frac{f(x | \xi)h(\xi)}{\int_\Omega f(x | \xi')h(\xi')d\xi'},$$

where h is the prior probability density function of ξ_m.

Show that the posterior p.d.f. for ξ_m is normal with mean and variance given by Equations (4.114) and (4.115).

5

Inflation and Asset Returns

The effects attributed to inflation range from output and employment effects and dynamic effects on capital accumulation and growth to effects on asset returns. In general, there is very little consensus on the magnitudes of these effects or how they should be modeled. Here we adopt the framework provided by the cash-in-advance model for this purpose. In a cash-in-advance model, it is assumed that some types of purchases must be made with cash acquired in advance of making the purchase.

The cash-in-advance model has been used to study the relationship among velocity, nominal interest rates, and output by Lucas [232, 233, 235], Svensson [322], and Lucas and Stokey [236], among others. We study some of these models in a later part of this chapter. From an asset pricing point of view, the cash-in-advance model allows us to price assets denominated in nominal terms and to define such concepts as the inflation premium in asset returns and inflation risk. In Section 2, we describe a model with cash and credit goods and a model that allows for consumption and leisure decisions and generates output effects of the stochastic inflation tax. In this section, we also describe a model that incorporates open market operations and a liquidity effect in bond returns. In Section 3, we describe some methods for testing the timing convention in these models.

1. The Basic Cash-in-Advance Model

We begin by describing versions of cash-in-advance models. The basic model is the asset pricing model described in Chapter 2 except that a constraint — the cash-in-advance constraint — is imposed that motivates the use of money. There are ways to justify this on some microeconomic foundations.

We begin by describing a version of the cash-in-advance model that incorporates the timing of trades and information in Lucas [233]. The two key features of the Lucas model are first, that all households observe realizations of endowment and money growth at the beginning of the period before any decisions are made and, second, that the asset market opens before the goods market.

The representative household has preferences over random sequences of the single consumption good given by:

$$E_0 \left\{ \sum_{t=0}^{\infty} \beta^t U(c_t) \right\}, \tag{5.1}$$

where $0 < \beta < 1$ is the discount factor.

The household holds nominal wealth in the form of currency and a portfolio of bonds and equities. The payment on maturing bonds and the lump-sum monetary transfer G_t are made prior to any trading. The asset market opens first and the household adjusts its portfolio and money holdings. Money required to make purchases of consumption goods in the goods market must be held at the close of the asset market. The constraint that applies in the asset market is:

$$M_t^d + Q_t^e z_t + Q_t B_t \leq H_t + Q_t^e z_{t-1},$$

where H_t denotes posttransfer money balances held at the beginning of the period after payments on one-period bonds have been made:

$$H_t \equiv P_{t-1} y_{t-1} z_{t-1} + B_{t-1} + M_{t-1}^d - P_{t-1} c_{t-1} + G_t.$$

In this expression, Q_t^e is the nominal price of the equity at date t, Q_t is the nominal price of bonds, P_t is the nominal price of the consumption good, M_t^d denotes the money balances held at the end of the asset market, z_t denotes the equity shares purchased in the asset market at time t, and B_t denotes the quantity of bonds purchased at time t. An equity share purchased in the current period is a claim to the nominal dividend stream, $P_t y_t$, paid at the end of period t so these funds are unavailable for spending in the current period.

The goods market opens after the asset market closes. The cash-in-advance constraint that applies in this market is:

$$P_t c_t \leq M_t^d.$$

Let s_t denote the vector of exogenous shocks to this economy. The consumer observes the current shock before the asset market opens and knows all past values of output and money supply. Since the consumer knows s_t, y_{t-1} and M_{t-1}, he also knows current ouput and the current

Figure 5.1. The Lucas Model.

	t	Asset Market	Goods Market	$t+1$
Decisions		z_t, M_t^d, B_t	c_t	
Information	y_t, s_t			
Receipts	B_{t-1}, G_t		$z_t P_t y_t$	
Portfolio	H_t, z_{t-1}			

money stock. The timing of trades and points at which various decisions are made are illustrated in Figure 5.1.

We prove the existence of equilibrium under the assumption that endowment and money supply are growing. When endowment is growing, we assume that preferences are of the constant relative risk aversion (CRR) variety. Later we consider models in which the money supply is growing but endowment is stationary. The vector of exogenous shocks $s_t \in S \subset \mathbb{R}^m$ follows a first-order Markov process with a stationary transition function $F : S \times S \to [0, 1]$ such that $F(s, s') \equiv \Pr(s_{t+1} \leq s' \mid s_t = s)$. The transition function F satisfies the following assumption.

Assumption 5.1 *The transition function F has the Feller property so that for any bounded, continuous function $h : S \to \mathbb{R}$, the function $Th(s) = \int_S h(s')F(s, ds')$ is continuous. The process defined by F has a stationary distribution Φ.*

Notice that this is the same assumption we made in Chapter 2.

The endowment y_t is exogenous and growing over time. The rate of growth is a function of the current shock. The endowment evolves as:

$$y_t = \lambda(s_t)y_{t-1}. \tag{5.2}$$

Money is injected into the economy as a lump-sum stochastic transfer. The law of motion for the money supply process is:

$$M_t^s = \omega(s_t)M_{t-1}^s. \tag{5.3}$$

The following assumption restricts money and endowment growth.

Assumption 5.2 *Define $\mathcal{L} \equiv [\underline{\lambda}, \bar{\lambda}]$ and $\mathcal{W} \equiv [\underline{\omega}, \bar{\omega}]$ where $\underline{\lambda} > 0$, $\underline{\omega} > 0$, $\bar{\lambda} < \infty$, and $\bar{\omega} < \infty$. The functions $\lambda : S \to \mathcal{L}$ and $\omega : S \to \mathcal{W}$ are continuous functions and both are bounded away from zero.*

The following assumption characterizes the utility function.

Assumption 5.3 *The utility function U is given by $(c^{1-\gamma} - 1)/(1 - \gamma)$ for $\gamma \geq 0$.*

In equilibrium, consumption equals endowment, $c_t = y_t$, money demand equals money supply, $M_t^d = M_t$, all bonds are held, $B_t = 0$, all shares are held, $z_t = 1$ and the lump-sum money transfer equals the net growth of money, $G_t = (1 - \omega_t)M_{t-1}$. To ensure that the consumer's utility is well defined in equilibrium, we make the following assumption.

Assumption 5.4 $\beta \int_S \lambda(s')^{1-\gamma} d\Phi(s') < 1$, $\gamma \neq 1$.

Define the quantity $\Upsilon(s) \equiv \lambda(s)^{1-\gamma}/\omega(s)$. The existence of a monetary equilibrium is established by making the following assumption.

Assumption 5.5 $0 < \beta \int_S \Upsilon(s') d\Phi(s') < 1$, $\gamma \neq 1$.

For notational convenience, also define $\omega_{t,\tau} \equiv M_{t+\tau}/M_t$ so that $\omega_{t,\tau}$ is the growth of the money supply between periods t and $t + \tau$.

We begin by formulating the household's problem as a dynamic programming problem. Because the money supply is growing, the household's nominal money holdings are growing in equilibrium. To make H_t and M_t stationary, we divide the (nominal) constraints by the current stock of money M_t. With this modification, the problem is now similar to the growing endowment case studied in Chapter 2. Define normalized money and bond holdings by $m_t^d \equiv M_t^d/M_t$, $b_t \equiv B_t/M_t$, and $h_t \equiv H_t/M_t$. The nominal price level and the nominal equity price are normalized by the level of money supply, $p_t \equiv P_t/M_t$ and $q_t^e \equiv Q_t^e/M_t$.[1] The normalized constraint in the asset market is:

$$m_t^d + q_t^e z_t + Q_t b_t \leq h_t + q_t^e z_{t-1}, \tag{5.4}$$

where

$$h_t \equiv \frac{1}{\omega(s_t)} [p_{t-1}y_{t-1}z_{t-1} + b_{t-1} + m_{t-1}^d - p_{t-1}c_{t-1} + (\omega_t - 1)].$$

The cash-in-advance constraint is

$$p_t c_t \leq m_t^d. \tag{5.5}$$

---

[1] In the versions of the cash-in-advance model where all the information is revealed at the beginning of the period, we can also divide the nominal constraints by the price level. We use the approach of normalizing by the money stock because it works even when some information is revealed after a market is closed.

Notice that as a result of this normalization, the level of the money held drops out of the constraints in equilibrium.

The household takes as given the nominal price of consumption goods and the nominal price of equities and bonds, which are all assumed to be continuous, strictly positive functions of the current shocks. As in Chapter 2, we can define an interval $Z = [0, \bar{z}]$ where $\bar{z} < \infty$ such that $z_t \in Z$. Likewise, $b_t \in B$ where $B = [-b, b]$ such that $b > 0$. Let $\mathcal{H} = [0, \bar{h}]$ where $\bar{h} > 1$ such that $h_t \in \mathcal{H}$. Finally, we know that in equilibrium all of the money will be held at the close of the assets market and because we have normalized by the money stock, $m^d = 1$. Hence, define $\mathcal{M} = [0, 1]$.

Notice that endowment y is strictly positive so that y is in $\mathbb{R}_{++}$. The prices are functions $p(s, y)$, $q^e(s, y)$, and $Q(s)$ and we assume that

$$p(s, y)y, \qquad \frac{q^e(s, y)}{p(s, y)y}$$

are *functions of s only*. Recall that $p(s, y)$ is the nominal price level divided by the money stock (the inverse of real balances) so that the restriction on $p(s, y)y$ says that real balances divided by endowment is a function of s only. Given the price functions p, q^e, and Q, the consumer's value function is defined by:

$$V(y, s, z, h) = \max_{c, m^d, z', b'} \left\{ U(c) + \beta \int_S V(y', s', z', h') F(s, ds') \right\},$$

subject to the constraints in Equations (5.4) and (5.5) and $m^d \in \mathcal{M}$, $z' \in Z$, and $b' \in B$. We have the following definition.

Definition 5.1 *A recursive competitive equilibrium is defined as a set of continuous, strictly positive price functions $p : S \times \mathbb{R}_{++} \to \mathbb{R}_{++}$, $q^e : S \times \mathbb{R}_{++} \to \mathbb{R}_{++}$, $Q : S \to \mathbb{R}_{++}$, and a value function $V : \mathbb{R}_{++} \times S \times Z \times \mathcal{H} \to \mathbb{R}_+$ such that (i) given $p(s, y)$, $q^e(s, y)$, and $Q(s)$, $V(y, s, z, h)$ solves the consumer's problem; (ii) markets clear.*

Under Assumption 5.4, we can show that V is well defined and finite. Recall that in Chapter 2, we restricted our attention to the space $\mathcal{B}$ of functions $g : \mathbb{R}_{++} \times S \times Z \times \mathcal{H} \to \mathbb{R}_+$ that are jointly continuous such that if $g \in \mathcal{B}$, then $\sup_{y, s, z, h} |g(y, s, z, h)|/y^{1-\gamma} < \infty$. We used this norm to verify the Weighted Contraction Mapping Theorem. We will not repeat this because the steps are identical to those proving Proposition 2.5 in Chapter 2 except to note that the modulus of the contraction in the proof is $\delta = \beta \int_S \lambda(s')^{1-\gamma} d\Phi(s')$ which, under Assumption 5.4, is always less than unity. (See Exercise 1.)

The main task is to construct the equilibrium price functions. Let $\mu(s, y)$ denote the multiplier on the cash-in-advance constraint and $\xi(s, y)$ denote the multiplier on the asset market constraint. Let $\phi(y, s) \equiv V(y, s, 1, 1)$ and define ϕ_i, $i = h, z$ as the partial derivative of $\phi(y, s)$ with respect to h and z. The first-order conditions with market-clearing with respect to c, m^d, z', and b' are:

$$U'(y) = \mu(s, y)p(s, y)$$
$$+ \beta E_s \left[\phi_h(y', s')p(s, y)/\omega(s') \right], \tag{5.6}$$

$$\xi(s, y) = \mu(s, y) + \beta E_s \left[\phi_h(y', s')/\omega(s') \right], \tag{5.7}$$

$$\xi(s, y)q^e(s, y) = \beta E_s[\phi_h(y', s')p(s, y)y/\omega(s') + \phi_z(y', s')], \tag{5.8}$$

$$\xi(s, y)Q(s) = \beta E_s \left[\phi_h(y', s')/\omega(s') \right], \tag{5.9}$$

where $E_s(\cdot) \equiv E(\cdot|s)$. The envelope conditions are:

$$\phi_h(s, y) = \xi(s, y), \tag{5.10}$$

$$\phi_z(s, y) = \xi(s, y)q^e(s, y). \tag{5.11}$$

Notice that the first two conditions do not involve the equity or bond price functions. We can solve first for the consumption price function and then solve for the asset prices. We can eliminate $\xi(s, y) = U'(y)/p(s, y)$ using Equations (5.6) and (5.7). After substituting the envelope condition in Equation (5.10) into Equation (5.6) and dividing both sides by $p(s, y)$, Equation (5.6) becomes:

$$\frac{U'(y)}{p(s, y)} = \mu(s, y) + \beta E_s \left[\frac{U'(y')}{p(s', y')\omega(s')} \right]. \tag{5.12}$$

To solve for the goods price function, we use the method in Giovannini and Labadie [152]. We start by defining implicitly a function Ψ, which is the inverse of velocity as a ratio of the money stock, such that for all $s \in S$ the cash-in-advance constraint in Equation (5.5) holds with equality. Recall that $m^d = 1$ in equilibrium so that the price level satisfies $1/p(s, y)y = \Psi(s)$. Since $y > 0$ for all s, studying the properties of the function Ψ is equivalent to studying the function p. This follows as an application of the implicit function theorem. We will show momentarily that Ψ is a function only of s.

The cash-in-advance constraint restricts $p(s,y)y \leq 1$ so that the value that the function Ψ can take for any s cannot fall below unity since this violates the lower bound on the inverse of the price level imposed by the constraint. For each y, s if $\Psi(s) > 1$, then the cash-in-advance constraint is nonbinding, while if $\Psi(s) = 1$, then the constraint is binding. Substituting for $p(s,y)$ in Equation (5.12), solving for $\mu(s,y)$, and dividing by $U'(y)y = y^{1-\gamma}$, we obtain:

$$\frac{\mu(s,y)}{y^{1-\gamma}} = \Psi(s) - \beta E_s \left[\frac{\lambda(s')^{1-\gamma}\Psi(s')}{\omega(s')} \right]. \tag{5.13}$$

Under the restrictions on the values that the function Ψ can take and using the definition of Υ, Equation (5.13) shows that Ψ satisfies the functional equation:

$$\Psi(s) = \max\{1, \beta E_s[\Upsilon(s')\Psi(s')]\} \tag{5.14}$$

for all s. Notice that Ψ is a function only of s. Define the operator T by:

$$(T\Psi)(s) = \max\{1, \beta E_s[\Upsilon(s')\Psi(s')]\}. \tag{5.15}$$

We now have the following theorem.

Theorem 5.1 *Under Assumptions 5.1, 5.2, and 5.5, there exists exactly one continuous and bounded function Ψ that solves Equation (5.15).*

PROOF
We first show that $T : \mathcal{C}(S) \rightarrow \mathcal{C}(S)$. Next, we show that T^n is a contraction. Hence we can conclude that there exists exactly one solution to Equation (5.15).

Under Assumption 5.1, the expectation operator maps continuous, bounded functions into continuous, bounded functions. Under Assumption 5.5 if Ψ^0 is in the space of bounded, continuous functions, then so is $\beta E_s[\Upsilon(s')\Psi^0(s')]$. If $f \in \mathcal{C}(S)$, then $\max[1, f(s)]$ is also because the max operator is linear and bounded and, because a linear operator is bounded if and only if it is continuous, it is also continuous. Hence T takes continuous, bounded functions into continuous, bounded functions.

The next step is to verify Blackwell's conditions for a contraction. For any $f, g \in \mathcal{C}(S)$ such that $f(s) > g(s)$ for all $s \in S$, $Tf(s) \geq Tg(s)$. Hence, T is monotone. To determine if T has the discounting property, notice that applying T to an arbitrary function in $\mathcal{C}(S)$ will <u>not</u> discount because

$$T(f+a)(s) = \max\left[1, \beta \int_S \Upsilon(s')(f(s')+a)F(s,ds')\right]$$

$$\leq \max\left[1, \beta \int_S \Upsilon(s')f(s')F(s,ds')\right]$$

$$+ \max\left[1, \beta \int_S \Upsilon(s')aF(s,ds')\right],$$

where we are using the conditional expectation. Under our assumptions, $\Upsilon(s')$ is a stationary process so that there is some $j < \infty$ such that $\beta E_t[\Upsilon(s_{t+j})] < 1$. Define $N(s_t)$ such that

$$\beta^{N(s_t)} E_t \left(\prod_{i=1}^{N(s_t)} \Upsilon(s_{t+i})\right) < 1.$$

Let N denote the maximum over the $N(s_t)$ or $N = \max_{s \in S} N(s)$. Start with an initial guess $\Psi^0 \in \mathcal{C}(S)$ and define:

$$\Psi^1(s_t) = (T\Psi^0)(s_t) = \max\left\{1, \beta E_s\left[\Upsilon(s_{t+1})\Psi^0(s_{t+1})\right]\right\}.$$

When T is applied M times,

$$T^M \Psi^0(s) = \max\left\{1, \beta E_s\left[\Upsilon(s')\Psi^{M-1}(s')\right]\right\}.$$

To determine if T^M has the discounting property, define:

$$T^M(\Psi^0 + a)(s_t) = T^{M-1} \max\left(1, \beta E_t\left\{\Upsilon(s_{t+1})[\Psi^0(s_{t+1}) + a]\right\}\right)$$

$$\leq T^{M-1} \max\left\{1, \beta E_t\left[\Upsilon(s_{t+1})\Psi^0(s_{t+1})\right]\right\} + a\beta^M E_t \prod_{i=1}^M \Upsilon(s_{t+i}).$$

If $M > N$, then $\beta^M E_t \left(\prod_{i=1}^M \Upsilon(s_{t+i})\right) a = \delta a$ where $0 < \delta < 1$. Hence T^M has the discounting property and is monotone so that T^M is a contraction mapping. By the N-Stage Contraction Mapping Theorem, Luenberger [237, p. 275], if T^M is a contraction for some positive integer M, then T has a unique fixed point in $\mathcal{C}(S)$, which can be found by the method of successive approximation. ■

Let $\Psi^\star$ denote the fixed point. We now study the properties of the equilibrium price-nominal dividend ratio, $q^e(s,y)/(p(s,y)y)$. Notice that we can derive a functional equation for this quantity from Equation (5.8) as follows:

$$\frac{q^e(s,y)}{p(s,y)y} = \beta E_s\left[\frac{U'(y')}{U'(y)p(s',y')y}\left(\frac{p(s,y)y}{\omega(s')} + q^e(s',y')\right)\right]. \tag{5.16}$$

Define the function $\psi(s) \equiv q^e(s,y)/p(s,y)y$; notice that we are assuming that it depends only on s. Using the definition of $\Psi^\star(s)$, we can rewrite Equation (5.16) as:

$$\psi(s) = \beta E_s \left[\lambda(s')^{1-\gamma} \left(\frac{\Psi^\star(s')}{\Psi^\star(s)\omega(s')} + \psi(s') \right) \right]. \tag{5.17}$$

Define the function $\Gamma : S \to \mathbb{R}_+$ by:

$$\Gamma(s) \equiv \beta \int_S \frac{\Upsilon(s')\Psi^\star(s')}{\Psi^\star(s)} F(s,ds')$$

where $\Upsilon(s) \equiv \lambda(s)^{1-\gamma}/\omega(s)$. For any $\psi \in \mathcal{C}(S)$, define an operator T_Ψ from the right side of Equation (5.17) as:

$$(T_\Psi \psi)(s) \equiv \Gamma(s) + \beta \int_S \lambda(s')^{1-\gamma}\psi(s')F(s,ds').$$

We have the following theorem.

Theorem 5.2 *There is a unique, bounded, continuous solution to $\psi^\star$ to $(T_\Psi \psi) = \psi$. For any $\psi_0 \in \mathcal{C}(S)$, $\lim_{n\to\infty} T^n \psi_0 = \psi^\star$.*

PROOF
Given the fixed point function $\Psi^\star \in \mathcal{C}(S)$, notice that under Assumption 5.1, the expectation operator maps continuous, bounded functions into continuous, bounded functions. By Assumption 5.5, if $\Psi^\star$ is in the space of bounded, continuous functions, then so is $\Gamma(s)$. If $\psi \in \mathcal{C}(S)$, then it follows by Assumption 5.4 that $\int_S \lambda(s')^{1-\gamma}\psi(s')F(s,ds')$ is bounded and by Assumption 5.1, it is continuous. Hence, $T_\Psi : \mathcal{C}(S) \to \mathcal{C}(S)$.

For any $f,g \in \mathcal{C}(S)$ such that $f(s) > g(s)$ for all $s \in S$, $T_\Psi f(s) \geq T_\Psi g(s)$ so that T_Ψ is monotone. Notice that T_Ψ applied to an arbitrary function in $\mathcal{C}(S)$ will not discount because

$$T_\Psi(\psi + a)(s) = \Gamma(s) + \beta \int_S \lambda(s')^{1-\gamma}[\psi(s') + a]F(s,ds').$$

However, proceeding as in Theorem 5.1, we can show that there exists an N such that when T_Ψ is applied M times,

$$T_\Psi^M(\psi_0 + a)(s_t) = (T_\Psi^M \psi_0)(s_t) + a\beta^M E_t \left(\prod_{i=1}^M \lambda(s_{t+i}) \right)$$

$$\leq (T_\Psi^M \psi_0)(s_t) + \delta a,$$

where $a\beta^M E_t \left(\prod_{i=1}^{M} \lambda(s_{t+i})\right) = \delta a$ and $0 < \delta < 1$ for $M > N$. Hence, T_Ψ^M is a contraction mapping and by the N-Stage Contraction Mapping Theorem, has a fixed point in $\mathcal{C}(S)$. ∎

Theorems 5.1 and 5.2 constitute the main results for the existence of the inverse velocity function and the equilibrium price-dividend ratio for the basic cash-in-advance model. Notice that if we make the assumption that $\beta \int_S \lambda(s')^{1-\gamma} F(s, ds') < 1$, which is stronger than Assumption 5.4, then we can show that the mapping T_Ψ satisfies Blackwell's conditions and is a contraction itself as opposed to showing that T_Ψ^M is a contraction. The proofs for the case with an endowment that is stationary in levels can be obtained by modifying these results and they are simpler because we do not need to account for growth in endowment, which requires us to make Assumption 5.4. In the next chapter, we describe two-country versions of the monetary models presented here. In many cases, existence of the inverse velocity functions and equity prices in these models can be accomplished using modifications of Theorems 5.1 and 5.2.

1.1. Velocity and Interest Rates

We first discuss the implications of this model for the relationship between velocity and nominal interest rates. Define the nominal interest rate as $R^1(s) \equiv 1/Q(s) - 1$.

The first-order condition in Equation (5.6) can be written as:

$$\frac{\mu(s,y)p(s,y)}{U'(y)} = 1 - \beta E_s \left[\Upsilon(s')\frac{\Psi^\star(s')}{\Psi^\star(s)}\right],$$

$$= 1 - Q(s).$$

From this expression, notice that the cash-in-advance constraint is binding (which occurs when $\mu(s,y) > 0$) only if $Q(s) < 1$ (so that nominal interest rates are positive), implying that velocity is constant. Yet in the data we do not observe such a close relationship between velocity and nominal interest rates since nominal interest rates are positive and velocity is not constant. The links among velocity, money growth, output growth, the nominal interest rate, and inflation for the basic cash-in-advance model are studied empirically by Hodrick, Kocherlakota, and Lucas [193] and Giovannini and Labadie [152]. Using quarterly data on consumption and money growth, Hodrick *et al.* conduct a calibration exercise similar to Mehra and Prescott [257]. They find that the cash-in-advance constraint almost always binds and that velocity is constant for the basic cash-in-advance model. They also find that the model is unable to match the sample moments of other endogenous variables for parameter values that result in reasonable values for the variability of velocity.

One way to weaken the relationship between velocity and nominal interest rates is by altering the nature of information households have available when they make decisions. Lucas [233] suggests a cash-in-advance model with an alternative timing of information to solve this problem. In particular, he assumes that the timing of trade is as described in the previous model: the asset market opens first and then the goods market opens but that the money supply shock is observed before trading occurs in the assets market, and the realization of the endowment is observed only after the asset market closes but before the goods market opens. Now the nominal price of consumption goods is determined in the goods market and depends in equilibrium on all information available at that point in time, including the information revealed by the realization of the endowment. Thus, households need to acquire cash for consumption purchases before knowing what the price level will be.

Another way to explain the relationship between inflation, nominal interest rates, and velocity is to use the Stockman-Svensson timing convention. In this case, the timing of trades is the reverse of that in the two versions of the Lucas model. This type of model has been studied by Stockman [314], who studies an exchange rate model which has the timing that the goods market opens first followed by the asset market, and by Svensson [322, 321]. The goods market opens first and consumption purchases must be made with currency acquired in the asset market from the previous period. After the goods market closes, the money transfers are made and the payoffs on bonds maturing in the current period are paid. In the asset market, the household adjusts his holdings of bonds, equities, and money balances. In this model, there is a precautionary motive for holding money because money balances must be acquired in period t in order to purchase consumption goods next period. Figure 5.2 describes the Stockman-Svensson timing conventions.

1.2.   Inflation Risk and the Inflation Premium

We now describe the implications of this framework for asset price behavior, including equity prices and the price of real and nominal risk-free assets. Unlike the real models considered earlier, we can use this framework to decribe the effects of changes in the nominal price level on equilibrium rates of return for assets that have nominal payoffs.

Returning to Equation (5.17) and reverting to time subscripts, we can

Figure 5.2. Stockman-Svensson Timing of Trades.

	Goods Market	Asset Market	
t			$t+1$
Decisions	c_t	$z_{t+1}, H_{t+1}, B_{t+1}$	
Information	y_t, s_t		
Receipts	$B_t, G_t, P_t z_t y_t$		
Portfolio	H_t, z_t, B_t	$H_{t+1}, z_{t+1}, B_{t+1}$	

derive an expression for the price-dividend ratio as:

$$\frac{q_t^e}{p_t y_t} = E_t \left[\sum_{i=1}^{\infty} \beta^i \frac{U'(y_{t+i})y_{t+i}}{U'(y_t)y_t} \frac{\Psi_{t+i}^{\star}}{\Psi_t^{\star}\omega_{t,i}} \right]$$

$$= E_t \left[\sum_{i=1}^{\infty} \beta^i \frac{U'(y_{t+i})p_t}{U'(y_t)p_{t+i}} \frac{1}{\omega_{t,i}} \right]. \tag{5.18}$$

Recall that the equity in this model is a claim to a nominal dividend $p_t y_t$. The price-dividend ratio is a claim to the purchasing power of a unit of currency at the end of the period. The purchasing power of money is defined as the inverse of the price level. Since there is money growth, the purchasing power of money falls by $\omega_{t,i}^{-1}$ between periods t and $t + i$. Unlike the real models of Chapters 2 and 4, the stochastic discount factor is the ratio of the marginal utility of the purchasing power of money $U'(y)/p(s,y)$ at adjacent periods or the *nominal MRS*. The stochastic discount factor converts \$1.00 received tomorrow into utility units today. Specifically, $\beta U'(y')/(p(s',y')\omega(s'))$ measures the utility value of \$1.00 held one period hence while $U'(y)/p(s,y)$ measures the utility value of \$1.00 held today; their ratio measures the intertemporal tradeoff.

The equilibrium price of a one-period nominal bond that pays one unit of currency at the beginning of the next period can be determined from Equations (5.9) and (5.10) as:

$$Q_t^1 = \beta E_t \left[\frac{U'(y_{t+1})p_t}{U'(y_t)p_{t+1}\omega_{t+1}} \right]. \tag{5.19}$$

As we can see, the price of a one-period nominal bond is just equal to the stochastic discount factor. The expected real return to a one-period nominal bond is:

$$E_t(1 + r_t^1) = (1 + R_t^1)E_t \left(\frac{p_t}{p_{t+1}\omega_{t+1}} \right). \tag{5.20}$$

This is a version of the Fisher equation, which divides the nominal interest rate into the expected real interest rate plus the expected rate of inflation. We can derive similar expressions for the expected real return on all assets denominated in nominal terms, including the nominal equity return.

When agents are risk averse, there is also a risk premium included in the Fisher equation. To derive the inflation risk premium, we consider assets that have real payoffs indexed by inflation. The price of an inflation-indexed bond maturing in one period is given by:

$$q_t^1 = \beta E_t \left[\frac{U'(y_{t+1})}{U'(y_t)} \right]. \tag{5.21}$$

The return to a one-period indexed bond is defined as $(1 + r_t^f) \equiv 1/q_t^1$. The difference between the nominal bond and the inflation-indexed bond is that the stochastic discount factor for the latter is the intertemporal MRS in consumption goods.

We define the *inflation risk premium* as the difference between the expected real return to a one-period nominal bond and the return to a one-period indexed bond, $E(r_t^1) - r_t^f$. Now the nominal interest rate satisfies the relation:

$$1 + R_t^1 = \left\{ \beta E_t \left[\frac{U'(y_{t+1})p_t}{U'(y_t)p_t\omega_{t+1}} \right] \right\}^{-1}. \tag{5.22}$$

Using a covariance decomposition, the term in braces can be written as:

$$\beta \mathrm{Cov}_t \left[\frac{U'(y_{t+1})}{U'(y_t)}, \frac{p_t}{p_{t+1}\omega_{t+1}} \right] + \frac{1}{1 + r_t^f} E_t \left[\frac{p_t}{p_{t+1}\omega_{t+1}} \right].$$

The conditional covariance measures the covariation between the intertemporal MRS in consumption with the expected deflation. If we substitute the above expression into Equation (5.20), notice that if conditional covariance above equals zero, then expected real return to the nominal bond equals the real interest rate. In this case, we say that the inflation risk premium is zero.

Fama and Schwert [126], Nelson [268], and Jaffe and Mandelker [204], among others, have studied the effects of inflation on asset returns. Fama and Schwert use versions of Equation (5.20) to test whether a given asset serves as a hedge against inflation, which they define in terms of a unit coefficient on the expected inflation term in a logarithmic approximation to Equation (5.20). Their tests are valid under the assumption that the expected real return and expected inflation are unrelated. One of their noteworthy findings is the negative covariation between stock returns and expected inflation, which is contrary to the role of equities as an inflation hedge. Notice that in our framework changes in endowment induce fluctuations in the price level and in the real intertemporal MRS in consumption. If we assume that fluctuations in the money supply are independent of the fluctuations in endowment growth, then an increase in expected money growth will affect the expected inflation only and will not affect the real rate of interest.

To determine the effects of stochastic inflation on the equity price and the equity premium, notice that we can rewrite Equation (5.16) as:

$$1 = \beta E_t \left[\frac{U'(y_{t+1})}{U'(y_t)} \left(\frac{p_t y_t}{p_{t+1} \omega_{t+1}} + \frac{q^e_{t+1}}{p_{t+1}} \right) \Big/ \frac{q^e_t}{p_t} \right]$$

$$1 = \beta E_t \left[\frac{U'(y_{t+1})}{U'(y_t)} (1 + r^e_{t+1}) \right],$$

where r^e_{t+1} is the (net) real equity return. The equity premium is defined as the difference between the expected real equity return and the return on a one-period inflation-indexed bond, $E_t(r^e_{t+1}) - r^f_t$. Stochastic inflation affects the real equity premium because dividends are paid in nominal terms. Thus, changes in the nominal price level or, equivalently, changes in the purchasing power of money affect the equity return through current dividends as well as through the future equity price, which depends on the whole future path of nominal price level changes. A second way that stochastic inflation can affect the measured equity premium is that in practice, the real equity premium must be computed as the difference between the expected real equity return and the expected real return on a one-period nominal bond, $E_t(r^e_{t+1}) - E_t(r^1_t)$. As long as $E_t(r^1_t)$ differs from r^f_t due to the inflation risk premium, there arises a second channel by which stochastic inflation affects the equity premium. Labadie [225] studies these effects empirically to determine whether they can account for the "equity premium puzzle." She finds that the magnitude of the equity premium is sensitive to the conditional variance of money and endowment growth.

The prices of a variety of other assets can also be determined, assuming that these assets are in zero net supply. Assuming that there is an active secondary market, the price today of a nominal bond paying one unit of currency at time $t + \tau$ is:

$$Q^\tau_t = \beta E_t \left[\frac{U'(y_{t+1}) p_t}{U'(y_t) p_{t+1} \omega_{t+1}} Q^{\tau-1}_{t+1} \right].$$

By repeated substitution for the bond price, notice that this is equivalent to:

$$Q_t^\tau = \beta^\tau E_t \left[\frac{U'(y_{t+\tau})p_t}{U'(y_t)p_{t+\tau}\omega_{t,\tau}} \right]. \tag{5.23}$$

Hence, the price of a nominal bond that pays one unit of currency at time $t + \tau$ is just the expected marginal rate of substitution in the purchasing power of money between periods t and $t + \tau$. The return to holding a bond maturing in τ periods for n periods and selling it in the secondary market is defined as $Q_{t+1}^{\tau-1}/Q_t^\tau$. The expected *real* return to a nominal bond maturing in τ periods is defined as:

$$E_t(1 + r_t^\tau) = E_t \left[\frac{Q_{t+1}^{\tau-1}}{Q_t^\tau} \frac{p_t}{p_{t+1}} \right]. \tag{5.24}$$

The expected *real* holding risk premium, defined as the difference between the expected real return to holding for one-period a nominal bond maturing in τ periods and the return to a one-period indexed bond is

$$E_t(r_t^\tau) - r_t^f = E_t(r_t^1) - r_t^f + E_t(r_t^\tau - r_t^1). \tag{5.25}$$

The holding risk premium can be divided into the *inflation risk premium*, defined as $E_t(r_t^1) - r_t^f$ and a *term risk premium*, $E_t(r_t^\tau - r_t^1)$. Jaffe and Mandelker [205] study the relationship between inflation and the holding period returns on bonds.

In actual capital markets, we typically observe assets with nominal payoffs being traded. Since the existence of changes in the nominal price level induce another type of risk that risk-averse agents would prefer to avoid, the question arises as to the welfare gains from issuing inflation-indexed bonds and why there are so few instances of this occurring. Fischer [131] studies the welfare gains of issuing inflation-indexed bonds in a multi-good model with price level uncertainty. In his framework, all bonds are in net zero supply.

2.   Variants of Cash-in-Advance Models

A basic feature of the cash-in-advance model is that the marginal value of liquidity — the value of the multiplier attached to the cash-in-advance constraint — is closely linked to the nonnegativity of nominal interest rates. We described above how this link could be broken by altering the informational assumptions in the basic cash-in-advance model. Another way to break the close link between velocity and nominal interest rates is to assume that only some goods are required to be purchased with currency while other goods can be purchased on credit. Velocity can then vary when interest rates are positive. This type of model is developed by Lucas [232] and Lucas and Stokey [236].

2.1. The Cash-Credit Model

We begin by describing the cash-credit model. In this model, the representative agent has preferences given by:

$$E\left\{\sum_{t=0}^{\infty} \beta^t U(c_{1,t}, c_{2,t})\right\}, \quad 0 < \beta < 1, \tag{5.26}$$

where $c_{1,t}$ is consumption of the cash good, $c_{2,t}$ is consumption of the credit good, and the expectation is over realizations of the shocks at time zero. To retain the assumption that there is only one type of good produced and yet make the distinction between cash and credit goods, Lucas and Stokey assume that there is a linear technology for transforming cash goods into credit goods on the production or supply side. Let y_t be the exogenous endowment. The linear technology constraint is:

$$x_{1,t} + x_{2,t} = y_t, \tag{5.27}$$

where $x_{1,t}$ is the production of the cash good and $x_{2,t}$ is the production of the credit good.

Assumption 5.1 on the shocks to the economy still holds and the money supply process satisfies Equation (5.3) but we now assume that the endowment process is stationary in levels. We also require that money growth takes values in a compact set.

Assumption 5.6 *Define* $W \equiv [\underline{\omega}, \bar{\omega}]$ *where* $\underline{\omega} > 0$ *and* $\bar{\omega} < \infty$ *and* $\mathcal{Y} = [\underline{y}, \bar{y}]$ *where* $\underline{y} > 0$ *and* $\bar{y} < \infty$. *The functions* $y : S \to \mathcal{Y}$ *and* $\omega : S \to W$ *are continuous functions that are bounded away from zero.*

The rate of contraction of the money supply satisfies the following assumption.

Assumption 5.7 *For all* $s \in S$, $\beta \int_S [1/\omega(s')] F(s, ds') < 1$.

Since the technology for transforming one good into the other is linear if their prices are equal, the agent will be indifferent to the proportion in which they are consumed. To ensure that both types of goods are consumed, we assume that the marginal rate of substitution between cash and credit goods is infinite at zero values for these goods.

Assumption 5.8 *(i) The utility function* $U : \mathbb{R}_+^2 \to \mathbb{R}$ *is continuously differentiable, strictly increasing, and strictly concave. For all* $y > 0$,

$$\lim_{c \to 0} \frac{U_1(c, y - c)}{U_2(c, y - c)} = \infty, \quad \lim_{y \to c} \frac{U_1(c, y - c)}{U_2(c, y - c)} = 0;$$

(ii) For all $y \geq 0$, $cU_2(c, y - c)$ *is strictly increasing in* c, *with*

$$\lim_{c \to 0} cU_2(c, y - c) = 0, \quad \lim_{c \to y} cU_2(c, y - c) = \infty,$$

and for some $A < \infty$, $cU_1(c, y - c) \leq A$ *for all* $0 \leq c \leq y$ *and all* $y \geq 0$.

At the beginning of the period, the agent starts with currency accumulated last period M_{t-1}, observes the realization of the current shocks s_t, and receives the lump-sum money transfer G_t. The agent's post-transfer money holdings are $H_t = M_{t-1} + G_t$ where $G_t = M_t - M_{t-1}$. To make the nominal variables stationary, we divide the agent's posttransfer balances by the money supply in period t so that

$$h_t \equiv m_{t-1} + [\omega(s_t) - 1]/\omega(s_t).$$

The agent's initial wealth takes the form of money holdings, an equity share z_t which is a claim to a stochastic nominal dividend stream, and one-period nominal bonds B_{t-1}, each of which is a claim to one unit of currency at time t. The goods market opens first and the agent's purchases of cash goods $p_t c_{1,t}$ are subject to the following constraint:

$$p_t c_{1,t} \leq h_t \tag{5.28}$$

where p_t is the price level as a ratio of the money stock. The agent also purchases credit goods in the amount $p_t c_{2,t}$, payment for which can be postponed until the asset market opens.

At the close of the goods market, the agent receives the nominal dividend payment $z_t p_t y(s_t)$ and the payment on one-period nominal bonds B_{t-1} purchased last period. Define $b_t \equiv B_t/M_t^s$. The agent's budget constraint in the asset market after normalization by the money stock is:

$$p_t c_{2,t} + m_t + q_t^e z_{t+1} + Q_t b_t \leq (y_t p_t + q_t^e) z_t$$

$$+ h_t - p_t c_{1,t} + b_{t-1}/\omega(s_t), \tag{5.29}$$

where Q^e is the nominal price of the equity share, $q^e \equiv Q^e/M^s$ and Q is the nominal price of the one-period bond.

Because there is one equity share outstanding, z_t will equal exactly one in equilibrium and so, for convenience, define an interval $Z \equiv [\epsilon, \bar{z}]$

Figure 5.3. The Cash-Credit Model.

	t	Goods Market	Asset Market	$t+1$
Decisions		$c_{1,t}, c_{2,t}$	z_{t+1}, m_t^d, b_t	
Information	s_t			
Receipts		$b_{t-1}, (\omega_t - 1)M_{t-1}$	$z_{t+1}p_t y_t, b_t$	
Portfolio		h_t, z_t, b_{t-1}		h_{t+1}, z_{t+1}, b_t

where $\epsilon > 0$ and $\bar{z} > 1$ such that $z_t \in Z$. One-period nominal bonds are assumed to be in zero net supply so that, in equilibrium, b_t will equal zero and so, without loss of generality, define an interval $B \equiv [-b, b]$ where $b > 0$ such that $b_t \in B$. Finally, we know that in equilibrium, $h = 1$ (the agent's posttransfer money holdings as a ratio of the current money supply). We can define any finite upper bound $\bar{h} > 1$ but because we permit the money supply to contract, the lower bound must be chosen so that if the agent has posttransfer balances of $\underline{h}$, he can choose end-of-period balances so that, for any shock s' next period, his beginning-of-period balances are at least $\underline{h}$.[2]

For any h, z, b, s, let $\Phi(h, z, b, s)$ denote the set (c_1, c_2, z', b', m') such that $c_1, c_2, z', b', m' \geq 0$ satisfying Equations (5.27), (5.28), and (5.29). If $p(s), \psi(s)$, and $Q(s)$ are strictly positive, then the correspondence Φ is compact-valued. It is also convex valued and is continuous in h. If p and q are continuous, then under Assumption 5.6, Φ is continuous in s. The household chooses $(c_1, c_2, z', m', b') \in \Phi(h, z, b, s)$ to solve:

$$V(h, z, b, s) = \max \left\{ U(c_1, c_2) + \beta \int_S V\left(h', z', b', s'\right) F(s, ds') \right\}.$$

Let $\mathcal{C}$ be the space of bounded, continuous, real-valued functions on $\mathcal{H} \times S$ with the norm $\|f\| = \sup_{h,s} |f(h, s)|$. Under Assumptions 5.1, 5.6, and 5.8(i), there exists a unique value function $V \in \mathcal{C}$ such that V is strictly increasing, strictly concave, and continuously differentiable. This follows as an application of Proposition 2.1 from Chapter 2.[3]

---

[2]This implies that $\underline{h} < [p(s)y(s)\epsilon + \omega(s') - 1 + \underline{h}]/\omega(s')$. If $\omega(s) > 1$ for all s, then let $\underline{h} = 0$; otherwise set the lower bound $\underline{h}$ to satisfy $\min_s[\epsilon y(s)p(s)] > (1 - \bar{\omega})(1 - \underline{h})$. Let $\mathcal{H} = [\underline{h}, \bar{h}]$ such that $h_t \in \mathcal{H}$.

[3]The remainder of the proof for the existence of equilibrium is identical to the proof for the consumption-leisure model that we consider next. Equivalently, we refer the reader to Lucas and Stokey [236].

Let $c(s)$ and $y(s) - c(s)$ denote the equilibrium quantities of good 1 and good 2. Let $\mu(s)$ and $\xi(s)$ be the multipliers associated with the cash-in-advance constraint and the wealth constraint when markets clear. Substituting the envelope conditions, the first-order conditions with market clearing are:

$$0 = U_1[c(s), y(s) - c(s)] - p(s)[\mu(s) + \xi(s)], \tag{5.30}$$

$$0 = U_2[c(s), y(s) - c(s)] - p(s)\xi(s), \tag{5.31}$$

$$\xi(s) = \beta E_s [(\xi(s') + \mu(s'))], \tag{5.32}$$

$$\xi(s)q^e(s) = \beta E_s \{\xi(s')[p(s')y(s') + q^e(s')]\}, \tag{5.33}$$

$$\xi(s)Q(s) = \beta E_s [\xi(s')/\omega(s')]. \tag{5.34}$$

We also have the slackness conditions associated with the two constraints:

$$0 = \xi(s)\{[y(s)p(s) + q^e(s)]z + m - p(s)c_1 +$$
$$\omega(s)^{-1}b - p(s)c_2 - h' - q^e(s)z' - Q(s)b'\},$$

$$0 = \mu(s)[p(s)c(s) - 1].$$

The first-order condition for nominal bonds is

$$Q(s) = \beta E_s \left[\frac{\xi(s')}{\xi(s)\omega(s')} \right]. \tag{5.35}$$

If we assume that the cash-in-advance constraint is always binding, then the bond price is:

$$Q_t = \beta E_t \left[\frac{U_{2,t+1}}{U_{2,t}} \frac{p_t}{\omega_{t+1}p_{t+1}} \right],$$

which is the intertemporal MRS in the purchasing power of money for the credit good. The nominal bond depends on the marginal utility of credit goods divided by the price level. The close link between the nominal interest rate and velocity has been severed in this model. To see this, suppose that the cash-in-advance constraint is binding. Consumption velocity v_t satisfies:

$$h_t v_t = p_t(c_{1,t} + c_{2,t}) = 1 + \frac{c_{2,t}}{c_{1,t}} = \frac{y}{c}$$

and, hence, consumption velocity varies as the proportion of credit to cash goods varies.

The equity price function satisfies:

$$\xi(s)q^e(s) = \beta E_s \left\{ \xi(s')[y(s')p(s') + q^e(s')] \right\}.$$

For discussion's sake, suppose that the cash-in-advance constraint is always binding. In that case,

$$\xi(s) = U_2[c(s), y(s) - c(s)]/p(s).$$

Define $U_{2,t} \equiv U_2[c(s_t), y(s_t) - c(s_t)]$ and let $p_t = p(s_t)$. Using time subscripts, the real equity price satisfies the relation:

$$\frac{q_t^e}{p_t} = \beta E_t \left[\frac{U_{2,t+1}}{U_{2,t}} \left(y_{t+1} + \frac{q_{t+1}^e}{p_{t+1}} \right) \right]. \tag{5.36}$$

Solving this forward:

$$\frac{q_t^e}{p_t} = E_t \left[\sum_{i=1}^{\infty} \frac{\beta^i U_{2,t+i}}{U_{2,t}} y_{t+i} \right]. \tag{5.37}$$

This formula for the real equity price is similar to the present-value formula we derived in Chapter 2 in an economy without money. This formula says that the real equity price is formed by discounting real dividends in period $t+i$ by the marginal rate of substitution for consumption between t and $t+i$. But notice that in this model, the relevant MRS is the MRS for consumption of credit goods. Since cash goods and credit goods are not perfect substitutes in consumption, the MRS for consumption of credit goods will be affected by the existence of the cash-in-advance constraint on cash goods, thus differentiating this model from the real, representative consumer asset pricing model with a single consumption good. Sill [309] presents some empirical evidence about the behavior of money demand equations implied by a cash-credit model with preference shocks.

2.2.   A Model with a Consumption-Leisure Choice

We now introduce a model that allows for a consumption-leisure choice by agents. Since consumption choices are constrained by cash holdings, a wedge is introduced that allows for the output effects of monetary growth shocks. An explicit government budget constraint is introduced, linking bond supply and the money supply. The government finances an exogenous and stochastic expenditure stream, which is distributed lump-sum to households, by collecting income taxes, seignorage, and borrowing.

Each agent is endowed with one unit of time per period which can be divided between labor n and leisure ℓ. There is an exogenous and stochastic capital stock κ owned by the firm which depreciates 100 percent each period. The firm issues one equity which is a claim to the return to capital and any profits. The equity is traded each period in a competitive stock market. Output y is produced by a linear homogeneous production function:

$$y_t = A\kappa_t^{1-\theta}n_t^{\theta}, \tag{5.38}$$

where $0 < \theta < 1$. The household owns the labor stock and is a price-taker in the factor market. Each factor is paid the value of its marginal product and these payments exhaust the revenue of the typical firm. The real wage is:

$$w_t = \theta y_t / n_t, \tag{5.39}$$

and the return to the exogenous and stochastic capital stock is:

$$r_t = (1 - \theta)y_t / \kappa_t. \tag{5.40}$$

The exogenous and stochastic expenditures G_t are financed by issuing currency $M_t - M_{t-1}$, setting the income tax τ_t, and by borrowing through the issue of one-period nominal bonds B_t^s which are sold at the price Q_t. The government's budget constraint is:

$$B_{t-1}^s + G_t = M_t - M_{t-1} + Q_t B_t^s + \tau_{t-1}(P_{t-1}y_{t-1}), \tag{5.41}$$

where P_{t-1} is the price level in period $t - 1$. Define $b^s = B^s/M$, $g = G/M$, and $p = P/M$. The growth of money defined as $M_t/M_{t-1} \equiv \omega(s_t)$ satisfies:

$$g_t = \frac{1}{\omega(s_t)}[\omega(s_t) - 1 - b_{t-1}^s + \tau_{t-1}(p_{t-1}y_{t-1})] + Q_t b_t^s. \tag{5.42}$$

The asset and factor markets open first followed by the goods market. In the factor market, the household decides how to allocate its time between labor n_t and leisure ℓ_t subject to the time constraint:

$$n_t + \ell_t \leq 1. \tag{5.43}$$

In the asset market, the household adjusts its holdings of currency, nominal bonds, and equity shares. We normalize by dividing the nominal constraints by the money stock at the beginning of the period. The agent's beginning-of-period money balances after receiving the lump-sum

Figure 5.4. The Consumption-Leisure Model.

t	Asset/Factor Market	Goods Market	$t+1$
Decisions	$\ell_t, z_{t+1}, m_t^d, b_t$	c_t	
Information	s_t		
Receipts	g_t, b_{t-1}	$n_t w_t p_t, z_{t+1} p_t d_t$	
Tax Payments		$\tau n_t w_t p_t + p_t d_t z_{t+1}$	
Portfolio	h_t, z_t, b_{t-1}		

transfer G_t are denoted H_t. The household's budget constraint in the asset market is:

$$m_t + Q_t b_t + q_t^e z_{t+1} \leq h_t + q_t^e z_t, \tag{5.44}$$

where m_t denotes money balances held at the close of the asset market and $h_t \equiv H_t/M_t$.

After the asset and labor markets close, consumption purchases are made with the currency acquired in the asset market. Because nominal factor payments are received after the goods market is closed, all consumption purchases must be financed with real balances held at the closing of the asset market. The normalized cash-in-advance constraint is

$$p_t c_t \leq m_t, \tag{5.45}$$

where c_t is consumption and p_t is its price.

After the goods market closes, the household receives the dividend payment $d_t z_{t+1} p_t$ and payment on labor supplied $w_t n_t p_t$, where w_t is the real wage, and pays taxes on this income. The law of motion for the agent's beginning-of-period money holdings is:

$$h_{t+1} = g_{t+1} + [b_t + p_t(w_t n_t + z_{t+1} d_t)(1 - \tau_t)$$
$$+ m_t - p_t c_t]/\omega(s_{t+1}). \tag{5.46}$$

At the time the agent decides on the amount of labor to supply, the real value next period of the factor payment is uncertain because inflation is uncertain. The timing of trade is summarized in Figure 5.4.

The representative household has preferences:

$$E_0 \left\{ \sum_{t=0}^{\infty} \beta^t U(c_t, \ell_t) \right\}, \quad 0 < \beta < 1. \tag{5.47}$$

We have the following assumption.

Assumption 5.9 *(i) The utility function is continuously twice differentiable, strictly increasing, and strictly concave; (ii) $U_{11} + U_{12} < 0$, $U_{22} + U_{21} < 0$, and $U_{12} > 0$;*

$$(iii)\ \lim_{\ell \to 1} \frac{U_1(A\kappa^{1-\theta}(1-\ell)^\theta, \ell)}{U_2(A\kappa^{1-\theta}(1-\ell)^\theta, \ell)} = \infty, \quad \lim_{\ell \to 0} \frac{U_2(A\kappa^{1-\theta}(1-\ell)^\theta, \ell)}{U_1(A\kappa^{1-\theta}(1-\ell)^\theta, \ell)} = \infty.$$

Part (ii) of this assumption says that current consumption and leisure are not inferior goods while part (iii) implies both goods will be consumed in equilibrium.

We assume that the shock to the economy s_t satisfies the conditions of Assumption 5.1 and the rate of contraction of the money supply satisfies the conditions of Assumption 5.7. In this model, the capital stock is exogenous. We have the following assumption.

Assumption 5.10 *The capital stock $\kappa : S \to \mathbb{R}_+$ is continuous, strictly bounded away from 0, and takes values on $K \equiv [\underline{\kappa}, \overline{\kappa}]$.*

We assume that there is one outstanding equity share traded in a competitive market that is a claim to the nominal return to capital and profits. Because the production function is Cobb-Douglas, the factor payments exhaust all revenue. Hence, there are no profits to be distributed and the firm's maximization problem is straightforward. The following assumption holds for government policy.

Assumption 5.11 *The income tax $\tau : S \to [0, \overline{\tau}]$, with $\overline{\tau} < 1$, is a continuous function. Government expenditure $g : S \to \mathbb{R}_+$ and the issue of one-period nominal bonds $b^s : S \to \mathbb{R}_+$ are continuous functions that satisfy Equation (5.42).*

After observing the realization s_t, the government transfers $g(s_t)$ as a lump-sum payment to households and pays $b^s(s_{t-1})$ to bondholders. It finances these expenditures through seignorage revenue and borrowing in the asset market.

The price functions $p : S \to \mathbb{R}_{++}$, $q^e : S \to \mathbb{R}_{++}$, $Q : S \to \mathbb{R}_{++}$, and $w : S \to \mathbb{R}_{++}$ are assumed to be continuous and strictly positive. The household takes as given the functions describing the government's expenditures, nominal bond supply, income tax rates, and money supply growth. The dynamic programming problem solved by the household is:

$$V(h, z, s) = \max_{\{c, \ell, m, z', b'\}} \left\{ U(c, \ell) + \beta \int_S V(h', z', s') F(s, ds') \right\} \quad (5.48)$$

subject to the time constraint (Equation 5.43), the asset market constraint (Equation 5.44), the cash-in-advance constraint (Equation 5.45), and the law of motion for money holdings (Equation 5.46). Assume as before that $z \in Z$ and that $h \in \mathcal{H} \equiv [0, \bar{h}]$ where $\bar{h} > 1$.

We can define an equilibrium as before. Define the equilibrium multiplier on the cash-in-advance constraint in Equation (5.45) as $\mu(s)$ and the equilibrium multiplier on the asset market constraint as $\xi(s)$. The first-order conditions with market-clearing for c, ℓ, m, b', z' are:

$$U_1(c, \ell) = \mu(s)p(s) + \beta E_s \left[\frac{U_1(c', \ell')p(s)}{p(s')\omega(s')} \right], \tag{5.49}$$

$$U_2(c, \ell) = \beta E_s \left[\frac{U_1(c', \ell')w(s)p(s)[1 - \tau(s)]}{\omega(s')p(s')} \right], \tag{5.50}$$

$$\xi(s) = \mu(s) + \beta E_s \left[\frac{U_1(c', \ell')}{\omega(s')p(s')} \right], \tag{5.51}$$

$$\xi(s)Q(s) = \beta E_s \left[\frac{U_1(c', \ell')}{\omega(s')p(s')} \right], \tag{5.52}$$

$$\xi(s)q^e(s) = \beta E_s \left\{ \frac{U_1(c', \ell')p(s)d(s)[1 - \tau(s)]}{\omega(s')p(s')} + \right. \tag{5.53}$$

$$\left. \frac{U_1(c', \ell')q^e(s')}{p(s')} \right\}. \tag{5.54}$$

This model allows the stochastic inflation tax and the income tax to have real output effects. Notice that if $\mu(s) = 0$, then $U_1(c, \ell)/p = U_2(c, \ell)/wp(1 - \tau)$ so that the cash-in-advance constraint creates a wedge not only in the consumption-leisure choice but also in the intertemporal substitution between leisure today and leisure tomorrow. It also has the feature that the government faces a tradeoff in creating real seignorage revenue. As the government increases the growth of the money supply, it generates real revenue by taxing the stock of real balances held by the private sector but it also decreases the real value of the tax revenue it collected at the end of the previous period.

The wedge introduced by the cash-in-advance constraint implies that we must solve simultaneously for the multiplier on the cash-in-advance constraint $\mu(s)$ and the equilibrium value of leisure $\ell(s)$. Define the functions $\hat{y}$ and $\hat{w}$ as: $\hat{y}(s, \ell) = A[\kappa(s)]^{1-\theta}(1-\ell)^\theta$ and $\hat{w}(s, \ell) = \theta \hat{y}(s, \ell)/(1-\ell)$. We begin with the following proposition.

Proposition 5.1 *(1) Under Assumption 5.9, $U_1(\hat{y}(s,\ell),\ell)$ is strictly increasing in ℓ.*
(2)

$$\frac{\partial}{\partial \ell}\left[\frac{U_2(\hat{y}(s,\ell),\ell)}{\hat{w}(s,\ell)[1-\tau(s)]}\right] < 0, \quad \lim_{\ell\to 0}\left[\frac{U_2(\hat{y}(s,\ell),\ell)}{\hat{w}(s,\ell)[1-\tau(s)]}\right] = \infty.$$

(3) There exists a unique $0 < \ell^*(s) < 1$ such that

$$U_1(\hat{y}(s,\ell),\ell) - \frac{U_2(\hat{y}(s,\ell),\ell)}{\hat{w}(s,\ell)[1-\tau(s)]} = 0$$

at $\ell = \ell^*$. Further, for $\ell > \ell^*$ the left side is strictly positive.

PROOF
Part (1) follows by differentiating with respect to ℓ and using the strict concavity and $U_{12} > 0$. Part (2) follows also by differentiating and using the concavity and conditions on U specified in the assumption. To prove part (3), we know from part (1) that the first term on the left side is strictly increasing and the second term is strictly decreasing. As $\ell \to 0$, the ratio $U_2/[U_1 w(1-\tau)]$ tends to ∞, while, as $\ell \to 1$, $y \to 0$ so that the ratio $[U_1 w(1-\tau)]/U_2$ tends to ∞. Hence, the functions cross at one and only one point, ℓ^* and for $\ell > \ell^*$, the difference is positive. ∎
    Next, define the function $\Lambda : S \to \mathbb{R}_+$ as:

$$\Lambda(s) \equiv \beta E_s\left[\frac{U_1(\hat{y}(s',\ell'),\ell')}{p(s')\omega(s')}\right].$$

Solve Equation (5.49) for $\mu(s)$ and Equation (5.50) for $p(s)$ and substitute the resulting solution for $p(s)$ into the equation for $\mu(s)$, leading to

$$\mu(s) = \Lambda(s)\left[\frac{U_1(\hat{y}(s,\ell),\ell),\hat{w}(s,\ell)[1-\tau(s)]}{U_1(\hat{y}(s,\ell),\ell)} - 1\right]. \tag{5.55}$$

The cash-in-advance constraint $p(s)\hat{y}(s,\ell) \leq 1$ and Equation (5.55) form a system of two equations in two unknowns (μ,ℓ).
    Choose a fixed value Λ such that $0 < \Lambda < \infty$. Under Assumption 5.9, the function $\hat{\ell}(s,\Lambda)$ satisfying

$$\frac{U_2\{\hat{y}(s,\hat{\ell}(s,\Lambda)),\hat{\ell}(s,\Lambda)\}}{\hat{w}(s,\hat{\ell}(s,\Lambda))} = \Lambda$$

is well defined. This follows because of the continuous differentiability of U_2 and the continuity of $\hat{y}$ and $\hat{w}$. From the cash-in-advance constraint, we know that the following inequality holds,

$$\hat{y}(s, \ell)\frac{U_2(\hat{y}(s, \ell), \ell)(1 - \ell)}{\hat{w}(s, \ell)[1 - \tau(s)]} \leq \Lambda, \tag{5.56}$$

and holds with equality when $\mu(s) = 0$. Define the function $\Lambda^\star(s)$ as:

$$\Lambda^\star(s) = \frac{\hat{y}(s, \ell^\star(s))U_2\{\hat{y}(s, \ell^\star(s)), \ell^\star(s)\}}{\hat{w}(s, \ell^\star(s))[1 - \tau(s)]}.$$

We have the following proposition.

Proposition 5.2 *Under Assumption 5.9 for any finite $\Lambda \geq 0$, the unique pair ℓ, μ satisfying Equations (5.55) and (5.56) is given by*

$$\ell(s, \Lambda) = \begin{cases} \hat{\ell}(s, \Lambda) & if\ 0 \leq \Lambda \leq \Lambda^\star(s) \\ \ell^\star(s) & if\ \Lambda \geq \Lambda^\star(s) \end{cases} \tag{5.57}$$

and μ is given by Equation (5.55).

PROOF
Because $\mu(s) \geq 0$, it follows from Equation (5.55) that $[U_1w(1-\tau)]/U_2 \geq 1$ which in turn implies that $\ell \geq \ell^\star$. Suppose that $0 \leq \Lambda(s) < \Lambda^\star(s)$. Then $\ell > \ell^\star(s)$ since Equation (5.56) would be violated if $\ell = \ell^\star(s)$ so that $[U_1w(1 - \tau)]/U_2 > 1$. If $[U_1w(1 - \tau)]/U_2 > 1$, then Equation (5.55) implies that $\mu > 0$. Hence, Equation (5.56) must hold with equality so that the solution is $\hat{\ell}(s, \Lambda)$. Suppose next that $\Lambda > \Lambda^\star(s)$. Since $\ell \geq \ell^\star(s)$, Equation (5.56) must hold as an inequality. Therefore $\mu = 0$ and $[U_1w(1 - \tau)]/U_2 = 1$ and $\ell = \ell^\star(s)$. ∎

We make the following assumption.

Assumption 5.12 *For all $s \in S$, $U_1(\hat{y}(s, \ell), \ell)\hat{y}(s, \ell)$ is increasing in ℓ.*

Next define the function $G : S \times \mathbb{R}_+ \to \mathbb{R}_+$ by:

$$G(s, \Lambda) = \begin{cases} \hat{y}(s, \hat{\ell}(s, \Lambda))U_1\{\hat{y}(s, \hat{\ell}(s, \Lambda)), \hat{\ell}(s, \Lambda)\} & if\ 0 \leq \Lambda \leq \Lambda^\star(s) \\ \Lambda^\star(s) & if\ \Lambda \geq \Lambda^\star(s). \end{cases}$$

A solution is a function Λ satisfying

$$\Lambda(s) = \beta \int_S G(s', \Lambda(s'))F(s', ds). \tag{5.58}$$

We have the following proposition.

Proposition 5.3 *For each* $s \in S$ *and* $\Lambda \geq 0$, $G(s,\Lambda) - \Lambda$ *is weakly decreasing in* Λ.

PROOF
Under Assumption 5.12, $y(s,\ell)U_1(y(s,\ell),\ell)$ is increasing in ℓ and, from Proposition 5.1, $\hat{\ell}(s,\Lambda)$ is nonincreasing in Λ, so that $G_2 \leq 0$. ∎
   We then have the following theorem.

Theorem 5.3 *Under Assumptions 5.9, 5.10, and 5.11, Equation (5.58) has a unique solution* $\Lambda \in \mathcal{C}$ *and for all* $\Lambda_0 \in \mathcal{C}$, $\lim_{n \to \infty} \|T^n \Lambda^0 - \Lambda\| = 0$.

PROOF
Define the operator T on $\mathcal{C}$ by:

$$(Tf)(s) = \beta \int_S G(s', f(s'))F(s', ds). \tag{5.59}$$

Because f, G are continuous and bounded, Tf is continuous and bounded. Hence $T : \mathcal{C} \to \mathcal{C}$. Finally, T is a continuous operator. Note that

$$\|Tf - Tf_n\| = \max_{s \in S} |Tf(s) - Tf_n(s)|$$

$$\leq \max_{s \in S} \beta \int_S |G(s', f(s')) - G(s', f_n(s'))|F(s, ds')$$

$$\leq \beta \max_{s' \in S} |G(s', f(s')) - G(s', f_n(s'))|.$$

We show that the operator T satisfies Blackwell's conditions. Under the assumptions above and from Proposition 5.1, G is nondecreasing in f, so that T is monotone. We need only verify the discounting property. From Proposition 5.1, $G(s,\Lambda) - \Lambda$ is weakly decreasing in Λ. For any $\Lambda \in \mathcal{C}$ and $a > 0$ $G(s, \Lambda + a) - (\Lambda + a) \leq G(s, \Lambda) - \Lambda$ or $G(s, \Lambda) \leq G(s, \Lambda) + a$. Then

$$T(f + a)(s) = \beta \int_S G(s', f(s') + a)F(s, ds')$$

$$\leq \beta \int_S \{G(s', f(s')) + a\}F(s, ds')$$

$$\leq Tf(s) + \beta a,$$

so that T is a contraction with modulus β. ∎
   Let $\ell(s)$ be the solution with the output equal to $y(s)$ when $\ell(s)$ is leisure. Define the stochastic discount factor as the intertemporal marginal rate of substitution in the purchasing power of money:

$$\mathcal{M}(s', s) \equiv \frac{\beta U_1 \{y(s'), \ell(s')\} p(s)}{U_1 \{y(s), \ell(s)\} \omega(s') p(s')}.$$

All assets denominated in nominal terms in this model are priced using this stochastic discount factor. The income tax and the stochastic inflation tax drive a wedge between consumption and leisure choices and increase the volatility of the stochastic discount factor that is used to price all assets with random payoffs. This wedge is similar to the wedge with cash and credit goods.

2.3. Liquidity Effects and Asset Prices

We now describe a model in which money is injected or withdrawn from the economy in two ways: by open market operations or by lump-sum transfers. The government does not collect taxes or purchase consumption goods. It merely prints currency or borrows by issuing new debt to pay off maturing debt in the current period. Introducing the government's budget constraint allows us to drop the assumption that the net supply of bonds is zero.

There are different cash-in-constraints for consumption and purchases of assets. Any net purchases of bonds and equities must be made with currency brought into the asset market. However, by swapping long-term for short-term bonds or bonds for stocks, an agent can rearrange the composition of his portfolio without using currency as long as the market value of the portfolio remains unchanged. A liquidity effect on asset prices emerges in this model because agents must divide their money balances between the goods market and the asset market before knowing the realizations of the government's policy. The model presented here is similar to Lucas [235] and has also been studied by Coleman, Gilles, and Labadie [74].[4]

The government's stock of debt outstanding at the beginning of the period is denoted $B_{\tau,t}$ where τ is the maturity length of the bond. We assume that the bonds pay no coupons and are sold at a discount. The supply of money held by the private sector at the beginning of the period is M_t. A bond issued in period t that matures in τ periods, denoted $D_{\tau,t}$, sells at a price $Q_{\tau,t}$ and is a claim to one unit of currency paid at time $t + \tau$. The law of motion for the outstanding stock of bonds is:

$$B_{\tau,t+1} = B_{\tau+1,t} + D_{\tau+1,t}$$

for $\tau \geq 0$. Note that $B_{0,t}$ is the stock of bonds maturing in the current

---

[4]A related model is described by Fuerst [140].

period. The government's current period budget constraint is:

$$M_{t+1} = M_t + \sum_{\tau=1}^{T} Q_{\tau,t} D_{\tau,t} - B_{0,t} + N_t,$$

where N_t is a lump-sum transfer made at the end of period t.

Define $d_{\tau,t} \equiv D_{\tau,t}/M_t$, and d as the vector of normalized new bond issues, $n_t \equiv N_t/M_t$, and $b_{\tau,t} \equiv B_{\tau,t}/M_t$. Money growth, $\omega(s_t) \equiv M_{t+1}/M_t$, satisfies:

$$\omega(s_t) = 1 + \sum_{\tau=1}^{T} Q_{\tau,t} d_\tau(s_t) + b_{0,t} + n(s_t). \tag{5.60}$$

The government chooses the values for any two of the three instruments (d, n, ω) with the third instrument determined so that Equation (5.60) is satisfied. We assume that the policy choices are well defined functions of s, $d(s), n(s)$, and $\omega(s)$. The law of motion of the government's outstanding stock of bonds normalized by the money stock is:

$$b_{\tau,t+1} = (b_{\tau+1,t} + d_{\tau,t})/\omega(s_t). \tag{5.61}$$

Let b denote the vector of government debt at the beginning of the period. Since b is a function of $d(s)$ and $\omega(s)$, it is also a well defined function of the exogenous shock s. Under the assumption that the shocks are first-order Markov, notice that s summarizes the current state of government policy.

At the beginning of period t, the realization s_t is not known but a signal $\hat{s}_t$ is announced. Let $\hat{v}_t \equiv (s_{t-1}, \hat{s}_t)$ be the information set at the beginning of the period. The endowment is stationary and it is a function of the shocks $s_{t-1}, \hat{s}_t$, $y_t \equiv y(s_{t-1}, \hat{s}_t)$. We assume that $y : S \times S \to [\underline{y}, \bar{y}]$ where $\underline{y} > 0$ and $\bar{y} < \infty$ is a continuous function that is bounded away from zero. The utility function $U : S \to \mathbb{R}_+$ is strictly increasing, strictly concave, and continuously differentiable.

The representative agent's nominal wealth consists of currency H_t, equity shares z_t, and a stock of bonds $A_{\tau,t}$ where $\tau = 0$ denotes holdings of bonds that mature in the current period. At the beginning of the period, the agent receives payment on bonds maturing in the current period. Based on the information set $\hat{v}_t$, he decides how to allocate his money holdings between the goods market and the asset market. Denote G_t as the currency allocated to the goods market so that currency allocated to the asset market is $H_t - G_t$. After choosing G_t, the agent observes s_t.[5]

---

[5]This setup differs slightly from that in Lucas [235] because we assume that information flows freely between the two markets, although money allocations cannot be altered after G is chosen.

Figure 5.5. The Liquidity Model.

	Goods Market		Asset Market	
t				$t+1$
Decisions	$g_t, h_t - g_t$	c_t	z_{t+1}, w_t	
Information	v_t		v_t, η_t	
Receipts	b_0			$z_{t+1} p_t y_t, n_t$

where $v_t = (s_{t-1}, \hat{s}_{t-1}, b_t)$ and $\eta_t = (b_t, s_t)$.

Define $h_t \equiv H_t/M_t$, $g_t \equiv G_t/M_t$, and $p_t \equiv P_t/M_t$. The cash-in-advance constraint in the goods market is:

$$p_t c_t \leq g_t. \qquad (5.62)$$

The agent's portfolio in the asset market consists of nominal bonds $A_{\tau,t}$, equity shares purchased last period z_t, and real balances $h_t - g_t$. The normalized cash-in-advance constraint in the asset market is:

$$\sum_\tau Q_{\tau,t} w_{\tau,t} + q_t^e(z_{t+1} - z_t) \leq h_t - g_t, \qquad (5.63)$$

where $w_{\tau,t}$ is the net purchases (positive) or sales (negative) of bonds maturing at time $t + \tau$. The normalized law of motion for an agent's stock of bonds is:

$$a_{\tau-1,t+1} = (a_{\tau,t} + w_{\tau,t})/\omega(s_t), \qquad (5.64)$$

where $\tau \geq 1$ and $w_{\tau,t}$ is net purchases at time t of bonds maturing in τ periods.

After both markets have closed, the agent receives the nominal dividend on the equity $z_{t+1} y_t p_t$ and the lump-sum money transfer. Notice that the nominal dividend on an equity share purchased in period t is paid at the end of period t. The normalized law of motion for the agent's money stock is:

$$h_{t+1} = b_{0,t+1} + [h_t - \sum_\tau Q_{\tau,t} w_{\tau,t} - p_t c_t - q_t^e(z_{t+1} - z_t)$$

$$+ z_{t+1} p_t y_t + n_t]/\omega(s_t). \qquad (5.65)$$

The agent takes all prices as given. The information set after s_t is revealed is $v_t \equiv (s_t)$ while recall that $\hat{v}_t \equiv (s_{t-1}, \hat{s}_t)$.

We consider only equilibria in which prices are continuous and strictly positive functions of the state s, $p(s), q^e(s), Q_\tau(s)$. Given the price functions $p(s), Q(s), q^e(s)$, the dynamic programming problem is:

$$V(h, a, z, \hat{v}) = \max_g E_{\hat{v}} \left\{ \max_{c,w,z'} [U(c) + \beta E_v V(h', a', z', v')] \right\} \quad (5.66)$$

subject to the cash-in-advance constraints (Equations 5.62 and 5.63), the laws of motion for the agent's bonds and money balances (Equations 5.64 and 5.65), and the government's policy functions d, n and law of motion for its debt, which are part of the state of the economy.

In equilibrium, markets clear so $h = 1$, $z = 1$, $c = y$, and $w = d$. Let $\xi(s)$ denote value of the equilibrium multiplier for the cash-in-advance constraint in the asset market and let $\mu(s)$ denote the value of the equilibrium multiplier for the cash-in-advance constraint in the goods market. Define $\phi(\hat{v}) \equiv V(1, b, 1, \hat{v})$. Let ϕ_h be the partial derivative of V with respect to money holdings, ϕ_a^τ is the partial derivative of V with respect to the τ'th element of its second argument, and ϕ_z is the partial derivative of V with respect to equity holdings.

The equilibrium first-order conditions corresponding to the optimal choice for equity shares, net purchases of bonds, and consumption are:

$$q^e(s) \{\xi(s) + \beta E_v [\phi_h(\hat{v}')/\omega(s)]\} =$$
$$\beta E_v [\phi_h(\hat{v}')yp(s)/\omega(s)] + \beta E_v [\phi_z(\hat{v}')], \quad (5.67)$$

$$Q_\tau(s) \{\xi(s) + \beta E_v [\phi_h(\hat{v}')/\omega(s)]\} = \beta E_v [\phi_a^\tau(\hat{v}')/\omega(s)] \quad (5.68)$$

$$\mu(s) + \beta E_v [\phi_h(\hat{v}')/\omega(s)] = U'(y(\hat{v}))/p(s). \quad (5.69)$$

The first-order condition with respect to the allocation of currency between the markets is:

$$E_{\hat{v}} [\mu(s)] = E_{\hat{v}} [\xi(s)]. \quad (5.70)$$

We also have the slackness conditions for the multipliers $\mu(s)$ and $\xi(s)$:

$$0 = [g(\hat{v}) - p(s)y]\mu(s), \quad (5.71)$$

$$0 = \{h - g - \sum_\tau [Q_\tau(s)d_\tau(s) + q^e(s)(z' - z)]\}\xi(s). \quad (5.72)$$

The envelope conditions with respect to holdings of money, stocks, and bonds are:

$$\phi_h(\hat{v}) = E_{\hat{v}} [U'(y)/p(s)], \quad (5.73)$$

$$\phi_z(\hat{v}) = E_{\hat{v}} \{\xi(s) + \beta E_{\hat{v}} [\phi_h(\hat{v}')/\omega(s)] q^e(s)\}, \quad (5.74)$$

$$\phi_a^\tau(\hat{v}) = \beta E_{\hat{v}} [\phi_a^{\tau-1}(\hat{v}')/\omega(s)]. \quad (5.75)$$

The existence and uniqueness of a fixed point to the functional equation in the unknown function V, Equation (5.66), can be established following the approach in Proposition 2.1 from Chapter 2.

We can use the approach described earlier to study the behavior of the normalized price level by defining a function Ψ that is related to the inverse of velocity. Suppose that we have a function $g(\hat{v})$ of cash allocated to the goods market where, for all $\hat{v}$, $0 < g(\hat{v}) \leq 1$. The cash-in-advance constraint in the goods market is $p(s)y \leq g(\hat{v})$ which is used to define the function Ψ by $p(s)y\Psi(s) = g(\hat{v})$. Substituting into Equation (5.69), we have:

$$\frac{U'(y)y\Psi(s)}{g(\hat{v})} = \mu(s) + \beta E_v \left[\frac{U'(y')y'\Psi(s')}{\omega(s)g(\hat{v}')} \right].$$

By construction, the function Ψ must satisfy $\Psi(s) \geq 1$ for all s. When $\mu(s) > 0$, $\Psi(s) = 1$. Define the function $\Gamma(s)$ by:

$$\Gamma(s) \equiv U'(y)y\Psi(s)/g(\hat{v}).$$

Because y is exogenous and strictly positive, $U'(y)y$ is strictly positive so that we can solve for the function Γ as well as the function Ψ. Let $\mathcal{C}(S)$ denote the space of real-valued, bounded, continuous functions on S with the sup norm. Define the operator $T_g : \mathcal{C}(S) \to \mathcal{C}(S)$ by:

$$T_g[\Gamma(s)] = \max \left[\frac{U'(y)y}{g(\hat{v})}, \beta E_s \left(\frac{\Gamma(s')}{\omega(s')g(\hat{v}')} \right) \right]. \tag{5.76}$$

The function Ψ is not the inverse of velocity although it is related to velocity. Notice that consumption velocity, defined as $V = Py/M$, is equal to $g(\hat{v})/\Psi(s)$. Hence, velocity varies through g even if the goods market cash-in-advance constraint is binding $[\Psi(s) = 1]$. The next step is to determine the function g. This is described by Coleman, Gilles and Labadie [74].

We now turn to a discussion of the liquidity effect in this model. Consider the effect of an unanticipated decrease in open market sales (a decrease in $d(s)$) that is sterilized by an offsetting increase in transfers $n(s)$ such that money growth $\omega(s)$ is unchanged. When only one-period bonds are issued, the asset market cash-in-advance constraint implies that

$$Q_1(s)d(s) = 1 - g(\hat{v}),$$

where we assume that the constraint is always binding. Notice that $g(\hat{v})$ is fixed. An unanticipated decrease in $d(s)$ necessarily increases bond prices and hence, decreases the nominal interest rate. The implication is that unanticipated open market shocks can affect the nominal and real interest rate; this is the liquidity effect. Because the realization of the signal $\hat{s}$ provides information about s, $E_{\hat{v}}[d(s)]$ is the expected open market operation. Agents will forecast the open market operation when making decisions about how to allocate their money balances.

We now turn to the general case when the government issues bonds of various maturities. For notational convenience, define the function:

$$\alpha(s) \equiv \xi(s) + \beta E_v \left[\phi_h(\hat{v}')/\omega(s) \right].$$

The function α measures the marginal value of liquidity in the asset market. It consists of two parts: the direct return on liquidity, measured by the multiplier ξ and the indirect return $\alpha - \xi$. The equilibrium first-order conditions of interest are:

$$Q_\tau(s)\alpha(s) = \beta E_v \left[\phi_a^\tau(\hat{v}')/\omega(s) \right],$$
$$\phi_a^\tau(\hat{v}) = \beta E_{\hat{v}} \left[\phi_a^{\tau-1}(\hat{v}')/\omega(s) \right].$$

We can solve this recursively by starting with $\tau = 1$. From the first-order condition, we have:

$$Q_1(s)\alpha(s) = \phi_a^1(s) = \beta E_v \left[U'(y')/p(s')\omega(s) \right]$$
$$= \beta E_v[\alpha(s')].$$

For $\tau = 2$, the envelope condition is:

$$\phi_a^2(s) = \beta E_v \left[\phi_a^1(x')/\omega(s) \right] = E_{\hat{v}} \left[\alpha(s')Q_1(s') \right].$$

Using the first-order condition for $\tau = 2$, we have:

$$Q_2(s)\alpha(s) = \beta E_v \left[\alpha(s')Q_1(s')/\omega(s) \right].$$

For any $\tau > 1$,

$$Q_\tau(s)\alpha(s) = \beta E_v \left[\alpha(s')Q_{\tau-1}(s')/\omega(s) \right].$$

Solving this for $Q_\tau(s)$ and rewriting with time subscripts, we have:

$$Q_\tau(s_t) = \frac{1}{\alpha(s_t)} E_t \left[\beta^\tau \frac{U'(y_{t+\tau})}{\omega_{t+\tau-1,t}p(s_{t+\tau})} \right]$$
$$= E_t \left[\beta^\tau \frac{\alpha(s_{t+\tau})}{\alpha(s_t)\omega_{t+\tau-1,t}} \right].$$

The price of a bond that matures in τ periods is determined by the marginal rate of substitution of liquidity services today for liquidity services at time $t + \tau$. Because the MRS of liquidity services systematically differs from the MRS in the purchasing power of money, the bond prices in this model are different from those derived from a standard model, such as the first model described in this chapter.

3. Timing of Information

We now discuss some ways of empirically distinguishing the timing of information and the sequence of trades that differentiate alternative versions of the basic cash-in-advance model. Singleton [312] and Finn, Hoffman, and Schlagenhauf [130] present Euler equation-based tests of these timing conventions.

Finn *et al.* use data on two monthly stock return series: one which is a value-weighted return and the other an equally weighted return. Let $R^d_{t+1,t}$ denote the measured nominal stock return between periods $t + 1$ and t. This series is computed using a price observed at the beginning of period t, denoted q^b_t, a dividend paid at the beginning of period $t + 1$, denoted d^b_{t+1}, and a price observed at the beginning of period $t + 1$. They measure the nominal interest rate using one-month Treasury Bill returns. Let i^d_t denote the nominal interest rate. Finn *et al.* note that, in discrete time models, a variable such as q^b_{t+1} measured at the beginning of period $t + 1$ can also be interpreted as a variable measured at the end of period t. Let the stock price observed at the end of period t be denoted q^e_t. It follows that $q^b_{t+1} = q^e_t$. Hence, the measured return $R^d_{t,t-1}$ can be interpreted as a return from the end of period $t - 1$ to the end of period t or else as a return from the beginning of period t to the beginning of period $t + 1$.

In the first version of the Lucas model, an equity share purchased in the asset market meeting at the beginning of period t is a claim to a dividend paid at the end of the period in which the claim is purchased. Hence, buying a claim at the beginning of period t means foregoing consumption in period t while the return on the claim can be spent on consumption next period. The information set at time t, denoted I^1_t, includes all $t - 1$ variables, c_t, and p_t. Thus, the Lucas model can be formulated empirically as:

$$1 = E_{I^1_t}\left[\frac{U'(c_{t+1})p_t}{U'(c_t)p_{t+1}} R^d_{t,t-1} \right], \tag{5.77}$$

$$1 = E_{I_t^1} \left[\frac{U'(c_{t+1})p_t}{U'(c_t)p_{t+1}} (1 + i_{t-1}^d) \right]. \tag{5.78}$$

Notice that the current equity price, which is an argument of $R_{t,t-1}^d$, is *not* part of the information set on which the expectation is conditioned although the current dividend c_t is part of that information set. The equity return $R_{t,t-1}^d$ is used because it includes the dividend paid in time t and, under our assumptions about the information set, the price at which the shares can be sold is unknown when the shares are purchased.

The second version of the Lucas model makes the assumption that the endowment is unknown at the time the equity and bonds are purchased. Purchasing an equity share at the beginning of period t entails foregoing an uncertain consumption at time t, receiving an uncertain dividend at the end of period t, and possibly spending the return on uncertain consumption next period. The information set includes all $t-1$ variables, the nominal equity price at time t, and the nominal interest rate at time t; let I_t^2 denote this information set. The empirical formulations are:

$$1 = E_{I_t^2} \left[\beta \frac{U'(c_{t+1})p_t}{U'(c_t)p_{t+1}} R_{t+1,t}^d \right], \tag{5.79}$$

$$1 = E_{I_t^2} \left[\beta \frac{U'(c_{t+1})p_t}{U'(c_t)p_{t+1}} (1 + i_t^d) \right]. \tag{5.80}$$

Notice that at the time the equity share is purchased, the buyer knows the current equity price but does not know the dividend or the resale price of the equity.

In the Svensson model, the dividend payment on an equity share purchased in period t is made in the asset market at the end of the next period and so agents do not know the value of the endowment or the price level next period when making their asset choices. An equity share purchased in the asset market at the end of period t means foregoing consumption in period $t + 1$ and receiving the uncertain equity payoff at the end of period $t + 1$, which makes it available for spending on consumption in period $t + 2$. The information set at the time the equity share and bonds are purchased includes all $t - 1$ variables, and the equity price and bond price at time t; let I_t^3 denote this information set. It turns out that the empirical formulation of the Svensson model is the same as that of the second version of the Lucas model in which the endowment realization is not observed until after the asset market closes.

The empirical formulation of the Svensson model is:

$$1 = E_{I_t^3}\left[\beta\frac{U'(c_{t+1})p_t}{U'(c_t)p_{t+1}}R_{t+1,t}\right], \tag{5.81}$$

$$1 = E_{I_t^3}\left[\beta\frac{U'(c_{t+1})p_t}{U'(c_t)p_{t+1}}(1+i_t)\right]. \tag{5.82}$$

Finn *et al.* use the GMM estimation technique to estimate the various versions of the model. They use monthly data over the sample period January 1958 to December 1986. They also use two measures of real consumption expenditures, an implicit price deflator for the consumption series, total population age 16 and over (to convert variables to per capita), and end-of-period, seasonally adjusted M1. Preferences are assumed to display constant relative risk aversion. Two parameters are estimated: the discount factor β and the risk aversion parameter. The instruments used for the first version of the Lucas model, Equations (5.77) and (5.78), are lagged consumption growth $c_t/c_{t-1}-1$, lagged real return $(p_{t-1}R_{t,t-1})p_t$, and a constant. The instruments used for the second version of the Lucas model and the Svensson model are consumption growth $c_{t-1}/c_{t-2}-1$, lagged stock return $(p_{t-1}R_{t,t-1})/p_t$, and deflation between periods $t-2$ and t (measured as p_{t-2}/p_t). One econometric difficulty they encounter is that M1 velocity, measured as real balances divided by consumption, is nonstationary.

In their study of the equity premium puzzle, Mehra and Prescott [257] construct a stock return from annual data. They use the average Standard and Poor's Composite Stock Price Index, denoted PSN, which is a nominal series, and the annual nominal dividend for the Stock Price Index, denoting the dividend that accrues over time period t and paid at the beginning of period $t+1$ as DS_t. The consumption series used to measure theoretical endowment is real per capita consumption of nondurables and services measured in constant (1972) dollars and the associated consumption deflator, denoted PC_t. The real return they compute is:

$$r_{t+1,t}^d = \left[\frac{PSN_{t+1}}{PC_{t+1}} + \frac{DS_t}{PC_t}\right]\left(\frac{PSN_t}{PC_t}\right) - 1.$$

This approach to measuring the return leads to an empirical formulation of the first version of the Lucas model as

$$1 = E_t\left[\frac{U'(c_{t+1})p_t}{U'(c_t)p_{t+1}}R_{t+1,t}^d\right],$$

where the information at time t includes all $t-1$ variables and the time t variables c_t, PSN_t, PC_t, and DS_t.

4.   Exercises

1. Consider the basic asset pricing model in Section 1.1. Define $\mathcal{B}$ as the space of bounded, continuous functions on $\mathbb{R}_{++} \times S \times Z \times \mathcal{H}$ such that $\sup_{y,s,z,h} |V(y,s,z,h)/y^{1-\gamma}|\infty$. For $V \in \mathcal{B}$, define the operator T:

$$(TV)(y,s,z,h) = \max_{c,m^d,z',b'} \left\{ U(c) + \beta \int_S V(y',s',z',h')F(s,ds') \right\},$$

subject to the constraints in Equations (5.4) and (5.5) and $m^d \in \mathcal{M}$, $z' \in Z$, and $b' \in B$.

Show that under Assumptions 5.1, 5.2, and 5.4, T has a unique fixed point in $\mathcal{B}$.

2. The Svensson Model

At the beginning of the period, the household observes the realization s_t. The money supply evolves as $M_{t+1} = \omega(s_t)M_t$ and endowment is stationary in levels. Money growth and endowment satisfy Assumption 5.6. The normalized money balances held at the beginning of the asset market are $m_t^d \equiv p_t y_t z_t + b_t + h_t - p_t c_t + \omega_t - 1$. The normalized budget constraint in the asset market is:

$$h_{t+1}\omega_t + q_t^e z_{t+1} + Q_t b_{t+1}\omega_t \le m_t^d + q_t^e z_t. \tag{5.83}$$

The normalized cash-in-advance constraint is

$$p_t c_t \le h_t. \tag{5.84}$$

The state vector for the representative household is (s_t, z_t, b_t, h_t).

a) Formulate the household problem in a stationary equilibrium in which prices $p(s)$, $q^e(s)$, and $Q(s)$ are continuous, strictly positive functions of the economy-wide state variables.

b) Derive the first-order conditions, envelope conditions, and specify the market-clearing conditions.

c) Show that the equilibrium bond price can be written as:

$$Q(s) = \frac{\beta E_s \left\{ [U'(y')/p(s') - \mu(s')]p(s) \right\}}{\beta E_s [U'(y)]}.$$

d) Discuss the relationship between a binding cash-in-advance constraint and strictly positive nominal interest rates. Are consumers willing to hold nominal money balances at a positive nominal interest rate?

3. Consumption and Leisure Choices

Use the labor-leisure model in Section 2.2 and assume that the utility function takes the form:

$$U(c_t, \ell_t) \equiv \beta^t \frac{1}{1-\gamma} (c_t^\alpha \ell_t^{1-\alpha})^{1-\gamma}.$$

Let $\rho \equiv 1 - \gamma$ for notational simplicity and assume that $\rho > 0$. Also assume that $0 < \alpha < 1$. For the utility function to be concave in both arguments, the following conditions must hold: $\alpha\rho < 1$ and $(1-\alpha)\rho < 1$. Also notice that, if $\rho > 0$, $U_{c\ell} > 0$ (so leisure and consumption are complements).

a) Derive the first-order conditions and the envelope conditions.

b) Next, use the basic structure of the consumption-leisure model but drop the cash-in-advance constraint to make it a real model. Construct the equilibrium for two cases: a zero tax rate τ and a positive tax rate. Compare the consumption and leisure streams for the three versions of the model.

4. A Cash-in-Advance Model with Storage[6]

There is a representative competitive firm that produces a nondurable consumption good y_t using an input x_t. The production function is $y_t = \lambda(s_t)x_t^\alpha$, where $\lambda : S \to \mathbb{R}_+$ is a technology shock. The intermediate good x_t depreciates at 100% when used in production. The firm buys the input from consumers in a competitive market at the real price of w_t. The firm solves:

$$\max_{x_t} \lambda(s_t)x_t^\alpha - x_t w_t.$$

The intermediate good is storable when held by households. The law of motion for the consumer's holdings of the intermediate good at the beginning of the period is given by:

$$k_{t+1} = \theta(s_{t+1})(k_t - x_t). \tag{5.85}$$

---

[6]This exercise is derived from Eichenbaum and Singleton [112].

The capital stock is assumed to be nonnegative ($k_{t+1} \geq 0$). If we assume that the storage shock θ is positive with probability one, then the nonnegativity assumption is equivalent to the constraint $k_t - x_t \geq 0$. The realization of the shock θ_{t+1} is unknown when x_t is chosen in period t.

The timing of trades is identical to the Svensson model. The asset market opens and equity shares are traded and money holdings adjusted. The normalized law of motion for money holdings at the beginning of the period is

$$h_{t+1} = \frac{1}{\omega(s_t)}[h_t - p_t c_t + b_t + (q_t^e + p_t d_t)z_t$$

$$-q_t^e z_{t+1} + w_t p_t x_t + \omega(s_t) - 1] - Q_t b_{t+1}. \tag{5.86}$$

The cash-in-advance constraint is identical to Equation (5.84).

The agent's preferences are:

$$E_0 \left\{ \sum_{t=0}^{\infty} \beta^t \nu_t \log(c_t) \right\}, \quad 0 < \beta < 1, \tag{5.87}$$

where $E_0(\cdot)$ denotes expectation conditional on information at time 0. The taste shock is assumed to follow the process $\nu_{t+1} = \nu_t^a \varepsilon_{t+1}$, where $|a| \leq 1$ and $\log \varepsilon$ is normally distributed with mean zero, variance σ_ε^2, and is not autocorrelated. We assume that ν_{t-1} and ε_t are part of s_t.

a) Derive the equilibrium wage rate and dividends.

b) The household's state variables are z_t, b_t, k_t, h_t, as well as s_t and the economy-wide capital stock, κ_t which takes values on an interval $\mathcal{K} \equiv [0, \bar{\kappa}]$ and evolves as $\kappa_{t+1} = \theta(s_{t+1})(\kappa_t - x_t)$. Formulate the household's problem as a dynamic program.

c) Derive the equilibrium first-order conditions and envelope conditions for $\{c, h', z', x, b'\}$.

d) Let $\tilde{x}(s, \kappa)$ be a fixed policy that satisfies the nonnegativity constraint and let $\tilde{y}(s, \kappa)$ be the output produced under this policy. Define a function Ψ such that, for all (s, κ), the price level satisfies $p(s, \kappa) = 1/\tilde{y}(s, \kappa)\Psi(s, \kappa)$. Show that Ψ satisfies the functional equation:

$$\nu\Psi(s, \kappa) = \max \left[\nu, \beta E_s \left(\nu' \frac{\Psi(s', \kappa')}{\omega(s)} \right) \right]. \tag{5.88}$$

e) Assume that the money supply rule is not a function of κ. Prove that there exists a fixed point for Equation (5.88) that is a function of s only. Denote this fixed point Ψ^*.

f) Define $\Lambda(s_{t+1}, s_t) \equiv \beta\left[\nu_{t+1}\Psi^*(s_{t+1})/\omega_t\Psi^*(s_t)\right]$. Use the equilibrium first-order conditions and the fact that $w_t/c_t = \alpha/x_t$ in equilibrium to show that $\Lambda(s_{t+1}, s_t)$ satisfies the equation:

$$\frac{\mu_k(s_t, \kappa_t)}{\beta\alpha} = E_t\left[\frac{\Lambda(s_{t+1}, s_t)}{x(s_t, \kappa_t)}\right] - \beta E_t\left[\frac{\Lambda(s_{t+2}, s_{t+1})\theta(s_{t+1})}{x(s_{t+1}, \kappa_{t+1})}\right].$$

g) Assume that $\beta E_t[\nu_{t+1}/\nu_t\omega_t] < 1$. Let $\zeta_t \equiv 1/\omega_t$ and assume that $\zeta_{t+1} = \zeta_t^\eta u_{t+1}$ where $|\eta| < 1$ and u_t is lognormally distributed with mean zero and variance σ_u^2. Show that the cash-in-advance constraint is always binding and $\Psi_t^* = 1$ for all t.

h) Show that the nonnegativity constraint on capital is not binding and find a closed-form expression for the intermediate good.

5. Find a closed-form solution for the one-period nominal bond in the storage model.

6. Construct the factor supply function for the storage model for a *real* version of the model; that is, assume that no money is required for trading to occur. Compare the solutions and provide some intuition for the wedge introduced by the cash-in-advance constraint.

6

International Asset Markets

As international asset markets have grown in size and importance, there has been a proliferation in the variety of assets that are traded. Paralleling the growth of these markets is the increased interest in testing their efficiency and examining the empirical behavior of assets denominated in alternative currencies. In this chapter, we study the behavior of such markets. For this purpose, we describe a two-country model with cash-in-advance constraints in which purchases of goods must be made with sellers' currencies. We certainly do not mean to suggest that this is the only model or even the most commonly accepted model of exchange rates and asset prices. We choose this model because it allows us to demonstrate the existence of equilibrium based on utility-maximizing behavior of agents and it provides a useful framework for examining a variety of observed relationships. We describe the basic model in Section 1 while in Section 2, we modify it to incorporate nontraded goods and investment and capital flows.

Earlier models in the exchange rate literature include the Dornbusch model [99] and the Mussa model [264], both of which emphasize differential speeds of adjustment and neither of which is based on utility-maximizing behavior. Obstfeld and Stockman [272] provide a useful survey that includes a description of these alternative models of exchange rate determination.[1]

In Section 3, we turn to a discussion of the empirical behavior of foreign exchange rate markets. We discuss tests of the hypothesis that forward exchange rates are unbiased predictors of future spot rates. Since the unbiasedness hypothesis is typically rejected for the floating exchange rate period, we describe alternative ways of modeling risk premia. The final topic of this chapter is methods for modeling the distribution of short-term changes in exchange rates.

---

[1] Exchange rate behavior has also been studied in money-in-the-utility function models (see Calvo [57] and Calvo and Rodriguez [58]) and in overlapping generations models (see Kareken and Wallace [216] and Greenwood and Williamson [162]).

1.   A Two-Country Model

We begin our discussion with a simple two-country version of the Lucas asset pricing model with a cash-in-advance constraint (see Lucas [232]). Agents from both countries are identical in terms of preferences so they can differ only in terms of initial endowments. In this model, we study what is typically referred to as a pooled equilibrium — if initial endowments are identical or if somehow the economy converges to an equilibrium with equal forms of wealth (so wealth is the same in all states); then we will show that the economy will stay in this equilibrium.

This is a two-country flexible exchange rate model with two goods, Y_1 and Y_2. Country 1 has a random endowment of good Y_1 and country 2 has a random endowment of good Y_2. Neither good is storable. Agents from both countries hold identical portfolios and have identical preferences. We assume that endowments are stationary in levels but that money supplies are growing. The case with growing endowments can be analyzed using an approach similar to that in Chapter 5, Section 1 but for expositional purposes, we consider the case when only money supplies are growing.

Let $s_t \in S \subseteq \mathbb{R}_+^m$ denote a vector of exogenous shocks that follows a first-order Markov process with a stationary transition function F. The transition function F satisfies Assumption 5.1 in Chapter 5. The outstanding stock of money of country i at time t is $M_{i,t}$ and the money supply process is:

$$M_{i,t} = \omega_i(s_t)M_{i,t-1}, \quad i = 1, 2. \tag{6.1}$$

At the beginning of the period, agents observe the current realization of the endowment of each country denoted $y_{i,t}$ for $i = 1, 2$. We assume that endowment is a time-invariant function of the exogenous shock, $y_{i,t} \equiv y_i(s_t)$.

Assumption 6.1 *Define* $\mathcal{W} \equiv [\underline{\omega}, \bar{\omega}]$ *and* $\mathcal{Y} \equiv [\underline{y}, \bar{y}]$ *where* $\underline{\omega} > 0$, $\underline{y} > 0$, $\bar{\omega} < \infty$, *and* $\bar{y} < \infty$. *The functions* $y_i : S \to \mathcal{Y}$ *and* $\omega_i : S \to \mathcal{W}$ *are continuous functions that are bounded away from zero for* $i = 1, 2$.

The following assumption restricts money growth in each country.

Assumption 6.2 *For all* $s \in S$, $0 < \beta \int_S [1/\omega_i(s')]F(s, ds') < 1$.

These assumptions are the counterparts of Assumptions 5.6 and 5.7 in Chapter 5.

The representative consumer in country j has preferences over random sequences $\{c_{1,t}^j, c_{2,t}^j\}_{t=0}^{\infty}$ defined by:

$$E_0\left\{\sum_{t=0}^{\infty}\beta^t U(c_{1,t}^j, c_{2,t}^j)\right\}, \quad 0 < \beta < 1. \tag{6.2}$$

We have the following assumption.

Assumption 6.3 *The utility function* $U : \mathbb{R}_+^2 \rightarrow \mathbb{R}$ *is continuously differentiable, strictly increasing, and strictly concave. For all* $c_1, c_2 > 0$,

$$\lim_{c_1 \to 0} \frac{U_1(c_1, c_2)}{U_2(c_1, c_2)} = \infty, \quad \lim_{c_2 \to 0} \frac{U_1(c_1, c_2)}{U_2(c_1, c_2)} = 0.$$

This requirement on the utility function ensures that both goods are consumed in equilibrium.

At the beginning of the period, the representative agent of country 1 receives one-half of the money transfer from its government denoted T_1^1 and one-half of the money transfer from country 2 denoted T_2^1. The representative agent from country 2 receives a similar set of transfers, T_i^2 for $i = 1, 2$.[2]

Country 1 is defined as the domestic country and good 1 is the numeraire good. The nominal exchange rate e_t converts nominal quantities defined in the currency of country 2 into units of the domestic currency. The nominal wealth of an agent in country j consists of the currency $M_{1,t-1}^j$ of country 1, currency $M_{2,t-1}^j$ of country 2, claims to a nominal dividend for good 1 denoted as $z_{1,t-1}^j$, which can be sold for a price $Q_{1,t}^e$, and claims to nominal dividend for good 2 denoted $z_{2,t-1}^j$, which can be sold for a price $Q_{2,t}^e$ and is denominated in units of country 2's currency. Later on, we introduce nominal bonds of various maturities that are in zero net supply and forward and futures contracts for foreign exchange.

The price of good 1 measured in units of M_1 is $p_{1,t}$ and the price of good 2 measured in units of M_2 is $p_{2,t}$. Thus, the representative agent in country j has posttransfer beginning-of-period nominal balances measured in units of country 1's currency equal to:

$$H_t^j \equiv M_{1,t-1}^j - p_{1,t-1}c_{1,t-1}^j + e_t(M_{2,t-1}^j - p_{2,t-1}c_{2,t-1}^j)$$

$$+ p_{1,t-1}y_{1,t-1}z_{1,t-1}^j + e_t p_{2,t-1}y_{2,t-1}z_{2,t-1}^j + T_{1,t}^j + e_t T_{2,t}^j, \tag{6.3}$$

---

[2]In Exercise 8, this assumption is dropped and, instead, we assume that claims in the transfers are traded just like any other security. In equilibrium, the representative agent from country 1 will hold one-half of the claims to the transfer of country 1 and one-half of the claims to the transfer from country 2, just as in the money transfers scheme just described.

where the last two terms are the transfers made to the representative agent in country j.

The asset market opens first. Agents trade in securities, bonds, and currency. While in the asset market, agents acquire the currency they need to make consumption purchases. It is assumed that domestic sellers will accept payment only in their domestic currency. This means that the buyer has no access to the foreign exchange market once the asset market has closed. Since there is no new information revealed after the asset market closes and before the goods market opens, this is similar to the cash-in-advance constraint in the one-country version of the model with the Lucas timing in which there is only a transactions demand and no liquidity or store of value demand for money.

The budget constraint in the asset market faced by the representative agent of country j is:

$$Q^e_{1,t}z^j_{1,t} + e_t Q^e_{2,t}z^j_{2,t} + M^j_{1,t} + e_t M^j_{2,t}$$

$$\leq H^j_t + Q^e_{1,t}z^j_{1,t-1} + e_t Q^e_{2,t}z^j_{2,t-1}. \tag{6.4}$$

The demand by agent j for units of currency i, $i \neq j$, is:

$$F^j_{i,t} \equiv M^j_{i,t} - [M^j_{i,t-1} + T^j_{i,t} + p_{i,t-1}(y^j_{i,t-1}z^j_{i,t-1} - c^j_{i,t-1})]. \tag{6.5}$$

In the goods market, the following cash-in-advance constraints apply to the purchases of goods 1 and 2 by the agent from country j:

$$p_{1,t}c^j_{1,t} \leq M^j_{1,t}, \tag{6.6}$$

$$e_t p_{2,t}c^j_{2,t} \leq e_t M^j_{2,t}. \tag{6.7}$$

After the goods market closes, the agent receives the nominal dividend payments on the claims from both countries.

Notice that the consumer's nominal wealth is growing because the money supply is growing. To eliminate the effects of such growth, we divide all nominal variables by the nominal price of good 1. We also define the relative price of good 2 in terms of good 1 as:

$$\zeta_t = \frac{e_t p_{2,t}}{p_{1,t}}. \tag{6.8}$$

This relative price is often called the *terms of trade* or the *real exchange rate*. Later on, we show that this relative price is independent of the money stocks.

Let lower case letters denote the nominal value divided by the appropriate price; that is, define $h_t \equiv H_t/p_{1,t}$, $q^e_{i,t} \equiv Q^e_{i,t}/p_{i,t}$, $m_{i,t} \equiv M_{i,t}/p_{i,t}$, and $\tau_{i,t} \equiv T_{i,t}/p_{i,t}$ for $i = 1, 2$. For notational convenience, also define the variable $\pi_{i,t} \equiv p_{i,t-1}/p_{i,t}$ for $i = 1, 2$. The normalized budget constraint in the asset market can be written as:

$$q_{1,t}^e z_{1,t}^j + \zeta_t q_{2,t}^e z_{2,t}^j + m_{1,t}^j + \zeta_t m_{2,t}^j \le$$

$$h_t^j + q_{1,t}^e z_{1,t-1}^j + \zeta_t q_{2,t}^e z_{2,t-1}^j, \tag{6.9}$$

where

$$h_t^j = \pi_{1,t}(m_{1,t-1}^j - c_{1,t-1}^j) + \zeta_t \pi_{2,t}(m_{2,t-1}^j - c_{2,t-1}^j)$$

$$+ \pi_{1,t} y_{1,t-1} z_{1,t-1}^j + \zeta_t \pi_{2,t} y_{2,t-1} z_{2,t-1}^j + \tau_{1,t}^j + \zeta_t \tau_{2,t}^j, \tag{6.10}$$

Likewise, we divide the cash-in-advance constraints in Equations (6.6) and (6.7) by $p_{1,t}$ to obtain:

$$c_{1,t}^j \le m_{1,t}^j, \tag{6.11}$$

$$\zeta_t c_{2,t}^j \le \zeta_t m_{2,t}^j. \tag{6.12}$$

Notice that dividing the nominal constraints by the price level has transformed the variables into real quantities or else ratios of prices for the same good at different points in time.

The market-clearing conditions for this economy for $i = 1, 2$ are:

$$c_{i,t}^1 + c_{i,t}^2 = y_{i,t}, \tag{6.13}$$

$$M_{i,t}^1 + M_{i,t}^2 = M_{i,t}, \tag{6.14}$$

$$z_{i,t}^1 + z_{i,t}^2 = 1, \tag{6.15}$$

$$e_t F_{2,t}^1 + F_{1,t}^2 = 0. \tag{6.16}$$

There are seven markets. Using Walras's Law, if six of them clear, then the seventh market — the foreign exchange market — will also clear.

Let primes denote future values and unprimed variables denote current values. We will seek an equilibrium in which the nominal price levels and the nominal exchange rate depend on the realization of the shock s and the stocks of money, $M \equiv (M_1, M_2)$, but the equity prices and the real exchange rate depend only on s. The price functions q_i^e, ζ are assumed to be continuous and strictly positive functions $q_i^e : S \to \mathbb{R}_{++}$, $i = 1, 2$ and $\zeta : S \to \mathbb{R}_{++}$. The nominal exchange rate e and the nominal price levels p_i for $i = 1, 2$ are assumed to be continuous and strictly positive functions $e : S \times \mathbb{R}_+^2 \to \mathbb{R}_{++}$, $p_i : S \times \mathbb{R}_+^2 \to \mathbb{R}_{++}$ for $i = 1, 2$.

Define the (gross) deflation rate by $\pi_i(s') \equiv p_i(s, M)/p_i(s', M')$. Notice that we assume that deflation is a function of s' and, in particular, does not depend on the stocks of money. This is a property that must be demonstrated.

Because agents are identical in equilibrium, we drop the index j. The consumer's state variables consist of his initial wealth h, his share holdings z_i for $i = 1, 2$, and the current exogenous shock s. Given the price functions ζ, e and q_i^e and p_i for $i = 1, 2$, the resident of each country chooses $(c_1, c_2, m_1, m_2, z_1', z_2')$ to solve:

$$V(h, z_1, z_2, s) = \max \{U(c_1, c_2) + \beta E_s[V(h', z_1', z_2', s')]\} \qquad (6.17)$$

subject to the asset market constraint (Equation 6.9), the law of motion for posttransfer real balances (Equation 6.10), and the cash-in-advance constraints (Equations 6.11 and 6.12). We can show the existence of a solution to the consumer's value function as an application of Proposition 2.1 in Chapter 2.

In equilibrium, agents are identical so that $c_i^1 = c_i^2 = (1/2)y_i$ and $z_i^1 = z_i^2 = 1/2$. When the market-clearing conditions are substituted into the law of motion for the posttransfer money holdings, these holdings become $h = (1/2)[(M_1/p_1) + \zeta(M_2/p_2)]$, which is just the world supply of real balances measured in units of good 1. Let $\mu_i(s)$ denote the multiplier for the cash-in-advance constraint on good i, and $\xi(s)$ denote the multiplier on the budget constraint in the asset market. Let U_i be the partial derivative of U with respect to to its i'th argument and define $U_i(s) \equiv U_i(y_1/2, y_2/2)$. Substituting the envelope conditions, the equilibrium first-order conditions with respect to $c_1, c_2, m_1, m_2, z_1', z_2'$ are:[3]

$$U_1(s) = \mu_1(s) + \beta E_s[\xi(s')\pi_1(s')], \qquad (6.18)$$

$$U_2(s) = \zeta(s)\mu_2(s) + \beta E_s[\xi(s')\pi_2(s')\zeta(s')], \qquad (6.19)$$

$$\xi(s) = \mu_1(s) + \beta E_s[\xi(s')\pi_1(s')], \qquad (6.20)$$

$$\zeta(s)\xi(s) = \mu_2(s)\zeta(s) + \beta E_s[\xi(s')\pi_2(s')\zeta(s')], \qquad (6.21)$$

$$q_1^e(s)\xi(s) = \beta E_s\{\xi(s')[\pi_1(s')y_1(s) + q_1^e(s')]\}, \qquad (6.22)$$

$$q_2^e(s)\zeta(s)\xi(s) = \beta E_s\{\xi(s')\zeta(s')[\pi_2(s')y_2(s) + q_2^e(s')]\}. \qquad (6.23)$$

We also have the slackness conditions with respect to the multipliers $\xi(s)$ and $\mu_i(s)$ for $i = 1, 2$.

---

[3]In Exercise 2, the reader is asked to derive the first-order conditions and envelope conditions for the agent's dynamic programming problem.

These equilibrium first-order conditions are similar to the first-order conditions that we derived for the basic cash-in-advance model in Chapter 5. The difference arises from the fact that we have to determine the relative price of country 2's good in terms of country 1's good, or the real exchange rate $\zeta(s)$. We also need to determine the nominal exchange rate $e(s, M)$. For this purpose, we need to determine the nominal price level in each country, $p_i(s, M)$ for $i = 1, 2$. We do this following the approach in the previous chapter by deriving the inverse of the velocity functions for each currency.

Adding the cash-in-advance constraints for the two types of agents and imposing market-clearing yields $y_i \leq M_i/p_i$. Define the variables:

$$\Psi_i \equiv M_i/p_i y_i \quad i = 1, 2.$$

Because M, y are exogenous and positive, solving for Ψ_i is equivalent to solving for p_i. Notice that the multipliers $\mu_i(s)$ satisfy the conditions:

$$\mu_i(s) = U_i(s) - \beta E_s[U_i(s')\pi_i(s')], \quad i = 1, 2.$$

But $\pi_i(s') \equiv p_i(s, M)/p_i(s', M')$ by definition. Substituting for $\pi_i(s')$ and recalling that $\mu_i(s) \geq 0$, the functions Ψ_i must satisfy:

$$U_i(s)y_i(s)\Psi_i(s) = \max \left[U_i(s)y_i(s), \beta E_s \left(\frac{U_i(s')y_i(s')\Psi_i(s')}{\omega_i(s')} \right) \right] \quad (6.24)$$

for $i = 1, 2$. Notice that these equations are expressed in terms of the stationary growth rates of money supplies and the stationary endowments so that Ψ_i is a function only of the shock s. Furthermore, Equation (6.24) can be solved separately from the other price functions and, in particular, does not depend on the exchange rate. To find a fixed point to these functional equations, define the functions:

$$\Gamma_i(s) \equiv U_i(s)y_i(s)\Psi_i(s), \quad i = 1, 2.$$

Since $y_i(s) > 0$ for all s, studying the properties of the function Γ_i is equivalent to studying the function Ψ_i. This follows as an application of the implicit function theorem. Using the definition of the functions Γ_i, define the operators $T_i\Gamma_i$ for $i = 1, 2$ by:

$$(T_i\Gamma_i)(s) \equiv \max \left[U_i(s)y_i(s), \beta E_s \left(\frac{\Gamma_i(s')}{\omega_i(s')} \right) \right]. \quad (6.25)$$

Notice that, under Assumptions 5.1 and 6.1, T_i maps $\mathcal{C}(S)$, the space of bounded and continuous, real-valued functions defined on S, into itself.

It is straightforward to verify that T_i is monotone. Under Assumption 6.2, $\beta E_s[\omega_i(s')^{-1}] < 1$ for all s so that T discounts,

$$\beta E_s \left\{ \omega_i(s')^{-1} [\Gamma_i(s') + a] \right\} \le \beta E_s[\Gamma_i(s')] + \delta a,$$

where $0 < \delta < 1$. Therefore, Contraction Mapping Theorem implies that T_i has a fixed point in $\mathcal{C}(S)$. Let Ψ_i^* denote this fixed point.

We can use these fixed points and the first-order conditions in Equations (6.22) and (6.23) to construct the equity price functions. Define the functions:

$$\phi_i(s) \equiv q_i^e(s) U_i(s), \quad i = 1, 2.$$

Notice that these functions satisfy the following mapping:

$$(T_i \phi_i)(s) = \beta E_s \left[\frac{U_i(s') y_i(s') \Psi_i^*(s')}{\omega_i(s') \Psi_i^*(s)} + \phi_i(s') \right], \tag{6.26}$$

where we have substituted for $\pi_i(s') = p_i / p_i'$ and $p_i = M_i / \Psi_i^* y_i$ for $i = 1, 2$. Under Assumptions 5.1, 6.1, and 6.2, it is straightforward to show that there exist functions $\phi_i^* \in \mathcal{C}(S)$ that are the fixed points of Equation (6.26).

1.1. The Terms of Trade and the Exchange Rate

We are now in a position to derive expressions for the equilibrium real and nominal exchange rate and to show the implications of the model for their behavior.

We use Equations (6.18) and (6.19) to express the terms of trade or the real exchange rate as:

$$\zeta(s) = \frac{U_2(s)}{U_1(s)}. \tag{6.27}$$

Fluctuations in the endowment of either good affect the real exchange rate while fluctuations in the money supply have no effect on the real exchange rate. This last result is known as *purchasing power parity* and it is the open economy counterpart of the quantity theory of money. It has been widely studied as an empirical phenomenon.

Given the solutions Ψ_i^*, we can use the definition of the real exchange rate to find a solution for the equilibrium nominal exchange rate as a function of M_1/M_2 and y_2/y_1 as:

$$e(s, M) = \frac{U_2(s)}{U_1(s)} \frac{\Psi_2^*(s)}{\Psi_1^*(s)} \frac{M_1 y_2(s)}{M_2 y_1(s)}. \tag{6.28}$$

Hence, the equilibrium exchange rate is affected by changes in relative velocity, changes in the MRS in consumption, and changes in the relative supplies of the goods and money stocks. Real disturbances affect both the exchange rate and the terms of trade so that we would expect these variables to be correlated. Notice that some standard results apply. An increase in the money supply of country 1 depreciates the exchange rate for currency 1 (increases e) while an increase in the money supply of country 2 appreciates it (decreases e).

Notice that the change in the nominal exchange rate satisfies:

$$\frac{e(s', M')}{e(s, M)} = \frac{U_2(s')y_2(s')}{U_2(s)y_2(s)} \frac{U_1(s)y_1(s)}{U_1(s')y_1(s')} \frac{\Psi_1^\star(s)}{\Psi_1^\star(s')} \frac{\Psi_2^\star(s')}{\Psi_2^\star(s)} \frac{\omega_1(s')}{\omega_2(s')}.$$

Since the growth rate of money supplies in each country is a stationary random variable, changes in nominal exchange rates are also stationary. We can multiply both sides of the expression in Equation (6.28) by M_2/M_1 to obtain

$$\frac{M_2}{M_1} e(s, M) = \frac{U_2(s)}{U_1(s)} \frac{\Psi_2^\star(s)}{\Psi_1^\star(s)} \frac{y_2(s)}{y_1(s)} = \zeta(s) \frac{\Psi_2^\star(s)}{\Psi_1^\star(s)} \frac{y_2(s)}{y_1(s)}.$$

Since the right side of this expression is stationary, notice that the nominal exchange rate times the ratio of the money supplies in the two countries is also a stationary random variable. Recall that we did not restrict the relative money supplies to be stationary. Nevertheless, the assumption that the equilibrium real exchange rate is a stationary variable implies restrictions for the time series behavior of the nominal exchange rate and the relative money supplies.

These expressions also allow us to discuss tests of alternative forms of purchasing power parity. The absolute version of purchasing power parity says that the real exchange rate or the relative price of the foreign versus domestic goods is just unity in the long run. Using the expression for the real interest rate, the absolute version of purchasing power parity can be expressed as:

$$\log(\zeta_t) = \log(e_t) - \log(p_{1,t}/p_{2,t}) = 0. \tag{6.29}$$

The relative version of purchasing power parity states that this relation holds in first differences:

$$\Delta \log(\zeta_t) = \Delta \log(e_t) - \Delta \log(p_{1,t}/p_{2,t}) = 0, \tag{6.30}$$

where Δ is the first difference operator.

Notice that if purchasing power parity holds in the long run, movements in nominal exchange rates should be offset by movements in relative price levels. A number of studies have argued that the real exchange rate follows a random walk (see Adler and Lehman [6]), which implies that deviations from purchasing power parity can be expected to be permanent. Mark [251] reports similar findings using monthly observations from June 1973 through February 1988. He uses consumer price index data taken from the International Monetary Fund publication *International Financial Statistics* to measure commodity prices. Exchange rate data are taken from Harris Bank's *Foreign Exchange Weekly Review*, which reports Friday closing prices in London. The countries chosen are Belgium, Canada, France, Germany, Italy, Japan, and the United Kingdom. Mark examines three sets of bilateral relationships, with the United States, the United Kingdom, and Germany serving as the home country, and finds that movements in nominal exchange rates and relative price levels are unrelated in the long run as well as in the short run.

Mark also suggests a test of purchasing power parity as a long-run relationship by testing whether $\log(e_t)$ and $\log(p_{1,t}/p_{2,t})$ are cointegrated series. According to this methodology, two sequences of random variables $\{x_t\}$ and $\{y_t\}$ are said to be *cointegrated* if (i) they are nonstationary in levels; (ii) they are stationary in first differences; and (iii) there exists a linear combination of the levels, $u_t = x_t + \alpha y_t$, which is stationary. The variable α is referred to as the cointegrating constant. To test for cointegration, we determine whether $\{x_t\}$ and $\{y_t\}$ are nonstationary in levels but stationary in first differences. Next, x_t is regressed on y_t, or vice versa. This is called the cointegrating regression and $\{u_t\}$ is defined as the residual from this regression. The cointegrating constant can be consistently estimated by least squares. Finally, an augmented Dickey-Fuller test is performed on the error sequence, $\{u_t\}$.[4]

Mark first tests for unit roots in $\log(e_t)$ and $\log(p_{1,t}/p_{2,t})$. He finds that the logarithms of the nominal exchange rate are nonstationary in levels but stationary in first differences. For some country pairs, the unit root hypothesis can be rejected for the logarithms of the relative

---

[4]To do this test, consider the regression

$$(1 - \theta_1 L - \theta_2 L^2)(1 - \rho L)u_t = v_t,$$

where $\{v_t\}$ is an i.i.d. sequence and L is the lag operator. We wish to test whether $\rho = 1$. We rewrite the above equation as $u_t = -\phi_1 u_{t-1} + \phi_2 \Delta u_{t-1} + \phi_3 \Delta u_{t-2} + v_t$, where $\phi_1 = (1 - \rho)(1 - \theta_1 - \theta_2)$. Under the null hypothesis of no cointegration, $\phi_1 = 0$. The distribution of the usual t-statistic is not standard. However, critical values tabulated by Engle and Granger [117] may be used.

price levels. Excluding these country pairs, he is unable to reject at conventional significance levels the null hypothesis of no cointegration for $\log(e_t)$ and $\log(p_{1,t}/p_{2,t})$ or, equivalently, that the real exchange rate has a unit root. He argues that while small departures from the null hypothesis may be hard to detect with existing data, there is evidence to suggest that shocks to the real exchange rate are persistent enough to prevent a return to purchasing power parity in the long run.

Huizinga [202] studies the long-run behavior of real exchange rates using an alternative set of statistical procedures. He considers the real exchange rates of the U.S. dollar, the British pound, and the Japanese yen against ten major currencies. His sample consists of monthly observations on the logarithm of the real exchange rate for the floating exchange rate period from 1974 to 1986. He finds the long-run behavior of real exchange rates differs from a random walk by having a notable mean-reverting component. In contrast to the serially uncorrelated changes implied by a random walk, there is substantial negative serial correlation of changes in real exchange rates, which he argues is a common feature among the real exchange rates of many countries. Despite the existence of a mean-reverting component, he finds that the permanent component accounts for between 52% and 77% of the variance of the actual change in the real exchange rate of the U.S. dollar against ten currencies. These results are in accord with Campbell and Clarida [60], who develop an empirical model of real exchange rates using Kalman filtering techniques.

A related empirical issue is the behavior of the real exchange rate across different nominal exchange rate regimes. For example, Mussa [265] argues that the behavior of the real exchange rate has become more variable in the floating exchange rate period since the breakdown of the Bretton Woods agreement in 1973. Grilli and Kaminsky [163] examine a variety of nominal exchange rate regimes since 1885, including the gold standard eras in the nintheenth century and in the interwar era, and the fixed and floating exchange rate eras since World War II. They find that transitory disturbances are important for the behavior of the real exchange rate in the pre–World War II era and that the behavior of the real exchange rate varies more by historical episode than by the exchange rate regime. Recall that in our model, the real exchange rate is a stationary random variable so that real shocks or shocks to endowments have only a temporary effect.

1.2.   Pricing Alternative Assets

We can derive the prices of a variety of assets using this framework, including equity prices, the price of pure discount bonds, and the prices of forward and futures contracts for foreign exchange.

We first briefly discuss the determinants of equity prices in the domestic and foreign country. We already described how to construct the equity price functions using the fixed points $\phi_i^\star$ for $i = 1, 2$. Using Equations (6.22) and (6.23), the equity prices satisfy:

$$q_{1,t}^e = \beta E_t \left[\frac{U_{1,t+1}}{U_{1,t}} (\pi_{1,t+1} y_{1,t} + q_{1,t+1}^e) \right]$$

$$q_{2,t}^e = \beta E_t \left[\frac{U_{1,t+1}}{U_{1,t}} \frac{\zeta_{t+1}}{\zeta_t} (\pi_{2,t+1} y_{2,t} + q_{2,t+1}^e) \right],$$

where $U_{1,t+k}$ is the marginal utility of consumption of the first good at date $t + k$ evaluated at equilibrium consumption. Notice that the nominal prices of goods 1 and 2 affect the equity pricing formulas only so far as they affect the term involving the dividend payment. The dividend on the claims to good 1 are paid in the currency of country 1 and likewise for equities issued by country 2. Because the nominal dividend $p_{1,t} y_{1,t}$ is paid at the end of period t, it can only be used to purchase consumption goods in period $t + 1$. Hence, we divide the nominal dividend by the nominal price of 1 in period $t + 1$ to convert it to a real quantity. The same arguments apply to the real price of claims to good 2: in this case, $q_{2,t}$ is the price of equities expressed in units of good 2. We convert the MRS for consumption in good 1 to units of good 2 by multiplying it with the ratio of the relative prices ζ_{t+1}/ζ_t.

We can also derive the price of pure discount bonds denominated in country i's currency. The equilibrium price of a k-period nominal bill for country i is given by:

$$Q_{t,k}^i = \beta^k E_t \left[\frac{U_{i,t+k}}{U_{i,t}} \pi_{i,t+k} \right], \quad i = 1, 2. \tag{6.31}$$

Define $R_{t,k}^i \equiv 1/Q_{t,k}^i$ as the (gross) return on the nominal bond. Notice that the nominal bond price depends on the nominal MRS, which is the MRS in consumption times the ratio of purchasing powers of money between periods t and $t + k$.

There are many other types of assets that can be priced in this economy. A particularly important one is a *forward contract* for foreign exchange, which is an obligation to deliver one unit of foreign exchange at some specified date in the future. It is bought or sold at a current price measured in units of domestic currency. Although a forward contract involves no expenditures in the current period, leaving the current period budget constraint unaffected, the agent's budget constraint is affected in the period in which the delivery occurs.

Assume that the delivery occurs at the beginning of the period. Let the domestic market price at date t of one unit of foreign currency at time $t + k$ be defined as $G_{t,k}$. Suppose that the agent has purchased $z^G_{t,k}$ contracts forward at price $G_{t,k}$. After the delivery, the agent's real balances at the beginning of period $t + k$ evaluated in units of good Y_1 are:

$$h_{t+k} + \frac{z^G_{t,k}}{p_{1,t+k}}(e_{t+k} - G_{t,k}),$$

where h_{t+k} is defined as in Equation (6.10). The total return (or loss) is equal to the difference between the spot exchange rate at the date the contract is delivered and the price at which the contracts are purchased, or $(e_{t+k} - G_{t,k})z^G_{t,k}$. Because no expenditure is required at time t, the first-order condition for the choice of $z^G_{t,k}$ is:

$$0 = \beta^k E_t\left[\frac{U_{1,t+k}}{U_{1,t}}\pi_{1,t+k}(e_{t+k} - G_{t,k})\right], \tag{6.32}$$

where we have multiplied both sides by $p_{1,t}/U_{1,t}$. As before, the nominal MRS is used to discount the return. Because $G_{t,k}$ is known at time t, we can rewrite this as:

$$\beta^k E_t\left[\frac{U_{1,t+k}}{U_{1,t}}\pi_{1,t+k}e_{t+k}\right] = \beta^k E_t\left[\frac{U_{1,t+k}}{U_{1,t}}\pi_{1,t+k}\right]G_{t,k}.$$

Using the expression for the bond price in Equation (6.31), we can write the forward price as:

$$G_{t,k} = \beta^k E_t\left[\frac{U_{1,t+k}}{U_{1,t}}\pi_{1,t+k}e_{t+k}\right]R^1_{t,k}, \tag{6.33}$$

where $R^1_{t,k} \equiv 1/Q^1_{t,k}$.

Using a covariance decomposition, we can rewrite Equation (6.33) as:

$$E_t(e_{t+k}) - G_{t,k} = -R^1_{t,k}\mathrm{Cov}_t\left(\frac{\beta^k U_{1,t+k}}{U_{1,t}}\pi_{1,t+k}, e_{t+k}\right). \tag{6.34}$$

The left side is the *expected profit* on a long position in the forward market, which involves a purchase of foreign currency in the forward market, while the right side is the *risk premium*. Notice that there are two sources of time-varying risk premia or expected profits in the forward market: the first derives from movements in the conditional covariance between the future spot rate and the nominal MRS and the second derives from movements in the nominal risk-free rate, $R_{t,k}^1$. Notice also that *if* the nominal MRS and the spot exchange rate were independent, then $G_{t,k} = E_t(e_{t+k})$, or the forward price is an unbiased predictor of the future spot rate. Thus, the forward rate is a biased predictor of the future spot rate as long as the conditional covariance between the future spot rate and the nominal MRS is different from zero.[5] We describe tests of the unbiasedness hypothesis and alternative ways of modeling risk premia in Section 3.

We now derive the risk premium in the forward market using interest rate arbitrage. This involves comparing the returns from purchasing foreign currency using an uncovered investment strategy versus a covered investment strategy in the market for foreign exchange. An *uncovered* one-period investment in a foreign-denominated bond is one in which an agent exchanges $e_t Q_{t,1}^2$ units of domestic currency for e_{t+1} units of domestic currency next period. Converting these nominal quantities into current units of good Y_1 and discounting the uncertain payoff next period, the equilibrium condition is:

$$1 = \beta E_t \left[\frac{U_{1,t+1}}{U_{1,t}} \pi_{1,t+1} R_{t,1}^2 \frac{e_{t+1}}{e_t} \right]. \tag{6.36}$$

Such an investment strategy is subject to exchange rate risk in the sense that the payoff on the bond at time $t + 1$ of one unit of country 2's currency has an uncertain value in units of country 1's currency. To eliminate the exchange rate risk, the investor can sell a forward contract at time t (so that he agrees to supply foreign currency in exchange for

---

[5]One might conclude that this biasedness is necessarily a result of risk aversion. To show that this conclusion is wrong, suppose that agents are risk neutral. In this case, we have a linear utility function and constant marginal utility of consumption. Thus, Equation (6.33) becomes

$$G_{t,k} = \beta^k E_t \left(\pi_{1,t+k} e_{t+k} \right) R_{t,k}^1$$

$$= E_t(e_{t+k}) + \beta^k \text{Cov}_t \left(\pi_{1,t+k}, e_{t+k} \right) R_{t,k}^1. \tag{6.35}$$

As long as the covariance between the future spot rate and the ratio of the purchasing powers of money is nonzero, the forward rate is a biased predictor of the future spot rate. This bias does not arise from the risk premium but from the covariance of changes in the nominal price of goods and the future exchange rate.

domestic currency at time $t + 1$). This is a covered position or a *covered one-period investment* and a *covered interest arbitrage* argument, which eliminates exchange rate risk, satisfies:

$$1 = \beta E_t \left[\frac{U_{1,t+1}}{U_{1,t}} \pi_{1,t+1} R_{t,1}^2 \frac{G_{t,1}}{e_t} \right]. \tag{6.37}$$

Using the expression for bond prices in Equation (6.31) and noting that $R_{t,1}^2$, $G_{t,1}$, and e_t are known at time t, Equation (6.37) implies that the ratio of current nominal interest rates is equal to the ratio of the forward rate and the spot exchange rate:

$$\frac{R_{t,1}^1}{R_{t,1}^2} = \frac{G_{t,1}}{e_t}. \tag{6.38}$$

This is a statement of *interest rate parity*, which says that an agent is indifferent between investing in a bond denominated in the domestic currency, or investing a unit of the domestic currency in the foreign-denominated bond and selling the foreign-denominated proceeds in the forward market. The return on the former strategy is $R_{t,1}^1$ while the return on the latter strategy is $(G_{t,1}/e_t)R_{t,1}^2$, which are equal by Equation (6.38).

The uncovered and covered investment strategies can be compared by subtracting Equation (6.36) from Equation (6.37):

$$0 = \beta E_t \left[\frac{U_{1,t+1}}{U_{1,t}} \pi_{1,t+1} R_{t,1}^2 \left(\frac{e_{t+1} - G_{t,1}}{e_t} \right) \right]. \tag{6.39}$$

Using the covariance decomposition and dividing by $R_{t,1}^2$, this equation can be rewritten in terms of the risk premium as in Equation (6.34).

Another related quantity is the *forward premium*, defined as $G_{t,k} - e_t$. We can derive an alternative expression for the forward premium by subtracting e_t from both sides of Equation (6.34) as:

$$G_{t,k} - e_t = E_t(e_{t+k}) - e_t + R_{t,k}^1 \text{Cov}_t \left(\frac{\beta^k U_{1,t+k}}{U_{1,t}} \pi_{1,t+k}, e_{t+k} \right). \tag{6.40}$$

This says that the forward premium is equal to the sum of expected depreciation on the domestic currency and the risk premium. In Section 3, we describe an empirical puzzle in the international asset pricing literature known as the negative covariation of expected depreciation and the risk premium that is due to Fama [124].

Now let us consider the pricing of *futures contracts* for foreign exchange. The difference between forward contracts and futures contracts for foreign exchange lies in the institutional features of the futures market. The key feature is the daily resettlement of profit and loss on a contract called "marking to market." The resettlement is accomplished by a clearinghouse in the futures exchange which stands between the buyer and seller of a futures contract. The clearinghouse takes no active position in the market. We assume that the daily resettlement occurs at the beginning of the period so that the agent's initial holdings of real balances are affected if the futures price changes.

Suppose that two parties have contracts at time t with the clearinghouse at the initial futures price $F_{t,k}$. The agent who sells a contract to deliver currency is in a short position and the agent who buys the contract is in a long position. If, in the next time period, the price rises (falls) to $F_{t+1,k-1}$, the amount $F_{t+1,k-1} - F_{t,k}$ is credited to (debited from) the account of the party who bought the contract and debited from (credited to) the account of the short party who sold the contract. The sequence of cash flows between the initial contract date and the date at which the contract is delivered is the major difference between futures contracts and forward contracts.

Let $z_{t,k}^F$ denote the quantity of futures contracts bought (sold) in period t to be delivered at time $t + k$. This decision doesn't alter the agent's budget constraint at time t but, at time $t + 1$, marking to market occurs and the agent's budget constraint at time $t + 1$ is affected. Thus, the quantity $(F_{t+1,k-1} - F_{t,k})z_{t,k}^F$ (which can be positive or negative) enters the agent's budget constraint at time $t + 1$. The first-order condition with respect to $z_{t,k}^F$ is:

$$0 = \beta E_t \left[\frac{U_{1,t+1}}{U_{1,t}} \pi_{1,t+1} \left(F_{t+1,k-1} - F_{t,k} \right) \right],$$

where we have multiplied both sides by $p_{1,t}/U_{1,t}$, The futures price is given by:

$$F_{t,k} = \beta E_t \left[\frac{U_{1,t+1}}{U_{1,t}} \pi_{1,t+1} R_{t,1}^1 F_{t+1,k-1} \right].^6 \tag{6.41}$$

For notational convenience, define the nominal MRS between periods t and $t + k$ as $\mathcal{M}_{t,k}^1 \equiv \beta^k (U_{1,t+k}/U_{1,t})\pi_{1,t+k}$. Substituting for $F_{t+i,k-i}$,

---

[6]Since $F_{t,k}$ is known at time t, we can simplify the first-order condition as:

$$\beta E_t \left[\frac{U_{1,t+1}}{U_{1,t}} \pi_{1,t+1} F_{t+1,k-1} \right] = Q_{t,1} F_{t,k},$$

and use the definition of $R_{t,1}^1$.

$i = 1, \cdots, k$ in the above expression and using an iterated expectation argument, we obtain:

$$F_{t,k} = E_t \left[\mathcal{M}_{t,k}^1 \left(\prod_{i=t}^{t+k-1} R_{i,1}^1 \right) e_{t+k} \right], \tag{6.42}$$

where the last line follows because $F_{t+k,0} = e_{t+k}$.

Using a covariance decomposition, we can write the futures price as:

$$F_{t,k} = E_t(e_{t+k}) + \text{Cov}_t \left[\mathcal{M}_{t,k}^1 \left(\prod_{i=t}^{t+k-1} R_{i,1}^1 \right), e_{t+k} \right]. \tag{6.43}$$

We are now in a position to compare the futures price and the forward price. Let us consider the difference:

$$F_{t,k} - G_{t,k} = E_t \left[\mathcal{M}_{t,k}^1 e_{t+k} \left(\prod_{i=t}^{t+k-1} R_{i,1}^1 - R_{t,k}^1 \right) \right].$$

The forward price $G_{t,k}$ differs from the futures price $F_{t,k}$ because the product of the one-period nominal rates of return (which are random as of time t) does not necessarily equal the k-period risk-free rate between t and $t + k$, which is $R_{t,k}^1$. This difference can be attributed to the sequence of cash flows that is generated by the futures contract but not by the forward contract.

2.   Variants of the Basic Model

In this section, we consider two variants of the basic two-country model with cash-in-advance constraints that we developed in the previous section. We first study the effects of nontraded goods on equilibrium exchange rates and asset prices. In the second variant of the basic model, we introduce capital flows and study a model with the Stockman–Svensson timing of trades.

2.1.   Nontraded Goods

In this section, we introduce nontraded goods in such a way that agents are no longer identical in terms of their wealth or asset holdings. Modifying the model in this way results in a richer velocity function and more interesting dynamics for asset prices. Our discussion is derived from the paper by Stockman and Dellas [315].

The setup is identical to the model just described aside from the fact that households living in country 1 receive not only an endowment of y_1

units of a traded good but also n_1 units of a nontraded good while households residing in country 2 receive an endowment of y_2 of a traded good and n_2 of a nontraded good. Goods Y_1 and Y_2 are traded costlessly while goods n_1 and n_2 are only traded domestically. All goods are perishable. The endowments of the nontraded goods are assumed to be stationary in levels. They are determined as $n_{i,t} = \eta_i(s_t)$. Let $\mathcal{N} \equiv [\underline{\eta}, \bar{\eta}]$ with $\underline{\eta} > 0$ and $\bar{\eta} < \infty$. Similar to Assumption 6.1, we assume that $\eta_i : S \to \mathcal{N}$ is a continuous function that is bounded away from zero.

The representative household in country j chooses consumption and end-of-period assets to maximize:

$$E_0 \left\{ \sum_{t=0}^{\infty} \beta^t [U(c_{1,t}^j, c_{2,t}^j) + W(c_{n,t}^j)] \right\}, \tag{6.44}$$

where U satisfies Assumption 6.3 and W is strictly increasing, strictly concave, continuously differentiable with $\lim_{c \to 0} W'(c) = \infty$ and $W(0) = 0$.

At the outset, we allow agents to hold claims to the endowment of the nontraded good of either country. The asset market opens first followed by the goods market. Let $q_{i,t}^n$ denote the real price of a claim to the nontraded good dividend in country i, denominated in units of Y_i, and let $x_{j,t}^i$ denote the beginning-of-period shares of the nontraded endowment in country j held by an agent from country i. Let the nominal price of n_1 in units of country 1's currency be p_1^n, the nominal price of n_2 in units of country 2's currency be p_2^n, and define $\zeta_{i,t}^n = p_{i,t}^n/p_{i,t}$ to be the relative price of the nontraded good measured in units of Y_i. The representative agent in country 1 has posttransfer beginning-of-period real balances, measured in units of good Y_1, equal to:

$$h_t^1 \equiv \pi_{1,t}[m_{1,t-1}^1 - c_{1,t-1}^1 - \zeta_{1,t-1}^n c_{n,t-1}^1] + \zeta_t \pi_{2,t}[m_{2,t-1}^1 - c_{2,t-1}^1]$$
$$+ \pi_{1,t}[y_{1,t-1}z_{1,t}^1 + \zeta_{1,t-1}^n n_{1,t-1}x_{1,t}^1] +$$
$$\zeta_t \pi_{2,t}[y_{2,t-1}z_{2,t}^1 + \zeta_{2,t-1}^n n_{2,t-1}x_{2,t}^1] + \tau_{1,t}^1 + \zeta_t \tau_{2,t}^1, \tag{6.45}$$

where the last two terms are the transfers made to the representative agent in country 1. The representative agent in country 2 has posttransfer beginning-of-period real balances, measured in units of good Y_1, equal to:

$$h_t^2 \equiv \pi_{1,t}[m_{1,t-1}^2 - c_{1,t-1}^2] + \zeta_t \pi_{2,t}[m_{2,t-1}^2 - c_{2,t-1}^2 - \zeta_{2,t-1}^n c_{n,t-1}^2]$$
$$+ \pi_{1,t}[y_{1,t-1}z_{1,t}^2 + \zeta_{1,t-1}^n n_{1,t-1}x_{1,t}^2]$$
$$+ \zeta_t \pi_{2,t}[y_{2,t-1}z_{2,t}^2 + \zeta_{2,t-1}^n n_{2,t-1}x_{2,t}^2] + \tau_{1,t}^2 + \zeta_t \tau_{2,t}^2. \tag{6.46}$$

The asset market opens first and agents trade in securities and currency. While in the asset market, agents acquire the currency they need to make consumption purchases in the subsequent goods market. It is assumed that domestic sellers will accept payment only in their domestic currency. The budget constraint in the asset market faced by the representative agent of country j is:

$$q_{1,t}^e z_{1,t+1}^j + q_{1,t}^n x_{1,t+1}^j + \zeta_t[q_{2,t}^e z_{2,t+1}^j + q_{2,t}^n x_{2,t+1}^j] + m_{1,t}^j + \zeta_t m_{2,t}^j$$

$$\leq h_t^j + q_{1,t}^e z_{1,t}^j + q_{1,t}^n x_{1,t}^j + \zeta_t[q_{2,t}^e z_{2,t}^j + q_{2,t}^n x_{2,t}^j], \tag{6.47}$$

where $q_{i,t}^n$ is the real price at time t of an equity share of the nontraded good in country i measured in units of good Y_i.

In the goods market, the following cash-in-advance constraints apply to the purchases of goods Y_1 and Y_2 by the agent from country 1:

$$c_{1,t}^1 + c_{n,t}^1 \zeta_{1,t}^n \leq m_{1,t}^1, \tag{6.48}$$

$$\zeta_t c_{2,t}^1 \leq \zeta_t m_{2,t}^1, \tag{6.49}$$

and for the agent from country 2,

$$c_{1,t}^2 \leq m_{1,t}^2, \tag{6.50}$$

$$\zeta_t[c_{2,t}^2 + c_{n,t}^2 \zeta_{2,t}^n] \leq \zeta_t m_{2,t}^2. \tag{6.51}$$

After the goods market closes, the agent receives the nominal dividend payments on the claims from both countries.

Define $\zeta : S \to \mathbb{R}_{++}$, $\zeta^n : S \to \mathbb{R}_{++}$, and $q_i^e : S \to \mathbb{R}_{++}$ for $i = 1, 2$ to be strictly positive, continuous functions. Also define the nominal price of traded and nontraded goods $p_i : S \times \mathbb{R}_+^2 \to \mathbb{R}_{++}$ and $p_i^n : S \times \mathbb{R}_+^2 \to \mathbb{R}_{++}$ for $i = 1, 2$, and the nominal exchange rate $e : S \times \mathbb{R}_+^2 \to \mathbb{R}_{++}$ to be strictly positive, continuous functions. For notational convenience, define the vector $\alpha^j \equiv (z_1^j, z_2^j, x_1^j, x_2^j)$. The consumer's state consists of h^j, α^j and the current shock s. Given the price functions ζ, ζ^n, e, q_i^e, p_i and p_i^n for $i = 1, 2$, the resident of country j chooses $(c_1^j, c_2^j, c_n^j, m_1^j, m_2^j, \alpha^{j\prime})$ to solve:

$$V(h^j, \alpha^j, s) = \max\left\{U(c_1^j, c_2^j) + W(c_n^j) + \beta E_s[V(h^{j\prime}, \alpha^{j\prime}, s\prime)]\right\}$$

subject to the asset market constraint (Equation 6.47), the law of motion for posttransfer real balances (Equation 6.45 or 6.46), and the cash-in-advance constraints (Equations 6.48 and 6.49 or 6.50 and 6.51). The market-clearing conditions require that $c_i^1 + c_i^2 = y_i$, $c_n^i = n_i$, $M_i^1 + M_i^2 = M_i$, $z_i^1 + z_i^2 = 1$, $x_i^1 + x_i^2 = 1$ for $i = 1, 2$.

In the first section, we assumed that agents are identical in equilibrium. In the presence of nontraded goods, we continue to assume that each consumer consumes half the endowment of each country and holds half the shares of the traded goods. To determine the holdings of equity shares of the nontraded endowments, substitute these conditions into the agents' holdings of money balances at the beginning of the period. For $i = 1$,

$$h_t^1 = \pi_{1,t}[m_{t-1}^1 + \zeta_{1,t-1}^n n_{1,t-1}(x_{1,t}^1 - 1)]$$

$$+ \zeta_t \pi_{2,t}[m_{2,t-1}^1 + n_{2,t-1} x_{2,t}^1] + \tau_{1,t}^1 + \zeta_t \tau_{2,t}^1.$$

We have a similar expression for h_t^2. Under the assumption that agents are identical in their consumption of traded goods and holdings of equity shares on traded goods, a stationary equilibrium requires that agents do not hold claims on the nontraded goods of the foreign country, $\hat{x}_2^1 = \hat{x}_1^2 = 0$ and $\hat{x}_1^1 = \hat{x}_2^2 = 1$. Under this allocation, $\hat{h}^1 = \hat{h}^2$, which equal world real balances $.5\left[(M_{1,t}/p_{1,t}) + \zeta_t(M_{2,t}/p_{2,t})\right]$.[7] Notice that in equilibrium, asset holdings are given by $\hat{\alpha}^1 = (.5, .5, 1, 0)$ for residents of country 1 and $\hat{\alpha}^2 = (.5, .5, 0, 1)$ for residents of country 2 while equilibrium consumption satisfies $\hat{c}_1^j = .5y_1$, $\hat{c}_2^j = .5y_2$, and $\hat{c}_n^j = n_j$ for $j = 1, 2$.

Let $\mu_i(s)$ denote the multiplier for the cash-in-advance constraint on good i, and $\xi(s)$ denote the multiplier on the budget constraint in the asset market. Define $U_i(s)$ as before and let $W_i(s)$ denote the marginal utility with respect to the i'th nontraded good. The equilibrium first-order conditions with respect to c_1, c_2, c_n, m_1, m_2, z_1, z_2, x_1, and x_2 for the representative consumer from country 1 are:

$$U_1(s) = \mu_1(s) + \beta E_s\left[\xi(s')\pi_1(s')\right], \tag{6.52}$$

$$U_2(s) = \zeta(s)\mu_2(s) + \beta E_s\left[\xi(s')\pi_2(s')\zeta(s')\right], \tag{6.53}$$

$$W_1(s) = \zeta_1^n(s)\mu_1(s) + \beta E_s\left[\xi(s')\pi_1(s')\zeta_1^n(s')\right], \tag{6.54}$$

$$\xi(s) = \mu_1(s) + \beta E_s\left[\xi(s')\pi_1(s')\right], \tag{6.55}$$

$$\zeta(s)\xi(s) = \zeta(s)\mu_2(s) + \beta E_s\left[\xi(s')\pi_2(s')\zeta(s')\right], \tag{6.56}$$

$$q_1^e(s)\xi(s) = \beta E_s\{\xi(s')[\pi_1(s')y_1(s) + q_1^e(s')]\}, \tag{6.57}$$

---

[7]If we set $x_j^i = .5$ for $i, j = 1, 2$, the real balances held by the two agents would no longer be equal ($h^1 \neq h^2$). In that case, we would be unable to sustain a perfectly pooled equilibrium in the traded goods and assets markets because the endowment processes for the nontraded goods are not identical while agents have the same utility function for consumption of the nontraded good.

$$q_2^e(s)\zeta(s)\xi(s) \;=\; \beta E_s\{\xi(s')\zeta(s')[\pi_2(s')y_2(s) + q_2^e(s)]\}, \qquad (6.58)$$

$$q_1^n(s)\xi(s) \;=\; \beta E_s\{\xi(s')[\pi_1(s')\zeta_1^n(s)n_1(s) + q_1^n(s')]\}, \qquad (6.59)$$

$$q_2^n(s)\zeta(s)\xi(s) \;=\; \beta E_s\{\xi(s')\zeta(s')[\pi_2(s')\zeta_2^n(s)n_2(s) + q_2^n(s')]\}. \qquad (6.60)$$

The slackness conditions can be derived in a straightforward manner.

A similar set of conditions characterizes the problem of a representative consumer from country 2. The only different condition involves the nontraded good from country 2:

$$W_2(s) = \zeta(s)\zeta_2^n(s)\mu_2(s) + \beta E_s\left[\xi(s')\pi_2(s')\zeta(s')\zeta_2^n(s')\right]. \qquad (6.61)$$

We now derive the implications of this model for equilibrium prices. The right side of Equation (6.52) equals the right side of Equation (6.55) so that $U_1(s) = \xi(s)$. Similarly, the right side of Equation (6.53) equals the right side of Equation (6.56) so that $U_2(s) = \zeta(s)\xi(s)$. Finally, using Equations (6.52) and (6.54) together yields a solution for $\zeta_1^n(s)$ as:

$$\zeta_1^n(s) = \frac{W_1(s)}{U_1(s)}. \qquad (6.62)$$

This says that the relative price of the nontraded good in country 1 is defined in terms of the MRS in consumption between the traded and nontraded good. We can derive a similar expression for $\zeta_2^n(s)$.

It is straightforward to demonstrate that the inverse of the velocity function for country i satisfies:

$$U_i(s)[y_i(s) + \zeta_i^n(s)n_i(s)]\Psi_i(s) = \max\{U_i(s)[y_i(s) + \zeta_i^n(s)n_i(s)],$$

$$\beta E_s\left(\frac{U_i(s')[y_i(s') + \zeta_i^n(s')n_i(s')]\Psi_i(s')}{\omega_i(s')}\right)\}. \qquad (6.63)$$

Introducing nontraded goods into this setup creates another way for velocity to fluctuate because it depends on the relative price of the traded to the nontraded good.

The nominal exchange rate is determined from Equations (6.53) and (6.56), from which it follows that $U_2(s) = \zeta(s)U_1(s)$. Hence,

$$e(s, M) = \frac{U_2(s)}{U_1(s)} \frac{M_1}{M_2} \frac{[y_2(s) + \zeta_2^n(s)n_2(s)]}{[y_1(s) + \zeta_1^n(s)n_1(s)]} \frac{\Psi_2^\star(s)}{\Psi_1^\star(s)}, \qquad (6.64)$$

where $\Psi_i^\star$ denotes the solution to Equation (6.63). Notice that the terms of trade ($\zeta = U_2/U_1$) and the relative price of nontraded goods affect the nominal exchange rate. The effect of an increase in the supply of the nontraded good on the exchange rate will depend on the sign of $W''n + W'$. If the supply of n_1 increases and if $W''n + W' < 0$, then the exchange rate increases (or depreciates).

The price of a one-period nominal bond that pays one unit of currency i next period with certainty satisfies:

$$Q_1^i(s) = \beta E_s \left[\frac{U_i(s')\Psi_i(s')[y_i(s') + \zeta_i^n(s')n_i(s')]}{U_i(s)\Psi_i(s)[y_i(s) + \zeta_i^n(s)n_1(s)]\omega_i(s')} \right]. \tag{6.65}$$

Notice that changes in the supply of the nontraded good affect the nominal interest rate. In this model, velocity is constant whenever interest rates are positive. The bond price can be substituted into the functional equation for Ψ and clearly if nominal interest rates are positive, then the cash-in-advance constraint is binding.

2.2. Exchange Rates and International Capital Flows

We now introduce a model with investment and international capital flows. Our discussion derives from the paper by Stockman and Svensson [316]. This model has the Stockman–Svensson timing convention which assumes that the goods market opens first and the consumer makes goods purchases using the sellers' currencies and then the asset market opens.

In this model, countries are completely specialized in production. Output of the domestic good denoted $x_{1,t}$ depends on the domestic capital stock denoted k_t and a random disturbance θ_t as:

$$x_{1,t} = f(k_t, \theta_t), \tag{6.66}$$

where $f(\cdot, \theta)$ is strictly increasing, strictly concave, and differentiable. The capital stock depreciates 100% each period. Output of the foreign good denoted $x_{2,t}$ is exogenous. Only the foreign good can be used for domestic investment. Investment at time t transforms the foreign goods into domestic capital at time $t + 1$ so that the quantity of foreign goods available for world consumption at time t is $x_{2,t} - k_{t+1}$.

The shocks to the economy s_t follow a first-order Markov process with a transition function F that satisfies the conditions of Assumption 5.1. The money supplies in each country evolve according to Equation (6.1) and satisfy Assumption 6.2. The endowment of country 2 at time t is a time-invariant function of the exogenous shock, $x_{2,t} \equiv x_2(s_t)$ and so is the disturbance to the production function of country 1 which we denote by $\theta_t \equiv \theta(s_t)$. Define $\mathcal{X} \equiv [\underline{x}_2, \bar{x}_2]$ and $\Theta \equiv [\underline{\theta}, \bar{\theta}]$, where $\underline{x}_2 > 0$, $\bar{x}_2 < \infty$, $\underline{\theta} > 0$ and $\bar{\theta} < \infty$. We assume that $x_2 : S \to \mathcal{X}$ and $\theta : S \to \Theta$ are continuous functions that are bounded away from zero. Since output takes values in a compact set and there is 100% depreciation, notice that k_{t+1} takes values in the compact set $\mathcal{K} \equiv [\underline{k}, \bar{k}]$ where $\underline{k} > 0$ and $\bar{k} < \infty$.

The household in country j begins the period with holdings of domestic and foreign currency denoted $M^j_{1,t}$ and $M^j_{2,t}$ and claims to dividends $z^j_{1,t}$ and $z^j_{2,t}$ for the production processes in each country. There is one outstanding equity share in each production process. The household is assumed to be the owner of the capital stock and, at the beginning of the period, it rents out the capital accumulated the previous period k^j_t in exchange for rental income paid by the firm after the goods market closes. We assume that there is a competitive rental market so that households and firms are price-takers.[8] Essentially the firm receives the nominal revenue from selling output in the goods market and, after the close of the market, it pays rent and dividends to households so that the firm holds no money between periods.

After the goods markets close, the asset markets open and all interest and dividend payments are made, factor payments are made to the owners of capital, and assets are traded. The consumer in country j also receives the lump-sum money transfers $T^j_{i,t}$ from the government of country i which equal the net growth of money, $T^j_{i,t} = [\omega_i(s_t) - 1]\bar{M}_{i,t}$. The constraint in the asset market for the representative consumer in country j at time t denominated in units of the domestic currency is:

$$p_t c^j_{1,t} + e_t p_{2,t}(c^j_{2,t} + k^j_{t+1}) + M^j_{1,t+1} + e_t M^j_{2,t+1} + Q^e_{1,t} z^j_{1,t+1} +$$

$$e_t Q^e_{2,t} z^j_{2,t+1} \leq (Q^e_{1,t} + p_{1,t} d_{1,t}) z^j_{1,t} + e_t(Q^e_{2,t} + p_{2,t} d_{2,t}) z^j_{2,t}$$

$$+ M^j_{1,t} + T^j_{1,t} + e_t(M^j_{2,t} + T^j_{2,t}) + R_t k^j_t,$$

where R_t is the nominal rent paid to owners of the capital stock. The cash-in-advance constraints are:

$$p_{1,t} c^j_{1,t} \leq M^j_{1,t},$$

$$e_t p_{2,t}(c^j_{2,t} + k^j_{t+1}) \leq e_t M^j_{2,t}.$$

Since the money supplies are growing, we divide the nominal constraints by the domestic currency price of country 1's goods to convert

---

[8]The assumption that households own the capital stock and rent it to the firm differs from the setup in Stockman and Svensson who assume that, when the consumer holds a share in the domestic firm, it receives the dividends $d_{1,t}$ from the firm but in addition, it agrees to deliver investment goods to the firm in each period equal to k_{t+1}.

nominal quantities into units of good 1. The asset market constraint
becomes:

$$c_{1,t}^j + \zeta_t(c_{2,t}^j + k_{t+1}^j) + \frac{M_{1,t+1}^j}{p_{1,t}} + \zeta_t \frac{M_{2,t+1}^j}{p_{2,t}} + q_{1,t}^e z_{1,t+1}^j +$$

$$\zeta_t q_{2,t}^e z_{2,t+1}^j \leq (q_{1,t}^e + d_{1,t}) z_{1,t}^j + \zeta_t (q_{2,t}^e + d_{2,t}) z_{2,t}^j +$$

$$\frac{M_{1,t}^j}{p_{1,t}} + \tau_{1,t}^j + \zeta_t \left(\frac{M_{2,t}^j}{p_{2,t}} + \tau_{2,t}^j \right) + r_t k_t^j, \qquad (6.67)$$

where $\zeta_t \equiv e_t p_{2,t}/p_{1,t}$, $r_t \equiv R_t/p_{1,t}$, $q_{i,t}^e \equiv Q_{i,t}^e/p_{i,t}$, and $\tau_{i,t} \equiv T_{i,t}/p_{i,t}$ for
$i = 1, 2$. Likewise, the cash-in-advance constraints become:

$$c_{1,t}^j \leq M_{1,t}^j/p_{1,t}, \qquad (6.68)$$

$$\zeta_t(c_{2,t}^j + k_{1,t+1}^j) \leq \zeta_t M_{2,t}^j/p_{2,t}. \qquad (6.69)$$

Consumers in both countries have identical information and portfolios
and their preferences are defined as in Equation (6.2), where the utility
function satisfies Assumption 6.3. The household observes the current
exogenous shock s and so observes the current disturbance to domestic
production, the endowment of country 2, and the money growth rates.
The consumer's state at time t is summarized by its money holdings
M_1^j, M_2^j, equity holdings z_1^j, z_2^j, and its stock of capital k^j. The aggregate
state consists of the aggregate capital stock k and the current shock s.

We will seek an equilibrium in which the terms of trade, the rental
rate, and the equity prices are time-invariant functions of k and s, and
the nominal exchange rate and nominal prices levels are time-invariant
functions of s, k, and $M \equiv (\bar{M}_1, \bar{M}_2)$. Define $\mathcal{S} \equiv S \times \mathcal{K}$. Define
$\zeta : \mathcal{S} \to \mathbb{R}_{++}$, $r : \mathcal{S} \to \mathbb{R}_{++}$, and $q_i^e : \mathcal{S} \to \mathbb{R}_{++}$ for $i = 1, 2$ to be
positive, continuous functions and $p_i : \mathcal{S} \times \mathbb{R}_+^2 \to \mathbb{R}_{++}$ for $i = 1, 2$ and
$e : \mathcal{S} \times \mathbb{R}_+^2 \to \mathbb{R}_{++}$ to be positive, continuous functions. For notational
convenience, define $\alpha^j \equiv (M_1^j, M_2^j, z_1^j, z_2^j, k^j)$. Given the price functions
ζ, e, r and q_i^e and p_i for $i = 1, 2$, the representative agent's problem in
country j is to solve:

$$V(\alpha^j, k, s) = \max_{c_1^j, c_2^j, \alpha^{j\prime}} \left\{ U(c_1^j, c_2^j) + \beta E_s[V(\alpha^{j\prime}, k, s')] \right\}$$

subject to the asset market constraint (Equation 6.67) and the cash-in-
advance constraints (Equations 6.68 and 6.69). We can show the existence to the consumer's value function using the methods defined earlier.

The market-clearing conditions are:

$$c_{1,t}^1 + c_{1,t}^2 = x_{1,t}, \tag{6.70}$$

$$c_{2,t}^1 + c_{2,t}^2 + k_{t+1}^1 + k_{t+1}^2 = x_{2,t}, \tag{6.71}$$

$$z_{i,t+1}^1 + z_{i,t+1}^2 = 1, \tag{6.72}$$

$$M_{i,t+1}^1 + M_{i,t+1}^2 = \omega_i(s_t)\bar{M}_{i,t}, \tag{6.73}$$

for $i = 1, 2$.

We assume that the optimal consumption and capital holdings by the representative consumer in country j can be expressed as time-invariant functions of the aggregate state, $c_1(k,s)$, $c_2(k,s)$, and $K(k,s)$. Define $U_i(k,s)$ as the partial derivative of U with respect to its i'th argument evaluated at $c_i(k,s)$ for $i = 1, 2$. Let $\xi(k,s)$ denote the Lagrange multiplier on the asset market constraint and $\mu_i(k,s)$ denote the Lagrange multiplier on the cash-in-advance constraints. Substituting the envelope conditions, the first-order conditions with respect to c_i, M_i', z_i' for $i = 1, 2$ and k' are:

$$U_1(k,s) = \xi(k,s) + \mu_1(k,s), \tag{6.74}$$

$$U_2(k,s) = \zeta(k,s)[\xi(k,s) + \mu_2(k,s)], \tag{6.75}$$

$$\xi(k,s) = \beta E_s\{\pi_1(k',s')[\xi(k',s') + \mu_1(k',s')]\}, \tag{6.76}$$

$$\zeta(k,s)\xi(k,s) = \beta E_s\{\pi_2(k',s')\zeta(k',s')[\xi(k',s') + \mu_2(k',s')]\}, \tag{6.77}$$

$$q_1^e(k,s)\xi(k,s) = \beta E_s\{\xi(k',s')[d_1' + q_1^e(k',s')]\}, \tag{6.78}$$

$$\zeta(k,s)q_2^e(k,s)\xi(k,s) = \beta E s\{\zeta(k',s')\xi(k',s')[d_2' + q_2^e(k',s')]\}, \tag{6.79}$$

$$\zeta(k,s)[\xi(s) + \mu_2(k,s)] = \beta E_s[\xi(s')r(k',s')]. \tag{6.80}$$

In these expressions, $\pi_i(k',s') \equiv p_i(k,s,M)/p_i(k',s',M')$ for $i = 1, 2$. We also have the slackness conditions with respect to the multipliers $\xi(k,s)$ and $\mu_i(k,s)$ for $i = 1, 2$.

For country 2, where the output of good 2 is determined exogenously, the dividend is equal to the amount of good 2 produced so that $d_2 = x_2(s)$. Now turn to the problem solved by a firm which produces good

1. The firm chooses the amount of capital k_t to rent that maximizes its profits; it solves:

$$d_{1,t} \equiv \max_{k_t}[f(k_t, \theta_t) - r_t k_t], \tag{6.81}$$

The firm rents capital up to the point where its marginal product equals the rental rate. When capital markets clear, the amount hired by firms just equals the amount held by the representative household. The profits of the firm are paid out as dividends to shareholders.

The first-order condition for investment, with the equilibrium condition $r_t = f_k(k_t, \theta_t)$ substituted in, is

$$\beta E_t[\xi_{t+1} f_k(k_{t+1}, \theta_{t+1})] = (\xi_t + \mu_{2,t})\zeta_t = U_{2,t}, \tag{6.82}$$

where f_k denotes the partial derivative of $f(k, \theta)$ with respect to k. The right side is just the marginal cost of investment at time t. The left side shows the expected marginal benefit at time $t + 1$: a higher value of capital at time $t + 1$ produces additional output at $t + 1$ and ξ_{t+1} is the marginal utility of this income.

We study the pooled equilibrium for this model. The pooled equilibrium requires that:

$$c_1 = x_1/2, \quad c_2 = [x_2 - K(k, s)]/2,$$

$$z_i' = 1/2, \quad M_i' = \omega_i(s)\bar{M}_i/2, \quad i = 1, 2.$$

We assume that the utility function in each country U is separable with respect to c_1 and c_2. In this case, we can use the conditions in Equations (6.74), (6.76), and (6.82) to solve for the function K and the inverse of the velocity function in country 1. Since U is separable, we can write U_1 and U_2 as functions of the equilibrium consumption of domestic and foreign goods only, $U_1(x_1/2)$ and $U_2[(x_2 - k')/2]$.

We add the cash-in-advance constraints for members of country 1 and 2 in the domestic and the foreign currency and define the functions:

$$\Psi_1 \equiv \bar{M}_1/p_1 x_1, \tag{6.83}$$

$$\Psi_2 \equiv \bar{M}_2/(p_2 x_2 + k'). \tag{6.84}$$

Notice that we can derive an expression for the multiplier on the cash-in-advance constraint for country 1 as:

$$U_1(k, s)\Psi_1(k, s)x_1 = \mu_1(k, s) + \beta E_s \left[\frac{U_1(k', s')\Psi_1(k', s')x_1'}{\omega_1(s')} \right].$$

In equilibrium, $x_1(k, s) = f(k, s)$ is given. It will be more convenient to derive a mapping for the function:

$$\Gamma(k, s) \equiv U_1(k, s)\Psi_1(k, s)x_1(k, s)$$

from the above expression by considering the cases when $\mu_1 = 0$ and $\mu_1 > 0$ as:

$$\Gamma(k, s) = \max\left[U_1(k, s)x_1(k, s), \beta E_s\left(\frac{\Gamma(k', s')}{\omega(s')}\right)\right]. \qquad (6.85)$$

Notice that k' is a decision variable. If the capital process were given exogenously, then we could define an operator with a fixed point $\Gamma^\star$ that satisfies Equation (6.85). Instead, we need to solve also for the equilibrium capital path. Here we will outline the steps that are necessary to solve this model.

Recall that the first-order condition for investment can be expressed as:

$$U_2[x_2(s) - k'] = \beta E_s[\xi(k', s')f_k(k', \theta')] \qquad (6.86)$$

Notice that U_2 is increasing in k' given s so that we can define k' from $\phi(k, s) = U_2[x_2(s) - k']$ for $\phi_1 > 0$ as:

$$k' = H(\phi, s) = x_2(s) - U_2^{-1}(\phi).$$

Notice also that H is increasing in its first argument. Let $K(k, s)$ be a feasible solution and define $\phi(k, s) \equiv U_2[x_2(s) - K(k, s)]$. We can then write Equation (6.86) as:

$$\phi(k, s) = \beta E_s\left\{\xi(H[\phi(k, s), s], s')f_k(H[\phi(k, s), s], \theta')\right\}. \qquad (6.87)$$

Notice that we evaluate ϕ at (k, s) on both sides of the equation. By assumption f_k is strictly decreasing in its first argument. For fixed (k, s), consider the solution scalar $\phi > 0$, that is, the solution to:

$$\phi = \beta E_s\{\xi[H(\phi, s), s']f_k[H(\phi, s), \theta']\}. \qquad (6.88)$$

If we assume that ξ is decreasing in its first argument, then for fixed (k, s) the left side is clearly increasing in ϕ and the right side is strictly decreasing so there exists a unique solution ϕ for each (k, s) pair. Let $(S\xi)(k, s)$ denote the solution ϕ to Equation (6.88).

Given the function Γ, we can define the multiplier function ξ using the following argument. Let $K(k, s)$ be given. When $\mu_1 = 0$, $\xi(k, s) = U_1(s)$ and $\Gamma(k, s) = \beta E_s[\Gamma(k', s')/\omega(s')]$. When $\mu_1 > 0$, then $\Gamma(k, s) =$

$U_1(s)x_1(s)$ and $\xi(k,s) = \beta E_s[\Gamma(k',s')/(x_1(s)\omega(s'))]$. From the definition of the function Γ, it follows that:

$$\xi(k,s) \equiv \min\left[U_1(k,s), \beta E_s\left(\frac{\Gamma(k',s')}{x_1(s)\omega(s')}\right)\right]. \tag{6.89}$$

Let T_2 be the operator that yields ξ from Γ or $\xi(k,s) = (T_2\Gamma)(k,s)$. Given $\xi(k,s) = (T_2\Gamma)(k,s)$, we can find the solution ϕ to Equation (6.88). Define the operator T_1 by:

$$\phi(k,s) \equiv (T_1\Gamma)(k,s)$$
$$= \beta E_s\left\{(T_2\Gamma)(H[\phi(k,s),s],s')f_k(H[\phi(k,s),s],\theta')\right\}. \tag{6.90}$$

We can now define the operator $\mathcal{T}_\infty$ as follows:

$$\Gamma^{n+1}(k,s) = (\mathcal{T}_\infty\Gamma^n)(k,s)$$
$$= \max\left[U_1(k,s)x_1(k,s), \beta E_s\left(\frac{\Gamma^n\{H[\phi(k,s)],s'\}}{\omega(s')}\right)\right], \tag{6.91}$$

where $\phi(k,s) = (T_1\Gamma)(k,s)$ is the solution to the previous mapping. The form of this mapping is different from the other mappings that we studied earlier. A proof can be constructed using the approach in Deaton and Laroque [86] but it is beyond the scope of our analysis to provide the entire derivation. Assuming a solution has been found, let $\xi^*(k,s)$ denote a fixed point and let $K^*(k,s)$ be the optimal investment function. Given the solution for $\Psi_1^*(k,s)$ and $K^*(k,s)$, we can use Equations (6.75) and (6.77) to solve for $\Psi_2(k,s)$ and Equations (6.78) and (6.79) to solve for the equity prices $q_1^e(k,s)$ and $q_2^e(k,s)$.

Since there is one equity share outstanding, the value of the firm is just $q_{1,t}^e$. We can derive an expression for firm value by solving Equation (6.78) forward:

$$q_{1,t}^e = \frac{1}{\xi_t}E_t\left(\sum_{\tau=t+1}^{\infty}\beta^{t-\tau}\{\xi^*(k_\tau^*,s_\tau)[x_1(k_\tau^*,s_\tau) - f_k(k_\tau^*,\theta_\tau)k_\tau^*]\}\right),$$

where we have made use of the fact that equilibrium dividends at each date τ are equal to domestic profits at that date.

We now use this framework to define a number of accounting identities involving international capital flows. The domestic country's *current account surplus* is defined as the change in its net holdings of foreign assets, which is also the *capital account deficit*. We denote the capital account deficit (current account surplus) in period t, measured in units of the domestic good, by C_t. The total world values of foreign assets $V_{2,t}$ and domestic assets $V_{1,t}$ are:

$$V_{1,t} = q_{1,t}^e + \omega_1(s_t)m_{1,t}, \qquad (6.92)$$

$$V_{2,t} = \zeta_t[q_{2,t}^e + \omega_2(s_t)m_{2,t}], \qquad (6.93)$$

where $m_{i,t} \equiv \bar{M}_{i,t}/p_{i,t}$ for $i = 1, 2$ denote the world real balances of the domestic and foreign currencies. Foreign assets consist of shares in the foreign firm and the real balances of foreign money. Domestic assets are the shares in the home firm and real balances of domestic money.

Households in the domestic country have a net foreign account asset position at the end of period t, denoted F_t, which is given by:

$$F_t = V_{2,t}/2 - V_{1,t}/2. \qquad (6.94)$$

The current account surplus in period t is:

$$C_t = \Delta F_t = (V_{2,t} - V_{2,t-1} - V_{1,t} + V_{1,t-1})/2, \qquad (6.95)$$

where Δ denotes the first difference operator. Define domestic saving S_t as the change in domestic wealth, $S_t = \Delta(V_{2,t}/2 + V_{1,t}/2)$, and domestic investment I_t as the change in the value of domestic assets, $I_t = \Delta V_{1,t}$. The current account surplus C_t can be written as:

$$C_t = S_t - I_t. \qquad (6.96)$$

We now define the balance-of-trade surplus and the service account surplus. The *trade account surplus* measured in domestic goods is defined as:

$$TA_t = c_{1,t}^2 - \zeta_t(c_{2,t}^1 + k_{t+1}) = x_{1,t}/2 - \zeta_t[x_{2,t} + K(k_t, s_t)]/2.$$

The first term shows exports, which equal half of domestic output. The second term shows imports of consumption goods and the third term shows imports of goods for investment.

The *service account surplus* consists of net dividends or interest payments and capital gains on all assets:

$$SA_t = [\zeta_t x_{2,t} - x_{1,t} + K(k_t, s_t) + \Delta(\zeta_t q_{2,t}^e - q_{1,t}^e) + \zeta_t(\omega_{2,t} - 1)m_{2,t}$$

$$-(\omega_{1,t} - 1)m_{1,t} + (\Delta\zeta_t p_{2,t}^{-1})\bar{M}_{2,t} - (\Delta p_{1,t}^{-1})\bar{M}_{1,t}]/2.$$

The first three terms are the net dividends from the foreign and domestic production processes received by the domestic country. The fourth and fifth terms show the capital gains on foreign equity minus foreigners' capital gains on domestic equity. The sixth and seventh terms show the receipt of foreign monetary transfers minus the payment of domestic monetary transfers. The last two terms show domestic capital gains on holdings of foreign currency minus foreign capital gains on holdings of domestic currency. Notice that $C_t = TA_t + SA_t$.

One difference between these measures and reported current-account data is that capital gains are arbitrarily excluded from the latter so that the sum of SA_t and TA_t does not equal the change in the net foreign asset position. Also, the definitions of saving and investment given above do not correspond to national-income-accounting (NIA) definitions. The NIA definitions of gross domestic savings is the difference between "income" defined as $[x_{1,t} + \zeta_t(x_{2,t} + k_{t+1})]/2$ and consumption:

$$[x_{1,t} + \zeta_t(x_{2,t} + k_{t+1})]/2 - c_{1,t}^1 - \zeta_t c_{2,t}^1 = k_{t+1}.$$

The NIA definition of gross domestic investment is k_{t+1} so savings minus investment is zero according to the NIA definitions and it is not equal to the change in the net foreign asset position.

Stockman and Svensson use the solution to the model to analyze the determinants of the current account surplus (the capital account deficit) and the covariation between capital flows C_t and such variables as investment (defined as $k_{t+1} - k_t$), national outputs, $x_{1,t}$ and $x_{2,t}$, the terms of trade ζ_t, and the rate of change in the exchange rate. For example, we can ask under what conditions real appreciation of the domestic currency is associated with a current account surplus versus a deficit. Stockman and Svensson find that these covariances depend on the degree of risk aversion (or the degree of intertemporal substitution in consumption), the size and magnitude of net foreign assets, the marginal product of capital, and the stochastic properties of the disturbances to productivity and money growth. To derive such results, we need to use the properties of the optimal investment policy $K^*(k, s)$, the inverse velocity functions $\Psi_i^*(k, s)$, and the equity price functions $q_i^e(k, s)$ for $i = 1, 2$.

3.   The Empirical Behavior of Foreign Exchange Markets

In this section, we discuss tests of efficiency in the markets for forward contracts for foreign exchange. These tests are motivated by the fact that if such markets are efficient, then forward exchange rates should be useful for predicting future spot rates. When investors are risk averse, the forward rate equals the expected spot rate plus a time-varying risk premium.

We first describe a set of tests that examine the efficiency of forward exchange markets under the assumption that this risk premium is constant over time. These tests are typically referred to as regression-based tests of unbiasedness. Next, we describe ways of allowing for a time-varying risk premium. The final topic of this chapter involves methods for modeling the distribution of short-term changes in exchange rates.

3.1. Regression-Based Tests

The model that we examined implies that if foreign exchange rate markets are efficient, then the equilibrium condition in Equation (6.32) should hold in the data. Regression-based tests of unbiasedness are typically obtained by imposing a set of auxiliary assumptions on the behavior of the variables entering this condition. These assumptions are not necessarily consistent with an equilibrium model but they allow us to examine observed relationships between forward rates and future spot rates.

One set of auxiliary assumptions involves imposing joint lognormality for the endogenous variables defined by the vector:

$$Z_t' = (e_t^1, \cdots, e_t^p, G_{t,k}^1, \ldots, G_{t,k}^p, \mathcal{M}_{t,k}^1),$$

where $e_t^j, j = 1, \cdots, p$ denote exchange rates measured in some numeraire currency, $G_{t,k}^j, j = 1, \cdots, p$ denote the forward exchange rates (which are the domestic currency prices of a unit of currency j established at date t for payment at $t + k$), and $\mathcal{M}_{t,k}^1$ is the nominal MRS.

Let $I_t^Z = (\tilde{z}_t, \tilde{z}_{t-1}, \ldots)$ be the subset of the agent's information set generated by current and past realizations of the logarithm of the vector Z_t and $E_t^Z(\cdot)$ the expectation conditional on I_t^Z. Since $I_t^Z \subset I_t$, the equilibrium condition in Equation (6.32) implies that

$$E_t^Z(\mathcal{M}_{t,k}^1 e_{t+k}^j) = E_t^Z(\mathcal{M}_{t,k}^1) G_{t,k}^j. \qquad (6.97)$$

If we assume that Z_t is lognormally distributed, then $\mathcal{M}_{t,k}^1$ and e_{t+k}^j are also lognormal random variables. Thus,

$$E_t^Z(\mathcal{M}_{t,k}^1 e_{t+k}^j) = \exp\left[E_t^Z(\tilde{e}_{t+k}^j) + E_t^Z(\tilde{\mathcal{M}}_{t,k}^1) + \frac{1}{2}V_t^Z(\tilde{e}_{t+k}^j)\right.$$
$$\left. + \frac{1}{2}V_t^Z(\tilde{\mathcal{M}}_{t,k}^1) + \mathrm{Cov}_t^Z(\tilde{e}_{t+k}^j, \tilde{\mathcal{M}}_{t,k}^1)\right] \qquad (6.98)$$

and

$$G_{t,k}^j E_t^Z(\mathcal{M}_{t,k}^1) = \exp\left[\tilde{G}_{t,k}^j + E_t^Z(\tilde{\mathcal{M}}_{t,k}^1) + \frac{1}{2}V_t^Z(\tilde{\mathcal{M}}_{t,k}^1)\right]. \qquad (6.99)$$

Substituting Equations (6.98) and (6.99) into Equation (6.97) and taking logarithms yields:

$$E_t^Z(\tilde{e}_{t+k}^j) - \tilde{G}_{t,k}^j = -\frac{1}{2}V_t^Z(\tilde{e}_{t+k}^j) - \mathrm{Cov}_t^Z(\tilde{e}_{t+k}^j, \tilde{\mathcal{M}}_{t,k}^1). \qquad (6.100)$$

We assume that the logarithm of Z_t denoted $\tilde{z}_t$ has an autoregressive representation given by $\tilde{z}_t = A_0 + A(L)\tilde{z}_{t-1} + \epsilon_t$, where A_0 is a vector of constants, $A(L)$ is a matrix whose elements may be infinite order polynomials in the lag operator L, and $\{\epsilon_t\}$ is a sequence of mean zero, independently distributed normal random vectors.[9] We also assume that the innovations ϵ_t are conditionally homoscedastic. Under these assumptions, the conditional variance of the spot rate and the conditional covariance between the spot rate and the nominal MRS that enter Equation (6.100) are both constant. This yields the testable implication that the conditional expectation of the logarithm of the future spot rate is equal to the logarithm of the forward rate plus a constant:

$$E_t^Z(\tilde{e}_{t+k}^j) = a_j + \tilde{G}_{t,k}^j. \qquad (6.101)$$

To derive an econometric model from Equation (6.101), let $u_{t,k}^j$ be the forecast error in predicting the logarithm of the future spot rate based on information contained in the information set I_t^Z, $u_{t,k}^j = \tilde{e}_{t+k}^j - E_t^Z(\tilde{e}_{t+k}^j)$. Then we know that $u_{t,k}^j$ is orthogonal to elements in the information set I_t^Z; that is, for any r-dimensional vector $\boldsymbol{x}_t \in I_t^Z$:

$$E(u_{t,k}^j \otimes \boldsymbol{x}_t) = 0. \qquad (6.102)$$

Assume that the first element of the vector $\boldsymbol{x}_t$ is equal to unity. Then, we can test the restrictions in Equation (6.101) by testing the null hypothesis that $b_{2,j} = \cdots = b_{r,j} = 0$ in the regressions:

$$\tilde{e}_{t+k}^j - \tilde{G}_{t,k}^j = \boldsymbol{x}_t'\boldsymbol{b}_j + u_{t,k}^j, \quad j = 1,\ldots,p. \qquad (6.103)$$

Notice that unless the sampling interval of the data is equal to the forecast interval, the error terms are serially correlated. More precisely,

$$E\left(u_{t+h,k}^j u_{t,k}^j\right) = E\left[E_{t+k}^Z\left(u_{t+h,k}^j\right)u_{t,k}^j\right] = 0$$

for $h \geq k$ because $u_{t,k}^j$ is an element of the information set at time $t + k$. Thus, the error terms $u_{t,k}^j$ follow a moving average process of order $k - 1$. For example, if we use weekly data on spot exchange rates and 3-month

---

[9]The roots of $\det[I - \delta A(\delta)] = 0$ are not necessarily assumed to be outside the unit circle to allow the logarithm of the spot exchange rate to contain unit roots.

or 13-week forward rates, the forecast interval is thirteen and the error terms follow a twelfth-order moving average process. One way to obtain a version of Equation (6.103) with serially uncorrelated errors is to set the forecast interval equal to the sampling interval so that $k = 1$.

Here we describe how GMM estimation can be used to estimate and test the restrictions in Equation (6.103).[10] Let us stack the equations in Equation (6.103) to obtain:

$$\boldsymbol{y}_j = \boldsymbol{X}\boldsymbol{b}_j + \boldsymbol{u}_j,$$

where $\boldsymbol{y}_j = (\tilde{e}^j_{1+k} - \tilde{G}^j_{1,k}, \ldots, \tilde{e}^j_{T+k} - \tilde{G}^j_{T,k})$, $\boldsymbol{u}_j = (u^j_{1,k}, \ldots, u^j_{T,k})'$ and the rows of the $T \times r$ matrix $\boldsymbol{X}$ are given by the transpose of the r-dimensional vectors $\boldsymbol{x}_t$ for $t = 1, \ldots, T$. Now it is easy to see that OLS will yield consistent estimates of $\boldsymbol{b}_j$, because $E(u^j_{t,k} \otimes \boldsymbol{x}_t) = \boldsymbol{0}$ implies that $E(\boldsymbol{X}'\boldsymbol{u}_j) = \boldsymbol{0}$, where $\boldsymbol{0}$ is the r-dimensional zero vector. Since $u^j_{t,k}$ is a moving average process of order $k-1$, however, the OLS standard errors will not be correct.

The sample counterpart of the orthogonality conditions implied by the condition $E(u^j_{t,k} \otimes \boldsymbol{x}_t) = \boldsymbol{0}$ can be expressed as:

$$g_T(\boldsymbol{b}_j) = \frac{1}{T} \sum_{t=1}^{T} u^j_{t,k} \otimes \boldsymbol{x}_t = \frac{1}{T}\boldsymbol{X}'\boldsymbol{u}_j.$$

The GMM criterion function used to derive the estimate of $\boldsymbol{b}_j$ is then given by:

$$g_T(\boldsymbol{b}_j)'W_T g_T(\boldsymbol{b}_j) = \left(\frac{1}{T} \sum_{t=1}^{T} u^j_{t,k} \otimes \boldsymbol{x}_t \right)' W_T \left(\frac{1}{T} \sum_{t=1}^{T} u^j_{t,k} \otimes \boldsymbol{x}_t \right)$$

$$= (\boldsymbol{y}_j - \boldsymbol{X}\boldsymbol{b}_j)' \boldsymbol{X} W_T \boldsymbol{X}' (\boldsymbol{y}_j - \boldsymbol{X}\boldsymbol{b}_j).$$

where W_T is an $r \times r$ positive, semidefinite weighting matrix that is chosen as a function of the data. Differentiating the above expression with respect to $\boldsymbol{b}_j$ yields the OLS estimate $\boldsymbol{b}_j = (\boldsymbol{X}'\boldsymbol{X})^{-1}\boldsymbol{X}'\boldsymbol{y}_j$. When the weighting matrix W_T is chosen optimally, we know that the asymptotic covariance matrix of the GMM estimator is given by $(D_0'S_w^{-1}D_0)^{-1}$, where

$$D_0 = E[\partial(u^j_{t,k} \otimes \boldsymbol{x}_t)/\partial\boldsymbol{b}_j],$$

---

[10]Hodrick [190] describes how maximum likelihood estimation can be implemented for the linear models considered here. Some examples that use maximum likelihood are Baillie, Lippens, and McMahon [24] and Hakkio [170].

and S_w is defined as

$$S_w = \sum_{i=-k+1}^{k-1} E[u_{t+i,k}^j u_{t,k}^j \otimes \boldsymbol{x}_{t+i} \boldsymbol{x}_t']. \tag{6.104}$$

Now $\partial(u_{t,k} \otimes \boldsymbol{x}_t)/\partial \boldsymbol{b}_j = \boldsymbol{x}_t \boldsymbol{x}_t'$. Thus, a consistent estimate of D_0 is provided by:

$$D_T = \frac{1}{T} \sum_{t=1}^{T} \boldsymbol{x}_t \boldsymbol{x}_t' = (\boldsymbol{X}'\boldsymbol{X}/T).$$

To find a consistent estimate for S_w, notice that S_w depends on a finite number of autocovariances because the forecast errors have a finite moving average representation. Thus, we need to use one of the kernel estimators described in Chapter 3.

Various authors have examined the restrictions in Equation (6.103). Hansen and Hodrick [175] examine the behavior of five currencies, measured as U.S. dollars per unit of currency: the Franch franc, the Japanese yen, the Swiss franc, the U.K. pound, and the Deutsche mark. They estimate a version of Equation (6.103) using a sample of semiweekly observations in which Tuesday forward rates are assumed to predict Thursday spot rates thirty days in the future and Friday forward rates are used to predict Monday spot rates. Their regressors include the lagged forecast error in predicting the future spot rate for a given currency and for four other currencies, $e_t^j - G_{t-k,k}^j$ for $j = 1, \ldots, 5$, and the forward premium for the currency and four other forward premia, $G_{t,k}^j - e_t^j$ for $j = 1, \ldots, 5$. The null hypothesis that the coefficients on the regressors are zero is rejected for the Japanese yen, the Swiss franc, and the Deutsche mark at all levels of significance greater than 0.02. Similar findings are reported by Hansen and Hodrick [174] who use weekly data on spot rates and a 3-month (or 13-week) forward rate.

Notice that the forecast error in such regressions involving overlapping data are serially correlated so that a serial correlation correction must be imposed. Furthermore, the forward rate must be matched with the future spot rate that a forward position in the foreign exchange rate market is intended to cover. The institutional features of the forward exchange rate market imply that delivery of spot foreign currency occurs two business days from the date at which it was purchased on what is called the *spot value date*. The delivery date of a one-month forward contract is determined by finding the appropriate spot value date and then checking to see if that date is a business date in both countries. If so, that date is the *forward value date*. If the spot value date in the future month is not a legitimate business date, then resettlement on the forward contract occurs on the next business day without going out of the month. Instead of going into the next month, the contract is settled on the first business date before the numerical date corresponding to the spot value date of the previous month. For example, in Hansen and Hodrick's [175] application, there is misalignment of the data because Friday forward rates should predict Tuesday spot rates.

Hsieh [199] and Cumby and Obstfeld [80] estimate a model of the forward exchange market with nonoverlapping data and allow the forecast errors to be conditionally heteroscedastic. They construct an implicit measure of the one-week forward rate by using data on Eurocurrency interest rates to increase the size of their sample of nonoverlapping data. This implicit measure of the one-week forward rate satisfies the relation $G_t^j = e_t^j Q_t^j / Q_t^0 = e_t^j R_t^0 / R_t^j$, where R_t^0 is the one-week interest rate in some numeraire currency and R_t^j is the one-period interest rate in the currency of country j. The use of nonoverlapping data implies that the relation between the implicit one-week forward rate and the spot rate one week into the future that it is intended to cover is given by:

$$y_{t+1}^j = \boldsymbol{x}_t' \boldsymbol{b}_j + u_{t+1}^j, \tag{6.105}$$

where $y_{t+1}^j = \tilde{e}_{t+1}^j - \hat{G}_t^j$ and u_{t+1}^j is a serially uncorrelated forecast in predicting y_{t+1}^j using information available at time t. Hsieh [199] considers eight exchange rates, including the U.S. dollar values of the currencies of France, Germany, the United Kingdom, Switzerland, the Netherlands, Canada, Italy, and Japan. When the forecast errors are assumed to be conditionally homoscedastic, only weak evidence against the null hypothesis is found. When the forecast errors are allowed to be conditionally heteroscedastic, seven out of the eight currencies have test statistics greater than the value at the ten percent level, and the Japanese yen has a test statistic greater than the value at the five percent level. Similar results are reported by Cumby and Obstfeld [80] who consider the U.S. dollar values of the U.K. pound, the Deutsche mark, the Swiss franc, the Canadian dollar, and the Japanese yen. They test and reject the hypothesis of conditional homoscedasticity of the forecast errors. They also reject the overidentifying restrictions of the regression of the rate of depreciation in currency j, $\tilde{e}_{t+k}^j - \tilde{e}_t^j$, on the forward premium $\hat{G}_{t,k}^j - \tilde{e}_t^j$ plus a constant, which is estimated using GMM with more instruments than a constant and the right side regressor. In addition, they estimate the coefficients on the forward premium to be negative for all currencies except the Canadian dollar.

3.2. Models of Risk Premia

These findings suggest that there exists a time-varying risk premium in foreign exchange markets. There have been different models proposed for describing such time-varying risk premia.

One way to express the risk premium is to derive a *risk-return model* from the equilibrium conditions that we examined earlier. To do this, let $R_{t,k}^b$ denote the return on the benchmark bond held from period t to $t + k$ and let $R_{t,k}^1$ denote the return on the risk-free bond also held from period t to $t + k$. We will show that the excess return on any asset j denoted $R_{t,k}^j$ can be expressed as:

$$E_t(R_{t,k}^j - R_{t,k}^1) = \beta_{t,k}^j E_t(R_{t,k}^b - R_{t,k}^1), \tag{6.106}$$

where

$$\beta_{t,k}^j = \frac{\text{Cov}_t(R_{t,k}^j, R_{t,k}^b)}{\text{Var}_t(R_{t,k}^b)}. \tag{6.107}$$

In the two-country model of the previous section, the stochastic discount factor used to value random payoffs is the nominal MRS for good 1, $\mathcal{M}_{t,k}^1$. The risk-free return has the property that it is uncorrelated with the stochastic discount factor. The return on the one-period nominal discount bond in country 1 satisfies this requirement because $R_{t,k}^1 = 1/E_t(\mathcal{M}_{t,k}^1)$. The benchmark bond has the property that its return is perfectly correlated with the stochastic discount factor. Hence, the benchmark return is defined as $R_{t,k}^b = \mathcal{M}_{t,k}^1/E_t(\mathcal{M}_{t,k}^1)^2$.

Notice that we can rewrite the expected profit on the forward contract in terms of these returns. Dividing Equation (6.34) by e_t and rewriting using the expressions for the benchmark return and the risk-free return yields:

$$E_t\left(\frac{e_{t+k} - G_{t,k}}{e_t}\right) = \beta_{t,k} E_t\left(R_{t,k}^b - R_{t,k}^1\right) \tag{6.108}$$

where $\beta_{t,k} \equiv \text{Cov}_t[(e_{t+k} - G_{t,k})/e_t, R_{t,k}^b]/\text{Var}_t(R_{t,k}^b)$. The same approach can also be used to study the risk premium in futures contracts. Without further assumptions, however, the relation in Equation (6.108) has little empirical content.

Hansen and Hodrick [175] show that if the benchmark return is treated as a latent variable, then the risk-return model can be estimated using data on forward and spot exchange rates and nominal bonds. To derive the latent variable risk-return model, define the vector:

$$\boldsymbol{Y}_{t+k} = (Y_{t+k}^1, \dots, Y_{t+k}^p)',$$

where $Y_{t+k}^j \equiv (e_{t+k}^j - G_{t,k}^j)/e_t^j$ and $\boldsymbol{R}_{t,k}^f$ denotes a vector of nominal risk-free returns in the p currencies. This set of returns satisfies:

$$E_t^Y(\boldsymbol{Y}_{t+k}) = \boldsymbol{\beta}_t^\star E_t(R_{t,k}^b - R_{t,k}^f), \tag{6.109}$$

where $\boldsymbol{\beta}_t^\star$ is a p-dimensional vector containing $\beta_t^{\star j}$ for $j = 1,\ldots,p$ and $\beta_t^{\star j} \equiv \mathrm{Cov}_t(Y_{t+k}^j, R_{t,k}^b)/\mathrm{Var}_t(R_{t,k}^b)$. The information set I_t^Y consists of current and past values of Y_t and $\boldsymbol{R}_{t,k}^f$. The vector $\boldsymbol{\beta}_t^\star$ is treated as a vector of constants and $E_t(R_{t,k}^b - R_{t,k}^f)$ as a latent variable.

The equations that are estimated are given by:

$$\boldsymbol{Y}_{t+k} = \boldsymbol{\beta}_t^\star x_t + \boldsymbol{u}_{t,k},$$

where $x_t \equiv E_t(R_{t,k}^b - R_{t,k}^f)$ and $\boldsymbol{u}_{t,k}$ is a vector of forecast errors that satisfy:

$$E(\boldsymbol{u}_{t,k}\boldsymbol{u}_{t-j,k}') = \begin{cases} \Omega_j & j = 0,\ldots,k-1 \\ 0 & j \geq k, \end{cases}$$

and $E(\boldsymbol{u}_{t,k}z_t) = 0$ for all $z_t \in I_t^Y$. Since x_t is unobservable, it is replaced with its best linear predictor of itself based on an observable subset of I_t^Y, namely, $x_t = \alpha_0^\star + \boldsymbol{\alpha}_1^{\star\prime}\boldsymbol{Y}_t + \epsilon_t$. Thus, the relation in Equation (6.109) becomes:

$$\boldsymbol{Y}_{t+k} = \boldsymbol{\beta}^\star\alpha_0^\star + \boldsymbol{\beta}^\star\boldsymbol{\alpha}_1^{\star\prime}\boldsymbol{Y}_t + \boldsymbol{v}_{t,k}, \tag{6.110}$$

where $\boldsymbol{v}_{t,k} = \boldsymbol{u}_{t,k} + \boldsymbol{\beta}^\star\epsilon_t$. Notice that, by construction, x_t is defined to be a function of the lagged forecast errors, $Y_t^j \equiv (e_t^j - G_{t-k,k}^j)/e_{t-k}^j$.

Hansen and Hodrick [175] estimate this model using GMM. They do not find evidence against this model even when the restrictions across the constant terms and the slope coefficents in the above regression are imposed. Latent variable risk-return models have also been estimated to describe risk premia in the forward market and in the term structure of interest rates and the stock market. These include the studies by Campbell and Clarida [61] and Giovannini and Jorion [150]. The former study considers uncovered investments in three-month EuroDeutschemark and Eurosterling deposits and excess returns in the Eurodollar term structure. The latter study considers excess returns computed as the difference between one-week Eurodeposits in U.K. pounds, German marks, Dutch guilders, and Swiss francs and the one-week Eurodollar deposit rate and the realized rate of return on the U.S. stock market in excess of the rate of return of the Eurodollar rate. The former study cannot reject the latent variable risk-return model, whereas the latter study finds strong evidence against the hypothesis of constant conditional covariances.

One problem with using the latent variable model to understand the nature of the risk premia in foreign exchange markets is that there is no economic interpretation placed on the latent variable. The single latent variable is, by construction, a linear function of the lagged forecast errors in the different currencies. Since the results of regression-based tests imply that the lagged forecast errors $(e_t^j - G_{t-k,k}^j)/e_{t-k}^j$ are useful in predicting the risk premia in the different currencies $(e_{t+k}^j - G_{t,k}^j)/e_t^j$, it is not surprising to find that the latent variable model is not rejected by the data for samples where this correlation holds.

3.3.   Risk Premia or Expectational Errors?

A finding that is related to rejections of tests of unbiasedness is the negative covariation between the expected depreciation of the domestic currency and the risk premium noted by Fama [124]. The puzzling aspect of this finding is that the higher the expected depreciation of the dollar, the higher the required expected nominal return on a dollar-denominated security. To describe this, let e_t be the spot exchange rate of U.S. dollars per unit of foreign currency and let G_t be the one-period forward rate. The risk premium P_t is defined to be the expected profit from buying U.S. dollars on the forward market, $P_t \equiv G_t - E_t(e_{t+1})$. The empirical findings suggest that when there is an increase in the expected rate of depreciation of the U.S. dollar relative to the foreign currency, that is, when $E_t[(e_{t+1} - e_t)/e_t]$ increases, there is a fall in the expected profit from buying U.S. dollars in the forward market, or P_t falls.

Hodrick and Srivastava [192] note that this negative covariation can be rationalized since the expected profit in the empirical work is denominated in the foreign currency. The appropriate dollar-denominated profit is $(e_{t+1} - G_t)$. This version is obtained by selling dollars in the forward market for foreign currency and using that foreign currency to buy dollars at the future spot rate. Hence, the covariation of $(-P_t)$ with the expected rate of depreciation of the dollar relative to foreign currencies is positive.

Fama has argued that an implication of the negative covariation between the expected depreciation of the domestic currency and the risk premium is that the variance of the risk premium exceeds the variance of expected depreciation. To demonstrate this result, recall that we can rewrite the equilibrium condition in Equation (6.33) as $G_t = E_t(e_{t+1}) + P_t$.

Subtracting e_t from both sides and dividing by e_t yields forward premium:

$$\frac{G_t - e_t}{e_t} = \frac{E_t(e_{t+1}) - e_t}{e_t} + \frac{P_t}{e_t}. \tag{6.111}$$

Let $g_t \equiv (G_t - e_t)/e_t$ and $p_t \equiv P_t/e_t$. Consider the covariance of these terms with $\delta e_{t+1} \equiv (e_{t+1} - e_t)/e_t$:

$$\text{Cov}(g_t, \delta e_{t+1}) = \text{Cov}[E_t(\delta e_{t+1}), \delta e_{t+1}] + \text{Cov}(p_t, \delta e_{t+1}). \tag{6.112}$$

Since $(e_{t+1} - e_t)/e_t = [E_t(e_{t+1}) - e_t]/e_t + \eta_{t+1}$, where η_{t+1} is a prediction error that is uncorrelated with information at time t, we can write Equation (6.112) as

$$\text{Cov}(g_t, \delta e_{t+1}) = \text{Var}[E_t(\delta e_{t+1})] + \text{Cov}[p_t, E_t(\delta e_{t+1})]. \tag{6.113}$$

The covariance between the forward premium and the actual rate of change of the spot rate can be measured from the left side of Equation (6.113). However, neither term on the right side of this equation is observable. Since $\text{Var}[E_t(\delta e_{t+1})]$ is positive, a negative value for $\text{Cov}(g_t, \delta e_{t+1})$ implies that $\text{Cov}[p_t, E_t(\delta e_{t+1})]$ is negative and greater in absolute value than $\text{Var}[E_t(\delta e_{t+1})]$. Following the reasoning in Fama, this implies that the variance of the risk premium must exceed the variance of expected depreciation. This can be demonstrated by considering the variance of both sides of Equation (6.111):

$$\text{Var}(g_t) = \text{Var}[E_t(\delta e_{t+1})] + \text{Var}(p_t) + 2\text{Cov}[p_t, E_t(\delta e_{t+1})].$$

Hodrick and Srivastava [192] use a parametric example to show that the theoretical model is consistent with the negative covariation documented by Fama. However, there is little evidence to suggest that the two-country model we described earlier can explain the size or variability of the risk premium. (See Macklem [240].)

Many have interpreted the rejections of the unbiasedness hypothesis and the negative covariation puzzle as evidence for systematic expectational errors in foreign exchange rate markets. To test this hypothesis directly, Froot and Frankel [138] use survey data on measured expectations from three surveys: the survey conducted by the American Express Banking Corporation of London irregularly between 1976 and 1985; a second survey conducted by the *Economist's Financial Report* from London; and a third survey conducted by Money Market Services of Redwood City, California. They present some evidence that the variance of the expected depreciation is greater than the variance of the risk premium and also that the bias is due to systematic expectational errors.

3.4. Modeling Short-Term Changes in Exchange Rates

There is a large body of evidence to suggest that short-term price changes on financial markets are nearly unpredictable given past prices and that the probability distribution of short-term changes in exchange rates and stock prices (in particular, daily changes in such prices) is non-Gaussian and leptokurtic. The latter implies that this probability distribution is excessively peaked around zero and too thick in the extreme tails relative to the Gaussian distribution.[11]

There is also a significant body of evidence for the existence of conditional heteroscedasticity and the dependence of higher order moments on time-varying conditioning sets in the distribution of daily price changes.[12] We now describe a model of a *serially correlated news arrival process* due to Gallant, Hsieh, and Tauchen [146] (hereafter referred to as Gallant *et al.*) to rationalize these features in the distribution of short-term exchange rate changes.

The non-Gaussian nature of daily price changes is considered something of a paradox. Typically, the daily price change is the sum of many within-day independent price movements, triggered by many new pieces of information about market fundamentals. By the central limit theorem, the distribution of daily price changes should converge to the Gaussian distribution in the data but it does not. As a way of resolving this paradox, Clark [70] noted that trading activity varies randomly from day to day. On some days, much new information flows to the market and the price takes many steps while on other days, trading activity is light and the price takes few steps within the day. Consequently, the daily price should be modeled as a mixture of Gaussian random variables such that the daily price is the sum of a random number of within-day changes. Since a mixture of random variables, even Gaussian random variables, is non-Gaussian and has a leptokurtic density, we obtain a resolution of the paradox.

Let e_t denote the exchange rate or stock price at the end of the trading day and let $\tilde{e}_t$ denote its logarithm. Thus, $\Delta \tilde{e}_t = \tilde{e}_t - \tilde{e}_{t-1}$ denotes the day-to-day log price change and price movements are interpreted as percentage changes. The mixture model postulates that the unpredictable part of price over the trading day is generated by new information about market fundamentals and that new information arrives in a stochastic fashion. Thus, the unpredictable part of the daily price change is the

---

[11]See, for example, Clark [69], Epps and Epps [119], and Tauchen and Pitts [325].

[12]This includes Engle and Bollerslev [116], Baillie and Bollerslev [23], Bollerslev [38], Diebold [94], Nelson [269], and Hsieh [200], among others.

sum of a random number of within-day independent price movements.
We can write this model as:

$$\Delta \tilde{e}_t = \mu_t + \sum_{i=T_{t-1}+1}^{T_t} \epsilon_i, \qquad (6.114)$$

where $\mu_t = E(\Delta \tilde{e}_t | \mathcal{E}_{t-1})$ is the expectation of daily price changes conditional on past daily exchange rates back to some initial period, namely, $\mathcal{E}_{t-1} \equiv (\tilde{e}_{t-1}, \dots, \tilde{e}_0)$, and $\{\epsilon_i\}$ is a serially independent Gaussian process with mean zero and variance σ^2 that is independent of $\mathcal{E}_{t-1}$. The parameter μ_t is included as the predictable part of the price change but typically changes in speculative prices are unpredictable given their past and thus, one would expect μ_t to equal a constant or to vary little with t. The process $\{T_t\}$ is called the *directing process* of the mixture model. It is a nondecreasing, integer-valued process with strictly stationary increments, $I_t \equiv T_t - T_{t-1}$, and $\{I_t\}$ is distributed independently of $\{\epsilon_i\}$. Here I_t will be referred to as the *mixing variable*.

There are different ways of modeling the process for the mixing variable I_t. If it is assumed that $\{I_t\}$ is a serially dependent process, then the resulting distribution of daily price changes will display conditional heteroscedasticity and conditional leptokurtosis, as we now demonstrate. Notice that the unpredictable part of the daily price change has expectation zero and variance equal to $\sigma^2 I_t$. Thus, we can write:

$$\Delta \tilde{e}_t = \mu_t + \sigma I_t^{1/2} U_t, \qquad (6.115)$$

where U_t is $N(0,1)$ and independent of $\{\tilde{e}_{t-j}, j \geq 1\}$ and $\{I_t\}$. Conditional on $(\mathcal{E}_{t-1}, I_t)$, $\Delta \tilde{e}_t$ is Gaussian with mean μ_t and variance $\sigma^2 I_t$. This is the Gaussian ARCH model denoted ARCH-n.

In the mixture model, $\{I_t\}$ is unobserved and, typically, the researcher conditions only on the past price process given by $\mathcal{E}_{t-1}$. In this case, however, $\Delta \tilde{e}_t$ given $\mathcal{E}_{t-1}$ is not Gaussian. For example, the kurtosis of the conditional distribution of $\Delta \tilde{e}_t$ given $\mathcal{E}_{t-1}$ is:

$$\begin{aligned}
\kappa(\Delta \tilde{e}_t | \mathcal{E}_{t-1}) &= \frac{E[(\Delta \tilde{e}_t - \mu_t)^4 | \mathcal{E}_{t-1}]}{\{E[(\Delta \tilde{e}_t - \mu_t)^2 | \mathcal{E}_{t-1}]\}^2} \\
&= \frac{E[I_t^2 U_t^4 | \mathcal{E}_{t-1}]}{\{E[I_t U_t^2 | \mathcal{E}_{t-1}]\}^2} = \frac{3 E[I_t^2 | \mathcal{E}_{t-1}]}{\{E[I_t | \mathcal{E}_{t-1}]\}^2} \\
&= 3(1 + c_t^2),
\end{aligned}$$

where $c_t = \sqrt{\mathrm{Var}(I_t | \mathcal{E}_{t-1})} / E(I_t | \mathcal{E}_{t-1})$ is the coefficient of variation of the conditional distribution of the mixing variable I_t given $\mathcal{E}_{t-1}$. Thus, the conditional distribution of $\Delta\tilde{e}_t$ given $\mathcal{E}_{t-1}$ is leptokurtic or has kurtosis greater than 3, which is the kurtosis of the Gaussian distribution. Notice that $\Delta\tilde{e}_t$ given $\mathcal{E}_{t-1}$ is leptokurtic even if $\{I_t\}$ is independent of past prices given in $\mathcal{E}_{t-1}$.[13] The distribution for $\Delta\tilde{e}_t$ conditional on $\mathcal{E}_{t-1}$ will be Gaussian only if I_t is perfectly predictable given $\mathcal{E}_{t-1}$.

Now we describe how the conditional mixture model is able to generate conditional heteroscedasticity through the serial dependence of the mixing process. For this purpose, define $w_t \equiv (\Delta\tilde{e}_t - \mu_t)^2$, the squared innovation in $\Delta\tilde{e}_t$, and notice that $E(w_t|\mathcal{E}_{t-1})$ is the variance of the conditional distribution of $\Delta\tilde{e}_t$. Now $w_t = \sigma^2 I_t U_t^2$, and for $j \neq 0$,

$$
\begin{aligned}
\text{Cov}(w_t, w_{t-j}) &= \sigma^4 E\left\{ [I_t U_t^2 - E(I_t)][I_{t-j}U_{t-j}^2 - E(I_{t-j})] \right\} \\
&= \sigma^4 \left[E(I_t I_{t-j}) - E(I_t)E(I_{t-j}) \right] \\
&= \sigma^4 \text{Cov}(I_t I_{t-j}).
\end{aligned}
$$

Thus, for $j > 0$, the autocovariance function of $\{w_t\}$ is exactly proportional to the autocovariance function of the mixing variable I_t. Thus, the size of past price changes, as captured by past w_t's, will convey information about the magnitude of the contemporaneous price change, as captured by the current value of w_t, whenever the rate of flow of new information to the market can be predicted using its own past. These effects are similar to ARCH effects.

Notice that $\text{Var}(\Delta\tilde{e}_t|\mathcal{E}_{t-1}) = E(w_t|\mathcal{E}_{t-1}) = \sigma^2 E(I_t|\mathcal{E}_{t-1})$. Provided $\{I_t\}$ is autocorrelated, then $\text{Var}(\Delta\tilde{e}_t|\mathcal{E}_{t-1})$ varies with elements of $\mathcal{E}_{t-1}$. However, it fails to be the case that lagged values of w_t are sufficient to predict I_t. In other words, $\text{Var}(\Delta\tilde{e}_t|\mathcal{E}_{t-1}) \neq \text{Var}(\Delta\tilde{e}_t|\mathcal{W}_{t-1})$ where $\mathcal{W}_{t-1} \equiv (w_{t-1}, \ldots, w_0)$, which is typically the assumption made in an ARCH-type model.

Now consider the conditionally Studentized innovation:

$$
z_t = \frac{\Delta\tilde{e}_t - \mu_t}{\sqrt{\text{Var}(\Delta\tilde{e}_t|\mathcal{E}_{t-1})}}.
$$

Using the representation for $\Delta\tilde{e}_t$, z_t can be written as:

$$
z_t = \frac{\sigma I_t^{1/2} U_t}{\sqrt{E(I_t|\mathcal{E}_{t-1})}} = \left(\frac{I_t}{E(I_t|\mathcal{E}_{t-1})} \right)^{1/2} U_t = q_t^{1/2} U_t,
$$

---

[13]In this case, the conditional kurtosis equals the unconditional kurtosis, $\kappa(\Delta\tilde{e}_t) = 3(1 + c^2)$ where c is the coefficient of variation of the unconditional distribution of I_t.

where $q_t \equiv I_t / E(I_t | \mathcal{E}_{t-1})$. Notice that $E(z_t | \mathcal{E}_{t-1}) = E(q_t^{1/2} | \mathcal{E}_{t-1}) E(U_t)$, which equals zero since $E(U_t) = 0$ and that

$$\mathrm{Var}(z_t | \mathcal{E}_{t-1}) = E(q_t | \mathcal{E}_{t-1}) E(U_t^2) - [E(q_t^{1/2} | \mathcal{E}_{t-1})]^2 [E(U_t)]^2,$$

which equals one. Recall that the random variable U_t is Gaussian but z_t is not since z_t will be leptokurtic and conditionally leptokurtic relative to the Gaussian distribution. This fact explains why an ARCH-n model in which the innovations are Gaussian does not fit short-term price changes very well. It also explains why an ARCH-t, which has innovations distributed as Student-t, may fit better because the t-distribution has fatter tails than the Gaussian.

Gallant *et al.* use the seminonparametric (SNP) method to fit the conditional density for daily changes in the British pound/U.S. dollar exchange rate. This method allows for conditional heteroscedasticity and conditional dependence in the higher order moments of the series but unlike variants of ARCH and GARCH models, it is not based on a specific parametric distributional assumption. The authors find that after accounting for systematic calendar effects, the mean of daily movements of the pound/dollar exchange rate is unpredictable, given current information. Second, there is strong evidence for conditional heteroscedasticity in the exchange rate. Third, the authors find overwhelming evidence against a Gaussian innovation density and their plots of the fitted density indicate that it has a sharp peak at the origin and side lobes in the tails.

4.   Exercises

1. Consider the following linear model:

$$\tilde{e}_{t+k} - \tilde{G}_{t,k} = \delta_0' x_t + u_{t,k}, \quad t = 1, \dots, T,$$

where $\tilde{e}_{t+k}$ and $\tilde{G}_{t,k}$ are logarithms of the future spot exchange rate and the forward rate and $u_{t,k}$ is a forecast error that is uncorrelated with variables known at time t, $E(u_{t,k} \otimes x_t) = 0$. Also x_t and δ_0 are r-dimensional vectors.

Suppose $k = 2$. Show that $E(u_{t,k} u_{t-j,k}) = 0$ for $j \geq 2$. Define $y_t \equiv \tilde{e}_{t+k} - \tilde{G}_{t,k}$ and $u_t \equiv u_{t,k}$. Show that u_t can be written as:

$$u_t = \nu_t - \lambda \nu_{t-1}, \quad |\lambda| < 1, \tag{6.116}$$

where ν_t is a serially uncorrelated white noise process.

Consider the estimates that are obtained by running OLS on the following filtered model:

$$(1 - \lambda L)^{-1} y_t = (1 - \lambda L)^{-1} \delta_o' x_t + (1 - \lambda L)^{-1} u_t.$$

Are these estimates consistent?

2. Consider the dynamic programming problem problem defined in Equation (6.17). Define $\phi(s) \equiv V(h(s), 0.5, 0.5, s)$ and let $\phi_h = V_h$, $\phi_1 = V_{z_1}$, and $\phi_2 = V_{z_2}$ denote the first partial derivative of the consumer's valuation function with respect to h, z_1 and z_2, respectively, evaluated at equilibrium money and asset holdings, and the current state.

Derive the equilibrium first-order conditions and envelope conditions for the consumer's problem and show that they yield the conditions described by Equations (6.18) through (6.23).

3. Siegel's Paradox

Siegel [308] argued that the proposition that the level of the forward rate was equal to the expected value of the level of the future spot rate would lead to a contradiction. If this were true for exchange rates quoted as the British pound per U.S. dollar, then it could not be true for the exchange rate quoted as U.S. dollar per British pound.

a) Using Jensen's inequality, state the nature of Siegel's paradox.

b) Comment on Siegel's paradox in an equilibrium model with risk-neutral consumers.

4. Derive the forward rate and the risk premium, the futures price, and the stock prices for the two-country model with the Stockman–Svensson timing.

5.[14] Modify the two-country model with the Stockman–Svensson timing in the previous exercise by assuming that the government does not consume any endowment and that money is injected by way of a lump-sum transfer at the beginning of the asset market. Assume, however, that agents can trade the two currencies taken to the goods market. For a representative agent who enters the good market with holdings $H_{1,t}$ and $H_{2,t}$, the following budget constraint holds:

$$H_{1,t} + \bar{e}_t H_{2,t} \geq \ell_{i,t} \bar{H}_{1,t} + \bar{e}_t \ell_{2,t} \bar{H}_{2,t}$$

---

[14]This exercise derived from Engel [114].

where $\bar{e}_t$ is the equilibrium exchange rate in the exchange market that meets at the same time as the goods market, ℓ_i is the nominal price of acquiring one more unit of currency i, and $\bar{H}_{1,t}$ and $\bar{H}_{2,t}$ are the adjusted money holdings. The agent now has two additional decision variables, $\bar{H}_{1,t}$ and $\bar{H}_{2,t}$.

a) Derive the first-order conditions for the new decision variables and determine the equilibrium price ℓ and the exchange rate.

b) Derive the equilibrium prices $\bar{p}_1$ and $\bar{p}_2$. Derive the forward exchange rate.

6.[15] Variations in the roles of national currencies in the international economy are studied. Assume that there is only one endowment good which is received by both countries. Let p_h denote the price of the good in units of the home country currency and let p_f denote the price of the good in units of the foreign country currency. Assume that the timing corresponds to that of the Lucas version of the model. If the endowment good of both countries is to be bought and consumed, then the law of one price must hold: $p_h = ep_f$.

Consider two monetary mechanisms. Under the first, the seller will accept only domestic currency. This is the mechanism that we have used throughout our discussion of international cash-in-advance models. Under the second mechanism, we assume that all transactions are constrained to take place with the buyer's domestic currency.

a) Derive the first-order conditions and equilibrium prices, real and nominal exchange rates, and equilibrium nominal interest rates under the first mechanism. Derive the forward rate.

b) Derive the first-order conditions and equilibrium prices, real and nominal exchange rates, and equilibrium nominal interest rates under the second mechanism. Derive the forward rate.

7.[16] Consider the Lucas two-country model and assume that preferences are given by:

$$U(c_1, c_2) = [\theta c_1^{1-\gamma} + (1-\theta)c_2^{1-\gamma}]/(1-\gamma), \quad \gamma \geq 0, \ 0 < \theta < 1.$$

a) Find expressions for the changes in the logs of the nominal and real exchange rates.

---

[15]This exercise derived from Helpman and Razin [189].
[16]This exercise is derived from Mark [251].

b) To be broadly consistent with actual experience, the model must produce real and nominal exchange rates that are of roughly equal variance and that are highly correlated. Using your answer to a), show that the Lucas model generally requires monetary variability to be more important than real variability for these results to obtain.

8. Assume that shares to the monetary transfers are traded in the Lucas version of the two-country model. Determine the equilibrium price of the shares under the assumption that there is a pooled equilibrium.

7

Asset Markets with
Heterogeneous Populations

We now study the implications of equilibrium frameworks with population heterogeneity. Unlike the previous chapters where we typically assumed a representative consumer, we consider populations that may be heterogeneous because of differences in *ex ante* characteristics or due to private information. In Section 1, we begin by discussing tests of the permanent-income hypothesis using panel data. We also discuss tests of borrowing constraints and the full risk-sharing hypothesis implied by the complete contingent claims equilibrium. We show how estimation methods that are derived from individuals' intertemporal optimization problems must be modified in panel data situations.

Next, we turn to a discussion of models with private information. Private information considerations are usually given as the rationale for market incompleteness and the absence of claims that pay off for each possible state of the world. One approach to studying models with market incompleteness is to specify the markets that are assumed to exist and to study the implications for the resulting equilibrium prices and allocation. Another approach is to derive the form of the optimal, incentive compatible allocations that account for the informational constraints. Here we study the properties of the optimal contract for an important class of private information models, namely, principal-agent models.

In Section 2, we derive the form of the optimal contract for the principal-agent model following the approach in Grossman and Hart [165]. As an application, we describe the model by Margiotta and Miller [250] who use this framework to study empirically the effects of moral hazard on managerial compensation. These authors embed a multiperiod principal-agent problem in a general equilibrium setting and use the form of the optimal contract to derive econometric tests of their model.

1. Equilibrium Models for Panel Data

In this section, we describe how a variety of hypotheses about the behavior of individual consumption and labor supply allocations implied by models of intertemporal optimization and equilibrium can be tested using panel data. The approach is to assume the existence of an equilibrium and to derive econometric implications using individuals' optimality conditions.

1.1. Applications

As a way of unifying our discussion throughout this section, we consider an environment for which there exist data on consumption and labor supply choices of individuals. We assume that the individual is alive between dates $t = \underline{n}$ and $t = \bar{n}$. Let $c_{i,t}$ and $\ell_{i,t}$ denote the consumption and leisure allocations for the i'th individual, respectively. If total leisure units are normalized as one, $\ell_{i,t}$ measures the proportion of time the i'th individual spends in nonmarket activities. Here $c_{i,t}$ represents consumption of a single homogeneous good. There is *ex ante* heterogeneity throughout the population, which implies that individuals are *ex ante* identical up to a vector of time-varying characteristics, $\theta_{i,t}$. Although all the elements of $\theta_{i,t}$ are known to the individual, there may exist components that are unobservable to the econometrician.

Suppose preferences have the form:

$$E_0 \left\{ \sum_{t=\underline{n}}^{\bar{n}} \beta^t U(\ell_{i,t}, c_{i,t}, \theta_{i,t}) \right\}, \quad 0 < \beta < 1, \tag{7.1}$$

where $E_0(\cdot)$ denotes expectation conditional on information at date zero. The utility function U is assumed to be concave and increasing in $(\ell_{i,t}, c_{i,t})$ for each $\theta_{i,t}$.

To further characterize the individual's choice problem, we need to make precise the nature of securities trading in which consumers can engage. We initially assume that there is a countable set R of one-period securities with random payoffs but that markets are not necessarily complete. Throughout our discussion, we also assume that spot labor markets exist. We let $z_{r,t}^i$ denote the quantity of asset r held by the i'th individual in period t, $q_{r,t}$ its price, and $d_{r,t}$ the associated dividend. In this case, the household faces the sequence of budget constraints:

$$c_{i,t} - (1 - \ell_{i,t})w_{i,t} \leq \sum_{r \in R} \left[q_{r,t}(z_{r,t}^i - z_{r,t+1}^i) + d_{r,t}z_{r,t}^i \right], \tag{7.2}$$

which must be satisfied for all $t \in \{\underline{n}, \cdots, \bar{n}\}$ and all events realized at those dates.[1]

The household maximizes the criterion function in Equation (7.1) by choosing sequences $\{\ell_{i,t}\}_{t=\underline{n}}^{\bar{n}}$, $\{c_{i,t}\}_{t=\underline{n}}^{\bar{n}}$, and $\{z_{r,t+1}^i\}_{t=\underline{n}}^{\bar{n}}$ for $r \in R$ subject to the constraint in Equation (7.2). Define the real return on the r'th asset at time t as $\pi_{r,t+1} \equiv (q_{r,t+1} + d_{r,t+1})/q_{r,t}$. If there are no borrowing constraints or short sales restrictions, the first-order conditions with respect to $\ell_{i,t}$, $c_{i,t}$, and $z_{r,t+1}^i$, $r \in R$, are

$$U_\ell(\ell_{i,t}, c_{i,t}, \theta_{i,t}) \geq \lambda_{i,t} w_{i,t}, \tag{7.3}$$

$$U_c(\ell_{i,t}, c_{i,t}, \theta_{i,t}) = \lambda_{i,t}, \tag{7.4}$$

$$\lambda_{i,t} = \beta E_t[\lambda_{i,t+1} \pi_{r,t+1}], \quad r \in R, \tag{7.5}$$

where $\beta^t \lambda_{i,t}$ is the period t Lagrange multiplier associated with the budget constraint in Equation (7.2), U_ℓ and U_c denote the partial derivatives of U with respect to ℓ and c, respectively, and Equation (7.3) holds with equality whenever $\ell_{i,t} < 1$.

We now use this framework to discuss issues that arise in testing the permanent-income hypothesis and lifecycle models of consumption and labor supply using panel data. In the literature on the permanent-income hypothesis, the assumption that is typically made is that there exist assets that allow consumers to smooth consumption over time. Tests of the permanent-income hypothesis implemented by Hall [171], Flavin [132], and others, for example, assume that individuals can borrow and lend at a constant interest rate against the alternative that they are constrained to consume out of current income.

To derive a version of this test, suppose that $\pi_{r,t+1} = 1 + r$ where r is the constant real interest rate, and further, that the real interest rate is equal to the rate of time preference so that $\beta(1 + r) = 1$. We can use Equations (7.4) and (7.5) to express the individual's intertemporal Euler equations as follows:

$$E_t \left[\frac{U'(\ell_{i,t+1}, c_{i,t+1}, \theta_{i,t+1})}{U'(\ell_{i,t}, c_{i,t}, \theta_{i,t})} \right] = 1, \tag{7.6}$$

or,

$$\frac{U'(\ell_{i,t+1}, c_{i,t+1}, \theta_{i,t+1})}{U'(\ell_{i,t}, c_{i,t}, \theta_{i,t})} = 1 + \epsilon_{i,t+1}, \tag{7.7}$$

---

[1]For simplicity, we assume that bequests and inheritances are zero in Equation (7.2).

where $\epsilon_{i,t+1}$ is a forecast error that is uncorrelated with variables known at time t, $E_t[\epsilon_{i,t+1}] = 0$.

To make our discussion more concrete, we assume that the single-period utility function has the form:

$$U(\ell_{i,t}, c_{i,t}, \theta_{i,t}) = \gamma^{-1}(u_{i,t}^c c_{i,t})^\gamma + \phi^{-1}(u_{i,t}^\ell \ell_{i,t})^\phi, \tag{7.8}$$

where $\gamma \leq 1$ and $\phi \leq 1$ and

$$\theta_{i,t} \equiv (u_{i,t}^c, u_{i,t}^\ell)'. \tag{7.9}$$

Here $u_{i,t}^j = \exp(u_i^j + \varepsilon_{i,t}^j)$ for $j = c, \ell$ are permanent or *fixed effects* to individual preferences. We assume that $\{\theta_{i,t}\}$ is known to the individual when he makes his decisions at each date but components of it may be unobserved by the econometrician. However, the econometrician views $\{\varepsilon_{i,t}^c\}$ and $\{\varepsilon_{i,t}^\ell\}$ as being drawn at time zero from a population that is independent and identically distributed over time with $E(\varepsilon_{i,t}^c) = 0$, $E(\varepsilon_{i,t}^\ell) = 0$, $\text{Var}(\varepsilon_{i,t}^c) = \sigma_c^2$, $\text{Var}(\varepsilon_{i,t}^\ell) = \sigma_\ell^2$, and $\{\varepsilon_{i,t}^c\}$ and $\{\varepsilon_{i,t}^\ell\}$ contemporaneously correlated.

Using Equations (7.8) and (7.9) , we can rewrite Equation (7.7) as:

$$(\gamma - 1)\Delta \log(c_{i,t+1}) = \epsilon_{i,t+1} - \gamma\Delta \log(u_{i,t+1}^c), \tag{7.10}$$

where Δ is the first difference operator. This representation is derived by assuming that $\log(1 + \epsilon_{i,t+1}) \approx \epsilon_{i,t+1}$. The *excess sensitivity test* of the permanent income hypothesis is based on the idea that if consumers are smoothing consumption over time in an optimal manner, consumption growth should be independent of income growth in a relationship similar to Equation (7.10). More precisely, the null hypothesis that is tested is that $b = 0$ in a regression of the form:

$$\Delta \log(c_{i,t+1}) = a + b\Delta \log(y_{i,t+1}) + \tilde{\epsilon}_{i,t+1}, \tag{7.11}$$

where $\tilde{\epsilon}_{i,t+1}$ is an error that is assumed to be uncorrelated with income growth, $E[\Delta \log(y_{i,t+1})\tilde{\epsilon}_{i,t+1}] = 0$. But notice that in our model, consumption growth and income growth at time t are correlated because individuals' consumption responds to transitory changes in the marginal utility of leisure. In other words, the composite error term in Equation (7.10) is correlated with the variable $\Delta \log(y_{i,t+1})$ because income at each date t is determined as a function of the shock to the marginal utility of leisure $u_{i,t}^\ell$, which is correlated with the shock to the marginal utility of consumption, $u_{i,t}^c$. As Hayashi [185] and others have noted, such regressions of consumption growth on income growth are valid only under the assumption that income is exogenously determined at time t. In Section 1.2, we describe a test of consumption insurance and consumption smoothing that does not rely on such assumptions and that allows consumers to trade in a rich array of assets with random payoffs.

We now turn to the issues that arise in using optimality conditions that are derived from individuals' intertemporal optimization problems to test lifecycle models of consumption and labor supply with panel data. Following MaCurdy [241, 242], various authors have used conditions characterizing individuals' optimal interior choices to identify and estimate parameters of preferences. Browning, Deaton and Irish [56] estimate the effects of family size and family composition on household consumption and leisure choices in an intertemporal model. Altonji [8] implements a test of the intertemporal substitution of leisure hypothesis using this framework. MaCurdy [242] shows how individuals' intratemporal marginal rate of substitution between consumption and leisure can be used to estimate parameters of preferences under weak assumptions about market structure. It has also been argued that individuals' intertemporal marginal rates of substitution for consumption at different dates can be used to identify models of individual behavior under similar assumptions. To illustrate the problems with following the latter approach, we will discuss the restrictions that can be tested for individual behavior using panel data with and without the assumption of complete markets.

Let us return to the first-order conditions in Equations (7.3)–(7.5) for the problem of maximizing the objective function in Equation (7.1) subject to the sequence of budget constraints in Equation (7.2). Typically, the approach taken in the literature cited above is to consider an estimation method that relies on an approximation to the individual's intertemporal Euler equation defined by Equation (7.5). Consider the logarithm of this equation as:

$$\Delta \log(\lambda_{i,t+1}) + \log(\beta) + \log(\pi_{r,t+1}) = \log(1 + \epsilon^i_{r,t+1}), \qquad (7.12)$$

where $\epsilon^i_{r,t+1}$ is the error from forecasting $\beta(\lambda_{i,t+1}/\lambda_{i,t})\pi_{r,t+1}$ given information available at time t and Δ denotes the first difference operator. Notice that this transformation requires that returns are always nonnegative and consequently, $\epsilon^i_{r,t} \geq -1$. Now, first difference the logarithm of Equation (7.4) and substitute for the right side using Equation (7.12):

$$
\begin{aligned}
\Delta \log\left[U_c(\ell_{i,t}, c_{i,t}, \theta_{i,t})\right] &= \Delta \log(\lambda_{i,t}) \\
&= \log(1 + \epsilon^i_{r,t}) - \log(\beta \pi_{r,t}). \qquad (7.13)
\end{aligned}
$$

Now, $E_t[(1 + \epsilon^i_{r,t+1})] = 0$ does not imply that $E_t[\log(1 + \epsilon^i_{r,t+1})] = 0$. Provided $-1 < \epsilon^i_{r,t} \leq 1$, however, we can use the expansion for $\log(1 + \epsilon^i_{r,t+1})$ to write Equation (7.13) as:

$$\Delta \log\left[U_c(\ell_{i,t}, c_{i,t}, \theta_{i,t})\right] = \sum_{k=1}^{\infty} (-1)^{k+1} \epsilon^i_{r,t}/k! - \log(\beta\pi_{r,t}). \qquad (7.14)$$

Suppose $E_{t-1}[\log(1 + \epsilon^i_{r,t})]$ exists and is known, up to a finite parameter vector, for some asset r. Then, the variable $\epsilon^{i*}_{r,t}$ defined by:

$$\begin{aligned}
\epsilon^{i*}_{r,t} &\equiv \log(1 + \epsilon^i_{r,t}) - E_{t-1}[\log(1 + \epsilon^i_{r,t})] \\
&= \Delta \log\left[U_c(\ell_{i,t}, c_{i,t}, \theta_{i,t})\right] + \log(\beta\pi_{r,t}) - E_{t-1}\left[\log(1 + \epsilon^i_{r,t})\right]
\end{aligned}$$

is zero in expectation. Then we could form orthogonality conditions from the condition $E_{t-1}(\epsilon^{i*}_{r,t}) = 0$ using the approach we described in Chapter 3, Section 1 to estimate alternative parameterizations of the utility function.

There are several problems with following this approach in a panel data setting, however. The first is that $E_{t-1}[\log(1+\epsilon^i_{r,t})]$ can be evaluated only under some simple assumptions such as lognormality for the forecast error $\epsilon^i_{r,t}$. The second difficulty arises from the fact that $\epsilon^{i*}_{r,t}$ typically depends on common shocks so that consistent estimates based on the above equation can only be obtained by using time series data but not cross-sectional data. Suppose we disregard the higher order moments in Equation (7.14) and approximate $\log(1 + \epsilon^i_{r,t})$ by $\epsilon^i_{r,t}$. Then $\epsilon^{i*}_{r,t}$ depends on $E_{t-1}(\epsilon^i_{r,t})$ which must be evaluated using a sample average. Now, the average of $\epsilon^i_{r,t}$ evaluated over time is zero but not over the cross section. Chamberlain [67] pointed this out when he noted that *"a time average of forecast errors over T periods should converge to zero as $T \to \infty$. But an average of forecast errors across N individuals surely need not converge to zero an $N \to \infty$. There may be common components in these errors, due to economy-wide innovations."*

The problem is that the time dimension of most panel data sets is very short. If we try to use $\epsilon^{i*}_{r,t}$ as the error for our estimation and average over the cross section, we run into the problem that Chamberlain raised. Put differently, Euler equation-based methods that were devised to estimate and test dynamic equilibrium models in a time series setting are not directly applicable in a panel data setting unless we make further assumptions about the nature of aggregate shocks or the nature of market structure or both. Clearly, in the absence of aggregate shocks, the procedure described above is valid.

Now suppose that markets are complete. Recalling our analysis from Chapters 1 and 2, notice that individuals' intertemporal MRS in consumption is equated to the common ratio p_{t+1}/p_t, implying that their forecast errors $\epsilon^i_{r,t+1}$ in Equation (7.5) are identical. In this case, Equation (7.5) can be written as:

$$p_t = \beta E\left[p_{t+1}\pi_{r,t+1}\right]. \tag{7.15}$$

Denote by $\epsilon_{r,t+1}$ the error from forecasting $\beta(p_{t+1}/p_t)\pi_{r,t+1}$ at time t. Equations (7.13) and (7.15) imply that for all $r \in R$,

$$\log(1 + \epsilon_{r,t}) - \log(\beta\pi_{r,t}) = \Delta\log(p_t)$$

$$= \Delta\log\left[U_c(\ell_{i,t}, c_{i,t}, \theta_{i,t})\right]. \tag{7.16}$$

Under the complete markets assumptions, it is possible to treat the term $\log(1 + \epsilon_{r,t}) - \log(\beta\pi_{r,t})$ as a time dummy and obtain consistent estimates of household preferences by using the cross-sectional aspects of the panel when there are aggregate shocks.

Now consider a slightly different problem. Consider the problem of maximizing the objective function in Equation (7.1) subject to the sequence of budget constraints in Equation (7.2) and a borrowing constraint of the form, $z^i_{r,t+1} \geq 0$. To simplify our discussion, we will drop the dependence of the utility function U on $\ell_{i,t}$ and assume that there is one asset available for trade so that $R = \{1\}$. Now the conditions in Equations (7.3), (7.4), and (7.5) are valid if consumers do not face short sales constraints or borrowing constraints. If they do, then Equation (7.5) must be replaced with the condition:

$$\lambda_{i,t} = \beta E_t\left[\lambda_{i,t+1}\pi_{t+1}\right] + \mu_{i,t}, \tag{7.17}$$

where $\mu_{i,t}$ satisfies the relation:

$$\mu_{i,t}z_{i,t+1} = 0, \quad \text{with } \mu_{i,t} = 0 \text{ if } z^i_{t+1} > 0. \tag{7.18}$$

We can further simplify this condition by substituting for $\lambda_{i,t}$ and $\lambda_{i,t+1}$ using the counterpart of Equation (7.4). In other words,

$$U_c(c_{i,t}, \theta_{i,t}) = \begin{cases} \beta E_t\left[U_c(c_{i,t+1}, \theta_{i,t+1})\pi_{t+1}\right] & \text{if } z^i_{t+1} > 0 \\ \beta E_t\left[U_c(c_{i,t+1}, \theta_{i,t+1})\pi_{t+1}\right] + \mu_{i,t} & \text{if } z^i_{t+1} = 0 \end{cases}$$

Define the variable $\mu'_{i,t}$ as:

$$\mu'_{i,t} = \frac{\mu_{i,t}}{\beta E_t[U_c(c_{i,t+1}, \theta_{i,t+1})\pi_{t+1}]}.$$

Notice that $\mu'_{i,t} = 0$ if households do not face any borrowing constraints at their optimum. Dividing both sides of the above expression by $U_c(c_{i,t}, \theta_{i,t})$ notice that we can express the first-order conditions as:

$$\left[\frac{\beta U_c(c_{i,t+1}, \theta_{i,t+1})}{U_c(c_{i,t}, \theta_{i,t})} \pi_{t+1} \right] = 1 + \epsilon_{i,t+1} \quad \text{if } z^i_{t+1} > 0 \tag{7.19}$$

$$\left[\frac{\beta U_c(c_{i,t+1}, \theta_{i,t+1})}{U_c(c_{i,t}, \theta_{i,t})} \pi_{t+1} \right] (1 + \mu'_{i,t}) = 1 + \epsilon''_{i,t+1} \quad \text{otherwise.} \tag{7.20}$$

Here $\epsilon_{i,t+1}$ and $\epsilon''_{i,t+1}$ are the errors in predicting the left side of Equations (7.19) and (7.20), respectively, using information held by the consumer at time t. Thus, $E_t[\epsilon_{i,t+1}] = 0$ and $E_t[\epsilon''_{i,t+1}] = 0$.

Notice that the multiplier on the borrowing constraint, $\mu'_{i,t}$, is not observable by the econometrician. Thus, we cannot directly test the overidentifying restrictions in Equation (7.20) because $\epsilon''_{i,t+1}$ depends on $\mu'_{i,t}$. However, suppose our panel data set can be split into two groups, those who are likely to face borrowing constraints and those who are not. The idea behind the test of borrowing constraints proposed by Zeldes [343] and others is that a currently binding borrowing constraint for some individual in the first group will lead to a rejection of the unconstrained Euler equation, namely, Equation (7.19).[2] Zeldes estimates his model using GMM methods. To deal with the problem posed by aggregate shocks, he assumes that the forecast error of individuals can be decomposed into a common component that depends on aggregate shocks and an idiosyncratic component. Although a similar approach is adopted by Hotz, Kydland, and Sedlacek [197], these authors note that such a decomposition of the forecast error cannot be justified on theoretical grounds.

To make this point more clearly, suppose that there are I types of consumers in the economy and the proportion of type i agents is equal to the *ex ante* probability of agents with type i characteristics. We also introduce aggregate shocks by assuming that the asset traded in equilibrium has a random dividend, $d_t = d(s_t)$, which is a function of the exogenous state variable $s_t \in S$, where S is a compact set. Let $F(s_t, s_{t+1})$ denote the stationary transition function of s_t. Let $x_{i,t}$ denote the average holdings of the asset by a representative agent of type i at time t. Also define the vector of asset holdings, $x_t \equiv (x_{1,t}, \ldots, x_{I,t})'$ and the vector of individual characteristics, $\theta_t \equiv (\theta_{1,t}, \ldots, \theta_{I,t})'$. The state of the economy is given by $\hat{s}_t = (x'_t, \theta'_t, d_t)'$. The individual's state vector consists of his own

---

[2] Runkle [293] implements a similar test.

asset holdings $x_{i,t}$, his characteristics at time t, $\theta_{i,t}$, and the aggregate state $\hat{s}_t$. We can express individual allocations by $c_{i,t} = \hat{c}_i(x_{i,t}, \theta_{i,t}, \hat{s}_t)$ and $z_{i,t+1} = \hat{z}_i(x_{i,t}, \theta_{i,t}, \hat{s}_t)$. We assume that the return at time $t + 1$ can be expressed as a time-invariant function of the current and future state, $\pi_{t+1} = \pi(\hat{s}_{t+1}, \hat{s}_t)$. Also let $H(x_{i,t}, \theta_{i,t})$ denote the distribution of endogenous and exogenous characteristics throughout the population in equilibrium and consider the population average of the forecast error:

$$\mathcal{E}_1(\hat{s}', \hat{s}) \equiv \int \int \left(\epsilon'_i - \int \epsilon'_i F(s, ds') \right) dH(x_i, \theta_i)$$

$$= \int \int \left\{ \frac{\beta U_c[c_i(x'_i, \theta'_i, \hat{s}'), \theta'_i]}{U_c[c_i(x_i, \theta_i, \hat{s}), \theta_i]} \pi(\hat{s}', \hat{s}) + \right.$$

$$\left. \left[\int_S \frac{\beta U_c[c_i(x'_i, \theta'_i, \hat{s}'), \theta'_i]}{U_c[c_i(x_i, \theta_i, \hat{s}), \theta_i]} \pi(\hat{s}', \hat{s}) F(s, ds') \right] \right\} dH(x_i, \theta_i).$$

In this expression, variables with primes denote future values and unprimed variables denote the current value. Notice that the population average of the forecast error varies with the state of the economy, $(\hat{s}, \hat{s}')$.

The studies considered above propose to treat the aggregate component of the forecast error as a time dummy. Suppose the utility function $U(c_{i,t}, \theta_{i,t})$ is of the form $\theta_{i,t} U(c_{i,t}; \gamma)$. Thus, there are only two parameters to estimate: the discount factor β, and the concavity parameter, γ. If we are to derive a test from Equation (7.19), then the number of instruments must be greater than the number of parameters. Thus, consider the 3×1 instrument vector $y_{i,t}$ such that $y_{i,t} = (1, c_{i,t}, c_{i,t-1})'$, where $c_{i,t}$ and $c_{i,t-1}$ are in agents' information set at time t. Now consider the population average of the forecast error times the second instrument:

$$\mathcal{E}_2(\hat{s}', \hat{s}) = \int \int \left\{ \frac{\beta U_c[c_i(x'_i, \theta'_i, \hat{s}'), \theta'_i]}{U_c[c_i(x_i, \theta_i, \hat{s}), \theta_i]} \pi(\hat{s}', \hat{s}) c_i(x, \theta_i, \hat{s}) + \right.$$

$$\left. \left[\int_S \frac{\beta U_c[c_i(x'_i, \theta'_i, \hat{s}'), \theta'_i]}{U_c[c_i(x_i, \theta_i, \hat{s}), \theta_i]} \pi(\hat{s}', \hat{s}) F(s, ds') \right] c_i(x, \theta_i, \hat{s}) \right\} dH(x_i, \theta_i).$$

Unless the equilibrium allocation is independent of the state of the economy, notice that $\mathcal{E}_2(\hat{s}', \hat{s}) \neq \mathcal{E}_1(\hat{s}', \hat{s}) E(c_i)$ where $E(\cdot)$ denotes the population average at time t. Thus, if we treat $\mathcal{E}_1(\hat{s}', \hat{s})$ as a time dummy, then $\mathcal{E}_2(\hat{s}', \hat{s})$ must also be treated as a time dummy since the consumption allocations of individuals at time t depend on aggregate shocks. However, given a single cross-section, it is not possible to identify more than one time dummy and thus, obtain consistent estimates with this method.

Now note what happens if we assume complete markets. Then individuals set their intertemporal marginal rate of substitution equal to the common ratio, p_{t+1}/p_t, which varies with the state of the economy as $\psi(\hat{s}_t, \hat{s}_{t+1})$. If we integrate individuals' forecast errors over the population, then $\psi(\hat{s}_t, \hat{s}_{t+1})$ can be treated as a constant with respect to the distribution of characteristics $H(x_{i,t}, \theta_{i,t})$. But this is equivalent to assuming that individuals set their forecast errors equal to the common error ϵ_{t+1}, which can be treated as a time dummy in cross-sectional averages with any individual-specific variable.

1.2.   A Factor Structure

The above discussion shows that it is possible to give a consistent interpretation to estimates derived from individuals' intertemporal optimality conditions in an economy with aggregate shocks if we make the complete markets assumption. These points have been made by Altuğ and Miller [12, 13] who also devise a test of the full risk-sharing hypothesis implied by the complete contingent claims equilibrium using data on individuals. Unlike tests of the permanent-income hypothesis that we described earlier, this test allows for unobservables in preferences and an endogenous labor-leisure choice.

Preferences are described by Equation (7.1) and there is *ex ante* heterogeneity among individuals. We assume that the individual's labor supply can be measured in efficiency units that depend on the time-varying characteristics, $\theta_{i,t}$. Thus $\hat{h}_{i,t}$ denotes the labor supply of the i'th individual in period t, weighted by an efficiency index $\gamma(\theta_{i,t})$:

$$\hat{h}_{i,t} = \gamma(\theta_{i,t})(1 - \ell_{i,t}). \tag{7.21}$$

Given the efficiency units assumption for individual labor supply, if the individual participates in the labor market, then

$$w_{i,t} = w_t \gamma(\theta_{i,t}), \tag{7.22}$$

where w_t is the real wage of a standard unit of labor in period t.

We now assume that markets are complete and that all information is public; thus, individuals can condition their choices at t on information that is publicly available at that date and they can purchase contingent claims to consumption that pay off for each possible state of the economy. The exogenous shocks to this economy are defined in terms of a first-order Markov process $s_t \in S \subset \mathbb{R}^m$ with transition function $F(s, s')$ defined on $S \times S$ and a strictly positive density function $f(s'|s)$. The state of the economy at time t is described in terms of the history of realizations of the exogenous shocks up to time t, $s^t \equiv (s_1, \ldots, s_t) \in S^t$. We define the price of a contingent claim that pays off conditional on the event $\bar{S} \subseteq S^t$ occurring at date t by $\bar{p}_t$:

$$\bar{p}_t(\bar{S}) = \beta^t \int_{\bar{S}} p(s^t) g(s^t) ds^t, \tag{7.23}$$

where $g(s^t)$ is the joint density of $s^t \equiv (s_1, \ldots, s_t)$ and $p(s^t)$ is a "price density" defined in a manner similar to that in Chapter 2, Section 1.3. Setting $\bar{S} = S^t$, for example, we see that $\beta^t E_0(p_t)$ is the price of a sure unit of consumption in period t.

Given the representation for the contingent claims prices in Equation (7.23), the individual maximizes Equation (7.1) at date 0 (when all trades occur) by choosing the vector $(\ell_{i,t}, c_{i,t})$ for each $t \in \{\underline{n}, \cdots, \bar{n}\}$ and for each possible event that can occur at that date subject to the lifetime budget constraint:

$$E_0 \left\{ \sum_{t=\underline{n}}^{\bar{n}} \beta^t p_t \left[c_{i,t} - (1 - \ell_{i,t}) w_{i,t} \right] \right\} \leq c_i, \tag{7.24}$$

where the exogenously determined quantity c_i denotes bequests net of inheritances. Let η_i denote the Lagrange multiplier associated with the budget constraint in Equation (7.24). The first-order conditions with respect to $\ell_{i,t}$ and consumption $c_{i,t}$ are:

$$U_\ell(\ell_{i,t}, c_{i,t}, \theta_{i,t}) \geq \eta_i p_t w_{i,t}, \tag{7.25}$$

$$U_c(\ell_{i,t}, c_{i,t}, \theta_{i,t}) = \eta_i p_t. \tag{7.26}$$

Here U_ℓ and U_c denote the partial derivatives of U with respect to ℓ and c, respectively, and Equation (7.25) holds with equality whenever $\ell_{i,t} < 1$. Notice that the condition in Equation (7.26) is an expression of the full risk-sharing hypothesis implied by the complete contingent claims equilibrium and it says that the weighted marginal utilities of consumption are equated across consumers. Notice that our formulation also allows for aggregate shocks; these affect individual allocations through the equilibrium (shadow) price of consumption, p_t, and the aggregate component of wages, w_t.

Suppose we have a panel data set that contains T observations on N individuals. By comparing Equation (7.26) with Equation (7.4), notice that the assumption of complete markets imposes a simple factor structure for the behavior of the individual Lagrange multipliers $\lambda_{i,t}$ defined in the previous section:

$$\lambda_{i,t} = \eta_i p_t, \quad i \in \{1, \ldots, N\}, \quad t \in \{1, \ldots, T\}. \tag{7.27}$$

The factor structure in Equation (7.27) imposes $NT - (N + T)$ restrictions for the behavior of $\lambda_{i,t}$. However, these restrictions cannot be tested directly because under the alternative hypothesis that markets are incomplete, the parameters $\lambda_{i,t}$ are unidentified. Nevertheless, certain parameters of the model are identified under much weaker assumptions about market structure and this provides a basis for testing the $\{p_t; \eta_i\}$ factor structure.

We describe these tests under the parametric specification for individual utilities described by Equations (7.8) and (7.9). Consider first the marginal rate of substitution between leisure and consumption for individual i who, we assume, invariably participates in the labor market:

$$\text{MRS}(\ell_{i,t}, c_{i,t}) \equiv \frac{U_\ell(\ell_{i,t}, c_{i,t}, \theta_{i,t})}{U_c(\ell_{i,t}, c_{i,t}, \theta_{i,t})} = w_{i,t}. \tag{7.28}$$

This condition holds provided there exists a spot market for labor services and consumption goods. In particular, it does not require that markets are complete. Using Equations (7.8) and (7.9), we can write the logarithm of Equation (7.28) as:

$$(\phi - 1)\log(\ell_{i,t}) - (\gamma - 1)\log(c_{i,t}) - \log(w_{i,t})$$
$$= \gamma \log(u_{i,t}^c) - \phi \log(u_{i,t}^\ell).$$

Notice that the permanent or fixed individual characteristics u_i^c and u_i^ℓ in preferences that enter this expression are correlated with all current and past choices of consumption, leisure, asset holdings, and so on. To eliminate such fixed effects, we difference the above expression as:

$$(\phi - 1)\Delta \log(\ell_{i,t}) - (\gamma - 1)\Delta \log(c_{i,t}) - \Delta \log(w_{i,t})$$
$$= \gamma \Delta \varepsilon_{i,t}^c - \phi \Delta \varepsilon_{i,t}^\ell,$$

where Δ denotes the first difference operator. Now define the errors $e_{i,t}^1 \equiv \gamma \Delta \varepsilon_{i,t}^c - \phi \Delta \varepsilon_{i,t}^\ell$. From the point of view of an econometrician, a testable implication of Equation (7.28) is that $E_t[e_{i,t}^1] = 0$. Let the identifiable parameters in Equation (7.28) be defined as $\alpha_1 = (\gamma, \phi)'$. Consider a q-dimensional instrument vector $y_{i,t}$ that satisfies the relation:

$$E_t[e_{i,t}^1 \otimes y_{i,t}] = 0. \tag{7.29}$$

Thus, $y_{i,t}$ includes any variables that are uncorrelated with changes in the idiosyncratic parts of the preference shocks at time t. This is a set of population orthogonality conditions that we can consistently estimate using GMM estimation methods.

Now suppose that markets are complete. Then we know from Equation (7.26) that households' first-order condition for consumption satisfies:

$$\text{MU}(c_{i,t}) \equiv U_c(\ell_{i,t}, c_{i,t}, \theta_{i,t}) = p_t \eta_i. \tag{7.30}$$

Using Equation (7.8), we can write this condition as

$$(1 - \gamma) \log(c_{i,t}) + \log(p_t) + \log(\eta_i) = \gamma \log(u^c_{i,t}).$$

Differencing to eliminate the fixed effect in preferences and the individual-specific Lagrange multiplier yields:

$$(1 - \gamma) \Delta \log(c_{i,t}) + \Delta \log(p_t) = \gamma \Delta(\varepsilon^c_{i,t}).$$

The growth rates of the contingent claims prices in this expression are estimated as time dummies. Now define the error term $e^2_{i,t} \equiv \gamma \Delta(\varepsilon^c_{i,t})$ and the identifiable parameters in $e^2_{i,t}$ as $\alpha_2 = [\Delta \log(p_t)/(1-\gamma)]$. We can construct orthogonality conditions from this error as in Equation (7.29):

$$E_t[e^2_{i,t} \otimes y_{i,t}] = 0. \tag{7.31}$$

The idea underlying the tests of risk-sharing proposed by Altuğ and Miller [12] is to note that the orthogonality conditions defined by Equation (7.29) hold provided there exist spot labor markets. On the other hand, the orthogonality conditions defined in Equation (7.31) hold only under the full insurance hypothesis implied by the complete contingent claims equilibrium. To implement this test, we first estimate the orthogonality conditions in Equation (7.29) separately. We then combine the orthogonality conditions in Equations (7.29) and (7.31) and test whether the additional orthogonality conditions implied by the complete markets assumption hold in the data. As long as the instrument vector in Equations (7.29) and (7.31) does not involve variables that may be correlated with the preference shocks, this test can avoid the problems that arise from tests of the permanent-income hypothesis based on regressions of consumption growth on income growth.

Notice that the population orthogonality conditions in Equations (7.29) and (7.31) hold for each individual at each date. The estimator we derive replaces the population orthogonality conditions with their sample counterparts evaluated across the cross-sectional aspects of the panel data set. To account for aggregate shocks (which can affect the co-variance properties of the disturbances times the instrument vector over time), we stack the terms $e^j_{i,t} \otimes y_{i,t}$ for each individual in terms of the $r_j qT$-dimensional vector $f_j(\alpha_j, i)$ as:

$$f_j(\alpha_j, i) = ((e^j_{i,1} \otimes y_{i,1})', \cdots, (e^j_{i,T} \otimes y_{i,T})')', \quad j = 1, 2, \tag{7.32}$$

and form sample orthogonality conditions by averaging Equation (7.32) over $i \in \{1, \ldots, N\}$. Thus, we estimate the ℓ_j-dimensional parameter vector α_j by minimizing the quadratic form V_j with respect to α_j:

$$V_j(\alpha_j) = \left\{ \left[\frac{1}{N} \sum_{i=1}^{N} f_j(\alpha_j, i) \right]' W_j \left[\frac{1}{N} \sum_{i=1}^{N} f_j(\alpha_j, i) \right] \right\} \tag{7.33}$$

for $j = 1, 2$. For our application, the smallest asymptotic covariance matrix within this class of estimators is found by making W_j the inverse of $\hat{W}_j = E[f_j(\alpha_j, i) f_j(\alpha_j, i)']$. In this case, the resulting estimator has an asymptotic covariance matrix of $(D'_j \hat{W}_j^{-1} D_j)^{-1}$, where $D_j = E[\partial f_j(\alpha_j, i)/\partial \alpha_j]$. Provided $r_j qT > \ell_j$, we can test the overidentifying restrictions in Equation (7.29) or Equation (7.31) by making use of the fact that N times the minimized value of the objective function in Equation (7.33) is asymptotically distributed as a χ^2-random variable with $r_j qT - \ell_j$ degrees of freedom.

To test the hypothesis that markets are complete, define the full set of orthogonality conditions in terms of the rqT-dimensional vector:

$$f(\alpha, i) = (f_1(\alpha_1, i)', f_2(\alpha_2, i)')',$$

where $\alpha' = (\alpha'_1, \alpha'_2)$ and $r = r_1 + r_2$, and calculate the value of the minimized objective function $V(\alpha)$ using $f(\alpha, i)$ in Equation (7.33). Let α^N and α_1^N denote the minimizers of $V(\alpha)$ and $V_1(\alpha_1)$, respectively. Consider the statistic:

$$C = N \left[V(\alpha^N) - V_1(\alpha_1^N) \right]. \tag{7.34}$$

Under the null hypothesis that markets are complete, C is asymptotically distributed as a χ^2-random variable with $rqT - \ell - (r_1 qT - \ell_1) = r_2 qT - \ell_2$ degrees of freedom.

Data on household consumption, husbands' and wives' leisure, and household characteristics derived from the Michigan Panel Study of Income Dynamics (PSID) are used to estimate conditions similar to

Equations (7.28) and (7.30). Altuğ and Miller use a parametric specification of preferences that allows for nonseparabilities between household consumption and the wife's leisure time as well as observed and unobserved characteristics that affect household preferences. In addition to estimating the intratemporal MRS between household consumption and husband's leisure and the marginal utility of consumption equation, they also estimate the equation for the husband's marginal utility of leisure. They consider an instrument vector that includes age and age squared, two- and three-times lagged values of the husband's wages and the wife's leisure, twice lagged values of the wife's wages, current and lagged values of family size, the value of a homeowner's house and rental value, and the current value of an aggregate stock index return.

Among other results, they cannot reject the intratemporal MRS between household consumption and male leisure. Nor do they find evidence against the full risk-sharing hypothesis when they consider orthogonality conditions implied by the intratemporal MRS and the marginal utility of household consumption or the intratemporal MRS and the marginal utility of husband's leisure. They estimate the elasticity of male leisure time to be about 0.11, which is consistent with estimates obtained by MaCurdy [241], Altonji [8], and others. They also find that the wife's leisure time is nonseparable with household food consumption. Finally, they find evidence for the effect of aggregate shocks on individual choices as transmitted through the aggregate component of wages w_t and the time-varying contingent claims prices p_t. They conclude that the hypothesis of full risk-sharing cannot be rejected for their sample of continuously married households but they do report evidence of model misspecification in terms of some implausible parameter estimates.

In Chapter 3, we described tests of the equilibrium asset pricing model that are implemented based on the intertemporal Euler equation characterizing consumption and asset returns. These tests assume a representative consumer and ignore exogenous and endogenous forms of heterogeneity throughout the population. A final test of the complete markets model can be derived from the intertemporal Euler equation without making such assumptions. For the purpose of this test, it is assumed that aggregate shocks are stationary and ergodic. This test is implemented by augmenting the orthogonality conditions derived from the individual's first-order conditions for leisure and consumption with those derived from Equation (7.5). We know that under complete markets, the ratio $\lambda_{i,t+1}/\lambda_{i,t}$ is equal to p_{t+1}/p_t. Using panel data on individuals, this common ratio is identified from individuals' marginal utility of consumption or marginal utility of leisure condition.

We noted in Chapter 3 that one reason for rejections obtained from tests using aggregate data may be due to rejections of the strong aggregation conditions underlying them. To see how the test described above allows for heterogeneity throughout the population that does not aggregate to a representative consumer, consider preferences of the form:

$$U(\ell_{i,t}, c_{i,t}, \theta_{i,t}) = \gamma^{-1}\delta(\theta_{i,t})c_{i,t}^{\gamma}\ell_{i,t}^{\rho},$$

where $\max(\gamma, \rho) \leq 1$ and $\delta(\theta_{i,t})$ is a time-varying utility index. Equation (7.25) implies that $\delta(\theta_{i,t})c_{i,t}^{(\gamma-1)}\ell_{i,t}^{\rho} = \eta_i p_t$. We can use this relation to find an expression for aggregate consumption:

$$c_t = p_t^{1/(\gamma-1)}E\left[\left(\frac{\eta_i}{\delta(\theta_{i,t})}\right)^{1/(\gamma-1)}(\ell_{i,t})^{\rho/(1-\gamma)}\right], \tag{7.35}$$

where $E(\cdot)$ denotes expectation over the population.

In a complete contingent claims equilibrium, we construct the stochastic discount factor from the ratio p_{t+1}/p_t. In a representative consumer model, we use the intertemporal MRS of the representative consumer. Notice that unless the expectation of the term in square brackets in Equation (7.35) is constant over time, a stochastic discount factor formed by choosing $(c_{t+1}/c_t)^{\gamma-1}$ will be incorrect. Notice that if preferences do not depend on leisure (so that $\rho = 0$) or if the exogenous characteristics of the population do not change (so that $\delta(\theta_{i,t})$ is constant over time), then the term in brackets in Equation (7.35) will be constant over time. If $\rho \neq 0$, an important source of heterogeneity is induced when some individuals do not participate in the labor market by setting $\ell_{i,t} = 0$.

1.3.   Tests of Risk-Sharing

Subsequent to this analysis, a number of authors have used regressions of consumption growth on income growth to test the full risk-sharing hypothesis with panel data. These include Cochrane [71], Mace [239], and Townsend [328]. Altonji, Hayashi, and Kotlikoff [9] test for full risk-sharing within families using a similar approach. In Section 1.1, we described the problems that arise from using such regressions to test versions of the permanent-income hypothesis using panel data. We now describe how the same problems apply to tests of risk-sharing implemented by the above authors.

Cochrane [71] tests for full risk-sharing or consumption insurance by using a specialization of the above framework. He omits the second term in Equation (7.8) and uses the ratios of the condition in Equation (7.26) for two consecutive periods to derive an expression for individual consumption growth from the condition:

$$\beta_i \frac{\theta_{i,t+1}}{\theta_{i,t}} \left(\frac{c_{i,t+1}}{c_{i,t}} \right)^{\gamma_i - 1} = \frac{p_{t+1}}{p_t}.$$

Here β_i is the individual-specific discount factor and p_{t+1}/p_t is constant across households. Taking logs of both sides and adding measurement error $\epsilon_{i,t+1}$ to consumption growth yields the representation:

$$\log(c_{i,t+1}/c_{i,t}) = a + \boldsymbol{X}'_{i,t+1} \boldsymbol{b} + \epsilon^*_{i,t+1}, \quad i = 1, \ldots, N, \tag{7.36}$$

where $\boldsymbol{X}_{i,t+1}$ are idiosyncratic variables that are cross-sectionally independent of the preference shifters $\log(\theta_{i,t+1}/\theta_{i,t})$, γ_i, β_i, and the measurement error $\epsilon_{i,t+1}$ and $\epsilon^*_{i,t+1}$ is a composite error term.[3] Cochrane uses data from the PSID and considers such variables as "days lost because of illness," a dummy variable for "involuntary job loss" as elements of the vector $\boldsymbol{X}'_{i,t+1}$ and tests for full risk-sharing by testing the null hypothesis $\boldsymbol{b} = 0$. The problem with this test is that it does not distinguish between *ex ante* heterogeneity across consumers and uninsurable idiosyncratic shocks. If an individual's *ex ante* marginal utility of consumption depends on the state of his health but the econometrician cannot observe the individual-specific variables in $\theta_{i,t}$ (one of which may correspond to health), then this test is invalid.

The tests that Cochrane implements do not contradict the full insurance assumption for such variables as "illness less than 100 days," "spells of unemployment following an involuntary job loss," "loss of work due to strikes," and an "involuntary move." On the other hand, he finds that variables such as "loss of more than 100 days of work due to illness" and "involuntary job loss" are significantly related to consumption growth. He also rejects the hypothesis that consumption growth is unrelated to income growth. Yet Cochrane himself notes that variables such as income growth and prolonged illness are likely to be correlated with unobserved preference shifters, as we argued above, so that these results do not necessarily provide evidence against consumption insurance.

Mace [239] and Townsend [328] implement tests of the full risk-sharing hypothesis by regressing consumption growth (or changes in the level of consumption) on income growth (or changes in the level of income). Mace uses data from the Consumer Expenditure Survey (CES). Townsend uses

---

[3]More precisely, $\epsilon^*_{i,t+1} = [\log(p_{t+1}/p_t) - \log(\theta_{i,t+1}/\theta_{i,t}) - \log(\beta_i)]/(\gamma - 1) + \epsilon_{i,t+1}$.

data on household consumption, income, and demographic characteristics for six villages in India. Restrictions for the behavior of individual consumption are obtained by considering the solution to a social planner's problem that involves maximizing the weighted sum of individual utilities subject to an aggregate resource constraint. Let I equal the finite number of consumers in the economy, $c_{i,t}$ and $y_{i,t}$ denote the consumption and exogenous endowment for individual i in period t, and $U(c_{i,t}, \theta_{i,t})$ the single-period utility function that depends on current consumption and the preference shock $\theta_{i,t}$. Let $\beta^t \lambda_t$ denote the Lagrange multiplier associated with the resource constraint in period t and $\omega^i > 0$ the social weight associated with each household i. It is straightforward to demonstrate that the first-order necessary conditions for the social planning problem require that the weighted marginal utility of consumption be equated across consumers:

$$\omega_i U'(c_{i,t}, \theta_{i,t}) = \lambda_t, \quad i = 1, \ldots, I. \tag{7.37}$$

Notice that these conditions are identical to the risk-sharing conditions that we derived in Section 1.2 provided $\omega_i = 1/\eta_i$ and $\lambda(s^t) = p(s^t)$ for any possible history of the economy at date t, s^t.[4]

Suppose the utility function is given by the exponential utility function, $U(c_{i,t}, \theta_{i,t}) = (1/\rho) \exp[-\rho(c_{i,t} - \theta_{i,t})]$, $\rho > 0$. Using Equation (7.37), it is straightforward to demonstrate that changes in individual consumption satisfy:

$$c_{i,t+1} - c_{i,t} = c_{a,t+1} - c_{a,t} + [(\theta_{i,t+1} - \theta_{i,t}) - (\theta_{a,t+1} - \theta_{a,t})], \tag{7.38}$$

where $c_{a,t} \equiv \sum_{i=1}^{I} c_{i,t}/I$ and $\theta_{a,t} \equiv \sum_{i=1}^{I} \theta_{i,t}/I$. For the power utility function $U(c_{i,t}, \theta_{i,t}) = \exp(\gamma\theta_{i,t})c_{i,t}^{\gamma}/\gamma$, $\gamma < 1$, we can derive a similar expression for the growth rate of consumption as:

$$\log(c_{i,t+1}) - \log(c_{i,t}) = \log(c_{a,t+1}) - \log(c_{a,t}) +$$
$$\frac{\gamma}{1-\gamma}[(\theta_{i,t+1} - \theta_{i,t}) - (\theta_{a,t+1} - \theta_{a,t})], \tag{7.39}$$

where $\log(c_{a,t+1}) - \log(c_{a,t}) = \sum_{i=1}^{I}[\log(c_{i,t+1}) - \log(c_{i,t})]/I$ and $\theta_{a,t}$ is defined as before. The main implication of these sharing rules (which admit exact aggregation to a representative consumer) is that changes in

---

[4]Townsend derives similar conditions by assuming that members of a village maximize a weighted sum of household utilities subject to a village resource constraint. This is equivalent to assuming that each village constitutes a separate Arrow-Debreu economy with its own set of (common) contingent claims prices.

individual consumption (or its growth rate) vary one-to-one with changes in aggregate consumption (or its growth rate).[5]

Mace and Townsend test the restrictions implied by these sharing rules by considering regressions such as:

$$\Delta c_{i,t} = a + b_1 \Delta c_{a,t} + b_2 \Delta y_{i,t} + u_{i,t} \qquad (7.40)$$

$$\Delta \log(c_{i,t}) = a + b_1 \Delta \log(c_{i,t}) + b_2 \Delta \log(y_{i,t}) + v_{i,t}, \qquad (7.41)$$

where $y_{i,t}$ denotes the income of individual i, and $u_{i,t}$ and $v_{i,t}$ include the time-varying component of both individual and aggregate preference shocks and may also include measurement errors from consumption and income data. The test of risk-sharing is implemented by testing the null hypothesis that $b_1 = 1$ and $b_2 = 0$. Notice that this test is identical to the excess sensitivity tests of the permanent-income hypothesis that we described in Section 1.1. In particular, it requires that changes in current income are uncorrelated with the error terms in Equations (7.40) and (7.41). But, as we showed above, this is a strong requirement. Even if preferences are separable with respect to consumption and leisure (an assumption that is not supported by evidence from microdata studies), changes in current income will be uncorrelated with changes in current consumption only if shocks to the marginal utility of consumption are uncorrelated with shocks to the marginal utility of leisure.

These sharing rules are estimated by pooling the first difference (or growth rate) observations across households. Townsend also considers time series regressions for each household. Mace runs regressions that include a dummy variable for the change in household employment status in place of the income variable. Townsend includes an aggregate leisure variable in his regressions to control for nonseparabilities with respect to leisure but this is valid only if all individuals choose to participate in market activities. Mace finds that for most measures of consumption, the results for the pooled first difference regressions are consistent with the restrictions of the sharing rules derived above. She cannot reject the hypothesis that $b_1 = 1$ and $b_2 = 0$ for 10 out of 12 goods, including total consumption, services, durables, food, housing, utilities, household furnishings, medical care, transportation, and recreation). For nondurables and clothing, the coefficient on changes in income are significant. Similar results are obtained when employment status dummies are included in

---

[5]Townsend also considers exponential and power utility functions but he assumes that the utility function depends on individual consumption per unit of a constructed age/sex index, $c_{i,t}/A_{i,t}$. He also allows for variation in household size and relates total household consumption to an average village consumption variable.

place of the income variables. The results for the power utility specification (which restricts the behavior of consumption growth rates) are less favorable, with rejections occurring for six goods (total consumption, services, nondurables, food, medical care, and recreation). In his empirical study of six villages in India, Townsend finds that variables such as sickness and unemployment do not matter for the determination of individual consumptions whereas current income, although statistically significant, does not have a large effect on current consumptions. While these results may be taken as evidence in favor of full risk-sharing, they are difficult to interpret because they fail to control for correlations between current consumption and current income or other demographic variables and fail to introduce nonseparabilities between consumption and leisure.

1.4. Extensions

In Section 1.1, we described how the assumption of complete markets can be used to control for aggregate shocks in individuals' forecast errors. There we assumed that preferences are additively separable over time. In situations where there are intertemporal inseparabilities in preferences or wages, the problem of correlated forecast errors arises even if we assume complete markets. This is the situation studied by Altuğ and Miller [13] and their solution to this problem is to develop a semiparametric estimator that uses the factor structure implied by complete markets to simulate forecast errors that are independent across the cross-section. We present a simplified version of their model and a brief discussion of the technique that they employ.

Suppose preferences for individual i have the form

$$E_0 \left\{ \sum_{t=\underline{n}}^{\bar{n}} \beta^t \left[U(c_{i,t}, \theta_{i,t}) - V(h_{i,t}, \theta_{i,t}) \right] \right\}, \tag{7.42}$$

where $h_{i,t}$ is time spent in market activities, and U and V are strictly concave, increasing, and differentiable. Unlike the application considered in Section 1, we will assume that past labor market experience affects current wages:

$$w_{i,t} = w_t \gamma(h_{i,t-1}, \theta_{i,t}). \tag{7.43}$$

We assume that there exist complete contingent claims markets. Thus the lifetime budget constraint for individual i has the form in Equation (7.24). Let η_i denote the Lagrange multiplier associated with this budget constraint. The first-order conditions with respect to $c_{i,t}$ and $h_{i,t}$ are as follows:

$$U'(c_{i,t}, \theta_{i,t}) = \eta_i p_t, \tag{7.44}$$

$$-V'(h_{i,t}, \theta_{i,t}) \geq \eta_i p_t w_{i,t} +$$
$$E_t[\eta_i p_{t+1} w_{t+1} \gamma'(h_{i,t}, \theta_{i,t+1}) h_{i,t+1}], \tag{7.45}$$

where the second term on the right side of Equation (7.45) derives the fact that labor supplied in period t will affect wages in period $t + 1$. Here $\gamma'(h_{i,t}, \theta_{i,t+1})$ shows the change in wages due to past labor market experience and is expected to have a positive sign.

If we had a long panel data set, we could estimate the intertemporal Euler equation for the optimal (interior) choice of hours described by Equation (7.45) using standard Euler equation techniques. In the absence of a long panel, we run into the problem of correlated forecast errors across cross sections. To devise an alternative approach, we put more structure on the problem by assuming that $\{\theta_{i,t}\}$ evolves as a first-order Markov process and that the ratios of the contingent claims prices $\{p_t w_t/(p_{t-1} w_{t-1})\}$ are identically and independently distributed with some distribution function G. Notice that the latter assumption restricts the equilibrium contingent claims price process.[6] Given these assumptions, notice that the state variables for the individual's problem in a competitive equilibrium are given by $(\eta_i p_t w_t, h_{t-1}, \theta_{i,t})$. The factor structure implied by the complete markets assumption implies that the individual-specific Lagrange multiplier and the shadow prices for consumption and a standardized unit of human capital always enter multiplicatively into the individual's choice of optimal hours and participation and it is this multiplicative representation that allows us to derive an estimator that accounts for aggregate shocks and achieves consistency from the cross-sectional aspects of the panel.

Suppose we could estimate the (common) expectation that enters inividuals' intertemporal Euler equation. Then the problem of correlated forecast errors in cross-sections would be eliminated. The idea behind the estimation method is to derive an estimate of this expectation by noting that the behavioral response of some individual to any aggregate shock, which may not have been realized in the data, systematically resembles some behavior of other individuals actually observed.

---

[6]Novales [271] follows a similar approach in his empirical study of consumption durability using aggregate data and assumes a process for the equilibrium stochastic real interest rate.

Consider some individual m who faces the aggregate shock $p_s w_s$ in period s. Consider some other individual n who faces the aggregate shock $p_t w_t$ in period t. If $(\eta_n p_t w_t, h_{t-1}, \theta_{n,t}) = (\eta_m p_s w_s, h_{s-1}, \theta_{m,s})$, then it must be the case that their optimal choices are identical, that is, $h_{m,s}^\star = h_{n,t}^\star$. Thus one can imagine inferring the behavior of some individual m in some future period s who responds to an aggregate shock $p_s w_s$ by forming an appropriate comparison group of choices actually observed in the earlier period t. For example, to predict the behavior of a highly valued individual in a slump (high η_n and low $p_t w_t$), we observe the behavior of an individual with a lower utility weight in a boom. Hence, the expected future behavior of an individual can be inferred by nonparametrically estimating the current behavior of individuals she may later mimic, weighted by the probability of the event actually occurring. Rather than estimate the whole probability distribution, however, simulation techniques are used to simulate a hypothetical sequence of aggregate shocks for each observation and to compute nonparametric estimates of their behavioral response to the simulated shocks. These nonparametric estimates are substituted for the actual expectations in sample counterparts of moments formed from the intertemporal Euler equations (Equation 7.45).

2.   Models with Private Information

We now turn to alternative ways of modeling individual choices in environments with private information. Private information can arise if individuals have superior information about their characteristics, in which case we say that there is adverse selection. The problem of adverse selection in competitive insurance markets with asymmetrically informed agents has been studied by Rothschild and Stiglitz [289] and Wilson [340], among others. When individuals have private information about their actions, we say that there is moral hazard due to the unobservability of actions. The problem of moral hazard has been used to rationalize the nature of labor contracts, firms' financial structure, and observed arrangements among shareholders, bondholders, and managers. It has been studied by Holmstrom [194, 195], Shavell [304], and Grossman and Hart [165], among others. In the financial economics literature, private information models have also been used to study the properties of rational expectations equilibria with informed and uninformed traders (Grossman [164], Grossman and Stiglitz [168]) and models of financial intermediation (Diamond [91] and Diamond and Dybvig [92]).

The existence of uninsurable idisyncratic risk and private information is often used to motivate models with alternative forms of market incompleteness and markets frictions. Bewley [31] presents a model with idiosyncratic risk and borrowing constraints. In the borrowing constraint model considered by Scheinkman and Weiss [301], idiosyncratic income risk is nondiversifiable because these shocks are not publicly observed. Hence, agents have limited opportunities to borrow against future income and cannot totally insure against all types of risks. Even in the absence of aggregate shocks, the model generates random fluctuations in aggregate output, the labor input, and the relative price of the asset that is traded in equilibrium. Another implication is that the cross-sectional distribution of nonhuman wealth is an important determinant of aggregate economic activity.

Several authors, including Bewley [32] and Mankiw [246], have noted that introducing market frictions can help to explain the equity premium. Mankiw uses a two-period model in which the risk-free rate is fixed and shows how the concentration of idiosyncratic shocks throughout the population affects the equity premium. This point has been further studied by Weil [334] who also models the risk-free rate. Other papers that use market incompleteness and market frictions to explain the behavior of asset returns include Aiyagari and Gertler [7], Heaton and Lucas [188], Brown [54], and Danthine, Donaldson, and Mehra [85].[7] Constantinides [76], Duffie and Sun [105], and Dumas and Luciano [107], among others, study models with market frictions such as transactions costs. These papers assume price processes and then derive the effect of transactions costs on optimal consumption and portfolio decisions. Grossman and Laroque [166] study optimal portfolio and consumption choices in the presence of an illiquid durable consumption good such as housing. They argue that the existence of an illiquid asset may be responsible for recent failures of the intertemporal Euler equation linking per capita consumption and asset returns.

Another approach to studying models with private information involves determining the nature of trading restrictions by decentralizing the optimal informationally constrained consumption and leisure alloca-

---

[7]Some of these papers include borrowing constraints and transactions costs to generate greater volatility in asset returns. Constantinides and Duffie [78] argue that such frictions are needed in these models because idiosyncratic labor income shocks are i.i.d. and hence, transient so that the permanent income of agents is almost equal across agents despite imperfect risk-sharing. Hence, trading in a risk-free bond is almost enough to yield the consumption smoothing opportunities attainable under full risk-sharing.

tions. Using this approach, Green [160] shows that the efficient allocation in an economy where agents have private information about their endowment shocks yields a version of Friedman's permanent income hypothesis, in which individuals' wealth follows a random walk and their consumption is a constant proportion of their wealth. Atkeson and Lucas [19] consider an economy with a continuum of agents whose preferences are affected by an idiosyncratic, serially independent taste shock at each date that is privately observed. The optimal allocations in an economy with private information are derived as the solution to a social planning problem that incorporates constraints on feasibility and incentive compatibility or truth-telling. The approach followed in these papers can be thought of in terms of a principal-agent problem. In the case of Green, Thomas and Worall [326], and others, the principal minimizes the total cost of providing a given level of utility to a group of consumers who are entitled to receive that utility, with resources at each date valued according to a given set of prices. These papers are interesting attempts at endogenously generating the form of trading restrictions that might emerge in economies with private information. However, they have generated few testable restrictions.

In what follows, we analyze the problem of private information in the context of a simple principal-agent model with an informed agent and an uninformed principal. Although this is one of the simplest frameworks for studying private information considerations, it can be used to derive testable implications for the behavior of observed variables such as managerial compensation schemes.

2.1. The Principal-Agent Problem

The principal-agent problem arises when there is moral hazard due to the unobservability of actions. The problem is to devise an incentive scheme so that the agent will take the right action when this action cannot be observed. A risk averse agent expends effort and produces output. The risk neutral principal must devise an optimal compensation scheme when he can only observe output but not the agent's action or the state of nature.

In a multiperiod environment where the principal and agent are involved in a long-term relationship, an important question arises as to the value of long-term contracts, which make the agent's payments functions of his past actions. Long-term contracts may have value if they help the agent to smooth consumption over time. In this case, the principal acts as an intermediary for a worker who might otherwise have limited opportunities to obtain such services on his own and the optimal contract provides consumption smoothing services to the agent at the same time that it sets up an efficient incentive scheme that determines his effort-compensation levels.

The problem of setting incentives over time in an optimal manner is studied in the literature on repeated principal-agent problems, which includes Rogerson [281], Lambert [226], Malcomson and Spinnewyn [243], and Fudenberg, Holmstrom, and Milgrom [139], among others. Recently, the latter two papers have shown that there exist conditions under which there are no gains to long-term contracts in the multiperiod principal-agent model and an optimal long-term contract may be implemented as a sequence of short-term contracts. Some key assumptions that yield this result are that both the principal and the agent share the same beliefs about the payoff-relevant future and that they both have access to perfect capital markets.

The first assumption rules out adverse selection from developing at points at which the long-term contract is due for renegotiation. Among other things, it requires that publicly observed outcomes at some date t convey no new information about the agent's past actions. In the static principal-agent problem, the contract is negotiated before the action is taken and both the principal and agent have the same beliefs about the probability distribution for output, conditional on the agent taking some action. As a result, both the agent and the principal are symmetrically informed. In a multiperiod context, the assumption that no new information becomes available about the agent's past actions at time t ensures that asymmetric information does not develop during the contract period. Since the agent knows his past action but the principal does not, if the probability distribution of publicly observed outcomes at time t such as output were to depend on the agent's past actions, then the principal and agent would not face the same probability distribution for output, conditional on the agent's action.

The assumption of perfect capital markets implies that the severity of the punishment that might be meted out to ensure that the agent take the right action is not limited by the ability to borrow and lend. If the agent's consumption (or wealth) is observable at each date or there are no wealth effects in preferences, then the optimal contract does not depend on the agent's consumption. Under these assumptions, the problem of consumption smoothing is separated from the problem of setting incentives optimally and the long-term contract decentralizes as a sequence of short-term contracts.

We initially study a static model and characterize the optimal contract using the approach Grossman and Hart [165]. In the next section, we use the results of Malcomson and Spinnewyn [243] and Fudenberg, Holmstrom, and Milgrom [139] to study the problem of moral hazard and managerial compensation in a multiperiod setting. In the earlier literature, the principal-agent model has been studied by assuming that the principal maximizes his expected utility subject to a constraint that the agent's expected utility is no lower than some prespecified level and the agent satisfies his first-order conditions with respect to his choice of action. As Mirrlees [262] has shown, this procedure requires that a certain property, known as the monotone likelihood property, holds for the distribution of output induced by the agent's actions. Here we follow the approach by Grossman and Hart for deriving the form of the optimal incentive compatible contract that does not rely on such assumptions.

2.1.1. The Optimal Contract

We consider an application in which the owner of a firm delegates the running of a firm to a manager. The owner is the principal and the manager is the agent. In the next section, we extend this framework to allow for a stock market and assume that shareholders are the principal. The principal cannot monitor the agent's actions but he can observe the outcome of these actions, which we take to be the firm's profit. There is also a random component that affects the firm's profit regardless of the agent's actions. When the principal observes a large profit in some state, he cannot tell if it is due to the agent's actions or to the state of nature.

We initially study this problem by assuming that there are a finite number of possible profit levels denoted $x_1, \ldots, x_n$ where $x_1 < \cdots < x_n$. In the next next section, we relax this assumption. The principal is risk neutral and is interested in profit minus the payment to the manager. The agent's actions take values in a compact set $A \subset \mathbb{R}$. Instead of modeling the production function for output in terms of the agent's action and the random state of nature, we model the probability distribution for output conditional on the agent's effort, or the probability distribution for output induced by the agent's actions. The probability that the i'th outcome x_i occurs, conditional on the action $a \in A$ being selected by the manager, is defined using the function $\pi : A \to \Delta$ where $\Delta \equiv \{\alpha \in \mathbb{R}^n | \alpha \geq 0, \sum_{i=1}^{n} \alpha_i = 1\}$. When the agent chooses action a, he knows the probability function π but not which outcome will occur.

The agent is risk averse and has expected utility preferences over random consumption c and effort levels a. We assume that the utility function has the form:

$$U(a, c) = \Gamma(a) + \Lambda(a)V(c). \tag{7.46}$$

When $\Lambda(a) = $ constant, notice that U is additively separable in a and c. When $\Gamma(a) = 0$ then U is multiplicatively separable in a and c. In what follows, we will study an application in which $V(c) = -\exp(-\rho c)$ and $\Lambda(a) = \exp(\rho a)$ so that $U(a, c) = -\exp[-\rho(c - a)]$. We have the following assumption.

Assumption 7.1 *(i) V is a real-valued, continuous, strictly increasing concave function defined on some open interval $C \equiv (\underline{c}, \infty)$; (ii) $\lim_{c \to \underline{c}} V(c) = -\infty$; (iii) Γ, Λ are real-valued, continuous functions defined on A and Λ is strictly positive; (iv) for $a_1, a_2 \in A$ and $c, \hat{c} \in C$, $\Gamma(a_1) + \Lambda(a_1)V(c) \geq \Gamma(a_2) + \Lambda(a_2)V(c) \Rightarrow \Gamma(a_1) + \Lambda(a_1)V(\hat{c}) \geq \Gamma(a_2) + \Lambda(a_2)V(\hat{c})$.*

The first part of this assumption says that the agent is risk averse. The last part of this assumption says that the agent's preferences over perfectly certain actions is independent of consumption. If $\Lambda(a)$ is not constant, then parts (ii) and (iv) imply that V is bounded above.

Notice that the agent can work for the principal or he can seek employment elsewhere. Let $\bar{U}$ be the agent's reservation price or the expected utility he can achieve by working elsewhere and $\mathcal{U} \equiv \{v | v = V(c) \text{ for some } c \in C\}$. The set $\mathcal{U}$ is just the set of utilities attainable at some consumption $c \in C$. We have the following assumption.

Assumption 7.2 $[\bar{U} - \Gamma(a)]/\Lambda(a) \in \mathcal{U}$ *for all $a \in A$.*

We can define the agent's first-best reservation price for picking the action a by $h\{[\bar{U} - \Gamma(a)]/\Lambda(a)\}$ where $h \equiv V^{-1}$. This reservation price gives the utility cost to the agent of taking some action $a \in A$ given that he can obtain total utility $\bar{U}$ elsewhere.

In the first-best situation when the agent's action is observable, the principal can ensure that the agent picks the action $a \in A$ by offering the following contract: if action a is chosen, the payment is $h\{[\bar{U} - \Gamma(a)]/\Lambda(a)\}$ and $\tilde{c}$ otherwise where $\tilde{c}$ is very close to $\underline{c}$. The expected benefit to the principal of getting the agent to pick the action a is defined by $B(a) = \sum_{i=1}^{n} \pi_i(a)x_i$, which is just expected output conditional on the action a being chosen. The first-best optimal action solves:

$$\max_{a \in A} \left\{ B(a) - h\{[\bar{U} - \Gamma(a)]/\Lambda(a)\} \right\}.$$

In situations where the principal cannot monitor the action a, the agent's compensation cannot depend on a. Instead payment is made contingent on the outcome of the action.

An *incentive scheme* is defined as an n-dimensional vector:

$$c \equiv (c_1, \ldots, c_n) \in C,$$

where c_i is the agent's compensation in the event that profit equals x_i. Given c, the agent chooses $a \in A$ to maximize his expected utility conditional on the action a, defined as $\sum_{i=1}^n \pi_i(a)U(a, c_i)$.

The principal knows the utility function $U(a, c)$, the set of possible actions A, and the function $\pi : A \to \Delta$. The incentive problem is due solely to the inability to monitor the agent's actions. Let $\mathcal{I}$ be the set of ordered pairs of incentive schemes c^* and actions a^* such that given c^*, the agent will be willing to work for the principal and find it optimal to choose a^*:

$$\max_{a \in A} \sum_{i=1}^n \pi_i(a)U(a, c_i^*) = \sum_{i=1}^n \pi_i(a)U(a^\star, c_i^*) \geq \bar{U}.$$

The principal chooses $(c, a) \in \mathcal{I}$ to maximize $\sum_{i=1}^n \pi_i(a)(x_i - c_i)$.

The optimal incentive compatible contract is characterized in two parts. Given that the principal wishes to implement the action a^*, what is the least cost of doing this, and second, which $a^\star$ should be implemented. The first problem involves solving:

$$\min_{c_1, \ldots, c_n} \sum_{i=1}^n \pi_i(a^\star)c_i \tag{7.47}$$

subject to

$$\sum_{i=1}^n \pi_i(a^\star)U(a^\star, c_i) \geq \sum_{i=1}^n \pi_i(a)U(a, c_i) \quad \text{for all } a \in A,$$

$$\sum_{i=1}^n \pi_i(a^\star)U(a^\star, c_i) \geq \bar{U}$$

$$c_i \in C \quad \text{for all } i.$$

The objective function is just the expected cost to the principal of getting the agent to choose the action a^*. The first constraint is the incentive-compatibility constraint, which says that the expected utility to the agent from choosing the action a^* is greater than the expected utility from choosing any other action $a \in A$. The second constraint says that the optimal contract must offer the agent at least as much utility as he can obtain by working elsewhere; it is known as the participation constraint.

Using Assumption 7.1, we can rewrite this problem in a simpler form. For this purpose, define $v_1 = V(c_1), \ldots, v_n = V(c_n)$ as the principal's choice variables. Recall that $\mathcal{U} = \{v | v = V(c) \quad \text{for some } c \in C\} = (-\infty, \bar{v})$. Using these results, we can rewrite the above problem as:

$$\min_{v_1, \ldots, v_n} \sum_{i=1}^{n} \pi_i(a^\star) h(v_i) \tag{7.48}$$

subject to

$$\Gamma(a^\star) + \Lambda(a^\star) \left(\sum_{i=1}^{n} \pi_i(a^\star) v_i \right) \geq \Gamma(a) + \Lambda(a) \left(\sum_{i=1}^{n} \pi_i(a) v_i \right)$$

$$\text{for all } a \in A,$$

$$\Gamma(a^\star) + \Lambda(a^\star) \left(\sum_{i=1}^{n} \pi_i(a^\star) v_i \right) \geq \bar{U},$$

$$v_i \in \mathcal{U} \quad \text{for all } i,$$

where $h \equiv V^{-1}$. Notice that the constraints in this problem are linear in v_i. Since V is concave, h is convex so that the objective function is convex in the v_i's. Thus, the problem is to minimize a convex function subject to a set of linear constraints. When the action set A is finite, the Kuhn-Tucker Theorem yields necessary and sufficient conditions for an optimum.

Define the n-tuple $c = (c_1, \ldots, c_n)$ or $v \equiv (v_1, \ldots, v_n)$. Consider the set of c's or the set of v's that satisfy the constraints in Equation (7.47) or Equation (7.48). We say that c (or v) implements the action $a^\star$ if it belongs to this set. (If the agent is indifferent between two actions, he is assumed to choose the action preferred by the principal.) If the set of v's that satisfies the constraints in Equation (7.48) is nonempty, then since h is convex,

$$\sum_{i=1}^{n} \pi_i(a^\star) h(v_i) \geq h \left(\sum_{i=1}^{n} \pi_i(a^\star) v_i \right) \geq h \left(\frac{\bar{U} - \Gamma(a^\star)}{\Lambda(a^\star)} \right),$$

so that the principal's objective function is bounded below on this set. Denote the greatest lower bound of this objective function by $C(a^\star)$; that is, $C(a^\star) = \inf \{\sum_{i=1}^{n} \pi_i(a^\star) h(v_i) | v \text{ implements } a^\star\}$. In the case where the constraint set is empty, we can write $C(a^\star) = \infty$.

The principal's problem is described as follows: First, for each $a \in A$, he computes $C(a)$. The second step is to choose which action to implement by choosing $a \in A$ to maximize $B(a) - C(a)$. The second problem is generally not a convex problem because $C(a)$ is generally not convex. However, it is possible to characterize the nature of the optimal contract by using information from the first step alone. We define a second-best optimal action $\hat{a}$ as one which maximizes $B(a) - C(a)$ on A. A second-best optimal incentive scheme $\hat{c}$ is one which implements a second-best optimal action $\hat{a}$ at least expected cost; that is, $\sum_{i=1}^{n} \pi_i(\hat{a})\hat{c}_i = C(\hat{a})$.

A final assumption is made to ensure that the greatest lower bound in the definition for $C(a)$ is achieved.

Assumption 7.3 *For all $a \in A$ and $i = 1, \ldots, n$, $\pi_i(a) > 0$.*

Since there are only a finite number of output levels, this assumption implies that $\pi_i(a)$ is bounded away from zero. Under Assumptions 7.1 through 7.3, Grossman and Hart show that there exists a second-best optimal action and a second-best optimal incentive scheme.

If $\Lambda(a)$ is a constant function on A or $\Gamma(a) = 0$ for all $a \in A$, we can show that the participation condition holds with equality:

$$\sum_{i=1}^{n} \pi_i(\hat{a})U(\hat{a}, \hat{c}_i) = \bar{U}.$$

To see this, consider the multiplicatively separable case and assume the contrary. Let $\hat{v}_i = V(\hat{c}_i)$. Then $\Gamma(\hat{a}) + \Lambda(\hat{a}) \sum_{i=1}^{n} \pi_i(\hat{a})\hat{v}_i > \bar{U}$. But in this case, we can reduce the principal's costs and satisfy all the remaining constraints in Equation (7.48) if we replace $\hat{v}_i$ by $v_i(1 + \epsilon)$ for all i where $\epsilon > 0$ is small.

The optimal contract involves tradeoffs between risk-sharing and the appropriate way to set incentives. In the first-best situation, if the agent is strictly risk averse and the principal risk neutral, then the principal bears all risk and the agent bears none. In the second-best situation, the agent is required to bear some risk to ensure that he will undertake the right action. Thus, the cost of implementing a second-best action and a second-best incentive scheme are greater than the first-best cost. We illustrate these costs in the next application.

2.2. Moral Hazard and Managerial Compensation

We now describe an application due to Margiotta and Miller [250], who use a structural model of the relationship between managers and shareholders to study the effects of moral hazard on managerial compensation.

In this model, there is a stock market and aggregate fluctuations. As a result, the manager's wealth may vary due to poor performance or due to aggregate shocks. As a way of modeling access to perfect capital markets, it is assumed that there exist complete contingent claims in the market for consumption goods. It is also assumed that shareholders can costlessly monitor the portfolio decisions a manager makes on his own account.

There is a single indivisible plant, which is owned by some well diversified shareholders. The output of the plant depends stochastically on the work effort of the manager. Individuals have finite lives but the plant, which is identical to the firm, is infinitely lived. Thus, a sequence of executives successively manage each firm. The manager works for the i'th firm between periods $\underline{n}$ and $\tilde{n}$, after which he retires.

The preferences of a manager are defined over lifetime consumption and leisure allocations. Let $c_{i,t} \in (-\infty, \infty)$ denote the consumption of the n'th manager at date t and assume that there are three levels of labor activity. Thus, the i'th manager's choice in period t may be described by the vector $\ell_{i,t} = (\ell_{i,t}^0, \ell_{i,t}^1, \ell_{i,t}^2)'$, where $\ell_{i,t}^j \in (0,1)$ for $j = 0, 1, 2$ and

$$\sum_{j=0}^{2} \ell_{i,t}^j = 1. \tag{7.49}$$

If $\ell_{i,t}^0 = 1$, the manager has retired and this is a publicly observable activity. The other two work effort levels, respectively called shirking (in which case $\ell_{i,t}^1 = 1$) and working diligently (in which case $\ell_{i,t}^2 = 1$), are private information to the manager. The manager's preferences are defined in terms of a time-additive utility function as:

$$E_0 \left\{ -\sum_{t=\underline{n}}^{\tilde{n}} \beta^t \sum_{j=0}^{2} \alpha_j \ell_{i,t}^j \exp(-\rho c_{i,t}) \right\}, \quad 0 < \beta < 1, \tag{7.50}$$

where $E_0(\cdot)$ is expectation conditional on information at date 0, ρ is the coefficient of absolute risk aversion, α_j is a utility parameter associated with choosing $\ell_{i,t}^j = 1$, and $\ell_{i,t}^0 = 1$ for all $t \in \{\tilde{n}, \cdots, \bar{n}\}$, the retirement phase. It is assumed that $\alpha_2 > \alpha_1$, or diligence is more distasteful than shirking but the ordering of α_2 versus α_0 and α_1 versus α_0 is unclear.

As in the principal-agent model we analyzed earlier, the agent's actions induce a probability distribution over the output of the firm which we define as $x_{i,t}$. This distribution depends on current level of effort expended by the manager but not on past effort levels. Output is measured relative to the size of the firm and it is identically and independently distributed across firms and over time. More precisely, conditional on effort level $\ell_{i,t}^j = 1$ for $j \in \{1,2\}$, $x_{i,t}$ has a truncated normal distribution denoted $f_j(x_{i,t})$, with support (ψ, ∞):

$$f_j(x_{i,t}) = \left\{ \Phi \left(\frac{\mu_j - \psi}{\sigma_j} \right) \sigma_j \sqrt{2\pi} \right\}^{-1} \exp \left[-\frac{(x_{i,t} - \mu_j)^2}{2\sigma_j^2} \right], \qquad (7.51)$$

where Φ is the standard normal distribution function and (μ_j, σ_j) denotes the mean and variance of the parent normal distribution. Notice that conditional on the agent's current action, the probability distribution of the return this period is independent of the past actions of the agent. Therefore, before the agent decides which action to take, at the beginning of each period, the principal and the agent are equally as well informed about the distribution of future payoffs.

2.2.1. A Managerial Compensation Scheme

Notice that this is a multiperiod principal-agent problem. In general, the optimal contract may involve current compensation being made dependent on information about the manager's past performance. However, the conditions in Fudenberg, Holmstrom, and Milgrom [139] and Malcomson and Spinnewyn [243] are satisfied in this model so that the optimal long-term contract can be implemented as a sequence of short-term contracts. Consequently, it is sufficient to study the one-period contract.[8]

We analyze the form of the short-term contract under the following assumptions.

Assumption 7.4 $\tilde{n} = \underline{n} + 1$.

This assumption says that the manager works for one period and then retires. Let I_0 denote information on all publicly observed variables at time zero.

Assumption 7.5 $E_0(p_{t+1}/p_t) \in I_0$.

According to this assumption, future interest rates are perfectly predictable. The approach to deriving the optimal contract is to derive the conditional valuation function for the manager who works for one period and then retires, given an arbitrary effort-payment schedule. This function is used to determine which contracts are feasible and can be implemented as part of the optimal contract. The final part of the derivation

---

[8]Recall that the agent has exponential utility (so that there are no wealth effects), there are a complete set of contingent claims markets, and the probability distribution of output is independent of the agent's past actions.

involves showing that Assumptions 7.4 and 7.5 do not change the form of the optimal contract.

The intertemporal consumption problem for a manager who works at some effort level $j \in \{0, 1, 2\}$ in period t and the (constant) effort level $k \in \{0, 1, 2\}$ in periods $t + s$ for $s = 0, \ldots, \bar{n} - t$ is given by:

$$\max_{\{c_{i,t+s}\}_{s=0}^{\bar{n}-t}} -E_t \left\{ \alpha_j \exp(-\rho c_{i,t}) + \alpha_k \sum_{s=1}^{\bar{n}-t} \beta^s \exp(-\rho c_{i,t+s}) \right\} \qquad (7.52)$$

subject to the budget constraint

$$E_t \left\{ \sum_{s=0}^{\bar{n}-t} \beta^s p_{t+s} c_{i,t+s} \right\} \leq p_t W_{i,t}, \qquad (7.53)$$

where p_{t+s} denote the "price densities" associated with the contingent claims prices defined as in Equations (7.23) and $W_{i,t}$ denotes the wealth of the manager at time t. Since the preferences considered here fall within the HARA class, only a small number of securities is needed to characterize the optimal financial portfolio and the optimal consumption stream for the manager. As we described in Chapter 2, Section 1.4, these securities can be defined as a bond which pays a unit of consumption periods $t+s$ for $s = 0, \cdots, \bar{n}-t$ and another bond which pays $\log(p_{t+s}/p_t)$ over the same period. Let $p_{i,t} \equiv p_t^{(\bar{n}-t)}$ and $q_{i,t} \equiv q_t^{(\bar{n}-t)}$ where $p_t^{(\bar{n}-t)}$ and $q_t^{(\bar{n}-t)}$ are defined as in Chapter 2, Proposition 2.4. Using these results, the indirect utility to the manager from choosing $\ell_{i,t}^j = 1$ for $j \in \{1, 2\}$ in period t and then retiring is given by:

$$V_{i,t}^{(j)} = -(1 + p_{i,t})\alpha_j^{1/(1+p_{i,t})}\alpha_k^{p_{i,t}/(1+p_{i,t})} \times$$
$$\exp\left[(-\rho W_{i,t} + q_{i,t})/(1 + p_{i,t})\right], \qquad (7.54)$$

where $\alpha_k = \alpha_0 E_t^j \{\exp[-\rho \omega_{i,t}/(1 + p_{i,t+1})]\}$ and E_t^j denotes the expectation operator conditional on information available at date t and given $\ell_{i,t}^j = 1$.[9]

To characterize the optimal contract, we need to specify the objective for shareholders. Margiotta and Miller assume that the return to the firm is given by:

$$\pi_{i,t} = \pi_t - \omega_{i,t}/s_{i,t} + x_{i,t}, \qquad (7.55)$$

where π_t is the equilibrium return on the market portfolio, $\omega_{i,t}/s_{i,t}$ which is managerial compensation weighted by firm size, and an idiosyncratic

---

[9]See Exercises 6 and 7.

factor $x_{i,t}$ which is mean independent of π_t. If the firm's assets are small relative to the size of the economy, then shareholders can also diversify away all idiosyncratic risk and minimize the discounted value of expected compensation $E_t(\beta^t p_t \omega_{i,t})$ on a period-by-period basis subject to the participation constraint and the incentive-compatibility constraint.

Let us momentarily suppose that the shareholders decided the manager should shirk. Then the shareholders must offer a contract to the manager which is at least as attractive as immediate retirement. Now the expected utility from retirement is obtained by setting α_j and α_k equal to α_0 in Equation (7.54):

$$- (1 + p_{i,t})\alpha_0 \exp[(-\rho W_{i,t} + q_{i,t})/(1 + p_{i,t})]. \tag{7.56}$$

Similarly, the expected utility from shirking and then retiring is:

$$-(1 + p_{i,t})\alpha_1^{1/(1+p_{i,t})} \left(\alpha_0 E_t^1 \{ \exp[-\rho \omega_{i,t}/(1 + p_{i,t+1})] \} \right)^{p_{i,t}/(1+p_{i,t})} \times$$

$$\exp[(-\rho W_{i,t} + q_{i,t})/(1 + p_{i,t})]. \tag{7.57}$$

Combining these results shows that the participation constraint when $\ell_{i,t}^1 = 1$ is:

$$E_t^1 \{ \exp[-\rho \omega_{i,t}/(1 + p_{i,t+1})] \} \le (\alpha_0/\alpha_1)^{1/p_{i,t}}. \tag{7.58}$$

Since the manager is risk averse and the shareholders behave as if they are risk neutral, it is optimal for them to pay the manager a constant wage which raises his wealth just enough to offset the nonpecuniary benefits of retirement. This scheme fully insures him against idiosyncratic fluctuations in $\pi_{i,t}$ about π_t. Furthermore, consumption after entering retirement is the same regardless of the retirement date. Using the participation constraint, we obtain:

$$\omega_{i,t}^1 = (\rho p_{i,t})^{-1}(1 + p_{i,t+1}) \log(\alpha_1/\alpha_0). \tag{7.59}$$

It is easy to see that any contract which pays the above quantity in expectation is cost-minimizing for $\ell_{i,t}^1 = 1$; the manager purchases contingent claims to offset any deviation of the contract from Equation (7.59). Since shareholders anticipate the manager to eliminate all idiosyncratic risk, there is no need to monitor his financial portfolio and there is separation between the compensation contract and decisions concerning the financial portfolio.

Now consider the case in which the shareholders decided the manager should work diligently. For the agent to participate in the contract, the expected utility from working diligently must be greater or equal to the expected utility from retirement. The expected utility from working diligently for one period and then retiring is:

$$-(1 + p_{i,t})\alpha_2^{1/(1+p_{i,t})} \left(\alpha_0 E_t^1 \{\exp[-\rho\omega_{i,t}/(1 + p_{i,t+1})]\}\right)^{p_{i,t}/(1+p_{i,t})} \times$$

$$\exp[(-\rho W_{i,t} + q_{i,t})/(1 + p_{i,t})]. \qquad (7.60)$$

As before, the participation condition can be expressed as:

$$E_t^2 \{\exp[-\rho\omega_{i,t}/(1 + p_{i,t+1})]\} \le (\alpha_0/\alpha_2)^{1/p_{i,t}}. \qquad (7.61)$$

The incentive-compatibility constraint is derived by noting that the expression in Equation (7.60) must exceed the expression in Equation (7.57) so that

$$E_t^1 \{\exp[-\rho\omega_{i,t}/(1 + p_{i,t+1})]\} -$$

$$(\alpha_2/\alpha_1)^{1/p_{i,t}} E_t^2 \{\exp[-\rho\omega_{i,t}/(1 + p_{i,t+1})]\} \ge 0,$$

which can be written equivalently as

$$\int_\psi^\infty \exp[-\rho\omega_{i,t}/(1 + p_{i,t+1})] \left[f_1(x_{i,t}) - \left(\frac{\alpha_2}{\alpha_1}\right)^{1/p_{i,t}} f_2(x_{i,t})\right] dx_{i,t} \ge 0.$$

Defining $g(x_{i,t}) = f_1(x_{i,t})/f_2(x_{i,t})$ as the ratio of the probability density functions from shirking versus working diligently, we can express the incentive-compatibility constraint as:

$$E_t^2 \{\exp[-\rho\omega_{i,t}/(1 + p_{i,t+1})] [g(x_{i,t}) - (\alpha_2/\alpha_1)^{1/p_{i,t}}]\} \ge 0. \qquad (7.62)$$

We consider the transformation

$$\nu_{i,t} \equiv \exp[-\rho\omega_{i,t}/(1 + p_{i,t+1})] \qquad (7.63)$$

to describe the shareholders' cost minimization problem for the case $\ell_{i,t}^2 = 1$. This transformation makes the objective function strictly convex and the constraints linear. It allows us to formulate the shareholders' problem using the approach of Grossman and Hart that is described in Equation (7.48). Under this transformation, the shareholders solve the problem:

$$\min_{\nu_{i,t}} E_t^2 \{-\log(\nu_{i,t})\}$$

subject to

$$E_t^2 \{\nu_{i,t} - (\alpha_0/\alpha_2)^{1/p_{i,t}}\} \le 0,$$

$$E_t^2 \{\nu_{i,t}[(\alpha_2/\alpha_1)^{1/p_{i,t}} - g(x_{i,t})]\} \le 0.$$

The first-order condition is:

$$v_{i,t}^{-1} = \eta_{i,t}^2[(\alpha_2/\alpha_1)^{1/p_{i,t}} - g(x_{i,t})] + \eta_{i,t}^1, \tag{7.64}$$

where $\eta_{i,t}^j$ are the Lagrange multipliers on the constraints defined from Equations (7.61) and (7.62). Since the utility function is multiplicatively separable in consumption and effort, we can show that the constraints are met with equality. Using the condition in Equation (7.64) to substitute for the $v_{i,t}$ in the incentive-compatibility constraint in Equation (7.62), the ratio of the Lagrange multipliers $\eta \equiv \eta_{i,t}^2/\eta_{i,t}^1$ is defined implicitly as the solution to the equation:

$$0 = \int \left\{ f_2(x)[(\alpha_2/\alpha_1)^{1/p_{i,t}} - g(x)]/[(\alpha_2/\alpha_1)^{1/p_{i,t}} - g(x) + \eta^{-1}] \right\} dx.$$

Multiplying both sides of the first-order condition by $v_{i,t}$ and adding and subtracting $\eta_{i,t}^1(\alpha_0/\alpha_2)^{1/p_{i,t}}$ yields:

$$1 = \eta_{i,t}^2 \int_\psi^\infty v_{i,t} \left[(\alpha_2/\alpha_1)^{1/p_{i,t}} - g(x_{i,t}) \right] f_2(x_{i,t})dx_{i,t} +$$

$$\eta_{i,t}^1 \int_\psi^\infty \left[v_{i,t} - (\alpha_0/\alpha_1)^{1/p_{i,t}} \right] f_2(x_{i,t})dx_{i,t} + \eta_{i,t}^1(\alpha_0/\alpha_2)^{1/p_{i,t}}.$$

The first two terms in this expression are the participation and incentive compatibility constraints and they hold with equality so that

$$\eta_{i,t}^1 = (\alpha_2/\alpha_0)^{1/p_{i,t}}.$$

Since $\eta_{i,t} \equiv \eta_{i,t}^2/\eta_{i,t}^1$, we have $\eta_{i,t}^2 = (\alpha_2/\alpha_0)^{1/p_{i,t}}\eta_{i,t}$. Using this result together with the definition of $v_{i,t}$ and the first-order condition yields the expression for the manager's optimal compensation when $\ell_{i,t}^2 = 1$ as:

$$\omega_{i,t}^2 = \rho^{-1}(1 + p_{i,t+1}) \left\{ \log(\alpha_2/\alpha_0)^{1/p_{i,t}} \right.$$

$$\left. + \log[1 + \eta_{i,t}(\alpha_2/\alpha_1)^{1/p_{i,t}} - \eta_{i,t}g(x_{i,t})] \right\}. \tag{7.65}$$

In this case, the manager is required to take on idiosyncratic risk, which cannot be undone by trading in contingent claims. This can be enforced provided the manager's trades are public information.

The optimal compensation in Equation (7.65) consists of two parts. The first part defined as

$$(\rho p_{i,t})^{-1}(1 + p_{i,t+1}) \log(\alpha_2/\alpha_0)^{1/p_{i,t}}$$

is the amount that the manager would be paid if he were required to work diligently and his effort could be observed. The second component

$$\rho^{-1}(1 + p_{i,t+1}) \log\{1 + \eta_i[(\alpha_2/\alpha_1)^{1/p_{i,t}} - g(x_{i,t})]\}$$

is attributable to moral hazard. The variable $\eta_{i,t}$ is the ratio of the Lagrange multipliers in the shareholders' minimization problem. As the shadow value of relaxing the incentive-compatibility constraint relative to the participation constraint approaches zero, this component disappears. Furthermore, $g(x_{i,t})$, the ratio of the probability distributions from shirking relative to working diligently, tends to decline if $x_{i,t}$ increases since it is proportional to $\exp[\sigma^{-1}(\mu_1 - \mu_2)x]$. Thus, managerial compensation is increasing in the measure of firm performance $x_{i,t}$.

2.2.2. Empirical Results

The paper by Margiotta and Miller uses the form of the optimal contract to derive an econometric test of the model. To implement this test, it is assumed that measured compensation, $\tilde{\omega}_{i,t}$, is a noisy measure of actual compensation:

$$\tilde{\omega}_{i,t} = \omega_{i,t} + \epsilon_{i,t},$$

where $\epsilon_{i,t}$ is an independent, identically distributed normal random variable with mean zero and variance σ^2. Notice that we can write the participation constraint, the incentive compatibility constraint, and the optimal contract as:

$$h_{i,t}^1 = \exp[-(\rho\tilde{\omega}_{i,t} + \phi)/(1 + p_{i,t+1})] - (\alpha_0/\alpha_2)^{1/p_{i,t}},$$

$$h_{i,t}^2 = [(\alpha_2/\alpha_1)^{1/p_{i,t}} - g(x_{i,t})] \exp[-(\rho\tilde{\omega}_{i,t} + \phi)/(1 + p_{i,t+1})],$$

$$h_{i,t}^3 = \exp[-(\rho\tilde{\omega}_{i,t} + \phi)/(1 + p_{i,t+1})] - (\alpha_2/\alpha_0)^{1/p_{i,t}}\{1 + $$

$$\eta_{i,t}[(\alpha_2/\alpha_1)^{1/p_{i,t}} - g(x_{i,t})]\},$$

where $\phi = \rho^2\sigma^2/2$. Since utility cannot be measured, we can only identify α_0, α_1 and α_2 up to a factor of proportionality. Thus, let us normalize $\alpha_0 = 1$. The unknown parameters consist of the preference parameters $(\alpha_1, \alpha_2, \rho)$, the variance of the measurement error on compensation, σ^2, and the parameters in $g(x_{i,t})$. Now form the vector of errors, $h_{i,t} \equiv (h_{i,t}^1, h_{i,t}^2, h_{i,t}^3)'$.

The restrictions of the cost-minimization problem that shareholders solve are given by:

$$E_t^2[h_{i,t}] = 0. \tag{7.66}$$

This says that, conditional on the agent working diligently, the participation and incentive-compatibility conditions and the optimal compensation schedule are satisfied for observed compensation and firm returns. The conditions in Equation (7.66) are population orthogonality conditions that allow us to test the null hypothesis that observed compensation levels and firm returns are generated as the outcome of an optimal contract between shareholders and the manager.

We stack these conditions over time as $h_i \equiv (h_{i,1}, \ldots, h_{i,T})'$. It is straightforward to derive a GMM estimator from the vector of errors h_i by considering some $q \times 1$ vector of instruments y_i which have the property that $E(h_i \otimes y_i) = 0$, provided $3q$ is greater or equal to the number of unknown parameters. Notice that this test extends Euler equation-based tests to a setting with private information.

This approach also yields quantitative measures of the importance of moral hazard. The first measure denoted $r_1(p_{i,t})$ is the reservation value of a perfect monitor to shareholders:

$$r_1(p_{i,t}) = E_t^2 \left[\omega_{i,t}^2 - (\rho p_{i,t})^{-1}(1 + p_{i,t}) \log(\alpha_2/\alpha_0) \right]$$

$$= \rho^{-1}(1 + p_{i,t}) \int \log\{1 + \eta_{i,t}[(\alpha_2/\alpha_1)^{1/p_{i,t}} - g(x_{i,t})]\} f_2(x) dx.$$

The first line shows the expected difference between optimally computed compensation $\omega_{i,t}^2$ and what shareholders would pay the manager if effort was perfectly monitored, namely, $(\rho p_{i,t})^{-1}(1 + p_{i,t}) \log(\alpha_2/\alpha_0)$. Since $\eta_{i,t}$ does not depend on ρ, the more risk averse the manager, the more costly the incentive compatibility constraint is to shareholders and the more they are willing to pay for perfect monitoring.

The second measure of the importance of moral hazard is the value the manager places on the nonpecuniary benefits from pursuing his own goals within the firm, which is described in terms of the compensating differential of working diligently versus shirking. It is the amount the manager would be paid to work hard if he was perfectly monitored and his utility remained at the reservation level less $\omega_{i,t}^1$, the shirking wage:

$$r_2(p_{i,t}) = (\rho p_{i,t})^{-1}(1 + p_{i,t}) \log(\alpha_2/\alpha_0) - \omega_{i,t}^1$$

$$= (\rho p_{i,t})^{-1}(1 + p_{i,t}) \log(\alpha_2/\alpha_1).$$

The third measure is based on the income the firm would gain from signing a contract with the manager that stipulated the manager would shirk (by selecting $\ell_{i,t}^j = 1$) and was compensated accordingly. It is defined as the difference between the expected output loss to the firm from the manager pursuing his own goals versus those of the firm:

$$r_3(p_{i,t}) = s_{i,t} \int x[1 - g(x)]f_2(x)dx.$$

Margiotta and Miller use data on compensation packages for the top three executives of 34 firms for the period 1948 through 1977 as well as time series data on stock returns, interest and inflation rates to estimate their model. The authors cannot reject the overidentifying restrictions implied by the orthogonality conditions described in Equation (7.66). Estimates of the alternative measures of moral hazard are obtained using the estimates of the structural parameters. These measures are calculated on an industry basis since the measures $r_j(p_{i,t})$ for $j = 1, 2, 3$ depend on $g(x)$, which is the ratio of the industry-specific probability densities for various effort levels.

They find that the shadow value for directly observing the activities of the CEO is about \$200,000 (in 1967 prices), whereas shareholders would not be willing to pay \$3000 to have his subordinates perfectly monitored. The second measure of the importance of moral hazard is r_2, the additional compensation needed to motivate high effort in the absence of private information. The magnitude of r_2 is very similar to r_1 for both CEOs and non-CEOs. The sum of r_1 and r_2 shows the additional cost of getting managers to work hard rather than shirk. They find that this value barely exceeds \$0.5 million. The final measure r_3 shows the benefits to the firm of getting the manager to work diligently. The magnitude of this measure varies from \$83 million to \$263 million, implying that from the shareholders' point of view, motivating the manager to act in the interests of the firm is cheap compared to the losses incurred from having the manager pursue his own goals on company time.

3. Exercises

1. A Model with Idiosyncratic Risk[10]

Consider an economy consisting of a countable infinity of agents. There are two types of agents, where α is the proportion of agents that are type 1 and $1 - \alpha$ the proportion of agents of type 2. The production function for an agent of type i is:

$$y_{i,t} = \theta_{i,t}\ell_{i,t}, \tag{7.67}$$

---

[10]This exercise is based on Scheinkman and Weiss [301].

where ℓ_i is the labor supply. We assume that the productivity of each agent at time t is defined in terms of an i.i.d. random variable $\theta_{i,t}$ with $\Pr(\theta_{i,t} = 1) = \pi$ and $\Pr(\theta_{i,t} = 0) = 1 - \pi$. The random variables $\theta_{1,t}$ and $\theta_{2,t}$ are *not* independent. If one type is productive (i.e., $\theta_{i,t} = 1$), then the other type is unproductive (i.e, $\theta_{j,t} = 0$ for $j \neq i$). Thus, $\theta_{1,t} + \theta_{2,t} = 1$ for all t.

In a complete contingent claims equilibrium, consumer i solves the problem:

$$\max_{\{c_{i,t}, \ell_{i,t}\}_{t=0}^{\infty}} E_0 \left\{ \sum_{t=0}^{\infty} \beta^t [U(c_{i,t}) - \ell_{i,t}] \right\}$$

subject to

$$E_0 \left\{ \sum_{t=0}^{\infty} \beta^t p_t [c_{i,t} - \theta_{i,t} \ell_{i,t}] \right\}$$

where U is strictly increasing, concave and differentiable and the contingent claims prices have the representation in Equation (7.23).

a) Show that the first-order conditions and market-clearing conditions for a complete contingent claims equilibrium are given by:

$$U'(c_{i,t}) = \lambda_i p_t,$$

$$1 = \lambda_i \theta_{i,t} p_t,$$

$$\alpha c_{1,t} + (1 - \alpha) c_{2,t} = \alpha \theta_{1,t} \ell_{1,t} + (1 - \alpha) \theta_{2,t} \ell_{2,t},$$

where λ_i is the Lagrange multiplier associated with budget constraint of agent i.

b) Show that the expected present value of lifetime earnings of a type 1 agent is:

$$E_0 \left\{ \sum_{t=0}^{\infty} p_t \theta_{1,t} \ell_{1,t} \right\} = \frac{1}{1 - \beta} \frac{\pi \ell_1}{\lambda_1}.$$

c) Define the function g as $g(x) = (U')^{-1}(x)$. Show that the expected present value of the type 1 agent's consumption stream is:

$$E_0 \left\{ \sum_{t=0}^{\infty} p_t c_{1,t} \right\} = \frac{1}{1 - \beta} \frac{\pi g(1)}{\lambda_1} + \frac{1}{1 - \beta} \left[\frac{(1 - \pi)}{\lambda_2} g(\lambda_1 / \lambda_2) \right].$$

Equating the two expressions and using the market-clearing condition when $\theta_{1,t} = 1$, solve for $\ell_1 - g(1)$ to obtain

$$\left(\frac{1-\alpha}{\alpha}\right) g\left(\frac{\lambda_2}{\lambda_1}\right) = \left(\frac{1-\pi}{\pi}\right)\left(\frac{\lambda_1}{\lambda_2}\right) g\left(\frac{\lambda_1}{\lambda_2}\right). \tag{7.68}$$

d) Define $x \equiv \lambda_1/\lambda_2$; then the equilibrium condition equation (7.68) becomes

$$\left(\frac{1-\alpha}{\alpha}\right) g\left(\frac{1}{x}\right) = \left(\frac{1-\pi}{\pi}\right) xg(x). \tag{7.69}$$

Suppose that $\pi = 2/3$ but retain the assumption that $\alpha = 1/2$. Then each period, one half of the agents are productive just as before. Is the expected present value of the lifetime earnings for a type 1 agent equal to that of a type 2 agent?

e) Suppose utility displays constant relative risk aversion so that $U'(c) = c^{-\gamma}$, $\pi = 2/3$ and $\alpha = 1/2$. Using Equation (7.69), show that the solution for x is $x = \left(\frac{1}{2}\right)^{\frac{\gamma}{2-\gamma}}$, the real interest rate r_1 when type 1 agents are productive $(s_t = 1)$ is

$$\frac{1}{1+r_1} = \pi\beta + \beta(1-\pi)x,$$

and the real interest rate r_2 when type 2 agents are productive $(s_t = 2)$ is

$$\frac{1}{1+r_2} = \pi x\beta + \beta(1-\pi).$$

f) Suppose $\pi = 1/2$ and $\alpha = 1/2$. Derive an expression for the real interest rate when type 1's versus type 2's are productive.

g) Comparing your answers to parts e) and f), describe the effects of *ex ante* heterogeneity on aggregate fluctuations for this economy.

2. Borrowing Constraints

Consider an economy populated by equal numbers of two types of consumers. The preferences of consumers of type i, $i = 1, 2$, over stochastic streams of consumption and labor hours are defined by:

$$E_0\left\{\sum_{t=0}^{\infty} \beta^t[\log(c_{i,t}) - \ell_{i,t}]\right\}, \tag{7.70}$$

where $0 < \beta < 1$, $c_{i,t} \geq 0$, $\ell_{i,t} \geq 0$ and E_0 denotes expectation conditional on information at time zero. The production function and the nature of individuals' productivity is the same as in the previous problem with $\pi = 1/2$ and $\alpha = 1/2$.

Suppose that consumers trade in a single asset, the quantity of which has been normalized to one. Initially, type 1 consumers hold $z_{1,0} = x_0$ units and type 2 consumers hold $z_{2,0} = 1 - x_0$ units where $z_{i,t}$ denotes the asset holdings of consumer i at date t. There is a borrowing constraint in that individuals' asset holdings must be nonnegative, $z_{i,t+1} \geq 0$. Let $\{q_t\}_{t=0}^{\infty}$ denote the stochastic process for the price of the asset.

a) The problem of individual i is to choose sequences for consumption, labor supply, and asset holdings to maximize the objective function in Equation (7.70) subject to the constraints:

$$z_{i,t+1} - z_{i,t} = (y_{i,t} - c_{i,t})/q_t,$$

$$y_{i,t} = \theta_{i,t}\ell_{i,t},$$

$$z_{i,t+1} \geq 0, \ell_{i,t} \geq 0, \ c_{i,t} \geq 0.$$

Specify the first-order conditions that type i's consumption, labor supply, and asset holdings must satisfy.

b) Suppose an econometrician uses the average real return on a risk-free nominal bill to measure the rate of time preference. Comment on this procedure in light of your answer to part b).

3. Family Risk-Sharing[11]

Consider a family that consists of K members. Let the utility function for the k'th individual in the i'th family be defined as:

$$E_0 \left\{ \sum_{t=\underline{n}}^{\overline{n}} \beta^t U(\ell_{i,t}^k, c_{i,t}^k, \theta_{i,t}^k) \right\}.$$

Let $I_{i,t}$ denote the set of all possible events that involve members of the i'th family and suppose that members of the family can trade claims that payoffs in events $\bar{S} \in I_{i,t}$. Define the prices of such claims as

$$\bar{\lambda}_i(\bar{S}) = \beta^t \int_{\bar{S} \in I_t} \lambda_{i,t}(s^t) g(s^t) ds^t.$$

---

[11]This exercise is derived from Altonji, Hayashi, and Kotlikoff [9].

a) Show that if the hypothesis of complete family risk-sharing holds, the marginal utility of consumption for the k'th member of the i'th family exhibits a factor structure:

$$U_c(\ell^k_{i,t}, c^k_{i,t}, \theta^k_{i,t}) = \eta^k_i \lambda_{i,t}.$$

b) Using the approach described in Section 1.2, describe how you would test this hypothesis.

c) Suppose the utility function for the k'th member of the i'th household has the form in Equation (7.8). If you regressed the consumption growth of the k'th individual on the change in current labor income for family i and obtained a coefficient that was significantly different from zero, would this be evidence against the hypothesis of family risk-sharing?

4.[12] Suppose that agents live two periods and that per capita consumption takes one of two values, μ or $(1 - \phi)\mu$ where $0 < \phi < 1$, with each state occurring with probability $1/2$. At time zero, agents choose their portfolio. At time 1, the uncertain endowment is realized, the payoff on the portfolio is made, and then agents consume. The portfolio pays -1 in the bad state and $1 + \pi$ in the good state where π is a risk premium.

Assume that all agents are identical. The representative consumer maximizes $EU(c)$. Let R denote the expected payoff on the portfolio so that the first-order condition is $E[RU'(c)] = 0$ which can be written as:

$$(1 + \pi)U'(\mu) - U'[(1 - \phi)\mu] = 0.$$

Let $U = c^{1-\gamma}/(1 - \gamma)$.

Solve for the risk premium π under this assumption.

5. We now introduce heterogeneity and incomplete markets using the setup in Exercise 4. Agents are identical *ex ante* but not *ex post*. In the bad state assume that the fall in aggregate consumption equal to $\phi\mu$ is concentrated among a fraction λ of the population. This implies that in the good state, which occurs with probability $1/2$, the agent consumes μ and the portfolio pays $1 + \pi$. In the bad state the portfolio pays -1 and his consumption is μ with probability $1 - \lambda$ and $(1 - \phi/\lambda)\mu$ with probability λ.

a) Derive the first-order condition and the premium π.

---

[12]This exercise is based on Mankiw [246].

b) Show that the premium depends not only on the size of the aggregate shock ϕ but also on its distribution within the population.

c) Assume that utility is constant relative risk aversion and show that a decrease in λ increases π (so the more concentrated the shock the larger the premium).

6. To derive the form of the valuation function in Equation (7.54), consider first the problem of a manager who is one period away from retirement and who chooses $(c_{i,t}, W_{i,t+1})$ to maximize:

$$-E_t^j \left\{ \alpha_j \exp(-\rho c_{i,t}) + \beta \alpha_k (1 + p_{i,t+1}) \exp \left[\frac{-\rho W_{i,t+1} + q_{i,t+1}}{1 + p_{i,t+1}} \right] \right\}$$

subject to

$$E_t \{ p_t c_t + p_{t+1} W_{i,t+1} \} \le p_t W_{i,t}.$$

Show that the valuation function satisfies:

$$V_{i,t} = -(1 + p_{i,t}) \alpha_j^{1/(1+p_{i,t})} \alpha_k^{p_{i,t}/(1+p_{i,t})} \times$$

$$\exp \left[(-\rho W_{i,t} + q_{i,t})/(1 + p_{i,t}) \right].$$

7. When next period's compensation is random, the manager chooses $(c_{i,t}, W_{i,t+1})$ to maximize:

$$-\alpha_j \exp(-\rho c_{i,t}) +$$

$$\beta \alpha_0 E_t^j \left\{ (1 + p_{i,t+1}) \exp \left[\frac{-\rho W_{i,t+1} + \rho \omega_{i,t} + q_{i,t+1}}{1 + p_{i,t+1}} \right] \right\}$$

subject to

$$E_t \{ p_t c_t + p_{t+1} W_{i,t+1} \} \le p_t W_{i,t}.$$

Show that the result is given by Equation (7.54) with α_k as defined in the text.

References

[1] Abel, A. (1980). "Empirical Investment Equations." *Carnegie-Rochester Conference Series on Public Policy* **12**, pp. 39–91.

[2] Abel, A. (1988). "Stock Prices Under Time-Varying Dividend Risk: An Exact Solution in an Infinite-Horizon General Equilibrium Model." *Journal of Monetary Economics* **22**, pp. 375–393.

[3] Abel, A. and O. Blanchard (1983). "An Intertemporal Model of Saving and Investment." *Econometrica* **51**, pp. 675–692.

[4] Abel, A. and O. Blanchard (1986). "The Present Value of Profits and Cyclical Movements in Investment." *Econometrica* **54**, pp. 249–273.

[5] Abramowitz, M. and I. Stegun (1964). *Handbook of Mathematical Functions: Applied Mathematics Series* **55**. Washington: National Bureau of Standards.

[6] Adler, M. and B. Lehman (1983). "Deviations from Purchasing Power Parity in the Long Run." *Journal of Finance* **38**, pp. 1471–1487.

[7] Aiyagari, S. and M. Gertler (1991). "Asset Returns with Transactions Costs and Uninsured Individual Risk." *Journal of Monetary Economics* **27**, pp. 311–331.

[8] Altonji, J. (1986). "Intertemporal Substitution in Labor Supply: Evidence from Micro Data." *Journal of Political Economy* **94**, pp. S176–S215.

[9] Altonji, J., F. Hayashi, and L. Kotlikoff (1993). "Risk-Sharing Between and Within Families." Unpublished Manuscript, University of Pennsylvania.

[10] Altuğ, S. (1989). "Time-to-Build and Aggregate Fluctuations: Some New Evidence." *International Economic Review* **30**, pp. 889–920.

[11] Altuğ, S. (1993). "Time-to-Build, Delivery Lags, and the Equilibrium Pricing of Capital Goods." *Journal of Money, Credit, and Banking* **25**, pp. 301–319.

[12] Altuğ, S. and R. Miller (1990). "Household Choices in Equilibrium." *Econometrica* **58**, pp. 543–570.

[13] Altuğ, S. and R. Miller (1991). "Human Capital, Aggregate Shocks and Panel Data Estimation." Discussion Paper 48, Institute for Empirical Macroeconomics, Federal Reserve Bank of Minneapolis.

[14] Amemiya, T. (1974). "The Nonlinear Two-Stage Least-Squares Estimator." *Journal of Econometrics* **2**, pp. 105–110.

[15] Andrews, D. (1991). "Heteroscedasticity and Autocorrelation Consistent Covariance Matrix Estimation." *Econometrica* **59**, pp. 817–858.

[16] Arrow, K. (1953). "Le Rôle des Valeurs Boursières pour la Répartition la Meilleure des Risques." *Econométrie*, pp. 41–48, Centre National de la Recherche Scientifique, Paris. Translated as: (1964) "The Role of Securities in the Optimal Allocation of Risk-Bearing." *Review of Economic Studies* **31**, pp. 91–96.

[17] Arrow, K. (1964). "Comment on 'The Portfolio Approach to the Demand for Money and Other Assets.'" by J. Duesenberry, *Review of Economics and Statistics* **45**, 24–27.

[18] Arrow, K. and G. Debreu (1954). "Existence of an Equilibrium for a Competitive Economy." *Econometrica* **22**, pp. 265–290.

[19] Atkeson, A. and R. Lucas (1992). "On Efficient Distribution with Private Information." *Review of Economic Studies* **59**, pp. 427–454.

[20] Atkinson, K. (1976). *A Survey of Numerical Methods for the Solution of Fredholm Integral Equations of the Second Kind.* Philadelphia: Society for Industrial and Applied Mathematics.

[21] Atkinson, K. (1989). *An Introduction to Numerical Analysis,* 2nd ed. New York: John Wiley and Sons.

[22] Backus, D., A. Gregory, and S. Zin (1989). "Risk Premiums in the Term Structure: Evidence from Artificial Economies." *Journal of Monetary Economics* **24**, pp. 371–399.

[23] Baillie, R. and T. Bollerslev (1989). "The Message in Daily Exchange Rates: A Conditional Variance Tale." *Journal of Business and Economic Statistics* **7**, pp. 297–305.

[24] Baillie, R., R. Lippens, and P. McMahon (1983). "Testing Rational Expectations and Efficiency in the Foreign Exchange Market." *Econometrica* **51**, pp. 553–563.

[25] Barsky, R. (1989). "Why Don't Prices of Stocks and Bonds Move Together?" *American Economic Review* **79**, pp. 1132–1145.

[26] Becker, R. (1985). "Capital Income Taxation and Perfect Foresight." *Journal of Public Economics* **26**, pp. 147–167.

[27] Benninga, S. and A. Protopapadakis (1991). "The Stock Market Premium, Production, and Relative Risk Aversion." *American Economic Review* **81**, pp. 591–599.

[28] Benveniste, L. and J. Scheinkman (1979). "On the Differentiability of the Value Function in Dynamic Models of Economics." *Econometrica* **47**, pp. 727–732.

[29] Bertsekas, D. (1976). *Dynamic Programming and Stochastic Control.* New York: Academic Press.

[30] Bertsekas, D. and S. Shreve (1978). *Stochastic Optimal Control: The Discrete Time Case.* New York: Academic Press.

[31] Bewley, T. (1977). "The Permanent Income Hypothesis: A Theoretical Formulation." *Journal of Economic Theory* **16**, pp. 252–292.

[32] Bewley, T. (1982). "Thoughts on the Intertemporal Asset Pricing Model." Unpublished Manuscript, Northwestern University.

[33] Bhattacharya, S. (1979). "Imperfect Information, Dividend Policy, and 'The Bird in the Hand' Fallacy." *Bell Journal of Economics* **10**, pp. 259–270.

[34] Bickel, P. and D. Freedman (1981). "Some Asymptotic Theory for the Bootstrap." *Annals of Statistics* **9**, pp. 1196–1217.

[35] Bizer, D. and K. Judd (1989). "Taxation and Uncertainty." *American Economic Review* **79**, pp. 331–336.

[36] Blackwell, D. (1965). "Discounted Dynamic Programming." *Annals of Mathematical Statistics* **36**, pp. 226–235.

[37] Blundell, R., S. Bond, M. Devereux, and F. Schiantarelli (1992). "Investment and Tobin's Q: Evidence from Company Panel Data." *Journal of Econometrics* **51**, pp. 233–257.

[38] Bollerslev, T. (1986). "Generalized Autoregressive Conditional Heteroskedasticity." *Journal of Econometrics* **31**, pp. 307–327.

[39] Bollerslev, T., R. Chou, and K. Kroner (1992). "ARCH Modeling in Finance: A Review of the Theory and Empirical Evidence." *Journal of Econometrics* **52**, pp. 5–59.

[40] Bollerslev, T., R. Engle, and J. Wooldridge (1988). "A Capital Asset Pricing Model with Time-Varying Covariances." *Journal of Political Economy* **96**, pp. 116–131.

[41] Boyd, J. (1988). "Capital Theory 1: Existence, Characterization and Stability." Unpublished Manuscript, University of Rochester.

[42] Breeden, D. (1979). "An Intertemporal Asset Pricing Model with Stochastic Consumption and Investment Opportunities." *Journal of Financial Economics* **7**, pp. 265–296.

[43] Breiman, L. (1968). *Probability.* Reading, MA: Addison-Wesley.

[44] Brock, W. (1979). "An Integration of Stochastic Growth Theory and The Theory of Finance, Part I: The Growth Model." In J. Green and J. Scheinkman (eds.), *General Equilibrium, Growth, and Trade.* New York: Academic Press, pp. 165–192.

[45] Brock, W. (1982). "Asset Prices in a Production Economy." In J. McCall (ed.), *The Economics of Information and Uncertainty.* Chicago: University of Chicago Press, pp. 1–43.

[46] Brock, W. (1986). "Distinguishing Random and Deterministic Systems: Abridged Version." *Journal of Economic Theory* **40**, pp. 168–195.

[47] Brock, W. (1988). "Nonlinearity and Complex Dynamics in Economics and Finance." In P. Anderson, K. Arrow, and D. Pines (eds.), *The Economy as an Evolving Complex System.* Santa Fe Institute Studies in the Sciences of Complexity, Vol. 5. Redwood City, CA: Addison-Wesley, pp. 77–97.

[48] Brock, W. and L. Mirman (1972). "Optimal Economic Growth and Uncertainty: The Discounted Case." *Journal of Economic Theory* **4**, pp. 479–513.

[49] Brock, W. and L. Mirman (1973). "Optimal Economic Growth and Uncertainty: The No Discounting Case." *International Economic Review* **14**, pp. 560–573.

[50] Brock, W. and S. Turnovsky (1981). "The Analysis of Macroeconomic Policies in Perfect Foresight Equilibrium." *International Economic Review* **22**, pp. 179–209.

[51] Brock, W., W. Dechert, and J. Scheinkman (1987). "A Test for Independence Based on the Correlation Dimension." Unpublished Manuscript, University of Wisconsin, Madison.

[52] Brock, W., D. Hsieh, and B. LeBaron (1991). *Nonlinear Dynamics, Chaos, and Instability.* Cambridge, MA: MIT Press.

[53] Brock, W., J. Lakonishok, and B. LeBaron (1992). "Simple Technical Trading Rules and the Stochastic Properties of Stock Returns." *Journal of Finance* **47**, pp. 1731–1764.

[54] Brown, D. (1988). "Implications of Nonmarketable Income for Consumption-Based Models of Asset Pricing." *Journal of Finance* **43**, pp. 867–880.

[55] Brown, D. and M. Gibbons (1985). "A Simple Econometric Approach for Utility-Based Asset Pricing Models." *Journal of Finance* **40**, pp. 359–381.

[56] Browning, M., A. Deaton, and M. Irish (1985). "A Profitable Approach to Labor Supply and Commodity Demands over the Life-Cycle." *Econometrica* **53**, pp. 503–543.

[57] Calvo, G. (1983). "Staggered Contracts and Exchange Rate Policy." In J. Frenkel (ed.), *Exchange Rates and International Macroeconomics.* Chicago: University of Chicago Press, pp. 235–252.

[58] Calvo, G. and C. Rodriguez (1977). "A Model of Exchange Rate Determination Under Currency Substitution and Rational Expectations." *Journal of Political Economy* **85**, pp. 617–625.

[59] Campbell, J. (1986). "Bond and Stock Returns in a Simple Exchange Model." *Quarterly Journal of Economics* **101**, pp. 785–803.

[60] Campbell, J. and R. Clarida (1987). "The Dollar and Real Interest Rates." *Carnegie-Rochester Conference Series on Public Policy* **27**, pp. 103–139.

[61] Campbell, J. and R. Clarida (1987). "The Term Structure of Euromarket Interest Rates: An Empirical Investigation." *Journal of Monetary Economics* **19**, pp. 25–44.

[62] Campbell, J. and N. Mankiw (1987). "Are Output Fluctuations Transitory?" *Quarterly Journal of Economics* **102**, pp. 857–880.

[63] Campbell, J. and R. Shiller (1987). "Cointegration and Tests of Present Value Models." *Journal of Political Economy* **95**, pp. 1062–1088.

[64] Campbell, J. and R. Shiller (1988). "Stock Prices, Earnings, and Expected Dividends." *Journal of Finance* **43**, pp. 661–676.

[65] Campbell, J. and R. Shiller (1989). "The Dividend-Price Ratio and Expectations of Future Dividends and Discount Factors." *Review of Financial Studies* **1**, pp. 175–228.

[66] Cass, D. (1965). "Optimum Growth in an Aggregative Model of Capital Accumulation." *Review of Economic Studies* **32**, pp. 233–240.

[67] Chamberlain, G. (1984). "Panel Data." In Z. Griliches and M. Intriligator (eds.), *Handbook of Econometrics, Vol. 2.* Amsterdam: North-Holland, pp. 1247–1318 (Chapter 22).

[68] Chamberlain, G. and M. Rothschild (1983). "Arbitrage, Factor Structure, and Mean-Variance Analysis on Large Asset Markets." *Econometrica* **51**, pp. 1281–1304.

[69] Clark, P. (1970). "A Subordinated Stochastic Process Model for Cotton Futures." Ph.D. Dissertation, Harvard University.

[70] Clark, P. (1973). "A Subordinated Stochastic Process Model with Finite Variance for Speculative Prices." *Econometrica* **41**, pp. 135–155.

[71] Cochrane, J. (1991). "A Simple Test of Consumption Insurance." *Journal of Political Economy* **99**, pp. 957–976.

[72] Cochrane, J. and L. Hansen (1992). "Asset Pricing Explorations in Macroeconomics." *NBER Macroeconomics Annual 1992*, pp. 115–165.

[73] Coleman, W. (1991). "Equilibrium in a Production Economy with an Income Tax." *Econometrica* **59**, pp. 1091–1104.

[74] Coleman, W., C. Gilles, and P. Labadie (1992). "The Liquidity Premium in Average Interest Rates." *Journal of Monetary Economics* **30**, pp. 449–465.

[75] Constantinides, G. (1982). "Intertemporal Asset Pricing with Heterogeneous Consumers and Without Demand Aggregation." *Journal of Business* **55**, pp. 253–267.

[76] Constantinides, G. (1986). "Capital Market Equilibrium with Transaction Costs." *Journal of Political Economy* **94**, pp. 842–862.

[77] Constantinides, G. (1990). "Habit Formation: A Resolution of the Equity Premium Puzzle." *Journal of Political Economy* **98**, pp. 519–543.

[78] Constantinides, G. and D. Duffie (1992). "Asset Pricing with Heterogeneous Consumers." Unpublished Manuscript, Stanford University.

[79] Cryer, C. (1982). *Numerical Functional Analysis.* New York: Oxford University Press.

[80] Cumby, R. and M. Obstfeld (1984). "International Interest-Rate and Price-Level Linkages Under Flexible Exchange Rates: A Review of Recent Evidence." In J. Bilson and R. Marston (eds.), *Exchange Rate Theory and Practice.* Chicago: University of Chicago Press for the National Bureau of Economic Research.

[81] Danthine, J.-P. and J. Donaldson (1981). "Stochastic Properties of Fast vs. Slow Growing Economies." *Econometrica* **49**, pp. 1007–1033.

[82] Danthine, J.-P. and J. Donaldson (1985). "A Note on the Effects of Capital Income Taxation on the Dynamics of a Competitive Economy." *Journal of Public Economics* **28**, pp. 255–265.

[83] Danthine, J.-P., J. Donaldson, and R. Mehra (1983). "On the Impact of Shock Persistence on the Dynamics of a Recursive Economy." *European Economic Review* **21**, pp. 147–166.

[84] Danthine, J.-P., J. Donaldson, and R. Mehra (1989). "On Some Computational Aspects of Equilibrium Business Cycle Theory." *Journal of Economic Dynamics and Control* **13**, pp. 449–470.

[85] Danthine, J.-P., J. Donaldson, and R. Mehra (1992). "The Equity Premium and the Allocation of Income Risk." *Journal of Economic Dynamics and Control* **16**, pp. 509–532.

[86] Deaton, A. and G. Laroque (1992). "On the Behavior of Commodity Prices." *Review of Economic Studies* **59**, pp. 1–24.

[87] Debreu, G. (1954). "Valuation Equilibrium and Pareto Optimum." *Proceedings of the National Academy of Sciences*, **40**, pp. 588–592.

[88] Debreu, G. (1959). *Theory of Value*. New Haven: Yale University Press.

[89] DeGroot, M. (1970). *Optimal Statistical Decisions*. New York: McGraw-Hill.

[90] Devine, T. and N. Kiefer (1991). *Empirical Labor Economics: The Search Approach*. Oxford: Oxford University Press.

[91] Diamond, D. (1984). "Financial Intermediation and Delegated Monitoring." *Review of Economic Studies* **51**, pp. 393–414.

[92] Diamond, D. and P. Dybvig (1983). "Bank Runs, Deposit Insurance and Liquidity." *Journal of Political Economy* **91**, pp. 401–419.

[93] Diamond, P. and J. Stiglitz (1974). "Increases in Risk and in Risk Aversion." *Journal of Economic Theory* **8**, pp. 337–360.

[94] Diebold, F. (1987). *Empirical Modeling of Exchange Rates*. Berlin: Springer-Verlag.

[95] Diebold, F. and P. Pauly (1988). "Endogenous Risk in a Portfolio Balance Rational Expectations Model of the Deutschmark-Dollar Rate." *European Economic Review* **32**, pp. 27–53.

[96] Domowitz, I. and C. Hakkio (1985). "Conditional Variance and the Risk Premium in the Foreign Exchange Market." *Journal of International Economics* **19**, pp. 47–66.

[97] Donaldson, J. and R. Mehra (1983). "Stochastic Growth with Correlated Production Shocks." *Journal of Economic Theory* **29**, pp. 282–312.

[98] Donaldson, J. and R. Mehra (1984). "Comparative Dynamics of an Equilibrium Intertemporal Asset Pricing Model." *Review of Economic Studies* **51**, pp. 491–508.

[99] Dornbusch, R. (1976). "Expectations and Exchange Rate Dynamics." *Journal of Political Economy* **84**, pp. 1161–1176.

[100] Dothan, M. (1990). *Prices in Financial Markets.* New York: Oxford University Press.

[101] Dotsey, M. (1990). "The Economic Effects of Production Taxes in a Stochastic Growth Model." *American Economic Review* **80**, pp. 1168–1182.

[102] Duffie, D. (1988). *Security Markets: Stochastic Models.* Boston: Academic Press.

[103] Duffie, D. (1989). *Futures Markets.* Englewood Cliffs, NJ: Prentice-Hall.

[104] Duffie, D. (1992). *Dynamic Asset Pricing Theory.* Princeton: Princeton University Press.

[105] Duffie, D. and T. Sun (1990). "Transactions Costs and Portfolio Choice in a Discrete-Continuous-Time Setting." *Journal of Economic Dynamics and Control* **14**, pp. 35–51.

[106] Dufour, J.-M., E. Ghysels, and A. Hall (1991). "Generalized Predictive Tests and Structural Change Analysis in Econometrics." Unpublished Manuscript, Université de Montréal.

[107] Dumas, B. and E. Luciano (1991). "An Exact Solution to a Dynamic Portfolio Choice Problem Under Transactions Costs." *Journal of Finance* **46**, pp. 577–595.

[108] Dunn, K. and K. Singleton (1986). "Modeling the Term Structure of Interest Rates Under Non-Separable Utility and Durability of Goods." *Journal of Financial Economics* **17**, pp. 27–55.

[109] Efron, B. (1982). *The Jackknife, the Bootstrap and Other Resampling Plans.* Philadelphia: Society for Industrial and Applied Mathematics.

[110] Eichenbaum, M. and L. Christiano (1990). "Unit Roots in Real GNP: Do We Know and Do We Care?" *Carnegie-Rochester Conference Series on Public Policy* **32**, pp. 7–62.

[111] Eichenbaum, M. and L. Hansen (1990). "Estimating Models with Intertemporal Substitution Using Aggregate Time Series Data." *Journal of Business and Economic Statistics* **8**, pp. 53–69.

[112] Eichenbaum, M. and K. Singleton (1986). "Do Equilibrium Real Business Cycle Theories Explain Postwar U.S. Business Cycles?" *NBER Macroeconomics Annual 1986*, pp. 91–135.

[113] Eichenbaum, M., L. Hansen, and K. Singleton (1988). "A Time Series Analysis of Representative Agent Models of Consumption and Leisure Choice Under Uncertainty." *Quarterly Journal of Economics* **103**, pp. 51–78.

[114] Engel, C. (1992). "The Risk Premium and the Liquidity Premium in Foreign Exchange Markets." *International Economic Review* **33**, pp. 871–879.

[115] Engle, R. (1982). "Autoregressive Conditional Heteroskedasticity with Estimates of the Variance of U.K. Inflation." *Econometrica* **50**, pp. 987–1008.

[116] Engle, R. and T. Bollerslev (1986). "Modeling the Persistence of Conditional Variances." *Econometric Reviews* **5**, pp. 1–50.

[117] Engle, R. and C. Granger (1987). "Co-integration and Error Correction: Representation, Estimation and Testing." *Econometrica* **55**, pp. 251–276.

[118] Engle, R., D. Lilien, and R. Robins (1987). "Estimating Time Varying Risk Premia in the Term Structure: The ARCH-M Model." *Econometrica* **55**, pp. 391–407.

[119] Epps, T. and M. Epps (1976). "The Stochastic Dependence of Security Price Changes and Transaction Volumes: Implications for the Mixture-of-Distributions Hypothesis." *Econometrica* **44**, pp. 305–321.

[120] Epstein, L. and S. Zin (1989). "Substitution, Risk Aversion, and the Temporal Behavior of Consumption and Asset Returns: A Theoretical Framework." *Econometrica* **57**, pp. 937–969.

[121] Epstein, L. and S. Zin (1990). "First-Order Risk Aversion and the Equity Premium Puzzle." *Journal of Monetary Economics* **26**, pp. 387–407.

[122] Epstein, L. and S. Zin (1991). "Substitution, Risk Aversion, and the Temporal Behavior of Consumption and Asset Returns: An Empirical Analysis." *Journal of Political Economy* **99**, pp. 263–286.

[123] Fama, E. (1965). "The Behavior of Stock Market Prices." *Journal of Business* **38**, pp. 34–105.

[124] Fama, E. (1984). "Forward and Spot Exchange Rates." *Journal of Monetary Economics* **14**, pp. 319–338.

[125] Fama, E. and K. French (1988). "Permanent and Temporary Components of Stock Prices." *Journal of Political Economy* **96**, pp. 246–273.

[126] Fama, E. and G. Schwert (1977). "Asset Returns and Inflation." *Journal of Financial Economics* **5**, pp. 115–146.

[127] Ferguson, T. (1958). "A Method of Generating Best Asymptotically Normal Estimates with Application to the Estimation of Bacterial Densities." *Annals of Mathematical Statistics* **29**, pp. 1046–1062.

[128] Ferson, W. and G. Constantinides (1991). "Habit Persistence and Durability in Aggregate Consumption." *Journal of Financial Economics* **29**, pp. 199–240.

[129] Ferson, W. and C. Harvey (1992). "Seasonality and Consumption-Based Asset Pricing." *Journal of Finance* **47**, pp. 511–552.

[130] Finn, M., D. Hoffman, and D. Schlagenhauf (1990). "Intertemporal Asset-Pricing Relationships in Barter and Monetary Economies: An Empirical Analysis." *Journal of Monetary Economics* **25**, pp. 431–451.

[131] Fischer, S. (1975). "The Demand for Index Bonds." *Journal of Political Economy* **83**, pp. 509–534.

[132] Flavin, M. (1981). "The Adjustment of Consumption to Changing Expectations About Future Income." *Journal of Political Economy* **89**, pp. 974–1009.

[133] Flavin, M. (1983). "Excess Volatility in the Financial Markets: A Reassessment of the Empirical Evidence." *Journal of Political Economy* **91**, pp. 929–956.

[134] Freedman, D. (1981). "Bootstrapping Regression Models." *Annals of Statistics* **9**, pp. 1218–1228.

[135] Freedman, D. (1984). "On Bootstrapping Two-Stage Least-Squares Estimates in Stationary Linear Models." *Annals of Statistics* **12**, pp. 827–842.

[136] Freedman, D. and S. Peters (1984). "Bootstrapping an Econometric Model: Some Empirical Results." *Journal of Business and Economic Statistics* **2**, pp. 150–158.

[137] Friedman, M. (1956). *A Theory of the Consumption Function.* Princeton: Princeton University Press.

[138] Froot, K. and J. Frankel (1989). "Forward Discount Bias: Is It an Exchange Risk Premium?" *Quarterly Journal of Economics* **104**, pp. 139–161.

[139] Fudenberg, D., B. Holmstrom, and P. Milgrom (1990). "Short-Term Contracts and Long-Term Agency Relationships." *Journal of Economic Theory* **51**, pp. 1–31.

[140] Fuerst, T. (1992). "Liquidity, Loanable Funds, and Real Activity." *Journal of Monetary Economics* **29**, pp. 3–24.

[141] von Furstenberg, G. (1977). "Corporate Investment: Does Market Valuation Matter in the Aggregate?" *Brookings Papers on Economic Activity*, pp. 347–397.

[142] Gallant, A. (1977). "Three-Stage Least-Squares Estimation for a System of Simultaneous, Nonlinear, Implicit Equations." *Journal of Econometrics* **5**, pp. 71–88.

[143] Gallant, A. (1987). *Nonlinear Statistical Models*. New York: John Wiley and Sons.

[144] Gallant, A. and H. White (1988). *A Unified Theory of Estimation and Inference for Nonlinear Dynamic Models*. New York: Basil Blackwell.

[145] Gallant, A., D. Hsieh, and G. Tauchen (1991). "On Fitting a Recalcitrant Series: The Pound/Dollar Exchange Rate, 1974–1983." In W. Barnett, J. Powell, and G. Tauchen (eds.), *Nonparametric and Semiparametric Methods in Econometrics and Statistics: Proceedings of the Fifth International Symposium in Economic Theory and Econometrics*. Cambridge: Cambridge University Press, pp. 199–240.

[146] Ghysels, E. and A. Hall (1990). "Are Consumption-Based Intertemporal Asset Pricing Models Structural?" *Journal of Econometrics* **45**, pp. 121–139.

[147] Ghysels, E. and A. Hall (1990). "A Test for Structural Stability of Euler Conditions Parameters Estimated via the Generalized Method of Moments Estimator." *International Economic Review* **31**, pp. 355–364.

[148] Gilles, C. and S. LeRoy (1991). "Econometric Aspects of the Variance-Bounds Tests: A Survey." *Review of Financial Studies* **4**, pp. 753–791.

[149] Giovannini, A. and P. Jorion (1987). "Interest Rates and Risk Premia in the Stock Market and in the Foreign Exchange Market." *Journal of International Money and Finance* **6**, pp. 107–123.

[150] Giovannini, A. and P. Jorion (1989). "The Time Variation of Risk and Return in the Foreign Exchange and Stock Markets." *Journal of Finance* **44**, pp. 307–325.

[151] Giovannini, A. and P. Labadie (1991). "Asset Prices and Interest Rates in Cash-in-Advance Models." *Journal of Political Economy* **99**, pp. 1215–1251.

[152] Gittins, J. and D. Jones (1974). "A Dynamic Allocation Index for the Sequential Design of Experiments." In J. Gani, K. Sarkadi, and I. Vineze (eds.), *Progress in Statistics*. Amsterdam: North-Holland.

[153] Golub, G. and J. Welsch (1969). "Calculation of Gaussian Quadrature Rules." *Mathematics of Computation* **23**, pp. 221–230.

[154] Gorman, T. (1953). "Community Preference Fields." *Econometrica* **21**, pp. 63–80.

[155] Gorman, T. (1980). "A Possible Procedure for Analyzing Quality Differentials in the Egg Market." *Review of Economic Studies* **47**, pp. 843–846.

[156] Gould, J.(1968). "Adjustment Costs in the Theory of the Investment of the Firm." *Review of Economic Studies* **35**, pp. 47–55.

[157] Granger, C. and A. Andersen (1978). *An Introduction to Bilinear Time Series Models*. Gottingen: Vandenhoeck & Ruprecht.

[158] Granger, C. and P. Newbold (1986). *Forecasting Economic Time Series*, 2nd ed. San Diego: Academic Press.

[159] Green, E. (1987). "Lending and the Smoothing of Uninsurable Income." In E. Prescott and N. Wallace (eds.), *Contractual Arrangements for Intertemporal Trade*. Minneapolis, MN: University of Minnesota Press.

[160] Greene, W. (1993). *Econometric Analysis*, 2nd ed. New York: McMillan.

[161] Greenwood, J. and S. Williamson (1989). "International Financial Intermediation and Aggregate Fluctuations Under Alternative Exchange Rate Regimes." *Journal of Monetary Economics* **23**, pp. 401–431.

[162] Grilli, V. and G. Kaminsky (1991). "Nominal Exchange Rate Regimes and the Real Exchange Rate: Evidence from the United States and Great Britain, 1885–1986." *Journal of Monetary Economics* **27**, pp. 191–212.

[163] Grossman, S. (1976). "On the Efficiency of Competitive Stock Markets Where Traders Have Diverse Information." *Journal of Finance* **31**, pp. 573–585.

[164] Grossman, S. and O. Hart (1983). "An Analysis of the Principal-Agent Problem." *Econometrica* **51**, pp. 7–45.

[165] Grossman, S. and G. Laroque (1990). "Asset Pricing and Optimal Portfolio Choice in the Presence of Illiquid Durable Consumption Goods." *Econometrica* **58**, pp. 25–51.

[166] Grossman, S. and R. Shiller (1981). "The Determinants of the Variability of Stock Market Prices." *American Economic Review Proceedings* **71**, pp. 222–227.

[167] Grossman, S. and J. Stiglitz (1980). "On the Impossibility of Informationally-Efficient Markets." *American Economic Review* **70**, pp. 393–408.

[168] Grossman, S., A. Melino, and R. Shiller (1987). "Estimating the Continuous-Time Consumption-Based Asset Pricing Model." *Journal of Business and Economic Statistics* **5**, pp. 315–327.

[169] Hakkio, C. (1981). "Expectations and the Forward Exchange Rate." *International Economic Review* **22**, pp. 663–678.

[170] Hall, R. (1978). "Stochastic Implications of the Life Cycle–Permanent Income Hypothesis: Theory and Evidence." *Journal of Political Economy* **86**, pp. 971–987.

[171] Hansen, G. (1985). "Indivisible Labor and the Business Cycle." *Journal of Monetary Economics* **16**, pp. 309–327.

[172] Hansen, L. (1982). "Large Sample Properties of Generalized Method of Moments Estimators." *Econometrica* **50**, pp. 1029–1054.

[173] Hansen, L. and R. Hodrick (1980). "Forward Exchange Rates as Optimal Predictors of Future Spot Rates: An Econometric Analysis." *Journal of Political Economy* **88**, pp. 829–853.

[174] Hansen, L. and R. Hodrick (1983). "Risk Averse Speculation in the Forward Foreign Exchange Market: An Econometric Analysis of Linear Models." In J. Frenkel (ed.), *Exchange Rates and International Macroeconomics*. Chicago: University of Chicago Press for the National Bureau of Economic Research, pp. 113–152.

[175] Hansen, L. and R. Jagannathan (1991). "Implications of Security Market Data for Models of Dynamic Economies." *Journal of Political Economy* **99**, pp. 225–262.

[176] Hansen, L. and T. Sargent (1980). "Formulating and Estimating Dynamic Linear Rational Expectations Models, *Journal of Economic Dynamics and Control* **2**, pp. 7–46.

[177] Hansen, L. and K. Singleton (1982). "Generalized Instrumental Variables Estimation of Nonlinear Rational Expectations Models." *Econometrica* **50**, pp. 1269–1286.

[178] Hansen, L. and K. Singleton (1983). "Stochastic Consumption, Risk Aversion and the Temporal Behavior of Asset Returns." *Journal of Political Economy* **91**, pp. 249–265.

[179] Harris, M. (1987). *Dynamic Economic Analysis.* New York: Oxford University Press.

[180] Harrison, J. and D. Kreps (1979). "Martingales and Arbitrage in Multiperiod Securities Markets." *Journal of Economic Theory* **20**, pp. 381–408.

[181] Hart, O. (1979). "On Shareholder Unanimity in Large Stock Market Economies." *Econometrica* **47**, pp. 1057–1083.

[182] Harvey, A. (1981). *Time Series Models.* New York: John Wiley and Sons.

[183] Hayashi, F. (1982). "Tobin's Marginal q and Average q: A Neoclassical Interpretation." *Econometrica* **50**, pp. 213–224.

[184] Hayashi, F. (1985). "Tests for Liquidity Constraints: A Critical Survey and Some New Observations." In T. Bewley (ed.), *Advances in Econometrics: Fifth World Congress, Vol. 2.* Cambridge: Cambridge University Press.

[185] Hayashi, F. and T. Inoue (1991). "The Relation Between Firm Growth and Q with Multiple Capital Goods: Theory and Evidence from Panel Data on Japanese Firms." *Econometrica* **59**, pp. 731–753.

[186] He, H. and D. Modest (1992). "Market Frictions and Consumption-Based Asset Pricing." Unpublished Manuscript, University of California, Berkeley.

[187] Heaton, J. and D. Lucas (1992). "The Effects of Incomplete Insurance Markets and Trading Costs in a Consumption-Based Asset Pricing Model." *Journal of Economic Dynamics and Control* **16**, pp. 601–620.

[188] Helpman, E. and A. Razin (1984). "The Role of Saving and Investment in Exchange Rate Determination Under Alternative Monetary Mechanisms." *Journal of Monetary Economics* **13**, pp. 307–325.

[189] Hodrick, R. (1987). *The Empirical Evidence on the Efficiency of Forward and Futures Foreign Exchange Markets.* London: Harwood Academic Publishers.

[190] Hodrick, R. (1989). "Risk, Uncertainty, and Exchange Rates." *Journal of Monetary Economics* **23**, pp. 433–459.

[191] Hodrick, R. and S. Srivastava (1986). "The Covariation of Risk Premiums and Expected Future Spot Exchange Rates." *Journal of International Money and Finance* **5**, pp. 5–21.

[192] Hodrick, R., N. Kocherlakota, and D. Lucas (1991). "The Variability of Velocity in Cash-in-Advance Models." *Journal of Political Economy* **99**, pp. 358–384.

[193] Holmstrom, B. (1979). "Moral Hazard and Observability." *Bell Journal of Economics* **10**, pp. 74–91.

[194] Holmstrom, B. (1982). "Moral Hazard in Teams." *Bell Journal of Economics* **13**, pp. 234–240.

[195] Hotz, V. and R. Miller (1993). "Conditional Choice Probabilities and the Estimation of Dynamic Models." *Review of Economic Studies* **60**, pp. 497–529.

[196] Hotz, V., F. Kydland, and G. Sedlacek (1988). "Intertemporal Preferences and Labor Supply." *Econometrica* **56**, pp. 335–360.

[197] Hotz, V., R. Miller, S. Sanders, and J. Smith (1993). "A Simulation Estimator for Dynamic Models of Discrete Choice." *Review of Economic Studies* **61**, pp. 265–289.

[198] Hsieh, D. (1984). "Tests of Rational Expectations and No Risk Premium in Forward Exchange Markets." *Journal of International Economics* **17**, pp. 173–184.

[199] Hsieh, D. (1988). "The Statistical Properties of Daily Foreign Exchange Rates: 1974–1983." *Journal of International Economics* **24**, pp. 129–145.

[200] Huang, C. and R. Litzenberger (1988). *Foundations of Financial Economics.* Amsterdam: North-Holland.

[201] Huizinga, J. (1987). "An Empirical Investigation of the Long-run Behavior of Real Exchange Rates." *Carnegie-Rochester Conference Series on Public Policy* **27**, pp. 149–214.

[202] Hull, J. (1993). *Options, Futures, and Other Derivative Securities,* 2nd ed. Englewood Cliffs, NJ: Prentice-Hall.

[203] Jaffe, J. and G. Mandelker (1976). "The 'Fisher Effect' for Risky Assets: An Empirical Investigation." *Journal of Finance* **31**, pp. 447–458.

[204] Jaffe, J. and G. Mandelker (1979). "Inflation and the Holding Period Returns on Bonds." *Journal of Financial and Quantitative Analysis* **14**, pp. 959–979.

[205] Jarrow, R. (1988). *Finance Theory.* Englewood Cliffs, NJ: Prentice-Hall.

[206] Jensen, M. and W. Meckling (1976). "Theory of the Firm: Managerial Behavior, Agency Costs and Ownership Structure." *Journal of Financial Economics* **3**, pp. 305–360.

[207] Jeong, J. and G. Maddala (1993). "A Perspective on Application of Bootstrap Methods in Econometrics." In G. Maddala, C. Rao, and H. Vinod (eds.), *Handbook of Statistics, Vol. 11.* Amsterdam: North-Holland.

[208] Jones, L. and R. Manuelli (1990). "A Convex Model of Equilibrium Growth: Theory and Policy Implications." *Journal of Political Economy* **98**, pp. 1008–1038.

[209] Jorgenson, D. and J. Laffont (1974). "Efficient Estimation of Nonlinear Simultaneous Equations Models with Additive Disturbances." *Annals of Economic and Social Measurement* **3**, pp. 615–640.

[210] Judd, K. (1985). "Redistributive Taxation in a Simple Perfect Foresight Model." *Journal of Public Economics* **28**, pp. 59–83.

[211] Judd, K. (1985). "Short-Run Analysis of Fiscal Policy in a Simple Perfect Foresight Model." *Journal of Political Economy* **93**, pp. 298–319.

[212] Judd, K. (1987). "Debt and Distortionary Taxation in a Simple Perfect Foresight Model." *Journal of Monetary Economics* **20**, pp. 51–72.

[213] Judd, K. (1987). "The Welfare Cost of Factor Taxation in a Simple Perfect-Foresight Model." *Journal of Political Economy* **95**, pp. 675–709.

[214] Judd, K. (1991). "Numerical Methods in Economics." Unpublished Manuscript, Hoover Institution.

[215] Kareken, J. and N. Wallace (1981). "On the Indeterminancy of Equilibrium Exchange Rates." *Quarterly Journal of Economics* **96**, pp. 207–222.

[216] Kim, E. (1989). "Discussion: Optimal Capital Structure in Miller's Equilibrium." In S. Bhattacharya and G. Constantinides (eds.), *Financial Markets and Incomplete Information.* Totowa, NJ: Rowman and Littlefield Publishers.

[217] Kimball, Miles S. (1990). "Precautionary Saving in the Small and in the Large." *Econometrica* **58**, pp. 53–73.

[218] Kleidon, A. (1986). "Bias in Small Sample Tests of Stock Price Rationality." *Journal of Business* **59**, pp. 237–261.

[219] Kleidon, A. (1986). "Variance Bounds Tests and Stock Price Valuation Models." *Journal of Political Economy* **94**, pp. 953–1001.

[220] Koopmans, T. (1965). "On the Concept of Optimal Economic Growth." In Semaine d'Étude sur le rôle de l'analysis économétrique dans la formulation de plans de développement, 225–300, Pontificau Academiae Scientiarum Scropta Varia, No. 28, Vatican.

[221] Kreps, D. and E. Porteus (1978). "Temporal Resolution of Uncertainty and Dynamic Choice Theory." *Econometrica* **46**, pp. 185–200.

[222] Kreyszig, E. (1978). *Introductory Functional Analysis with Applications.* New York: John Wiley and Sons.

[223] Kydland, F. and E. Prescott (1982). "Time-to-Build and Aggregate Fluctuations." *Econometrica* **50**, pp. 1345–1370.

[224] Labadie, P. (1989). "Stochastic Inflation and the Equity Premium." *Journal of Monetary Economics* **24**, pp. 277–298.

[225] Lambert, R. (1983). "Long-Term Contracts and Moral Hazard." *Bell Journal of Economics* **14**, pp. 441–452.

[226] Lancaster, K. (1966). "A New Approach to Consumer Theory." *Journal of Political Economy* **47**, pp. 132–157.

[227] LeRoy, S. and R. Porter (1981). "The Present-Value Relation: Tests Based on Implied Variance Bounds." *Econometrica* **49**, pp. 555–574.

[228] Lintner, J. (1965). "The Valuation of Risky Assets and the Selection of Risky Investment in Stock Portfolios and Capital Budgets." *Review of Economics and Statistics* **47**, pp. 13–37.

[229] Lucas, R. (1967). "Adjustment Costs and the Theory of Supply." *Journal of Political Economy* **75**, pp. 321–334.

[230] Lucas, R. (1978). "Asset Prices in an Exchange Economy." *Econometrica* **46**, pp. 1429–1445.

[231] Lucas, R. (1982). "Interest Rates and Currency Prices in a Two-Country World." *Journal of Monetary Economics* **10**, pp. 335–359.

[232] Lucas, R. (1984). "Money in a Theory of Finance." *Carnegie-Rochester Conference Series on Public Policy* **21**, pp. 9–45.

[233] Lucas, R. (1988). "On the Mechanics of Economic Development." *Journal of Monetary Economics* **22**, pp. 3–42.

[234] Lucas, R. (1990). "Liquidity and Interest Rates." *Journal of Economic Theory* **50**, pp. 237–264.

[235] Lucas, R. and N. Stokey (1987). "Money and Interest in a Cash-in-Advance Economy." *Econometrica* **55**, pp. 491–513.

[236] Luenberger, D. (1969). *Optimization by Vector Space Methods*. New York: John Wiley and Sons.

[237] Luttmer, E. (1993). "Asset Pricing in Economies with Frictions." Unpublished Manuscript, Northwestern University.

[238] Mace, B. (1991). "Full Insurance in the Presence of Aggregate Uncertainty." *Journal of Political Economy* **99**, pp. 928–956.

[239] Macklem, T. (1991). "Forward Exchange Rates and Risk Premiums in Artificial Economies." *Journal of International Money and Finance* **10**, pp. 365–391.

[240] MaCurdy, T. (1981). "An Empirical Model of Labor Supply in a Life-Cycle Setting." *Journal of Political Economy* **89**, pp. 1059–1085.

[241] MaCurdy, T. (1983). "A Simple Scheme for Estimating an Intertemporal Model of Labor Supply and Consumption in the Presence of Taxes and Uncertainty." *International Economic Review* **24**, pp. 265–289.

[242] Malcomson, J. and F. Spinnewyn (1988). "The Multiperiod Principal-Agent Problem." *Review of Economic Studies* **55**, pp. 391–408.

[243] Malliaris, A. and W. Brock (1982). *Stochastic Methods in Economics and Finance.* Amsterdam: North-Holland.

[244] Mandelbrot, B. (1963). "The Variation of Certain Speculative Prices." *Journal of Business* **36**, pp. 394–419.

[245] Mankiw, N. (1986). "The Equity Premium and the Concentration of Aggregate Shocks." *Journal of Financial Economics* **17**, pp. 211–219.

[246] Mankiw, N., D. Romer, and M. Shapiro (1985). "An Unbiased Reexamination of Stock Market Volatility." *Journal of Finance* **40**, pp. 677–689.

[247] Mankiw, N., D. Romer, and M. Shapiro (1991). "Stock Market Forecastability and Volatility: A Statistical Appraisal." *Review of Economic Studies* **58**, pp. 455–477.

[248] Mankiw, N., J. Rotemberg, and L. Summers (1985). "Intertemporal Substitution in Macroeconomics." *Quarterly Journal of Economics* **100**, pp. 225–252.

[249] Margiotta, M. and R. Miller (1993). "Managerial Compensation and the Cost of Moral Hazard." Unpublished Manuscript, Carnegie-Mellon University.

[250] Mark, N. (1990). "Real and Nominal Exchange Rates in the Long Run: An Empirical Investigation." *Journal of International Economics* **28**, pp. 115–136.

[251] Marsh, T. and R. Merton (1986). "Dividend Variability and Variance Bounds Tests for the Rationality of Stock Market Prices." *American Economic Review* **76**, pp. 483–498.

[252] McCallum, B. (1976). "Rational Expectations and the Natural Rate Hypothesis: Some Consistent Estimates." *Econometrica* **44**, pp. 43–52.

[253] McCallum, B. (1986). "On 'Real' and 'Sticky-Price' Theories of the Business Cycle." *Journal of Money, Credit, and Banking* **18**, pp. 397–414.

[254] McKenzie, L. (1959). "On the Existence of General Equilibrium for a Competitive Economy." *Econometrica* **27**, pp. 54–71.

[255] Mehra, R. (1988). "On the Existence and Representation of Equilibrium in an Economy with Growth and Nonstationary Consumption." *International Economic Review* **29**, pp. 131–135.

[256] Mehra, R. and E. Prescott (1985). "The Equity Premium: A Puzzle." *Journal of Monetary Economics* **15**, pp. 145–161.

[257] Merton, R. (1973). "An Intertemporal Capital Asset Pricing Model." *Econometrica* **41**, pp. 867–887.

[258] Miller, M. (1977). "Debt and Taxes." *Journal of Finance* **32**, pp. 261–275.

[259] Miller, R. (1984). "Job Matching and Occupational Choice." *Journal of Political Economy* **92**, pp. 1086–1120.

[260] Mirman, L. and I. Zilcha (1975). "On Optimal Growth Under Uncertainty." *Journal of Economic Theory* **11**, pp. 329–339.

[261] Mirrlees, J. (1975). "The Theory of Moral Hazard and Unobservable Behavior – Part I." Unpublished Manuscript, Nuffield College, Oxford.

[262] Modigliani, F. and M. Miller (1958). "The Cost of Capital, Corporation Finance, and the Theory of Investment." *American Economic Review* **48**, pp. 261–297.

[263] Mussa, M. (1982). "A Model of Exchange Rate Dynamics." *Journal of Political Economy* **90**, pp. 74–104.

[264] Mussa, M. (1986). "Nominal Exchange Rate Regimes and the Behavior of Real Exchange Rates: Evidence and Implications." *Carnegie-Rochester Conference Series on Public Policy* **25**, pp. 117–213.

[265] Myers, S. (1977). "Determinants of Corporate Borrowing." *Journal of Financial Economics* **5**, pp. 147–175.

[266] Naylor, A. and G. Sell (1982). *Linear Operator Theory in Engineering and Science.* New York: Springer-Verlag.

[267] Nelson, C. (1976). "Inflation and Rates of Return on Common Stocks." *Journal of Finance* **31**, pp. 471–483.

[268] Nelson, D. (1991). "Conditional Heteroskedasticity in Asset Returns: A New Approach." *Econometrica* **59**, pp. 347–370.

[269] Newey, W. and K. West (1987). "Hypothesis Testing with Efficient Method of Moments Estimation." *International Economic Review* **28**, pp. 777–787.

[270] Novales, A. (1990). "Solving Nonlinear Rational Expectations Models: A Stochastic Equilibrium Model of Interest Rates." *Econometrica* **58**, pp. 93–111.

[271] Obstfeld, M. and A. Stockman (1985). "Exchange-Rate Dynamics." In R. Jones and P. Kenen (eds.), *Handbook of International Economics, Vol. 2.* Amsterdam: North-Holland, pp. 917–977.

[272] Ogaki, M. (1993). "Generalized Method of Moments: Econometric Applications." In G. Maddala, C. Rao, and H. Vinod (eds.), *Handbook of Statistics, Vol. 11: Econometrics.* Amsterdam: North-Holland.

[273] Papoulis, A. (1984). *Probability, Random Variables, and Stochastic Processes.* New York: McGraw-Hill.

[274] Pratt, J. (1964). "Risk Aversion in the Small and in the Large." *Econometrica* **32**, pp. 122–136.

[275] Priestley, M. (1988). *Non-Linear and Non-Stationary Time Series Analysis.* London: Academic Press.

[276] Quenoille, M. (1956). "Notes on Bias in Estimation." *Biometrika* **43**, pp. 353–360.

[277] Radner, R. (1974). "A Note on Unanimity of Stockholders' Preferences Among Alternative Production Plans: A Reformulation of the Ekern-Wilson Model." *Bell Journal of Economics* **5**, pp. 181–184.

[278] Robinson, P. (1977). "The Estimation of a Nonlinear Moving Average Model." *Stochastic Processes and Their Applications* **5**, pp. 81–90.

[279] Rogerson, R. (1988). "Indivisible Labor, Lotteries and Equilibrium." *Journal of Monetary Economics* **21**, pp. 3–16.

[280] Rogerson, W. (1985). "Repeated Moral Hazard." *Econometrica* **53**, pp. 69–76.

[281] Roll, R. (1977). "A Critique of the Asset Pricing Theory's Tests. Part 1. On Past and Potential Testability of the Theory." *Journal of Financial Economics* **5**, pp. 129–176.

[282] Romer, P. (1986). "Increasing Returns and Long-Run Growth." *Journal of Political Economy* **94**, pp. 1002–1037.

[283] Ross, S. (1976). "The Arbitrage Theory of Capital Asset Pricing." *Journal of Economic Theory* **13**, pp. 341–360.

[284] Ross, S. (1977). "The Determination of Financial Structure: The Incentive-Signalling Approach." *Bell Journal of Economics* **8**, pp. 23–40.

[285] Ross, S. (1978). "A Simple Approach to the Valuation of Risky Streams." *Journal of Business* **51**, pp. 453–475.

[286] Rothschild, M. and J. Stiglitz (1970). "Increasing Risk I: A Definition." *Journal of Economic Theory* **2**, pp. 225–243.

[287] Rothschild, M. and J. Stiglitz (1971). "Increasing Risk II: Its Economic Consequences." *Journal of Economic Theory* **3**, pp. 66–84.

[288] Rothschild, M. and J. Stiglitz (1976). "Equilibrium in Competitive Insurance Markets: An Essay on the Economics of Imperfect Information." *Quarterly Journal of Economics* **90**, pp. 630–649.

[289] Rubinstein, M. (1974). "An Aggregation Theorem for Securities Markets." *Journal of Financial Economics* **1**, pp. 225–244.

[290] Rubinstein, M. (1981). "A Discrete-Time Synthesis of Financial Theory." *Research in Finance* **3**, pp. 53–102.

[291] Rubinstein, M. and J. Cox. (1985). *Options Markets.* Englewood Cliffs, NJ: Prentice-Hall.

[292] Runkle, D. (1991). "Liquidity Constraints and the Permanent-Income Hypothesis: Evidence from Panel Data." *Journal of Monetary Economics* **27**, pp. 73–98.

[293] Rust, J. (1987). "Optimal Replacement of GMC Bus Engines: An Empirical Model of Harold Zurcher." *Econometrica* **55**, pp. 999–1033.

[294] Salyer, K. (1990). "The Term Structure and Time Series Properties of Nominal Interest Rates: Implications from Theory." *Journal of Money, Credit, and Banking* **22**, pp. 478–490.

[295] Sandmo, A. (1969). "Capital Risk, Consumption and Portfolio Choice." *Econometrica* **37**, pp. 586–599.

[296] Sargan, J. (1958). "The Estimation of Economic Relationships Using Instrumental Variables." *Econometrica* **26**, pp. 393–415.

[297] Sargent, T. (1980). "'Tobin's q' and the Rate of Investment in General Equilibrium." *Journal of Monetary Economics* **12** (Supplement), pp. 107–154.

[298] Sargent, T. (1987). *Dynamic Macroeonomic Theory.* Cambridge, MA: Harvard University Press.

[299] Sargent, T. and C. Sims (1977). "Business Cycle Modeling Without Pretending to Have Too Much A Priori Economic Theory." In *New Methods in Business Cycle Research: Proceedings from a Conference*. Minneapolis, MN: Federal Reserve Bank of Minneapolis, pp. 45–109.

[300] Scheinkman, J. and L. Weiss (1986). "Borrowing Constraints and Aggregate Economic Activity." *Econometrica* **54**, pp. 23–45.

[301] Sharpe, W. (1964). "Capital Asset Prices: A Theory of Market Equilibrium Under Conditions of Risk." *Journal of Finance* **19**, pp. 425–442.

[302] Shavell, S. (1979). "On Moral Hazard and Insurance." *Quarterly Journal of Economics* **93**, pp. 541–562.

[303] Shiller, R. (1979). "The Volatility of Long-Term Interest Rates and Expectations Models of the Term Structure." *Journal of Political Economy* **87**, pp. 1190–1219.

[304] Shiller, R. (1981). "Do Stock Prices Move Too Much to be Justified by Subsequent Changes in Dividends?" *American Economic Review* **71**, pp. 421–436.

[305] Shiller, R. (1990). "The Term Structure of Interest Rates." In B. Friedman and F. Hahn (eds.), *Handbook of Monetary Economics, Vol. 1*. Amsterdam: Elsevier Science Publishers.

[306] Siegel, J. (1972). "Risk, Information, and Forward Exchange." *Quarterly Journal of Economics* **86**, pp. 303–309.

[307] Sill, K. (1990). "An Empirical Examination of Money Demand in an Intertemporal Optimizing Framework." Unpublished Manuscript, University of Virginia.

[308] Singh, K. (1981). "On the Asymptotic Accuracy of Efron's Bootstrap." *Annals of Statistics* **9**, pp. 1187–1195.

[309] Singleton, K. (1980). "Expectations Models of the Term Structure and Implied Variance Bounds." *Journal of Political Economy* **88**, pp. 1159–1176.

[310] Singleton, K. (1985). "Testing Specifications of Economic Agents' Intertemporal Optimum Problems in the Presence of Alternative Models." *Journal of Econometrics* **30**, pp. 391–413.

[311] Stock, J. (1990). "A Comment on 'Unit Roots in Real GNP: Do We Know and Do We Care?' " *Carnegie-Rochester Conference Series on Public Policy* **32**, pp. 63–82.

[312] Stockman, A. (1980). "A Theory of Exchange Rate Determination." *Journal of Political Economy* **88**, pp. 673–698.

[313] Stockman, A. and H. Dellas (1989). "International Portfolio Non-diversification and Exchange Rate Variability." *Journal of International Economics* **26**, pp. 271–289.

[314] Stockman, A. and L. Svensson (1987). "Capital Flows, Investment, and Exchange Rates." *Journal of Monetary Economics* **19**, pp. 171–201.

[315] Stokey, N. and R. Lucas, with E. Prescott (1989). *Recursive Methods in Economic Dynamics*. Cambridge, MA: Harvard University Press.

[316] Stoll, H. and R. Whaley (1993). *Futures and Options: Theory and Applications*, Ohio: South-Western Publishing.

[317] Stroud, A. (1971). *Approximate Calculation of Multiple Integrals*. Englewood Cliffs, NJ: Prentice-Hall.

[318] Summers, L. (1986). "Some Skeptical Observations on Real Business Cycle Theory." *Federal Reserve Bank of Minneapolis Quarterly Review* **10**, pp. 23–27.

[319] Svensson, L. (1985). "Currency Prices, Terms of Trade, and Interest Rates: A General Equilibrium Asset-Pricing, Cash-in-Advance Approach." *Journal of International Economics* **18**, pp. 17–42.

[320] Svensson, L. (1985). "Money and Asset Prices in a Cash-in-Advance Economy." *Journal of Political Economy* **93**, pp. 919–944.

[321] Tauchen, G. (1986). "Finite State Markov-Chain Approximations to Univariate and Vector Autoregressions." *Economics Letters* **20**, pp. 177–181.

[322] Tauchen, G. and R. Hussey (1991). "Quadrature-Based Methods for Obtaining Approximate Solutions to Nonlinear Asset Pricing Models." *Econometrica* **59**, pp. 371–396.

[323] Tauchen, G. and M. Pitts (1983). "The Price Variability-Volume Relationship on Speculative Markets." *Econometrica* **51**, pp. 485–505.

[324] Thomas, J. and T. Worrall (1990). "Income Fluctuation and Asymmetric Information: An Example of a Repeated Prinicipal-Agent Problem." *Journal of Economic Theory* **51**, pp. 367–390.

[325] Tong, H. and K. Lim (1980). "Threshold Autoregression, Limit Cycles, and Cyclical Data." *Journal of the Royal Statistical Society, Series B,* **42**, pp. 245–292.

[326] Townsend. R. (1994). "Risk and Insurance in Village India." *Econometrica* **62**, pp. 539–591.

[327] Treadway, A. (1969). "On Rational Entrepreneurial Behavior and the Demand for Investment." *Review of Economic Studies* **36**, pp. 227–239.

[328] Turnbull, S. and F. Milne (1991). "A Simple Approach to Interest-Rate Option Pricing." *Review of Financial Studies* **4**, pp. 87–120.

[329] Watson, M. (1993). "Measures of Fit for Calibrated Models." *Journal of Political Economy* **101**, pp. 1011–1041.

[330] Weil, P. (1989). "The Equity Premium Puzzle and the Riskfree Rate Puzzle." *Journal of Monetary Economics* **24**, pp. 401–421.

[331] Weil, P. (1990). "Nonexpected Utility in Macroeconomics." *Quarterly Journal of Economics* **105**, pp. 29–42.

[332] Weil, P. (1992). "Equilibrium Asset Prices with Undiversifiable Labor Income Risk." *Journal of Economic Dynamics and Control* **16**, pp. 769–790.

[333] Weitzman, M. (1979). "Optimal Search for the Best Alternative." *Econometrica* **47**, pp. 641–654.

[334] West, K. (1988). "Dividend Innovations and Stock Price Volatility." *Econometrica* **56**, pp. 37–61.

[335] White, H. (1980). "A Heteroskedasticity-Consistent Covariance Estimator and a Direct Test for Heteroskedasticity." *Econometrica* **48**, pp. 817–838.

[336] White, H. (1982). "Maximum Likelihood Estimation of Misspecified Models." *Econometrica* **50**, pp. 1–25.

[337] Whittle, P. (1983). *Prediction and Regulation by Linear Least-Squares Methods*, 2nd ed. Minneapolis, MN: University of Minnesota Press.

[338] Wilson, C. (1977). "A Model of Insurance Markets with Incomplete Information." *Journal of Economic Theory* **16**, pp. 167–207.

[339] Wilson, G. (1973). "The Estimation of Parameters in Multivariate Time Series Models." *Journal of the Royal Statistical Society, Series B,* **35**, pp. 76–85.

[340] Wilson, R. (1968). "The Theory of Syndicates." *Econometrica* **36**, pp. 119–132.

[341] Zeldes, S. (1989). "Consumption and Liquidity Constraints: An Empirical Investigation." *Journal of Political Economy* **97**, pp. 305–346.

Index

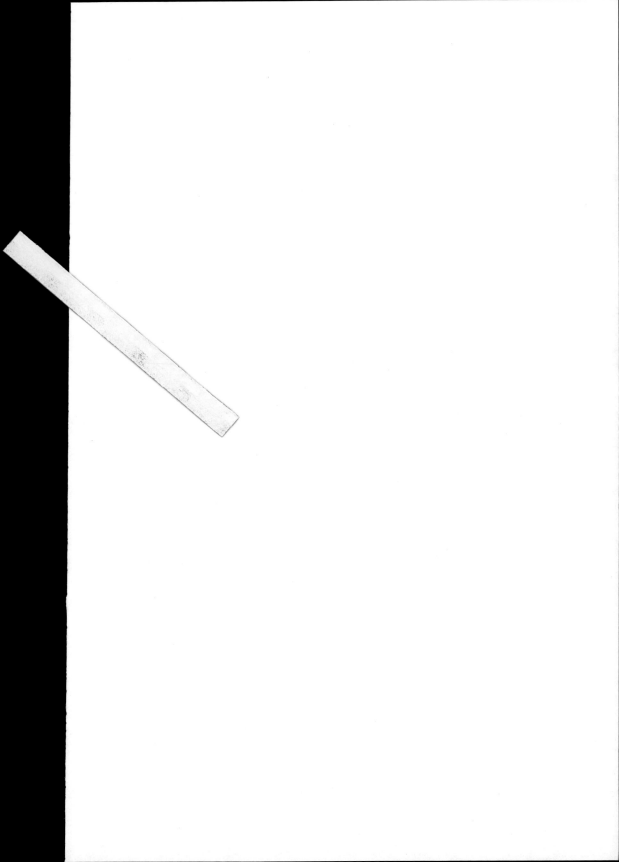